D0986547

The Complete WW2 MILITARY JEEP MANUAL

ISBN 1 85520 1216

Brooklands Books Ltd.
PO Box 146, Cobham,
Surrey, KT11 1LG. UK

In conjunction with

Portrayal Press, PO Box 1190,
Andover, New Jersey,
07821, USA

Printed in Hong Kong

Other Military Titles available from Brooklands/Portrayal

US Military Vehicles 1941-1945

Allied Military Vehicles Collection No.1

Allied Military Vehicles Collection No.2

Dodge Military Vehicles Collection No.1

Hail to the Jeep

Military Jeeps 1941-1945

Off Road Jeeps 1944-1971

Jeep Collection No.1

U.S. Army Military Vehicles WW2
(TM9-2800/SEPT 1943)

DISTRIBUTED BY

Brookland Books Limited, PO Box 146, Cobham, Surrey KT11 1LG, England.
Telephone: 0932 865051 Fax: 0932 868803

Brooklands Books, Unit 1, 81 Darley Street, Mona Vale, NSW 2109, Australia.
Telephone: (02) 997 8428 Fax: (02) 452 4679

Portrayal Press, PO Box 1190, Andover, NJ 07821, USA.
Telephone: (201) 579 5781

Printed in Hong Kong

ABOUT THIS MANUAL

In one compact volume, we have made available again all three basic service manuals on the standardized jeep of World War II – the Willys model MB and the Ford model GPW.

In addition, we have included a supplemental manual of corrections and updating information, and the appropiate section from the carburetor service manual.

Part 1

TM9-803 Covering operation and basic vehicle maintenance.

Part 2

Change One – Important corrections and updating of TM 9-803.

Part 3

TM9-1803A Covering the engine and clutch.

Part 4

Carburetor service. Excerpts from TM9-1826A of 1952.

Part 5

TM9-1803B Covering power train, body, frame and special tools.

TM 9-803

WAR DEPARTMENT TECHNICAL MANUAL

¼-TON 4x4 TRUCK (WILLYS-OVERLAND MODEL MB and FORD MODEL GPW)

WAR DEPARTMENT • FEBRUARY 1944

WAR DEPARTMENT TECHNICAL MANUAL

TM 9-803

**This manual supersedes TB 9-803-4, 5 January 1944. For supersession of Quartermaster Corps 10-series technical manuals, see paragraph 1*

¼-TON 4 x 4 TRUCK (WILLYS-OVERLAND MODEL MB and FORD MODEL GPW)

WAR DEPARTMENT • FEBRUARY 1944

United States Government Printing Office

Washington : 1947

WAR DEPARTMENT
Washington 25, D. C., 22 February 1944

TM 9-803, ¼-ton 4 x 4 Truck (Willys-Overland Model MB and Ford Model GPW), is published for the information and guidance of all concerned.

[A. G. 300.7 (17 November 43)]

BY ORDER OF THE SECRETARY OF WAR:

G. C. MARSHALL,
Chief of Staff.

OFFICIAL:

J. A. ULIO,
Major General,
The Adjutant General.

DISTRIBUTION: C & H (1).

(For explanation of symbols, see FM 21-6)

¼-TON 4 x 4 TRUCK (WILLYS-OVERLAND MODEL MB and FORD MODEL GPW)

CONTENTS

PART ONE—OPERATING INSTRUCTIONS

PART TWO—VEHICLE MAINTENANCE INSTRUCTIONS

¼-TON 4 x 4 TRUCK (WILLYS-OVERLAND MODEL MB and FORD MODEL GPW)

PART ONE—OPERATING INSTRUCTIONS

Section I

INTRODUCTION

1. SCOPE.

a. This technical manual* is published for the information and guidance of the using arm personnel charged with the operation and maintenance of this materiel.

b. In addition to a description of the ¼-ton 4 x 4 Truck (Willys-Overland model MB and Ford GPW), this manual contains technical information required for the identification, use, and care of the materiel. The manual is divided into two parts. Part One, sections I through VII, contains vehicle operating instructions. Part Two, sections VIII through XXXII, contains vehicle maintenance instructions to using arm personnel charged with the responsibility of doing maintenance work within their jurisdiction, including radio suppression and shipment and temporary storage information.

c. In all cases where the nature of the repair, modification, or adjustment is beyond the scope of facilities of the unit, the responsible ordnance service should be informed so that trained personnel with suitable tools and equipment may be provided, or proper instructions issued.

d. This manual includes operating and organizational maintenance instructions from the following Quartermaster Corps 10-series technical manuals. Together with TM 9-1803A and TM 9-1803B, this manual supersedes them:

(1) TM 10-1103, 20 August 1941.

(2) TM 10-1207, 20 August 1941.

(3) TM 10-1349, 3 January 1942.

(4) TM 10-1513, Change 1, 15 January 1943.

---

*To provide operating instructions with the materiel, this technical manual has been published in advance of complete technical review. Any errors or omissions will be corrected by changes or, if extensive, by an early revision.

Figure 1—1/4-Ton 4 x 4 Truck—Left Front

RA PD 305250

Figure 2—1/4-Ton 4 x 4 Truck—Right Rear

RA PD 305163

Figure 3—1/4-Ton 4 x 4 Truck—Right Side

RA PD 305164

Figure 4—1/4-Ton 4 x 4 Truck—Right Front

Section II

DESCRIPTION AND TABULATED DATA

2. DESCRIPTION.

a. Type. This vehicle is a general purpose, personnel, or cargo carrier especially adaptable for reconnaisance or command, and designated as 1/4-ton 4 x 4 Truck. It is a four-wheel vehicle with four-wheel drive. The engine is a 4-cylinder gasoline unit located in the conventional place, under the hood at the front of the vehicle. A conventional three-speed transmission equipped with a transfer case provides additional speeds for traversing difficult terrain. The body is of the open type with an open driver's compartment. The folding top can be removed and stowed; and, the windshield tilted forward on top of the hood, or opened upward and outward. A spare wheel equipped with a tire is mounted on the rear of the body, and a pintle hook is provided to haul trailed loads. Specifications of the vehicle are given under "Data" (par. 3). General physical characteristics are shown in figures 1 through 4.

b. Identification. The manufacturer's chassis serial number is stamped on a plate inside the left frame side member at the front end, and on the name plate (fig. 6). The engine serial number is stamped on the right side of the cylinder block, front upper corner. The U.S.A. registration number is painted on both sides of the hood.

3. DATA.

a. Vehicle Specifications.

Wheelbase	80 in.
Length, over-all	132 1/4 in.
Width, over-all	62 in.
Height, over-all–top up	69 3/4 in.
–top down	52 in.
Wheel size	combat 16 x 4.50 E
Tire size	16 x 6.00 in.
Tire pressure (front and rear)	35 lb
Tire type	mud and snow
Tire plies	6
Tread (center-to-center)–front	49 in.
–rear	49 in.
Crew, operating	2
Passenger capacity including crew	5

DESCRIPTION AND TABULATED DATA

Weights:
- Road, including gas and water .... 2,453 lb
- Gross (loaded) .... 3,253 lb
- Shipping (less water and fuel) .... 2,337 lb
- Boxed gross .... 3,062 lb
- Maximum pay load .... 800 lb
- Maximum trailed load .... 1,000 lb

Ground clearance .... 8¾ in.
Pintle height (loaded) .... 21 in.
Kind and grade of fuel (octane rating) .. Gasoline (68 min)
Approach angle .... 45 deg
Departure angle .... 35 deg
Shipping dimensions—cubic feet 331
—square feet 57

b. Performance.

Maximum allowable speeds (mph) with transfer case in "HIGH" range:
- High gear (3rd) 65
- Intermediate gear (2nd) 41
- Low gear (1st) 24
- Reverse gear 18

Maximum allowable speeds (mph) with transfer case in "LOW" range:
- High gear (3rd) 33
- Intermediate gear (2nd) 21
- Low gear (1st) 12
- Reverse gear 9

Maximum grade ability .... 60 pct
Minimum turning radius—right .... 17½ ft
—left .... 17½ ft
Maximum fording depth .... 21 in.
Towing facilities—front .... none
—rear .... pintle hook
Maximum draw-bar pull .... 1,930 lb
Engine idle speed .... 600 rpm
Miles per gallon—(high gear—high range)
average conditions 20
Cruising range—(miles) average conditions 20

c. Capacities.

Engine crankcase capacity—dry .... 5 qt
—refill .... 4 qt
Transmission capacity .... ¾ qt
Transfer case capacity .... 1½ qt

¼-TON 4 x 4 TRUCK (WILLYS-OVERLAND MODEL MB and FORD MODEL GPW)

Front axle capacity (differential)	1¼ qt
Rear axle capacity (differential)	1¼ qt
Front axle steering knuckle universal joint	¼ qt
Steering gear housing	¼ qt
Air cleaner (oil bath)	⅝ qt
Fuel tank capacity	15 gal
Cooling system capacity	11 qt
Brake system (hydraulic brake fluid)	¼ qt
Shock absorbers--front	5 oz
—rear	5¾ oz

d. Communications.

(1) RADIO OUTLET BOX. A radio outlet box is provided on the later vehicles to use the vehicle battery (6-volt current supply). This outlet is located against the body side panel at the right front seat.

(2) AUXILIARY GENERATOR. A 12-volt, 55-ampere auxiliary generator is furnished on some vehicles. The generator is driven by a V-belt from a power take-off unit on the rear of the transfer case. Instructions for operation and care accompany those vehicles.

Section III

DRIVING CONTROLS AND OPERATION

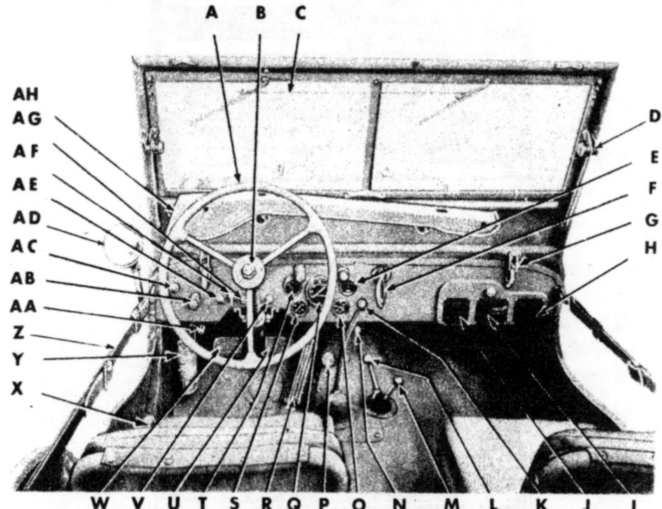

A STEERING WHEEL
B HORN BUTTON
C WINDSHIELD WIPERS
D WINDSHIELD ADJUSTING ARMS
E AMMETER
F HAND BRAKE
G WINDSHIELD CLAMPS
H CAUTION PLATE
I NAME PLATE
J SHIFT PLATE
K TRANSMISSION GEAR SHIFT LEVER
L TRANSFER CASE SHIFT LEVER—FRONT AXLE DRIVE
M TRANSFER CASE SHIFT LEVER—AUXILIARY RANGE
N STARTING SWITCH
O TEMPERATURE GAGE
P ACCELERATOR FOOT REST
Q SPEEDOMETER
R ACCELERATOR (FOOT THROTTLE)
S OIL PRESSURE GAGE
T FUEL GAGE
U BRAKE PEDAL
V INSTRUMENT PANEL LIGHT SWITCH
W CLUTCH PEDAL
X FUEL TANK
Y FIRE EXTINGUISHER
Z SAFETY STRAP
AA HEADLIGHT FOOT SWITCH (BEAM CONTROL)
AB BLACKOUT LIGHT SWITCH
AC BLACKOUT DRIVING LIGHT SWITCH
AD REAR VISION MIRROR
AE CHOKE CONTROL
AF IGNITION SWITCH
AG HAND THROTTLE
AH RIFLE HOLDER

RA PD 334753

Figure 5—Instruments and Controls

4. INSTRUMENTS AND CONTROLS.

a. Instruments.

(1) Ammeter (fig. 5). The ammeter on the instrument panel indicates the rate of current flow when the generator is charging the battery, and also indicates the amount of current being consumed when the engine is idle.

(2) Fuel Gage (fig. 5). The fuel gage on the instrument panel

WILLYS
NOMENCLATURE TRUCK ¼ TON 4 X 4
SUPPLY ARM OR SERVICE
MAINTAINING VEHICLE ORDNANCE DEPT
MAKE AND MODEL WILLYS MB.
SERIAL NUMBER:
GROSS WEIGHT LBS.
MAXIMUM PAYLOAD 800 LBS.
MAXIMUM TRAILEDLOAD 1000 LBS.
DATE OF DELIVERY
RECOMMENDED BY MANUFACTURER
OCTANE RATING OF GASOLINE 68 MIN.
S.A.E. GRADE OF OIL BELOW 32° F USE 10W S.A.E.
S.A.E. GRADE OF OIL ABOVE 32° F USE 30 S.A.E.
PUBLICATIONS APPLYING TO THIS VEHICLE
PARTS LIST
TECHNICAL MANUAL T/M

Ford
NOMENCLATURE TRUCK 1/4 TON 4X4
SUPPLY ARM OR SERVICE
MAINTAINING VEHICLE ORDNANCE DEPARTMENT
MAKE AND MODEL FORD-GPW
SERIAL NUMBER
GROSS WEIGHT LBS
MAXIMUM PAYLOAD 800 LBS
MAXIMUM TRAILED LOAD 1000 LBS
DATE OF DELIVERY
RECOMMENDED BY MANUFACTURER
OCTANE RATING OF GASOLINE 68 MIN.
S.A.E. GRADE OF OIL ABOVE 32°F. 30 S.A.E.
S.A.E. GRADE OF OIL BELOW 32°F. 10 S.A.E.
PUBLICATIONS APPLYING TO THIS VEHICLE
PARTS LIST T/M 10- 1348
MAINTENANCE MANUAL T/M 10- 1349

RA PD 330838

Figure 6—Name Plate

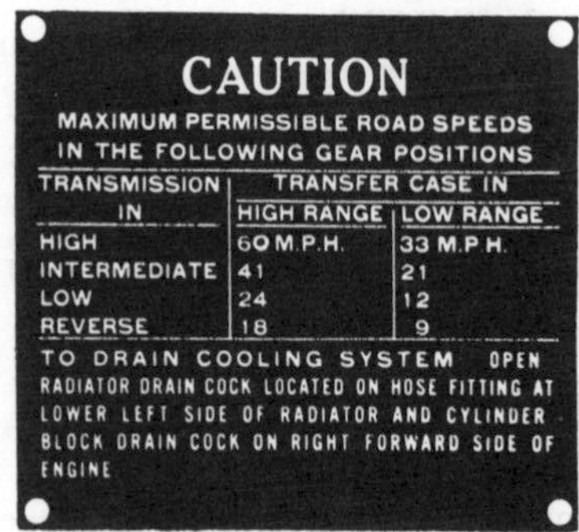

CAUTION
MAXIMUM PERMISSIBLE ROAD SPEEDS
IN THE FOLLOWING GEAR POSITIONS
TRANSMISSION IN
TRANSFER CASE IN
HIGH RANGE
LOW RANGE
HIGH 60 M.P.H. 33 M.P.H.
INTERMEDIATE 41 21
LOW 24 12
REVERSE 18 9
TO DRAIN COOLING SYSTEM OPEN RADIATOR DRAIN COCK LOCATED ON HOSE FITTING AT LOWER LEFT SIDE OF RADIATOR AND CYLINDER BLOCK DRAIN COCK ON RIGHT FORWARD SIDE OF ENGINE

RA PD 305162

Figure 7—Caution Plate

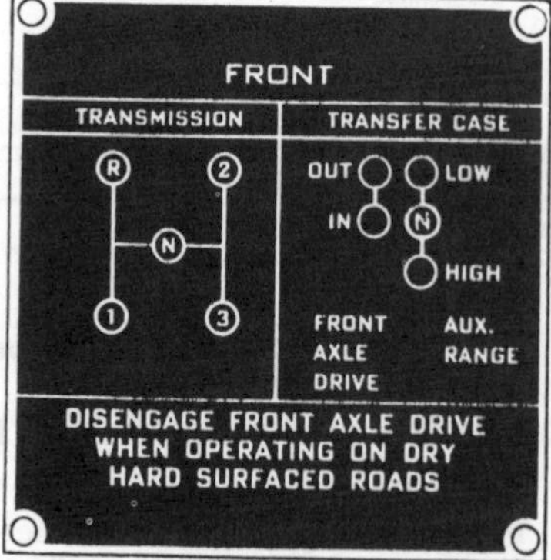

RA PD 305161

Figure 8—Shift Plate

is an electrical unit which indicates the fuel level in the tank, and only registers while the ignition switch is turned on.

(3) Oil Pressure Gage (fig. 5). The oil pressure gage located on the instrument panel indicates the oil pressure when the engine is running.

(4) Speedometer (fig. 5). The speedometer on the instrument panel indicates in miles per hour the speed at which the vehicle is being driven. The odometer (in upper part of speedometer face) registers the total number of miles the vehicle has been driven. A trip indicator (in lower part of speedometer face) gives distance covered on any trip. Set trip indicator by turning the knurled control shaft extending through back of the speedometer.

(5) Temperature Gage (fig. 5). The temperature gage registers the temperature of the solution in the cooling system.

b. Controls.

(1) Blackout Driving Light Switch (fig. 5). The blackout driving light switch (B.O. DRIVE) on the instrument panel controls the blackout driving light located on the left front fender, to furnish additional light during blackout periods. To operate light, first pull the blackout *light* switch button to the first position, then pull blackout *driving* light switch knob. To switch off the light, push in blackout *driving* light switch knob.

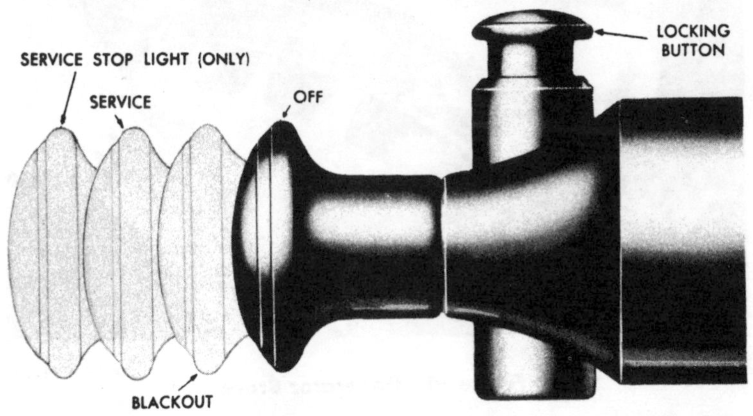

Figure 9—Blackout Light Switch Operating Positions

(2) Blackout Light Switch (fig. 5). The knob on the instrument panel (LIGHTS) controls the entire lighting system, including the instrument panel lights, blackout driving light, and stop lights. A circuit-breaker type fuse, on the back of the switch, opens when a short circuit occurs, and closes when the thermostatic element cools. The light switch is a four-position push-pull type with a safety lock (fig. 9). When the control knob is pulled out to the first position, the blackout headlights and blackout stop and taillights are turned on.

The switch control knob travel is automatically locked in this position by the lock-out button to prevent accidentally turning on of the service (bright) lights in a blackout area. To obtain service lights, push in on lock-out control button on the left side of the switch, and pull out control knob to second position. When switch is in this position service headlights, service stop and taillights are turned on, and the panel lights can be turned on by pulling out on the knob (PANEL LIGHTS). CAUTION: *When driving during the day, press in lock-out control button, and pull control knob out to the last or stop light position to cause only the regular stop light to function.*

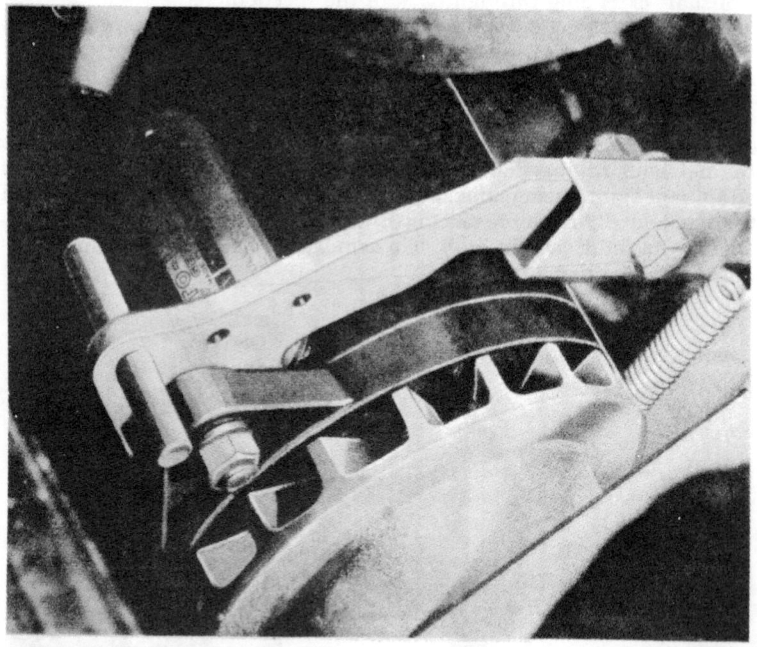

RA PD 305165

Figure 10—Generator Brace

(3) PANEL LIGHT SWITCH (fig. 5). The panel light switch knob (PANEL LIGHTS), located on the instrument panel, controls the lights to illuminate the panel instruments and controls. The blackout light switch (subpar. **b** (2) above) must be in service (bright light) position for this switch to control the panel lights.

(4) FIRE EXTINGUISHER (fig. 5). The fire extinguisher is mounted inside the left cowl panel. To remove, pull outward on the clamp release lever. To operate extinguisher, hold body in one hand and with the other, turn handle to left one-quarter turn, which releases plunger lock. Use pumping action to force liquid on base of fire. Read instructions on fire extinguisher plate.

(5) HAND BRAKE (fig. 5). The hand brake is applied by pulling out on the handle at the center of the instrument panel. Pull the handle out in a vertical position when the vehicle is parked. The brake is released by turning the handle one-quarter turn.

(6) WINDSHIELD ADJUSTING ARMS (fig. 5). The windshield adjustment arms are mounted on each end of the windshield frame. To open windshield, loosen knobs and push forward on lower part, then set by tightening the knobs.

(7) WINDSHIELD CLAMPS (fig. 5). The windshield clamps are located on the lower part of the windshield. Pull up on both clamps and unhook them, after which the windshield can be lowered on top of the hood. Be sure to hook down the windshield, using the hold-down catches on both sides of the hood.

(8) GENERATOR BRACE (fig. 10). The generator brace can be pulled up to release tension on the fan belt and stop the fan from throwing water over the engine when crossing a stream. Pull generator out to running position as soon as possible thereafter, and it will lock in place. CAUTION: *Be sure fan belt is on pulleys.*

(9) OTHER INSTRUMENTS AND CONTROLS. Other instruments and controls are of the conventional type, and are shown in figure 5.

5. USE OF INSTRUMENTS AND CONTROLS IN VEHICULAR OPERATION.

a. Before-operation Service. Perform the services in paragraph 13 before attempting to start the engine.

b. Starting Engine. To start the engine proceed as follows:

(1) Put transmission gearshift lever in neutral position (fig. 8).

(2) Pull out hand throttle button about ¾ inch to 1 inch.

(3) Pull out choke button all the way. NOTE: *Choking is not necessary when engine is warm.*

(4) Turn ignition to "ON" position.

(5) Depress clutch pedal to disengage clutch, and hold pedal down while engine is started.

(6) Step on starting switch to crank again. Release switch as soon as engine starts.

(7) Adjust choke and throttle control buttons to obtain proper idling speed. As engine warms up, push choke button all the way in.

(8) Check oil pressure gage reading; at idle speed the indicator hand should show at least 10 on the gage.

(9) Check ammeter for charge reading. Check fuel gage for indication of fuel supply.

(10) After engine has operated a few minutes, check temperature gage reading. Normal operating temperature is between 160°F and 185°F.

(11) In extremely cold weather refer to paragraph 7.

c. Placing Vehicle in Motion.

(1) For daytime driving turn on service stop light (par. 4 **b** (2)).

(2) Place transfer case right-hand shift lever in rear position to

engage "HIGH" range, then place center shift lever in forward position to disengage front axle (fig. 8).

(3) Depress clutch pedal, and move transmission shift lever toward driver and backward to engage low (1st) gear (fig. 8).

(4) Release parking (hand) brake.

(5) Slightly depress accelerator to increase engine speed, and at the same time slowly release clutch pedal, increasing pressure on accelerator as clutch engages and vehicle starts to move. NOTE: *During the following operations perform procedures outlined in paragraph 14.*

(6) Increase speed to approximately 10 miles per hour, depress clutch pedal, and at the same time release pressure on accelerator. Move transmission shift lever out of low gear into neutral, and then into second gear. No double clutching is required. Release clutch pedal and accelerate engine.

(7) After vehicle has attained a speed of approximately 20 miles per hour, follow the same procedure as outlined above in order to shift into high (3rd) gear, moving the gearshift lever straight back.

d. Shifting to Lower Gears in Transmission. Shift to a lower gear before engine begins to labor, as follows: Depress clutch pedal quickly, shift to next lower gear, increase engine speed, release clutch pedal slowly, and accelerate. When shifting to a lower gear at any rate of vehicle speed, make sure that the engine speed is synchronized with vehicle speed before clutch is engaged.

e. Shifting Gears in Transfer Case (fig. 8). The transfer case is the means by which power is applied to the front and rear axles. In addition, the low gear provided by the transfer case further increases the number of speeds provided by the transmission. The selection of gear ratios depends upon the road and load conditions. Shift gears in the transfer case in accordance with the shift plate (fig. 8), and observe the instructions on the caution plate (fig. 7). The transmission gearshift does not in any way affect the selection or shifting of the transfer case gears. Vehicle may be driven by rear axle, or by both front and rear axles. The front axle cannot be driven independently.

(1) FRONT AXLE ENGAGEMENT. Front axle should be engaged only in off-the-road operation, slippery roads, steep grades, or during hard pulling. Disengage front axle when operating on average roads under normal conditions.

(a) Engaging Front Axle with Transfer Case in "HIGH" Range. With transfer case in "HIGH" range, move front axle drive shift lever to "IN" position. Depressing the clutch pedal will facilitate shifting.

(b) Disengaging Front Axle with Transfer Case in "HIGH" Range. Move front axle drive shift lever to "OUT" position. Depress the clutch pedal to facilitate shifting.

(c) Disengaging Front Axle when Transfer Case is in "LOW."

1. Depress clutch pedal, then shift transfer case lever into "HIGH."

2. Shift front axle drive lever into "OUT" position.

3. Release clutch pedal and accelerate engine to desired speed.

(2) ENGAGING TRANSFER CASE LOW RANGE. Transfer case LOW range cannot be engaged until front axle drive is engaged.

(a) Engage front axle drive (subpar. e (1) above).

(b) Depress clutch pedal and move transfer case shift lever into "N" (neutral) position.

(c) Release clutch pedal and accelerate engine.

(d) Depress clutch pedal again and move transfer case shift lever forward into "LOW" position.

(e) Release clutch pedal, and accelerate engine to desired speed.

(3). ENGAGING TRANSFER CASE—"LOW" to "HIGH." This shift can be made regardless of vehicle speed.

(a) Depress clutch pedal and move transfer case shift lever into "HIGH" position.

(b) Release clutch pedal, and accelerate engine to desired speed.

f. Stopping the Vehicle. Remove foot from accelerator, and apply brakes by depressing brake pedal.

(1) When vehicle speed has been reduced to engine idle speed, depress clutch pedal and move transmission shift lever to "N" (neutral) position (fig. 8).

(2) When vehicle has come to a complete stop, apply parking (hand) brake, and release clutch and brake pedals.

g. Reversing the Vehicle. To shift into reverse speed, first bring the vehicle to a complete stop.

(1) Depress clutch pedal.

(2) Move transmission shift lever to the left and forward into "R" (reverse) position.

(3) Release clutch pedal slowly, and accelerate as load is picked up.

h. Stopping the Engine. To stop the engine turn the ignition switch to "OFF" position. NOTE: *Before a new or reconditioned vehicle is first put into service, make run-in tests as outlined in section 10.*

6. TOWING THE VEHICLE.

a. Attaching Tow Line. To tow vehicle attach the chain, rope or cable to the front bumper bar at the frame side rail gusset (fig. 11). Do not tow from the middle of the bumper. To attach tow line, loop chain, rope, or cable over top of bumper, bring tow line up across front of bumper, and back on opposite side of frame, then hook or tie.

b. Towing to Start Vehicle. Place transfer case (aux. RANGE) shift lever of towed vehicle to the rear ("HIGH"). Place front axle drive shift lever in "OUT" (forward) position. Depress clutch pedal and engage transmission in high (3rd) speed. Switch ignition "ON," pull out choke control knob (if engine is cold), pull out throttle knob about 1 inch, release parking (hand) brake, and tow vehicle. After vehicle is under way, release clutch pedal slowly. As engine starts, regulate choke and throttle controls and disengage clutch, being careful to avoid overrunning towing vehicle or tow line.

c. Towing Disabled Vehicle. When towing a disabled vehicle exercise care so that no additional damage will occur.

(1) ALL WHEELS ON GROUND.

(a) If transfer case is *not* damaged, shift transmission and transfer case into neutral position and follow steps *(c)* and *(d)* below.

(b) If transfer case *is* damaged, disconnect both propeller shafts at the front and rear axles by removing the universal joint U-bolts, being careful not to lose the bearing races and rollers. Securely fasten the shafts to the frame with wire or remove dust cap and pull apart at the universal joint splines. Place bolts, nuts, rollers, and races in the glove compartment.

Figure 11—Chain Tow

(c) If the front axle differential or propeller shaft is damaged, remove front axle shaft driving flanges. Place front axle drive shift lever in "OUT" (forward) position and drive vehicle under own power.

(d) If the rear axle differential is damaged, remove the rear axle shafts; remove rear propeller shaft at rear universal joint U-bolts and front universal joint snap rings in forward flange, then drive out bearing cups. Place front axle drive shift lever in "IN" (rear) position and this will allow front axle drive to propel vehicle under own power.

(e) If rear propeller shaft only is damaged, remove as described in step *(d)* above.

(2) TOWING VEHICLE WITH FRONT OR REAR WHEELS OFF GROUND. If vehicle is to be towed in this manner be sure that transfer case shift lever is placed in "N" (neutral) position and front axle drive shift lever is placed in "OUT" (disengaged) position.

Section IV

OPERATION UNDER UNUSUAL CONDITIONS

Paragraph

7. OPERATION IN COLD WEATHER.

a. Purpose. Operation of automotive equipment at subzero temperatures presents problems that demand special precautions and extra careful servicing from both operation and maintenance personnel, if poor performance and total functional failure are to be avoided.

b. Gasoline. Winter grade of gasoline is designed to reduce cold weather starting difficulties; therefore, the winter grade motor fuel should be used in cold weather operation.

c. Storage and Handling of Gasoline. Due to condensation of moisture from the air, water will accumulate in tanks, drums, and containers. At low temperatures, this water will form ice crystals that will clog fuel lines and carburetor jets, unless the following precautions are taken:

(1) Strain the fuel through filter paper, or any other type of strainer that will prevent the passage of water. CAUTION: *Gasoline flowing over a surface generates static electricity that will result in a spark, unless means are provided to ground the electricity. Always provide a metallic contact between the container and the tank, to assure an effective ground.*

(2) Keep tank full, if possible. The more fuel there is in the tank, the smaller will be the volume of air from which moisture can be condensed.

(3) Add ½ pint of denatured alcohol, Grade 3, to the fuel tank each time it is filled. This will reduce the hazard of ice formation in the fuel.

(4) Be sure that all containers are thoroughly clean and free from rust before storing fuel in them.

(5) If possible, after filling or moving a container, allow the fuel to settle before filling fuel tank from it.

(6) Keep all closures of containers tight to prevent snow, ice, dirt, and other foreign matter from entering.

(7) Wipe all snow or ice from dispensing equipment and from around fuel tank filler cap before removing cap to refuel vehicle.

d. Lubrication.

(1) TRANSMISSION AND DIFFERENTIAL.

(a) Universal gear lubricant, SAE 80, where specified on figure 14, is suitable for use at temperatures as low as −20°F. If consistent temperature below 0°F is anticipated, drain the gear cases while warm, and refill with Grade 75 universal gear lubricant, which is suitable for operation at all temperatures below +32°F. If Grade 75 universal gear lubricant is not available, SAE 80 universal gear lubricant diluted with the fuel used by the engine, in the proportion of one part fuel to six parts universal gear lubricant, may be used. Dilute make-up oil in the same proportion before it is added to gear cases.

(b) After engine has been warmed up, engage clutch, and maintain engine speed at fast idle for 5 minutes, or until gears can be engaged. Put transmission in low (first) gear, and drive vehicle for 100 yards, being careful not to stall engine. This will heat gear lubricants to the point where normal operation can be expected.

(2) CHASSIS POINTS. Lubricate chassis points with general purpose grease, No. 0.

(3) STEERING GEAR HOUSING. Drain housing, if possible, or use suction gun to remove as much lubricant as possible. Refill with universal gear lubricant, Grade 75, or, if not available, SAE 80 universal gear lubricant diluted with fuel used in the engine, in the proportion of one part fuel to six parts SAE 80 universal gear lubricant. Dilute make-up oil in the same proportion before it is added to the housing.

(4) OILCAN POINTS. For oilcan points where engine oil is prescribed for above 0°F, use light lubricating, preservative oil.

e. Protection of Cooling Systems.

(1) USE ANTIFREEZE COMPOUND. Protect the system with antifreeze compound (ethylene-glycol type) for operation below +32°F. The following instructions apply to use of new antifreeze compound.

(2) CLEAN COOLING SYSTEM. Before adding antifreeze compound, clean the cooling system, and completely free it from rust. If the cooling system has been cleaned recently, it may be necessary only to drain, refill with clean water, and again drain. Otherwise the system should be cleaned with cleaning compound.

(3) REPAIR LEAKS. Inspect all hoses, and replace if deteriorated. Inspect all hose clamps, plugs, and pet cocks and tighten if necessary. Repair all radiator leaks before adding antifreeze compound. Correct all leakage of exhaust gas or air into the cooling system.

(4) ADD ANTIFREEZE COMPOUND. When the cooling system is clean and tight, fill the system with water to about one-third capacity. Then add antifreeze compound, using the proportion of antifreeze compound to the cooling system capacity indicated below. Protect the system to at least 10°F below the lowest temperature expected to be experienced during the winter season.

OPERATION UNDER UNUSUAL CONDITIONS

ANTIFREEZE COMPOUND CHART
(for 11-quart capacity cooling system)

Temperature	Antifreeze Compound (ethylene-glycol type)
+10°F	3 qt
0°F	3¾ qt
−10°F	4½ qt
−20°F	4¾ qt
−30°F	5½ qt
−40°F	6 qt

(5) WARM THE ENGINE. After adding antifreeze compound, fill with water to slightly below the filler neck; then start and warm the engine to normal operating temperature.

(6) TEST STRENGTH OF SOLUTION. Stop the engine and check the solution with a hydrometer, adding antifreeze compound if required.

(7) INSPECT WEEKLY. In service, inspect the coolant weekly for strength and color. If rusty, drain and clean cooling system thoroughly, and add new solution of the required strength.

(8) CAUTIONS.

(a) Antifreeze compound is the only antifreeze material authorized for ordnance materiel.

(b) It is essential that antifreeze solutions be kept clean. Use only containers and water that are free from dirt, rust, and oil.

(c) Use an accurate hydrometer. To test a hydrometer, use one part antifreeze compound to two parts water. This solution will produce a hydrometer reading of 0°F.

(d) Do not spill antifreeze compound on painted surfaces.

f. Electrical Systems.

(1) GENERATOR AND CRANKING MOTOR. Check the brushes, commutators, and bearings. See that the commutators are clean. The large surges of current which occur when starting a cold engine require good contact between brushes and commutators.

(2) WIRING. Check, clean, and tighten all connections, especially the battery terminals. Care should be taken that no short circuits are present.

(3) COIL. Check coil for proper functioning by noting quality of spark.

(4) DISTRIBUTOR. Clean thoroughly, and clean or replace points. Check the points frequently. In cold weather, slightly pitted points may prevent engine from starting.

(5) SPARK PLUGS. Clean and adjust or replace, if necessary. If it is difficult to make the engine fire, reduce the gap to 0.005 inch less than that recommended for normal operation (par. 67 **b**). This will make ignition more effective at reduced voltages likely to prevail.

(6) TIMING. Check carefully. Care should be taken that the spark is not unduly advanced nor retarded.

(7) BATTERY.

(a) The efficiency of batteries decreases sharply with decreasing temperatures, and becomes practically nil at −40°F. Do not try to start the engine with the battery when it has been chilled to temperatures below −30°F until battery has been heated, unless a warm slave battery is available. See that the battery is always fully charged, with the hydrometer reading between 1.275 and 1.300. A fully charged battery will not freeze at temperatures likely to be encountered even in arctic climates, but a fully discharged battery will freeze and rupture at +5°F.

(b) Do not add water to a battery when it has been exposed to subzero temperatures unless the battery is to be charged immediately. If water is added and the battery not put on charge, the layer of water will stay at the top and freeze before it has a chance to mix with the acid.

(8) LIGHTS. Inspect the lights carefully. Check for short circuits and presence of moisture around sockets.

(9) ICE. Before every start, see that the spark plugs, wiring, or other electrical equipment is free from ice.

g. Starting and Operating Engine.

(1) INSPECT CRANKING MOTOR MECHANISM. Be sure that no heavy grease or dirt has been left on the cranking motor throwout mechanism. Heavy grease or dirt is liable to keep the gears from being meshed, or cause them to remain in mesh after the engine starts running. The latter will ruin the cranking motor and necessitate repairs.

(2) USE OF CHOKE. A full choke is necessary to secure the rich air-fuel mixture required for cold weather starting. Check the butterfly valve to see that it closes all the way, and otherwise functions properly.

(3) CARBURETOR AND FUEL PUMP. The carburetor, which will give no appreciable trouble at normal temperatures, is liable not to operate satisfactorily at low temperatures. Be sure the fuel pump has no leaky valves or diaphragm, as this will prevent the fuel pump from delivering the amount of fuel required to start the engine at low temperatures, when turning speeds are reduced to 30 to 60 revolutions per minute.

(4) AIR CLEANERS. At temperatures below 0°F do not use oil in air cleaners. The oil will congeal and prevent the easy flow of air. Wash screens in dry-cleaning solvent, dry, and replace. Ice and frost formations on the air cleaner screens can cause an abnormally high intake vacuum in the carburetor air horn hose, resulting in collapse.

(5) FUEL SYSTEM. Remove and clean sediment bulb, strainers, etc., daily. Also drain fuel tank sump daily to remove water and dirt.

(6) STARTING THE ENGINE. Observe the following precautions in addition to the normal starting procedure (par. 5 **a** and **b**).

(a) Clean ignition wires and outside of spark plugs of dirt and frost.

(b) Free distributor point arm on post and clean points.

(c) Be sure carburetor choke closes fully.

(d) Operate fuel pump hand lever to fill carburetor bowl (fig. 12).

(e) Free up engine with hand crank or use slave battery.

(f) Stop engine if no oil pressure shows on gage.

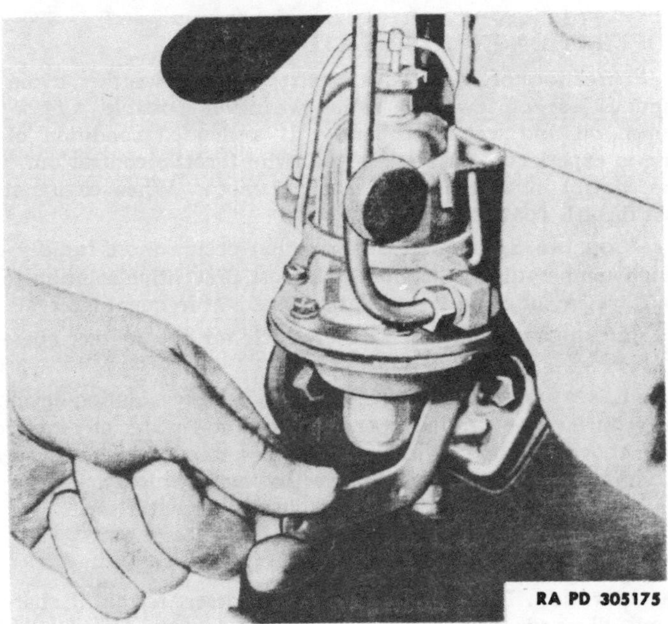

Figure 12—Fuel Pump, Hand Operation

(g) Engage clutch to warm up transmission oil before attempting to move vehicle.

(h) Check engine operation for proper condition (par. 13 **b** (22)).

h. Chassis.

(1) BRAKE BANDS. Brake bands, particularly on new vehicles, have a tendency to bind when they are very cold. Always have a blowtorch handy to warm up these parts, if they bind prior to moving, or attempting to move, the vehicle. Parking the vehicle with the brake released will eliminate most of the binding. Precaution must be taken, under these circumstances, to block the wheels or otherwise prevent movement of the vehicle.

(2) EFFECT OF LOW TEMPERATURES ON METALS. Inspect the vehicle frequently. Shock resistance of metals, or resistance against breaking, is greatly reduced at extremely low temperatures. Operation of vehicles on hard, frozen ground causes strain and jolting which will result in screws breaking, or nuts jarring loose.

(3) SPEEDOMETER CABLE. Disconnect the oil-lubricated speedometer cable at the drive end when operating the vehicle at temperatures of −30°F and below. The cable will often fail to work properly at these temperatures, and sometimes will break, due to the excessive drag caused by the high viscosity of the oil with which it is lubricated.

8. OPERATION IN HOT WEATHER.

a. **Protection of Vehicle.** In extremely hot weather avoid the continuous use of low gear ratios whenever possible. Check and replenish oil and water frequently. If a flooded condition of the engine is experienced in starting, pull the throttle control out, push choke control in, and use the cranking motor. When engine starts, adjust throttle control.

(1) COOLING SYSTEM. Rust formation occurs more rapidly during high temperatures; therefore, add rust preventive solution to the cooling system, or clean and flush the system at frequent intervals.

(2) LUBRICATION. Lubricate the vehicle for hot weather operation (par. 8).

(3) ELECTRICAL SYSTEM. Check the battery solution level frequently during hot weather operation, and add water as required to keep it above the top of the plates. If hard starting is experienced in hot, damp weather or quick changes in temperature, dry the spark plugs, wires, and both inside and outside of distributor cap.

9. OPERATION IN SAND.

a. **Operation.** Reduce tire pressures in desert terrain if character of sand demands this precaution. When operating in sand deep enough to cause the use of a lower gear, do not exceed the speed specified on the caution plate for the particular gear ratio (fig. 7).

b. **Starting the Vehicle.** When starting the vehicle in sand, gravel, or soft terrain, engage the front wheel drive (par. 5 e (1)). Release clutch pedal slowly so the wheels will not spin and "dig in," necessitating a tow or "winch-out."

c. **Clutch.** Do not attempt to "jump" or "rock" the vehicle out with a quick engagement of the clutch, particularly if a tow or winch is available. Racing the engine usually causes the wheels to "dig in" farther.

d. **Air Cleaner.** In sandy territory clean the carburetor air cleaner more often. The frequency of cleaning depends upon the severity of the sandy condition.

e. Radiator. In desert operation check the radiator coolant supply frequently, and see that the air passages of the core do not become clogged.

f. For additional information on technique of operating the vehicle in sand, refer to FM 31-25.

10. OPERATION IN LANDING.

a. Inspection. As soon as possible after completing a landing or operation in water, inspect the vehicle for water in the various units.

(1) ENGINE. Drain the engine crankcase oil. If water or sludge is found, flush the engine, using a mixture of half engine oil SAE 10 and half kerosene. Before putting in new oil, clean the valve chamber, drain and clean the oil filter, and install a new filter element.

(2) FUEL SYSTEM. Inspect the carburetor bowl, fuel strainers, fuel pump, filter, fuel tank, and lines. Clean the air cleaner and change the oil.

(3) POWER TRAIN. Inspect the front and rear axle housings, wheel bearings, transmission, and transfer case lubricant for presence of sludge. If sludge is found, renew the lubricant after cleaning the units with a mixture of half engine oil SAE 10 and half kerosene. Lubricate the propeller shaft universal joints and spring shackles to force out any water which might damage parts.

11. DECONTAMINATION.

a. Protection. For protective measures against chemical attacks and decontamination refer to FM 17-59.

Section V

FIRST ECHELON PREVENTIVE MAINTENANCE SERVICE

12. PURPOSE.

a. To ensure mechanical efficiency it is necessary that the vehicle be systematically inspected at intervals each day it is operated, also weekly, so that defects may be discovered and corrected before they result in serious damage or failure. Certain scheduled maintenance services will be performed at these designated intervals. The services set forth in this section are those performed by driver or crew before operation, during operation, at halt, and after operation and weekly.

b. Driver preventive maintenance services are listed on the back of "Driver's Trip Ticket and Preventive Maintenance Service Record," W.D. Form No. 48, to cover vehicles of all types and models. Items peculiar to specific vehicles, but not listed on W.D. Form No. 48, are covered in manual procedures under the items to which they are related. Certain items listed on the form that do not pertain to the vehicle involved are eliminated from the procedures as written into the manual. Every organization must thoroughly school each driver in performing the maintenance procedures set forth in manuals, whether they are listed specifically on W.D. Form No. 48 or not.

c. The items listed on W.D. Form No. 48 that apply to this vehicle are expanded in this manual to provide specific procedures for accomplishment of the inspections and services. These services are arranged to facilitate inspection and conserve the time of the driver, and are not necessarily in the same numerical order as shown on W.D. Form No. 48. The item numbers, however, are identical with those shown on that form.

d. The general inspection of each item applies also to any supporting member or connection, and generally includes a check to see whether the item is in good condition, correctly assembled, secure, or excessively worn.

(1) The inspection for "good condition" is usually an external visual inspection to determine whether the unit is damaged beyond safe or serviceable limits. The term "good condition" is explained further by the following: not bent or twisted, not chafed or burned, not broken or cracked, not bare or frayed, not dented or collapsed, not torn or cut.

(2) The inspection of a unit to see that it is "correctly assembled" is usually an external visual inspection to see whether or not it is in its normal assembled position in the vehicle.

(3) The inspection of a unit to determine if it is "secure" is usually an external visual examination, a hand-feel, wrench, or pry-bar check for looseness. Such an inspection should include any brackets, lock washers, lock nuts, locking wires, or cotter pins used in assembly.

(4) "Excessively worn" will be understood to mean worn, close to or beyond, serviceable limits, and likely to result in failure if not replaced before the next scheduled inspection.

e. Any defects or unsatisfactory operating characteristics beyond the scope of the first echelon to correct must be reported at the earliest opportunity to the designated individual in authority.

13. BEFORE-OPERATION SERVICE.

a. This inspection schedule is designed primarily as a check to see that the vehicle has not been tampered with or sabotaged since the After-operation Service was performed. Various combat conditions may have rendered the vehicle unsafe for operation, and it is the duty of the driver to determine whether or not the vehicle is in condition to carry out any mission to which it is assigned. This operation will not be entirely omitted, even in extreme tactical situations.

b. Procedures. Before-operation Service consists of inspecting items listed below according to the procedure described, and correcting or reporting any deficiencies. Upon completion of the service, results should be reported promptly to the designated individual in authority.

(1) ITEM 1, TAMPERING AND DAMAGE. Examine exterior of vehicle, engine, wheels, brakes, and steering control for damage by falling debris, shell fire, sabotage, or collision. If wet, dry the ignition parts to ensure easy starting.

(2) ITEM 2, FIRE EXTINGUISHER. Be sure fire extinguisher is full, nozzle is clean, and mountings secure.

(3) ITEM 3, FUEL, OIL, AND WATER. Check fuel tank, crankcase, and radiator for leaks or tampering. Add fuel, oil, or water as needed. Have value of antifreeze checked. If, during period when antifreeze is used, it becomes necessary to replenish a considerable amount of water, report unusual losses.

(4) ITEM 4, ACCESSORIES AND DRIVES. Inspect carburetor, generator, regulator, cranking motor, and water pump for loose connections and security of mountings. Inspect carburetor and water pump for leaks.

(5) ITEM 6, LEAKS, GENERAL. Look on ground under vehicle for indications of fuel, oil, water, brake fluid, or gear oil leaks. Trace leaks to source, and correct or report to higher authority.

(6) ITEM 7, ENGINE WARM-UP. Start engine, observe cranking motor action, listen for unusual noise, and note cranking speed. Idle engine only fast enough to run smoothly. Proceed immediately with following services while engine is warming up.

(7) ITEM 8, CHOKE. As engine warms, push in choke as required for smooth operation, and to prevent oil dilution.

(8) ITEM 9, INSTRUMENTS.

(a) Fuel Gage. Fuel gage should indicate approximate amount of fuel in tank.

(b) Oil Pressure Gage. Normal oil pressure should not be below 10 with engine idling, and should range from 40 to 50 at running speeds (at normal operating temperature). If gage fails to register within 30 seconds, stop engine, and correct or report to higher authority.

(c) Temperature Indicator. Temperature should rise slowly during warm-up. Normal operating temperature range is 160°F to 185°F.

(d) Ammeter. Ammeter should show high charge for short period after starting and positive (plus) reading above 12 to 15 miles per hour with lights and accessories off. Zero reading is normal with lights and accessories on.

(9) ITEM 10, HORN AND WINDSHIELD WIPERS. Sound horn, tactical situation permitting, for proper operation and tone. Check both wipers for secure attachment and normal full contact operation through full stroke.

(10) ITEM 11, GLASS AND REAR VIEW MIRROR. Clean windshield and rear view mirror and inspect for cracked, discolored, or broken glass. Adjust mirror.

(11) ITEM 12, LIGHTS AND REFLECTORS. Try switches in each position and see if lights respond. Lights and warning reflectors must be securely mounted, clean, and in good condition. Test foot control of headlight beams.

(12) ITEM 13, WHEEL AND FLANGE NUTS. Observe whether or not all wheel and flange nuts are present and tight.

(13) ITEM 14, TIRES. If time permits, test tires with gage, including spare; normal pressure is 35 pounds with tires cold. Inspect tread and carcass for cuts and bruises. Remove imbedded objects from treads.

(14) ITEM 15, SPRINGS AND SUSPENSION. Inspect springs for sagged or broken leaves, shifted leaves, and loose or missing rebound clips.

(15) ITEM 16, STEERING LINKAGE. Examine steering gear case, connecting links, and Pitman arm for security and good condition. Test steering adjustment, and free motion of steering wheel.

(16) ITEM 17, FENDERS AND BUMPERS. Examine fenders and bumpers for secure mounting and serviceable condition.

(17) ITEM 18, TOWING CONNECTIONS. Examine pintle hook for secure mounting and serviceable condition. Be sure pintle latches properly and locks securely.

(18) ITEM 19, BODY AND LOAD. Examine body and load (if any) for damage. Be sure there is a cap on front drain hole under fuel tank. See that rear drain hole cap is available in glove compartment. CAUTION: *Rear drain hole cap should be installed when about to pass through deep water.*

(19) ITEM 20, DECONTAMINATOR. Examine decontaminator for full charge and secure mountings.

(20) ITEM 21, TOOLS AND EQUIPMENT. See that tools and equipment are all present, properly stowed, and serviceable.

(21) ITEM 23, DRIVER'S PERMIT AND FORM 26. Driver must have his operator's permit on his person. See that vehicle manuals, Lubrication Guide, Form No. 26 (accident report) and W.D. AGO Form No. 478 (MWO and Major Unit Assembly Replacement Record) are present, legible, and properly stowed.

(22) ITEM 22, ENGINE OPERATION. Accelerate engine and observe for unusual noises indicating compression or exhaust leaks; worn, damaged, loose, and inadequately lubricated parts or misfiring.

(23) ITEM 25, DURING-OPERATION SERVICE. Begin the During-operation Service immediately after the vehicle is put in motion.

14. DURING-OPERATION SERVICE.

a. While vehicle is in motion, listen for any sounds such as rattles, knocks, squeals, or hums that may indicate trouble. Look for indications of trouble in cooling system, and smoke from any part of the vehicle. Be on the alert to detect any odor of overheated components or units such as generator, brakes, or clutch; check for fuel vapor from a leak in fuel system, exhaust gas, or other signs of trouble. Any time the brakes are used, gears shifted, or vehicle turned, consider this a test and notice any unsatisfactory or unusual performance. Watch the instruments frequently. Notice promptly any unusual instrument indication that may signify possible trouble in system to which the instrument applies.

b. Procedures. During-operation Service consists of observing items listed below according to the procedures following each item, and investigating any indications of serious trouble. Notice minor deficiencies to be corrected or reported at earliest opportunity, usually at next scheduled halt.

(1) ITEM 27, FOOT AND HAND BRAKES. Foot brakes must stop vehicle smoothly without side pull and within reasonable distance. There should be at least 1/3 reserve brake pedal travel and 1/2-inch free travel. Hand brake must securely hold vehicle on reasonable incline with 1/3 reserve ratchet travel. There must be 1/2-inch clearance (on cable) between relay crank and lower end of hand brake conduit.

(2) ITEM 28, CLUTCH. Clutch must operate smoothly without chatter, grabbing, or slipping. Free clutch pedal travel of three-quarter inch is normal.

(3) ITEM 29, TRANSMISSION. Gearshift mechanism must operate smoothly, and not creep out of mesh.

(4) ITEM 29, TRANSFER CASE. Gearshift mechanism must operate smoothly and not creep out of mesh.

(5) ITEM 31, ENGINE AND CONTROLS. Observe whether or not engine responds to controls, and has maximum pulling power without unusual noises, stalling, misfiring, overheating or unusual exhaust smoke. If radio noise is reported during operation of the vehicle, the driver will cooperate with the radio operator in locating the interference. See paragraph 178.

(6) ITEM 32, INSTRUMENTS. During operation observe the readings of all instruments frequently to see if they are indicating properly.

(a) Fuel Gage. Fuel gage must register approximate amount of fuel in tank.

(b) Oil Pressure Gage. Oil pressure gage should register 10 with engine running idle, and 40 to 50 at operating speeds.

(c) Temperature Indicator. Temperature indicator should show a temperature of 160°F to 185°F after warm-up under normal conditions.

(d) Speedometer. Speedometer should show speed of vehicle without noise or fluctuation of indicator needle. Odometer should register accumulating trip and total mileage.

(e) Ammeter. Ammeter should show zero reading with lights on, zero or positive (plus) charge with lights off, and slightly higher positive (plus) charge for short time immediately after starting.

(7) ITEM 33, STEERING GEAR. Observe steering for excessive pulling of vehicle to either side, wandering, or shimmy.

(8) ITEM 34, CHASSIS. Listen for unusual noises from wheel or axles.

(9) ITEM 35, BODY. Observe body for sagging springs, loose or torn top or windshield cover, if in use.

15. AT-HALT SERVICE.

a. At-halt Service may be regarded as the minimum maintenance procedure, and should be performed under all tactical conditions, even though more extensive maintenance services must be slighted or omitted altogether.

b. Procedures. At-halt Service consists of investigating any deficiencies noted during operation, inspecting items listed below according to the procedures following the items, and correcting any deficiencies found. Deficiencies not corrected should be reported promptly to the designated individual in authority.

FIRST ECHELON PREVENTIVE MAINTENANCE SERVICE

(1) ITEM 38, FUEL, OIL AND WATER. Check fuel supply, oil, and coolant; add, as required, for complete operation of vehicle to the next refueling point. If, during period when antifreeze is used, an abnormal amount of water is required to refill radiator, have coolant tested with hydrometer, and add antifreeze if required.

(2) ITEM 39, TEMPERATURES. Feel each brake drum and wheel hub, transmission, transfer case, and front and rear axles for overheating. Examine gear cases for excessive oil leaks.

(3) ITEM 40, AXLE AND TRANSFER CASE VENTS. Observe whether axle and transfer case vents are present, and see that they are not damaged or clogged.

(4) ITEM 41, PROPELLER SHAFT. Inspect propeller shaft for looseness, damage, or oil leaks.

(5) ITEM 42, SPRINGS. Look for broken spring leaves or loose clips and U-bolts.

(6) ITEM 43, STEERING LINKAGE. Examine steering control mechanism and linkage for damage or looseness. Investigate any irregularities noted during operation.

(7) ITEM 44, WHEEL AND FLANGE NUTS. Observe whether or not all wheel and axle flange nuts are present and tight.

(8) ITEM 45, TIRES. Inspect tires, including spare, for flats or damage, and for cuts or foreign material imbedded in tread.

(9) ITEM 46, LEAKS, GENERAL. Check around engine and on ground beneath the vehicle for excessive leaks. Trace to source, and correct cause or report to higher authority.

(10) ITEM 47, ACCESSORIES AND BELTS. See that fan, water pump and generator are securely mounted, that fan belt is adjusted to 1-inch deflection, and is not badly frayed. If radio noise during operation of the engine was observed, examine all radio noise suppression capacitors, at coil, ignition and starting switches, generator, regulator, and radio terminal box; suppressors at spark plugs and distributor, and all bond straps for damage, and loose mountings or connections.

(11) ITEM 48, AIR CLEANER. If dusty or sandy conditions have been encountered, examine oil sump for excessive dirt. Service if required. CAUTION: *Do not apply oil to element after cleaning.*

(12) ITEM 49, FENDERS AND BUMPERS. Inspect fenders and bumpers for looseness or damage.

(13) ITEM 50, TOWING CONNECTIONS. Inspect pintle hook and trailer light socket for serviceability.

(14) ITEM 51, BODY LOAD AND TARPAULIN. Inspect vehicle and trailed vehicle loads for shifting; see that tarpaulins are properly secured and not damaged.

(15) ITEM 52, APPEARANCE AND GLASS. Clean windshield, mirror, light lenses, and inspect vehicle for damage.

16. AFTER-OPERATION AND WEEKLY SERVICE.

a. After-operation Service is particularly important because at this time the driver inspects his vehicle to detect any deficiencies that may have developed, and corrects those he is permitted to handle. He should report promptly, to the designated individual in authority, the results of his inspection. If this schedule is performed thoroughly, the vehicle should be ready to roll again on short notice. The Before-operation Service, with a few exceptions, is then necessary only to ascertain whether the vehicle is in the same condition in which it was left upon completion of the After-operation Service. The After-operation Service should never be entirely omitted, even in extreme tactical situations, but may be reduced, if necessary, to the bare fundamental services outlined for the At-halt Service.

b. Procedures. When performing the After-operation Service the driver must remember and consider any irregularities noticed during the day in the Before-operation, During-operation, and At-halt Services. The After-operation Service consists of inspecting and servicing the following items. Those items of the After-operation Service that are marked by an asterisk (*) require additional Weekly Service, the procedures for which are indicated in step *(b)* of each applicable item.

(1) ITEM 54, FUEL, OIL, AND WATER. Check coolant and oil levels, and add as needed. Fill fuel tank. Refill spare cans. During period when antifreeze is used, have hydrometer test made of coolant if loss from boiling or other cause has been considerable. Add antifreeze with water if required.

(2) ITEM 55, ENGINE OPERATION. Listen for miss, backfire, noise, or vibration that might indicate worn parts, loose mountings, faulty fuel mixture, or faulty ignition.

(3) ITEM 56, INSTRUMENTS. Inspect all instruments to see that they are securely connected, and not damaged.

(4) ITEM 57, HORN AND WINDSHIELD WIPERS. Test horn for sound, if tactical situation permits. See that horn is securely mounted and properly connected. Operate both windshield wipers. See that blades contact the glass effectively throughout full stroke.

(5) ITEM 58, GLASS AND REAR VIEW MIRROR. Clean glass of windshield and rear view mirror. Examine for secure mounting and damage.

(6) ITEM 59, LIGHTS AND REFLECTORS. Observe whether or not lights operate properly with the switch in "ON" positions, and go out when switch is off. See that stop light operates properly. Clean lenses and warning reflectors.

(7) ITEM 60, FIRE EXTINGUISHER. Be sure fire extinguisher is full, nozzle is clean, and that extinguisher is mounted securely.

(8) ITEM 61, DECONTAMINATOR. Examine decontaminator for good condition and secure mounting.

FIRST ECHELON PREVENTIVE MAINTENANCE SERVICE

(9) ITEM 62, *BATTERY.

(a) See that battery is clean, securely mounted, and not leaking. Inspect electrolyte level, which should be ½ inch above plates with caps in place and vents open. Clean cables as required.

(b) Weekly. Clean top of battery. Remove battery caps, and add water to ½ inch above plates. (Use distilled water if available; if not use clean, drinkable water.) CAUTION: *Do not overfill.* Clean posts and terminals if corroded, and apply light coat of grease. Tighten terminals as needed. Tighten hold-down assembly. Clean battery carrier if corroded.

(10) ITEM 63, *ACCESSORIES AND BELTS.

(a) Test fan belt for deflection of 1 inch. Examine belt for good condition; it must not be frayed. Timing hole cover must be closed and tightened.

(b) Weekly. Tighten all accessories such as carburetor, generator, regulator, cranking motor, fan, water pump, and hose connections; examine fan belt for fraying, wear, cracking, or presence of oil.

(11) ITEM 64, *ELECTRICAL WIRING.

(a) See that all ignition wiring and accessible low voltage wiring is in good condition, clean, correctly and securely assembled and mounted.

(b) Weekly. Tighten all loose wiring connections or electrical unit mountings. Pay particular attention to radio noise suppression units such as: capacitors, bond straps, and spark plug and distributor suppressors.

(12) ITEM 65, *AIR CLEANER.

(a) Examine oil in air cleaner oil cup to see that it is at proper level, and not excessively dirty. Clean element and refill oil cup as required. CAUTION: *Do not apply oil to element after cleaning.*

(b) Weekly. Remove, clean, and dry air cleaner element and oil cup. Fill cup to indicated oil level (approximately ⅝ qt). Do not apply oil to element after cleaning.

(13) ITEM 66, *FUEL FILTERS.

(a) Examine fuel filter for leaks.

(b) Weekly. Remove plug from bottom of dash-mounted fuel filter. Allow water and sediment to drain out. Be sure plug is replaced tightly, and does not leak.

(14) ITEM 67, ENGINE CONTROLS. Examine engine controls for wear or disconnected linkage.

(15) ITEM 68, *TIRES.

(a) Inspect tires for cuts or abnormal tread wear; remove foreign bodies from tread; inflate to 35 pounds when tires are cold.

(b) Weekly. Replace badly worn or otherwise unserviceable tires.

(16) ITEM 69, *SPRINGS.

(a) Examine springs for sag, broken or shifted leaves, loose or missing rebound clips, or shackles.

(b) Weekly. Aline springs, and tighten U-bolts and shackles as required.

1/4-TON 4 x 4 TRUCK (WILLYS-OVERLAND MODEL MB and FORD MODEL GPW)

(17) ITEM 70, STEERING LINKAGE. Examine steering wheel column, gear case, Pitman arm, drag link, tie rod, and steering arm to see if they are bent, loose, or inadequately lubricated.

(18) ITEM 71, PROPELLER SHAFT. Inspect propeller shaft and universal joints for loose connections, lubrication leaks, or damage.

(19) ITEM 72, *AXLE AND TRANSFER VENTS.

(a) See that axle and transfer case vents are in good condition, clean, and secure.

(b) Weekly. Remove, clean, and replace vents.

(20) ITEM 73, LEAKS, GENERAL. Check under hood and beneath the vehicle for indications of fuel, oil, water, or brake fluid leaks.

(21) ITEM 74, GEAR OIL LEVELS. After units have cooled, inspect differential transmission and transfer unit lubricant levels. Lubricant should be level with bottom of filler hole. Observe gear cases for leaks.

(22) ITEM 76, FENDERS AND BUMPERS. Fenders and bumpers must be in good condition and secure.

(23) ITEM 77, *TOWING CONNECTIONS.

(a) Inspect pintle hook and towed-load connections for looseness or damage.

(b) Weekly. Tighten pintle hook mounting bolts, and lubricate pintle hook as required.

(24) ITEM 78, BODY AND TARPAULINS. Inspect body, top, and windshield cover for damage and proper stowage. Make sure rear drain below fuel tank is open, and that cap is in glove compartment.

(25) ITEM 82, *TIGHTEN.

(a) Tighten any loose wheel, axle drive flange, and spring U-bolt nuts.

(b) Weekly. Tighten all vehicle assembly or mounting nuts or screws that inspection indicates require tightening.

(26) ITEM 83, *LUBRICATE AS NEEDED.

(a) Lubricate spring shackles and steering linkage, if lubrication is needed.

(b) Weekly. Lubricate points indicated on current vehicle Lubrication Guide as requiring weekly attention, also points that experience and operating conditions indicate need lubrication. Observe latest lubrication directives.

(27) ITEM 84, *CLEAN ENGINE AND VEHICLE.

(a) Clean dirt and trash from inside of body. Keep sump under fuel tank cleaned of dirt and water. Remove excessive dirt or grease from exterior of the engine.

(b) Weekly. Wash vehicle if possible. If not possible, wipe off thoroughly; clean engine.

(28) ITEM 85, TOOLS AND EQUIPMENT. Check to see that all tools and equipment assigned to vehicle are present and secure.

Section VI

LUBRICATION

17. LUBRICATION GUIDE.

a. War Department Lubrication Guide No. 501 (figs. 13 and 14) prescribes lubrication maintenance for the $\frac{1}{4}$-ton 4 x 4 truck.

b. A Lubrication Guide is placed on or is issued with each vehicle and is to be carried with it at all times. In the event the vehicle is received without a Guide, the using arm shall immediately requisition a replacement from the Commanding Officer, Fort Wayne Ordnance Depot, Detroit 32, Mich.

c. Lubrication instructions on the Guide are binding on all echelons of maintenance and there shall be no deviations from these instructions.

d. Service intervals specified on the Guide are for normal operation conditions. Reduce these intervals under extreme conditions such as excessively high or low temperatures, prolonged periods of high speed, continued operation in sand or dust, immersion in water, or exposure to moisture, any one of which may quickly destroy the protective qualities of the lubricant and require servicing in order to prevent malfunctioning or damage to the materiel.

e. Lubricants are prescribed in the "Key" in accordance with three temperature ranges; above +32°F, +32°F to 0°F, and below 0°F. Determine the time to change grades of lubricants by maintaining a close check on operation of the vehicle during the approach to change-over periods. Be particularly observant when starting the engine. Sluggish starting is an indication of thickened lubricants and the signal to change to grades prescribed for the next lower temperature range. Ordinarily it will be necessary to change grades of lubricants *only when air temperatures are consistently in the next higher or lower range*, unless malfunctioning occurs sooner due to lubricants being too thin or too heavy.

18. DETAILED LUBRICATION INSTRUCTIONS.

a. Lubrication Equipment. Each piece of materiel is supplied with lubrication equipment adequate to maintain the materiel. Be sure to clean this equipment both before and after use. Operate lubricating guns carefully and in such manner as to insure a proper distribution of the lubricant.

b. Points of Application.

(1) Red circles surrounding lubrication fittings, grease cups, oilers and oil holes make them readily identifiable on the vehicle. Wipe clean such lubricators and the surrounding surface before lubricant is applied.

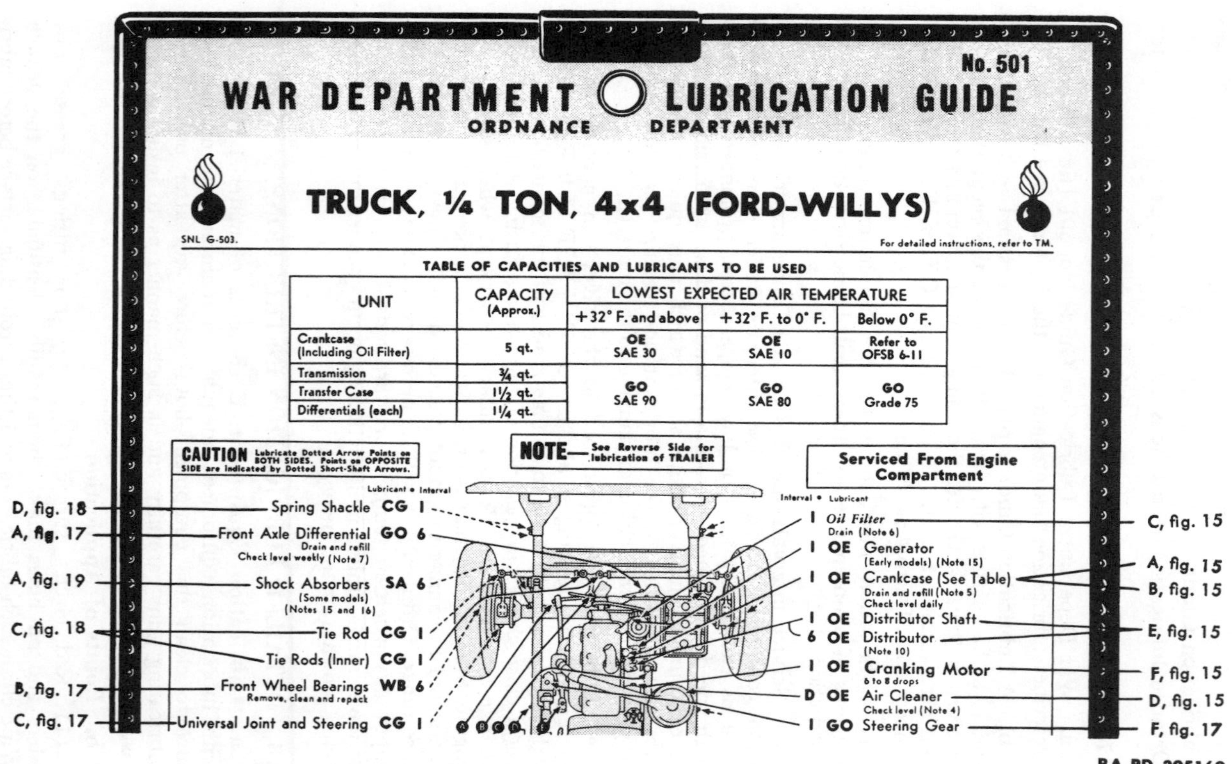

UNIT	CAPACITY (Approx.)	LOWEST EXPECTED AIR TEMPERATURE		
		+32° F. and above	+32° F. to 0° F.	Below 0° F.
Crankcase (Including Oil Filter)	5 qt.	OE SAE 30	OE SAE 10	Refer to OFSB 6-11
Transmission	¾ qt.	GO SAE 90	GO SAE 80	GO Grade 75
Transfer Case	1½ qt.			
Differentials (each)	1¼ qt.			

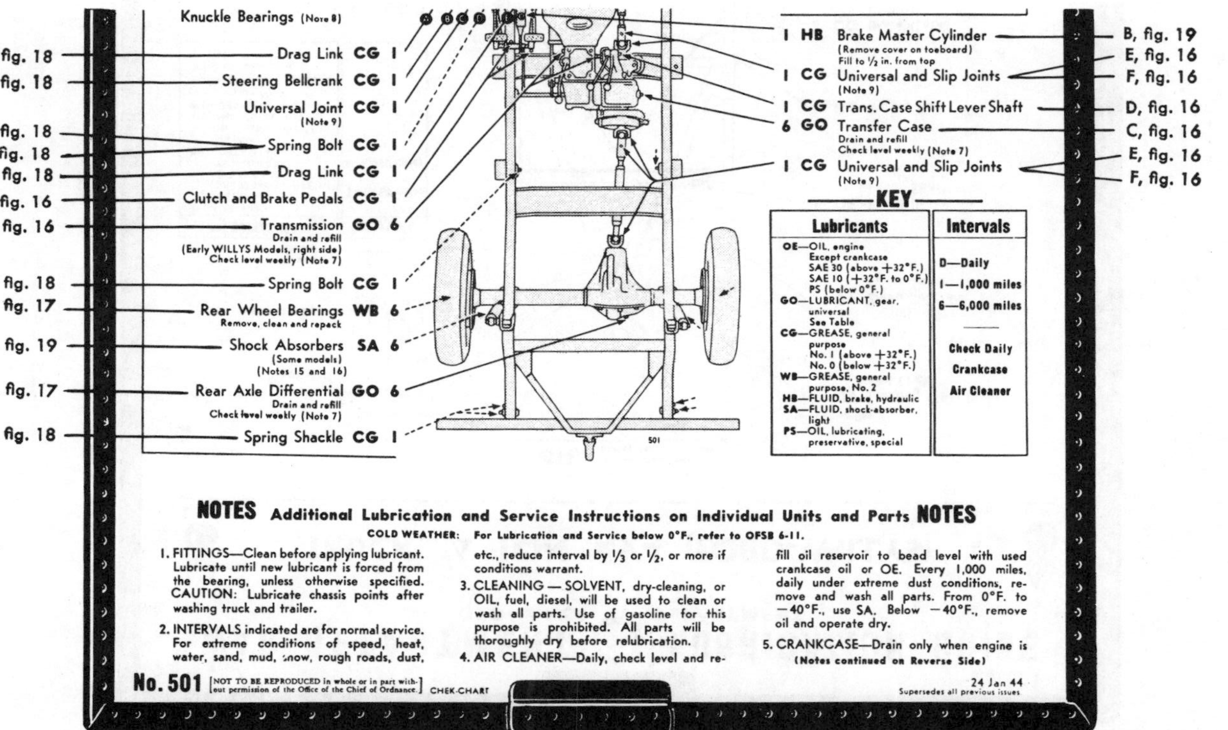

KEY

Lubricants	Intervals
OE—OIL, engine Except crankcase SAE 30 (above +32°F.) SAE 10 (+32°F. to 0°F.) PS (below 0°F.) GO—LUBRICANT, gear, universal See Table CG—GREASE, general purpose No. 1 (above +32°F.) No. 0 (below +32°F.) WB—GREASE, general purpose, No. 2 HB—FLUID, brake, hydraulic SA—FLUID, shock-absorber, light PS—OIL, lubricating, preservative, special	D—Daily 1—1,000 miles 6—6,000 miles Check Daily Crankcase Air Cleaner

NOTES Additional Lubrication and Service Instructions on Individual Units and Parts **NOTES**

COLD WEATHER: For Lubrication and Service below 0°F., refer to OFSB 6-11.

1. FITTINGS—Clean before applying lubricant. Lubricate until new lubricant is forced from the bearing, unless otherwise specified. CAUTION: Lubricate chassis points after washing truck and trailer.
2. INTERVALS indicated are for normal service. For extreme conditions of speed, heat, water, sand, mud, snow, rough roads, dust, etc., reduce interval by 1/3 or 1/2, or more if conditions warrant.
3. CLEANING — SOLVENT, dry-cleaning, or OIL, fuel, diesel, will be used to clean or wash all parts. Use of gasoline for this purpose is prohibited. All parts will be thoroughly dry before relubrication.
4. AIR CLEANER—Daily, check level and refill oil reservoir to bead level with used crankcase oil or OE. Every 1,000 miles, daily under extreme dust conditions, remove and wash all parts. From 0°F. to −40°F., use SA. Below −40°F., remove oil and operate dry.
5. CRANKCASE—Drain only when engine is

(Notes continued on Reverse Side)

No. 501 [NOT TO BE REPRODUCED in whole or in part without permission of the Office of the Chief of Ordnance.] CHEK-CHART

24 Jan 44
Supersedes all previous issues

Figure 13—Lubrication Guide—Truck, 1/4-Ton, 4 x 4 (Ford-Willys)

RA PD 305160B

¼-TON 4 x 4 TRUCK (WILLYS-OVERLAND MODEL MB and FORD MODEL GPW)

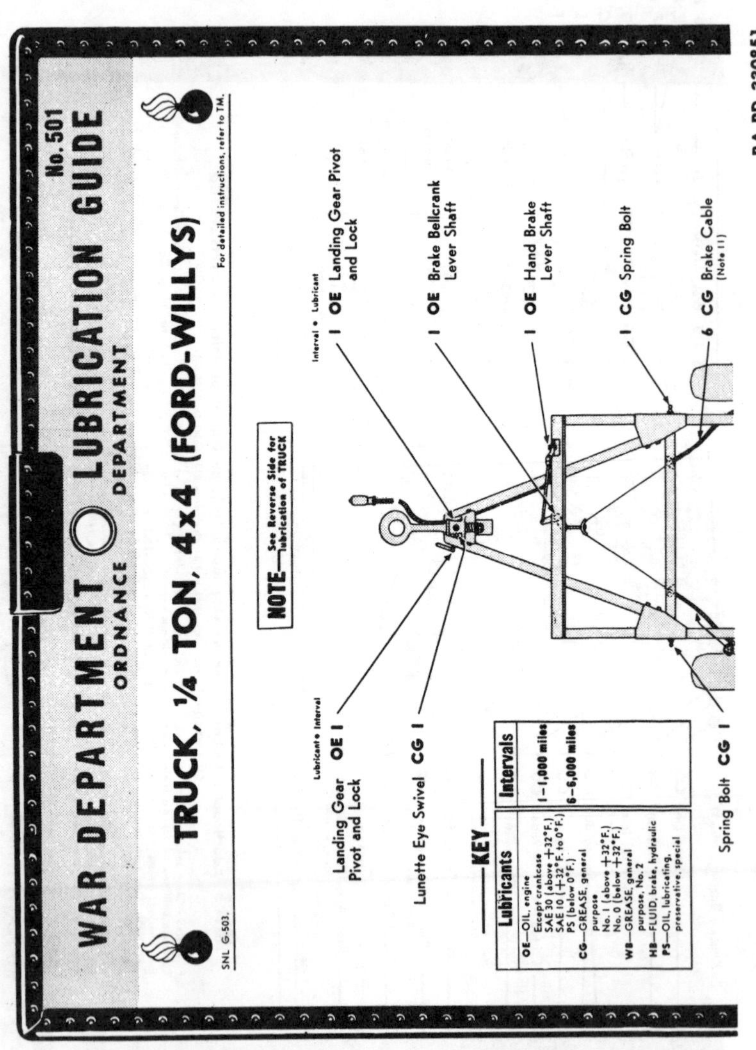

RA PD 330851

LUBRICATION

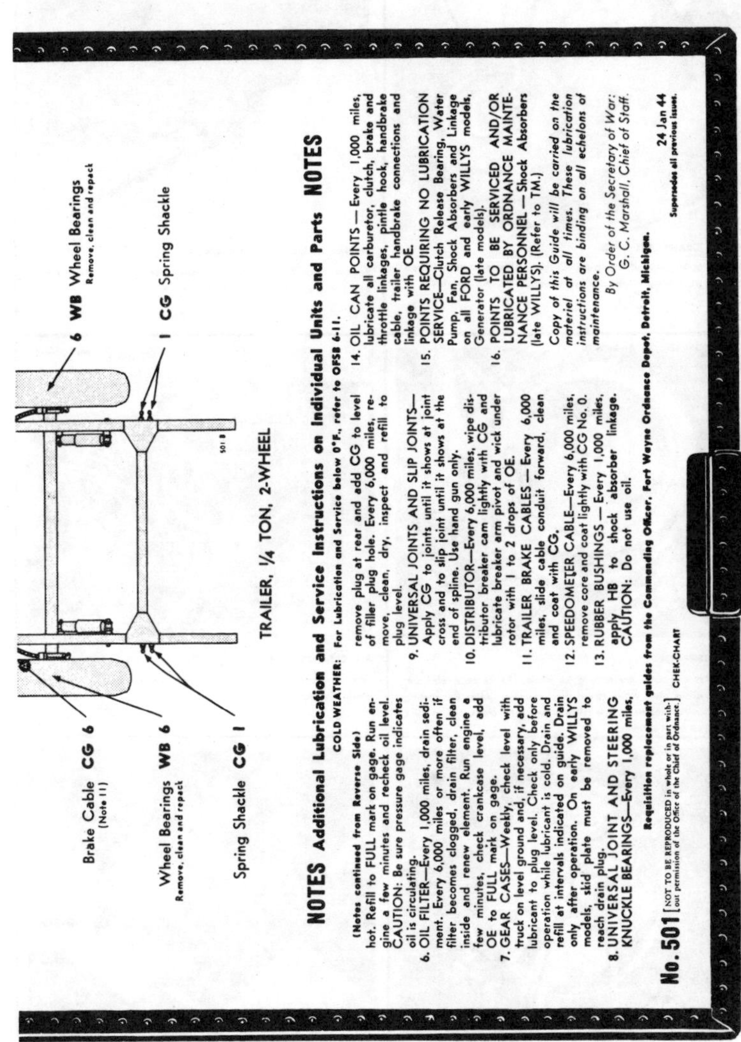

NOTES Additional Lubrication and Service Instructions on Individual Units and Parts NOTES

COLD WEATHER: For Lubrication and Service below 0°F., refer to OFSB 6-11.

(Notes continued from Reverse Side)

hot. Refill to FULL mark on gage. Run engine a few minutes and recheck oil level. CAUTION: Be sure pressure gage indicates oil is circulating.

6. OIL FILTER—Every 1,000 miles, drain sediment. Every 6,000 miles or more often if filter becomes clogged, drain filter, clean inside and renew element. Run engine a few minutes, check crankcase level, add OE to FULL mark on gage.
7. GEAR CASES—Weekly, check level with truck on level ground and, if necessary, add lubricant to plug level. Check only before operation while lubricant is cold. Drain and refill at intervals indicated on guide. Drain only after operation. On early WILLYS models, skid plate must be removed to reach drain plug.
8. UNIVERSAL JOINT AND STEERING KNUCKLE BEARINGS—Every 1,000 miles, remove plug at rear and add CG to level of filler plug hole. Every 6,000 miles, remove, clean, dry, inspect and refill to plug level.
9. UNIVERSAL JOINTS AND SLIP JOINTS—Apply CG to joints until it shows at joint cross and to slip joint until it shows at the end of spline. Use hand gun only.
10. DISTRIBUTOR—Every 6,000 miles, wipe distributor breaker cam lightly with CG and lubricate breaker arm pivot and wick under rotor with 1 to 2 drops of OE.
11. TRAILER BRAKE CABLES—Every 6,000 miles, slide cable conduit forward, clean and coat with CG.
12. SPEEDOMETER CABLE—Every 6,000 miles, remove core and coat lightly with CG No. 0.
13. RUBBER BUSHINGS—Every 1,000 miles, apply HB to shock absorber linkage. CAUTION: Do not use oil.
14. OIL CAN POINTS—Every 1,000 miles, lubricate all carburetor, clutch, brake and throttle linkages, pintle hook, handbrake cable, trailer handbrake connections and linkage with OE.
15. POINTS REQUIRING NO LUBRICATION SERVICE—Clutch Release Bearing, Water Pump, Fan, Shock Absorbers and Linkage on all FORD and early WILLYS models, Generator (late models).
16. POINTS TO BE SERVICED AND/OR LUBRICATED BY ORDNANCE MAINTENANCE PERSONNEL—Shock Absorbers (late WILLYS). (Refer to TM.)

Copy of this Guide will be carried on the materiel at all times. These lubrication instructions are binding on all echelons of maintenance.

By Order of the Secretary of War:
G. C. Marshall, Chief of Staff.

Requisition replacement guides from the Commanding Officer, Fort Wayne Ordnance Depot, Detroit, Michigan.

No. 501 [NOT TO BE REPRODUCED in whole or in part without permission of the Office of the Chief of Ordnance.] CHEK-CHART

24 Jan 44
Supersedes all previous issues.

RA PD 330851B

Figure 14—Lubrication Guide—Trailer, 1/4-Ton, 2-wheel

ENGINE CRANKCASE—OE
Oil level indicator in oil filler pipe. Check level at least daily. Keep oil up to FULL mark. Capacity five quarts; refill four quarts.

ENGINE CRANKCASE DRAINING—
Remove drain plug to drain. At least once a year, remove the oil pan and clean floating oil intake screen.

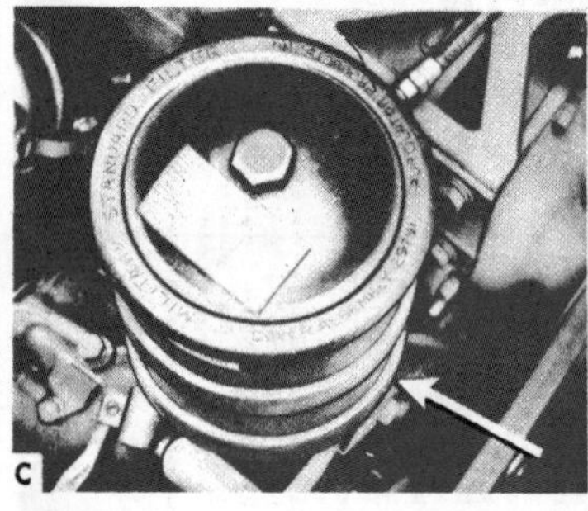

OIL FILTER—OE
One filter—Remove drain plug to drain. To replace element, remove drain plug, filter cover then element. After completing installation run engine a few minutes and refill crankcase to FULL mark on oil level indicator.

AIR CLEANER—OE
One air cleaner. Clean cleaner and refill reservoir to indicated level. Capacity ⅝ quart.

DISTRIBUTOR—OE
One distributor. Total places—four. Use oil can for oiler and lubricate sparingly wick and post; grease cam lightly.

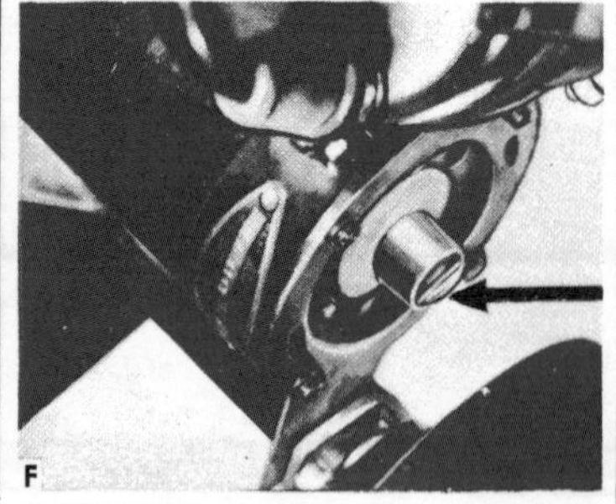

CRANKING MOTOR—OE
Total oilers—one. Use oil can, push aside oil hole cover. Oil and replace cover.

RA PD 305166

Figure 15—Engine Lubrication Points

LUBRICATION

CLUTCH AND BRAKE PEDAL SHAFT—CG

One pedal shaft. Total fittings—two. Use pressure gun on fittings until grease shows.

TRANSMISSION—GO

One transmission. Total plugs—two (filler and drain). Use gear oil pump. Drain and refill to bottom of filler plug hole. Capacity ¾ quart.

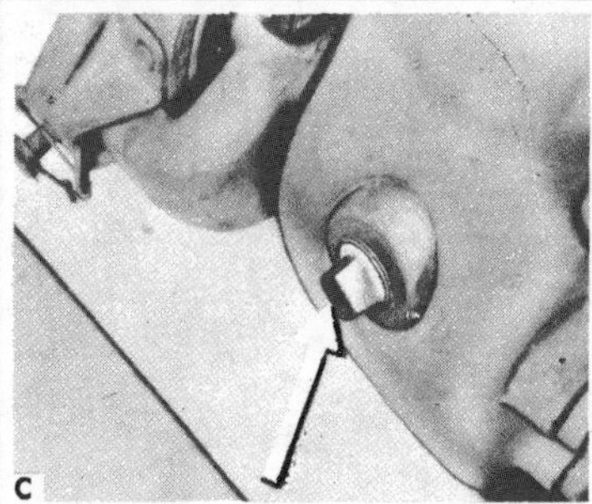

TRANSFER CASE—GO

One transfer case. Total plugs—two (filler and drain). Use gear oil pump. Drain and refill to bottom of filler plug hole. Capacity 1½ quarts.

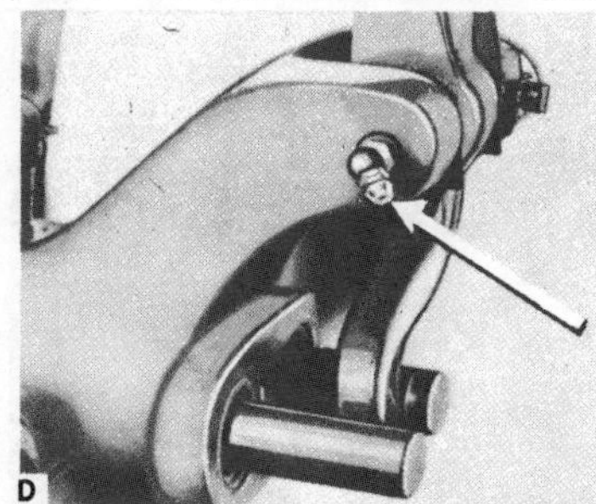

TRANSFER CASE SHIFT LEVER SHAFT—CG

One shift lever shaft. Total fittings—one. Use pressure gun on fitting until grease shows.

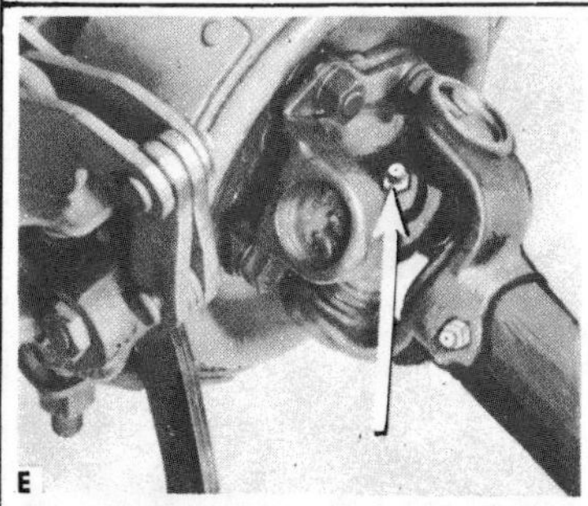

PROPELLER SHAFT UNIVERSAL JOINTS—CG

Four universal joints. Total fittings—four. Use pressure gun (hand) with adaptor. CAUTION: Do not use high pressure grease gun because of damage to seals.

PROPELLER SHAFT SLIP JOINT—CG

Two slip joints. Total fittings—two. Use pressure gun on fittings until grease shows.

RA PD 305167

Figure 16—Pedal Shafts and Power Train Lubrication Points

¼-TON 4 x 4 TRUCK (WILLYS-OVERLAND MODEL MB and FORD MODEL GPW)

AXLE HOUSINGS—GO

Two axle housings. Total plugs—four (filler and drain). Use gear oil pump. Drain and refill to bottom of filler plug hole. Capacity 1¼ quarts.

WHEEL BEARINGS—WB

Four wheels. Total bearings—eight. Use bearing lubricator or hand pack thoroughly. Apply grease also around outside of cage and rollers. Clean out wheel hub, inspect bearing races, put three ounces of grease in each hub.

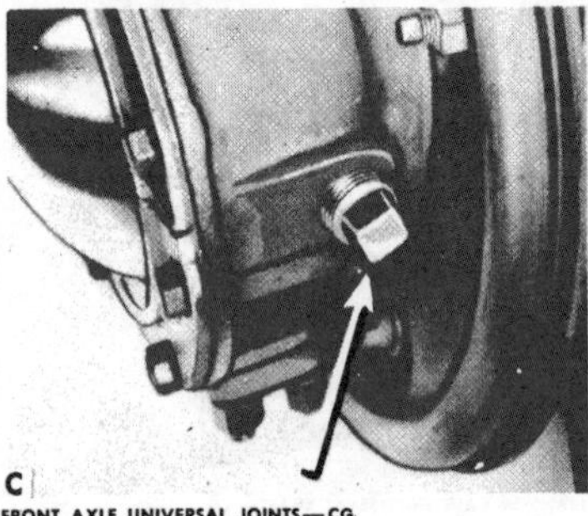

FRONT AXLE UNIVERSAL JOINTS—CG

Two universal joints. Total plugs—two. Use pressure gun (hand) and fill housing slowly to level of filler plug hole.

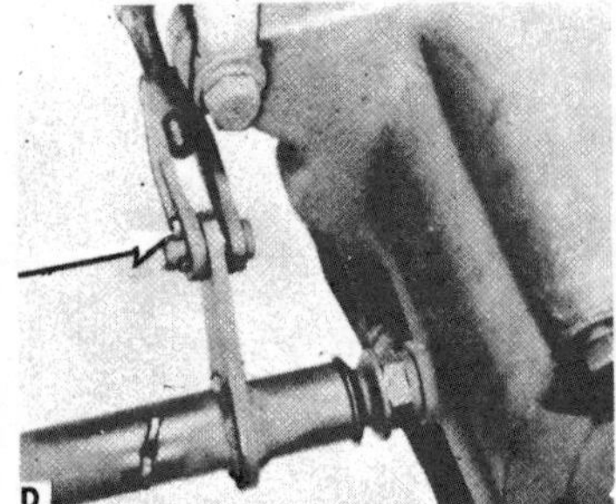

LINKAGE CLEVIS PINS—OE

All clevis pins and hood and windshield catches. Use oil can and apply in proper quantity.

PINTLE HOOK—OE

One hook—With an oil can lubricate pins, connections and sliding surfaces.

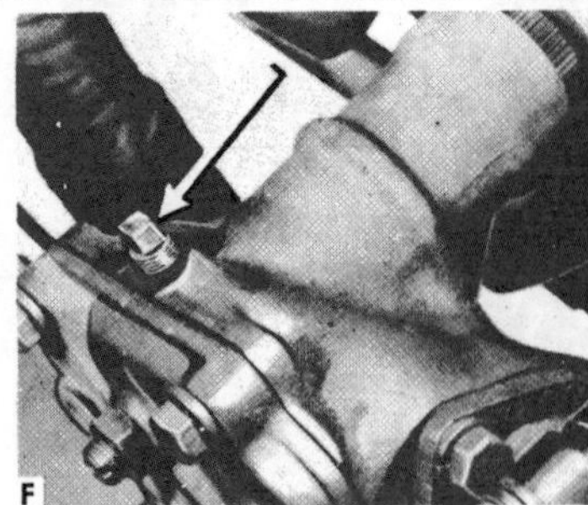

STEERING GEAR HOUSING—GO

One housing. Total plugs—one. Use pressure gun (hand) and fill housing slowly until full.

RA PD 305168

Figure 17—Axle, Wheel, Pintle, and Steering Gear Housing Lubrication Points

LUBRICATION

STEERING DRAG LINK—CG

One drag link. Total fittings—two. Use pressure gun on fittings until grease shows.

STEERING BELLCRANK—CG

One bellcrank. Total fittings—one. Use pressure gun on fittings until grease shows.

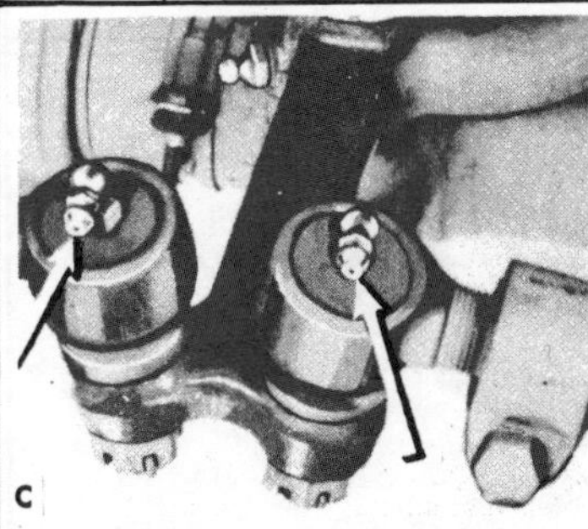

STEERING TIE ROD—CG

Two tie rods. Total fittings—four. Use pressure gun on fittings until grease shows.

SPRING SHACKLES—CG

Four spring shackles. Total fittings—eight. Use pressure gun on fittings until new grease shows.

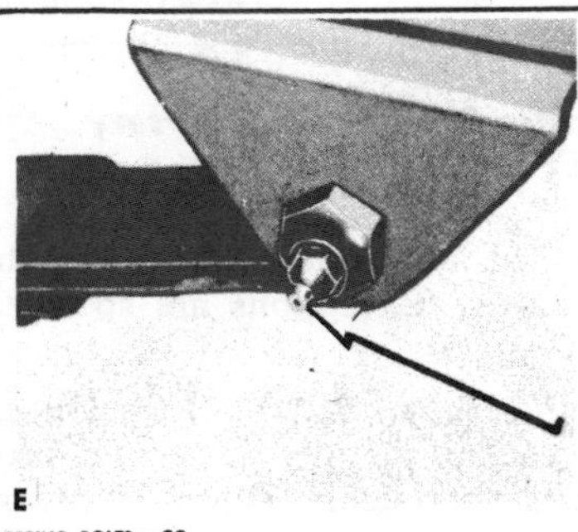

SPRING BOLTS—CG

Four spring bolts. Total fittings—four. Use pressure gun on fittings until grease shows.

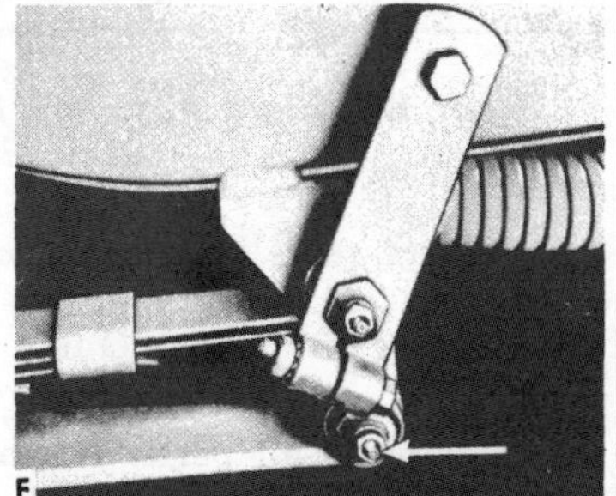

TORQUE REACTION SPRING BOLT—CG

One spring bolt. Total fittings—one (on vehicles equipped with this spring on the left front spring). Use pressure gun on fitting until grease shows.

RA PD 305169

Figure 18—Steering Gear and Spring Lubrication Points

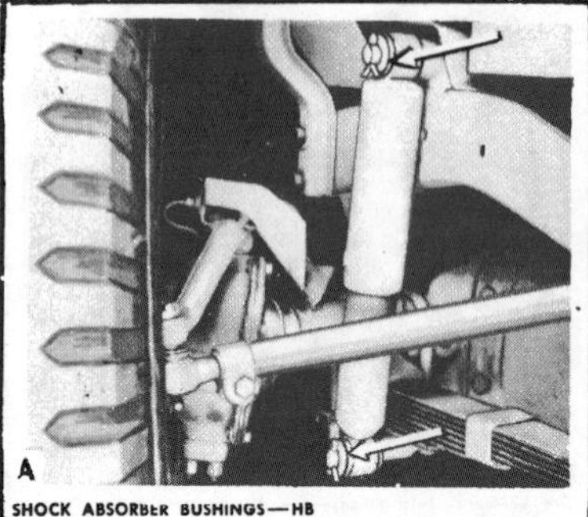

SHOCK ABSORBER BUSHINGS—HB
Four shock absorbers. Total rubber bushings—eight. Apply brake fluid to preserve rubber.

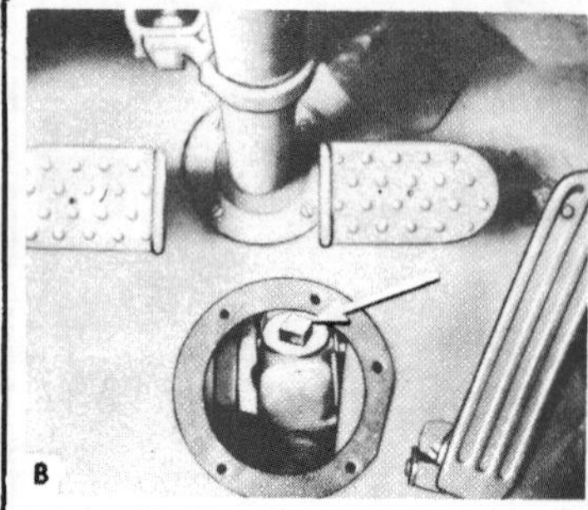

BRAKE SYSTEM—HB
Clean top of brake master cylinder and remove plug. Fill reservo to ¼ inch from top.

BATTERY—CG
One battery. Total terminals—two. Check condition. Remove and clean if necessary. Coat with grease. Check water level to keep it above plates.

RA PD 305170

Figure 19—Shock Absorber, Master Cylinder, and Battery Lubrication Points

(2) Where relief valves are provided, apply new lubricant until the old lubricant is forced from the vent. Exceptions are specified in notes on the Lubrication Guide.

c. Cleaning. Use SOLVENT, dry-cleaning, or OIL, fuel, Diesel, to clean or wash all parts. Use of gasoline for this purpose is prohibited. After washing, dry all parts thoroughly before applying lubricant.

d. Lubrication Notes on Individual Units and Parts. The following instructions supplement those notes on the Lubrication Guide which pertain to lubrication and service of individual units and parts. All note references in the Guide itself are to the paragraph below having the corresponding number.

LUBRICATION

(1) FITTINGS. Clean before applying lubricant. Lubricate until new lubricant is forced from the bearing, unless otherwise specified. CAUTION: *Lubricate chassis points after washing truck and trailer.*

(2) INTERVALS. Intervals indicated are for normal service. For extreme conditions of speed, heat, water, sand, mud, snow, rough roads, dust, etc., reduce interval by one-third or one-half, or more if conditions warrant.

(3) CLEANING. SOLVENT, dry-cleaning, or OIL, fuel, Diesel, will be used to clean or wash all parts. Use of gasoline for this purpose is prohibited. All parts will be thoroughly dry before relubrication.

(4) AIR CLEANER. Daily, check level and refill oil reservoir to bead level with used crankcase oil or OIL, engine, SAE 30 above +32°F or SAE 10 from +32°F to 0°F. Every 1,000 miles, daily under extreme dust conditions, remove and wash all parts. From 0°F to −40°F, use FLUID, shock-absorber, light. Below −40°F, remove oil and operate dry.

(5) CRANKCASE. Drain only when engine is hot. Refill to "FULL" mark on gage. Run engine a few minutes and recheck oil level. CAUTION: *Be sure pressure gage indicates oil is circulating.*

(6) OIL FILTER. Every 1,000 miles, drain sediment. Every 6,000 miles or more often if filter becomes clogged, drain filter, clean inside and renew element. Run engine a few minutes, check crankcase level, add OIL, engine, to "FULL" mark on gage. (SAE 30 above +32°F; SAE 10 from +32°F to 0°F; below 0°F, refer to OFSB 6-11.)

(7) GEAR CASES. Weekly, check level with truck on level ground and, if necessary, add lubricant to plug level. Check only before operation while lubricant is cold. Drain and refill at intervals indicated on Guide. Drain only after operation. On early Willys models, skid plate must be removed to reach drain plug.

(8) UNIVERSAL JOINT AND STEERING KNUCKLE BEARINGS. Every 1,000 miles, remove plug at rear and add GREASE, general purpose, No. 1 above +32°F or No. 0 below +32°F, to level of filler plug hole. Every 6,000 miles, remove, clean, dry, inspect and refill to plug level.

(a) Remove brake tube and brake backing plate screws. This permits the removal of the axle spindle, the complete axle shaft, and the universal joint assembly. Care should be taken not to injure the outer oil seal assembly in the housing.

(b) Wash the axle shaft and universal joint thoroughly in SOLVENT, dry-cleaning, and dry.

(c) Clean and repack upper and lower steering spindle bearings within the universal housing and reassemble entire unit.

(9) UNIVERSAL JOINTS AND SLIP JOINTS. Apply GREASE, general purpose, No. 1, above +32°F, or No. 0 below +32°F, to joints until it shows at joint cross, and to slip joint until it shows at the end of spline. Use hand gun only.

¼-TON 4 x 4 TRUCK (WILLYS-OVERLAND MODEL MB and FORD MODEL GPW)

(10) DISTRIBUTOR. Every 6,000 miles, wipe distributor breaker cam lightly with GREASE, general purpose, No. 1, above +32°F or No. 0, below +32°F, and lubricate breaker arm pivot and wick under rotor with 1 to 2 drops of OIL, engine, SAE 30 above +32°F; SAE 10 from +32°F to 0°F; OIL, lubricating, preservative, special, below 0°F.

(11) TRAILER BRAKE CABLES. Every 6,000 miles, slide cable conduit forward, clean and coat with GREASE, general purpose, No. 1 above +32°F and No. 0 below +32°F.

(12) SPEEDOMETER CABLE. Every 6,000 miles, remove core and coat lightly with GREASE, general purpose, No. 0.

(13) RUBBER BUSHINGS. Every 1,000 miles, apply FLUID, brake, hydraulic, to shock absorber linkage. CAUTION: *Do not use oil.*

(14) OILCAN POINTS. Every 1,000 miles, lubricate all carburetor, clutch, brake and throttle linkages, pintle hook and hand brake cable with OIL, engine, SAE 30, above +32°F; SAE 10, +32°F to 0°F; OIL, lubricating, preservative, special, below 0°F.

(15) POINTS REQUIRING NO LUBRICATION SERVICE. These are the clutch release bearing, water pump, fan, shock absorbers and linkage on all Ford and early Willys models, generator (late models), speedometer cable.

(16) POINTS TO BE SERVICED AND/OR LUBRICATED BY ORDNANCE MAINTENANCE PERSONNEL ONLY. These are the shock absorbers (late Willys). Every 6,000 miles, remove and disassemble the shock absorbers. Unscrew linkage eye and refill with FLUID, shock-absorber, light.

(17) WHEEL BEARINGS. Remove bearing cone assemblies from hub and wash spindle and inside of hub. Inspect bearing races and replace if necessary. Wet the spindle and inside of hub and hub cap with GREASE, general purpose, No. 2, to a maximum thickness of 1/16 inch only to retard rust. Wash bearing cones and grease seals. Inspect and replace if necessary. Lubricate bearings with GREASE, general purpose, No. 2, with a packer or by hand, kneading lubricant into all spaces in the bearing. Use extreme care to protect bearings from dirt and immediately reassemble and replace wheel. The lubricant in the bearings is sufficient to provide lubrication until the next service period. Do not fill hub or hub cap. Any excess might result in leakage into the brake drum.

e. **Reports and Records.** If lubrication instructions are closely followed, proper lubricants used, and satisfactory results are not obtained, make a report to the ordnance officer responsible for the maintenance of the materiel. A complete record of lubrication servicing may be kept in the Duty Roster (W.D., A.G.O Form No. 6).

f. **Localized Views.** The localized views of lubrication points (figs. 15, 16, 17, 18, and 19) supplement the instructions on the Guide and in the notes.

Section VII

TOOLS AND EQUIPMENT STOWAGE ON THE VEHICLE

19. VEHICLE TOOLS.

a. Unless the vehicle is equipped with extra tool equipment, the following are supplied (one of each unless otherwise specified):

Tool	Federal Stock No.	Where Carried
HAMMER, machinist's, ball peen, 16 oz	41-H-523	Tool bag
JACK, screw type, 1½-ton, w/handle	41-J-66	Tool compartment
PLIERS, combination, slip joint, 6-in.	41-P-1650	Tool bag
PULLER, wheel hub	41-P-2962-700	Tool compartment
WRENCH, drain plug	41-W-1962-50	Tool bag
WRENCH, engineer's open-end, ⅜- x 7/16-in.	41-W-991	Tool bag
WRENCH, engineer's open-end, ½- x 19/32-in.	41-W-1003	Tool bag
WRENCH, engineer's open-end, 9/16- x 11/16-in.	41-W-1005-5	Tool bag
WRENCH, engineer's open-end, ⅝- x 25/32-in.	41-W-1008-10	Tool bag
WRENCH, engineer's open-end, ¾- x ⅞-in.	41-W-1012-5	Tool bag
WRENCH, hydraulic brake, bleeder screw	41-W-1596-125	Tool bag
WRENCH, adjustable, auto type, 11-in.	41-W-449	Tool bag
WRENCH, socket, screw fluted	41-W-2459-500	Tool bag
WRENCH, socket, spark plug, w/handle	41-W-3335-50	Tool bag
WRENCH, wheel bearing nut, 2⅛-in. hex	41-W-3825-200	Tool compartment
WRENCH, wheel stud nut, 49/64-in. hex	41-W-3837-55	Tool compartment

20. VEHICLE EQUIPMENT.

a. Unless vehicle is equipped with special equipment, the following are supplied (one of each unless otherwise specified):

Tool	Federal Stock No.	Where Carried
ADAPTER, lubr. gun	....	Tool bag
APPARATUS, decontaminating, 1½ qt	....	Driver's compartment
AX, chopping, single-bit	41-A-1277	Body left side
BAG, tool	41-B-15	Tool compartment
CATALOG, ord. std. nom. list	SNL-G-503	Glove compartment
CHAINS, tire, 6.00 x 16	8-C-2358	Tool compartment (4)
CONTAINER, 5-gallon	....	Bracket on rear
COVER, headlight	....	Under right seat (2)
COVER, windshield	....	Under right seat
CRANK, starting	....	Under rear seat
EXTINGUISHER, fire	58-E-202	Inside cowl, left
GAGE, tire pressure	8-G-615	Tool compartment
GUN, lubr., hand-type	41-G-1330-60	Tool compartment
MANUAL, technical	TM 9-803	Glove compartment
NOZZLE, flexible tube	....	....
OILER, straight spout, ½-pt	13-O-1530	Front of dash
PUMP, tire, w/chuck	8-P-5000	Behind rear seat
RIFLE	....	On dash
SHOVEL, D-handle, rd. pt.	41-S-3170	Body, left side
TAPE, friction, roll	17-T-805	Parts bag
WIRE, iron, roll	22-W-650	Parts bag

21. VEHICLE SPARE PARTS.

a. Unless the vehicle is equipped with a special assortment of parts, the following are supplied (one of each unless otherwise specified):

Name of Spare Part	Federal Stock No.	Where Carried
BAG, spare parts	8-B-11	Glove compartment
BELT, fan	33-B-76	Parts bag
CAPS, tire valve (boxed)	8-C-650	Parts bag (5)
CORES, tire valve (boxed)	8-C-6750	Parts bag (5)

TOOLS AND EQUIPMENT STOWAGE ON THE VEHICLE

Name of Spare Part	Federal Stock No.	Where Carried
LAMP, elec. incand. 6-8V sing-tung-fil., 3 cp (MZ63)	17-L-5215	Parts bag
LAMP-UNIT, blackout, stop, sealed, one opng., 6-8V, 3 cp	8-L-421	Parts bag
LAMP-UNIT, blackout, tail, sealed, 4 opngs., 6-8V, 3 cp	8-L-415	Parts bag
LAMP-UNIT, service tail and stop, sealed, 6-8V, 21-3 cp	8-L-419	Parts bag
PIN, cotter, split, s. type B boxed ass't.	42-P-5347	Parts bag
PLUG, spark, with gasket	17-P-5365	Parts bag

PART TWO

VEHICLE MAINTENANCE INSTRUCTIONS

Section VIII

RECORD OF MODIFICATIONS

Paragraph

22. MWO AND MAJOR UNIT ASSEMBLY REPLACEMENT RECORD.

a. Description. Every vehicle is supplied with a copy of A.G.O. Form No. 478 which provides a means of keeping a record of each MWO completed or major unit assembly replaced. This form includes spaces for the vehicle name and U.S.A. registration number, instructions for use, and information pertinent to the work accomplished. It is very important that the form be used as directed, and that it remain with the vehicle until the vehicle is removed from service.

b. Instructions for Use. Personnel performing modifications or major unit assembly replacements must record clearly on the form a description of the work completed, and must initial the form in the columns provided. When each modification is completed, record the date, hours and/or mileage, and MWO number. When major unit assemblies, such as engines, transmissions, transfer cases, are replaced, record the date, hours and/or mileage, and nomenclature of the unit assembly. Minor repairs and minor parts and accessory replacements need not be recorded.

c. Early Modifications. Upon receipt by a third or fourth echelon repair facility of a vehicle for modification or repair, maintenance personnel will record the MWO numbers of modifications applied prior to the date of A.G.O. Form No. 478.

Section IX

SECOND ECHELON PREVENTIVE MAINTENANCE

23. SECOND ECHELON PREVENTIVE MAINTENANCE SERVICES.

a. Regular scheduled maintenance inspections and services are a preventive maintenance function of the using arms and are the responsibility of commanders of operating organizations.

(1) FREQUENCY. The frequency of the preventive maintenance services outlined herein is considered a minimum requirement for normal operation of vehicles. Under unusual operating conditions such as extreme temperatures, and dusty or sandy terrain, it may be necessary to perform certain maintenance services more frequently.

(2) FIRST ECHELON PARTICIPATION. The drivers should accompany their vehicles and assist the mechanics while periodic second echelon preventive maintenance services are performed. Ordinarily the driver should present the vehicle for a scheduled preventive maintenance service in a reasonably clean condition: that is, it should be dry and not caked with mud or grease to such an extent that inspection and servicing will be seriously hampered; however, the vehicle should not be washed or wiped thoroughly clean, since certain types of defects, such as cracks, leaks, and loose or shifted parts or assemblies are more evident if the surfaces are slightly soiled or dusty.

(3) INSTRUCTIONS. If instructions other than those which are contained in the general procedures in step (4), or in the specific procedures in step (5) which follow, are required for the correct performance of a preventive maintenance service or for correction of a deficiency, other sections of the vehicle operators' manual pertaining to the item involved, or a designated individual in authority should be consulted.

(4) GENERAL PROCEDURES. These general procedures are basic instructions which are to be followed when performing the services on the items listed in the specific procedures. NOTE: *The second echelon personnel must be thoroughly trained in these procedures so that they will apply them automatically.*

(a) When new or overhauled subassemblies are installed to correct deficiencies, care should be taken to see that they are clean, correctly installed, and properly lubricated and adjusted.

(b) When installing new lubricant retainer seals, a coating of the lubricant should be wiped over the sealing surface of the lip of the seal. When the new seal is a leather seal, it should be soaked in engine oil SAE 10 (warm if practicable) for at least 30 minutes, then, the leather lip should be worked carefully by hand before installing the seal. The lip must not be scratched or marred.

(c) The general inspection of each item applies also to any supporting member or connection, and usually includes a check to see

whether or not the item is in good condition, correctly assembled, secure, or excessively worn. The mechanics must be thoroughly trained in the following explanations of these terms.

1. The inspection for "good condition" is usually an external visual inspection to determine if the unit is damaged beyond safe or serviceable limits. The term "good condition" is explained further by the following: not bent or twisted, not chafed or burned, not broken or cracked, not bare or frayed, not dented or collapsed, not torn or cut.

2. The inspection of a unit to see that it is "correctly assembled" is usually an external visual inspection to see if it is in its normal assembled position in the vehicle.

3. The inspection of a unit to determine if it is "secure" is usually an external visual examination, a hand-feel, wrench, or a pry-bar check for looseness. Such an inspection should include any brackets, lock washers, lock nuts, locking wires, or cotter pins used in assembly.

4. "Excessively worn" will be understood to mean worn, close to or beyond serviceable limits, and likely to result in a failure if not replaced before the next scheduled inspection.

(d) Special Services. These are indicated by repeating the item numbers in the columns which show the interval at which the services are to be performed, and show that the parts or assemblies are to receive certain mandatory services. For example, an item number in one or both columns opposite a *Tighten* procedure means that the actual tightening of the object must be performed. The special services include:

1. Adjust. Make all necessary adjustments in accordance with the pertinent section of the vehicle operator's manual, special bulletins, or other current directives.

2. Clean. Clean units of the vehicle with dry-cleaning solvent to remove excess lubricant, dirt, and other foreign material. After the parts are cleaned, rinse them in clean fluid and dry them thoroughly. Take care to keep the parts clean until reassembled, and be certain to keep cleaning fluid away from rubber or other material which it will damage. Clean the protective grease coating from new parts, since this material is not a good lubricant.

3. Special lubrication. This applies both to lubrication operations that do not appear on the vehicle Lubrication Guide and to items that do appear on such charts, but which should be performed in connection with the maintenance operations if parts have to be disassembled for inspection or service.

4. Serve. This usually consists of performing special operations, such as replenishing battery water, draining and refilling units with oil, and changing the oil filter cartridge.

5. Tighten. All tightening operations should be performed with sufficient wrench-torque (force on the wrench handle) to tighten the unit according to good mechanical practice. Use torque-indicating wrench where specified. Do not overtighten, as this may strip threads or cause distortion. Tightening will always be understood to include the correct installation of lock washers, lock nuts, and cotter pins provided to secure the tightening.

(e) *Conditions.* When conditions make it difficult to perform the complete preventive maintenance procedures at one time, they can sometimes be handled in sections, planning to complete all operations within the week, if possible. All available time at halts and in bivouac areas must be utilized, if necessary, to assure that maintenance operations are completed. When limited by the tactical situation, items with special services in the columns should be given first consideration.

(f) The numbers of the preventive maintenance procedures that follow are identical with those outlined on W.D., A.G.O. Form No. 461, which is the Preventive Maintenance Service Work Sheet for Wheeled and Half-track Vehicles. Certain items on the work sheet that do not apply to this vehicle are not included in the procedures in this manual. In general, the numerical sequence of items on the work sheet is followed in the manual procedures, but in some instances there is deviation for conservation of the mechanic's time and effort.

(5) SPECIFIC PROCEDURES. The procedures for performing each item in the 1,000-mile (monthly) and 6,000-mile (6-month) maintenance procedures are described in the following chart. Each page of the chart has two columns at the left edge corresponding to the 6,000-mile and the 1,000-mile maintenance respectively. Very often it will be found that a particular procedure does not apply to both scheduled maintenances. In order to determine which procedure to follow, look down the column corresponding to the maintenance due, and wherever an item appears, perform the operations indicated opposite the number.

ROAD TEST

MAINTENANCE		
6000 Mile	1000 Mile	
		NOTE: *When the tactical situation does not permit a full road test, perform those items which require little or no movement of the vehicle, namely, items 3, 4, 5, 6, 9, 10, and 14. Make a full road test of 5, but not more than 10 miles, over varied terrain if possible.*
1	1	**Before-operation Service.** Perform Before-operation Service as outlined in paragraph 13.
3	3	**Dash Instruments and Gages.** Observe instruments frequently during road test.
		AMMETER. Ammeter should show high charge for short time after starting, then zero or slight positive (plus) reading above speeds of 12 to 15 miles per hour with lights and accessories off. Zero reading is normal with lights and accessories on.
		SPEEDOMETER. See that speedometer indicates vehicle speed, operates without excessive fluctuation or noise, and that odometer registers accumulating trip and total mileage correctly.

MAINTENANCE		
6000 Mile	1000 Mile	
		TEMPERATURE INDICATOR. Temperature indicator should gradually increase to normal operating range of 160°F to 180°F.
		FUEL GAGE. Fuel gage must indicate the approximate amount of fuel in tank.
4	4	**Horn, Mirror, and Windshield Wiper.** Test horn for proper operation and tone, tactical situation permitting. Adjust mirror, and inspect for broken or discolored glass. Wiper should have sufficient arm tension to stay in "UP" position. Examine blade for good condition and full contact with glass throughout entire stroke.
5	5	**Brakes.** Test brakes for smooth, even stop, excessive pedal travel before application, "spongy" pedal, or loss of pedal pressure when brakes are held on. Brakes must not squeak or require excessive pedal pressure. Test pedal free travel, which should be ½ inch. Hand brake must hold vehicle on a reasonable grade, must have positive ratchet action and ⅓ reserve handle travel. There should be ½-inch reserve clearance between hand brake relay crank and lower end of hand brake cable conduit.
6	6	**Clutch.** Clutch must have free pedal travel of three-quarter inch. Test clutch for slip, grab, gear clash, or rattle. Listen for noises that would indicate dry or defective release bearing or pilot bushing.
7	7	**Transmission and Transfer Case.** Shift through entire range of transmission and transfer, noting whether the levers move easily and snap into each position. With shifting levers in each position, accelerate and decelerate engine, noting any unusual noises or tendency of levers to slip into neutral. Inspect for loose mountings.
8	8	**Steering.** Steering gear must not bind. There should be no excessive free play with wheels in straightahead position. Test for existence of front-end shimmy, wander, or side pull.
9	9	**Engine.** Engine must idle smoothly without stalling. Test acceleration and pulling power in each transmission speed. Listen for detonation and "ping," misses, popping, spitting, or other noises that might indicate need for engine repair.
10	10	**Unusual Noises.** Listen for noises that might indicate loose, damaged, or faulty parts.
13	13	**Temperatures.** Feel brake drums and wheel hubs for abnormally high temperatures. Overheated brake drum or wheel hub may indicate dragging brake or defective, dry, or improperly adjusted wheel bearing. Examine

MAINTENANCE 6000 Mile	MAINTENANCE 1000 Mile	
		differentials, transmission, and transfer case for too-high running temperature. NOTE: *Transfer case operates at a higher temperature than other cases.*
14	14	**Leaks.** Look on ground under vehicle for indications of coolant, fuel, oil, or hydraulic fluid leaks.
16	16	**Gear Oil Level and Leaks.** Examine lubricant levels of transmission, transfer case, and differentials. Inspect cases for leaks. Safe level when cold is even with filler plug. If an oil change is due, drain and refill, according to Lubrication Guide (par. 18). Capacities: transmission, 3/4 quart; transfer case, 1 1/2 quarts; front differential, 1 1/4 quarts; rear differential, 1 1/4 quarts.
		MAINTENANCE OPERATIONS
17	17	**Unusual Noises.** With engine running, proceed as follows: Accelerate and decelerate engine slightly, and listen for unusual engine noises. With transmission in third gear, front wheel drive engaged, and engine at fast idle, listen for unusual noises in operating units. Observe propeller shaft and universal joints, wheels, and axles for excessive vibration and run-out.
22	22	**Battery.** Inspect battery case for cracks and leaks. Inspect cables, terminals, bolts, posts, straps, and hold-downs for good condition and secure mounting. Clean top of battery. Test specific gravity and voltage, and record on W.D., A.G.O. Form No. 461. Specific gravity readings below 1.225 indicate battery should be recharged or replaced. Electrolyte level should be above top of plates, and may extend 1/2 inch above plates.
22	22	SERVE. Perform high-rate discharge test according to instructions for "condition" test which accompany test instrument, and record voltage on W.D., A.G.O. Form No. 461. Cell variation should not be more than 30 percent. NOTE: *Specific gravity must be above 1.225 to make this test.*
		CLEAN. Clean entire battery and carrier, and repaint carrier if corroded. Clean battery cable terminals, terminal bolts and nuts, and battery posts; grease lightly; inspect bolts for serviceability. Tighten terminals and hold-downs carefully to avoid damage to battery. Add clean water to 1/2 inch above plates.
18	18	**Cylinder Head and Gasket.** Look for cracks, and indications of water or compression leaks. Tighten cylinder head (only if leaks are indicated and after performing item 21) with torque wrench; tighten head-screws to from 65 to 75 foot-pounds; head stud nuts

MAINTENANCE 6000 Mile	MAINTENANCE 1000 Mile	
		to from 60 to 65 foot-pounds. Tighten in correct order (fig. 25). Be sure cylinder head to dash bond strap is in good condition and securely connected.
	19	**Valve Mechanism.** Adjust valves only if noisy.
19		ADJUST. Check clearance and adjust valves. Proper clearances are: intake valve, 0.014 inch when hot or cold; exhaust valve, 0.014 inch when hot or cold.
	20	**Spark Plugs.** Wipe off plugs without removing; inspect for insulator cracks and leakage through insulators and gaskets. Service if required.
20		SERVE. Clean and adjust plugs to gap of 0.030 inch, using round gage. Plugs with broken insulators, excessive carbon deposits, electrodes burned thin or otherwise unserviceable, must be replaced. Correct plug (AN-7). NOTE: *If sand blast cleaner is not available install new or reconditioned plugs.*
21	21	**Compression.** Test compression with all plugs removed, and with throttle and choke wide open. Standard pressure is approximately 110 pounds at cranking speed; minimum pressure is 70 pounds. Maximum variation between cylinders must not be more than 10 pounds. If variation is greater than 10 pounds, recheck weak cylinders, using oil test, and report to higher authority. Record all readings.
23	23	**Crankcase.** Observe vehicle for crankcase, valve cover, timing case, or flywheel housing oil leaks. Check oil level. Drain and refill crankcase if change is due. See Lubrication Guide (par. 18).
23		CAUTION: *Do not start engine until completion of item 24.*
24	24	**Oil Filters and Lines.** Inspect filters, lines, and connections for good condition or leaks.
24		SERVE: Remove filter cartridge, clean filter case and install new cartridge and gaskets. Refill crankcase (5 quarts with new filter cartridge). Again inspect for leaks with engine running and check oil level after engine is stopped.
25	25	**Radiator.** Observe radiator core, hose, cap and gaskets for good condition and inspect for leaks. CAUTION: *System operates under 3¼ to 4¼ pounds pressure (be careful in removing cap).* Examine air passages and guards for obstructions and clean out any dirt, insects, or trash. Test and record antifreeze value (as climate demands). Examine coolant for oil, rust, or foreign

MAINTENANCE 6000 Mile	MAINTENANCE 1000 Mile	
		material. Clean and flush radiator as needed. CAUTION: *Save and filter coolant if antifreeze is present.* Add inhibitor and antifreeze if needed.
25		TIGHTEN. Tighten hose clamps. Inspect radiator cap and gasket for tight seal.
26	26	**Water Pump and Fan.** Loosen fan belt; test water pump shaft and bearing for play. Inspect pump for secure attachment, good condition, and for leaks. Inspect fan for alinement and secure mounting.
27	27	**Generator, Cranking Motor, and Switch.** Inspect these units to see if they are in good condition, clean and securely connected or mounted; particularly radio noise suppression capacitor on generator and starting switch terminal, and bond straps from generator and cranking motor.
27		SERVE. Inspect commutators and brushes for good condition and wear. Brushes should be free in holders, and have full contact with commutator. Clean commutators with 2/0 flint paper if needed. Blow out with compressed air. Replace generator or cranking motor when commutator is scored, rough, worn, or brushes are less than half their original length.
29	29	**Drive Belt and Pulleys.** Inspect fan belt for fraying, wear, and deterioration. Inspect pulleys for cracks and misalinement. Replace or adjust belt as needed. Adjust to deflection of 1 inch between pulleys.
31	31	**Distributor.** Clean and remove distributor cap. Examine cap and rotor arm for cracks, corrosion and burned conductors. Clean breaker plate assembly, if dirty. Inspect breaker points for burning, pitting, alinement, and adjustment. Replace and aline burned or badly pitted points. Feel to determine excessive distributor shaft play. Turn distributor shaft (with rotor), and release to test centrifugal advance for binding.
31		SPECIAL LUBRICATION. Sparingly lubricate cam surfaces, movable breaker arm pin, wick and camshaft according to Lubrication Guide (par. 18). Adjust breaker point gap to 0.020 inch.
32	32	**Coil and Wiring.** Examine coil, high tension, and exposed low voltage wiring for cleanliness, and secure connections and attachment. Clean and tighten as required. Pay particular attention to see that spark plug

MAINTENANCE		
6000 Mile	1000 Mile	
		and coil to distributor wire, radio noise suppressors, and coil terminal capacitor are in good condition, and securely mounted or connected.
33	33	**Manifolds and Heat Control.** Tighten manifold stud nuts as required to from 31 to 35 foot-pounds. Inspect for gasket leaks. Heat control valve must be free and bimetal spring must be in good condition.
34	34	**Air Cleaner.** Examine air cleaner for good condition and secure mounting. Examine oil cup. If dirty, remove and clean filter element; do not apply oil to element after cleaning. Clean oil cup and refill (⅝ qt).
36	36	**Carburetor.** Make certain that the choke and throttle open and close fully. Lubricate linkage, and inspect for worn parts.
37	37	**Fuel Filter, Screens, and Lines.** Clean fuel pump screen, renew gaskets, inspect unit for leaks. Remove disk filter element from fuel filter mounted on dash; clean element and bowl. Reinstall with new gasket. Inspect for leaks after unit has been refilled.
38	38	**Fuel Pump.** Observe fuel pump for leaks, secure mounting, and pressure reading. Pressure should be 1½ to 2½ pounds with engine running at approximately 30 miles per hour vehicle road speed.
39	39	**Cranking Motor.** Start engine and observe cranking motor for positive action, normal speed, and unusual noise. Make sure oil pressure gage and ammeter readings are satisfactory.
40	40	**Leaks.** Look around engine and on ground under engine for oil, fuel, coolant, or hydraulic fluid leaks.
41	41	**Ignition Timing.** With neon light, check ignition timing. Observe if spark advances automatically. Adjust timing as required (par. 65). CAUTION: *Close timing hole cover and tighten screw.*
42	42	**Engine Idle and Vacuum Test.** Adjust engine to smooth idle, using vacuum gage; obtain highest possible steady vacuum reading.
	43	**Regulator Unit.** See that regulator and radio noise capacitors are in good condition, and that all connections and mounting are secure.
43		TEST. Connect low voltage circuit tester and test voltage regulator, current regulator, and cut-out for output control.
47	47	**Tires and Rims.** Inspect valve stems for correct position and missing caps. Inspect tires for cuts, bruises, blisters, irregular and excessive tread wear. Remove imbedded glass, nails, or stones. Directional and non-

SECOND ECHELON PREVENTIVE MAINTENANCE

MAINTENANCE		
6000 Mile	1000 Mile	
		directional tires should not be installed on same vehicle. If equipped with directional tires, open end of chevron should meet ground first on front tires, and last on rear tires. Tires should match on all wheels within ¾-inch over-all circumference, and as to type of tread. Take measurements with all tires equally inflated. Inspect tire carrier for looseness and damage. Tighten all lug nuts securely. Inflate tires to 35 pounds (cold).
48	48	**Rear Brakes.** Remove grease and dirt from brake drums and backing plates, and inspect for excessive wear or scoring and loose mounting bolts. Inspect brake hose for proper fit and for deterioration. Inspect wheel cylinders (exterior) for good condition, secure mounting, and for leaks. Tighten brake support and drum mounting bolts securely.
49	49	**Rear Brake Shoes.** Remove right rear wheel and inspect linings for wear, oil, and dirt, and possibility of rivets scoring drum before next 1,000-mile inspection. If lining on right rear wheel requires replacement, remove all wheels for lining inspection.
49		SERVE. Remove all wheels and drums. Observe linings for wear, oil, and dirt, and determine if shoes are secure and guided by anchor pins. Inspect return springs for good action. Lightly lubricate anchor pins. Adjust brake shoes to 0.005 inch at heel, and 0.008 inch at toe.
	52	**Rear Wheels.** Inspect wheel for good condition and, without removal, test for evidence of looseness of wheel bearing adjustment, and dry or damaged bearings. Inspect around drive flanges, brake supports, and drums for lubricant or brake fluid leaks. Tighten drive flange and wheel nuts. CAUTION: *If it is known that vehicle has operated in deep water which may have entered wheel bearings, inspect right wheel bearing for contamination. Remove, clean, repack, and adjust as for 6,000-mile service. If contamination of lubricant has occurred, service other wheel bearings likewise.*
52		CLEAN. Disassemble wheel bearings and seals, clean, and inspect for damage.
		SPECIAL LUBRICATION. Pack wheel bearings, install new seals, and adjust bearings.
53	53	**Front Brakes.** Examine brake hose for chafing, leakage, and deterioration. Inspect wheel cylinders (exterior) for good condition, secure mounting, and leaks.
53		DRUMS AND SUPPORTS. Clean drums and backing plates thoroughly, and tighten backing plate bolts. Inspect drums for damage, looseness, excessive wear, and scoring. Lightly lubricate anchor pins.
54		**Front Brake Shoes.** Inspect brake shoes, linings, and anchors for damage or looseness. Replace worn parts

MAINTENANCE 6000 Mile	MAINTENANCE 1000 Mile	
		and worn linings. Clean dust from linings. Adjust brake shoes to 0.005-inch clearance at heel, and 0.008-inch clearance at toe.
55	55	**Steering Knuckles.** Inspect steering knuckle housings and oil seals for serviceable condition. Check lubricant for contamination. Refill to bottom of filler hole.
56	56	**Front Springs.** Inspect front springs for good condition, correct alinement, and excessive deflection. Inspect springs for excessive wear of spring bushing and clips. Tighten U-bolts securely and uniformly. Examine U-shackles and pivot bolts for wear.
57	57	**Steering.** Observe steering gear, Pitman arm, drag link, tie rod, and steering connecting rods for good condition, correct assembly, and secure mounting.
57		TIGHTEN. Tighten and adjust assembly mounting nuts and screws, arms, tie rods, drag link, Pitman arm, and gear, and steering wheel nuts. Replace broken seals or worn parts.
58	58	**Front Shock Absorbers.** Inspect shock absorbers to see if they are in good condition and secure, if bodies are leaking fluid, and if rubber bushings have deteriorated. If rubber bushings are hard or cracked, apply a film of brake fluid. NOTE: *If fluid is leaking or bodies are defective, shock absorber must be replaced.*
60	60	**Front Wheels.** Inspect for good condition, security, end play, and lubricant leaks. Rotate wheels and observe for loose, broken, or dry bearings.
60		CLEAN AND LUBRICATE. Remove, clean, inspect, lubricate, and replace bearings. Adjust bearings and test for wheel shake before removing jack.
61	61	**Front Axle.** Examine front axle housing for good condition and lubricant leaks. Inspect pinion shaft for end play and grease leaks. Inspect axle for apparent alinement, and see that vent is open.
62	62	**Front Propeller Shaft.** Inspect propeller shaft for damage and incorrect assembly, excessive wear, and lubricant leaks. Inspect universal and slip joints for alinement, wear, and leakage.
62		TIGHTEN. Tighten flange yoke bolts.
63	63	**Engine Mountings and Braces.** See that engine mountings and bond straps are in good condition and secure, and that rubber mountings are not separated from metal backing. Tighten front mountings if loose. Adjust rear

MAINTENANCE		
6000 Mile	1000 Mile	
		mounting bolts to from 38 to 42 foot-pounds with torque wrench. Tighten radio noise suppression bond strap mountings securely.
64	64	**Parking (Hand) Brake.** See that drum is not scored or oily; that lining is not oil-soaked nor worn thin. Inspect ratchet for positive holding action. Lubricate upper end of conduit tube at cable with engine oil.
64		ADJUST. Adjust clearance between drum and lining to from 0.005 inch to 0.010 inch. Reserve lever travel should be one-third the ratchet range. There must be ½-inch reserve clearance (on cable) between relay crank and lower end of hand brake conduit.
65	65	**Clutch Pedal.** Clutch pedal linkage must be secure and not worn; return spring must be operative; clutch should have free pedal travel of ¾ inch.
65		ADJUST. Adjust clutch pedal free travel to ¾ inch.
66	66	**Brake Pedal.** Test brake pedal operation; brake linkage must be secure and not worn excessively; return spring must be operative; brake should have ⅓ reserve travel.
66		ADJUST. Adjust brake pedal free travel to ½ inch.
67	67	**Brake Master Cylinder.** Inspect master cylinder for good condition and secure mounting; check master cylinder boot for good condition and correct installation; inspect stop light switch for terminal attachment and correct operation. Look for brake fluid leaks; clean out filler plug vent. Fill master cylinder reservoir to ¼ inch below plug.
71	71	**Transmission.** Inspect oil seals and gaskets for leakage. Test control for looseness, excessive wear, and improper operation. Inspect mounting and assembly bolts and cap screws for looseness.
71		TIGHTEN. Tighten mounting and assembly bolts and cap screws.
72	72	**Transfer Case.** Inspect oil seals and gaskets for leakage. Test controls for looseness, excessive wear, and improper operation. Inspect mounting and assembly bolts and cap screws for looseness. Clean vent.
72		TIGHTEN. Tighten mounting and assembly bolts, nuts, and cap screws.
73	73	**Rear Propeller Shaft.** Remove any trash that may be wrapped around shaft or universal joints. Inspect

MAINTENANCE 6000 Mile	1000 Mile	
		mounting of universal and slip joints for misalinement, wear, and grease leaks.
73		TIGHTEN. Tighten flange yoke cap screws.
75	75	**Rear Axle.** Inspect rear axle housing for leaks; feel for excessive play in pinion shaft; clean vent. Make sure differential carrier mounting cap screws are tight.
77	77	**Rear Springs.** Check springs for shifted leaves due to broken center bolt, loose spring clips, or U-bolts. If found loose, tighten U-bolts to from 50 to 55 foot-pounds. Tighten spring pivot bolt nut to from 29 to 30 foot-pounds.
78	78	**Rear Shock Absorbers.** Inspect in the same manner as for item 58.
80	80	**Frame.** Examine frame for loose side rails and cross members. Tighten loose bolts. If frame appears to be bent, or out of alinement, report condition to higher authority.
81	81	**Wiring, Conduits and Grommets.** Inspect all wiring for looseness and broken insulation; check conduits and grommets for proper position and good condition.
82	82	**Fuel Tank and Lines.** Inspect tank and lines for good condition, secure mounting, and leaks; check cap for defective gasket or clogged vent.
82		SERVE. Remove fuel tank drain plug briefly, and drain off accumulated water and sediment.
83	83	**Brake Lines and Connections.** Inspect brake lines for proper mounting, cracks, worn spots in lines, leaks, deteriorated or damaged hose and connections.
84	84	**Exhaust Pipe and Muffler.** Inspect exhaust pipe and muffler for secure mounting, rusted condition, damage or leaks. Inspect tail pipe for stoppage.
85	85	**Vehicle Lubrication.** Lubricate according to Lubrication Guide (par. 18) in this manual. Observe latest issued lubrication directives.
		LOWER VEHICLE TO GROUND
86	86	**Toe-in and Turning Stops.** With front wheels on ground, straight-ahead position, use wheel alining gage, and check toe-in. Normal toe-in range is $\frac{3}{64}$-inch to $\frac{3}{32}$-inch. Turn front wheels fully in both right and left

SECOND ECHELON PREVENTIVE MAINTENANCE

MAINTENANCE		
6000 Mile	1000 Mile	
		directions, and determine if turning stops hold tires clear of all parts of vehicle in these positions. Examine axle for loose turn stops.
91	91	**Lights.** Determine that switches for head, tail, instrument, and blackout lights operate properly. Operate stop light by depressing brake pedal. Test foot switch, noting whether beam is controlled for high and low positions. Inspect all lights; these must be clean, securely mounted, and in good condition; lenses must not be broken, cracked, or discolored; reflectors must not be discolored; blackout lights must be in good condition with shield in proper position.
91		ADJUST. Adjust and aim headlight beams.
92	92	**Safety Reflectors.** Safety reflectors must be present, clean, and secure. Replace if cracked or broken.
93	93	**Front Bumper and Grille.** Front bumper and grille must be present, in good condition, and securely mounted.
94	94	**Hood, Hinges and Fasteners.** Examine hood for alinement and secure mounting when fastened; see that fasteners are present, secure, undamaged, and not excessively worn or bent. Lubricate hinges and fasteners lightly. See that radio noise bond straps from hood to dash and grille are secure.
95	95	**Front Fenders.** Inspect front fenders for good condition and secure mounting.
96	96	**Body Hardware.** Inspect body of vehicle according to following standards: Hardware should operate properly and be adequately lubricated; top should be clean, having no holes or tears, and all grommets must be present and in good condition. Windshield should be free from cracks or discoloration; windshield frame and hold-down hooks at hood should be in good condition. Seats and upholstery should be clean and undamaged; safety straps should be present and in place; body handles should be present, secure, and undamaged; floor drain plugs (2) should be present, and in good condition.
98	98	**Circuit Breaker, Terminal Blocks, or Boxes.** Inspect points of thermal circuit breaker (30 amperes, located on main light switch) for pitting or corrosion. Be sure all radio noise suppression bond straps and capacitor on radio terminal box (if so equipped) are in good condition and secure.
101	101	**Rear Bumpers and Pintle Hook, Latch and Lock Pin.** Inspect rear bumpers and pintle hook to see if they are

MAINTENANCE		
6000 Mile	1000 Mile	
		present, in good condition, and secure. Pintle hook safety latch should be free, and lock securely.
103	103	**Paint and Markings.** Inspect paint of entire vehicle for good condition and bright spots that might cause glare or reflection. Vehicle markings and identification must be legible. Inspect identification plates and their mountings (if furnished) for good condition, secure mounting, and legibility.
104	104	**Radio Bonding (Suppressors, Filters, Condensers, and Shielding).** See that all units not covered in the foregoing specific procedures are in good condition, and securely mounted and connected. Be sure all additional noise suppression bond straps and toothed lock washers listed in paragraph 177, are inspected for looseness or damage, and see that contact surfaces are clean. NOTE: *If objectionable radio noise from vehicle has been reported, make tests in accordance with paragraph 178. If cleaning and tightening of mountings and connections, and replacement of defective radio noise suppression units does not eliminate the trouble, the radio operator will report the condition to the designated individual in authority.*
105	105	**Armament.** Examine gun mounts and covers (if present) for good condition, cleanliness, and secure attachment. NOTE: *Guns, parts, and covers are to be referred to armorer or gun commanders for all inspections or service.*
		TOOLS AND EQUIPMENT
131	131	**Tools and Equipment.** Standard vehicle tools, Pioneer tools, and equipment must be present, clean, serviceable, and securely mounted. Sharpen cutting tools and darken bright parts of exposed tools in combat areas. Check against stowage list (par. 19).
132	132	**Fire Extinguisher.** Inspect fire extinguisher for full charge and secure mounting. See that nozzle is clean.
133	133	**Decontaminator.** Inspect decontaminator for damage, secure mounting, and full charge. Make latter check by removing filler plug. Drain and refill with fresh solution every 90 days. See date of last filling on attached tag.
143	143	**First Aid Kit.** Examine contents of first aid kit for good condition, completeness, and satisfactory packing. Report any deficiency.
135	135	**Publications and Form No. 26.** See that the vehicle manuals and Lubrication Guide, Form No. 26 (Acci-

SECOND ECHELON PREVENTIVE MAINTENANCE

MAINTENANCE		
6000 Mile	1000 Mile	
		dent Report) and W.D., A.G.O. Form No. 478 (MWO and Major Unit Assembly Replacement Record), are present, legible, and properly stowed.
136	136	**Traction Devices.** Inspect tire chains for broken or worn links, missing cross chains, or damaged fasteners.
139	139	**Fuel Can and Bracket.** Inspect fuel can and bracket for damage, leaks, loose mounting, and presence of cap on chain.
140	140	**Fuel Can Nozzle and Bucket.** See that fuel can nozzle and bucket are not damaged, are clean, and properly stowed.
141	141	**Modifications (Completed).** Inspect entire vehicle to be sure all Modification Work Orders have been completed, and enter any modifications or major unit replacements made at time of this service, on Form No. 478.
142	142	**Final Road Test.** Road test, rechecking items 2 to 16. Recheck transmission, transfer case, and differentials for lubricant level and for leaks. Confine this test to minimum distance necessary to satisfactory observations. NOTE: *Correct or report all defects found during final road test to higher authority.*

Section X

NEW VEHICLE RUN-IN TEST

Paragraph

24. PURPOSE.

a. When a new or reconditioned vehicle is first received at the using organization, it is necessary for second echelon personnel to determine whether or not the vehicle will operate satisfactorily when placed in service. For this purpose, inspect all accessories, subassemblies, assemblies, tools, and equipment to see that they are in place and correctly adjusted. In addition, they will perform a run-in test of at least 50 miles as directed in AR 850-15, paragraph 25, table III, according to procedures in paragraph 26 below.

25. CORRECTION OF DEFICIENCIES.

a. Deficiencies disclosed during the course of the run-in test will be treated as follows:

(1) Correct any deficiencies within the scope of the maintenance echelon of the using organization before the vehicle is placed in service.

(2) Refer deficiencies beyond the scope of the maintenance echelon of the using organization to a higher echelon for correction.

(3) Bring deficiencies of serious nature to the attention of the supplying organization.

26. RUN-IN TEST PROCEDURES.

a. Preliminary Service.

(1) FIRE EXTINGUISHER. See that portable extinguisher is present and in good condition. Test it momentarily for proper operation, and mount it securely.

(2) FUEL, OIL, AND WATER. Fill fuel tank. Check crankcase oil and coolant supply; add oil and coolant as necessary to bring to correct levels. Allow room for expansion in fuel tank and radiator. During freezing weather, test value of antifreeze, and add as necessary to protect cooling system against freezing. CAUTION: *If there is a tag attached to filler cap or steering wheel concerning engine oil in crankcase, follow instructions on tag before driving the vehicle.*

(3) FUEL FILTER. Inspect main fuel filter for leaks, damage, and secure mountings and connections. Drain sediment bowl. Clean fuel pump filter screen and bowl. If any appreciable amount of dirt or water is present, remove main filter bowl and clean bowl and element

in dry-cleaning solvent. Also, drain accumulated dirt and water from bottom of fuel tank. Drain only until fuel runs clean.

(4) BATTERY. Make hydrometer and voltage test of battery, and add clean water to bring electrolyte 3/8 inch above plate.

(5) AIR CLEANER. Examine carburetor air cleaner to see if it is in good condition and secure. Remove element and wash thoroughly in dry-cleaning solvent. Fill oil cup to indicated level with fresh oil, and reinstall securely. Be sure oil cup and body gaskets are in good condition, and that air horn connection is tight.

(6) ACCESSORIES AND BELT. See that accessories such as carburetor, generator, regulator, cranking motor, distributor, water pump, fan, and oil filter, are securely mounted. Make sure that fan and generator drive belt is in good condition, and adjusted to have 1-inch finger-pressure deflection.

(7) ELECTRICAL WIRING. Examine all accessible wiring and conduits to see if they are in good condition, securely connected, and properly supported.

(8) TIRES. See that all tires, including spare, are properly inflated to 35 pounds, cool; that stems are in correct position; all valve caps present and finger-tight. Inspect for damage, and remove objects lodged in treads and carcasses.

(9) WHEEL AND FLANGE NUTS. See that all wheel mounting and axle flange nuts are present and secure.

(10) FENDERS AND BUMPER. Examine fenders and front bumper for looseness and damage.

(11) TOWING CONNECTIONS. Examine towing shackles and pintle hook for looseness and damage, and see that pintle latch operates properly and locks securely.

(12) BODY. See that all body mountings are secure. Inspect attachments, hardware, glass, seats, grab rails and safety straps, top and frame, curtains and hood, to see if they are in good condition, correctly assembled, and securely mounted or fastened. Examine body paint or camouflage pattern for rust, or shiny surfaces that might cause glare. See that vehicle markings are legible.

(13) LUBRICATE. Perform a complete lubrication service of the vehicle, covering all intervals, according to instructions on Lubrication Guide (par. 18), except gear cases, wheel bearings, and other units already lubricated or serviced in items (1) to (12). Check all gear case oil levels, and add as necessary to bring to proper levels. Change only if condition of oil indicates the necessity, or if gear oil is not of proper grade for existing atmospheric temperatures. NOTE: *Perform following items* (14) *through* (17) *during lubrication.*

(14) SPRINGS AND SUSPENSIONS. Inspect front and rear springs and shocks to see that they are in good condition, correctly assembled, secure, and that bushings and shackle pins are not excessively loose, or damaged.

(15) STEERING LINKAGE. See that all steering arms, rods, and connections are in good condition and secure; and that gear case is securely mounted and not leaking excessively.

(16) PROPELLER SHAFTS. Inspect all shafts and universal joints to see if they are in good condition, correctly assembled, alined, secure, and not leaking excessively.

(17) AXLE AND TRANSFER VENTS. See that axle housing and transfer case vents are present, in good condition, and not clogged.

(18) CHOKE. Examine choke to be sure it opens and closes fully in response to operation of choke button.

(19) ENGINE WARM-UP. Start engine and note if cranking motor action is satisfactory, and if engine has any tendency toward hard starting. Set hand throttle to run engine at fast idle during warm-up. During warm-up, reset choke button so that engine will run smoothly, and to prevent overchoking and oil dilution.

(20) INSTRUMENTS.

(a) Oil Pressure Gage. Immediately after engine starts, observe if oil pressure is satisfactory. (Normal operating pressure, hot, at running speeds is 40 to 50 pounds; at idle, 10 pounds). Stop engine if pressure is not indicated in 30 seconds.

(b) Ammeter. Ammeter should show slight positive (+) charge. High charge may be indicated until generator restores to battery current used in starting.

(c) Temperature Gage. Engine temperature should rise gradually during warm-up period to normal operating range, 160°F to 185°F

(d) Fuel Gage. Fuel gage should register "FULL" if tank has been filled.

(21) ENGINE CONTROLS. Observe if engine responds properly to controls, and if controls operate without excessive looseness or binding.

(22) HORN AND WINDSHIELD WIPERS. See that these items are in good condition and secure. If tactical situation permits, test horn for proper operation and tone. See if wiper arms will operate through their full range, and that blade contacts glass evenly and firmly.

(23) GLASS AND REAR VIEW MIRROR. Clean all body glass, curtain windows, and mirror, and inspect for looseness and damage. Adjust mirror for correct vision.

(24) LAMPS (LIGHTS) AND REFLECTORS. Clean lenses and inspect all units for looseness and damage. If tactical situation permits, open and close all light switches to see if lamps respond properly.

(25) LEAKS, GENERAL. Look under vehicle, and within engine compartment, for indications of fuel, oil, coolant, and brake fluid leaks. Trace to source any leaks found, and correct or report them to designated authority.

(26) TOOLS AND EQUIPMENT. Check tools and On Vehicle Stowage Lists, paragraphs 19 and 20, to be sure all items are present, and see that they are serviceable, and properly mounted or stowed.

NEW VEHICLE RUN-IN TEST

b. Run-in Test. Perform the following procedures, steps (1) to (11) inclusive, during the road test of the vehicle. On vehicles which have been driven 50 miles or more in the course of delivery from the supplying to the using organization, reduce the length of the road test to the least mileage necessary to make observations listed below. CAUTION: *Continuous operation of the vehicle at speeds approaching the maximum indicated on the caution plate should be avoided during the test.*

(1) DASH INSTRUMENTS AND GAGES. Do not move vehicle until engine temperature reaches 135°F. Maximum safe operating temperature is 200°F. Observe readings of ammeter, oil temperature, and fuel gages to be sure they are indicating the proper function of the units to which they apply. Also see that speedometer registers the vehicle speed, and that odometer registers accumulating mileage.

(2) BRAKES: FOOT AND HAND. Test service brakes to see if they stop vehicle effectively, without side pull, chatter, or squealing; and observe if pedal has at least ½-inch free travel before meeting push rod-to-piston resistance. Parking brake should hold vehicle on reasonable incline, leaving one-third lever ratchet travel in reverse. CAUTION: *Avoid long application of brakes until shoes become evenly seated to drums.*

(3) CLUTCH. Observe if clutch operates smoothly without grab, chatter, or squeal on engagement, or slippage (under load) when fully engaged. See that pedal has ¾-inch free travel before meeting resistance. CAUTION: *Do not ride clutch pedal at any time, and do not engage and disengage new clutch severely or unnecessarily.*

(4) TRANSMISSION AND TRANSFER. Gearshift mechanism should operate easily and smoothly, and gears should operate without excessive noise, and not slip out of mesh. Test front axle declutching for proper operation.

(5) STEERING. Observe steering action for binding or looseness, and note any excessive pull to one side, wander, shimmy, or wheel tramp. See that column, bracket, and wheel are secure.

(6) ENGINE. Be on the alert for any abnormal engine operating characteristics or unusual noise, such as lack of pulling power or acceleration, backfiring, misfiring, stalling, overheating, or excessive exhaust smoke. Observe if engine responds properly to all controls.

(7) UNUSUAL NOISE. Be on the alert throughout road test for any unusual noise from body and attachments, running gear, suspension, or wheels, that might indicate looseness, damage, wear, inadequate lubrication, or underinflated tires.

(8) HALT VEHICLE AT 10-MILE INTERVALS FOR SERVICES (steps (9) and (10) below).

(9) TEMPERATURES. Cautiously hand-feel each brake drum and wheel hub for abnormal temperatures. Examine the transmission, transfer case, and differential housing for indications of overheating

and excessive lubricant leaks at seals, gaskets, or vents. NOTE: *Transfer case temperatures are normally higher than other gear cases.*

(10) LEAKS. With engine running, and fuel, engine oil, and cooling systems under pressure, look within engine compartment and under vehicle for indications of leaks.

c. Upon completion of run-in test, correct or report any deficiencies noted. Report general condition of vehicle to designated individual in authority.

Section XI

ORGANIZATION TOOLS AND EQUIPMENT

27. STANDARD TOOLS AND EQUIPMENT.

a. All standard tools and equipment available to second echelon are listed in SNL N-19, and their availability is determined by the table of equipment for any particular organization.

28. SPECIAL TOOLS.

a. The special tools available to second echelon for repair of this vehicle are listed in the Organizational Spare Parts and Equipment List of SNL G-503. The special tools required for the operations described in this manual are listed below:

Tool	Federal Stock No.
COMPRESSOR, shock absorber grommet	41-C-2554-400
WRENCH, tappet, double-end, $^{11}/_{32}$- x $^{17}/_{32}$-in.	41-W-3575

Section XII

TROUBLE SHOOTING

29. GENERAL.

a. The following listed possible vehicle troubles and remedies will assist in determining the cause of unsatisfactory operation. A separate list is provided for each unit. If the remedy is not given, reference is made to a paragraph where more complete information will be found.

b. The information in this section applies to operation of the vehicle under normal conditions. If extreme conditions are encountered, it is assumed the vehicle has received the attention outlined in section IV.

30. ENGINE.

a. Diagnosing Troubles. Determine troubles in a general way first as follows:

(1) CHECK MECHANICAL CONDITION. Check for mechanical trouble such as broken or deficient parts in engine or cylinder compression.

TROUBLE SHOOTING

(2) CHECK IGNITION SYSTEM. Remove spark plug wire at a plug. Hold terminal end of wire about ¼ inch from a metal part of engine, and check for a good spark by having someone turn ignition switch on and operate cranking motor. If no spark is obtained, check ammeter operation to determine condition of ignition primary circuit. Ammeter must show slight deflection from zero to discharge side (with lights off) when cranking motor is operated and ignition switch is on. If ammeter drops to zero when starting switch is pressed, starting system is defective, or battery is discharged.

(3) CHECK FUEL SYSTEM. Operate priming lever on rear side of fuel pump; to determine if fuel is reaching carburetor. Resistance to operation indicates carburetor is empty or no fuel; no resistance indicates carburetor is full. A flooded carburetor and engine may prevail so the spark plugs are shorted.

b. Cranking Motor Will Not Crank Engine.

(1) AMMETER DROPS TOWARD ZERO WHEN STARTING SWITCH IS PRESSED.

Possible Cause	Possible Remedy
Battery discharged.	Replace or charge battery (par. 97).
Battery terminals or ground cables loose or corroded.	Remove and clean.
Cranking motor drive gear jammed in flywheel teeth.	Rock vehicle backwards or loosen cranking motor (par. 89).
Excessive engine friction due to seizure or improper oil.	Change oil to proper grade (par. 18); if seizure has occurred, report to higher authority.

(2) AMMETER REMAINS UNCHANGED WHEN STARTING SWITCH IS PRESSED.

Battery cable terminal corroded or broken.	Clean or replace.
Poor starting switch contacts.	Replace switch (par. 90).

(3) CRANKING MOTOR RUNS BUT FAILS TO CRANK ENGINE WHEN SWITCH IS PRESSED.

Cranking motor gear does not engage flywheel.	Remove cranking motor and clean gear (par. 89).
Cranking motor or drive gear faulty.	Replace cranking motor (par. 89).

c. Engine Will Not Start.

(1) NO SPARK.

(a) Ammeter Shows No Discharge (Zero Reading) with Ignition Switch "ON."

Ignition switch partly on.	Turn on fully.
Ignition switch faulty.	Replace switch (par. 68).

Possible Cause	Possible Remedy
Ignition primary wires, or cranking motor cables broken, or connections loose.	Repair or replace and tighten
Ignition coil primary winding open.	Replace coil (par. 66).
Distributor points burned, pitted, or dirty.	Clean or replace and adjust (par. 64).
Distributor points not closing.	Clean and adjust; put one drop of oil on arm post (par. 63).
Loose or corroded ground or battery cable connections.	Clean or replace and tighten.
Open circuit in suppression filter.	Test for trouble by removing ignition switch and coil wires, and connect together; if filter is faulty, report to higher authority.

(b) Ammeter Reading Normal.

Possible Cause	Possible Remedy
High tension wire from coil to distributor broken, grounded, or out of terminals.	Repair or replace (par. 69).
Short-circuited secondary circuit in coil.	Replace coil (par. 66).
Short-circuited condenser.	Replace condenser (par. 64).
Short-circuited or burned distributor cap or rotor.	Replace part (par. 64).
Spark plugs, distributor cap, or wires wet (shorted).	Dry and clean thoroughly.
Spark plug gaps wrong.	Reset gaps (par. 67).
Ignition timing incorrect.	Set timing (par. 65).
Ignition wires installed wrong in distributor cap.	Put in proper places (par. 69).

(c) Ammeter Indicates Abnormal Discharge.

Possible Cause	Possible Remedy
Short-circuited wire between ammeter and ignition switch or coil.	Repair or replace wire.
Short-circuited primary winding in ignition coil.	Install new coil (par. 66).
Radio filter short-circuited.	Disconnect temporarily, and report to higher authority.
Short-circuited condenser or broken lead.	Repair lead or replace condenser (par. 64).

TROUBLE SHOOTING

Possible Cause	Possible Remedy
Distributor points not opening.	Clean or replace and adjust (par. 63).
Distributor does not operate cam to open points.	Report to higher authority.
(2) WEAK SPARK.	
Distributor points pitted or burned.	Clean or replace and adjust (par. 64).
Distributor condenser weak.	Replace (par. 64).
Ignition coil weak.	Replace (par. 66).
Primary wire connections loose.	Tighten.
High tension or spark plug wires or distributor cap wet.	Dry thoroughly.
High tension or spark plug wires or distributor cap damaged.	Replace (par. 69).
Distributor rotor burned or broken.	Replace (par. 64).
(3) GOOD SPARK.	
Fuel tank empty.	Refill tank (par. 75).
Dirt or water in carburetor or float stuck.	Report to higher authority.
Carburetor and engine flooded by excessive use of choke.	Pull out throttle; crank engine with motor; when engine starts, regulate throttle; leave choke control "IN."
Choke control not operating properly.	Adjust (par. 72).
Fuel does not reach carburetor.	Check for damaged or leaky lines; air leak into line between tank and fuel pump.
Dirt in fuel lines or tank.	Disconnect drain tank and blow out lines.
Fuel line pinched.	Repair or replace.
Fuel strainer clogged.	Dismantle and clean (par. 76).
Fuel pump does not pump.	Clean screen; replace pump if inoperative (par. 74).
Lack of compression.	Report to higher authority.
(4) BACKFIRING.	
Ignition out of time.	Retime (par. 65).
Spark plug wires in wrong places in distributor cap or at spark plugs.	Install in proper places (par. 69).

¼-TON 4 x 4 TRUCK (WILLYS-OVERLAND MODEL MB and FORD MODEL GPW)

Possible Cause	Possible Remedy
Distributor cap cracked or shorted.	Replace (par. 64).
Valve holding open—due to lack of compression.	Report to higher authority.

d. Engine Runs but Backfires and Spits.

Possible Cause	Possible Remedy
Overheated engine.	Check (subpar. l below).
Improper ignition timing.	Reset (par. 65).
Spark plug wires in wrong place in distributor cap.	Install in proper places (par. 69).
Dirt or water in carburetor.	Clean and adjust (par. 72).
Carburetor improperly adjusted.	Check idle adjustment (par. 72).
Carburetor float level low.	Report to higher authority.
Valve sticking or not seating properly, burned, or pitted.	Report to higher authority.
Excessive carbon in cylinders.	Remove carbon (par. 54).
Valve springs weak.	Report to higher authority.
Heat control valve not operating.	Free-up and check thermostat spring position (par. 53).
Fuel pump pressure low.	Clean screen; replace pump, if faulty (par. 74).
Fuel strainer clogged.	Dismantle and clean (par. 76).
Partly clogged or pinched fuel line.	Clean or repair.
Intake manifold leak.	Check gaskets (par. 52).
Distributor cap cracked or shorted.	Replace (par. 64).

e. Engine Stalls on Idle.

Possible Cause	Possible Remedy
Carburetor throttle valve closes too far, or idle mixture incorrect.	Adjust (par. 72).
Carburetor choke valve sticks closed.	Free-up and lubricate.
Dirt or water in idle passages of carburetor.	Replace carburetor (par. 72).
Air leak at intake manifold.	Tighten manifold stud nuts or replace gaskets (par. 52).
Heat control valve faulty.	Free-up and adjust (par 53).
Spark plugs faulty, gaps incorrect.	Clean or replace, set gaps (par. 67).
Ignition timing too early.	Reset (par. 65).
Low compression.	Report to higher authority.

TROUBLE SHOOTING

Possible Cause	Possible Remedy
Water leak in cylinder head or gasket.	Replace gasket, or report cylinder head leak to higher authority.
Crankcase ventilator valve stuck open.	Clean (par. 59).

f. Engine Misfires on One or More Cylinders.

Possible Cause	Possible Remedy
Dirty spark plugs.	Clean and adjust or replace (par. 67).
Wrong type spark plugs.	Replace with correct type (par. 67).
Spark plug gap incorrect.	Reset gap (par. 67).
Cracked spark plug porcelain.	Replace spark plug (par. 67).
Spark plug or distributor suppressors faulty.	Replace (par. 67).
Spark plug wires grounded.	Replace.
Spark plug wires in wrong places in cap or at spark plugs.	Install correctly (par. 69).
Distributor cap or rotor burned or broken.	Replace (par. 64).
Valve tappet holding valve open.	Service (par. 56).
Compression poor—valve trouble.	Report to higher authority.
Leaky cylinder head gasket.	Replace gasket (par. 54).
Cracked cylinder block or broken valve tappet or tappet screw.	Report to higher authority.

g. Engine Does Not Idle Properly—(Erratic).

Possible Cause	Possible Remedy
Ignition timed too early.	Reset (par. 65).
Dirty spark plugs or gaps too close.	Clean and adjust (par. 67).
Ignition coil or condenser weak.	Replace (par. 66).
Distributor points sticking, dirty or improperly adjusted.	Adjust or replace (par. 64).
Distributor rotor or cap cracked or burned.	Replace (par. 64).
Weak or broken valve spring.	Report to higher authority.
Leaky cylinder head gasket.	Replace (par. 54).
Uneven cylinder compression.	Report to higher authority.
High tension or spark plug wires leaky—cracked insulation.	Replace.
Dirt or water in carburetor, or float level incorrect.	Report to higher authority.
Carburetor adjustment or choke not set right.	Adjust (par. 72).

Possible Cause	Possible Remedy
Fuel pump pressure low.	Clean screen; replace pump (par. 74).
Crankcase ventilator valve leaks.	Clean (par. 59).
Leaky intake manifold.	Tighten manifold stud nuts or replace gaskets (par. 52).

h. Engine Misses On Acceleration.

Dirty spark plugs or gaps too wide.	Clean and adjust (par. 67).
Wrong type spark plug.	Replace (par. 67).
Ignition coil or condenser weak.	Replace (par. 66).
Distributor breaker points sticking, dirty or improperly adjusted.	Adjust or replace (par. 64).
Distributor cap or rotor cracked or burned.	Replace (par. 64).
Distributor cap, spark plugs or wire wet or dirty.	Clean and dry thoroughly.
High tension or spark plug wires leaky—cracked insulation.	Replace (par. 69).
Carburetor choke not adjusted.	Adjust (par. 72).
Carburetor accelerating pump system faulty, dirt in metering jets or float level incorrect.	Report to higher authority.
Fuel pump faulty—lack of fuel.	Clean screen; replace faulty pump (par. 74).
Air cleaner dirty.	Clean and reoil (par. 73).
Heat control valve faulty.	Check and adjust (par. 53).
Valves sticking—weak or broken valve springs.	Report to higher authority.
Overheated engine.	Check (subpar. l below).
Fuel strainer clogged.	Dismantle and clean (par. 76).

i. Engine Misses at High Speeds.

Distributor points sticking, adjusted too wide or burned.	Clean and adjust (par. 64).
Weak distributor arm spring.	Replace (par. 64).
Incorrect type of spark plugs.	Replace (par. 67).
Excessive play in distributor shaft bearing.	Replace distributor (par. 64).
Spark plugs faulty, dirty or incorrect gap.	Clean, adjust or replace (par. 67).
Weak ignition coil or condenser.	Replace (par. 66).

TROUBLE SHOOTING

Possible Cause	Possible Remedy
Valves sticking—weak or broken springs.	Report to higher authority.
Fuel supply lacking at carburetor.	Check fuel system (par. 71 **a**).
Heat control valve faulty.	Free-up and adjust (par. 53).
Air cleaner dirty.	Clean and reoil (par. 73).
Carburetor metering rod incorrectly set.	Report to higher authority.

j. Engine Pings (Spark Knock).

Possible Cause	Possible Remedy
Ignition timing early.	Reset (par. 65).
Distributor automatic spark advance stuck in advance position or spring broken.	Replace distributor (par. 64).
Overheated engine.	Check (subpar. **l** below).
Excessive carbon deposit in cylinders.	Remove cylinder head and clean (par. 54).
Heat control valve faulty.	Free-up and adjust (par. 53).
Wrong type spark plug.	Replace (par. 67).
Old or incorrect fuel.	Drain and use correct fuel (par. 3).

k. Engine Lacks Power.

Possible Cause	Possible Remedy
Ignition timing late.	Reset (par. 65).
Ignition system faulty.	Check (subpar. **c** above).
Old or incorrect fuel.	Use correct gasoline.
Leaky gaskets.	Replace.
Engine overheated.	Check (subpar. **l** below).
Excessive carbon formation.	Remove cylinder head and clean (par. 54).
Engine too cold.	Test thermostat (par. 85); in cold weather, cover radiator.
Insufficient oil or improper grade.	Use correct grade (par. 18).
Oil system failure.	Report to higher authority.
Air cleaner dirty.	Clean; change oil in reservoir (par. 73).
Spark plug gaps too wide.	Reset (par. 67).
Choke valve partially closed or throttle does not open fully.	Adjust (par. 72).
Manifold heat control inoperative.	Check valve operation; see that spring is in proper position (par. 53).

Possible Cause	Possible Remedy
Exhaust pipe, muffler or tail pipe damaged or clogged.	Service or replace (par. 78).
Low compression—broken valve springs or sticking valves or improper tappet adjustment.	Report to higher authority.
Lack of fuel.	Clean filter (par. 76) check fuel pump (par. 74) check carburetor for water or dirt (par. 72).

l. **Engine Overheats.**

Possible Cause	Possible Remedy
Cooling system deficient.	Water low; air flow through radiator core restricted, clean from engine side; clogged core, clean or replace radiator (par. 81).
Radiator or water pump leaky.	Replace (par. 82).
Leaky cylinder head gasket.	Tighten or replace gasket (par. 54).
Damaged or deteriorated hose or fan belt.	Replace (par. 83).
Loose fan belt.	Adjust, or generator brace not hooked (par. 83).
Cylinder block, head or core hole plugs leaky.	Report to higher authority.
Ignition timing incorrect.	Reset (par. 65).
Damaged muffler; bent or clogged exhaust pipe.	Service or replace (par. 78).
Excessive carbon in cylinders.	Remove cylinder head and clean (par. 54).
Insufficient oil or improper grade.	Use correct grade (par. 18).
Air cleaner restricted.	Clean and renew oil (par. 73).
Inoperative thermostat or radiator cap.	Replace (par. 85).
Ignition system faulty.	Check (subpar. **c** above).
Water pump impeller broken.	Replace pump (par. 82).
Poor compression or valve timing wrong.	Report to higher authority.
Oil system failure (clogged screen).	Check (subpar. **p** below).

m. **Low Fuel Mileage.**

Possible Cause	Possible Remedy
High engine speeds (unnecessary and excessive driving in lower gear range).	Correct driving practice.

TROUBLE SHOOTING

Possible Cause	Possible Remedy
Air cleaner clogged.	Clean and renew oil (par. 73).
Carburetor float level too high. Metering rod, accelerating pump not properly adjusted.	Report to higher authority.
Fuel line leaks.	Tighten or replace.
Overheated engine.	Check (subpar. l above).
Carburetor parts worn or broken.	Replace carburetor (par. 72).
Fuel pump pressure too high or leaky diaphragm.	Replace fuel pump (par. 74).
Engine running cold.	Check thermostat (par. 85); cover radiator.
Heat control valve inoperative.	Free-up and put spring on bracket (par. 53).
Choke partially closed.	Adjust (par. 72).
Ignition timed wrong.	Reset (par. 65).
Spark advance stuck.	Replace distributor (par. 64).
Leaky fuel pump bowl gasket.	Replace gasket (par. 74).
Low compression.	Report to higher authority.
Carburetor controls sticking.	Free-up and lubricate.
Engine idles too fast.	Adjust carburetor throttle stop screw (par. 72).
Spark plugs dirty.	Clean or replace (par. 67).
Weak coil or condenser.	Replace (par. 64).
Clogged muffler or bent exhaust pipe.	Service or replace (par. 78).
Loose engine mountings permitting engine to shake and raise fuel level in carburetor.	Tighten; if damaged replace.

n. Low Oil Mileage.

Possible Cause	Possible Remedy
High engine speeds or unnecessary and excessive driving in low gear ranges.	Correct driving practice.
Oil leaks.	Replace leaky gaskets.
Improper grade or diluted oil.	Use new oil of proper grade (par. 18).
Overheating of engine causing excessive temperature and thinning of oil.	Check (subpar. l above).
Oil filter clogged.	Clean; replace element (par. 58).

Possible Cause	Possible Remedy
Faulty pistons, or rings or rear bearing oil return clogged; excessive clearance of intake valves in guides; cylinder bores worn (scored, out-of-round, tapered); excessive bearing clearance; misalined connecting rods.	Report to higher authority.

o. Poor Compression.

Possible Cause	Possible Remedy
Incorrect tappet adjustment.	Adjust (par. 56).
Leaky, sticking or burned valves; sticking tappets; valve springs weak or broken; valve stems and guides worn; piston ring grooves worn or rings worn, broken or stuck; cylinders scored or worn excessively.	Report to higher authority.

p. Low Oil Pressure.

Possible Cause	Possible Remedy
Insufficient oil supply.	Check oil level.
Improper grade of oil or diluted oil foaming at high speeds.	Change oil; check crankcase ventilator (par. 59); check for water in oil by inspecting dip stick.
High oil temperature causing oil to be thin.	Check (subpar. l above).
Oil too heavy (funneling in cold weather).	Dilute engine oil (par. 18).
Floating oil intake loose or gasket leaky.	Renew gasket, tighten (par. 57).
Oil screen clogged.	Remove oil pan and clean screen (par. 57).
Oil leak causing lack of oil.	Inspect and service.
Faulty oil pump or pressure regulator valve stuck or spring broken.	Report to higher authority.
Oil filter restriction hole too large.	Replace oil filter (par. 58).
Oil pressure too high.	Faulty oil pump regulator valve stuck closed or improperly adjusted, report to higher authority.

q. Faulty Valves.

Possible Cause	Possible Remedy
Incorrect tappet adjustment.	Adjust tappets (par. 56).
Other valve troubles.	Report to higher authority.

TROUBLE SHOOTING

r. Abnormal Engine Noises.

Possible Cause	Possible Remedy
Loose fan, fan pulley or belt, heat control valve, or noisy generator brush.	Tighten or service.
Leaky intake or exhaust manifold or gaskets, cylinder head gasket or spark plug.	Replace or tighten (pars. 52 and 54).
Overheated engine; clogged exhaust system.	Remove obstruction from muffler tail pipe. Check (subpar. 1 above).
Other abnormal engine noises.	Report to higher authority.

31. CLUTCH.

a. Clutch Slips.

Possible Cause	Possible Remedy
Improper pedal adjustment.	Adjust pedal free travel (par. 109).
Release linkage binding.	Free-up and lubricate.
Clutch facings burned or worn, torn loose from plate, or oil-soaked.	Replace clutch driven plate (pars. 110 and 111).
Weak pressure spring.	Report to higher authority.
Sticking pressure plate.	Report to higher authority.

b. Clutch Grabs or Chatters.

Possible Cause	Possible Remedy
Control linkage binding.	Free-up and lubricate.
Loose engine mountings.	Tighten.
Engine stay cable not adjusted.	Adjust; just taut.
Facings burned, worn, or loose on driven plate; driven plate crimped or cushion flattened out, worn, or binding on splined shaft.	Replace clutch driven plate (pars. 110 and 111).
Pressure plate or flywheel face scored or rough; pressure plate broken; improper clutch lever (finger) adjustment; excessive looseness in power train.	Report to higher authority.

c. Clutch Drags.

Possible Cause	Possible Remedy
Too much pedal play.	Adjust pedal free play (par. 109).
Driven plate warped; facings torn or loose.	Replace clutch driven plate (pars. 110 and 111).
Pressure plate warped or binds in bracket; improper finger adjustment; excessive friction in flywheel bushing.	Report to higher authority.

d. Clutch Rattles.

Possible Cause	Possible Remedy
Clutch pedal return spring is broken or disconnected.	Replace or connect.
Release fork loose on ball stud.	Adjust clutch pedal free travel to ¾ inch (par. 109).
Driven plate springs broken. Worn release bearing.	Replace (pars. 110 and 111).
Worn pressure plate or broken return springs at driving lugs; worn driven plate hub on splined shaft; worn release bearing; fingers improperly adjusted; pilot bushing worn in flywheel.	Report to higher authority.

32. FUEL SYSTEM.

a. Fuel Does Not Reach Carburetor.

No fuel in tank.	Fill tank.
Fuel filter clogged.	Service fuel filter (par. 76).
Fuel pump inoperative.	Replace.
Fuel line air leak between tank and fuel pump.	Locate and correct.
Fuel line clogged.	Disconnect and blow out lines.
Fuel tank cap not functioning.	Replace cap.

b. Fuel Reaches Carburetor but Does Not Enter Cylinders.

Choke does not close.	Free-up and lubricate; inspect for proper operation.
Fuel passages in carburetor clogged.	Replace carburetor (par. 72).
Carburetor float valve stuck closed.	Report to higher authority.

c. Low Fuel Mileage.

Engine at fault.	Check (par. 30 m above).
Lubricant in power train too heavy.	Use correct lubricant (par. 18).
Tires improperly inflated.	Inflate (par. 3).
Vehicle overloaded.	Reduce to 500 pounds if possible.

d. Low Fuel Pressure.

Air leak in fuel lines.	Tighten connections; repair if damaged; hand-tighten fuel pump dome nut.

TROUBLE SHOOTING

Possible Cause	Possible Remedy
Fuel pump faulty; diaphragm broken; valves leaky; linkage worn.	Replace fuel pump (par. 74).
Fuel lines clogged.	Clean or replace lines.

e. Engine Idles Too Fast.

Possible Cause	Possible Remedy
Improper carburetor throttle adjustment.	Adjust throttle stop screw (par. 72).
Carburetor control sticking.	Free-up and lubricate.
Control return spring weak.	Replace.

f. Fuel Gage Does Not Register.

Possible Cause	Possible Remedy
Loose wire connection at instrument panel or tank units.	Tighten connection.
Instrument panel unit or tank unit inoperative.	Replace (pars. 75 and 77).

33. INTAKE AND EXHAUST SYSTEMS.

a. Intake System.

Possible Cause	Possible Remedy
Leaky gaskets, sand hole or crack in manifold.	Replace (par. 52).
Leaky crankcase ventilator valve.	Replace (par. 59).

b. Exhaust System.

Possible Cause	Possible Remedy
Leaky gaskets, sand hole or crack in manifold.	Replace (par. 52).
Exhaust pipe and connections loose or leaking.	Service and/or replace (par. 78).
Muffler leaks or rattles.	Replace (par. 78).
Exhaust system or muffler restricted; exhaust pipe kinked or tail pipe plugged.	Service or replace parts.
Heat control valve inoperative, causing miss on acceleration or slow warm-up.	Free-up; install spring in place on bracket (par. 53).

34. COOLING SYSTEM.

a. Overheating.

Possible Cause	Possible Remedy
Abnormal conditions.	Check (par. 30 l).

b. Loss of Cooling Solution.

Possible Cause	Possible Remedy
Loose hose connection.	Tighten.
Damaged or deteriorated hose.	Replace.

Possible Cause	Possible Remedy
Leaky radiator.	Replace (par. 81).
Radiator cap inoperative.	Replace.

c. Engine Running Too Cool.

Possible Cause	Possible Remedy
Thermostat stuck open.	Replace (par. 85).
Low air temperatures.	Cover radiator; refer to operation under unusual conditions (par. 7).

d. Noises.

Possible Cause	Possible Remedy
Frayed or loose fan belt.	Replace or adjust (par. 83).
Water pump faulty.	Replace (par. 82).
Fan blades striking.	Aline blades.

35. IGNITION SYSTEM.

a. Ignition System Troubles.

Possible Cause	Possible Remedy
No spark.	Refer to paragraph 30 **c** (1).
Weak spark.	Refer to paragraph 30 **c** (2).
Timing incorrect.	Retime ignition (par. 65); refer to paragraph 30 **j** for other causes.
Moisture on distributor wires, coil, or spark plugs.	Dry and clean thoroughly with cloth dampened with carbon tetrachloride.
Ignition switch "OFF."	Turn "ON" fully.
Ignition switch does not make contact.	Replace switch (par. 68).
Primary or secondary wiring loose, broken, or grounded.	Service.
Primary or secondary wiring wrong.	Check against wiring diagram (par. 62 and fig. 30); install secondary wires correctly in distributor cap and on spark plugs.
Ground strap connections (engine to frame) loose or dirty.	Clean and tighten.
Coil faulty.	Refer to subparagraph **b** below.
Distributor faulty.	Refer to subparagraph **c** below.
Spark plug or distributor suppressors faulty.	Replace (par. 67).
Filter unit open or grounded.	Replace filter (par. 69).

TROUBLE SHOOTING

b. Ignition Coil Troubles.

Possible Cause	Possible Remedy
Connections loose; dirty or broken external wire; wet.	Clean and tighten or repair; dry thoroughly.
Coil internal fault.	Replace coil (par. 66).

c. Distributor Troubles.

Possible Cause	Possible Remedy
Distributor breaker points dirty or pitted; gap incorrect.	Clean or replace and adjust (par. 64).
Distributor breaker point arm spring weak.	Replace breaker point arm (par. 64).
Distributor breaker points stuck open.	Free-up and lubricate arm on post.
Distributor automatic advance faulty.	Lubricate and free up; if "frozen" replace distributor (par. 64).
Distributor cap or rotor shorted, cracked, or broken.	Replace.
Distributor rotor does not turn.	Report to higher authority.
Distributor cap cracked or shorted.	Replace cap (par. 64).
Condenser or lead wire faulty.	Replace condenser (par. 64).

d. Spark Plug Troubles.

Possible Cause	Possible Remedy
Cracked, broken, leaky, or improper type.	Replace spark plug (par. 67).
Spark plug wires installed on wrong plugs, or in distributor cap.	Install in correct place (par. 69).
Spark plugs dirty; gaps incorrect.	Clean or replace; set gaps (par. 67).
Spark plug porcelain cracked or broken.	Replace plug.
Spark plugs wrong type.	Replace with correct type (par. 67).

36. STARTING AND GENERATING SYSTEMS.

a. Cranking Motor Troubles.

(1) CRANKING MOTOR CRANKS ENGINE SLOWLY.

Possible Cause	Possible Remedy
Engine oil too heavy.	Change to proper seasonal grade (par. 18).
Battery low.	Replace or recharge (par. 97).
Battery cell shorted.	Replace battery (par. 97).

¼-TON 4 x 4 TRUCK (WILLYS-OVERLAND MODEL MB and FORD MODEL GPW)

Possible Cause	Possible Remedy
Battery connections corroded, broken, or loose; or engine ground strap to frame connections dirty or loose.	Clean and tighten or replace (par. 97).
Dirty commutator.	Clean (par. 89).
Poor brush contact.	Free-up brush or replace cranking motor (par. 89).
Cranking motor internal fault.	Replace cranking motor.
Starting switch faulty.	Replace switch (par. 90).

(2) CRANKING MOTOR DOES NOT CRANK ENGINE.

Possible Cause	Possible Remedy
Engine oil too heavy.	Change to proper seasonal grade (par. 18).
Cranking motor, starting switch or cables faulty; loose connections.	Replace; tighten loose connections.

b. Generator Troubles.

(1) NO OUTPUT.

Possible Cause	Possible Remedy
Generator faulty.	Replace generator (par. 93).
Filter unit or suppressors faulty.	Replace (par. 93).
Regulator faulty.	Replace (par. 94).

(2) LOW OR FLUCTUATING OUTPUT.

Possible Cause	Possible Remedy
Loose fan belt.	Adjust (par. 83); generator brace not hooked (par. 4 **b** (8)).
Poor brush contact, weak brush springs; worn commutator; broken or loose connections.	Replace generator (par. 93).
Dirty commutator.	Clean (par. 93).
Regulator faulty.	Replace (par. 94)
Loose or dirty connections in charging circuit.	Clean and tighten.
Ground strap (engine to frame) broken.	Replace.
Filter unit faulty.	Replace (par. 93).

(3) EXCESSIVE OUTPUT.

Possible Cause	Possible Remedy
Short circuit between field coil and armature leads.	Replace generator (par. 93).
Regulator faulty.	Replace regulator (par. 94).

(4) NOISY.

Possible Cause	Possible Remedy
Loose pulley or generator mounting.	Tighten.

TROUBLE SHOOTING

Possible Cause	Possible Remedy
Faulty bearings, improperly seated brushes, or armature rubbing on field poles.	Replace generator (par. 93).

c. Generator Regulator Troubles.

Possible Cause	Possible Remedy
Loose connections or mounting.	Clean and tighten.
Regulator internal defect.	Replace regulator (par. 94).

37. TRANSMISSION.

a. Excessive Noise.

Possible Cause	Possible Remedy
Incorrect driving practice.	Correct practice (par. 5).
Insufficient lubricant.	Add lubricant (par. 18).
Incorrect lubricant.	Use correct lubricant (par. 18).
Gears or bearings broken or worn; shift fork bent; gears worn on splines.	Replace transmission (pars. 115 and 116).
Overheated transmission.	Check lubricant grade and supply (par. 18).

b. Hard Shifting.

Possible Cause	Possible Remedy
Clutch fails to release.	Adjust clutch pedal free travel (par. 109).
Clutch driven plate binds on splines, or pressure plate faulty.	Report to higher authority.
Gearshift binding in housing.	Lubricate and free-up.
Shift rods binding in case.	Report to higher authority.
Transmission loose on bell housing.	Tighten.
Clutch shaft pilot binding in bushing case or shift housing damaged.	Report to higher authority.

c. Slips Out of Gear.

Possible Cause	Possible Remedy
Weak or broken poppet spring.	Report to higher authority.
Interlock plunger not in place.	Install plunger (par. 116).
Transmission gears or bearings worn.	Replace transmission (pars. 115 and 116).
Shift fork bent, causing partial gear engagement.	Report to higher authority.
Transmission loose on bell housing.	Tighten.
Damaged bell housing.	Report to higher authority.

d. Loss of Lubricant.

Possible Cause	Possible Remedy
Worn or damaged seals or gaskets.	Report to higher authority.

Possible Cause	Possible Remedy
Overfilled with lubricant.	Drain to proper level.
Loose bolts and screws.	Tighten.

38. TRANSFER CASE.

a. Slips Out of Gear.

Possible Cause	Possible Remedy
Shift rod poppet spring weak or broken; gears not fully engaged; shift fork bent; end play in sliding gear shaft.	Report to higher authority.
Parts damaged or worn.	Replace transfer case (pars. 119 and 120).

b. Hard Shifting.

Possible Cause	Possible Remedy
Improper driving practice.	Use correct procedure (par. 5).
Lack of lubrication.	Replenish supply.
Shift lever seizing on shaft.	Lubricate and free-up.
Shift rod tight in case; poppet scored or stuck; shift fork bent, or parts worn or damaged.	Report to higher authority.
Low or uneven tire pressures; odd tires on (front and rear) wheels.	Service.

c. Oil Leaks.

Possible Cause	Possible Remedy
Leaks at gaskets or seals.	Report to higher authority.
Lubricant level too high.	Reduce to correct level.
Vent on top of unit clogged.	Clean.

d. Excessive Noise.

Possible Cause	Possible Remedy
Insufficient lubricant.	Replenish supply.
Incorrect lubricant.	Drain and refill with correct lubricant (par. 18).
Gears or bearings worn, improperly adjusted, or damaged.	Replace transfer case (pars. 119 and 120).

e. Overheats.

Possible Cause	Possible Remedy
Insufficient lubricant.	Replenish supply.
Vent on top of unit clogged.	Clean.
Bearings adjusted too tight.	Report to higher authority.

f. Backlash.

Possible Cause	Possible Remedy
Universal joint yoke loose on output shaft.	Report to higher authority.

TROUBLE SHOOTING

Possible Cause	Possible Remedy
Transfer case loose on transmission or snubbing rubber.	Tighten.
Parts worn or damaged.	Report to higher authority

39. PROPELLER SHAFTS.

a. Excessive Vibration or Noise.

Foreign material around shaft.	Clean out.
Universal joints not in same plane.	Match arrows on joint and propeller shaft (par. 125).
Lack of lubricant.	Lubricate (par. 18).
Universal joint parts worn, or propeller shaft sprung.	Replace shaft.

b. Universal Joint Leaks.

Overfilled.	Lubricate correctly (par. 18).
Oil seals leak.	Report to higher authority.
Lubricant fitting leaks.	Replace fitting.

40. FRONT AXLE.

a. Steering trouble.	Refer to paragraph 45.
b. Noisy gears or backlash.	Report to higher authority.
c. Damaged axle.	Replace axle (pars. 136 and 137).
d. Abnormal tire wear.	Inflate tires (par. 13 **b** (13)) (do not use front wheel drive except where needed); correct toe-in; report to higher authority incorrect caster or camber.
e. Lubrication leaks.	Replace steering knuckle oil seals; for other remedies refer to paragraph 41 **c**.

41. REAR AXLE.

a. Noisy gears or backlash.	Report to higher authority.
b. Damaged axle.	Replace axle (par. 145).
c. Lubrication leaks.	Drain excessive lubricant; clean housing vent; replace wheel bearing grease seals; remove excessive grease in wheel hubs; tighten or replace housing cover gasket.

42. BRAKE SYSTEM.

a. All Brakes Drag.

Possible Cause	Possible Remedy
Improper pedal adjustment.	Adjust brake pedal free travel (par. 148).
Clogged master cylinder port.	Replace (par. 150).
Brake pedal return spring broken or weak.	Replace.
Brakes improperly adjusted.	Adjust (par. 148).
Rubber parts swollen from use of mineral oil in brake fluid.	Report to higher authority.

b. One Brake Drags.

Possible Cause	Possible Remedy
Brake shoe adjustment faulty.	Adjust (par. 148).
Brake shoe anchor pin tight in shoes.	Free-up and lubricate lightly.
Brake shoe return spring broken or weak.	Replace.
Brake hose clogged or pinched.	Replace.
Loose or damaged wheel bearings.	Adjust or replace (pars. 128 and 141).
Wheel cylinder pistons or cups faulty.	Replace wheel cylinder (par. 150).

c. One Brake Grabs (Vehicle Pulls to One Side).

Possible Cause	Possible Remedy
Tires underinflated.	Inflate tires (par. 13).
Tires worn unequally.	Replace.
Insufficient brake shoe clearance or brake anchor pin adjustment faulty.	Adjust (par. 148).
Axle spring clips or brake backing plate loose.	Tighten.
Brake shoes binding on anchor pin.	Free-up and lubricate lightly.
Weak or broken shoe return spring.	Replace spring.
Grease or brake fluid on linings.	Correct leakage; clean up and install new shoes and lining assemblies.
Dirt imbedded in linings or rivet holes.	Clean with wire brush.
Drums scored or rough.	Replace drums and brake shoe and lining assemblies.

TROUBLE SHOOTING

Possible Cause	Possible Remedy
Primary and secondary brake shoes reversed in one wheel.	Change shoes to proper place and adjust brakes (par. 148).
Odd kinds of brake lining on opposite wheels.	Replace shoe and lining assemblies in both wheels.
Loose or broken wheel bearings.	Adjust or replace (pars. 128 and 141).
Obstruction in brake line.	Clean or replace tube (par. 152).

d. Severe Brake Action on Light Pedal Pressure.

Possible Cause	Possible Remedy
Brake shoes improperly adjusted.	Adjust (par. 148).
Grease or brake fluid on linings.	Correct leakage, clean up and replace shoe and lining assemblies.
Loose brake shoe anchor.	Adjust and tighten (par. 148).
Improper linings.	Replace shoe and lining assemblies (par. 148).

e. Brakes Locked.

Possible Cause	Possible Remedy
Brake pedal lacks free travel.	Adjust pedal free travel (par. 148).
Bleed hole in master cylinder clogged.	Replace master cylinder (par. 150).
Dirt in brake fluid.	Flush system (par. 151).
Wheel cylinder stuck.	Replace cylinder (par. 150).
Brakes frozen to drums (cold weather).	Break loose by driving vehicle.

f. Brakes Noisy or Chatter.

Possible Cause	Possible Remedy
Brake lining worn out.	Replace shoe and lining assemblies (par. 148).
Grease or brake fluid on linings.	Correct leakage, clean up and replace shoe and lining assemblies (par. 148).
Improper adjustment of anchor bolts.	Adjust (par. 148).
Dirt imbedded in linings and rivet holes.	Clean with wire brush.
Improper or loose linings.	Replace shoe and lining assemblies (par. 148).
Brake shoes, drums, or backing plate distorted.	Straighten or replace.
Loose spring clips or shackles.	Tighten.

g. Excessive Pedal Travel.

Possible Cause	Possible Remedy
Normal lining wear.	Adjust brake eccentrics only (par. 148).
Lining worn out.	Replace shoe and lining assemblies (par. 148).
Brake not properly adjusted.	Adjust (par. 148).
Improper pedal adjustment.	Adjust (par. 148).
Brake line leaky or broken.	Locate and tighten or repair.
Low fluid level in master cylinder or air in brake system.	Fill master cylinder and bleed lines (par. 151).
Scored brake drums.	Replace (pars. 131 and 144).
Incorrect brake lining.	Replace with correct shoe and lining assemblies.
Pedal goes to floorboard (disconnected from master cylinder).	Connect or replace faulty part (par. 149).
Leaky piston cup in master or wheel cylinders.	Replace cylinder.

h. Excessive Pedal Pressure.

Possible Cause	Possible Remedy
Grease or brake fluid on linings; worn or glazed lining.	Correct cause, clean up and replace shoe and lining assemblies (par. 148).
Warped shoes or improper brake linings.	Replace shoe and lining assemblies (par. 148).
Shoes improperly adjusted.	Adjust (par. 148).
Brake drums scored or distorted.	Replace damaged parts.
Improper brake fluid.	Clean system and fill with correct fluid.
Obstructed main brake line.	Locate and correct.

i. Spongy Brake Pedal Action.

Possible Cause	Possible Remedy
Air or insufficient fluid in brake system.	Fill master cylinder and bleed lines (par. 149).
Brake anchor adjustment faulty.	Adjust (par. 148).

j. No Brakes—Pedal Will Pump Up.

Possible Cause	Possible Remedy
Brake shoe clearance excessive.	Adjust brake eccentrics (par. 148).
Leaky master or wheel cylinder piston cup.	Replace cylinder.
Leaky brake line or hose.	Locate and tighten or replace.

k. Pedal Goes to Floor Slowly When Brakes Are Applied.

Possible Cause	Possible Remedy
Leaky master cylinder piston cup.	Replace master cylinder (par. 149).
Leaky brake line or hose.	Tighten or replace part.

43. WHEELS, WHEEL BEARINGS, AND RELATED PARTS.

a. Wheel Troubles.

Wheel wobbles; bent.	Check mounting on hub; replace bent wheel.
Wheel loose on hub.	Tighten.
Wheel out of balance.	Remount tire correctly.
Wheel bearings run hot (pull vehicle to one side).	Adjust (pars. 128 and 141).
Wheels misalined.	Refer to paragraph 135.
Excessive or uneven tire wear.	Refer to paragraph 45.
Diameter of front tires not the same in size or wear.	Replace or match up.

44. SPRINGS AND SHOCK ABSORBERS.

a. Broken Springs.

Improper handling of vehicle on rough terrain.	Use correct practice when possible (par. 5).
Overloaded vehicle.	Reduce load (par. 3).
Overlubricated springs.	Do not lubricate unless rusty.
Rebound clips off or out of place.	Service.
Shackles or pivot bolts too tight.	Free-up and lubricate.
Main leaf broken at end.	Replace spring (par. 156).
Axle clips loose (spring broken at center).	Keep clips tight.
Shock absorbers not adjusted correctly, lack fluid, or damaged.	Adjust or replace shock absorbers (par. 157).
Clutch or brakes grab.	Service.

b. Noisy Springs.

Worn shackles, pivot pins, or bushings.	Replace worn parts (par. 155).
Spring clips loose on axle or leaves.	Tighten.
Spring hangers loose on frame.	Report to higher authority.
Spring shackle bushing loose; inner spring eye opened up.	Replace spring (par. 156).

Possible Cause	Possible Remedy
No fluid in shock absorbers, or bushings worn out.	Replace (par. 157).

c. Bottomed Springs.

Possible Cause	Possible Remedy
Overloaded vehicle.	Reduce load (par. 3).
Overlubricated springs.	Do not lubricate unless rusty.
Broken spring leaves.	Replace spring (par. 156).
Shock absorbers broken, lack fluid or proper adjustment.	Replace shock absorbers (par. 159).

d. Overflexible Springs.

Possible Cause	Possible Remedy
Overlubrication causes springs to bottom.	Do not lubricate springs.
Shock absorbers not adjusted right, lack fluid, or are broken.	Service, adjust, or replace shock absorbers (par. 157).
Rebound clips damaged or lost.	Replace.
Broken spring.	Replace spring (par. 156).

e. Stiff Springs.

Possible Cause	Possible Remedy
Rusted spring leaves.	Lubricate.
Shackle or pivot bolts too tight.	Free-up and lubricate.
Shock absorber adjustment not right.	Adjust (par. 157).

f. Noisy Shock Absorbers.

Possible Cause	Possible Remedy
Rubber bushings worn out.	Replace bushing (par. 157).
Mounting bracket loose.	Report to higher authority.
Shock absorber faulty.	Replace (par. 157).

g. Shock Absorber Control Too Stiff or Too Soft.

Possible Cause	Possible Remedy
Shock absorber adjustment wrong.	Adjust (par. 157).
Shock absorber damaged or lacks fluid.	Replace shock absorber (par. 157).

45. STEERING SYSTEM.

a. Steering Difficult.

Possible Cause	Possible Remedy
Lack of lubrication.	Lubricate (par. 18).
Tire pressures low.	Inflate (par. 13).
Tight steering system connections.	Lubricate and adjust (par. 159).
Tight steering gear; misalined front wheels (caster or camber); or bent frame.	Report to higher authority.

TROUBLE SHOOTING

Possible Cause	Possible Remedy
Improper front wheel toe-in.	Adjust (par. 135).
Bent steering connecting parts.	Straighten or replace.
Misalined steering gear mounting.	Adjust mounting.

b. Wander or Weaving.

Possible Cause	Possible Remedy
Improper toe-in	Adjust (par. 135).
Improper camber or caster (axle twisted).	Report to higher authority.
Front springs settled or broken.	Replace spring (par. 156).
Axle shifted (spring center bolt broken).	Replace part.
Loose or lost spring clips.	Tighten or replace.
Loose or worn spring shackles or bolts.	Replace or tighten.
Tire pressures uneven.	Inflate (par. 13).
Steering system connections or king pin bearings not properly adjusted.	Lubricate and adjust (par. 159).
Loose wheel bearings.	Adjust (pars. 128 and 141).
Faulty shock absorbers.	Replace (par. 157).
Steering gear worn or out of adjustment.	Report to higher authority.
Steering gear mounting loose.	Tighten.
Steering Pitman arm loose.	Tighten.

c. Low Speed Shimmy or Wobble.

Possible Cause	Possible Remedy
Loose steering connections.	Adjust.
Spring clips or shackles loose.	Adjust or replace.
Front axle loose on spring (broken spring center bolt).	Replace bolt.
Insufficient toe-in.	Adjust (par. 135).
Improper caster or twisted axle.	Report to higher authority.
Steering gear worn, or adjustments too loose.	Report to higher authority.
Loose wheel or king pin bearings.	Adjust (par. 128).

d. High Speed Shimmy or Tight Wheel (Refer to remedies listed in subparagraph c above).

Possible Cause	Possible Remedy
Tire pressures low or uneven.	Inflate (par. 13).
Wheels and tires out of balance.	Check tire mounting; report other trouble to higher authority.

Possible Cause	Possible Remedy
Wheel run-out; tire radial run-out or wheel camber incorrect.	Report to higher authority.
Front springs settled or broken.	Replace spring (par. 156).
Bent steering knuckle arm.	Report to higher authority.
Shock absorbers not effective.	Adjust or replace.
Steering gear loose in frame.	Tighten.
Front springs too flexible.	Do not lubricate.
Worn spring bolts, shackles, or bushings.	Replace (par. 155).
Axle housing or frame damaged.	Report to higher authority.

e. Wheel Tramp (High Speed).

Possible Cause	Possible Remedy
Wheels and tires out of balance.	Check tire mounting; report other trouble to higher authority.
Uneven tire wear.	Shift tires.
Shock absorbers ineffective.	Replace or adjust (par. 157).

f. Vehicle Pulls to One Side.

Possible Cause	Possible Remedy
Tires not inflated evenly.	Inflate (par. 13).
Unequal caster or camber (bent axle).	Report to higher authority.
Odd size, or new and old tires on opposite front wheels.	Switch tires.
Tight wheel bearing.	Adjust (pars. 128 and 141).
Bent steering arm or connection.	Straighten or replace.
Brake drag.	Adjust brakes (par. 148).

g. Road Shock.

Possible Cause	Possible Remedy
Tightness in steering connecting parts.	Adjust (par. 159).
Excessive spring flexibility.	Do not lubricate.
Loose wheel bearings.	Adjust.
Loose Pitman arm or mounting.	Tighten.
Looseness in steering gear.	Report to higher authority.
Shock absorbers out of adjustment or faulty.	Adjust or replace (par. 157).

h. Steering Dive.

Possible Cause	Possible Remedy
Steering gear loose on frame.	Tighten.
Broken front spring leaves.	Replace.
Worn spring shackles, bushings or bolts.	Replace.

TROUBLE SHOOTING

Possible Cause	Possible Remedy
Spring hangers loose on frame.	Report to higher authority.
Spring clips loose, broken, or lost.	Tighten or replace.
Spring center bolt broken and/or clips loose.	Replace.
Axle housing on frame damaged.	Report to higher authority.

i. Unequal Steering (Right and Left).

Possible Cause	Possible Remedy
Pitman arm not installed in proper position on steering gear.	Remove and install in correct position (par. 162).
Drag link bent.	Straighten or replace.

46. BODY AND FRAME.

a. Body.

Possible Cause	Possible Remedy
Worn or damaged seat cushion.	Replace.
Badly damaged fender, radiator guard, hood, fuel can rack, seats, top, or windshield.	Replace; report minor damage to higher authority.
Windshield wiper faulty.	Service or replace.

b. Frame.

Possible Cause	Possible Remedy
Badly damaged bumpers and pintle hook.	Replace; report minor damage to higher authority.
Damaged frame.	Report to higher authority.

47. BATTERY AND LIGHTING SYSTEM.

a. Battery.

(1) BATTERY DISCHARGED.

Possible Cause	Possible Remedy
Battery solution level low.	Add distilled water to bring level above plates; check for cracked case.
Short in battery cell.	Replace battery (par. 97).
Generator not charging.	Check generator, fan belt and regulator (par. 92).
Loose or dirty connections; broken cables.	Clean and tighten connections; replace cables.
Excessive use of cranking motor.	Tune up engine; charge battery.
Idle battery, or excessive use of lights.	Replace or charge battery.

(2) BATTERY (OTHER TROUBLES.)

Possible Cause	Possible Remedy
Overheated battery.	Check for short circuit or excessive generator charge.

Possible Cause	Possible Remedy
Case bulged or out of shape.	Check for overcharging and too tight hold-down screws.

b. Switch.

Loose or dirty connections or broken wire.	Clean and tighten; replace broken wire.
Internal fault.	Replace switch.

c. Fuse (Circuit Breaker).

Points dirty.	Clean.
Other troubles.	Replace fuse assembly (par. 104).

d. Wiring.

Loose or dirty connections, broken wire or terminal.	Clean, tighten or replace.

e. Lights do Not Light.

Switch not fully on.	Turn switch on fully.
Loose or dirty connection, or broken wire or terminal.	Clean and tighten; replace or repair wire or terminal.
Wiring circuit shorted or open.	Localize and repair.
Headlight, blackout driving light, tail or stop light burned out.	Replace lamp-unit (par. 96).
Blackout headlight burned out.	Replace lamp (par. 100).

f. Lights Dim.

Loose or dirty connection or poor ground connection.	Clean and tighten.
Wire grounding.	Localize and replace (par. 98).
Poor switch contact.	Replace switch.
Headlight aim not right.	Adjust lights (par. 99).

g. Trailer Connection Trouble.

No current supply.	Tighten loose wires; connect to correct terminals.

h. Horn Troubles.

Loose or dirty connections.	Clean and tighten.
Sounds continuously (short circuit in wiring between horn and horn button).	Replace wire.
Improper tone.	Adjust points; tighten cover or bracket screws; clean and tighten loose or dirty wiring connections.

TROUBLE SHOOTING

Possible Cause	Possible Remedy
Internal defect.	Replace horn.
Battery low.	Charge or replace battery.

48. RADIO SUPPRESSION.

a. Radio Interference.

Possible Cause	Possible Remedy
Faulty ignition.	Check distributor, spark plugs, and suppressors. Tighten braided bonding straps. Tighten radiator and fender supporting bolts. Check high-tension insulation. Tighten loose wiring connections, or replace corroded distributor cap towers. Replace defective switches or gages (par. 178).
Faulty generator.	Tighten generator to regulator bond. Check for faulty commutator, brushes, or holders. If defective, replace generator. Check for discharged battery causing high charging rate (par. 178).
Erratic noises.	Tighten or clean loose or dirty lock washer ground. Install lock washers in correct position (par. 178).

49. INSTRUMENTS.

a. Faulty Instruments.

Possible Cause	Possible Remedy
Dirty or loose connections.	Clean and tighten.
Internal defects.	Replace instrument.
Broken speedometer cable.	Replace (par. 166).

Section XIII

ENGINE—DESCRIPTION, DATA, MAINTENANCE, AND ADJUSTMENT IN VEHICLE

Paragraph

50. DESCRIPTION AND TABULATED DATA.

a. Description. The engine (figs. 20 and 21) is of the conventional 4-cylinder, L-head, internal-combustion type. The engine with the clutch, transmission, and transfer case is built into a unit power plant which is mounted at four points in the chassis. For identification refer to paragraph 2 **b**.

b. Tabulated Data.

Type .... L-head
Number of cylinders 4
Bore .... 3⅛ in.
Stroke .... 4⅜ in.
Piston displacement .... 134.2 cu in.
Compression ratio .... 6.48 to 1
Net horsepower .... 54 at 4,000 rpm
Compression .... 110 lb per sq in. at 185 rpm
SAE horsepower 15.63
Maximum torque .... 95 ft-lb
Firing order 1-3-4-2
Tappet clearance—intake and exhaust
(hot or cold) .... 0.014 in.

51. ENGINE TUNE-UP.

a. Procedure.

(1) Perform preventive maintenance and corrective operations listed in paragraph 16.

(2) Remove spark plugs and clean. Adjust gaps (par. 67).

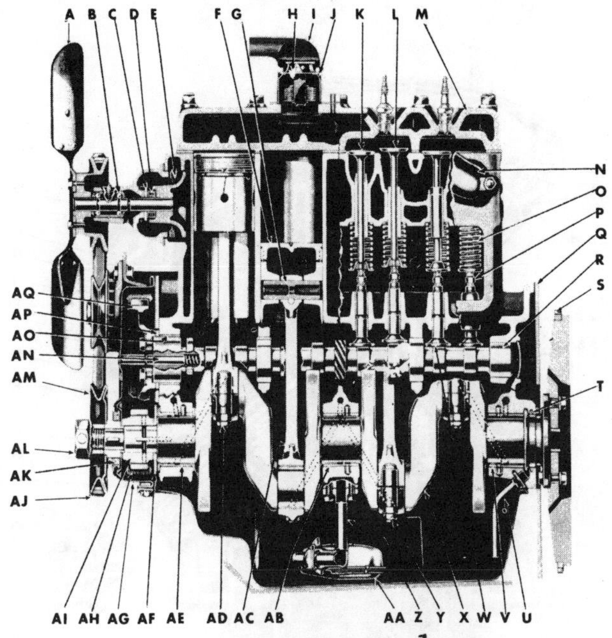

A FAN
B WATER PUMP BEARING AND SHAFT
C WATER PUMP SEAL WASHER
D WATER PUMP SEAL
E WATER PUMP IMPELLER
F PISTON
G PISTON PIN
H THERMOSTAT
I WATER OUTLET ELBOW
J THERMOSTAT RETAINER
K EXHAUST VALVE
L INLET VALVE
M CYLINDER HEAD
N EXHAUST MANIFOLD
O VALVE SPRING
P VALVE TAPPET ADJUSTING SCREW
Q ENGINE PLATE—REAR
R CAMSHAFT
S FLYWHEEL RING GEAR
T CRANKSHAFT PACKING—REAR
U CRANKSHAFT REAR BEARING DRAIN PIPE
V CRANKSHAFT BEARING—REAR LOWER
W VALVE TAPPET
X CRANKSHAFT
Y CONNECTING ROD CAP BOLT
Z OIL FLOAT SUPPORT
AA OIL FLOAT
AB CRANKSHAFT BEARING—CENTER LOWER
AC CONNECTING ROD
AD CONNECTING ROD BOLT NUT LOCK
AE CRANKSHAFT BEARING—FRONT LOWER
AF CRANKSHAFT THRUST WASHER
AG TIMING CHAIN COVER
AH TIMING CHAIN
AI CRANKSHAFT SPROCKET
AJ FAN BELT
AK CRANKSHAFT PACKING—FRONT END
AL STARTING CRANK NUT
AM FAN AND GENERATOR DRIVE PULLEY
AN CAMSHAFT THRUST PLUNGER
AO CAMSHAFT BUSHING—FRONT
AP CAMSHAFT THRUST WASHER
AQ CAMSHAFT SPROCKET

RA PD 305283

Figure 20—Sectional View of Engine

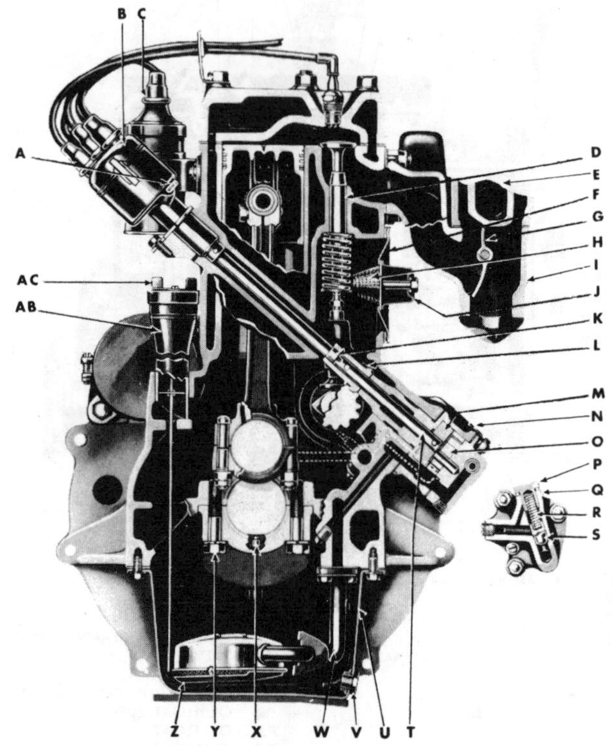

A	DISTRIBUTOR OILER	O	OIL PUMP PINION
B	IGNITION DISTRIBUTOR	P	OIL RELIEF PLUNGER SPRING RETAINER
C	IGNITION COIL	Q	OIL RELIEF PLUNGER SPRING SHIMS
D	EXHAUST VALVE GUIDE	R	OIL RELIEF PLUNGER SPRING
E	INTAKE MANIFOLD	S	OIL RELIEF PLUNGER
F	VALVE SPRING COVER	T	OIL PUMP SHAFT AND ROTOR
G	HEAT CONTROL VALVE	U	OIL PAN
H	CRANKCASE VENTILATOR BAFFLE	V	OIL PAN DRAIN PLUG
I	EXHAUST MANIFOLD	W	OIL FLOAT SUPPORT
J	CRANKCASE VENTILATOR	X	CRANKSHAFT BEARING DOWEL
K	DISTRIBUTOR SHAFT FRICTION SPRING	Y	CRANKSHAFT BEARING CAP TO CRANKCASE SCREW
L	OIL PUMP DRIVEN GEAR	Z	OIL FLOAT
M	OIL PUMP ROTOR DISK	AB	OIL FILLER TUBE
N	OIL PUMP	AC	OIL FILLER CAP AND LEVEL INDICATOR

RA PD 305284

Figure 21—Sectional View of Engine

Figure 22—Manifolds

(3) Test cylinder compression with gage. The gage must read more than 70 pounds, and the variation between cylinders remain less than 10 pounds. Normal compression is approximately 110 pounds per square inch at cranking speed. Report lack of compression to higher authority.

(4) Make sure that ground strap at engine left front support is in good condition and tight.

(5) Remove distributor cap and rotor. Check for cracks and leaks. Clean or replace breaker points and adjust (par. 64).

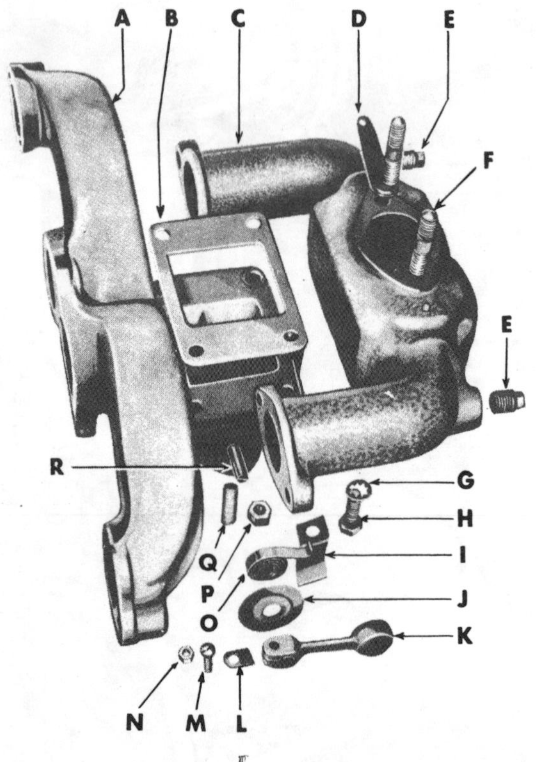

A EXHAUST MANIFOLD
B INTAKE TO EXHAUST MANIFOLD GASKET
C INTAKE MANIFOLD
D ACCELERATOR SPRING CLIP
E INTAKE MANIFOLD PLUG
F INTAKE MANIFOLD TO CARBURETOR STUD
G INTAKE TO EXHAUST MANIFOLD SCREW LOCKWASHER
H INTAKE TO EXHAUST MANIFOLD SCREW
I HEAT CONTROL VALVE BI-METAL SPRING STOP
J HEAT CONTROL VALVE BI-METAL SPRING WASHER
K HEAT CONTROL VALVE COUNTERWEIGHT LEVER
L HEAT CONTROL VALVE LEVER KEY
M HEAT CONTROL VALVE LEVER CLAMP SCREW
N HEAT CONTROL VALVE LEVER CLAMP SCREW NUT
O HEAT CONTROL VALVE BI-METAL SPRING
P EXHAUST PIPE TO EXHAUST MANIFOLD STUD NUT
Q EXHAUST PIPE TO EXHAUST MANIFOLD STUD
R HEAT CONTROL VALVE SHAFT

RA PD 334754

Figure 23—Manifolds, Disassembled

(6) Check ignition timing (par. 65).

(7) Check valve tappet clearance (par. 56).

(8) Install spark plugs, assemble distributor, start engine, and allow to run until normal temperature is reached; then set throttle valve stop screw so that engine will idle at 600 revolutions per minute (vehicle speed 8 mph).

(9) Adjust idle adjustment screw until engine idles smoothly. If carburetor float level, accelerating pump, or metering rod require adjustment, report to higher authority.

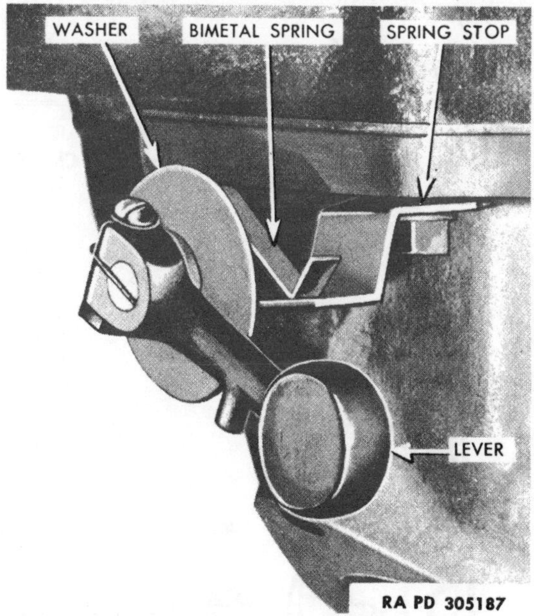

Figure 24—Heat Control Valve

(10) Tighten cylinder head screws and nuts, using torque wrench (par. 54).

(11) Check operation of manifold heat control (par. 53).

52. INTAKE AND EXHAUST MANIFOLDS.

a. Description. The intake and exhaust manifolds (figs. 22 and 23) are attached to each other with four screws, making a unit in which a heat control valve is used to regulate the intake manifold temperature (par. 53).

b. Remove Intake and Exhaust Manifolds. Remove carburetor air horn at top of carburetor, and disconnect hand throttle, choke,

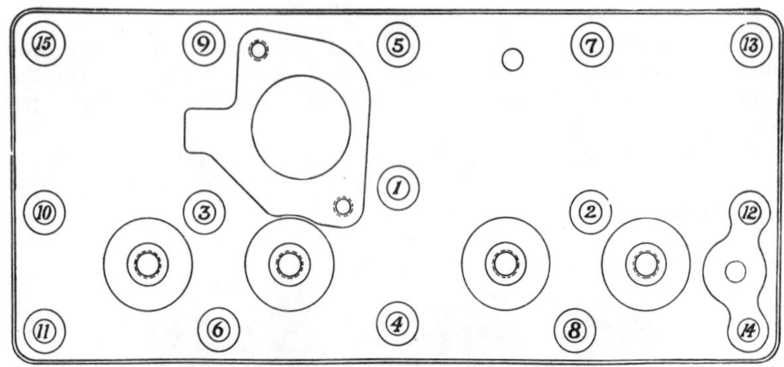

Figure 25—Cylinder Head Tightening Chart

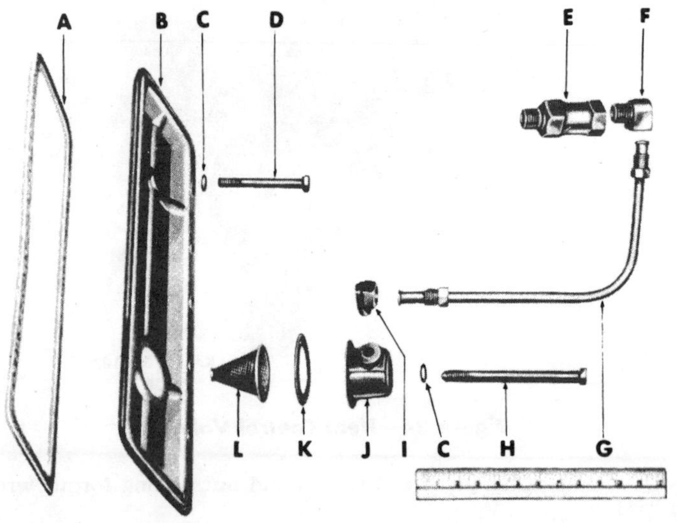

A	VALVE SPRING COVER GASKET	G	CRANKCASE VENTILATOR TUBE
B	VALVE SPRING COVER	H	VALVE SPRING COVER SCREW—FRONT
C	VALVE SPRING COVER SCREW GASKET	I	CRANKCASE VENTILATOR BODY ELBOW
D	VALVE SPRING COVER SCREW—REAR	J	CRANKCASE VENTILATOR BODY
E	CRANKCASE VENTILATOR VALVE	K	CRANKCASE VENTILATOR BODY GASKET
F	CRANKCASE VENTILATOR VALVE ELBOW	L	CRANKCASE VENTILATOR BAFFLE

RA PD 334755

Figure 26—Valve Spring Cover, Disassembled

and accelerator at carburetor. Loosen fuel line at fuel pump, and disconnect at carburetor. Remove two nuts attaching carburetor to intake manifold, and remove carburetor with accelerator spring clip. Loosen the valve spring cover front screw to relieve any pull on crankcase ventilator tube, and then remove the tube. Disconnect exhaust pipe at the manifold. Remove all nuts and washers from manifold studs in cylinder block, remove manifolds as an assembly, and remove ventilator valve.

c. **Separate Intake Manifold from Exhaust Manifold.** Remove four screws holding intake and exhaust manifolds together, and remove intake to exhaust manifold gasket.

d. **Assemble Intake Manifold to Exhaust Manifold.** Attach intake manifold to exhaust manifold loosely, using a new gasket. Tighten screws only slightly until manifolds are installed on cylinder block. Install ventilator valve.

e. **Install Intake and Exhaust Manifolds.** Clean contact surfaces of manifolds and cylinder block. Place new gasket on studs in cylinder block, and install manifold. Install washers and nuts with convex side of washers against manifolds, and tighten evenly (torque wrench reading 31 to 35 ft-lb). Tighten the four screws attaching intake manifold to exhaust manifold. Attach exhaust pipe to manifold, using new gasket, and tighten in place with nut and screw. Install ventilator tube, and tighten valve spring cover front screw. Install carburetor, accelerator clip, and spring. Attach fuel line at carburetor, and tighten at fuel pump. Connect accelerator rod, hand throttle, and choke at carburetor. Push controls in on instrument panel (throttle closed and choke fully open). Install carburetor air horn and secure in place. Operate fuel pump priming lever to put fuel in carburetor, then start engine, and check for leaky gaskets.

53. MANIFOLD HEAT CONTROL VALVE.

a. **Description.** The heat control valve (figs. 23 and 24) is controlled thermostatically by a bimetal spring. This valve diverts exhaust gases around the central portion of the intake manifold during the warm-up period of the engine. NOTE: *The manifold heat control valve is an integral part of the exhaust manifold. For replacement follow procedure outlined in paragraph 52.*

54. CYLINDER HEAD GASKET.

a. **Removal.** Drain the cooling system by opening the drain cock under the radiator at the left front. If there is antifreeze in the cooling system, drain into a pan so it can be used again. Disconnect spark plug wires at the plugs, and remove distributor cap from distributor. Remove two nuts on cylinder studs holding air cleaner tube bracket, and remove bracket with wires and distributor cap. Remove radiator upper tube with hoses attached. Disconnect oil filter upper tube, remove two nuts holding filter to engine, and remove filter. Remove all cylinder head screws and nuts. Remove cylinder head and bonding strap, taking care not to damage oil filler tube, and discard gasket.

b. Installation. Clean cylinder head, tops of pistons, and cylinder block thoroughly. Place cylinder head gasket in position on cylinder block. NOTE: *The front and rear center studs are pilot studs to correctly position the gasket.* Install cylinder head. CAUTION: *Do not damage oil filler pipe.* Install rear bonding strap, oil filter, and air cleaner tube bracket. Install cylinder head bolts and nuts. Tighten cylinder screws and nuts evenly and in sequence (fig. 25), using a

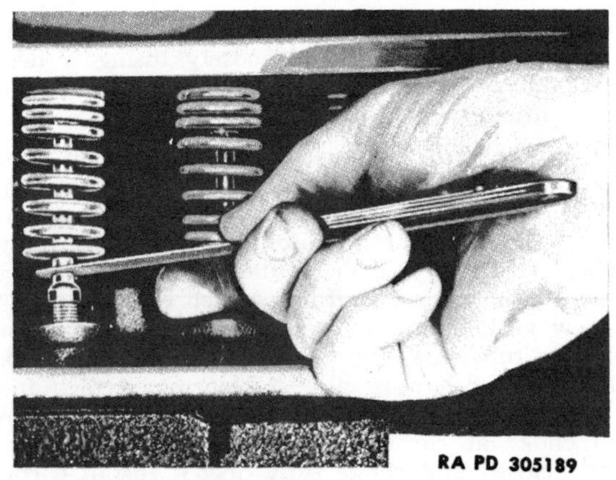

Figure 27—Valve Tappet Adjustment

torque-type wrench (screws, 65 to 70 ft-lb; nuts, 60 to 65 ft-lb). Connect oil filter tube, install distributor cap, and attach spark plug wires to correct plugs. Install radiator upper tube, tighten hose clamps, and close radiator drain cock. Fill the cooling system, giving due attention to antifreeze, if required (par. 7). Start engine, and check cooling system for leaks. See that cooling solution level has not gone down; replenish if necessary.

55. VALVE COVER GASKET.

a. Removal. Remove front valve spring cover bolt (fig. 26). Remove crankcase ventilator tube at ventilator valve, and remove tube and cap. Remove rear valve spring cover bolt, and slide valve spring cover forward, up, and out over the fuel pump. Discard gasket.

b. Installation. Clean cover and gasket seat on cylinder block. Cement cork gasket to cover. Position cover on cylinder block by sliding it to the rear over fuel pump. Install cover rear screw and copper gasket, but do not tighten. Install cover front screw and copper gasket, with ventilator cap, baffle, and gasket. Connect ventilator tube to valve, and tighten both cover screws evenly. Start engine and check for oil leaks.

56. VALVE TAPPET ADJUSTMENT.

a. Adjustment. Remove the valve spring cover (par. 55). Adjust the self-locking tappet screws while they are cold (or warm) to 0.014 inch (fig. 27). Set tappet screws, starting with No. 1 cylinder on compression stroke at top center, then adjust valves in cylinder firing order (par. 62 **b**), turning the crankshaft one-half turn for each cylinder. NOTE: *The valve tappets will then be on the heel of the cam.* After adjusting, replace valve spring cover (par. 55).

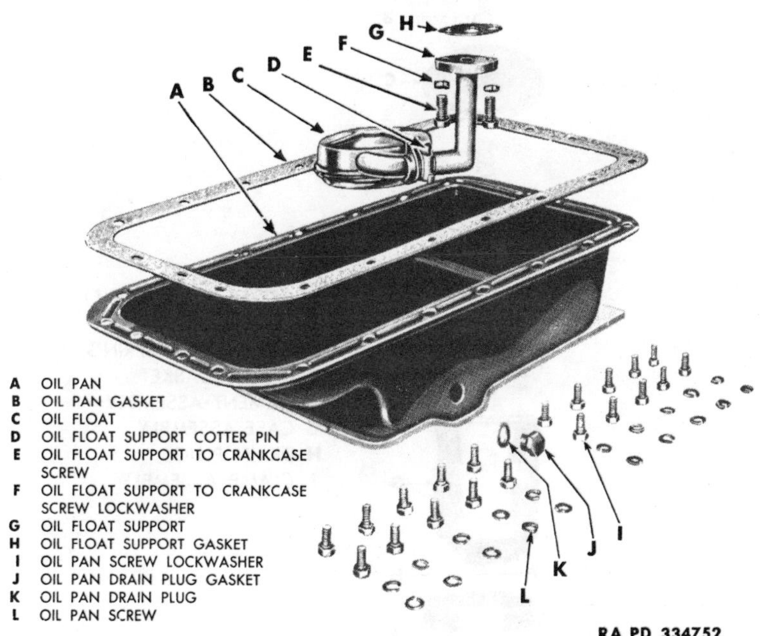

Figure 28—Floating Oil Intake and Oil Pan

57. OIL PAN GASKET.

a. Removal. Drain oil by removing drain plug in lower left side of oil pan (fig. 28). Remove oil pan screws, exercising care not to lose spacers under fan belt guard. Remove oil pan, then remove gasket.

b. Installation. First clean oil pan thoroughly. Check condition of floating oil intake screen and if dirty, clean in dry-cleaning solution. Clean face of oil pan and crankcase where gasket is installed, and cement gasket to oil pan. Put oil pan in position, and install screws. Be sure that spacers under belt guard are in position, and tighten all screws evenly. Torque wrench reading must be 10 to 14 foot-pounds.

58. OIL FILTER.

a. Description. The oil filter is the military standard type located on the right front side of the engine (fig. 36). Part of the oil circulated through the oiling system is sent through the filter. The filter-

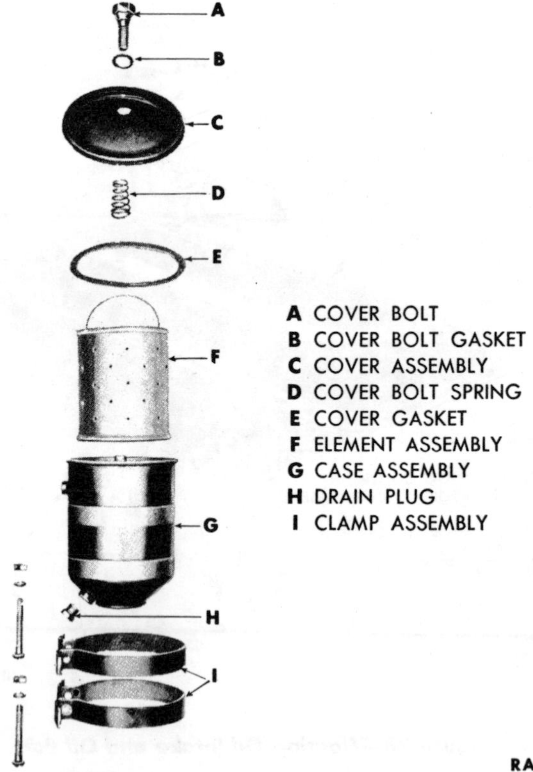

Figure 29—Oil Filter, Disassembled

ing element is a cylindrical replaceable unit which should be changed each 6,000 miles, more often if the oil gets dirty quickly. The inlet line at the top of the filter connects to the oil distribution line at the plug in the left front side of the engine. The outlet or oil return line connects to the timing chain cover.

b. Remove Element. Unscrew cover bolt in top of unit and remove cover, exercising care not to damage gasket (fig. 29). Remove drain plug in lower side of filter to drain filter, then lift out element.

c. Installing Element. Clean filter thoroughly. Install drain plug, and put new element in filter. Inspect cover gasket, and replace if necessary. Install cover and tighten in place with cover bolt. Start engine, and check filter for oil leaks. Add enough oil to crankcase to bring level up to "FULL" mark on gage.

d. Remove Filter. Drain filter by removing drain plug in lower side. Disconnect upper and lower tubes at filter. Remove four bolts holding filter in bracket, and remove filter. Remove tube fittings, using care not to distort them; then install drain plug.

e. Install Filter. Install tube fittings, exercising care not to damage them. Mount filter in bracket, and tighten in place. Connect tubes, being careful not to cross threads. Start the engine and check for oil leaks after which check engine oil level in crankcase and replenish supply to "FULL" mark on gage.

59. CRANKCASE VENTILATOR VALVE.

a. Description. The crankcase ventilator valve (fig. 22) is located at the center of the intake manifold. This valve is spring-loaded, and is operated by the intake manifold vacuum. The valve is closed when the engine is idling (manifold vacuum high). When the engine speed is increased the manifold vacuum is lowered, and the valve opens to allow clean air to be drawn from the air cleaner tube through the engine oil filler pipe to ventilate the crankcase. If this valve fails to seat properly, an engine operating condition will occur similar to a leaky intake manifold.

b. Remove Valve. Loosen valve spring cover front screw. Remove ventilator tube at valve, and remove ventilator valve (fig. 22).

c. Installing Valve. Place ventilator valve in a vise and remove top. Clean the valve and seat. Be sure that spring operates freely, and reassemble valve. Install valve in manifold and attach tube. Tighten valve spring cover front screw.

Section XIV

ENGINE—REMOVAL AND INSTALLATION

60. REMOVAL.

a. Open Hood. Unhook hood by pulling up catches at forward sides of hood. Raise hood and lay back against windshield. Hook or tie hood to windshield to avoid accidental closing.

b. Drain Cooling System. Open drain cocks at lower left-hand corner of radiator, and at right-front lower corner of cylinder block.

c. Remove Battery. Disconnect battery cables. Remove two wing nuts and washers from hold-down bolts. Remove battery hold-down frame, and lift out battery.

d. Remove Radiator. Remove upper and lower radiator hoses. Remove radiator stay rod nuts and remove rod. Remove two radiator stud nuts on bottom of radiator, and lift off radiator. Do not lose radiator pads.

e. Remove Air Cleaner. Disconnect air cleaner flexible hose at cleaner. Loosen wing nuts on side toward engine. Remove nuts on the opposite side, and remove cleaner. CAUTION: *Do not tip and spill oil from reservoir.*

f. Remove Cranking Motor. Disconnect cranking motor wires. Remove two bolts in engine rear plate, and one screw in side of crankcase. Remove motor.

g. On Right Side of Vehicle. Disconnect wires on generator. Disconnect ignition switch wire at ignition coil. Loosen fuel tank cap to relieve any pressure, and disconnect fuel line at flexible connection on right side of engine. Unscrew heat indicator unit from cylinder head. Remove two bolts holding engine front support insulator to frame, and disconnect bond strap.

h. On Left Side of Vehicle. Remove horn from bracket by removing two screws. Remove rear center cylinder head stud nut, and detach bond strap. Disconnect throttle and choke controls at carburetor. Remove fuel line (fuel pump to carburetor). Disconnect oil gage line at upper end of flexible tube on front of dash. Disconnect accelerator rod at lower end of bell crank on back of engine. Remove one bolt and one screw to separate exhaust pipe from manifold. Remove two engine front support bolts in frame, and disconnect engine ground strap from frame.

i. Disconnect Bell Housing. Remove bell housing upper bolts. Wrap a rope or cable around front and rear end of engine, attach chain hoist, and pick up weight of engine. Underneath vehicle, remove the remaining bell housing bolts, and disconnect engine stay cable at the frame crossmember. Drive out two bell housing bolts at side of engine. Raise engine and guide out of frame.

61. INSTALLATION.

a. Installing Engine. Wrap rope or cable around front and rear end of engine, and attach chain hoist. Raise engine and lower into position. Insert transmission shaft in clutch driven plate hub, and work engine back into place. Install dowel bolts from engine side. Install bell housing bolts and tighten. Install engine front support insulator bolts in frame. Attach engine ground strap at left support and bond strap at right support. Install engine stay cable. Run rear adjusting nut up to the bracket, then with cable just taut, tighten lock nut on the front side of bracket.

b. On Right Side of Vehicle. Install cranking motor and attach wires. Attach ignition coil wire. Install heat indicator unit in cylinder head. Attach generator wires and ground strap. Connect flexible fuel line. Check air cleaner oil in reservoir, and install cleaner on dash with wing nuts. Tighten air flexible connection. Install battery, and secure in place with hold-down frame and wing nuts. Clean cable connections, grease, and attach to battery posts.

c. On Left Side of Vehicle. Install accelerator rod with cotter pin. Connect oil gage tube. Attach exhaust pipe to manifold with bolt and screw. Gasket must be in good condition. Install bond strap on cylinder head rear stud, and tighten nut to from 60 to 65 foot-pounds. Install carburetor choke and throttle wires. NOTE: *Controls on instrument panel must be all the way in, the throttle in the carburetor in the closed position, and the choke fully open.* Install fuel line between pump and carburetor. Attach horn to bracket.

d. Installing Radiator. See that radiator pads are in place, and install radiator on frame. Install upper and lower radiator hoses. Install radiator stay rod. Fill radiator, giving due attention to anti-freeze, if required.

e. Inspection. Tighten fuel tank cap. Check engine oil (par. 18 c). Start engine, check for leaks, tune-up, and finally check level of solution in radiator. Close hood and hook properly.

Section XV

IGNITION SYSTEM

Paragraph

62. DESCRIPTION AND DATA.

a. **Description.** The ignition system (fig. 30) is a 6-volt system and consists of the spark plugs, high- and low-tension ignition wires,

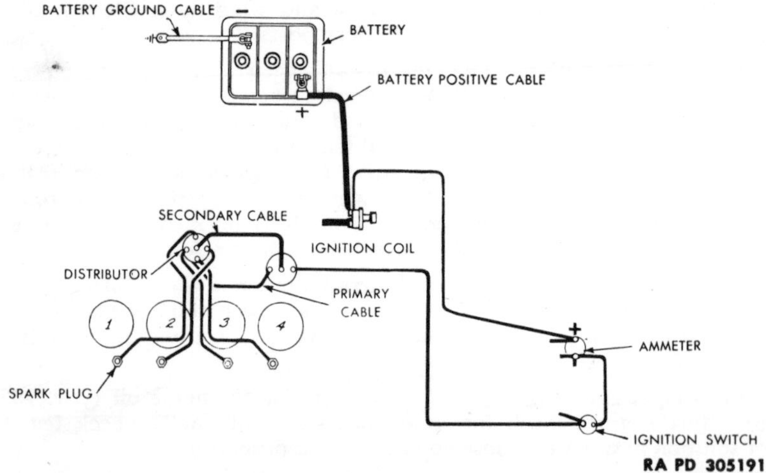

Figure 30—Ignition System Circuit

distributor, coil, and an ignition switch through which it is connected to the electrical system of the vehicle. There are two separate circuits in the ignition system (primary and secondary) which combine to develop the high-voltage current necessary to make a spark jump the plug gaps in the engine combustion chambers, and ignite the fuel mixture. In operation, with the ignition switch turned on, and the distributor points closed, current flows through the primary winding of the ignition coil and builds up a strong magnetic field. When the distributor points open, the magnetic field collapses and induces a high-voltage current in the secondary winding of the coil. This

IGNITION SYSTEM

happens each time the points open. This high-voltage current is delivered to the spark plugs at the correct time by the distributor rotor, cap, and secondary wires. To prevent burning of the distributor points by current arcing across the open points, a condenser is connected across the points (in parallel). This provides a place (capacity) for current to go until the points open enough to prevent arcing. Discharge of this condenser current back through the primary winding of the coil causes the magnetic field to collapse much faster in developing the high-voltage current for the spark plugs.

b. Data.

Distributor

Make and model	Auto-Lite IAD-4008
Type advance	Centrifugal
Rotation	Counterclockwise
Firing order	1-3-4-2
Point gap	0.020 in.
Breaker arm spring tension	17 to 20 oz
Condenser capacity	0.18 to 0.26 mfd

Ignition coil

Make and model	Auto-Lite IG-4070L
Voltage	6-8
Draw (engine stopped)	5 amps at 6.4 volts
Draw (engine idling)	2.5 amps

Spark plugs

Make and model	Auto-Lite AN-7
Thread size	14-mm
Gap	0.030 in.

Ignition switch

Make and model	Douglas No. 6282

Ignition wires

Primary (gage)	No. 14
Secondary (gage)	No. 16

c. Tests. The following procedure will assist in localizing trouble in the ignition system without the use of instruments:

(1) First check the brilliancy of the headlights and operate cranking motor, to judge the condition of the battery and connections as far as the ammeter.

(2) Remove an ignition wire at a spark plug and hold about three-eighths inch away from a bare metal part of the engine. A good spark should result when the cranking motor is operated with the ignition switch on. If spark is weak or absent, proceed as follows:

(3) Pull coil wire out of center of distributor cap; remove cap and crank engine until distributor points are fully closed. Turn on ignition switch, hold cap end of coil secondary wire about three-eighths inch away from cylinder block, and open breaker points with

the fingers, or rock the distributor cam. If a good spark occurs, fault is located in distributor cap, rotor, or wires; inspect cap and rotor for cracks or carbon runners and ignition wires for short circuits. To test distributor cap place wire back in cap and operate cranking motor. Short circuit will be evidenced by a spark within or outside the cap. To check rotor, remove from distributor; put end of coil secondary wire in rotor, and hold top against cylinder block; operate distributor points (spark will show where "short" occurs). If no spark occurs in preceding test, proceed as follows:

(4) Open distributor points and notice if a slight spark is obtained. If spark occurs, current is reaching points. If no spark occurs, detach condenser, and repeat above operation. If spark is obtained, condenser is at fault, and must be replaced. If no spark is obtained, determine if coil primary wires are faulty, as follows:

(5) Remove switch wire at ignition coil, and strike wire terminal against cylinder block. If no spark is obtained, check wiring up to ammeter for loose connection or open circuit. If spark is obtained, current is reaching coil, and this indicates coil is faulty. Replace coil.

63. MAINTENANCE.

a. The distributor requires periodic lubrication at various points (par. 18). Keep coil and distributor wires pushed down in towers. Keep distributor cap and spark plug porcelains free from dirt and grease. All wire terminals must be clean and tight. Replace any wires that are frayed or have cracked insulation. Clean and adjust spark plugs and distributor points (par. 67).

64. DISTRIBUTOR.

a. Description. The distributor (fig. 32) is mounted on the right side of the engine. A full automatic spark advance is mechanically governed by two counterweights which advance the spark as the engine speed increases. The distributor is driven by a shaft extending into the oil pump driven gear, which is driven by a gear on the camshaft. The lower end of the distributor shaft has an offset tongue which must be in correct relation to the oil pump shaft before the two can be assembled. A friction spring on the distributor shaft (fig. 21) engages in the oil pump gear to prevent backlash at this point, and uneven engine performance.

b. Removal. After raising hood, remove wires from distributor cap and primary wire from terminal on side of distributor. Remove screw holding advance arm to crankcase, and pull out distributor assembly.

c. Installation. Remove distributor cap. Insert distributor in crankcase, pushing it down into place, turn rotor until offset tongue on lower end of distributor shaft fits into oil pump shaft, then push farther down into position. Some resistance will be experienced, caused by friction of the spring on the lower end of the distributor shaft fitting into the oil pump gear (fig. 21). Install screw in advance arm loosely. Attach primary wire to distributor. Set timing (par. 65). Install distributor cap and wires (fig. 32).

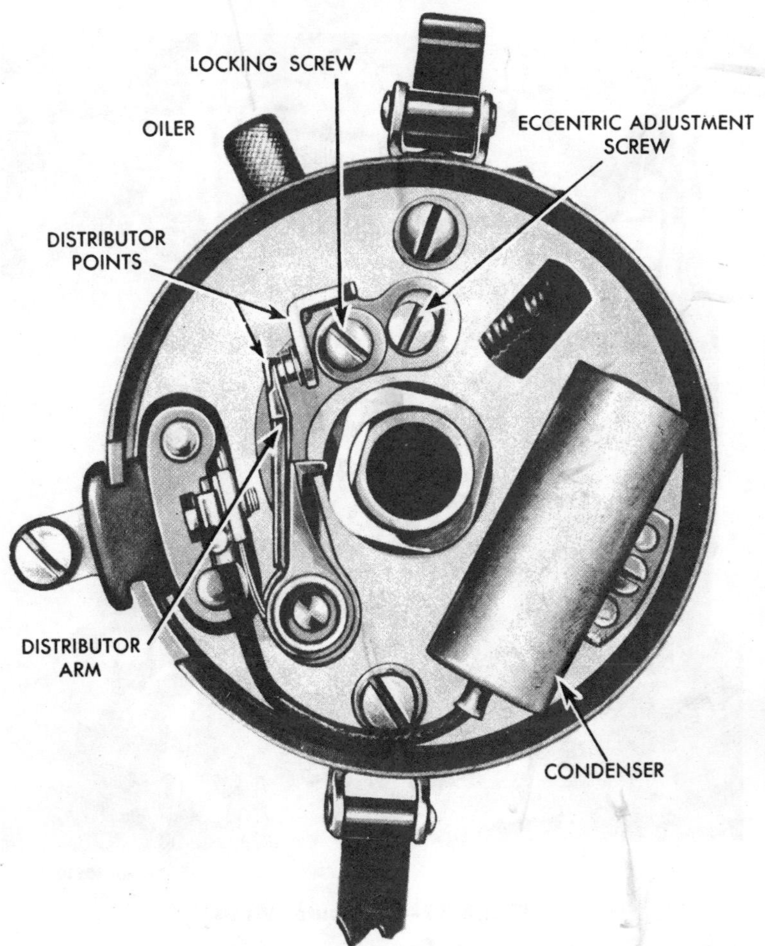

Figure 31—Distributor Points and Condenser

d. Distributor Points.

(1) ADJUSTMENT. Slip off the two clips holding the distributor cap in place and remove cap. Lift off rotor. Crank engine until point arm rubbing block is on top of a cam. Loosen lock screw (fig. 31), and turn eccentric screw until point gap is 0.020 inch measured with a thickness gage. Tighten lock screw and recheck gap. Install rotor and cap. Push wires well down into cap.

(2) REMOVAL. Slip off the two clips holding the distributor cap in place and lift off cap, then remove rotor (fig. 31). Using a small screwdriver, unscrew condenser lead which will release breaker arm

RA PD 305195

Figure 32—Distributor Wires

spring, then lift off breaker arm. Remove screw in stationary breaker point, and lift out point.

(3) INSTALLATION. Place stationary breaker point in distributor, and install locking screw loosely. Lightly lubricate breaker arm pivot pin, and install breaker arm. Place spring in position with condenser lead, insert screw, and tighten securely in place. Aline points if necessary. To adjust points refer to step (1) above.

e. Distributor Condenser.

(1) DESCRIPTION. The condenser is attached by one screw to the support plate in the distributor, and connected by a short flexible wire across the distributor points. The condenser functions to absorb momentarily any current which has a tendency to arc across the points when they open. The condenser must be firmly attached to the

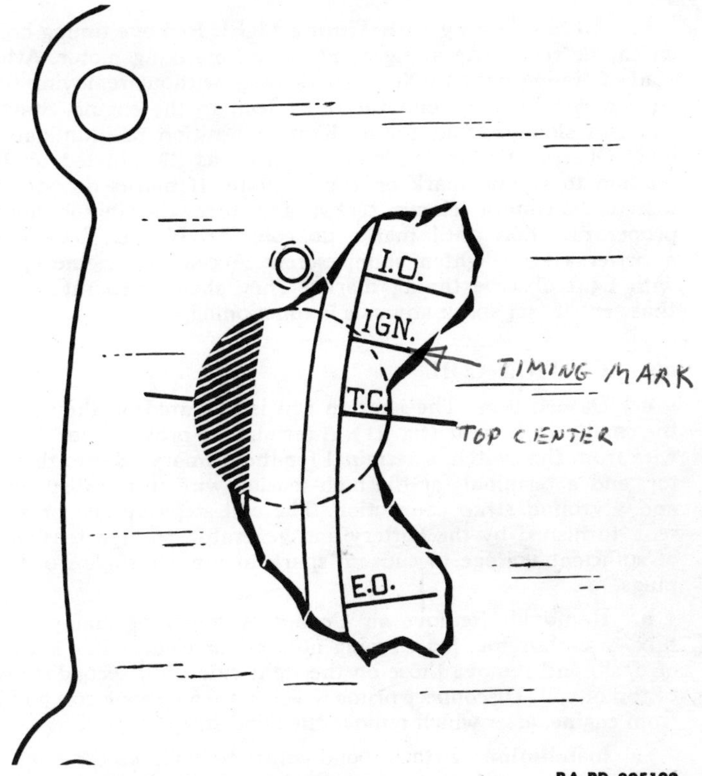

Figure 33—Timing Marks (Flywheel)

support plate, and the cable in good condition. Refer to paragraph 62 c for tests. Test condenser on a condenser tester, if available.

(2) REMOVAL. Slip off distributor cap clips and remove cap. Lift off rotor. Remove screw holding condenser to support plate. Remove screw in lead and remove condenser.

(3) INSTALLATION. Position condenser on plate and attach with screw. Attach lead. NOTE: *Determine if distributor points have been disturbed.* Install rotor and cap.

65. IGNITION TIMING.

a. To Set Timing without Timing Light. Remove timing hole cover on engine rear plate at right side under cranking motor. Remove distributor cap. Crank engine to No. 1 cylinder firing stroke (distributor rotor toward lower front corner of distributor). Set flywheel with ignition mark (fig. 33) in center of timing hole. Turn distributor housing so that breaker points are just opening, and tighten screw holding distributor to engine. Install timing hole cover.

b. To Set Timing with Timing Light. Remove timing hole cover on engine rear plate at right side under cranking motor. Attach one lead of timing light to No. 1 spark plug, without removing the high-tension wire, and ground the other lead to the engine. Start engine and run slowly. Hold timing light in position to illuminate timing hole. Observe timing mark on flywheel, as illuminated by light, in relation to timing mark on engine plate. If marks do not coincide, loosen distributor clamp screw, and turn distributor housing in proper direction until marks do coincide. NOTE: *Use mirror for a better view.* Tighten clamp screw. Accelerate engine speed, and with light observe timing marks. They should separate to indicate that centrifugal spark advance is functioning.

66. IGNITION COIL.

a. Description. The ignition coil is mounted on the right side of the engine at the rear (fig. 21). A terminal is provided for the primary wire from the switch, a terminal for the primary wire to the distributor, and a terminal for the high-tension wire to the distributor cap, and a ground strap connection. The coil steps up the primary current, furnished by the battery and generator, to high-tension current of sufficient voltage to cause a spark to jump the gaps of the spark plugs.

b. Removal. Remove air cleaner by loosening clamp on flexible tube to carburetor; loosen wing nuts on air cleaner bracket at center of dash, and remove those on the right side. Pull secondary wire out of top of coil. Disconnect primary wires, then remove coil and bracket from engine, after which remove the bond strap.

c. Installation. Attach bond strap to coil, and mount coil on engine with bond strap on coil bracket front stud, and tighten securely. Attach primary wires, and push secondary wire into top of coil. Install air cleaner, and tighten hose clamp.

67. SPARK PLUGS.

a. Description. Spark plugs (fig. 22) are located in the top of the cylinder head at the left side. The plugs are of the one-piece type. A copper-silver alloy gasket is used on each plug for heat transfer to the cylinder head, and to prevent leakage of compression. Push-on type wire terminals are used with radio filters at each plug. A spark plug insulator cap is fitted on each plug to protect the plugs from water and dirt. No shielding is used on the plugs.

b. Adjustment. To adjust the gap, bend the side electrode only, and gage the plug with a round thickness gage to a gap of 0.030 inch.

c. Removal. To avoid breakage of the porcelain, remove the plugs with the socket wrench and handle furnished in the vehicle tool equipment.

d. Installation. Install new plug gaskets if available. Tighten spark plugs snug so that gasket will compress.

68. IGNITION SWITCH.

a. Description. On the earlier production, a key-type ignition switch was used which has been superseded by an interchangeable lever-type switch (fig. 5). Turn the switch lever clockwise for "ON" position.

b Removal. Disconnect battery positive cable at battery. Unscrew retaining nut against face of instrument panel, and remove switch from panel. Disconnect wires and remove switch.

c. Installation. Install the wires on proper terminals, then fit the switch into the hole in the instrument panel, screw on retaining nut, and tighten securely.

69. IGNITION WIRING.

a. Description. The ignition wiring (fig. 30) consists of low-tension and high-tension wires. The low-tension, or primary wires, carry the current from the ignition switch, which is connected to the electrical system of the vehicle, to the ignition coil, and from the coil to the distributor. The high-tension or secondary wires carry the high-voltage current generated in the secondary wires of the coil, to the distributor, where it is distributed to the spark plugs. No shielding harness is used.

b. Removal. Before removing ignition switch wire, disconnect the battery negative (ground) cable. It is not necessary to disconnect the battery cable to replace the coil-to-distributor primary wire or the secondary wires. Disconnect wires at terminals, and remove wire or harness, opening wire clips on the harness in which the switch wire is a part. When removing secondary wires mark terminal tower in distributor cap for No. 1 cylinder spark plug. Pull wires out of distributor cap and off spark plug terminals.

c. Installation. To install primary wires, run wire or harness through clips, and attach terminals securely. Install secondary wires, for spark plugs, through support bracket. Push terminals down well into the proper distributor towers (fig. 32). Push rubber secondary wire tip down in place on distributor towers. Push terminals down on proper spark plugs. Refer to firing order (par. 62 **b**).

Section XVI

FUEL AND AIR INTAKE AND EXHAUST SYSTEMS

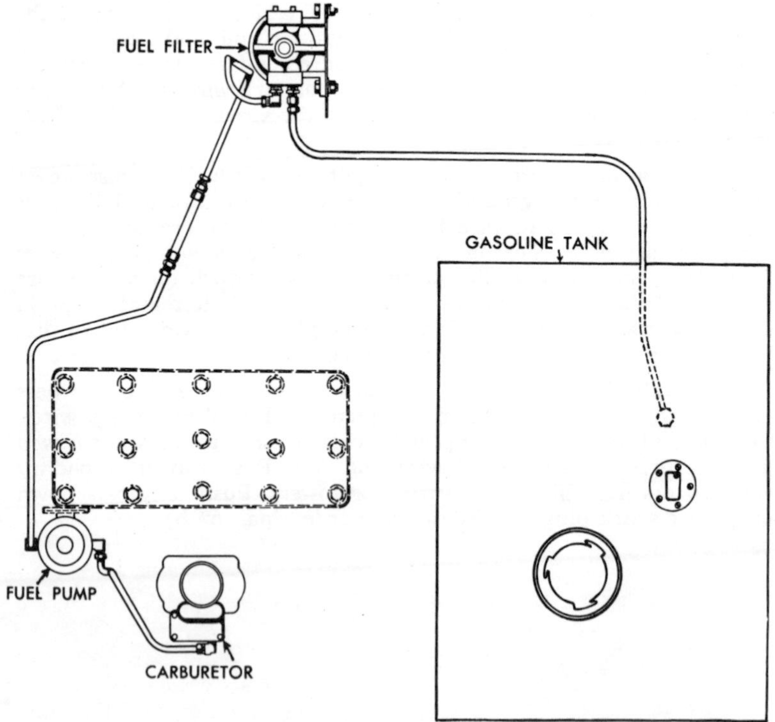

Figure 34—Fuel System RA PD 305196

70. DESCRIPTION AND DATA.

a. **Description.** The fuel system (fig. 34) consists of the fuel tank, fuel lines, fuel strainer, fuel pump, carburetor, and air cleaner. In addition to these units an electric-type fuel gage is mounted on the instrument panel, and is connected by one wire to a fuel tank unit.

b. Data.

Carburetor	Carter WO-539S
Air cleaner	Oakes 613300
Fuel pump	AC 1538312
Fuel pump static pressure	4.5 lb at 1,800 rpm
Fuel tank capacity	15 gal
Fuel strainer	Type T-2; AC1595848
Fuel gage	Electric actuation

c. Operation. Fuel in the tank is drawn through the fuel strainer by the action of a pump mounted on the forward left side of the engine. The pump also forces the fuel into the carburetor bowl until the flow is shut off by the carburetor float valve. In the carburetor, the fuel is proportioned and mixed with air drawn through the carburetor, from the oil-bath type air cleaner, by the action of the engine pistons. The fuel system must be inspected and cleaned periodically (par. 16). Tighten connections which show signs of leakage, and replace kinked or damaged lines.

71. MAINTENANCE.

a. The carburetor requires attention only to the idle adjustment. Fuel lines and vacuum connections must be tight. All mounting screws must be tight. Choke and throttle control clamp screws must be tight. Exterior of carburetor must be kept clean. All linkage must be lubricated at regular intervals, and be free to operate.

b. The air cleaner requires periodic check of correct oil level and condition of oil. Element must be kept clean and free from dirt. Mounting screws and clamps must be tight.

c. The fuel pump requires periodic cleaning of screen. Mounting screws and fuel line connections must be tight. Failure to function properly requires replacement of unit.

d. Drain fuel tank periodically to remove dirt and water. All connections and mounting bolts must be tight. Filler cap must be kept clean, and gasket checked for seat. Filler neck screen must be cleaned at regular intervals.

e. Clean fuel strainer at regular intervals. Gasket must be replaced if damaged. All connections and mounting bolts must be tight.

f. Fuel gage requires no attention other than that mounting screws must be tight. Replace damaged or frayed wires. Electrical connections must be clean and tight. Failure to operate requires replacement of unit.

72. CARBURETOR.

a. Description. The carburetor (fig. 35) is of the conventional downdraft, plain-tube type, with a throttle operated accelerator pump and economizer device. The carburetor is a precision instru-

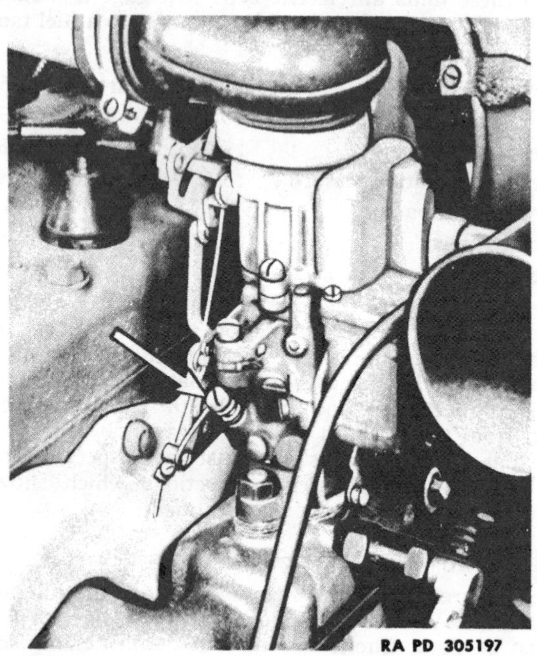

RA PD 305197

Figure 35—Carburetor Idle Adjustment

ment which delivers the proper fuel and air mixture for all speeds and operating requirements of the engine.

b. Adjustment. The idle adjustment screw indicated in figure 35 is the only service adjustment provided on the carburetor. To obtain the approximate correct setting, turn the adjustment screw to the right and all the way in, but do not jam the screw against the seat, then, back out adjustment screw between one and two turns. To make the final adjustment, warm up the engine, and adjust the screw until the engine runs smoothly. Set the throttle stop screw so the engine will idle at 600 revolutions per minute (vehicle speed, 8 mph). Replace carburetor if it requires other attention.

c. Removal. Loosen clamp on air horn and flexible air hose, and remove air horn. Remove throttle and choke control wires. Disconnect throttle control rod at throttle lever. Disconnect fuel line at carburetor. Remove carburetor flange nuts and retracting spring clip, and lift off carburetor.

d. Installation. Inspect condition of gaskets between carburetor and manifold, and install new gaskets, if required. Install carburetor retracting spring clip, and carburetor flange nuts. Tighten nuts evenly. Connect throttle control rod, and throttle and choke wires. Install carburetor air horn, and tighten clamp screws. Adjust carburetor (subpar. **b** above).

Figure 36—Air Cleaner and Oil Filter

73. AIR CLEANER.

a. Description. The air cleaner (fig. 36) is of the oil-bath type, and mounted on the right-front side of the dash. Air enters through louvers in the dash side of the unit, passes down and across the surface of the oil, up through the filtering element, then to the carburetor. For servicing of air cleaner refer to subparagraph **d** below.

b. Removal of Oil Cup. Hold one hand under cup and spring loose the two retaining clamps. Remove cup, clean, and refill to indicated oil level.

c. Installation. Place cup in position on bottom of cleaner, push up into place, and lock with the retaining clamps.

d. Removal and Servicing of Air Cleaner. Loosen the hose clamp and two wing nuts at the center of the dash. Remove two wing nuts on right side of dash, and lift out cleaner assembly. Unfasten the two clamps holding oil cup in place, and remove cup (fig. 37). Unscrew element wing bolt in bottom center of cleaner, and pull out cleaner element. Plunge the element up and down in dry-cleaning solvent to wash out any dirt, then dry with compressed air.

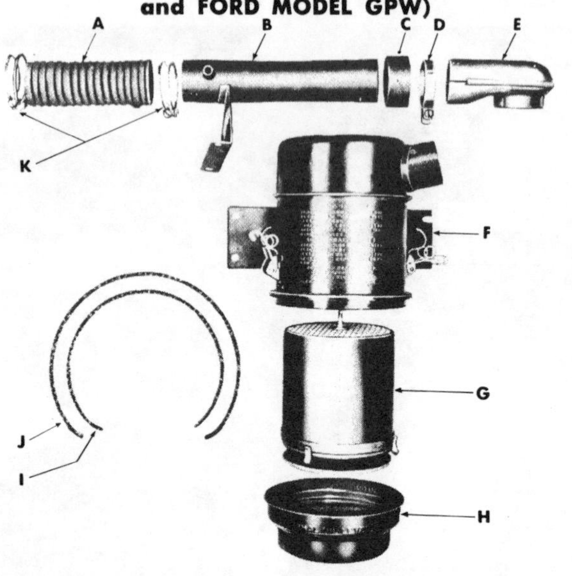

A FLEXIBLE HOSE CONNECTION
B TUBE AND BRACKET ASSEMBLY
C BUSHING
D HOSE CLAMP
E CARBURETOR AIR CLEANER HORN
F BODY ASSEMBLY
G ELEMENT AND WING BOLT ASSEMBLY
H CUP
I LOWER GASKET
J BODY GASKET
K HOSE CLAMP

RA PD 305281

Figure 37—Air Cleaner, Disassembled

e. **Installation.** Install the element in cleaner housing, and secure in place with retaining bolt. Clean and refill oil cup to indicated level, and clamp into place on cleaner. Mount cleaner on dash, install and tighten mounting nuts, and tighten air hose clamp in place.

74. FUEL PUMP.

a. **Description.** The fuel pump (fig. 38) located on the forward, left side of the engine is a diaphragm type, operated by a lever against an eccentric on the engine camshaft. The pump is equipped with a hand lever on the rear side which can be used to operate the pump for priming the carburetor bowl. Lever must be placed down for camshaft to operate pump. A filter screen in incorporated in the fuel bowl, and should be cleaned periodically (subpar. **b** below).

b. **To Clean Screen.** Unscrew knurled nut on bowl clamp, swing clamp aside and lift off bowl. Clean screen with dry-cleaning solvent and small brush. Dry with compressed air. Blow out fuel chamber lightly with compressed air and install screen in place. Install new bowl gasket or turn over old one if serviceable. Install bowl, place bail clamp in position and tighten securely.

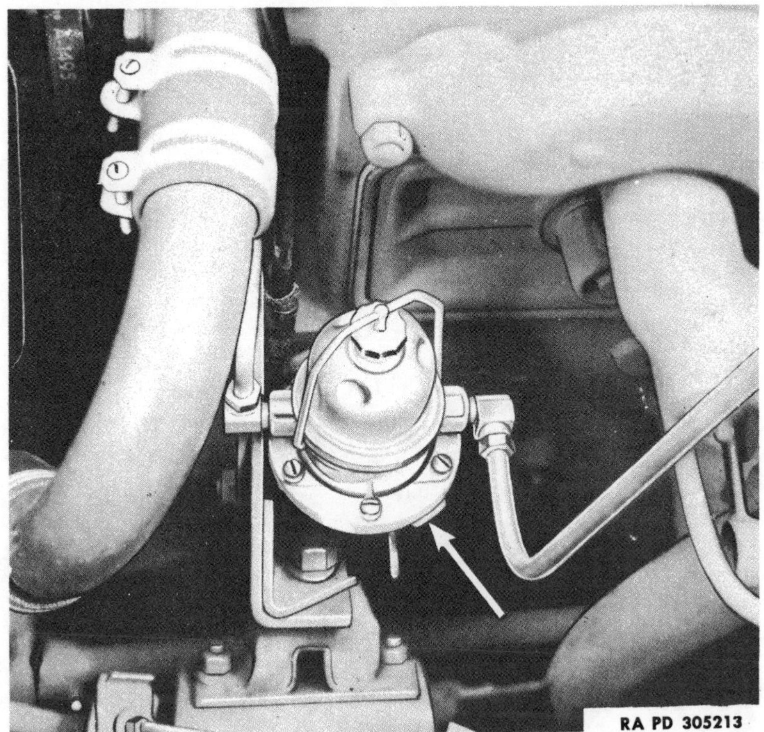

Figure 38—Fuel Pump

c. **Removal.** Remove the inlet and outlet lines, remove two screws holding pump to side of engine and remove pump.

d. **Installation.** Install pump in place on crankcase and tighten securely with two screws. Inspect gasket and replace if unserviceable. Attach inlet and outlet lines and tighten. Prime pump by operating priming lever, start engine, and check connections for leaks.

75. FUEL TANK.

a. **Description.** The fuel tank (fig. 39) is located under the driver's seat. An extension filler neck can be pulled up to facilitate filling the tank from a container. After removing the filler cap, pull up on the filler extension, and turn to the right to lock it in place. To remove the filler extension from the tank turn it to the left and pull up.

b. **Removal.** Drain fuel by removing drain plug in left side of tank. Remove bolts in seat rear flange and front legs, then lift out seat. Remove filler cap. Disconnect fuel gage wire and remove fuel

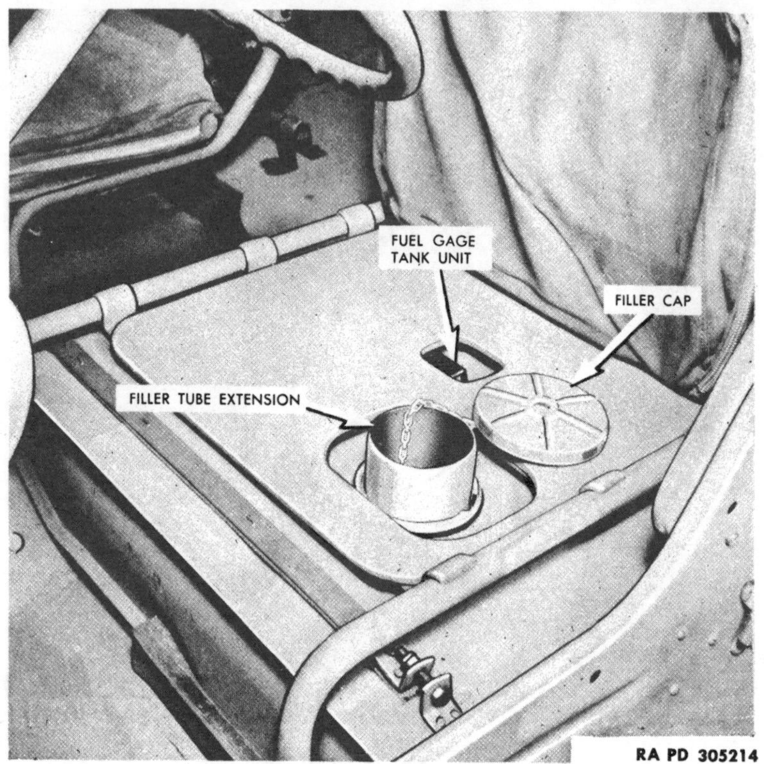

Figure 39—Fuel Tank

gage unit by taking out five screws. Disconnect fuel line from tank, under vehicle. Remove bolt holding tank to wheel housing, remove bolts in tank straps, and lift out tank.

c. **Installation.** Clean out fuel tank sump in body, and install tank in place. Attach tank straps and bolts, also bolt holding tank to wheel housing. Connect fuel line to tank. Install fuel gage in tank, and attach wire to gage. Set seat in position and secure in place with bolts in front legs and seat flange. Fill tank, install cap and check tank and connections for leaks.

76. FUEL STRAINER.

a. **Description.** The fuel strainer (fig. 41) has a disk-type (laminated) element, and a settling bowl for dirt and water. It is located between the fuel tank and the pump, and is mounted on the right-front side of the dash. Service this unit in accordance with preventive maintenance procedure (par. 16).

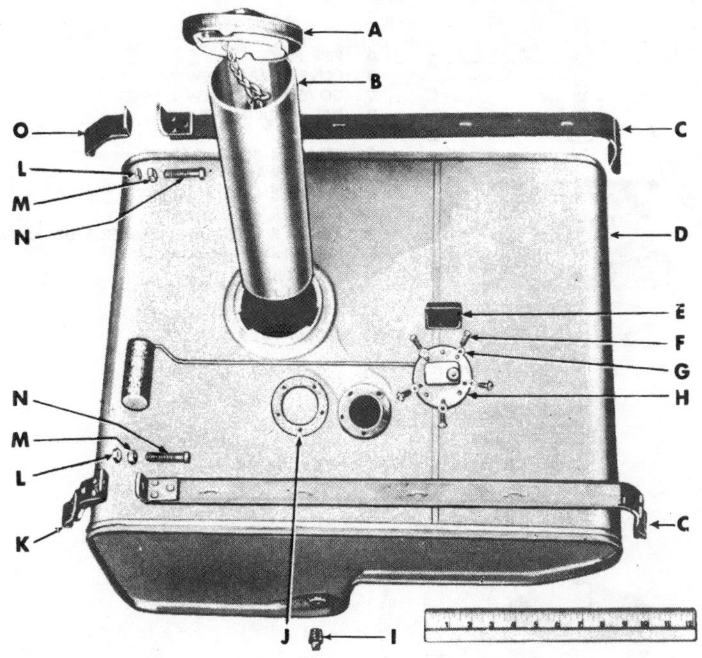

A	CAP	H	GAGE TANK UNIT ASSEMBLY
B	FILLER TUBE EXTENSION	I	DRAIN PLUG
C	HOLD DOWN STRAP	J	GAGE GASKET
D	FUEL TANK ASSEMBLY	K	HOLD DOWN CLAMP
E	GAGE TANK UNIT PROTECTOR	L	HOLD DOWN STRAP LOCK NUT
F	GAGE TO TANK SCREW	M	HOLD DOWN STRAP NUT
G	GAGE TO TANK SCREW LOCKWASHER	N	STRAP CLAMP SCREW
		O	STRAP CLAMP

RA PD 334756

Figure 40—Fuel Tank, Disassembled

b. To Clean Strainer. Remove drain plug and allow strainer to drain into a container. NOTE: *Do not allow fuel to drain onto cranking motor.* Unscrew cover bolt and remove strainer bowl and element. Do not damage bowl gasket. Remove element from bowl, and clean thoroughly in dry-cleaning solvent. Be sure all dirt particles are removed from between disks of the element. Blow element dry with compressed air, but do not use extreme pressure. Wash strainer bowl, and dry with clean cloth. Install element spring and element in bowl. Check condition of element gasket, bowl gasket and cover bolt gasket, and replace, if damaged. Install gaskets in position, and assemble bowl to cover. Install cover bolt and gasket, and tighten securely. Install drain plug. Start engine, run a few minutes, stop engine, and check for leaks.

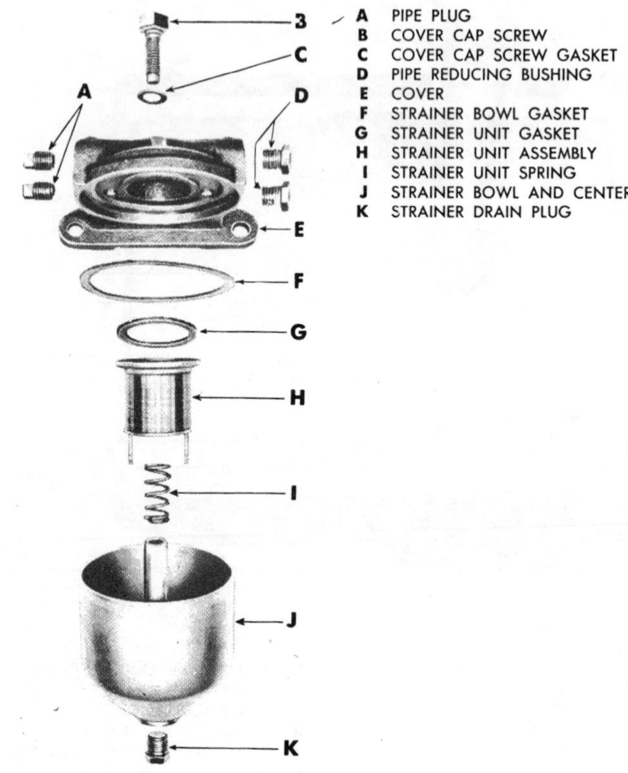

Figure 41—Fuel Strainer, Disassembled

c. Removal. Disconnect inlet and outlet lines from strainer (fig. 36). Open glove compartment door, and remove mounting bolt nuts, then remove strainer.

d. Installation. Place mounting bolts in strainer bracket, and reinstall on dash. Install nuts on bolts through glove compartment. Attach inlet and outlet lines to strainer. Start engine, run a few minutes, stop engine, and check for leaks.

77. FUEL GAGE.

a. Description. The fuel gage consists of an electrical indicating unit located in the instrument panel, and a tank unit in the fuel tank, for actuating the instrument panel unit. A float in the tank operates a rheostat, which governs the current flowing through the instrument panel gage. The gage registers only while the ignition switch is on. The fuel gage wiring circuit is shown in figure 42.

b. Removal of Tank Unit. Remove bolts in seat rear flange and front legs. Take out seat. Disconnect fuel gage wire, and remove tank unit, by unscrewing five screws.

c. Installation of Tank Unit. Inspect gasket, and replace if damaged. Install tank unit, and secure with five screws. Attach wire to fuel gage. Check operation of gage by turning ignition switch to "ON" position; gage must register amount of fuel in tank. Turn off ignition

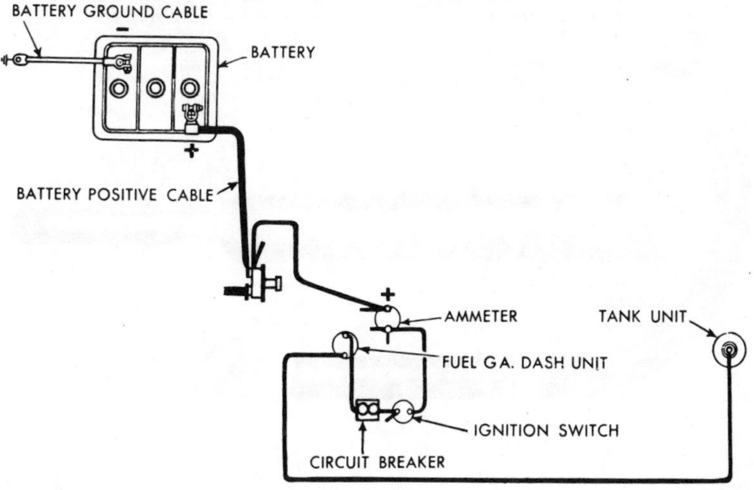

Figure 42—Fuel Gage Wiring Circuit

switch. Install seat, and secure in place with bolts in front legs and seat rear flange.

d. Removal of Fuel Gage (Instrument Panel). Disconnect positive terminal cable at battery. Remove wires on back of gage, and two retaining nuts on the retaining bracket. Remove bracket and take gage out through front of panel.

e. Installation of Fuel Gage (Instrument Panel). Place gage in panel, and install retaining clamp and nuts. Position gage correctly, and tighten retaining clamp nuts. Attach wires (wire to tank unit is attached to left terminal; wire from circuit breaker attaches to right-hand terminal). Clean terminal, and install positive cable on battery.

78. EXHAUST SYSTEM.

a. Description. The exhaust system (fig. 43) consists of the exhaust pipe which, for maximum road clearance, passes under the vehicle to the muffler located under the right side of the body. A flexible section of the exhaust pipe permits movement of the engine in the frame. The muffler is mounted on brackets with fabric inserts.

b. Removal of Exhaust Pipe. Remove three bolts in exhaust pipe shield at right frame member and remove shield. Remove two exhaust pipe clamp bolts in skid plate under transmission. Loosen clamp on exhaust pipe, at front end of muffler. Remove bolt and

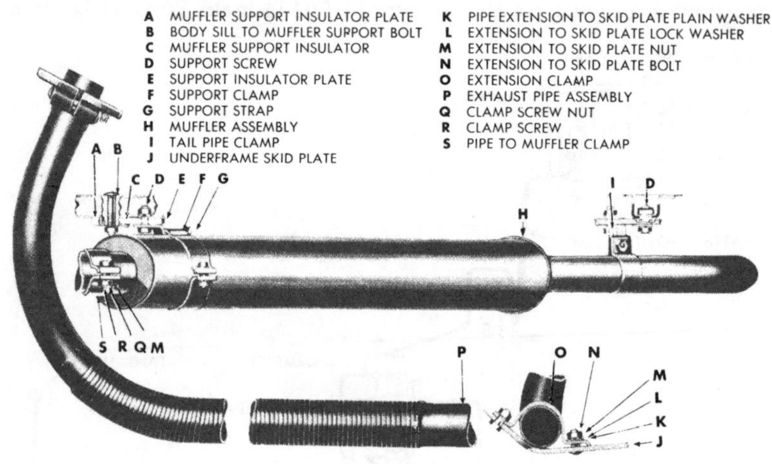

Figure 43—Exhaust System

screw in exhaust pipe flange at exhaust manifold. Drop front end of exhaust pipe, and remove from the left side of vehicle. Discard gasket.

c. Installation of Exhaust Pipe. Install pipe in position, and insert rear end in muffler. Install exhaust pipe manifold flange gasket, and attach pipe to manifold with screw and nut, and tighten evenly. Attach clamp at muffler, and attach exhaust pipe shield with three bolts.

d. Removal of Muffler. To remove the muffler, loosen exhaust pipe clamp. Remove muffler front support bolt and tail pipe support bolt. Remove muffler assembly, after which, remove muffler strap and tail pipe clamp.

e. Installation of Muffler. Loosely install tail pipe clamp and support clamp on muffler. Place muffler on exhaust pipe. Install bolt through tail pipe clamp and flexible mounting. Tighten tail pipe clamp bolt. Install bolt in muffler support and flexible mounting. Tighten muffler strap bolt and exhaust pipe clamp.

Section XVII

COOLING SYSTEM

79. DESCRIPTION AND DATA.

a. Description. The cooling system (fig. 44) consists of the radiator, pressure-type filler cap, fan, fan belt, water pump, thermostat, and temperature gage. The system is of the sealed type, operating under pressure when the engine is warmed up. When in proper condition, the units of the cooling system automatically maintain the engine at the proper operating temperature. The filler pipe is in the top of the radiator at the right side. There are two drain cocks, one in the radiator outlet at the lower left corner, and the other in the right side of the cylinder block at the forward end. In operation the water pump draws the coolant from the bottom of the radiator through the hose connection, and forces it through the cylinder block, past the thermostat, and back to the radiator, where it is cooled by the action of the fan drawing air through the radiator core. The cooling system capacity is 11 quarts.

b. Data.

Cooling system
- Capacity .... 11 qt

Radiator
- Type .... Fin and tube
- Filler cap .... Pressure type

Water pump
- Type .... Centrifugal
- Drive .... Fan belt
- Bearings .... Prelubricated ball

Fan belt
- Type .... Vee
- Length .... 44⅛ in.
- Width .... $^{11}/_{16}$ in.
- Angle of Vee .... 42 deg

Fan
- Blades 4
- Diameter .... 15 in.

Thermostat
  Opens .... 145° to 155°F
  Fully open .... 170°F
Temperature gage type .... Capillary

80. MAINTENANCE.

a. The cooling system must be inspected in accordance with preventive maintenance procedures (pars. 13 and 16). When draining the cooling system refer to caution plate on the instrument panel (fig. 7). General maintenance of the cooling system consists of the following procedures.

(1) Keep sufficient coolant in the system. Use clean water to which must be added the specified rust inhibitor; at temperatures below 32°F, add proper quantity of antifreeze solution (par. 7).

(2) Drain, flush, and refill system whenever inspection reveals any accumulation of rust or scale. Clean system seasonally as well as before and after using antifreeze solution.

(3) If engine overheats due to lack of coolant in the system, do not add cold water immediately. Let engine cool so that radiator does not boil, start engine, and add water slowly to prevent damage to cylinder block and head.

(4) Do not overfill radiator. Fill radiator to bottom of baffle visible through the radiator filler hole.

(5) Keep cylinder head, water pump, hose clamps, and connections leakproof. Replace deteriorated or leaky hose.

(6) Adjust fan belt and replace as required.

(7) Test periodically for air suction and exhaust gas leaking into system (subpars. **c** and **d** below).

b. Draining and Refilling System.

(1) Drain the cooling system, when required, by opening the drain cocks at the lower left corner of the radiator, and at the right front corner of the cylinder block. Loosen the pressure-type radiator cap to break any vacuum which might prevent proper draining. If solution is to be saved, catch it in a clean container. If system is not to be refilled immediately, attach a tag to the steering wheel, warning personnel about the system being drained.

(2) Refill the cooling system by first closing the two drain cocks tightly. Use clean water available, preferably soft water (water with low alkali content or other substances that promote rust and scale). Fill system through radiator filler pipe until level is up to lower edge of baffle visible through filler hole. Install radiator cap, and turn clockwise to tighten. Start engine and warm up. Check coolant level in radiator, and add more if required.

c. Air Suction Test. The air suction test is used to determine if air is entering the coolant, possibly due to low coolant level in the radiator, leaky water pump, or loose hose connections. To make test,

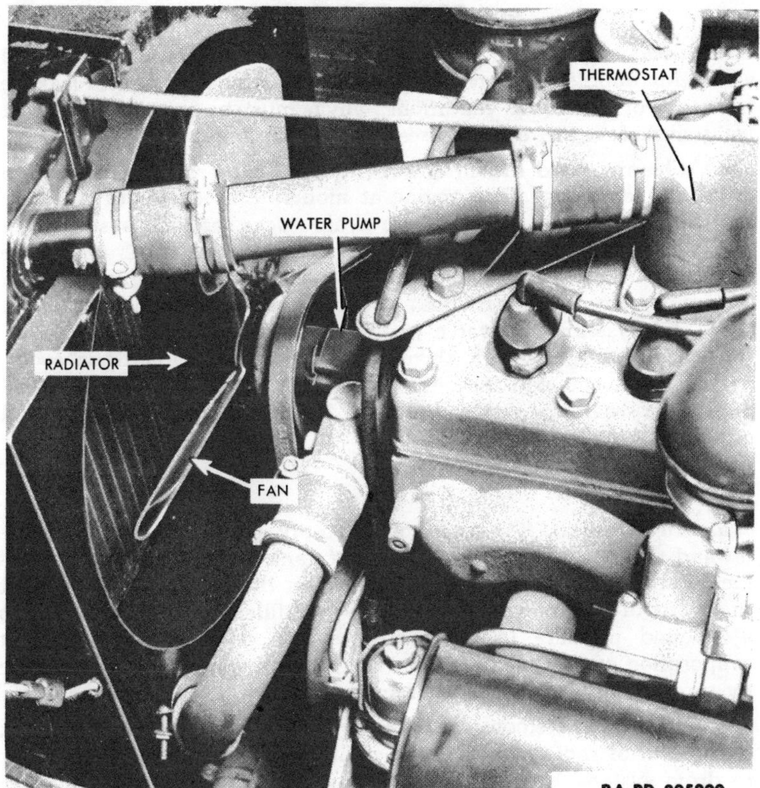

Figure 44—Cooling System

fill system to bottom edge of baffle in top of radiator. Replace pressure type cap with plain cap, and tighten securely (airtight). Attach length of rubber tubing to lower end of overflow pipe (this connection must be airtight). Run engine, with transmission in neutral, at a moderate speed until warmed up. Place tubing in glass container of water, and without changing engine speed, watch for bubbles in water. Continuous appearance of bubbles indicates that air is entering coolant. The cause will be one of the above, and must be corrected.

d. **Exhaust Gas Leakage Test.** The exhaust gas leakage test is used to determine if gas is entering the coolant, possibly due to leaky cylinder block, cylinder head, or gasket. NOTE: *Make this test with engine cold.* Remove fan belt. Open radiator drain cock until coolant is below cylinder head water outlet. NOTE: *Determine by loosening three screws holding outlet to head.* Remove water outlet, and fill cylinder head with coolant until level is up to top of head. With transmission in neutral, start engine, "gun" it several times, and watch for bubbles in water. Appearance of bubbles indicates leakage from one of the above conditions, which must be corrected. Replace leaky gasket; report other causes to higher authority.

e. **Cleaning and Flushing Procedure.** This procedure is used to clean out loose rust. Run engine at moderate speed to stir up loose rust. Drain cooling system. Close drain cocks, and fill system with specified cleaning compound. Install radiator cap. Operate engine as directed for prescribed solution. Stop engine and completely drain system by opening both drain cocks. To flush system close drain cocks, fill system with water, run engine until warmed up again, or run water through system, then completely drain. Close drain cocks, refill system, and add inhibitor corrosion compound to prevent formation of rust and scale. Inhibitor compound must be renewed periodically to be effective.

81. RADIATOR.

a. **Description.** The radiator assembly (fig. 44) consists of the fin-and-tube type core with a coolant tank at the top, and a sediment tank at the bottom. It is located in the conventional place at the front of the vehicle. A pressure-type filler cap maintains up to 4¼-pound pressure to give better engine efficiency, and prevent evaporation of the coolant. When the engine is warm, release pressure by turning cap slightly before removal.

b. **Removal.** Remove the radiator filler cap. Open the drain cock on bottom of radiator outlet and right front corner of cylinder block to drain system. Remove radiator stay rod nut at front end. Loosen hose clamp on upper hose at front end. Loosen hose connection at water pump. Remove two radiator hold-down nuts and lift off radiator, then remove drain cock and pads.

c. **Installation.** Install drain cock and place pads on bracket; set radiator in place. NOTE: *A light coating of grease in hose connections will facilitate assembly.* Install stay rod and tighten lock nut. Tighten upper and lower hose clamps. Install hold-down nuts and bond strap. Close radiator drain cock and cylinder block drain cock. Fill radiator, install cap, and check system for leaks. Start engine, check coolant level after engine is warmed up, and fill, if needed, to proper level.

82. WATER PUMP.

a. **Description.** The water pump (fig. 44) is of the centrifugal-impeller type and is located in the front end of the cylinder block. A double-row ball bearing is integral with the shaft, and is packed with lubricant when it is made. No lubrication attention is required. A packless self-sealing gland is used to prevent water leakage, and requires no attention. The water pump with the generator and fan is driven by a belt from the engine crankshaft fan pulley.

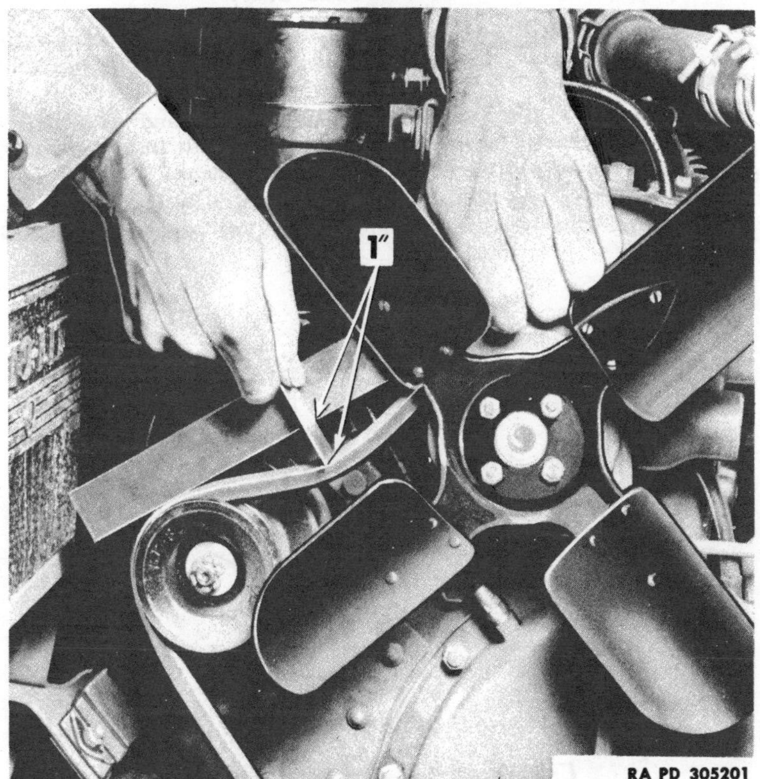

Figure 45—Fan Belt Deflection

b. Removal. Open the radiator drain cock in outlet pipe at lower left corner of radiator, and also drain cock in right side of cylinder block at forward end. Remove radiator filler cap. Pull up on handle of generator brace to loosen fan belt, and slip off belt. Loosen pump hose clamp and remove hose. Remove fan blade screws. Remove screws holding water pump in cylinder block, and remove water pump.

c. Installation. Check condition of pump to cylinder block gasket. Replace if damaged. Install pump in cylinder block, and tighten with screws. Install fan and screws. Install fan belt, and pull out generator until brace drops into position. Attach hose connection. Fill radiator, install cap, and check system for leaks. Start engine and check radiator coolant level after engine is warmed up.

83. FAN BELT.

a. Description. The fan belt (fig. 45) is of the V-type and drives the fan, water pump, and generator. Proper adjustment is necessary for efficient operation and maximum life of belt. Do not adjust the belt extremely tight, causing excessive wear on water pump and generator bearings.

b. Removal. Pull up on generator brace handle, and move generator toward engine as far as it will go. Remove belt from generator, pump, and crankshaft pulleys, and lift over fan blades.

c. Installation and Adjustment. Place belt over fan and crankshaft pulleys, then over the generator pulley. Pull generator out until

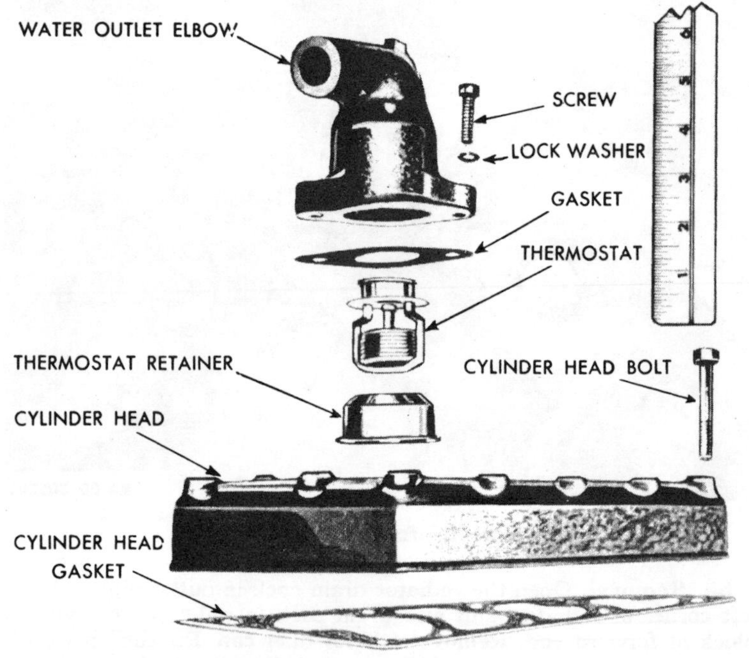

Figure 46—Thermostat, Disassembled

generator brace locks in position. To adjust fan belt tension, loosen generator brace nut, and move generator until fan belt has about one-inch deflection midway between fan and generator pulleys (fig. 45), then tighten nut.

84. FAN.

a. Description. A four-blade, 15-inch fan (fig. 44) draws air through the radiator core. It is mounted on the front end of the water pump shaft and is driven from the crankshaft by the same belt which drives the generator.

b. Removal. Remove four screws holding fan on fan pulley, and lift fan out of shroud.

c. Installation. Place fan in position on fan pulley, install four screws, and tighten securely.

85. THERMOSTAT.

a. Description. The thermostat (fig. 44) is of the bellows-type, and located in the water outlet elbow on top of the cylinder head. It is designed to open between 140°F and 155°F, and is fully open at 170°F.

b. Removal. Drain the cooling system by opening drain cock at lower left side of radiator. Loosen hose clamp at cylinder head water outlet elbow; remove three screws, and lift off elbow. Pull out thermostat retaining ring in elbow, and take out thermostat (fig. 46).

c. Installation. Place thermostat in water outlet elbow with bellows down, so that coolant can reach bellows, to cause valve to operate. Install retaining ring with flanged edge against thermostat. Check condition of gasket and cylinder head surface. Install new gasket if necessary. Insert outlet elbow in hose connection. Install outlet elbow on cylinder head, and tighten in place with three screws. Tighten hose connection. Close radiator drain cock, and fill cooling system, giving due attention to antifreeze, if required. Start engine, and check for leaky connections after engine is warmed up.

86. TEMPERATURE GAGE.

a. Description. The temperature gage (fig. 5) is of the Bourdon-type with a capillary tube connecting it to an expansion bulb in the right side of the cylinder head. The entire system is sealed into one assembly; if any difficulty is experienced, the whole assembly must be replaced.

b. Removal. Drain the cooling system by opening drain cock under left side of radiator. Remove engine unit in right side of cylinder head by unscrewing retaining nut in reducing bushing. Remove two nuts holding retaining bracket on back of gage. Remove grommet around tube through dash and draw out gage assembly, tube, and engine unit through hole in panel.

c. Installation. Insert engine unit through hole in panel, mounting bracket, and dash. Position gage correctly, install mounting bracket and nuts; tighten securely. Insert grommet in dash. Install engine unit, and tighten retaining nut. Fill cooling system, and check for leaks.

Section XVIII

STARTING SYSTEM

87. DESCRIPTION AND DATA.

a. **Description.** The starting system (fig. 47) is a 6-volt system. It consists of the starting switch, cranking motor, and the cables through which they are connected to the battery of the electrical system. When the starting switch is pressed with the right foot, the battery current energizes the cranking motor, causing the armature to turn. This results in the inertia-type cranking motor gear engaging the teeth on the outer circumference of the flywheel. When the engine starts, the gear is automatically thrown out of engagement with the flywheel teeth.

b. **Data.**

System voltage	6
Cranking motor	
Normal engine cranking speed	185 rpm
Make and model	Auto-Lite MZ-4113
Bearings	3
Brushes	4
Brush spring tension	42 to 53 oz
Drive (direct)	R.H. outboard Bendix
Starting switch	
Make and model	Auto-Lite SW-4015

88. MAINTENANCE.

a. The cranking motor requires lubrication only at the forward end. Check tightness of mounting screws. Wire terminals must be in good condition, clean, and tight. As part of the starting system, check the battery condition periodically. Clean the cranking motor drive periodically (par. 89).

89. CRANKING MOTOR.

a. **Description.** The cranking motor is a 6-volt, four-brush type, located at the right-rear side of the engine. The drive is transmitted to the engine from an inertia-type gear to the teeth on a removable ring gear on the circumference of the flywheel. Rotation of the cranking motor shaft causes the pinion of the cranking motor drive to advance and mesh with the gear on the flywheel. After the engine starts, and the speed of the flywheel exceeds that of the cranking motor, the flywheel disengages the pinion automatically. A removable cover at the front end of the cranking motor permits inspection of the brushes and commutator.

b. Removal. Remove cable from motor. Remove screw from front support bracket, and remove two attaching screws at flywheel. Remove cranking motor. Remove front bracket.

c. Installation. Clean cranking motor gear. *Do not oil drive.* Install front bracket and place cranking motor in position on engine. Insert attaching screws, also bracket screw, and tighten securely. Attach cable.

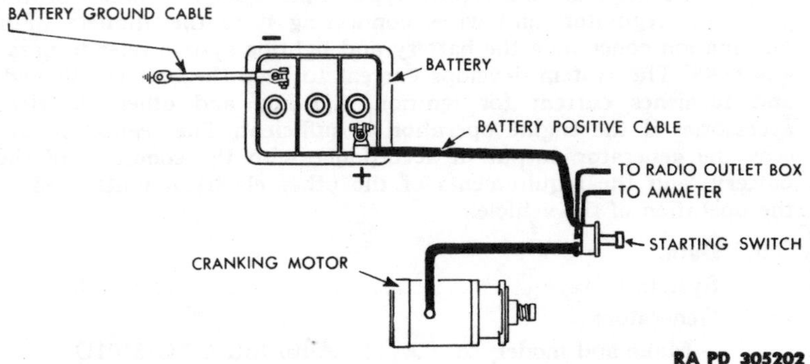

Figure 47—Starting System Circuit

90. STARTING SWITCH.

a. Description. The starting switch is a push-button type operated with the right foot, and located to the right of the accelerator treadle on the toeboard (fig. 5). Press the button to close the switch and cause the cranking motor to operate.

b. Removal. Remove battery cable at negative post of battery. Remove air cleaner (par. 73). Remove cable terminal nuts on switch, and remove cables and wires. Remove two screws holding switch to toeboard, and remove switch from underneath.

c. Installation. Remove cable terminal nuts, place switch in position under toeboard, and tighten in place with two screws. Attach cables and wires. NOTE: *Battery positive cable and wires to radio outlet box, filter, and ammeter are attached to top terminal.* Install air cleaner (par. 73), and connect battery cable to negative post on battery.

Section XIX

GENERATING SYSTEM

91. DESCRIPTION AND DATA.

a. **Description.** The generating system (fig. 49) is a 6-volt system, single-wire, ground-return type. This system consists of the generator, regulator, and wires connecting it to the ammeter. For information concerning the battery and lighting system refer to paragraph 95. The system develops current to keep the battery charged, and furnishes current for ignition, lighting, and other electrical accessories if the engine operation is sufficient. The regulator governs the generator output in accordance with the condition of the battery, and the requirements of the other electrical units used in the operation of the vehicle.

b. **Data.**

System voltage .... 6 to 8

Generator:

Make and model .... Auto-Lite GEG-5101D
Ground polarity .... Negative
Controlled output .... 40 amps
Rotation (drive end) .... Clockwise
Control .... Current voltage regulator
Brushes 2
Output .... 8.0 amps; 7.6 volts; 955 rpm
40.0 amps; 7.6 volts; 1460 rpm
40.0 amps; 8.0 volts; 1465 rpm

Regulator:

Make and model .... Auto-Lite VRY-4203 A
Type .... Current voltage
Volts 6
Amperes 40
Ground polarity .... Negative

92. MAINTENANCE.

a. The generator requires attention to lubrication of those generators provided with oilers. Properly adjust the drive belt. Check mounting screws and bracket attached to engine. Generator brace must be in position. Wire terminals must be in good condition, clean, and tight. External connecting wires with damaged or cracked insulation must be replaced. Bond straps must be cleaned and securely tightened. If trouble is experienced with the generator, report to higher authority.

93. GENERATOR.

a. Description. The generator is located on the right side of the engine at the forward end (fig. 49). It is a 6-8 volt, shunt-wound, two-brush unit rotating clockwise as viewed from the drive pulley end. It has a controlled output of 40 amperes, and is air-cooled by a fan built into the drive pulley. Air is drawn in at the back of the generator, and discharged at the fan.

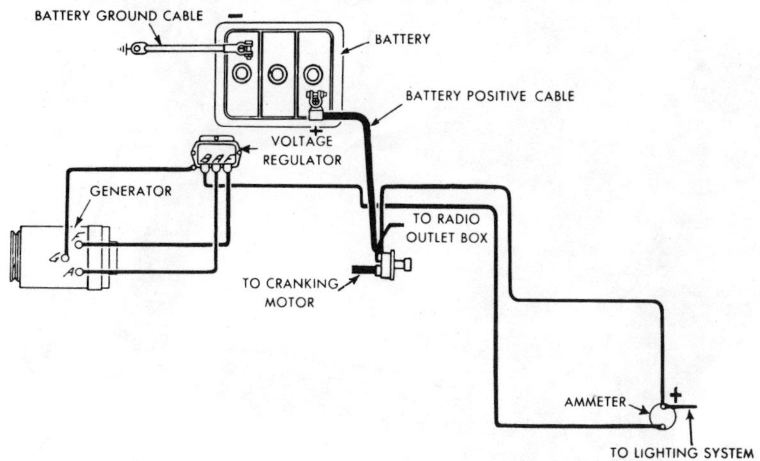

Figure 48—Generating System Circuit

b. Removal. Remove generator brace spring (fig. 10) and slip fan belt off pulley. Disconnect wires at generator; remove radio filter and ground strap. Remove two generator support bolts and remove generator.

c. Installation. Place generator in position, and install a drift or pin through front hole as a pilot. Install flat washer and bushing at rear support, and install bolt through hole. Remove drift, and install washer and bolt in front hole. Install generator brace spring. Install fan belt, and adjust if necessary (par. 83). Attach wires, filter, and ground strap. Start engine and check charging rate on ammeter in instrument panel (fig. 5).

94. REGULATOR.

a. **Description.** The regulator (fig. 49) automatically governs the output of the generator in accordance with the condition of the battery and the current requirements in the operation of the vehicle, thus, when the battery is low the output is increased, and as the

Figure 49—Generator and Regulator

battery becomes fully charged the generator develops less current to avoid overcharging. The regulator is mounted inside the splasher of the right front fender. It is a precision instrument, sealed at the factory, and no attempt should be made to adjust it. The regulator consists of three separate units: the cut-out or circuit breaker, the voltage regulator, and the current regulator. The circuit breaker automatically closes the circuit between the generator and the battery when the generator voltage rises above that of the battery, and opens the circuit when the generator current falls below that of the battery.

The voltage regulator governs the generator so that it will not develop more voltage than the value for which the voltage regulator is set. The current regulator controls the generator current (amperage) output so that it will develop enough to keep the battery charged (providing the engine is run sufficiently), and also prevent damage to the generator due to an overload.

b. Removal. Remove battery cable at battery negative post. Remove wires from regulator terminals. Mark wires to assure correct installation. Remove bond strap, and remove four bolts holding regulator to fender.

c. Installation. Place regulator in position on fender, and tighten securely with four bolts. Install bond strap. Connect wires to proper terminals. Install battery cable on post, and tighten securely. Start engine and check charging rate of ammeter in instrument panel.

¼-TON 4 x 4 TRUCK (WILLYS-OVERLAND MODEL MB and FORD MODEL GPW)

Section XX

BATTERY AND LIGHTING SYSTEM

95. DESCRIPTION AND DATA.

a. **Description.** The lighting system (fig. 50) functions on 6 volts supplied by a three-cell storage battery. The system consists of two service headlights, two blackout headlights, one blackout driving light, service and blackout stop and taillights, two instrument panel lights, and operating switches and battery. The entire lighting system is controlled by the blackout (main) light switch on the instrument panel. When the blackout light switch is set in the proper operating position, other light switches such as blackout driving light, instrument panel, stop lights and dimmers, are controlled by the respective switches. The lighting system is protected by a thermal-type fuse on the back of the blackout switch.

b. **Data.**

Battery:

Make and model	Auto-Lite-TS-2-15 Willard SW-2-119
Volts	6
Plates per cell	15
Capacity (ampere hours)	116
Length	10 in.
Width	7 in.
Height	$8\frac{5}{16}$ in.
Ground terminal	Negative

Wiring system:

Volts	6
Wiring identification reference	Fig. 50

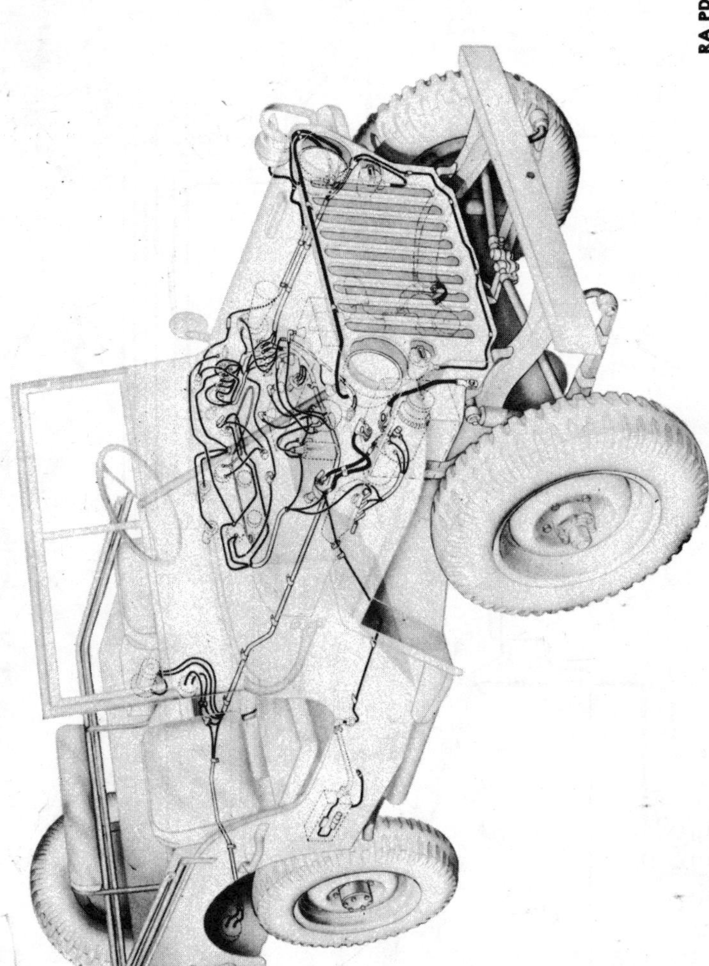

Figure 50—Wiring System—Phantom View

¼-TON 4 x 4 TRUCK (WILLYS-OVERLAND MODEL MB and FORD MODEL GPW)

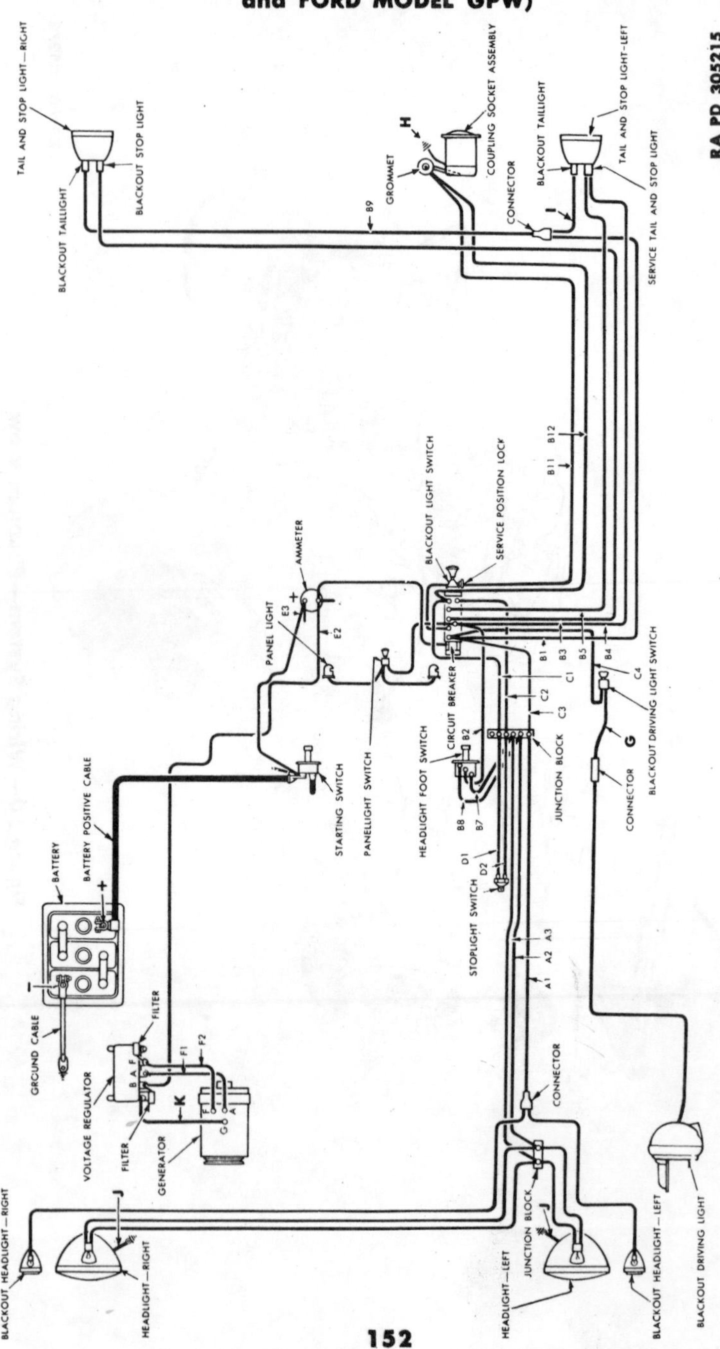

Figure 51—Lighting Circuits

		GAGE	COLOR
A—HEADLIGHT WIRING HARNESS			
A-1	BLACKOUT HEADLIGHT JUNCTION BLOCK TO JUNCTION BLOCK	14	YELLOW—2 BLACK TR.
A-2	HEADLIGHT JUNCTION BLOCK TO JUNCTION BLOCK (UPPER BEAM)	12	RED—3 WHITE TR.
A-3	HEADLIGHT JUNCTION BLOCK TO JUNCTION BLOCK (LOWER BEAM)	14	BLACK—2 WHITE TR.
B—BODY WIRING HARNESS—LONG			
B-1	LIGHT SWITCH TERMINAL "B H T" TO BLACKOUT TAIL CONNECTION	14	YELLOW—2 BLACK TR.
B-2	LIGHT SWITCH TERMINAL "H T" TO FOOT DIMMER SWITCH CENTER TERMINAL	12	BLUE—3 WHITE TR.
B-3	LIGHT SWITCH TERMINAL "B S" TO BLACKOUT STOPLIGHT	14	WHITE—2 BLACK TR.
B-4	LIGHT SWITCH TERMINAL "H T" TO SERVICE TAILLIGHT AND INSTRUMENT LIGHT SWITCH	14	BLUE—2 WHITE TR.
B-5	LIGHT SWITCH TERMINAL "S" TO SERVICE STOPLIGHT	14	RED—2 WHITE TR.
B-6	HORN CIRCUIT BREAKER TO HORN	14	BLACK—2 RED TR.
B-7	JUNCTION BLOCK TO FOOT DIMMER SWITCH (LOWER BEAM)	14	BLACK—2 WHITE TR.
B-8	JUNCTION BLOCK TO FOOT DIMMER SWITCH (UPPER BEAM)	12	RED—3 WHITE TR.
B-9	CONNECTOR TO BLACKOUT TAILLIGHT	14	YELLOW—2 BLACK TR.
B-11	LIGHT SWITCH TERMINAL "T T" TO COUPLING SOCKET TERMINAL "T L"	14	GREEN—2 BLACK TR.
B-12	LIGHT SWITCH TERMINAL "S S" TO COUPLING SOCKET TERMINAL "S L"	14	RED—2 BLACK TR.
C—BODY WIRING HARNESS—LEFT SIDE—SHORT			
C-1	JUNCTION BLOCK TO LIGHT SWITCH TERMINAL "S S"	14	RED—2 WHITE TR.
C-2	JUNCTION BLOCK TO LIGHT SWITCH TERMINAL "S W"	14	GREEN—2 BLACK TR.
C-3	JUNCTION BLOCK TO LIGHT SWITCH TERMINAL "B H T"	14	YELLOW—2 BLACK TR.
C-4	BLACKOUT LIGHT SWITCH TO LIGHT SWITCH TERMINAL "B H T"	14	BLACK—2 WHITE TR.
D—CHASSIS WIRING HARNESS—LEFT			
D-1	STOPLIGHT SWITCH TO JUNCTION BLOCK	14	RED—2 WHITE TR.
D-2	STOPLIGHT SWITCH TO JUNCTION BLOCK	14	GREEN—2 BLACK TR.
E—BODY WIRING HARNESS—RIGHT			
E-1	COIL TO IGNITION SWITCH TO GASOLINE GAGE CIRCUIT BREAKER	14	BLACK—2 WHITE TR.
E-2	VOLTAGE REGULATOR TERMINAL "B H T" TO AMMETER	12	RED—3 WHITE TR.
E-3	STARTING SWITCH TO AMMETER	12	BLACK—3 WHITE TR.
E-4	AMMETER TO HORN CIRCUIT BREAKER	14	BLACK—2 RED TR.
F—GENERATOR TO VOLTAGE REGULATOR AND FILTER HARNESS			
F-1	GENERATOR TO REGULATOR ARMATURE	12	RED—3 WHITE TR.
F-2	GENERATOR TO REGULATOR FIELD	14	GREEN—2 BLACK TR.
G—BLACKOUT DRIVING LIGHT CONNECTOR TO SWITCH		14	BLACK—2 WHITE TR.
H—COUPLING SOCKET TO GROUND		14	BLACK—2 WHITE TR.
I—CONNECTOR TO BLACKOUT TAILLIGHT		14	YELLOW—2 WHITE TR.
J—HEADLIGHT GROUND		12	BLACK—3 WHITE TR
K—GENERATOR TO VOLTAGE REGULATOR—GROUND			FLEXIBLE BRAIDED STRAP

RA PD 305215B

Legend for Figure 51—Lighting Circuits

Lamps:

Headlights	Sealed unit
Blackout headlights	Mazda No. 1245
Blackout driving light	Sealed unit
Taillights and stop lights	Sealed unit
Instrument lights	Mazda No. 51

Trailer connections:

Make	Wagner
Socket model	No. 3604
Plug model	No. 3544

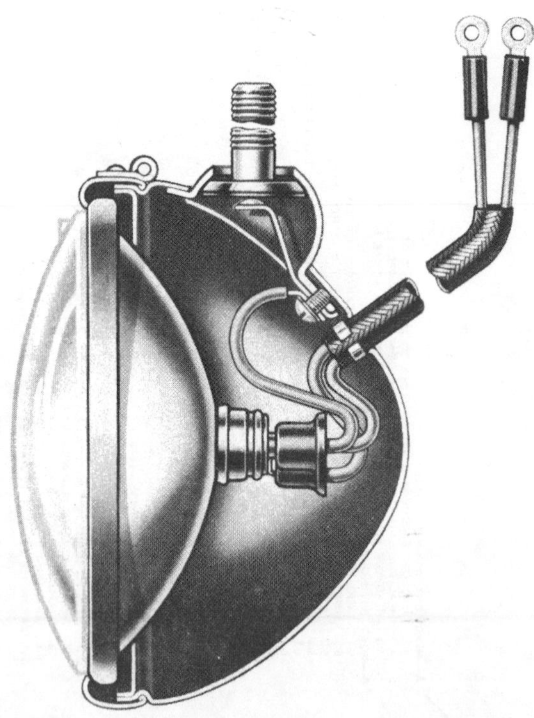

Figure 52—Headlight

RA PD 305216

96. MAINTENANCE.

a. The battery requires periodic checking of the proper level of electrolyte. Battery case must be kept clean. All vent plugs must be tight and breather holes kept open. Keep battery terminals and posts clean and securely tightened. Clean battery carrier when corroded. Tighten battery hold-down clamps. All light mounting screws and nuts must be kept clean and tight. Light lenses and reflectors must be kept clean and securely fastened. Headlights must be aimed properly. All loose and dirty electrical connections must be cleaned and tightened. All damaged or frayed wires must be replaced. Bond straps must be clean and securely tightened.

97. BATTERY.

a. Description. The battery (fig. 36) is a 6-volt, 116-ampere-hour storage battery consisting of three side-by-side cells of 15 plates each. The battery is located under the hood at the right side,

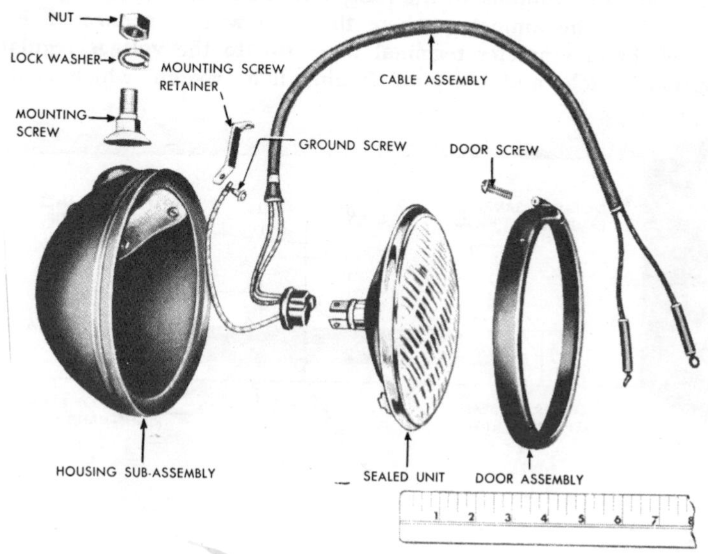

Figure 53—Headlight, Disassembled

and has the negative (small) post grounded. In normal temperatures the battery should be recharged when the specific gravity reads 1.175 or lower, and is fully charged when the specific gravity is 1.275 to 1.285.

b. Removal. Loosen bolts in cable terminals, and remove terminals from battery. Loosen two nuts holding frame on battery, and remove hold-down frame. Lift out battery.

c. Installation. Place battery in position with positive post to rear. Place hold-down frame in position, and tighten securely with nuts. Clean cable terminals; if necessary; grease and install on battery posts. Check level and specific gravity of electrolyte in battery. Electrolyte level must be ½ inch above plates, and specific gravity must be 1.275 to 1.285 at 80°F.

98. WIRING SYSTEM.

a. **Description.** The entire vehicle wiring system is shown in figure 50, and the circuits of the lighting system are shown in figure 51. A single-wire system is used, and the negative terminal of the battery is grounded. A single cable connects the battery positive post to the upper terminal of the starting switch, to which are also attached wires running to the radio outlet box, filter, and right-hand terminal of the ammeter, where the horn wire is connected. From the left-hand ammeter terminal wires run to the voltage regulator, ignition switch, and blackout (main) light switch, which controls

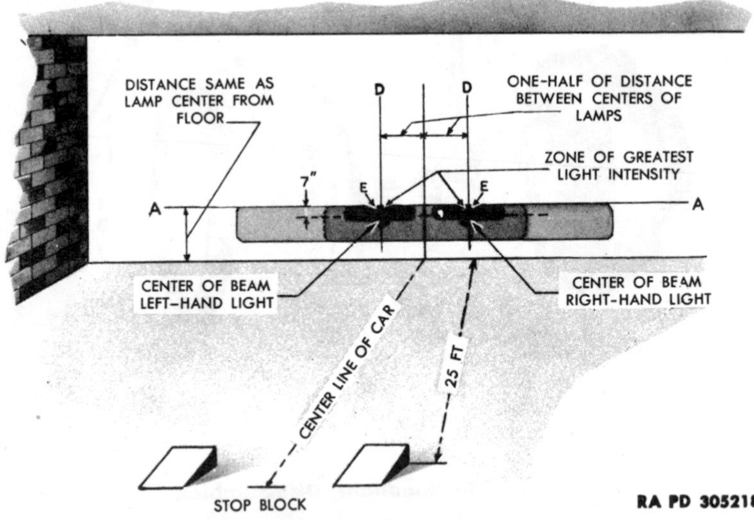

Figure 54—Headlight Aiming Chart

all lights in the lighting system. The wiring system consists of the harnesses and wires which are identified by colors and tracers as shown in figure 50, and described in the accompanying legend.

b. **Removal.** When necessary to renew wires in the wiring system, remove grounded (negative) cable at battery. Note location of wires; disconnect wires at terminals; loosen clips along harness, and remove wires.

c. **Installation.** When installing wires and harnesses see that all connections are correctly located and secure. Double-check location and tightness of connections; install retaining clips along wires.

99. HEADLIGHTS.

LO = BEAM IS TOP FILAMENT
HI = BEAM IS BOT FILAMENT

a. **Description.** Two headlights (fig. 52) are mounted at the front of the vehicle and are protected by the radiator guard. Each headlight is mounted on a hinged bracket. By loosening the wing nut, the light can be swung over and used as a trouble light in the engine compartment. The headlights are of the double filament sealed beam-unit type consisting of reflector, lamp, and lens, which can be

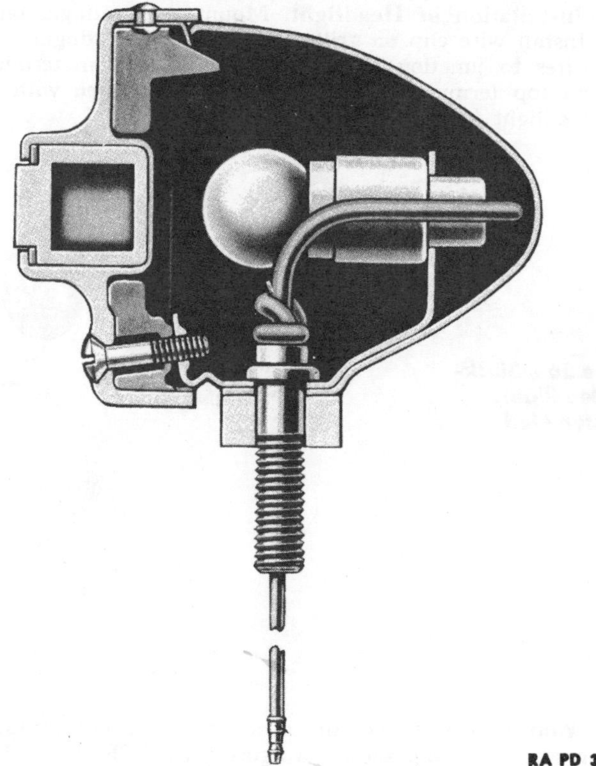

Figure 55—Blackout Headlight

replaced only as a unit (Mazda No. 2400). The headlights light when the blackout lighting switch is in service position. The upper and lower beams are controlled by the foot-operated dimmer switch. The lower beam filament is positioned slightly to one side of the focal point deflecting the beam slightly to illuminate the right side of the road.

b. **Removal of Sealed Beam-unit.** Remove door clamp screw and remove door (fig. 53). Remove sealed beam assembly, and pull connector from back of unit.

c. Installation of Sealed Beam-unit. Attach connector to back of unit. Place unit in position in headlight housing. Install door, and secure in place with screw.

d. Removal of Headlight. Disconnect headlight wires at junction block on left fender splash under hood. Remove clip on radiator grille (two on right headlight wire). Remove nut on headlight. Loosen headlight support wing nut, raise support, and remove headlight.

e. Installation of Headlight. Mount the headlight on the support. Install wire clip on grille (two on right headlight wire). Connect wires to junction block (red wire on bottom terminal; black wire on top terminal). Lower support, and fasten with wing nut. Aim headlight (subpar. f below).

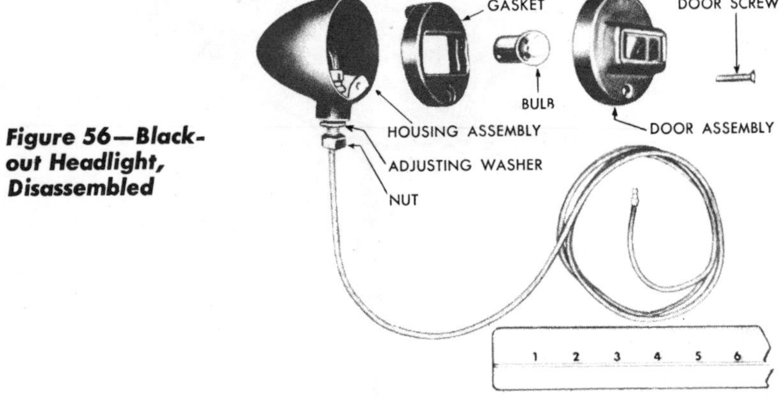

Figure 56—Blackout Headlight, Disassembled

RA PD 305220

f. Aiming Headlights. Aim headlights by using headlight aimer, aiming screen, or wall shown in figure 54. NOTE: *Use a light background with black center line for centering vehicle on screen. Mark two vertical lines on each side of center line equal to the distance between headlight centers. Mark screen 7 inches less than the height of centers of headlights.* Inflate all tires to recommended pressure (par. 3). Set vehicle so headlights are 25 feet away from screen and center line of vehicle is in line with center line of screen. To determine center line of vehicle, stand at rear and sight through windshield down across cowl and hood. Turn on headlight upper beam, cover one headlight, and observe location of upper beam on screen. Adjust headlight so that center of bright light area is on intersection of vertical and horizontal lines. Tighten headlight mounting nut. Cover headlight just aimed, and adjust other in same manner.

100. BLACKOUT HEADLIGHTS.

a. Description. There are two blackout headlights (fig. 55) with lens which permit only horizontal rays to pass through. These headlights are illuminated only when the blackout (main) light switch is in blackout position. Mazda No. 1245 lamps are used.

b. Removal of Lamp. Remove door screw in lower side of rim and remove door by pulling out on lower side (fig. 56). NOTE: *The door and lens are in one unit.* Push in on lamp, turn lamp to left and remove.

c. Installation of Lamp. Insert lamp in socket, push in and turn lamp to right. Replace door gasket, if damaged. Replace door and tighten door screw.

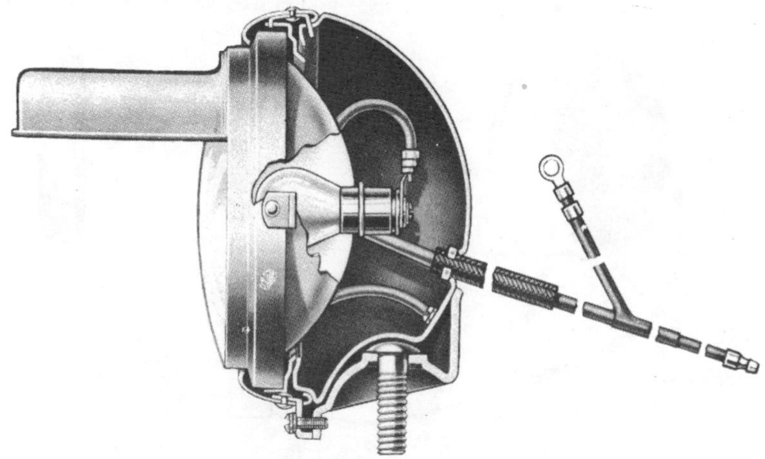

RA PD 305221

Figure 57—Blackout Driving Light

d. Removal of Blackout Headlight. Pull wire out of connection just behind left headlight. (For right headlight remove three clips across bottom of grille.) Remove mounting nut by reaching in from the rear and lift out headlight.

e. Installation of Blackout Headlight. Put light in position and tighten in place with mounting nut. (Attach three clips for right headlight.) Attach wire in connector.

101. BLACKOUT DRIVING LIGHT.

a. Description. The blackout driving light (fig. 57) is a hooded light having a sealed unit which throws a horizontal diffused beam to illuminate any vertical object. This light is mounted on the left front fender, and is controlled by a push-pull type switch (marked "B.O. DRIVE") in the instrument panel. The blackout driving light can be illuminated only when the blackout (main) light switch is in blackout position.

b. Removal of Sealed Unit. Remove screw at bottom of light door (fig. 58). Pull bottom of door forward and up to remove. Disconnect socket wire, and remove door by releasing mounting ring.

c. Installation of Sealed Unit. Place sealed unit in door, and install unit mounting ring. Attach wire connection. Install door on housing, and tighten retaining screw.

d. Removal of Blackout Driving Light. Pull wire out of connector at dash. Remove three wire clips, and pull wire through fender. Remove mounting nut on bottom of light, and lift off light.

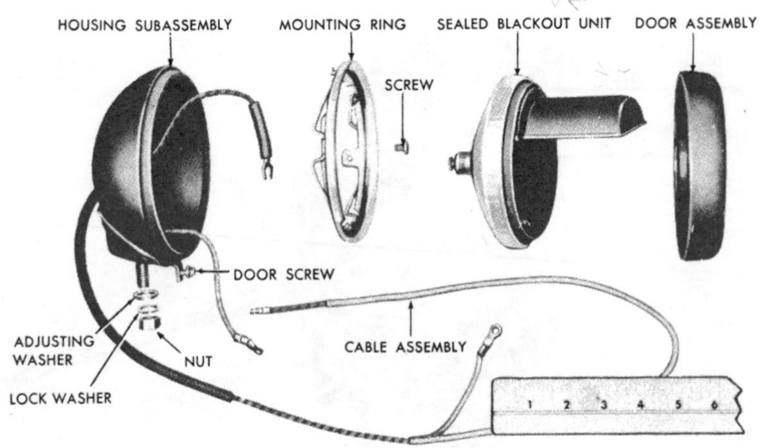

Figure 58—Blackout Driving Light, Disassembled

e. Installation of Blackout Driving Light. Install light on bracket and tighten nut; run wire through fender and splasher; attach three clips, and push wire into connector at dash.

f. Adjustment. The light is aimed with vehicle on a level surface and loaded. Hold a 4-foot wood stick on floor close to the light, and mark stick where bright spot appears. Move stick 10 feet ahead of light; bright spot should be 2.1 inches lower than mark.

102. TAILLIGHTS AND STOP LIGHTS.

a. Description. Two combination taillights and stop lights (fig. 59) are located in the rear panel of the body. Each light consists of two separate units in a housing. The left-hand light contains a combination service tail and stop light unit in the upper part, and a blackout taillight in the lower part. The upper unit consists of the taillight lens, gasket, reflector, and a 21-3-candlepower lamp. The lower unit consists of blackout lens, gasket, reflector, and 3-candlepower lamp. The right-hand light contains a blackout stop light unit in the upper part, and a blackout taillight in the lower part. The upper unit consists of the blackout stop light lens, gasket, reflector, and 3-candlepower lamp. The lower unit is the same as the lower unit in the left light. When a lamp burns out, the unit must be replaced. These lights are controlled by the blackout (main) light switch.

b. Removal of Light Unit. Remove two screws in light door, and remove door (fig. 60). Pull each unit straight out of socket.

c. Installation of Light Unit. Be sure that unit is correct type, and push into socket. Install light door and screws.

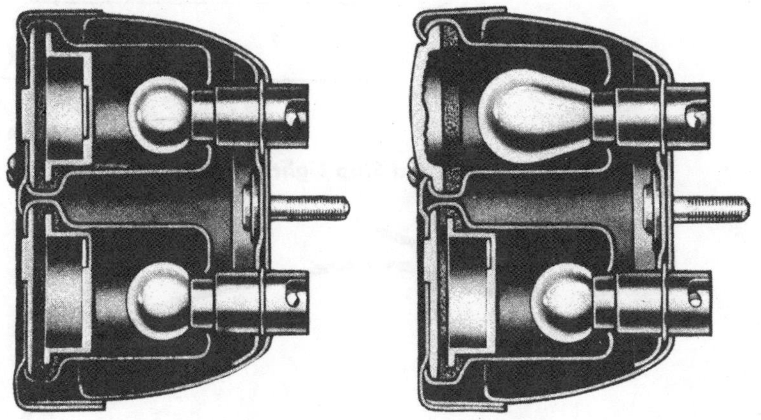

RA PD 305223

Figure 59—Taillights and Stop Lights

d. Removal of Light. Reach up under body and disconnect wire connector; push in on connector, turn counterclockwise and pull connector out of socket. Remove two nuts holding light to bracket, and remove light.

e. Installation of Light. Place light in position and secure with nuts. Attach connectors. Double contact connector goes in upper socket of left light. Turn on blackout (main) light switch to blackout position to see if right blackout taillight (lower unit) lights; if not, interchange connectors in sockets.

103. INSTRUMENT PANEL LIGHTS.

a. Description. There are two instrument panel lights (fig. 5) located above instruments and on the outside of the instrument panel. They are controlled by the panel light switch when the blackout (main) light switch is in service position.

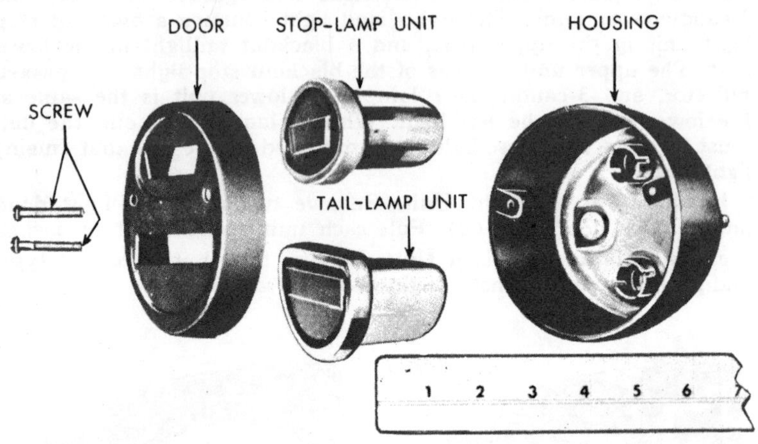

Figure 60—Taillights and Stop Lights, Disassembled

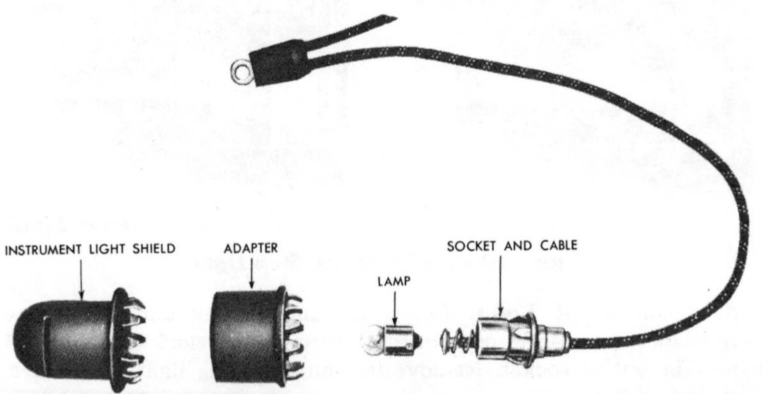

Figure 61—Instrument Light, Disassembled

b. Removal of Lamp. Pry off shield by using a sharp tool behind flange (fig. 61). Pull light socket out of shield; press in on lamp, turn lamp counterclockwise, and remove.

c. Installation of Lamp. Put lamp in socket, push lamp in, and turn clockwise. Push socket into shield, and push shield into instrument lamp adapter.

d. Removal of Instrument Light. Disconnect wire on back of light switch, and dismantle as outlined in subparagraph **b** above. Remove wire and sockets for both lamps under instrument panel.

e. Installation of Instrument Light. Attach wire terminal to panel light switch, and place sockets through holes in instrument panel. Assemble light as outlined in subparagraph **c** above.

104. BLACKOUT (MAIN) LIGHT SWITCH.

a. Description. The blackout light switch is a push-pull type (fig. 62), mounted in the instrument panel to the left of the steering gear (fig. 5). The switch controls all the lights, and has four positions (fig. 9). With the knob all the way in, all lights are off. Pull knob out to first (blackout) position to illuminate blackout headlights,

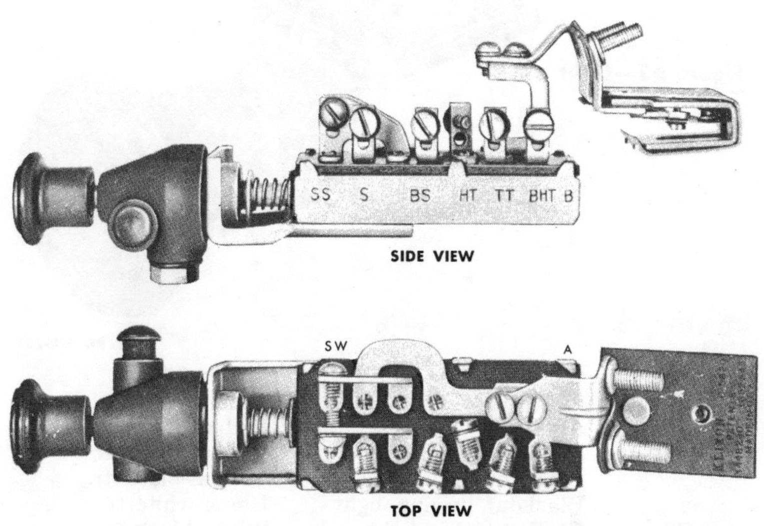

Figure 62—Blackout (Main) Light Switch

blackout taillights, and establish connection so blackout stop light will function when foot brake is applied. Press lockout control button, and pull switch knob out to second (service) position to illuminate service headlights and taillight, and to establish connections so service stop light will function when foot brake is applied. Pull knob out to third (service stop light) position, when vehicle is operated during daylight, to cause stop light only to function when foot brake is applied. A thermal-type fuse is mounted on the back of the switch having a bimetal spring, which causes a set of contact points to open and close, if a short circuit occurs in the lighting system.

b. Removal. Disconnect ground cable at negative post of battery. Loosen set screw in switch knob and unscrew knob. Loosen hexagon head screw at side of switch bushing on front of panel; press lockout control button, and pull off bushing. Remove mounting nut, and take switch out from under panel. Remove wire terminal screws. As wires are removed, mark them for identification.

c. Installation. Attach wires to proper terminals. NOTE: *Switch terminals are marked for easy identification.* Wires are to be attached as outlined below:

Figure 63—Light Switch

RA PD 305227

Terminal	Circuit	Wire Color
A	... Extra	Not used
B	... Ammeter	Red–white tr.
BHT	... Blackout headlights	Yellow–black tr.
	... Blackout taillights	Yellow–black tr.
	... Blackout driving light ..	Black–white tr.
BS	... Blackout stop light	White–black tr.
HT	... Service headlight	Blue–white tr.
	... Service taillight	Blue–white tr.
	... Panel lights	Blue–white tr.
S	... Service stop light.......	Red–white tr.
SS	... Blackout driving light...	Red–white tr.
	... Trailer coupling socket..	Red–black tr.
SW	... Stop light	Green–black tr.
TT	... Trailer coupling socket..	Green–black tr.

Install switch in panel and secure in place with mounting nut. Install bushings and tighten screw. Install knob and tighten set screw. Attach ground cable to battery.

105. PANEL AND BLACKOUT DRIVING LIGHT SWITCHES.

a. Description. The panel and blackout driving light switches

BATTERY AND LIGHTING SYSTEM

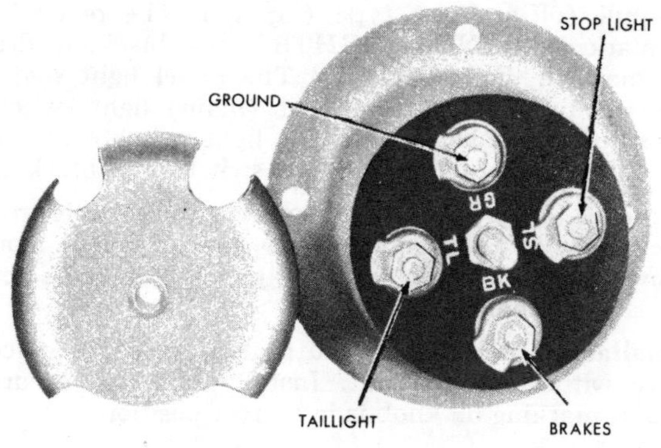

Figure 64—Trailer Socket Terminals

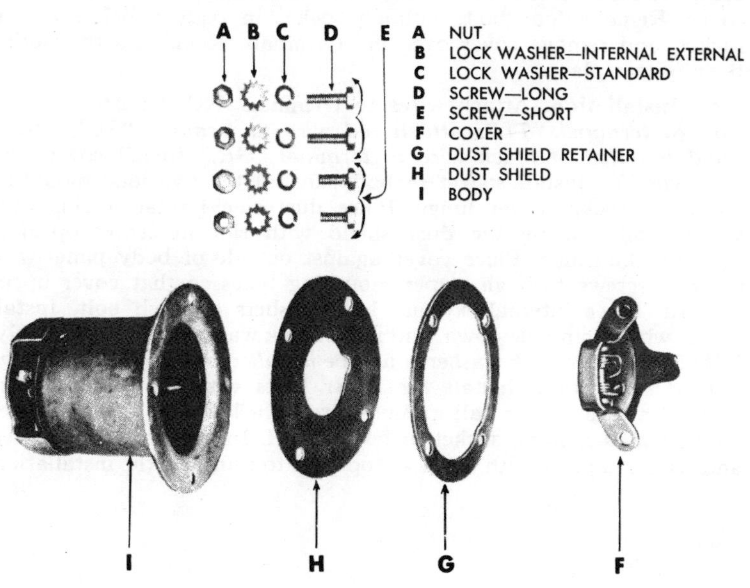

Figure 65—Trailer Socket, Disassembled

are push-pull (off-and-on) type (fig. 63). The panel light switch knob is marked "PANEL LIGHTS"; the blackout driving light switch is marked "B.O. DRIVE." The panel light switch controls these lights only when the blackout (main) light switch is in the service position. The blackout driving light switch controls that light only when the blackout (main) light switch is in blackout position.

b. Removal. As a precaution remove ground cable from battery. Loosen set screw in knob and unscrew knob. Remove mounting nut, and remove switch from in back of panel. Remove screws in wire terminals, and disconnect wires.

c. Installation. Attach wires to switch, install in place in panel, and secure with mounting nut. Install knob and secure with set screw so that marking on knob is in correct position.

106. TRAILER CONNECTION.

a. Description. The trailer connection is a socket located in the body rear panel at the left side (fig. 2). The blackout (main) light switch controls the current to socket and trailer lights.

b. Removal. Remove equipment from left rear tool compartment. Remove screw at top edge of protecting cover, and remove cover. Remove four bolts holding socket in body panel. Pull out socket, and remove cover over the terminals. Remove wires, noting their proper place.

c. Installation. Attach wires to terminals. NOTE: *Attach green wire to terminal "TL"; attach red wire to terminal "SL"; attach small terminal of black wire to terminal "GR."* Install cover over terminals. To install socket in body, install the two long mounting screws in socket cover hinge. Place dust shield retainer ring over screws, followed by the dust shield with slot in center opening, opposite the hinge. Place cover against outside of body panel with the two screws through upper mounting holes so that cover opens upward. Place internal-external lock washers on each bolt. Install socket with drain hole down, and install lock washers and nuts loosely. NOTE: *Toothed lock washers must be installed as directed for a good ground connection.* Install the lower bolts with the lock washers in correct position. Install ground wire on a lower bolt, and tighten all four nuts holding socket in body panel. Install protecting cover, and secure in place with screw at top edge to complete the installation.

Section XXI

CLUTCH

107. DESCRIPTION AND DATA.

a. Description. The clutch (fig. 66) located between the engine and the transmission is a single plate, dry-disk type. The clutch consists principally of two units, the clutch driven plate which has a spring-center vibration neutralizer, and the clutch pressure plate unit, which is bolted to the flywheel. The controlled pressure of the driven plate against the flywheel provides a means of engaging and disengaging the engine power to the transmission. A ball-type release bearing operates three clutch release levers to control the clutch. The release bearing is controlled by a rod and cable to the clutch pedal. This type clutch has only one service adjustment. This adjustment is for the foot pedal, and regulates the amount of free pedal travel. As the clutch facings wear, adjust the free pedal travel to three-quarters of an inch (fig. 68).

b. Data.

Type .... Dry single plate
Torque capacity driven plate .... 132 foot-pounds
  Make .... Borg and Beck No. 11123
  Size .... 7⅞ in.
Facings .... 1 woven and 1 molded
  Diameter .... 5⅛ in. inside, 7⅞ in. outside
  Thickness .... ⅛ in. (0.125)
Pressure plate:
  Make .... Atwood No. TP-2B-7-1
  Number of springs 3
Clutch release bearing type .... Prelubricated ball
Clutch shaft bushing (in flywheel) size .... I.D. 0.628 in.
Clutch pedal adjustment (free play) .... ¾ in.

108. MAINTENANCE.

a. The clutch requires attention to pedal adjustment. Pedal adjustment must be periodically checked, due to the natural wear of lining. Report grabbing or slipping condition of clutch to higher authority.

109. PEDAL ADJUSTMENT.

a. Adjust Pedal. Loosen clutch control cable adjusting yoke lock nut (figs. 67 and 68). Using a wrench, unscrew cable until clutch pedal has ¾ inch free play. Tighten lock nut.

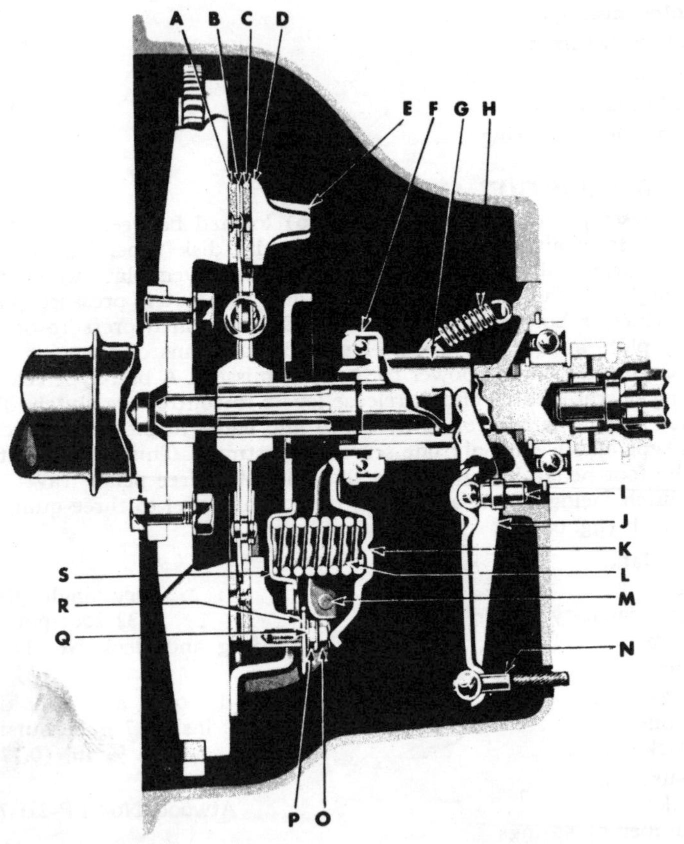

A	FACING—FRONT	J	CLUTCH CONTROL LEVER
B	DRIVEN PLATE ASSEMBLY	K	CLUTCH LEVER
C	FACING—REAR	L	PRESSURE SPRING
D	PRESSURE PLATE	M	CLUTCH LEVER PIVOT PIN
E	CLUTCH PRESSURE PLATE ASSEMBLY	N	CONTROL LEVER CABLE
F	RELEASE BEARING	O	ADJUSTING SCREW
G	RELEASE BEARING CARRIER	P	ADJUSTING SCREW LOCK NUT
H	RELEASE BEARING CARRIER SPRING	Q	ADJUSTING SCREW WASHER
I	CLUTCH CONTROL LEVER FULCRUM	R	PRESSURE PLATE RETURN SPRING
		S	PRESSURE SPRING CUP

RA PD 305274

Figure 66—Clutch—Sectional View

CLUTCH

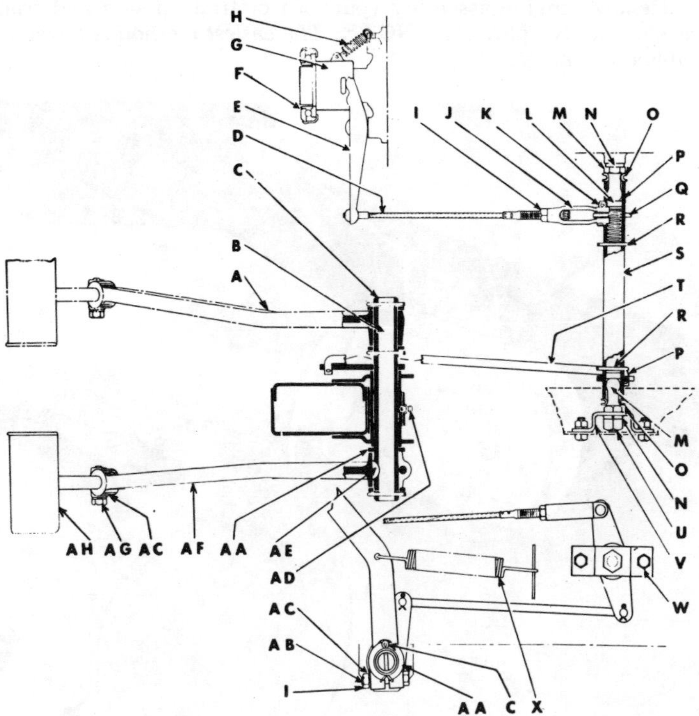

A	BRAKE PEDAL	Q	SPRING
B	PEDAL SHAFT ASSEMBLY	R	TUBE SPRING COTTER PIN
C	PEDAL SHAFT COTTER PIN	S	LEVER AND TUBE ASSEMBLY
D	LEVER CABLE	T	PEDAL ROD
E	LEVER	U	BALL STUD NUT
F	RELEASE BEARING	V	FRAME BRACKET
G	RELEASE BEARING CARRIER	W	FRAME BRACKET SCREW
H	RELEASE BEARING CARRIER SPRING	X	PEDAL RETRACTING SPRING
I	LEVER CABLE YOKE END LOCK NUT	AA	PEDAL SHAFT WASHER
J	LEVER CABLE YOKE END	AB	PEDAL CLAMP BOLT
K	LEVER CABLE CLEVIS PIN	AC	PEDAL CLAMP BOLT LOCK WASHER
L	TUBE WASHER	AD	PEDAL SHAFT HYDRAULIC GREASE FITTING
M	BALL STUD	AE	PEDAL TO SHAFT KEY
N	BALL STUD LOCK WASHER	AF	PEDAL
O	TUBE DUST WASHER	AG	PEDAL CLAMP BOLT
P	TUBE FELT WASHER	AH	PEDAL PAD

RA PD 305286

Figure 67—Clutch Control

110. REMOVAL.

a. Remove engine assembly (par. 60) or transmission and transfer case assembly (par. 115). NOTE: *The easiest method is to remove the engine assembly.*

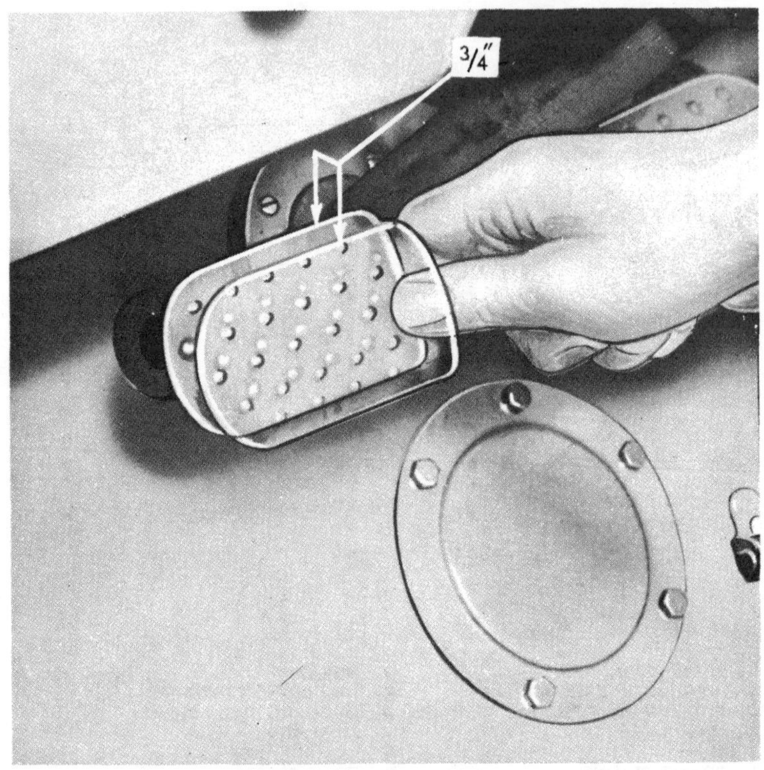

RA PD 305239

Figure 68—Clutch Pedal Free Travel

b. Mark clutch pressure plate and flywheel to assure correct position when installing. Loosen evenly and remove screws holding pressure plate to flywheel Remove pressure plate; remove driven plate.

111. INSTALLATION.

a. Clean flywheel and clutch. Install small amount of light grease in clutch shaft flywheel bushing. Install driven plate against flywheel with short end of hub toward flywheel. Install clutch pressure plate loosely with screws. Use a clutch shaft or clutch pilot arbor to aline driven plate, and tighten clutch pressure plate screws evenly. Remove pilot and check adjustment of clutch fingers (fig.

69), which should be $^{27}/_{32}$ inch. To adjust clutch fingers, loosen lock nut on adjusting screws, and turn screws until measurements from face of fingers (release bearing contacts) to face of clutch bracket measures $^{27}/_{32}$ inch; set lock nuts. Install engine (par. 61), or transmission and transfer case assembly (par. 116), as required.

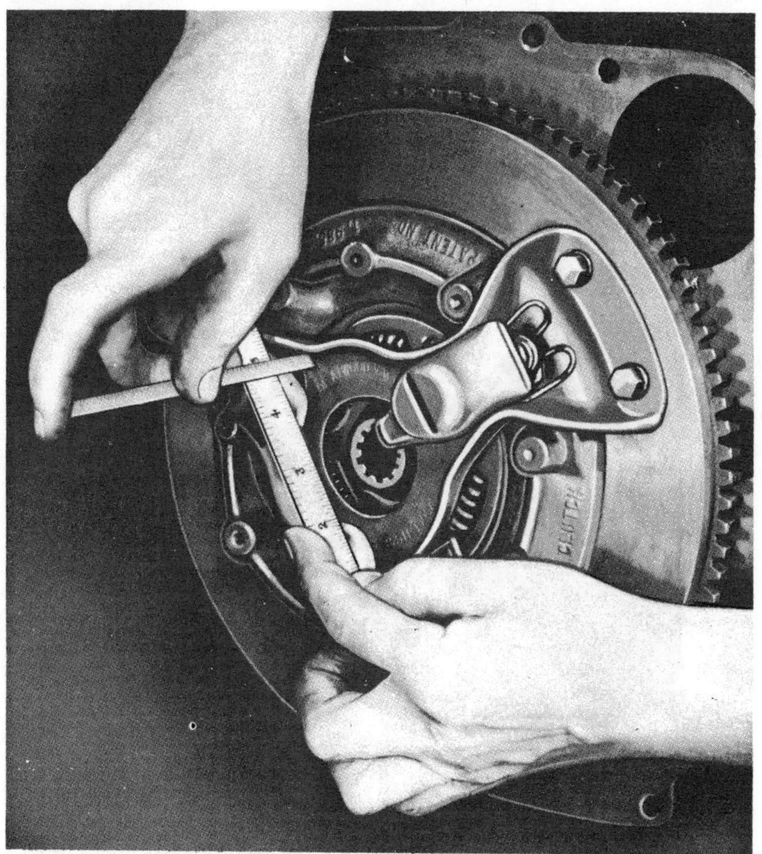

Figure 69—Clutch Finger Adjustment RA PD 305229

112. CLUTCH RELEASE BEARING.

a. Removal. Follow procedure outlined in paragraph 60 for removing engine. After release bearing can be reached, unhook release bearing carrier spring, and pull off bearing and carrier (fig. 66). Press carrier out of bearing.

b. Installation. Press carrier into bearing. Slip bearing and carrier onto transmission bearing retainer, install release lever on fulcrum, and hook spring to bearing carrier. Follow the procedure outlined in paragraph 61 for completion of assembly.

Section XXII

TRANSMISSION

Paragraph

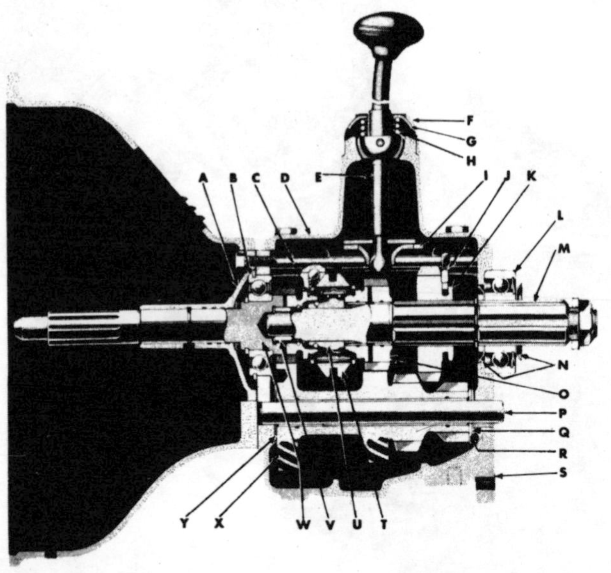

A MAIN DRIVE GEAR BEARING RETAINER
B MAIN DRIVE GEAR BEARING
C SHIFT RAIL—LOW AND REVERSE
D CONTROL HOUSING ASSEMBLY
E CONTROL LEVER ASSEMBLY
F CONTROL HOUSING CAP
G CONTROL HOUSING CAP WASHER
H CONTROL LEVER SUPPORT SPRING
I SHIFT PLATE
J LOW AND REVERSE SHIFT FORK
K LOW AND REVERSE SLIDING GEAR
L MAIN SHAFT BEARING
M MAIN SHAFT
N OIL RETAINING WASHER
O MAIN SHAFT SECOND SPEED GEAR ASSEMBLY
P COUNTERSHAFT
Q REAR COUNTERSHAFT THRUST WASHER (STEEL)
R REAR COUNTERSHAFT THRUST WASHER (BRONZE)
S CASE
T SECOND AND DIRECT SPEED CLUTCH SLEEVE
U HIGH AND INTERMEDIATE CLUTCH HUB
V MAIN SHAFT PILOT ROLLER BEARING
W MAIN DRIVE GEAR
X COUNTERSHAFT GEAR ASSEMBLY
Y COUNTERSHAFT THRUST WASHER-FRONT

RA PD 305285

Figure 70—Transmission—Sectional View

113. DESCRIPTION AND DATA.

a. Description. The transmission (fig. 70) is a selective, 3-speed, synchromesh type with synchronized second and high speed gears.

It is located in the power plant unit with the engine, clutch, and transfer case. Third speed is a direct drive through the transmission; all other speeds are through gears of various sizes to obtain the necessary gear reduction. The gears are shifted by a lever extending out of the top of the transmission, and through the floor at the right of the driver. For shifting instructions, refer to paragraph 5 e.

b. Data.

Make and model	Warner T-84-J
Type	Synchromesh
Speeds	3 forward—1 reverse
Ratios:	
Low (1st)	2.665 to 1
Intermediate (2nd)	1.564 to 1
High (3rd)	1 to 1
Reverse	3.554
Lubricant capacity	¾ qt
Lubricant grade reference	par. 18

114. MAINTENANCE.

a. The transmission requires periodic checking of lubrication level. Mounting screws must be tight. Gearshift ball cap must be removed and cleaned as required. Keep all bond straps clean and securely tightened. Vent hole in transmission control housing must be kept clean at all times. Report transmission gear noise to higher authority.

115. REMOVAL.

a. Raise hood and fasten to windshield to prevent accidental closing. Open drain cock at bottom of radiator and drain cooling system. Remove radiator upper hose. Unscrew balls on shift levers. Remove bolts around transmission cover on floor, and remove cover. Remove transmission shift lever by unscrewing retainer collar at top of shift housing. Remove transfer case shift lever pin set screw. Remove lubricator in right end of shift shaft. Drive out shaft and remove levers. Place jack under engine oil pan. Remove exhaust pipe guard. Remove exhaust pipe clamp on skid plate. Remove skid plate. Remove bolts in front and rear propeller shaft universal joint flanges at transfer case end, and tie propeller shafts up to frame. Disconnect speedometer cable at transfer case. Remove transfer case support (snubber) bolt at cross member (fig. 73). Remove clevis pin in lower end of hand brake cable, and remove hand brake retracting spring. Remove clevis pin in clutch release cable yoke at cross tube lever. Disconnect engine stay cable at cross member. Remove bonding strap on transfer case and transmission. Unhook clutch pedal pull-back spring. Remove nuts on engine rear support insulator studs in cross member. Place a second jack under the transmission. Remove frame to cross member bolts at each end, and remove cross member. Place rope around the transmission. Push transmission to right, and remove clutch release lever tube from ball joint on transfer case. Remove four bolts holding transmission to bell housing. Remove two screws in inspection cover. Remove core and clutch release fork. Hold weight of assembly with rope, and remove jack from under transmission. Slide transmission assembly back until clutch shaft clears bell housing, lowering jack under engine just enough so that transmission will clear floor pan. Remove assembly from under vehicle.

b. Remove Transmission from Transfer Case. Clean outside of units. Drain lubricant from transmission and transfer case. Remove screws holding rear cover on transfer case, and remove cover and gasket. Remove cotter pin, nut, and washer on rear end of transmission main shaft. Pull off main shaft gear and oil slinger.

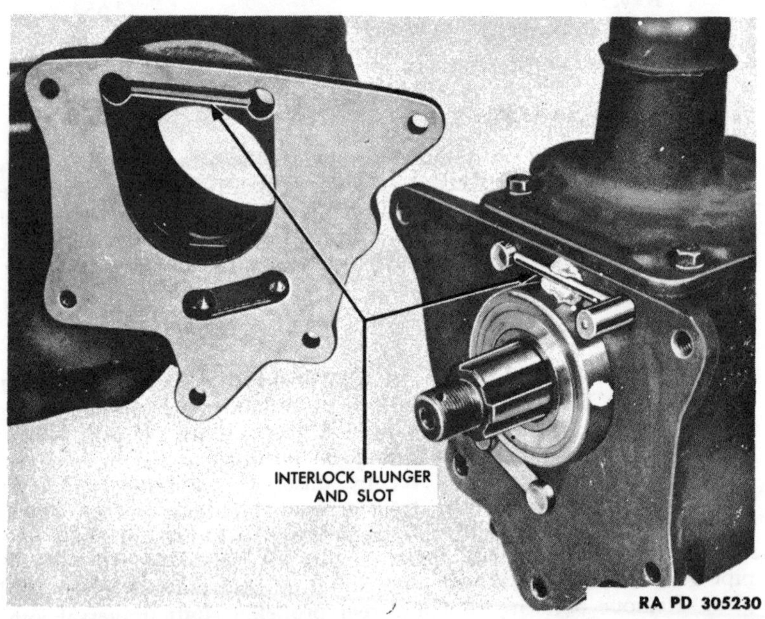

Figure 71—Gearshift Interlock Plunger

Remove four screws holding control housing on top of transmission, and remove housing. Remove shifter plate spring, and remove shifter plate. Loop piece of wire around main shaft to the rear of second speed gear, and attach wire tightly to front of transmission. Remove five screws holding transfer case to rear of transmission. Support transfer case, and tap lightly on end of transmission main shaft; at the same time draw transfer case away from transmission. NOTE: *Do not lose transmission gearshift interlock plunger* (fig. 71).

116. INSTALLATION.

a. **Assemble Transmission to Transfer Case.** Install transmission shift interlock plunger in position, using grease to hold it temporarily (fig. 71). Attach transfer case to transmission with five screws. Install shifter plate and spring. Install control housing on top of transmission with four screws. Using new gasket, install oil retaining washer on transmission main shaft in transfer case, with open face to rear. Install main drive gear with small power take-off gear to rear. Install washer, nut, and cotter pin. Install rear cover with screws and lock washers, using new gasket. Put lubricant in transmission and transfer case (par. 18).

b. **Install in Vehicle.** Place unit under vehicle. Place rope around transmission. Raise transmission, and insert transmission main drive gear shaft (clutch shaft) in hub of clutch plate and flywheel. Push transmission forward into position. Place jack under transmission to take the weight. Install clutch release fork on pivot ball, and install clutch release cable in end. Install transmission to bell housing bolts. Remove rope. Raise transmission with jacks. Push transmission to the right, and install clutch release tube on ball on transfer case. Install frame cross member. Remove jack under transmission. Install engine support insulator stud nuts at cross member. Place transfer case support rubber in place, and install bolt through cross member. Attach bond straps. Connect clutch release cable to lever. Connect hand brake cable and spring. Install engine stay cable and adjust so it is just taut. Install pedal pull-back spring. Adjust clutch release cable for pedal play (par. 109). Remove jack under engine. Connect speedometer cable at transfer case. Install transfer case shift levers and springs, driving shaft in from right side. Install shaft lock screw, and wire in place. Install lubricator in right end of shaft. Attach front and rear propeller shafts at transfer case. Install transmission skid plate. Install exhaust pipe clamp on skid plate. Install exhaust pipe guard. Install transmission shift lever in top of housing. Install transmission floor cover. Install gearshift lever balls. Install radiator upper hose. Fill cooling system, giving due attention to antifreeze, if required. Run engine until warm, and check coolant supply. Check cooling system for leaks. Lower hood and hook into place.

1/4-TON 4 x 4 TRUCK (WILLYS-OVERLAND MODEL MB and FORD MODEL GPW)

Section XXIII

TRANSFER CASE

117. DESCRIPTION AND DATA.

a. **Description.** The transfer case (fig. 72) is an auxiliary gear unit attached to the rear of the transmission. The transfer case is essentially a two-speed transmission which provides an additional

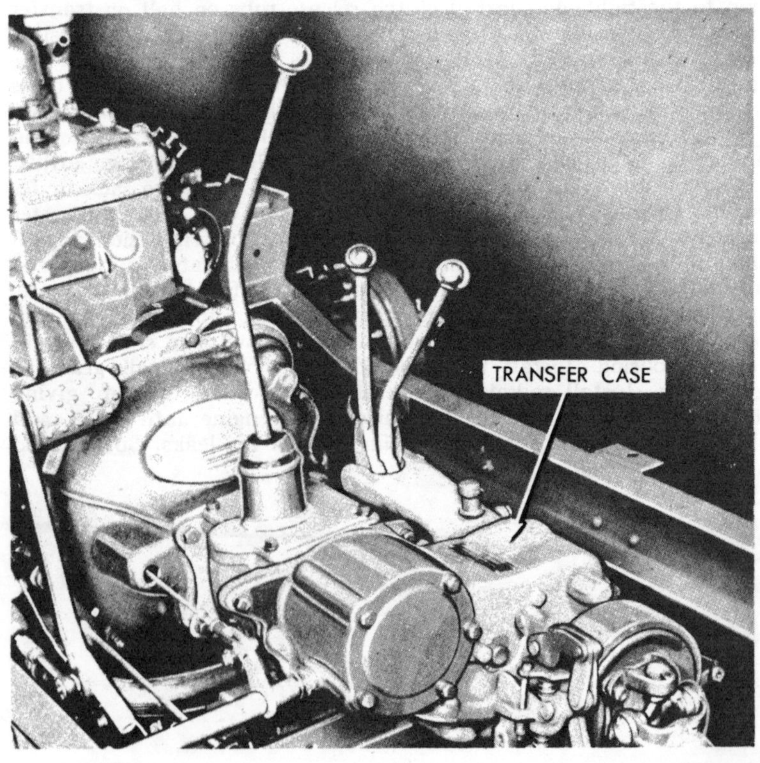

RA PD 305231

Figure 72—Transfer Case—Rear View

gear reduction for any selection of the transmission gears, also a means of engaging and disengaging power to drive the front axle. The shifting mechanism (fig. 73) is operated by two levers on the top of the case. A power take-off aperture is located at the rear just behind the transmission main shaft. The speedometer drive gear is located in the output shaft housing for the drive to the rear axle, and a hand brake is located on the same housing.

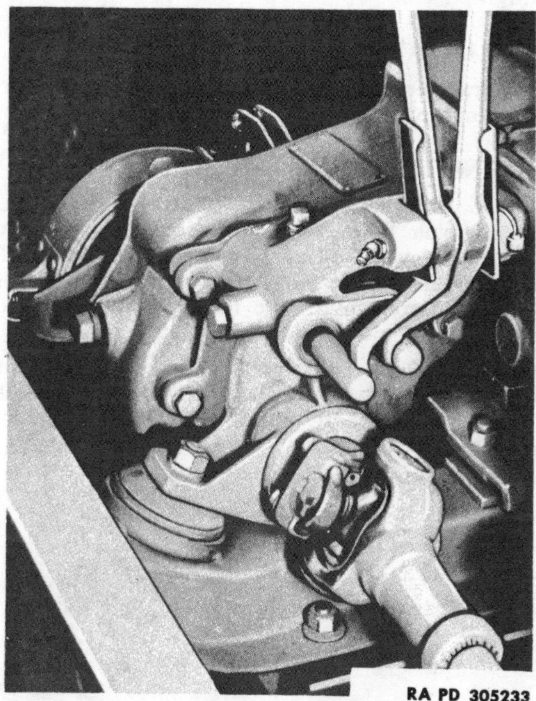

RA PD 305233

Figure 73—Transfer Case Shifting Mechanism

b. Data.

Make and model	Spicer–18
Ratio–high	1 to 1
–low	1.97 to 1
Speedometer teeth–drive gear	4
–driven gear	14
Lubricant capacity	1½ qt

118. MAINTENANCE.

a. The transfer case requires lubrication at regular intervals. All mounting bolts must be kept tight. Universal joint yoke and companion flange nuts must be tight. Bond strap must be clean and tightened securely. Tighten drain and filler plugs. Report failure to stay in gear and noisy gears to higher authority.

119. REMOVAL.

a. Remove transmission and transfer case as an assembly as outlined in paragraph 115.

120. INSTALLATION.

a. Attach transfer case to transmission, and install in vehicle as outlined in paragraph 116.

121. SHIFTING LEVERS.

a. Removal. Unscrew accelerator footrest and remove 10 screws holding transmission floor cover, also remove two screws holding transfer case shift lever housing cover. Remove covers. Raise hood and secure to windshield. Remove transfer case shift lever set screw and lock wire. Unscrew hydraulic fitting from right end of shaft. Drive out shaft, and remove levers (fig. 73).

b. Installation. Place shift levers and springs in position. Drive in shaft. Install shaft set screw, and wire in place. Install hydraulic fitting in right end of shaft. Install transmission floor cover and accelerator footrest.

Section XXIV

PROPELLER SHAFTS AND UNIVERSAL JOINTS

122. DESCRIPTION AND DATA.

a. Description. Two propeller shafts are used, one to drive each axle. Two universal joints are used on each shaft (fig. 74). A splined slip joint is used at the rear of the front shaft, and, at the front of the rear shaft. NOTE: *The slip joint is marked with an arrow on the spline shaft and on the sleeve yoke, and these arrows must aline*

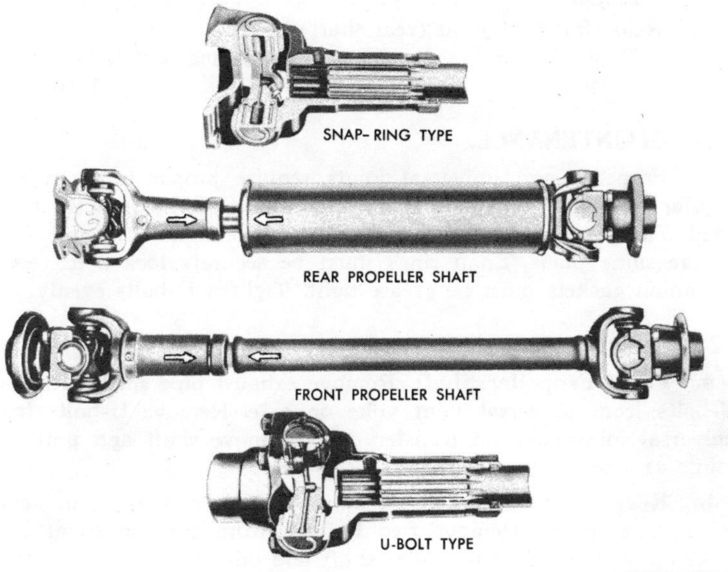

Figure 74—Propeller Shafts and Universal Joints

for correct assembly (fig. 74). The propeller shaft connecting the transfer case to the front axle has U-bolt type joints at both ends. The rear propeller shaft has a U-bolt type joint at the rear where it attaches to the rear axle, and a snap-ring type joint at the front end. The trunnion bearings are of the needle bearing type which are lubricated through a hydraulic fitting and an X-channel in the trunnion. Refer to lubrication instructions in paragraph 18.

b. Data.

Propeller shafts
- Make .... Spicer
- Installed length normal load-joint center to center
  - Front .... $21\frac{25}{32}$ in.
  - Rear .... $21\frac{5}{8}$ in.

Front Universal Joint (front shaft)
- Type .... Snap-ring and U-bolt
- Model 1268

Rear Universal Joint (front shaft)
- Type .... Snap-ring and U-bolt
- Model 1261

Front Universal Joint (rear shaft)
- Type .... Snap-ring
- Model 1261

Rear Universal Joint (rear shaft)
- Type .... Snap-ring and U-bolt
- Model 1268

123. MAINTENANCE.

a. Propeller and universal joints require proper lubrication at regular intervals. Attaching bolts and nuts must be securely tightened. The yokes of front and rear universal joints must be assembled in the same plane. Snap rings must be securely locked in recess. Trunnion gaskets must be grease-tight. Tighten U-bolts evenly.

124. REMOVAL.

a. **Front Propeller Shaft.** Remove exhaust pipe shield. Remove U-bolts from universal joint yoke on axle. Remove U-bolts from universal joint yoke on transfer case. Remove shaft and universal joints as a unit.

b. **Rear Propeller Shaft.** Remove four bolts in front universal joint yoke flange. Remove two U-bolts from rear universal joint yoke on axle. Remove propeller shaft and universal joints as a unit.

125. INSTALLATION.

a. **Front Propeller Shaft.** Install propeller shaft and universal joint assembly in position on vehicle. Install U-bolts at axle. Install U-bolts at transfer case. NOTE: *Tighten U-bolts evenly.* Install exhaust pipe shield. Lubricate universal joints (par. 18 c).

b. **Rear Propeller Shaft.** Install propeller shaft and universal joint assembly in position. Install U-bolts in rear universal joint, and tighten evenly. Attach front universal joint flange at transfer case with four bolts. Lubricate universal joints (par. 18 c).

Section XXV

FRONT AXLE

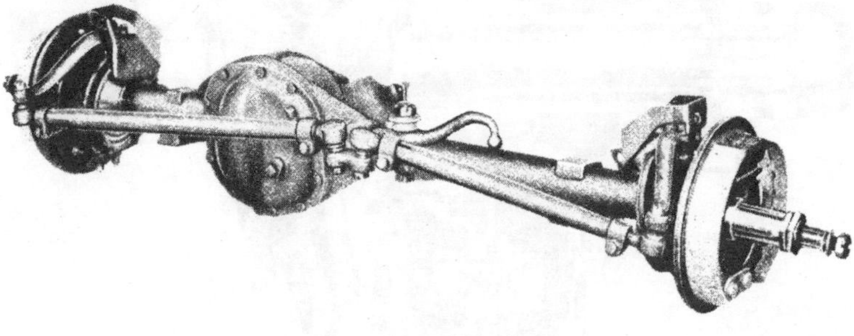

RA PD 305253

Figure 75—Front Axle

126. DESCRIPTION AND DATA.

a. Description. The front axle (fig. 75) is a full-floating type enclosing a front wheel driving unit having a single-reduction, two-pinion differential, and hypoid drive gears. The differential carrier housing is offset to the right so that the propeller shaft is located to the right of the engine for maximum ground clearance. A cover provides easy access to the differential unit. The front wheels are driven by axle shafts, each equipped with a constant-velocity type universal joint enclosed within a steering knuckle at the outer end of the axle housing. The differential assembly is the same as used in the rear axle. Power is transmitted by a propeller shaft from the transfer case, where a shift lever permits the vehicle operator to engage or disengage the drive.

b. Data.

Make and model .... Spicer—25
Drive gear ratio .... 4.88 to 1

Drive	Hotchkiss (through springs)
Type	Full floating
Road clearance	8$\frac{7}{16}$ in.
Differential type	2 pinion
Differential drive gears	Hypoid
Differential bearings	Tapered roller
Turning angle	26 deg

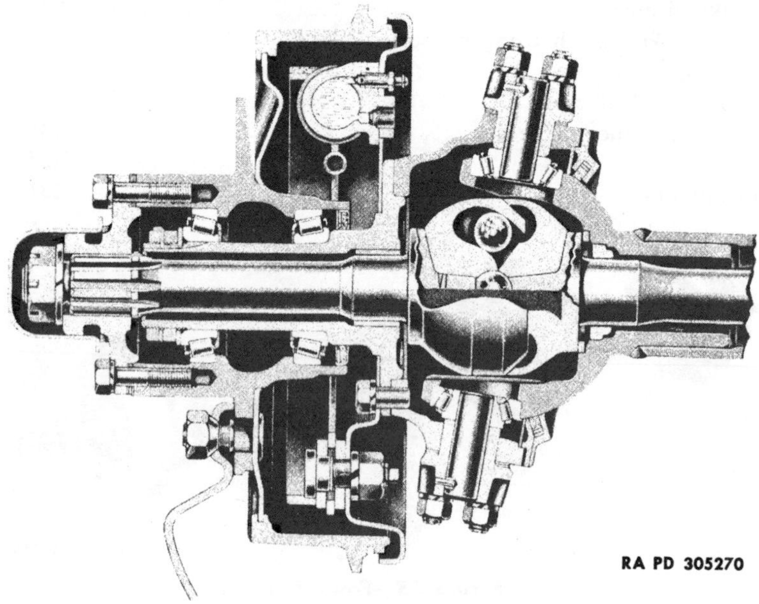

Figure 76—Front Wheel Hub

Tie rods:

Number	2
Right-hand length, center-to-center	24¼ in.
Left-hand length, center-to-center	17$\frac{11}{32}$ in.

Steering geometry:

King pin inclination	7½ deg
Wheel camber	1½ deg
Wheel caster	3 deg
Wheel toe-in	$\frac{3}{64}$ in. to $\frac{3}{32}$ in.

Bearings:

Differential side	Tapered roller
Pinion shaft	Tapered roller
Wheel hub	Tapered roller

Steering knuckle	Tapered roller
Steering bell crank	Tapered roller
Lubricant capacity	1¼ qt

127. MAINTENANCE.

a. Correct any lubricant leakage. Lubricate differential and steering housings, wheel bearings, and steering control as required (par.

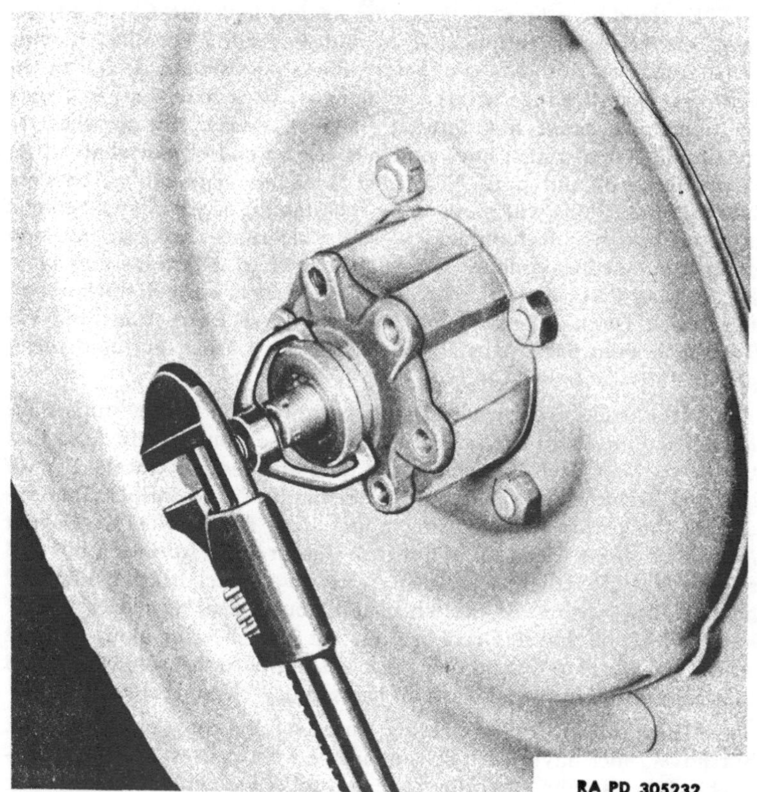

Figure 77—Removing Driving Flange, Using Puller (41-P-2905-60)

18). Keep vent cleared of dirt. Wheel bearings must be properly adjusted (par. 128). Replace damaged brake drums and hubs, and steering control rods (par. 133). Check wheel toe-in periodically, and correct if necessary (par. 135). Keep all mounting bolts tight. Report to higher authority any caster and camber trouble, or unusual noises.

128. WHEEL BEARINGS.

a. Adjustment. Raise front of vehicle so that tire clears floor. Pry off hub cap (fig. 76). Remove axle shaft nut cotter pin, nut, and washer. Remove driving flange screws. With puller, pull off flange (fig. 77). NOTE: *Do not lose flange shims.* Bend lip of nut lock washer away from nut. Remove lock nut with box-type socket wrench (fig. 78). Remove lock washer. Spin wheel and tighten wheel bearing nut until wheel binds. Back off nut about one-sixth turn, or more if necessary, until wheel turns freely. Install lock washer and lock nut. NOTE: *Bend over lip of lock washer against lock nut.* Check adjustment of bearings by gripping front and rear side of tire and moving it from side to side. A slight perceptible shake should be felt in the bearings. Install flange shims and flange. Check axle shaft end play by tightening flange nut without the lock washer. Swing wheel to maximum left or right; have punch mark on end of axle shaft up or down. Back off nut until 0.050-inch thickness gage will go between hub and nut. Shaft will move in by the amount of end play when end is tapped with soft hammer. Measure clearance between nut and flange, and deduct amount from 0.050 inch to determine end play. If less than 0.015 inch or more than 0.035 inch, correct thickness of shim pack (with Rzeppa joint disregard these instructions and use 0.060-inch shim pack). Install axle shaft lock washer, nut, and cotter pin. Install new hub cap.

b. Removal. Loosen wheel stud nuts. NOTE: *Wheel studs have left-hand threads on left side of vehicle.* Raise front of vehicle so that tire clears floor. Remove wheel stud nuts and remove wheels. Pry off hub cap. Remove axle shaft nut cotter pin, nut, and washer. Remove driving flange screws and using puller, pull flange. NOTE: *Do not lose flange shims.* Bend lip of nut lock washer away from lock nut and remove nut. Remove lock washer. Remove wheel bearing nut and bearing lock washer. Shake wheel until outer bearing comes free of hub, and lift off wheel. Drive or press out inner bearing along with oil seal. Turn wheel over, and drive or press out outer bearing cup. Clean lubricant out of hub, and wash all parts in dry-cleaning solvent.

c. Installation. Press bearing cups solidly into place in hub. Spread $\frac{1}{16}$-inch layer of lubricant inside hub to prevent rust. Thoroughly lubricate inner bearing cone and roller assembly. NOTE: *Pack lubricant thoroughly into bearing rollers and cage.* Install bearing in hub. Press oil seal into hub (with lip of seal toward bearing), until seal is even with end of hub. NOTE: *Before installation, soak seal in oil to soften leather.* Lubricate outer bearing cone and roller assembly. Install wheel on axle. Install outer bearing, lock washer, and nut. Adjust wheel bearings, and complete installation of parts (subpar. **a** above).

129. WHEEL GREASE RETAINER.

a. Removal. Remove retainer as outlined in paragraph 128 **b**.

b. Installation. Install retainer as outlined in paragraph 128 **c**.

FRONT AXLE

130. WHEEL HUB.

a. Removal. Remove wheel and hub (par. 128 **b**). Support brake drum inside at hub, and drive out studs. Remove brake drum.

b. Installation. Assemble brake drum on hub. Install new wheel studs. NOTE: *Left-hand thread studs are used in wheels for left side of vehicle.* Support studs and swedge shoulder over against tapered hole in hub. Install hub on axle and mount wheel (par. 128 **c**).

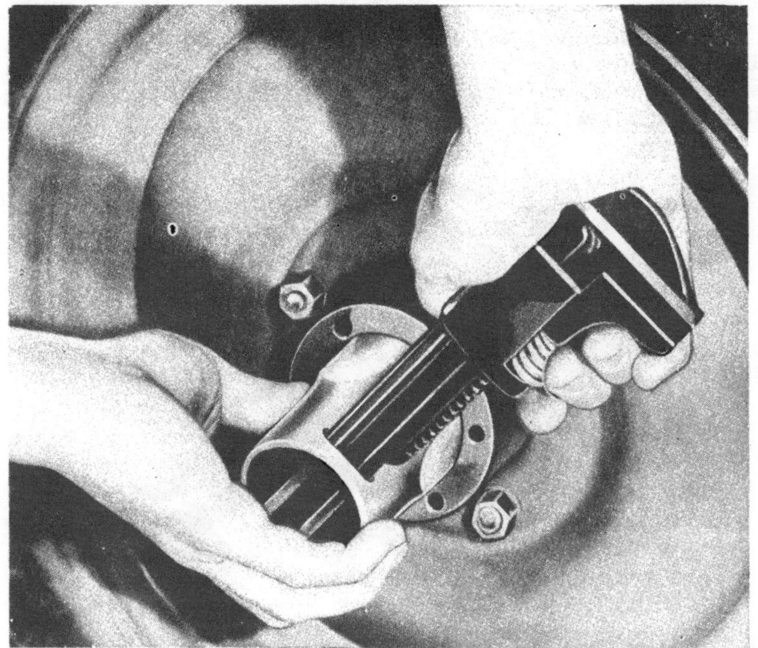

RA PD 305235

Figure 78—Removing Lock Nut, Using Wrench (41-W-3825-200)

131. BRAKE DRUMS.

a. Removal. Remove wheel hub and drum as outlined in paragraph 130 **a**.

b. Installation. Install drum and wheel hub as outlined in paragraph 130 **b**. Adjust brakes (par. 148).

132. STEERING KNUCKLE HOUSING OIL SEAL.

a. Removal. Raise front of vehicle. Remove screws holding oil seal in place, and remove both halves of oil seal assembly (fig. 79).

b. Installation. NOTE: *Before installing new oil seal smooth spherical surface of axle with aluminum oxide abrasive cloth.* Grease spherical surface of axle, also oil seal. Install seal in place so that ends fit snugly together, and tighten in place. Check lubricant level in steering knuckle housing, and replenish if necessary (par. 18).

133. STEERING TIE ROD.

a. Removal. Remove tie rod cotter pins and nuts from tie rod ends (fig. 75). Drive out tie rod ends from steering arms, and remove dust washers and springs.

b. Installation. Install dust washers and springs on tie rod ends. Install tie rod ends in steering knuckle arm and bell crank, and secure with nuts and cotter pins. Check wheel alinement, and adjust if necessary (par. 135).

RA PD 305240

Figure 79—Steering Knuckle Oil Seal

134. DRAG LINK BELL CRANK.

a. Removal. Remove cotter pin in front end of steering connecting rod. Remove slotted adjusting plug (ball seat). Lift rod off bell crank ball. Remove cotter pins and nuts on tie rod ends at bell crank. Drive tie rod ends out of bell crank. NOTE: *Do not lose dust washers and springs.* Remove cotter pin in bell crank stud and remove nut, dust washer, and thrust washer. Remove bell crank. Clean all parts in dry-cleaning solvent. To remove bell crank stud, remove thrust washer, and drive out tapered lock pin toward left front wheel. Drive stud up out of axle.

b. Installation. If bell crank has been removed, drive stud into axle so that slot will line up with tapered pin hole. Drive tapered pin into position, and stake edge of hole at large end. Install thrust washer on stud. Lubricate roller bearings, and install on stud. Install thrust washer, dust washer, nut, and cotter pin. Install steering connecting rod. Install tie rod ends in bell crank arm, and secure each with nut and cotter pin. Check front wheel toe-in, and adjust if necessary (par. 135).

135. WHEEL ALINEMENT (TOE-IN).

a. Caster and Camber. Caster is the backward tilt of the axle. Camber is the outward tilt of the wheels at the top. If these conditions require attention, notify higher authority.

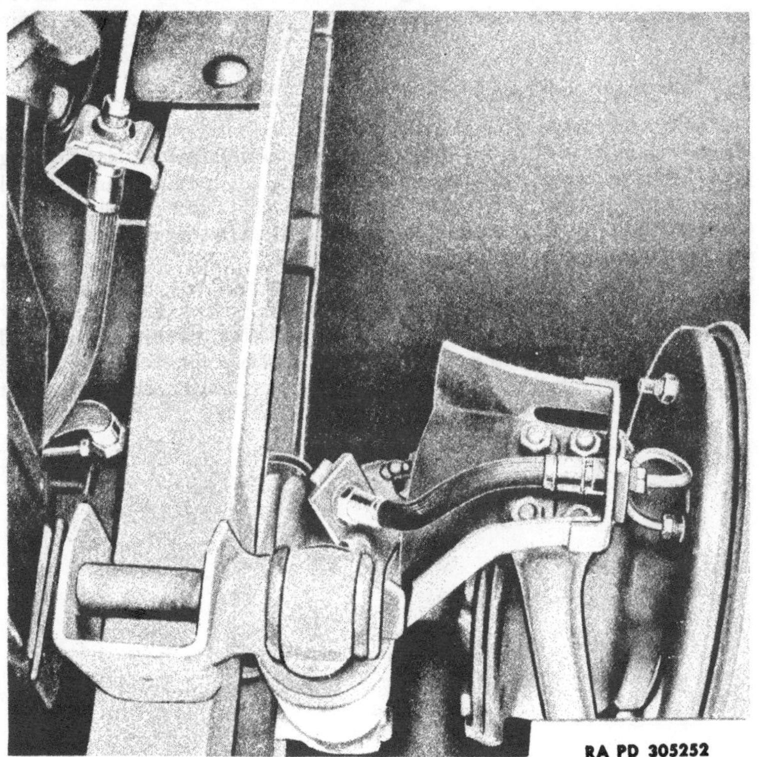

Figure 80—Brake Hose

b. Toe-in. Wheel toe-in is the difference in distance between the front wheels at the front and at the rear of the axle. To adjust toe-in, set tie rod arm of steering bell crank at right angles to front axle. Use straightedge or line against outside of left wheels, as a guide. Adjust left tie rod so that left wheel is straight ahead. While bell crank remains at right angle to axle, check right front wheel, and adjust tie rod if necessary. Set toe-in of front wheels at $^{3}/_{64}$ inch to $^{3}/_{32}$ inch by shortening right tie rod approximately one turn.

136. REMOVAL.

a. Loosen wheel stud nuts. Raise front of vehicle, and support underframe side members at rear of spring pivot brackets. Remove wheels. Disconnect brake line at front cross member (fig. 80). Remove universal joint U-bolts at front axle. Jack up front springs. Remove axle spring clip nuts and clips. Remove spring pivot bolt at rear end of right spring. Remove jacks from under springs. Disconnect steering connecting rod at bell crank. Install a jack between left spring and frame. Spread spring until axle assembly will clear. Move axle assembly to the right, and remove. Remove brake hose from axle.

137. INSTALLATION.

a. Attach brake hose at axle. Install axle assembly on springs. Remove jack from between left spring and frame. Install right spring pivot bolt. Position axle on springs. Jack up springs, and install spring clips, plates, and nuts. Remove jacks from under springs. Connect brake hose at cross member. Install dust cover on bell crank, and attach steering connecting rod. Attach propeller shaft. Draw universal joint U-bolts up evenly. Lubricate front axle universal joints, and check axle lubricant (par. 18). Adjust brakes if necessary (par. 147). Remove master cylinder inspection cover on toeboard between foot pedals. Fill master cylinder, and bleed brakes (par. 151). Replace master cylinder inspection cover. Install wheels and adjust (par. 128 **a**). Lower vehicle to floor.

Section XXVI

REAR AXLE

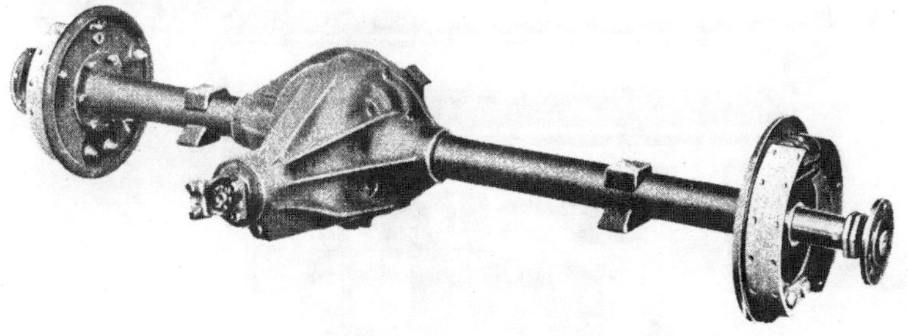

RA PD 305254

Figure 81—Rear Axle

138. DESCRIPTION AND DATA.

a. **Description.** The rear axle (fig. 81) is a full-floating type enclosing a single-reduction driving unit, two-pinion differential, and hypoid-drive gears. The differential carrier housing is offset to the right so that the propeller shaft will have a straight drive from the transfer case. A cover provides easy access to the differential unit. The axle shafts are splined to fit into the differential side gears, and flanged at the outer end where they attach to the wheel hub. The wheel bearings are adjusted by two nuts threaded onto the axle tube.

b. **Data.**

Make and model	Spicer 23-2
Drive gear ratio	4.88 to 1
Drive	Hotchkiss (through springs)
Type	Full floating
Road clearance	8 7/16 in.
Differential type	Two-pinion
Differential bearings	Tapered roller

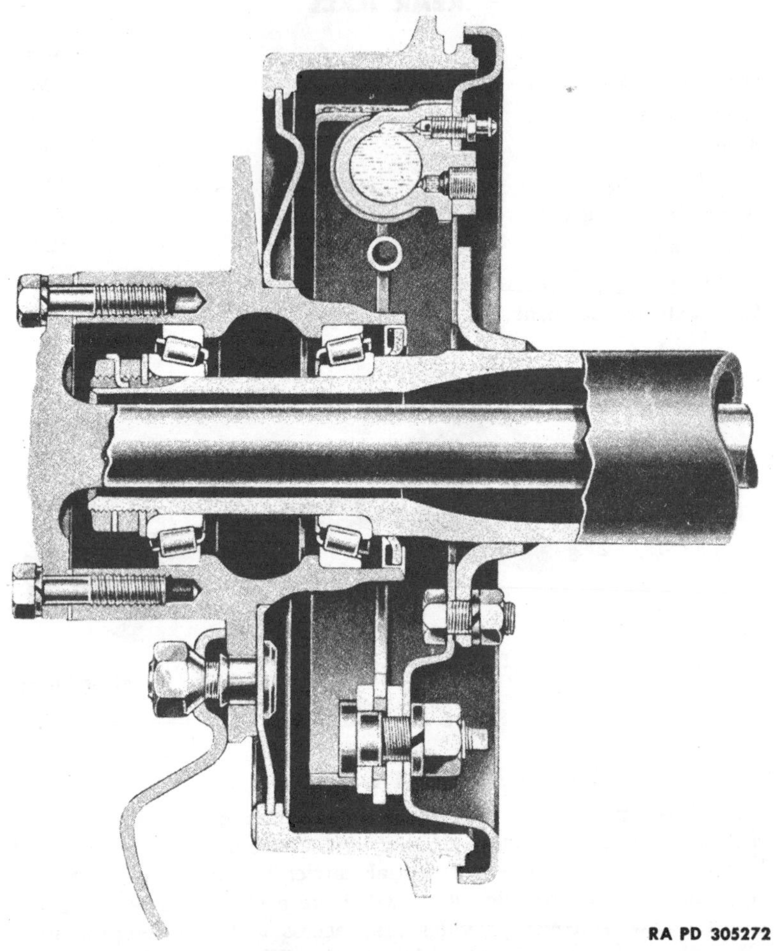

Figure 82—Rear Wheel Hub

139. MAINTENANCE.

a. Correct any lubricant leakage. Lubricate differential and wheel bearings as required (par. 18). Keep vent cleared of dirt. Wheel bearings must be properly adjusted (par. 141). Replace damaged drums and hubs (par. 143). Keep all mounting bolts tight. Report unusual noise to higher authority.

140. AXLE SHAFT.

a. Removal. Remove six axle shaft flange screws and lock washers. Pull out axle shaft (fig. 82), and remove flange gasket.

b. Installation. Install new axle shaft flange gasket. Install axle shaft in axle housing, rotating shaft so that shaft will enter differential side gear. Take care not to damage inner oil seal in axle housing. Install axle flange screws and lock washers, and tighten securely.

141. WHEEL BEARINGS.

a. Adjustment. Place jack under axle housing, and raise wheel so that tire clears floor. Remove axle shaft (par. 140 **a**). Bend lip of lock washer away from lock nut, and remove nut with box-type socket wrench (fig. 78). Remove lock washer. Spin wheel, and tighten wheel bearing nut until wheel just binds. Back off nut one-sixth turn or more, if necessary, until wheel turns freely. Install lock washer and lock nut. NOTE: *Bend over lip of lock washer against lock nut.* Check adjustment by shake of wheel. Install axle shaft (par. 140 **b**). Lower vehicle to floor.

b. Removal. Loosen wheel stud nuts. NOTE: *Wheel studs have left-hand threads on left side of vehicle.* Raise vehicle so that tire clears floor. Remove wheel stud nuts, and remove wheels. Remove axle shaft (par. 140 **a**). Bend lip of lock washer away from lock nut, and remove nut with box-type socket wrench (fig. 78). Remove lock washer. Remove bearing adjusting nut and bearing lock washer. Shake wheel until outer bearing comes free of hub, and lift off wheel. Drive or press out inner bearing along with oil seal from wheel hub. Drive or press out bearing cups from hub. Clean old lubricant out of hub, and wash all parts in dry-cleaning solvent Examine parts for excessive wear or damage, and replace if unserviceable.

c. Installation. Press bearing cups solidly into place in hub. Spread $^1/_{16}$-inch layer of lubricant inside of hub to prevent rust. Thoroughly lubricate inner bearing cone and roller assembly. NOTE: *Pack lubricant into bearing cage.* Install bearing in hub. Press oil seal into hub (with lip of seal toward bearing) until seal is even with end of hub. NOTE: *Before installation, soak seal in oil to soften leather.* Lubricate outer bearing cone and roller assembly. Install wheel on axle. Install outer bearing lock washer and nut. Adjust wheel bearings, and complete installation of parts (par. 141 **a**).

142. WHEEL BEARING GREASE RETAINER.

a. Removal. Remove retainer as outlined in paragraph 141 **b**.

b. Installation. Install retainer as outlined in paragraph 141 **c**.

143. WHEEL HUB.

a. Removal. Remove wheel and hub as outlined in paragraph 141 **b**. To remove brake drum from hub, support brake drum at hub, and drive out studs.

b. Installation. Place brake drum on hub. Install new wheel studs. NOTE: *Left-hand thread studs are used in wheels on left side of vehicle.* Support studs and swedge shoulder over against tapered hole in hub. Install hub on axle and mount wheel (par. 141 **c**). Tighten wheel stud nuts securely. Check brake action.

144. BRAKE DRUM.

a. Removal. Remove wheel hub and drum as outlined in paragraph 143 **a**.

b. Installation. Install drum and wheel hub as outlined in paragraph 143 **b**.

145. REAR AXLE REPLACEMENT.

a. Loosen wheel stud nuts. Raise rear of vehicle and support underframe side member just ahead of spring pivot brackets. Remove wheels. Remove universal joint U-bolts at rear axle. Disconnect brake hose at frame cross member. Remove brake hose at axle. Place jack under each rear spring. Remove spring clip nuts, clips, and plates. Remove jacks from under springs, place between frame and spring, and spread spring. Remove axle, sliding it to left until right end clears spring, then slide to right and remove.

b. Installation. Install axle assembly on springs. Remove jacks from between springs, and place under each spring. Position axle on springs. Install spring clips, plates, lock washers, and nuts. Tighten nuts securely. Remove jacks from under springs. Attach propeller shaft. Draw universal joint U-bolts up evenly. Attach brake hose at axle, then at frame cross member. Check axle lubricant. Remove master cylinder inspection cover on toeboard between foot pedals. Fill master cylinder, and bleed brakes (par. 151). Replace master cylinder inspection cover. Adjust brakes if necessary (par. 148). Install wheels. Lower vehicle to floor.

Section XXVII

BRAKES

146. DESCRIPTION AND DATA.

a. Description. The service, or foot brake, system is of the hydraulic type with brakes in all four wheels (fig. 83). The parking, or hand brake, is cable-controlled and mounted on the rear side of the transfer case (fig. 84). The service, or foot brakes, are of the two-shoe, double-anchor type. The brake pedal, through a connection, operates a piston in the master cylinder to force brake fluid through the lines to the brake cylinders in the wheels. The fluid enters the wheel cylinders between two pistons of equal diameter, forcing them apart to apply the brake shoes against the drums. Releasing the brake pedal permits the brake fluid to flow back through the lines to the master cylinder. Adjustments are provided to compensate for wear of the brake linings. The hand brake is designed for parking the vehicle, or as an emergency brake. The hand brake lever is located at the center of the instrument panel. Pulling out on the lever draws a flexible cable through a conduit to actuate an external contracting brake band at the rear of the transfer case. The brake cable is of a predetermined length, and cannot be adjusted. When adjustment is required, the brake band lining will be worn to the point where replacement is necessary. Adjustments are provided on the brake to set the band correctly, and to limit the release action.

b. Data.

Service brakes:
- Type .... Four-wheel, hydraulic
- Size .... 9 in. x 1¾ in.
- Fluid capacity .... ¼ qt

Master cylinder:
- Type .... Combination reservoir and cylinder
- Size .... 1 inch

Wheel cylinders:
- Type .... Straight bore
- Size .... Front, 1 in.; rear, ¾ in.

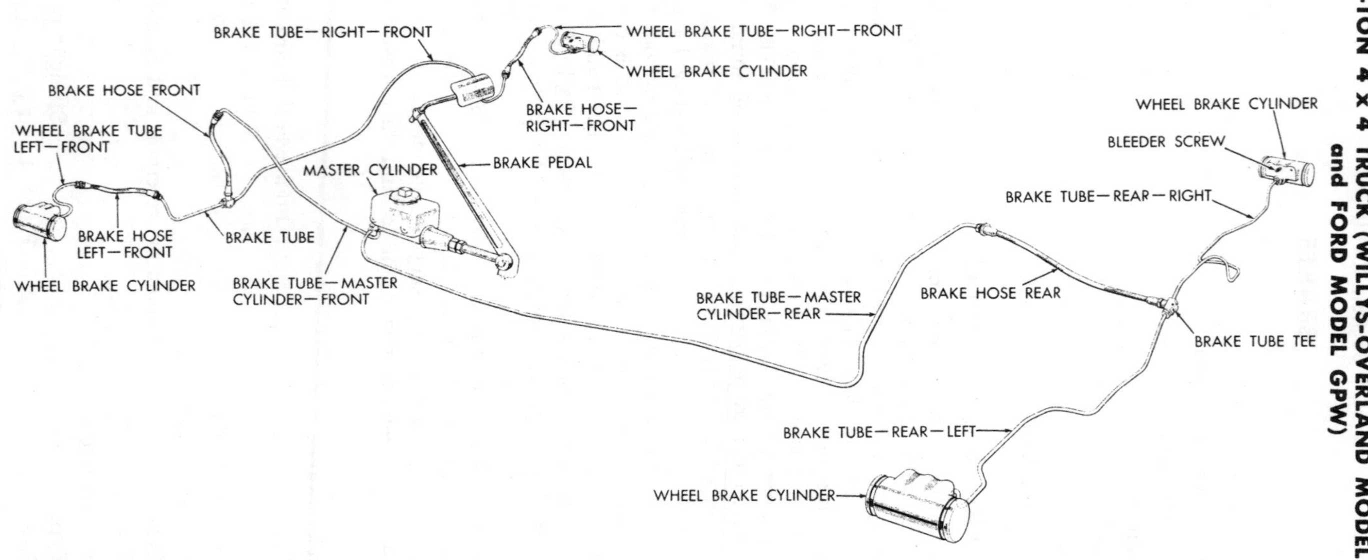

Figure 83—Service (Foot) Brake System

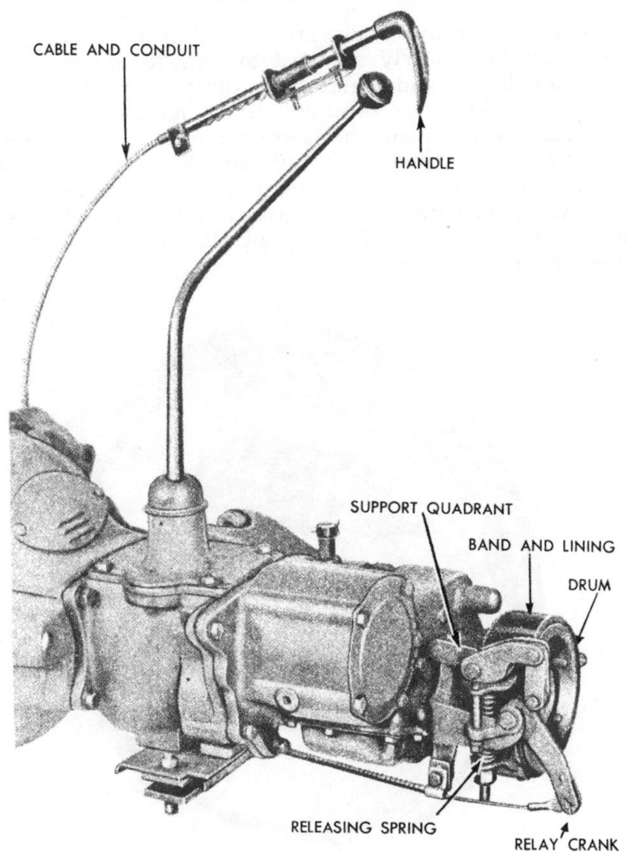

Figure 84—Parking (Hand) Brake System

Brake shoes:
- Lining length—forward shoe (moulded) .... 10 7/32 in.
- Lining length—reverse shoe (moulded) .... 6 39/64 in.
- Width .... 1 3/4 in.
- Thickness .... 3/16 in.

Hand brake:
- Type .... Mechanical
- Lining length (woven) .... 18 9/16 in.
- Width .... 2 in.
- Thickness .... 5/32 in.

147. MAINTENANCE AND ADJUSTMENT.

a. The service, or foot, brakes require periodic checking of the brake fluid supply in the master cylinder. Keep master cylinder supplied with fluid to avoid air entering the lines. Wheel bearings and brakes must be properly adjusted to provide emergency stops. All brake lines, hoses, and connections must be tight and leakproof. Scored brake drums or saturated brake linings must be replaced. Clean brake drums when wheels are removed. Brake anchor bolt and eccentric adjustment bolt lock nuts must be kept tight. Brake backing plate screws and axle spring clips must be kept tight. Brake pedal must have ½-inch free travel to assure full release of brakes. Brake control linkage must be free to operate, and should be inspected periodically for condition.

RA PD 305260

Figure 85—Wheel Brake

b. Adjustment. Adjust brake pedal free travel by lengthening or shortening brake master cylinder eyebolt so that pedal has ½-inch free play (par. 148). Follow procedure outlined in paragraph 148 to adjust brakes when lining has worn so that brake pedal goes almost to the toeboard. Three adjustments are provided on the hand brake (par. 152).

148. SERVICE (FOOT) BRAKES.

a. Adjustment (minor). Adjust brake pedal free play to one-half inch by lengthening or shortening brake master cylinder eyebolt. Set lock nut securely. Raise vehicle until tires clear floor. NOTE: *Do not adjust brakes when drums are hot.* Loosen eccentric lock nut on forward shoe of one brake (fig. 86). Place wrench on eccentric so

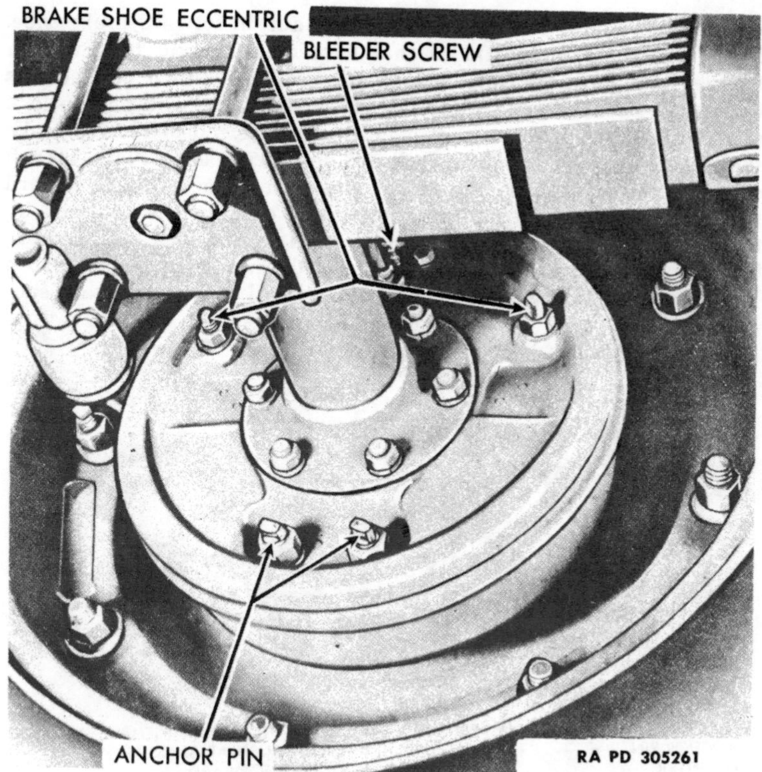

Figure 86—Wheel Brake Adjustment Points

that handle extends up. Rotate wheel, and turn wrench handle toward wheel rim, or forward, until brake drags. Turn wrench in opposite direction until wheel turns freely. Hold wrench on eccentric, and tighten lock nut. Loosen eccentric lock nut on reverse shoe. Place wrench on eccentric with handle up. Rotate wheel, and turn wrench toward wheel rim, or to the rear, until brake drags. Turn wrench in opposite direction until wheel turns freely. Hold wrench on eccentric, and tighten lock nut. Make the same adjustment on the other wheel brakes. Replenish brake fluid in master cylinder (par. 149). Lower vehicle to floor. Apply brake pedal to test brakes.

b. Adjustment (major). Adjust brake pedal free play to one-half inch by lengthening or shortening brake master cylinder eye-bolt. Set lock nut securely. Raise vehicle until tires clear floor. NOTE: *Do not adjust brakes when drums are hot.* Remove wheel stud nuts, and remove wheels from hubs. Insert 0.008-inch thickness gage through slot in brake drum, and turn drum so that gage is at upper (toe) end of forward brake lining. NOTE: *Check clearance 1 inch* *from end of lining*. Loosen eccentric lock nut on forward brake shoe. Place wrench on eccentric so that handle is up, and turn wrench handle toward wheel rim, or forward, until 0.008-inch clearance is obtained by feel of gage. Hold wrench on eccentric, and tighten lock nut. Turn brake drum so that gage is at upper end of reverse brake shoe lining. Loosen eccentric lock nut on reverse shoe. Place wrench on eccentric so that handle is up, and turn wrench handle toward wheel rim, or to the rear, until 0.008-inch clearance is obtained by feel of gage. Hold wrench on eccentric, and tighten lock nut. Remove 0.008-inch thickness gage, and insert 0.005-inch gage in slot. Turn brake drum so that gage is at lower (heel) end of forward brake shoe

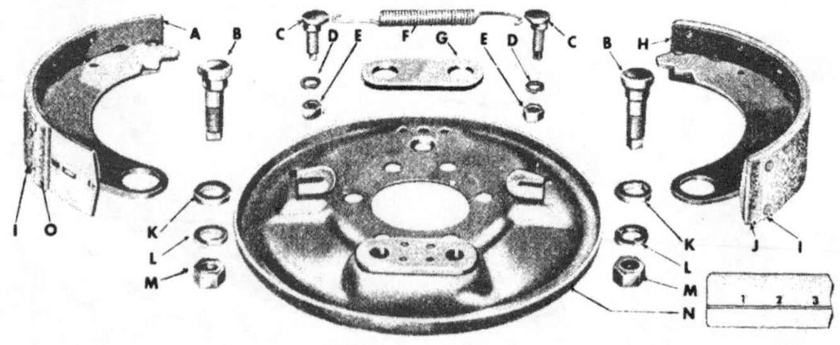

A SHOE AND LINING ASSEMBLY—REVERSE
B ANCHOR PIN
C ECCENTRIC
D ECCENTRIC LOCK WASHER
E ECCENTRIC NUT
F RETURN SPRING
G ANCHOR PIN PLATE
H SHOE AND LINING ASSEMBLY—FORWARD
I LINING TUBULAR BRASS RIVET
J LINING—FORWARD
K ANCHOR PIN CAM
L ANCHOR PIN LOCK WASHER
M ANCHOR PIN NUT
N BACKING PLATE ASSEMBLY
O LINING—REVERSE

RA PD 305277

Figure 87—Wheel Brake Shoes, Disassembled

lining. Loosen lock nut on anchor pin of forward shoe. Place wrench on anchor pin with handle down, and punch marks on ends of anchor pins toward each other; turn wrench toward rim, or forward, until 0.005-inch clearance is obtained by feel of gage. Hold anchor pin and tighten lock nut. Turn brake drum so gage is at lower end of reverse brake shoe lining. Loosen anchor pin lock nut on reverse shoe. Place wrench on anchor pin with handle down, and punch mark on end of anchor pin toward other anchor pin; turn wrench handle toward rim, or to the rear, until 0.005-inch clearance is obtained by feel of gage. Hold anchor pin and tighten lock nut. Follow same procedure on the other three brakes. Check amount of fluid in master cylinder (par.

149), and apply foot brake pedal to test brakes. Bleed brakes if *soft* pedal is experienced (par. 151). Install wheel. Lower vehicle to floor.

c. **Removal of Brake Shoes and Linings.** Raise vehicle. Remove wheel hubs (pars. 128 and 141). Loosen eccentric lock nuts (fig. 87). Turn eccentric so that low side is against the shoes. Install brake cylinder clamp to hold pistons in place. Remove brake shoe return spring. Remove anchor pin nuts, lock washers, anchor pins, and anchor pin plate from backing plate. Remove brake shoes. Remove brake shoe anchor pin cam. Inspect exterior of wheel brake cylinder for leakage of brake fluid. If leakage is apparent, replace cylinder assembly (par. 150).

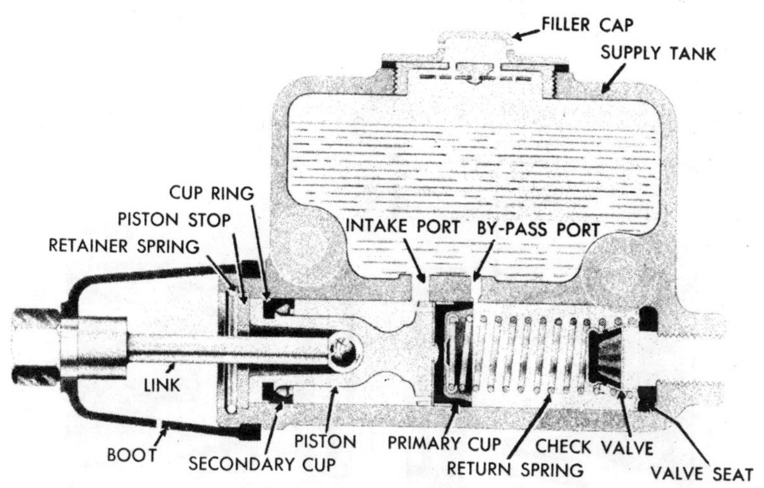

Figure 88—Master Cylinder

d. **Installation of Brake Shoes and Linings.** Install cam in brake shoes. Install anchor pin plate on anchor pins; install pins in brake shoes, and mount assembly on brake backing plate. NOTE: *Forward shoe has longest lining.* Install brake return spring, and remove brake cylinder clamp. Install brake anchor pin lock washers and nuts. NOTE: *Turn brake anchor pins so that punch marks on ends are toward each other. Do not tighten anchor nuts.* Install hubs (pars. 128 and 141). Make major brake adjustment (par. 149 **b**).

149. MASTER CYLINDER.

a. **Removal.** Raise hood and disconnect battery ground at battery terminal. Remove two bolts holding master cylinder shield and remove shield. Pull stop light switch wires out of terminal on switch. Remove stop light switch. Remove outlet fitting screw. Remove master cylinder front screw attaching cylinder to frame. Remove master cylinder rear bolt nut. Remove cotter pin holding master cylinder tie bar on pedal cross shaft. Remove master cylinder boot (fig. 88). Remove master cylinder and tie bar. Remove tie bar from master cylinder.

b. Installation. Fill master cylinder with brake fluid. Install tie bar and rear bolt on master cylinder, and install master cylinder in frame with tie bar on pedal shaft. Install cotter pin in pedal shaft. Install eyebolt link in cylinder. Install master cylinder front screw,

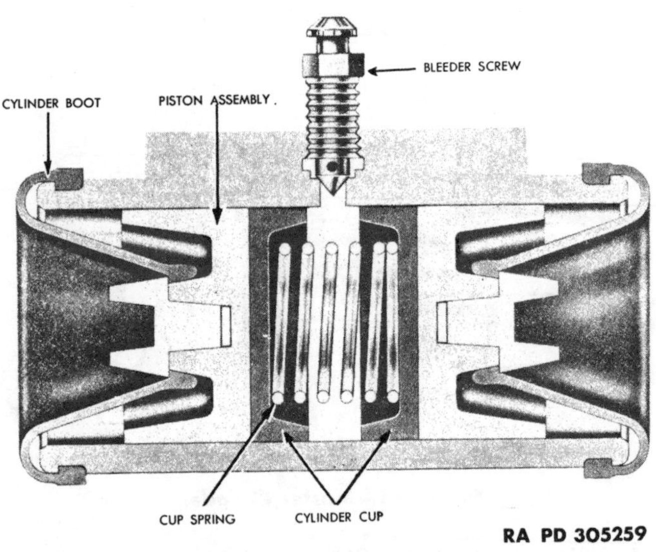

Figure 89—Wheel Cylinder

and tighten rear bolt. Install master cylinder boot with drain hole down. Install outlet fitting bolt. Install stop light switch. Insert stop light wires in terminals.. Install master cylinder shield with two bolts. Bleed brakes (par. 151). Attach battery ground cable. Lower hood and hook.

150. WHEEL CYLINDER.

a. Removal. Raise vehicle so that tire clears floor. Remove wheel and hub (pars. 128 and 141). Remove brake shoe return spring. Spread shoes until clear of brake cylinder. Disconnect brake tube at backing plate. Remove two screws holding cylinder to backing plate, and remove cylinder.

b. Installation. Place cylinder in position on backing plate, and attach with two screws and lock washers. Attach brake tube. Enter brake shoes in slots of cylinder pistons (fig. 89). Install brake shoe return spring. Replace wheel and hub (pars. 128 and 141). Bleed brake (par. 151). Apply foot brake pedal to test brakes. If soft pedal is experienced, bleed all brakes. Lower vehicle to floor.

151. FLEXIBLE LINES, HOSES, AND CONNECTIONS.

a. Removal of Brake Hose at Front Wheels. Remove brake tube connections at each end. With screwdriver slip hose lock off ends of hose fitting, and remove hose.

b. Installation of Brake Hose at Front Wheels. Place hose in brackets and drive locks into place in the fittings. Attach brake tube connections. Bleed brake. Press brake pedal; if soft pedal is experienced, bleed all brakes (subpar. s below).

c. Removal of Brake Hose at Frame and Front Axle. Remove brake tube connection at frame bracket, upper end of hose. With screwdriver, remove hose spring lock from fitting at bracket. Remove fitting from bracket. Unscrew brake hose lower fitting from T-connection on axle and remove.

d. Installation of Brake Hose at Frame and Front Axle. Screw brake hose lower fitting into T-connection on axle. Insert upper fitting into bracket, and install spring lock. Attach brake tube connection. Bleed both front brakes (subpar. s below). Press brake pedal; if soft pedal is experienced, bleed all brakes.

e. Removal of Rear Brake Hose. Remove brake tube connection frame cross member. With screwdriver, drive brake hose spring lock off hose fitting. Remove hose from frame. Unscrew hose fitting from T-connection on rear axle housing.

f. Installation of Rear Brake Hose. Screw brake hose into T-connection on rear axle housing. Insert hose fitting into frame, and drive spring lock into fitting. Attach tube connection. Bleed both rear brakes (subpar. s below). Press brake pedal; if soft pedal is experienced, bleed all brakes.

g. Removal of Master Cylinder to Front Hose Brake Tube. Remove clip from frame. Disconnect tube from brake hose fitting (frame to axle). Disconnect tube from master cylinder connection, and remove tube.

h. Installation of Master Cylinder to Front Hose Brake Tube. Connect tube at master cylinder. Connect tube at brake hose (frame to front axle). Install tube clip at frame. Bleed front brakes (subpar. s below). Press brake pedal; if soft pedal is experienced, bleed all brakes.

i. Removal of Master Cylinder to Rear Hose Brake Tube. Remove clip on underside of frame rear cross member. Remove clip on frame side member. Disconnect tube at rear brake hose. Remove master cylinder shield. Disconnect tube at master cylinder. Withdraw tube to rear of vehicle.

j. Installation of Master Cylinder to Rear Hose Brake Tube. Install tube in frame side member. Connect tube to master cylinder, and install master cylinder shield. Install tube in frame rear cross member, and attach to hose fitting. Install tube clips on frame side member and rear cross member. Bleed rear brakes (subpar. s below). Press brake pedal; if soft pedal is experienced, bleed all brakes.

k. Removal of Tee to Front Hose Brake Tube—Left. Disconnect brake tube at tee connection. Disconnect tube at brake hose fitting and remove tube.

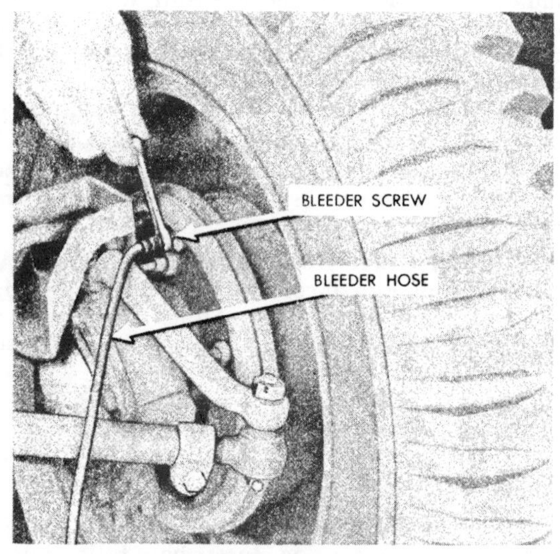

RA PD 305263

Figure 90—Bleeding Brakes

l. Installation of Tee to Front Hose Brake Tube—Left. Connect brake tube at tee connection. Connect tube at hose fitting. Bleed left brake (subpar. s below). Press brake pedal; if soft pedal is experienced, bleed all brakes.

m. Removal of Tee to Front Hose Brake Tube—Right. Remove clips and clamps on axle. Disconnect tube at tee connection. Disconnect tube at hose fitting and remove tube.

n. Installation of Tee to Front Hose Brake Tube—Right. Connect brake tube at tee connection. Connect tube at brake hose fitting. Install clips and clamps on axle. Bleed right front brake (subpar. s below). Press brake pedal; if soft pedal is experienced, bleed all brakes.

o. Removal of Front Wheel Cylinder to Hose Brake Tube. Disconnect tube at brake hose. Disconnect tube at wheel cylinder and remove tube.

p. Installation of Front Wheel Cylinder to Hose Brake Tube. Attach brake to wheel cylinder. Attach tube to hose fitting. Bleed brake (subpar. s below). Press brake pedal; if soft pedal is experienced, bleed all brakes.

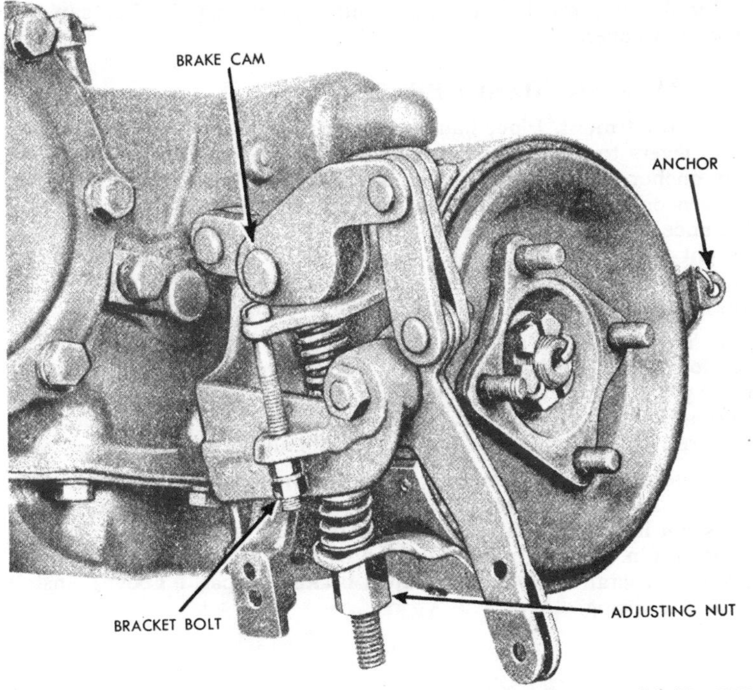

Figure 91—Parking (Hand) Brake

q. Removal of Tee to Rear Brake Tube—Right. Disconnect brake tube at tee connection. Disconnect tube at wheel cylinder. Remove tube clamp on axle. Bend tube slightly and remove.

r. Installation of Tee to Rear Brake Tube. Attach brake tube to wheel cylinder. Attach tube to tee connection. Install clamp on axle. Bleed brake (subpar. s below). Press brake pedal; if soft pedal is experienced, bleed all brakes.

s. Bleeding Brakes. Remove screws holding brake master cylinder inspection cover to toeboard between foot pedals and remove cover. Reach through hole, and clean around master cylinder filler cap. Remove cap and fill master cylinder with brake fluid. Replace cap temporarily. Clean all bleeder connections at wheel cylinders (fig. 90). Attach bleeder hose to *right rear* wheel cylinder bleeder screw, and place end in a glass jar or bottle so that the end is submerged in brake fluid. Open bleeder screw a three-quarter turn. Press brake pedal by hand, allowing it to return slowly. Continue action until air bubbles cease to appear at end of bleeder hose. Tighten bleeder screw and remove hose. Follow the same procedure on the *right front* brake, then the *left rear,* and finally, the *left front* brake. Replenish master cylinder brake fluid supply. Install filler cap and inspection cover.

152. PARKING (HAND) BRAKE.

a. Adjustment. Place hand brake grip in released position. Check brake levers to see that cable is free and released. Remove lock wire from anchor adjusting screw (fig. 91). Place 0.005-inch thickness gage between band and drum at anchor screw, and adjust screw to secure clearance. Install lock wire. Tighten adjusting nut until brake band is tight around drum. Loosen bracket bolt lock nut and rear nut. Back nut off two turns and set lock nut. Loosen adjusting nut so that brake band has approximately 0.010-inch clearance on drum.

b. Removal of Parking (Hand) Brake Band. Remove anchor bolt lock wire. Remove anchor bolt. Remove bracket bolt. Remove cotter pin from brake cam clevis pin and remove pin. Remove brake band adjusting nut. Remove brake adjusting bolt and spring. Remove retracting spring, and remove brake band assembly.

c. Installation of Parking (Hand) Brake Band. Install brake band on drum. Install brake release spring and adjusting bolt. Install clevis pin in brake cam and head of adjusting bolt. Install cotter pin in clevis pin. Install brake band adjusting nut. Install bracket bolt and nuts. Install anchor bolt. Adjust brake (subpar. **a** above). Install retracting spring.

Section XXVIII

SPRINGS AND SHOCK ABSORBERS

153. DESCRIPTION AND DATA.

a. **Description.** The springs (figs. 92 and 93) are of the semi-elliptic type with the second leaf wrapped around the spring eye of the first (main) leaf. The front springs appear to be identical, but

RA PD 305265

Figure 92—Left Front Spring

have different load carrying ability. The left spring has an "L" painted on the underside of the second leaf at the front end. Four spring leaf clips keep the leaves in alinement, and hold the leaves together to take the rebound. The front spring is shackled at the front end; the rear spring is shackled at the rear end. A spring pivot bolt attaches the opposite end of the spring to the frame. The shackles are of the threaded U-bolt type with threaded bushings having right- and left-hand threads. The left-hand threaded shackle ends and bushings are used in the spring eye of the left front spring and right rear spring. Left-hand threaded shackles have a small forged boss on the lower shank of the shackle. The left-hand threaded bushings have a groove cut around the hexagon head. The left front spring is equipped with a torque reaction spring to stabilize the front axle in extremely rough service. The shock absorbers are of the hydraulic-cylinder type, direct-acting, two-way control, adjustable, and refillable.

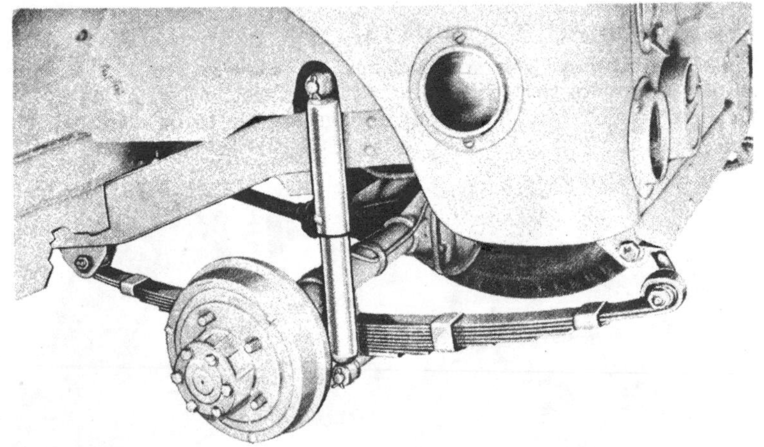

RA PD 305266

Figure 93—Left Rear Spring

b. Data.

Front Springs

Length—center line of eyebolts	36¼ in.
Width	1¾ in.
Number of leaves	8
Spring center bolt	At center
Spring eye bushed	Rear

Rear Springs

Length—center line of eyes	42 in.
Width	1¾ in.
Number of leaves	9
Spring center bolt	At center
Spring eye bushed	Front

SPRINGS AND SHOCK ABSORBERS

Shock Absorbers

Type	Hydraulic
Action	Double
Length—compressed—front	$10\frac{9}{16}$ in.
Length—compressed—rear	$11\frac{9}{16}$ in.
Length—extended—front	$16\frac{1}{8}$ in.
Length—extended—rear	$18\frac{1}{8}$ in.
Adjustable	Yes
Refillable	Yes
Mountings	Rubber bushings

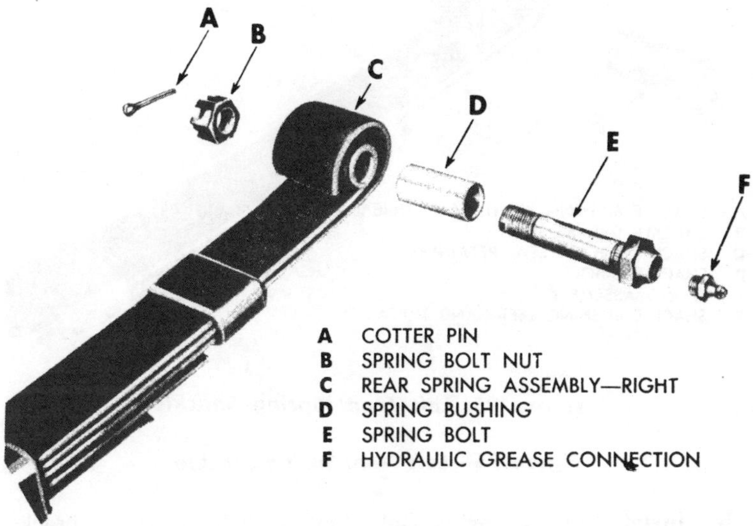

Figure 94—Right Rear Spring Bolt

154. MAINTENANCE.

a. The springs and shock absorbers should be inspected periodically in accordance with preventive maintenance (par. 23). Lubricate springs to prevent breakage, and excessive wear of spring pivot bolts and shackles (par. 18). Spring bushings and shackles must be free to move. Adjust shock absorbers correctly (par. 157). Replace worn or damaged shock absorber mounting bushings (par. 157).

155. SPRING SHACKLES AND BOLTS.

a. Removal of Spring Bolt. Raise vehicle frame until tires just rest on floor. Pull cotter pin in spring pivot bolt nut. Remove nut and drive out bolt (fig. 94).

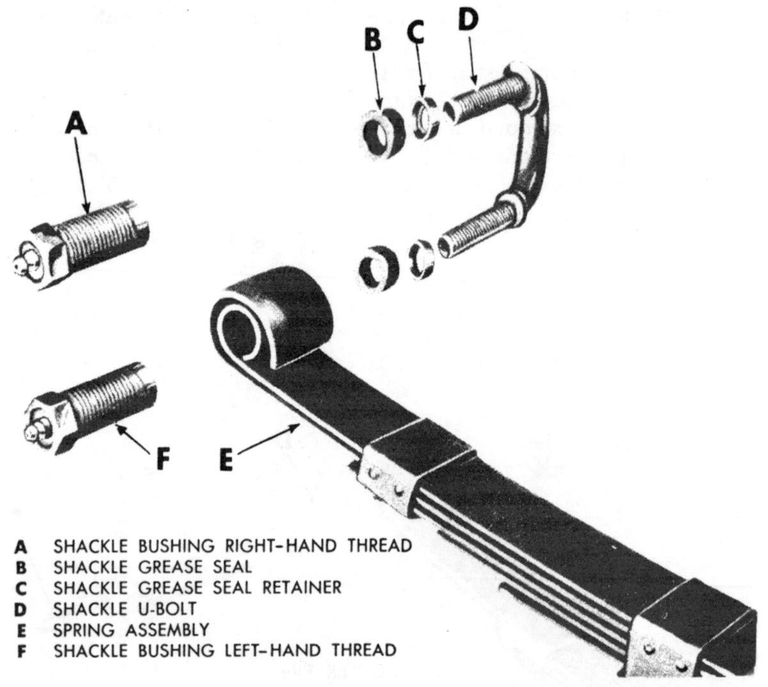

Figure 95, Left Front Spring Shackle

RA PD 305279

Figure 95—Left Front Spring Shackle

b. Installation of Spring Bolt. Line up holes in spring bracket and spring. Drive spring pivot bolt into place with oil groove *up.* Install nut and cotter pin. Lubricate with high pressure grease gun. Lower vehicle to floor.

c. Removal of Spring Shackle. Raise vehicle frame until tires just rest on floor. Remove shackle bushings (fig. 95). NOTE: *Left-hand threaded bushings are used in spring end of shackles on left front spring and right rear spring.*

d. Installation of Spring Shackle. Install shackle grease seal and retainer over threaded end, and up to the shoulder. Insert shackle through frame bracket and eye of spring, giving due attention to right- and left-hand threads. Hold shackle tightly against frame, and start upper bushing on shackle. Run in about half-way, then start lower bushing, holding shackle tightly against spring eye. Run bushing in about half-way. Then alternately tighten bushings until upper bushing is tight against frame bracket, and lower bushing hexagon head is about $\frac{1}{32}$ inch away from spring eye. Lubricate bushings, and try flex of shackle, which must be free. If tight, remove bushings and reinstall.

156. SPRINGS.

a. Removal. Remove spring shackle and pivot bolt (par. 155). Remove four axle spring clip bolt, nuts, and lock washers. Remove spring plate, or torque spring, and pivot bolt lock. Remove spring.

Figure 96—Shock Absorber

b. Installation. Install spring pivot bolt (par. 155 **b**). Install shackle (par. 155 **d**). Raise vehicle, and place center bolt in spring saddle on axle. Install axle spring clips and nuts. NOTE: *Axle spring clip nut torque wrench reading should be 50 to 55 foot-pounds; spring pivot bolt nut, 27 to 30 foot-pounds; torque reaction spring bolt, 60 to 65 foot-pounds.*

157. SHOCK ABSORBERS.

a. Removal. Pull cotter pins holding upper and lower washers against rubber bushing on mounting brackets. Remove washers, and pull off shock absorbers and rubber bushings (fig. 96).

b. Installation. Check shock absorber adjustment; compress shock absorber, and turn one end to engage adjusting keys in slots. Turn end in clockwise direction until limit of adjustment is reached, then turn end counterclockwise two turns for average adjustment. NOTE: *Turn end clockwise for firmer control, and counterclockwise for softer control, allowing faster spring action.* Install inner mounting rubber bushing on upper and lower bracket pins. Install shock absorber. Install outer bushing and flat washer. Use bushing compressor (41-C-2554-400) to compress bushing, and install cotter pin. Spread both ends of cotter pin to hold washer evenly in proper position.

Section XXIX

STEERING GEAR

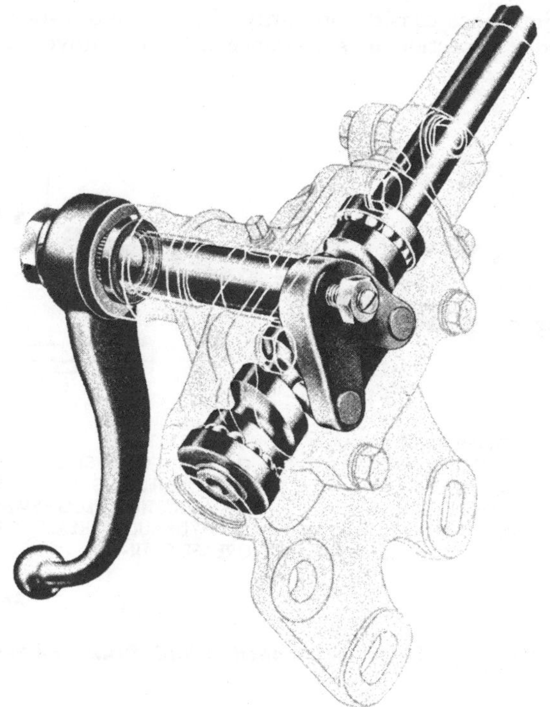

RA PD 305269

Figure 97—Steering Gear—Phantom View

158. DESCRIPTION AND DATA.

a. Description. The steering gear (figs. 97 and 99) is of the conventional type, mounted on the left frame side member, and connected to the front axle steering ball crank by a Pitman arm and steering connecting rod (fig. 98). The steering gear is of the cam and lever type with a variable-ratio cam. The steering wheel is of the

3-spoke, safety type, with 17¼-inch diameter. The steering connecting rod is of the adjustable, ball-and-socket type.

b. Data.

Make and model	Ross T-12
Type	Cam and twin pin lever
Ratio	Variable; 14-12-14 to 1
Wheel	3-spoke; safety type; 17¼ in.

159. MAINTENANCE.

a. Maintenance consists primarily of proper lubrication (par. 18) and periodic inspection in accordance with preventive maintenance

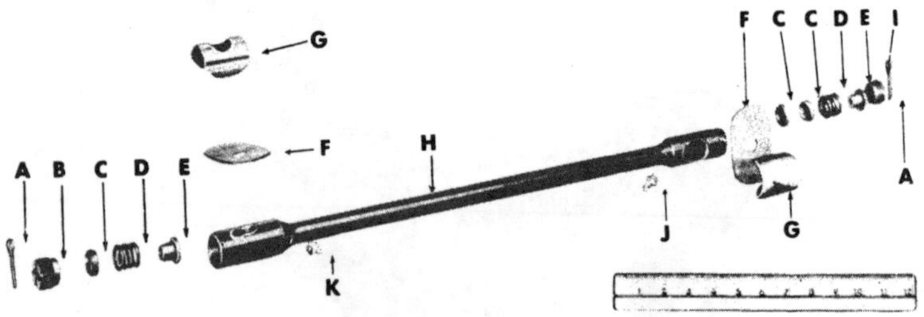

A COTTER PIN
B ADJUSTING PLUG—LARGE
C BALL SEAT
D SPRING
E SAFETY PLUG
F DUST COVER
G DUST COVER SHIELD
H CONNECTING ROD ASSEMBLY
I ADJUSTING PLUG—SMALL
J HYDRAULIC GREASE FITTING
K HYDRAULIC GREASE FITTING

RA PD 305278

Figure 98—Steering Connecting Rod, Disassembled

procedures (par. 23) to include the Pitman arm and steering connecting rod. A systematic inspection for steering troubles is as follows:

(1) Equalize tire pressures and set car on level floor.
(2) Inspect king pin and wheel bearing for looseness.
(3) Check wheel run-out.
(4) Check for spring sag.
(5) Inspect brakes and shock absorbers.
(6) Check steering assembly and connecting rod.
(7) Check toe-in.
(8) Check toe-out on turns.

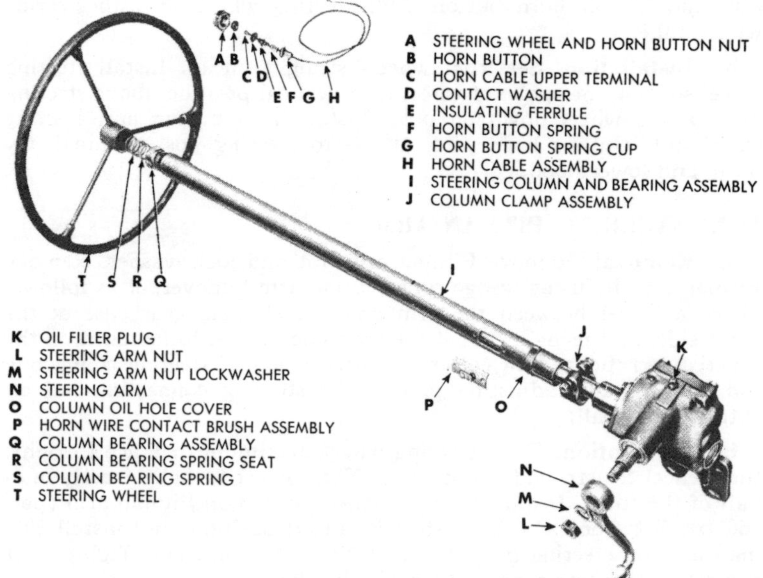

Figure 99—Steering Gear, Disassembled

(9) Check tracking of front and rear axle.

(10) Check frame alinement.

b. If steering difficulty is experienced after checking and correcting the above items, report to higher authority, because the trouble may be due to wheel balance, caster, camber, or king pin inclination.

160. STEERING CONNECTING ROD.

a. Removal. Pull cotter pin at each end of rod. Unscrew plugs and remove rod.

b. Installation. Correct end of connecting rod to be attached to front axle bell crank will have the lubrication hydraulic fitting to the right. Install safety plug, spring, and ball seat in this end of rod. Install rod on bell crank ball. Install adjusting plug. Screw plug in firmly against ball, back off one-half turn, and lock with cotter pin. Insert ball seat in other end of rod. Install rod on steering Pitman arm. Install second ball seat, spring, safety plug, and adjusting plug in order. Screw plug in firmly against ball, back off one-half turn, and lock with cotter pin. Lubricate with high pressure gun.

161. STEERING WHEEL.

a. Removal. Raise hood, remove horn wire at steering post terminal, and tape end so it will not ground. Remove steering wheel nut, and lift off horn button. Pull steering wheel off with steering wheel puller.

b. Installation. Set front wheels straight ahead. Install steering wheel so that one spoke of wheel is in vertical position above steering post. Drive wheel down on post. Install horn button and steering wheel nut. Untape horn wire, attach to steering post terminal, try horn, and lower hood.

162. STEERING PITMAN ARM.

a. Removal. Remove Pitman arm nut and lock washer. Remove Pitman arm by using wedge type Pitman arm remover, or as follows: Drive a chisel between the arm and the steering gear case at the front side, and using a bar, strike rear side of arm to loosen it on the tapered serrations. Pull cotter pin in rear end of steering connecting rod, and remove adjusting plug. Take steering connecting rod off Pitman arm ball.

b. Installation. Turn steering wheel maximum distance to right; turn wheel to left, and count turns. Turn wheel to right exactly one-half of the turns. Install steering connecting rod on Pitman arm (par. 160 **b**). Set front wheels in straight-ahead position, and install Pitman arm on steering gear. Install lock washer and nut. Tighten nut securely. Lubricate connecting rod hydraulic fitting.

163. STEERING GEAR.

a. Removal. Raise hood and tie to windshield. Remove battery ground cable at post on battery. Release headlight bracket wing nut and tilt headlight away from fender. Remove headlight wires from junction block on fender splasher. Remove blackout headlight wire clip on fender. Remove horn from bracket. Remove headlight wires from junction block on dash. Disconnect blackout driving light wire from slip connector at dash. Remove two screws attaching horn wire contact brush assembly to steering column. Loosen steering column clamp bolt. Remove bolts attaching fender to body, frame, and radiator grille. Remove fender support bolts in frame and remove fender. Remove cotter pin from rear end of steering connecting rod, unscrew adjusting plug, and remove from Pitman arm ball. Remove steering wheel nut and horn button. Pull steering wheel with steering wheel puller. Remove steering column bracket. Remove bolts in steering column floor seal, and remove seal and retainer. Pull steering column up off tube. Remove steering column to frame bolts. Lower upper end of steering column, and lift lower end out over frame side member.

b. Installation. Check steering gear lubricant; replenish if necessary. Insert upper end of steering gear through toeboard, and position in chassis. Install steering gear to frame bolts, but do not tighten. Install steering column floor seal, retainer, and screws. Install steering column over tube, with horn contact brush opening up. Tighten steering column clamp. Install horn wire contact brush, and tighten screws. Attach steering column bracket, and tighten steering gear to frame bolts. Install steering wheel (par. 161 **b**). Install steering connecting rod (par. 160 **b**). Install fender and support bolts, also screws and bolts to frame, body, and radiator grille. Install blackout headlight wire clip on fender. Attach headlight wires to junction block on fender splasher. Connect blackout headlight wire at slip connector. Attach headlight wire to junction block on dash. Connect blackout driving light wire in slip connector at dash. Install horn on bracket. Tilt headlight, and tighten wing nut. Attach battery cable. Check operation of horn and lights. Lower hood and lock.

c. Adjustment. Loosen lock nut on side adjusting screw. With front wheels straight ahead, adjust screw for minimum backlash of studs in cam groove. Tighten lock nut. For other adjustments, report to higher authority.

Section XXX

BODY AND FRAME

164. DESCRIPTION AND DATA.

a. Description. The body (figs. 1 to 4) is of the open type, identified by a name plate located on the instrument panel (figs. 5 and 6). There are two individual tubular frame front seats and a rear seat. The left front seat cushion can be raised to fill the fuel tank; the right front seat can be raised forward for stowage of the vehicle removable top, curtains, and windshield and light covers. The rear seat can be raised to reach the tire pump. Tools and accessories are stowed in two compartments in the rear corners of the body. The windshield is equipped with dual, hand-operated wipers, and can be opened forward or folded down on top of the hood. A fire extinguisher and an adjustable rear vision mirror are mounted on the left side of the cowl. Safety straps are provided in the entrance ways. A rifle holder is mounted on the lower panel of the windshield over the instrument panel. A strap and sheath carry a shovel and ax on the left side of the body. Hand grips on the side of the body facilitate lifting. The fuel tank sets in a sump in the floor pan under the driver's seat. The vehicle top is supported by top bows which can be folded down along the body sides to form a hand rail. A fuel can rack, trailer connection, and spare tire and wheel are mounted on the body rear panel. The chassis has five cross members; the rear intermediate cross member having a gun platform. Box-type, reinforced frame side members are used for maximum strength. Bumpers at the front and rear, and a radiator guard provide protection against damage. A pintle hook at the rear provides a means of hauling a trailed load.

b. Data.

Body type	Open	Windshield type	Folding
Driver's position	Left side	Cross members	5
Chassis frame type	Double drop		

165. MAINTENANCE.

a. General maintenance of the body requires periodic tightening of all loose parts, and lubrication of wearing parts. Keep the body clean and touch up bare spots to prevent rust. Keep the sump under the fuel tank free of dirt, stones, and water. Keep the sump front drain hole cover on so that dirt and water thrown by the front wheel will not enter. Keep the rear drain hole cover in the glove compartment in the instrument panel except when crossing water, when it must be installed. Water in the body can be drained by removing drain plugs in the floor at the side of the cowl. Chassis maintenance concerns primarily, proper lubrication of connecting parts (par. 18).

166. INSTRUMENTS.

a. Procedure for the removal and installation of the various panel instruments is identical, and as follows:

b. Removal. Remove battery ground cable at battery post as a safety precaution. Remove connecting wires or tubes. Remove two nuts holding retaining clamp in place, and remove instrument through face of instrument panel.

c. Installation. Install instrument in place in panel. Install retaining clamp and nuts. Attach tubes or wires.

167. SEATS AND CUSHIONS.

a. Removal of Seat Cushions and Backs. Remove five screws holding front seat cushion to frame at rear side, and remove cushion. Remove 10 screws holding seat back to frame, and remove seat back. Lift up back edge of rear seat cushion, remove five screws holding front edge of cushion to frame, and remove cushion. Remove five screws in top edge of seat back and two in lower edge, and remove seat back.

b. Installation of Seat Cushions and Backs. Place rear seat back in position, and install two lower screws. Pull edge of seat back up in place, and install five screws in top side. Place rear seat cushion in position, top side down. Install screws, and turn cushion over into place. Place front seat back in position, and install screws. Place seat cushions in position, and install screws.

c. Removal of Front Seats. Remove three screws holding back of driver's seat to floor. Remove screw in wheel housing holding seat. Remove two bolts holding front of seat frame to floor, and lift out seat. Remove two bolts holding right front seat bracket to floor, and lift out seat.

d. Installation of Front Seats. Place seat in position. Install bolts in place at front of seat. On driver's seat install screws and bolts holding seat back to floor and wheel housing.

e. Removal of Rear Seat. Pull up front edge of seat to fold seat. Remove bolt in tool compartment holding retainer bracket at seat bracket. On same side remove two bolts holding seat back bracket. Raise end of seat and lift out.

f. Installation of Rear Seat. Place seat in position in brackets. Install retainer bracket. Install seat back bracket and bolts.

168. WINDSHIELD WIPER.

a. Removal. Remove nuts holding wiper handle, and remove handles. Remove plain washer, and remove wiper blades.

b. Installation. Install blades and arms in place through windshield frame. Install plain washers, handles, and nuts.

169. WINDSHIELD.

a. Removal. Unhook windshield clamps on instrument panel (fig. 5). Remove wing screws at sides of cowl, and lift off windshield.

b. Installation. Place windshield in position, and install wing screws at sides of cowl. Clamp windshield to instrument panel.

170. TOP.

a. Installation. Loosen the two wing screws at the pivot brackets (fig. 4). Slide tubular bows back out of front bracket. Install front ends in rear brackets, and tighten winged screws. Allow front bow to drop down over seats. Remove top from under right front seat. Attach top to fasteners at top of windshield. Stretch top over bow and down to body back panel. Place straps in metal loops, and attach to body panel; stretch top, and buckle straps. Raise front bow into position at bow flaps, and snap flaps around bow. The curtains are attached in the conventional way with snap fasteners.

b. Removal. Remove curtains by releasing snap fasteners. Unsnap bow flaps, and lower front bow on front seat. Unbuckle top straps at body rear panel. Unsnap top at top of windshield, and remove. Fold top and stow under right front seat. Loosen wing screws in top rear brackets. Fold front bow against rear bow. Raise bows out of rear brackets, and insert lower ends in front brackets. Tighten rear bracket screws.

171. RIFLE HOLDER.

a. Removal. Swing the rifle bumper to the right, at the right end of holder, and remove rifle. Remove two bolts holding rifle holder to windshield lower panel, and remove holder (fig. 5).

b. Installation. Place rifle holder in position on windshield panel with butt end to the left, insert bolts, and tighten securely. Swing rifle bumper to the right. With barrel up, insert butt end of rifle in holder at the left. Push rifle up against spring pressure, and turn bumper to left under rifle.

172. SHOVEL AND AX.

a. Removal. Release straps and remove shovel or ax individually.

b. Installation. Turn bit, or blade, of ax up. Insert handle in front clamp. Insert blade in sheath. Pull up clamp under ax head, and strap in place. Turn face of shovel against cowl and place in strap on cowl side. Wrap fabric strap, through handle, over grip, between grip and side of body, through loop, over outside of grip, and buckle. NOTE: *This will hold the shovel forward in the strap on the cowl side (fig. 100).*

173. HOOD.

a. Removal. Unhook hood and raise against windshield. Remove screws in hinge at cowl, and disconnect bond strap.

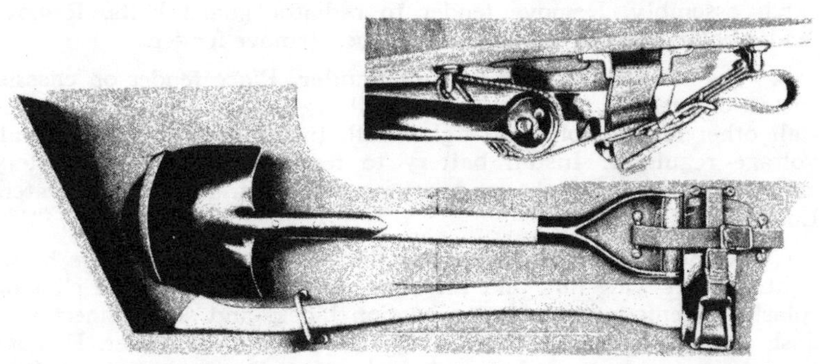

RA PD 305271

Figure 100—Shovel and Ax Mounting

b. Installation. Place hood in position and install hinge screws in cowl, but do not tighten. NOTE: *Install bonded screws last as follows:* Install flat washer on screw. Install screw through bond strap. Install flat washer. Install washer between hinge and hood. Install screw through hinge, and tighten to cowl. Lower hood for alinement. Raise hood and tighten screws. Lower hood and hook down both sides.

174. RADIATOR GUARD.

a. Removal. Raise hood. Remove headlight hinge bolts. Remove headlight wire clips on guard. Remove blackout headlight wire clip on left front fender. Remove wires from slip connector at left front fender. Remove fender to guard bolts. Remove guard from chassis. Remove blackout headlight wires, clips, and loom. Remove rubber shield at headlight. Remove blackout headlight nut and washer, and remove both light and wire assemblies.

b. Installation. Install both blackout headlight, spacer, and wire assemblies on guard. Install washer and nut. Install shield over wire. Install loom on wire. Install wire clips on loom and clips on guard. Install frame bolts in guard. Install guard on chassis. Install fender to guard bolts loosely. Install guard to frame bolt nuts. Tighten fender to guard bolts. Install headlight hinge bolts. Install headlight wire clips on guard. Install blackout headlight wire clip on fender. Connect wires to slip connector. Check operation of lights. Lower hood and lock down.

175. FENDERS.

a. Removal of Right Front Fender. Raise hood. Loosen wing nut on headlight bracket, and tilt light up. Remove battery to front fender strap. Remove battery ground cable at battery post. Remove voltage regulator bolts. Remove fuel line clip to fender. Remove hood catch assembly. Remove fender to radiator guard bolts. Remove fender bolts in support, body, and frame. Remove fender.

b. Installation of Right Front Fender. Place fender on chassis. Install one fender to body bolt. Install one fender to guard bolt. Install other fender bolts and tighten all. Install fuel line clip. Install voltage regulator. Install battery to fender strap. Install battery cable. Position headlight, and tighten wing nut. Install hood catch. Lower hood and lock.

c. Removal of Left Front Fender. Raise hood. Remove headlight bracket wing nut, and tilt lamp up. Remove two wire clips on splasher. Remove wires from junction block, and slip connector at dash. Remove blackout driving light clip on top of fender. Remove three bolts in blackout driving light bracket. Remove blackout driving light wire grommet and clips from fender. Remove junction block on fender. Remove blackout headlight wire clip. Remove hood catch. Remove fender shield to frame bolt. Remove bolts between fender and guard support, body, and frame. Remove fender.

d. Installation of Left Front Fender. Place fender on chassis. Install guard upper bolt. Install all fender bolts loosely. Install blackout headlight wire clip (front) on fender. Install junction block to fender. Install blackout driving light wire through fender and splasher. Install three bolts in blackout driving light bracket and fender. Install blackout headlight wire clip on fender. Install wire grommet in fender. Install two wire clips to fender splasher. Connect wires to junction block at dash and slip connector. Install hood catch. Place headlight in position, and secure with wing nut. Check operation of lights. Lower hood and lock down.

Section XXXI

RADIO INTERFERENCE SUPPRESSION SYSTEM

176. DESCRIPTION.

a. **Description.** Radio noise suppression is the elimination, or minimizing, of electrical disturbances which interfere with radio reception, or disclose the location of the vehicle to sensitive electrical detectors. Electrical disturbances or radio frequency waves may originate as static discharges between adjoining parts of the vehicle, or may be given off by the electrical systems during operation of the vehicle. These waves are actually radiated as disturbing signals that interfere with any radio receiving apparatus that may be operating in the vehicle or immediate vicinity. Each disturbance (at plugs, breaker points, generator brushes, or elsewhere) creates a surge of electricity, which produces interfering radio waves. Their origin can generally be determined by the nature of the noise heard in the receiver. Radio interference suppression, therefore, involves the suppression of these waves at their sources, or confining them within an area where they cannot be picked up by the antenna of a radio-equipped vehicle. Suppression is accomplished by the use of resistor-suppressors, and condensers. In addition, the hood and other metal parts in the vicinity of the engine are made to form a shield by the use of internal-external toothed lock washers and bond straps; thus, the hood and side panels form a box within which radio frequency waves are confined to prevent their acting on the antenna of receiving equipment. Wiring that may carry interfering surges to a point where interference will affect radio reception, is shielded. In attaching condensers and bond straps, the lock washers must be placed between the parts to be grounded, and tinned spots must be cleaned, but not painted. This is necessary to obtain good connections between the component parts, and to permit electrical energy to dissipate without causing electrical disturbances. The suppression components have no effect on engine performance as long as they are maintained in good condition. The sources of electrical noise interference may be basically divided into three groups: the ignition system, including coil, distributor, and spark plugs; the generator system, including generator and regulator; and the wiring.

177. DATA.

a. **Ignition** (both high-tension and primary-circuit suppression).

(1) High-tension suppression is of the resistor-suppressor type and consists of:

(a) Coil to distributor high-tension wire at distributor, resistance 10,000 ohms.

(b) Spark plug high-tension wire at spark plugs, resistance 10,000 ohms.

(2) Primary circuit suppression is of the capacitive-filter type and consists of:

(a) Ignition coil terminal (+) to cylinder block, capacity 0.10 microfarad.

(b) Ignition switch terminal (lower) to instrument panel, capacity 0.01 microfarad.

b. Charging Circuits (includes generator, regulator, ammeter, and battery).

(1) Generator suppression is of the capacitive-filter type and consists of generator armature terminal (A) to ground on generator, capacity 0.10 microfarad.

(2) Regulator suppression is of the capacitive-filter type and consists of:

(a) Regulator field terminal (F) to ground, capacity 0.01 microfarad.

(b) Regulator field terminal (B) to ground, capacity 0.25 microfarad.

c. Miscellaneous Circuits (including radio box and starting circuits).

(1) Radio terminal box suppression is of the capacitive-filter type and consists of:

(a) Radio box terminal to ground, capacity 0.50 microfarad.

(b) Starting switch battery terminal to floor, capacity 0.50 microfarad.

d. Bonding.

(1) BOND STRAPS (ground straps) (figs. 101 and 102). Bond straps are installed from:

(a) Hood to dash, right side (D).

(b) Hood to dash, left side (I).

(c) Cylinder head stud to dash (H).

(d) Cables (hand brake, speedometer, heat indicator) to dash (E).

(e) Generator mounting bolt to cranking motor bracket to engine support bracket (A).

(f) Generator to regulator wire shield to ground on generator and regulator (B).

(g) Front engine bracket to frame, left side (J).

(h) Hood ground to grille, left side (L).

(i) Hood ground to grille, right side (N).

(j) Radio terminal box to ground wire (F).

(2) TOOTHED LOCK WASHERS (figs. 101 and 102). Toothed lock washers are supplied from:

(a) Radiator to frame, right side (O).

(b) Radiator to frame, left side (K).

(c) Body bracket ground to frame, right side (S).

(d) Body bracket ground to frame, left side (R).

(e) Fender splasher ground to frame, right side (U).

(f) Fender splasher ground to frame, left side (T).

(g) Air cleaner mounting (C).

(h) Body hold-down bolts (G).

(i) Radiator grille to cross member (M).

(j) Fender to cowl, left side (P).

(k) Fender to cowl, right side (Q).

178. TESTS.

a. General. Electrical disturbances which cause radio interference are loose bonds, loose toothed lock washers, broken or cracked resistor-suppressors, loose connections, or faulty filters. Following are tests which can be made to determine the cause of interference. The radio equipment in the vehicle may be used as a test instrument to localize troubles, and to determine when faulty parts or conditions have been eliminated or corrected. If the vehicle has no radio equipment, utilize a radio-equipped vehicle placed about 10 feet from the vehicle under test. Here the cooperation of the radio operator is required. Determine the circuits causing the noise by checking as follows:

(1) Operate engine while listening to radio. A regular clicking which varies with engine speed, and ceases the instant the ignition is shut off, is caused by the ignition circuit.

(2) An irregular clicking which continues a few seconds after the ignition is shut off, is caused by the regulator.

(3) A whining noise which varies with engine speed, and continues a few seconds after the ignition is shut off, is caused by the generator.

b. Noise Caused by Ignition Circuit.

(1) Make certain ignition system is functioning properly (section XV). Improper plug gaps, late timing, poor adjustment of breaker points, and damaged or worn distributor, will affect the suppression system.

(2) Inspect resistor-suppressors in spark plug leads. Replace any that are scorched, cracked, or otherwise faulty. Be sure wires are screwed in tightly.

(3) Inspect resistor-suppressor at distributor. Replace if necessary.

(4) Inspect and tighten all bonds in engine compartment.

(5) Inspect capacitive-type filters in primary circuit at ignition coil and ignition switch. Make certain mounting bolts are tight. Replace filter and test for noise.

c. Noise Caused by Regulator.

(1) Check all connections to regulator.

(2) Check capacitive-type filter mounting bolts for tightness and correct placement of lock washers.

(3) Check regulator mounting bolts for tightness and correct placement of lock washers.

(4) Test for noise.

(5) If noise is still present, replace battery circuit filter attached to regulator (B) terminal. Test for noise.

(6) Replace field circuit filter attached to regulator (F) terminal. Test for noise.

(7) Replace armature circuit filter attached to generator (A) terminal.

(8) Test for noise.

d. Noise Caused by Generator.

(1) Check to make certain there is no excessive sparking at brushes. Correct if necessary.

(2) Inspect filter mounting, and check placement of lock washers. Tighten.

(3) Inspect ground strap.

(4) Replace filter.

(5) Test for noise.

e. Noise Caused by Miscellaneous Circuits (radio box and starting switch).

(1) Inspect mounting of filter attached to circuit. Tighten and test.

(2) Replace filter.

(3) Test for noise.

f. Noise Observed While Vehicle Is in Motion, but Not When Stopped.

(1) Inspect and tighten all body bonds (par. 177 **d** (1) above and figs. 101 and 102).

(2) Inspect and tighten all points where toothed lock washers are used (par. 177 **d** (2) above and figs. 101 and 102).

(3) Test for noise.

179. MAINTENANCE.

a. General. General maintenance of the radio suppression system (par. 23 **a** (5), item 104) must be made in connection with preventive maintenance items, particularly in regard to spark plugs, distributor and wires, late ignition timing, generator brushes, loose switch contacts, and discharged battery causing high generator charging rate.

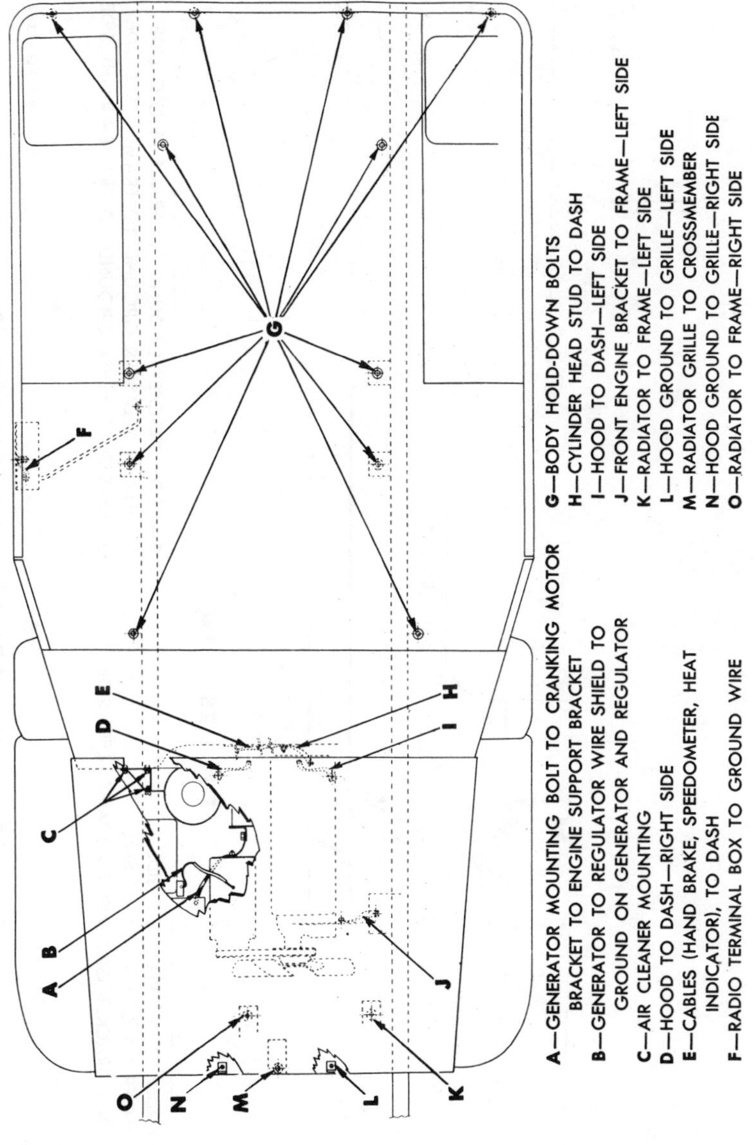

RA PD 305295

Figure 101—Location of Bond Straps and Fastenings (1)

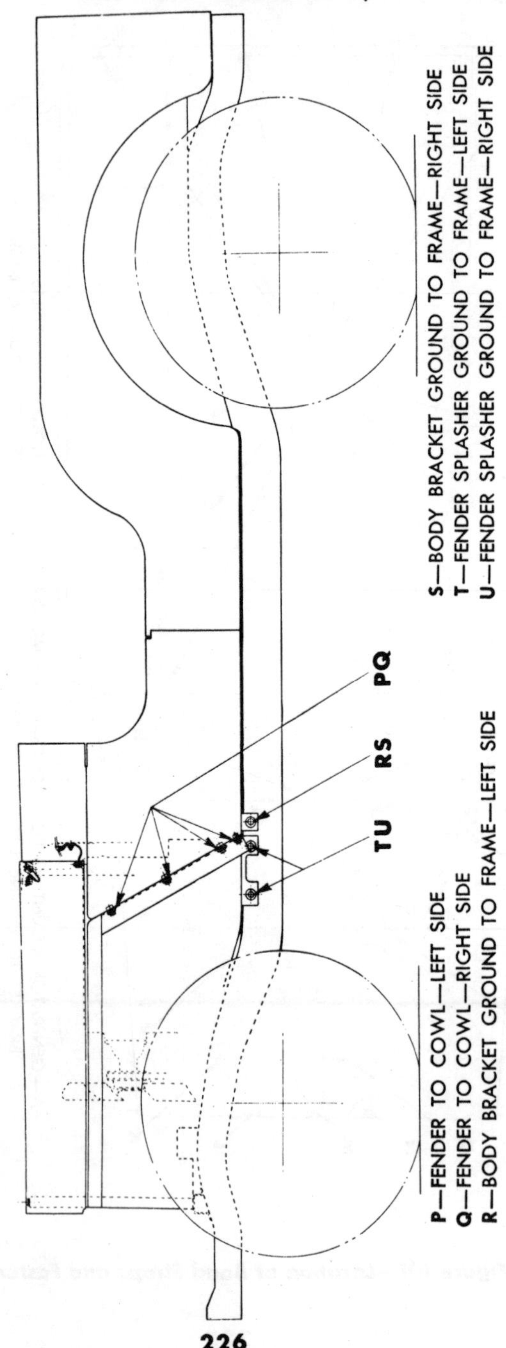

Figure 102—Location of Bond Straps and Fastenings (2)

b. Ignition Circuits.

(1) Resistor-suppressors, of which there are five (one at each spark plug and one at the distributor), consist of a high resistance element in an insulated housing. Inspect each suppressor for cracked or broken housing. Each suppressor must be threaded tightly into end of spark plug wire so that screw enters strands of cable. Wire terminals must be tight, well pushed down into place, and free of corrosion or dirt.

(2) Capacitive-filters, of which there are two in the ignition circuit, are located at the ignition coil and ignition switch. Replace if faulty by disconnecting wire at terminal, removing mounting nut or screw, and removing filter. Install coil filter with toothed lock washer between filter bracket and mounting nut. Install ignition switch filter with toothed lock washer between filter bracket and panel; also between bracket and mounting nut.

c. Charging Circuit.

(1) A capacitive-filter is mounted on the generator, and attached to the armature (A) terminal. The mounting screw must be tight with the internal-external toothed lock washer between the filter bracket and the generator housing, and the external toothed lock washer under the screw head.

(2) Two capacitive-filters are used on the regulator; one between the battery terminal and ground, the other between the field coil terminal and ground. The mounting screw must be tight with the internal-external toothed lock washer between the filter bracket and the regulator base.

(3) For battery removal and replacement, refer to paragraph 97.

d. Miscellaneous Circuits (radio box and starting circuits). The capacitive-filter used in the radio box between the terminal and the ground wire must be tight with the lock washer under the head of the mounting screw. The capacitive-filter in the starting circuit is mounted on the bottom of the starting switch with the connection on the "live" terminal. The filter bracket is located under the left mounting bolt with an internal-external toothed lock washer between the bolt head and the bracket, and an internal-external toothed lock washer between the nut and the rear side of the dash.

e. Bonding. Bonding points indicated in paragraph 117 **d** must be clean and tight. Tinned spots must be clean but not painted. Where bonding is obtained by use of an internal-external toothed lock washer, the lock washer must be between the parts to be grounded.

Section XXXII

SHIPMENT AND TEMPORARY STORAGE

180. GENERAL INSTRUCTIONS.

a. Preparation for domestic shipment of the vehicle is the same as preparation for temporary storage or bivouac. Preparation for shipment by rail includes instructions for loading and unloading the vehicle, blocking necessary to secure the vehicle on freight cars, number of vehicles per freight car, clearance, weight, and other information necessary to properly prepare the vehicle for rail shipment. For more detailed information, and for preparation for indefinite storage refer to AR 850-18.

181. PREPARATION FOR TEMPORARY STORAGE OR DOMESTIC SHIPMENT.

a. Vehicles to be prepared for temporary storage or domestic shipment are those ready for immediate service but not used for less than 30 days. If vehicles are to be indefinitely stored after shipment by rail, they will be prepared for such storage at their destination.

b. If the vehicles are to be temporarily stored or bivouacked, take the following precautions:

(1) LUBRICATION. Lubricate the vehicle completely (par. 18).

(2) COOLING SYSTEM. If freezing temperature may normally be expected during the limited storage or shipment period, test the coolant with a hydrometer, and add the proper quantity of antifreeze compound to afford protection from freezing at the lowest temperature anticipated during the storage or shipping period. Completely inspect the cooling system for leaks.

(3) BATTERY. Check battery and terminals for corrosion and if necessary, clean and thoroughly service battery (par. 97).

(4) TIRES. Clean, inspect, and properly inflate all tires. Replace with serviceable tires, tires requiring retreading or repairing. Do not store vehicles on floors, cinders, or other surfaces which are soaked with oil or grease. Wash off immediately any oil, grease, gasoline, or kerosene which comes in contact with the tires under any circumstances.

(5) ROAD TEST. The preparation for limited storage will include a road test of at least 5 miles, after the battery, cooling system, lubrication, and tire service, to check on general condition of the vehicle. Correct any defects noted in the vehicle operation, before the vehicle

is stored, or note on a tag attached to the steering wheel, stating the repairs needed or describing the condition present. A written report of these items will then be made to the officer in charge.

(6) FUEL IN TANKS. It is not necessary to remove the fuel from the tanks for shipment within the United States, nor to label the tanks under Interstate Commerce Commission Regulations. Leave fuel in the tanks except when storing in locations where fire ordinances or other local regulations require removal of all gasoline before storage.

(7) EXTERIOR OF VEHICLES. Remove rust appearing on any part of the vehicle with flint paper. Repaint painted surfaces whenever necessary to protect wood or metal. Coat exposed polished metal surfaces susceptible to rust, such as winch cables, chains, and in the case of track-laying vehicles, metal tracks, with medium grade rust-preventive lubricating oil. Close firmly all cab doors, windows, and windshields. Vehicles equipped with open-type cabs with collapsible tops will have the tops raised, all curtains in place, and the windshield closed. Make sure paulins and window curtains are in place and firmly secured. Leave rubber mats, such as floor mats, where provided, in an unrolled position on the floor; not rolled or curled up. Equipment such as Pioneer and truck tools, tire chains, and fire extinguishers will remain in place in the vehicle.

(8) INSPECTION. Make a systematic inspection just before shipment or temporary storage to insure all above steps have been covered, and that the vehicle is ready for operation on call. Make a list of all missing or damaged items, and attach it to the steering wheel. Refer to "Before-operation Service" (par. 13).

(9) ENGINE. To prepare the engine for storage, remove the air cleaner from the carburetor. Start the engine, and set the throttle to run the engine at a fast idle. Pour 1 pint of medium grade, preservative lubricating oil, Ordnance Department Specification AXS-674, of the latest issue in effect, into the carburetor throat, being careful not to choke the engine. Turn off the ignition switch as quickly as possible after the oil has been poured into the carburetor. With the engine switch off, open the throttle wide, and turn the engine five complete revolutions by means of the cranking motor. If the engine cannot be turned by the cranking motor with the switch off, turn it by hand, or disconnect the high-tension lead and ground it before turning the engine by means of the cranking motor. Then reinstall the air cleaner.

(10) BRAKES. Release brakes and chock the wheels.

c. **Inspections in Limited Storage.** Vehicles in limited storage will be inspected weekly for conditions of tires and battery. If water is added when freezing weather is anticipated, recharge the battery with a portable charger, or remove the battery for charging. Do not attempt to charge the battery by running the engine.

182. LOADING AND BLOCKING FOR RAIL SHIPMENT.

a. Preparation. In addition to the preparation described in paragraph 181, when ordnance vehicles are prepared for domestic shipment, the following preparations and precautions will be taken:

(1) EXTERIOR. Cover the body of the vehicle with a canvas cover supplied as an accessory.

(2) TIRES. Inflate pneumatic tires from 5 to 10 pounds above normal pressure.

(3) BATTERY. Disconnect the battery to prevent its discharge by vandalism or accident. This may be accomplished by disconnecting the positive lead, taping the end of the lead, and tying it back away from the battery.

(4) BRAKES. The brakes must be applied and the transmission placed in low gear after the vehicle has been placed in position, with a brake wheel clearance of at least 6 inches (fig. 101 "A"). The vehicles will be located on the car in such a manner as to prevent the car from carrying an unbalanced load.

(5) All cars containing ordnance vehicles must be placarded "DO NOT HUMP."

(6) Ordnance vehicles may be shipped on flat cars, end-door box cars, side-door box cars, or drop-end gondola cars, whichever type car is the most convenient.

b. Facilities for Loading. Whenever possible, load and unload vehicles from open cars under their own power, using permanent end ramps and spanning platforms. Movement from one flat car to another along the length of the train is made possible by cross-over plates or spanning platforms. If no permanent end ramp is available, an improvised ramp can be made from railroad ties. Vehicles may be loaded in gondola cars without drop ends by using a crane. In case of shipment in side-door cars, use a dolly-type jack to warp the vehicles into position within the car.

c. Securing Vehicles. In securing or blocking a vehicle, three motions, lengthwise, sidewise, and bouncing, must be prevented. There are two approved methods of blocking the vehicles on freight cars, as described below. When blocking dual wheels, all blocking will be located against the outside wheel of the dual.

(1) METHOD 1 (fig. 101). Locate eight blocks "B", one to the front and one to the rear of each wheel. Nail the heel of each block to the car floor, using five 40-penny nails to each block. That portion of the block under the tread will be toenailed to the car floor with two 40-penny nails to each block. Locate two blocks "D" against the outside face of each wheel. Nail the lower block to the car floor with three 40-penny nails, and the top block to the lower block with three 40-penny nails. Pass four strands, two wrappings, of No. 8 gage, black annealed wire "C" around the bumper support bracket at the front of the vehicle, and then through a stake pocket on the railroad car. Perform the same operation at the rear of the vehicle, passing the

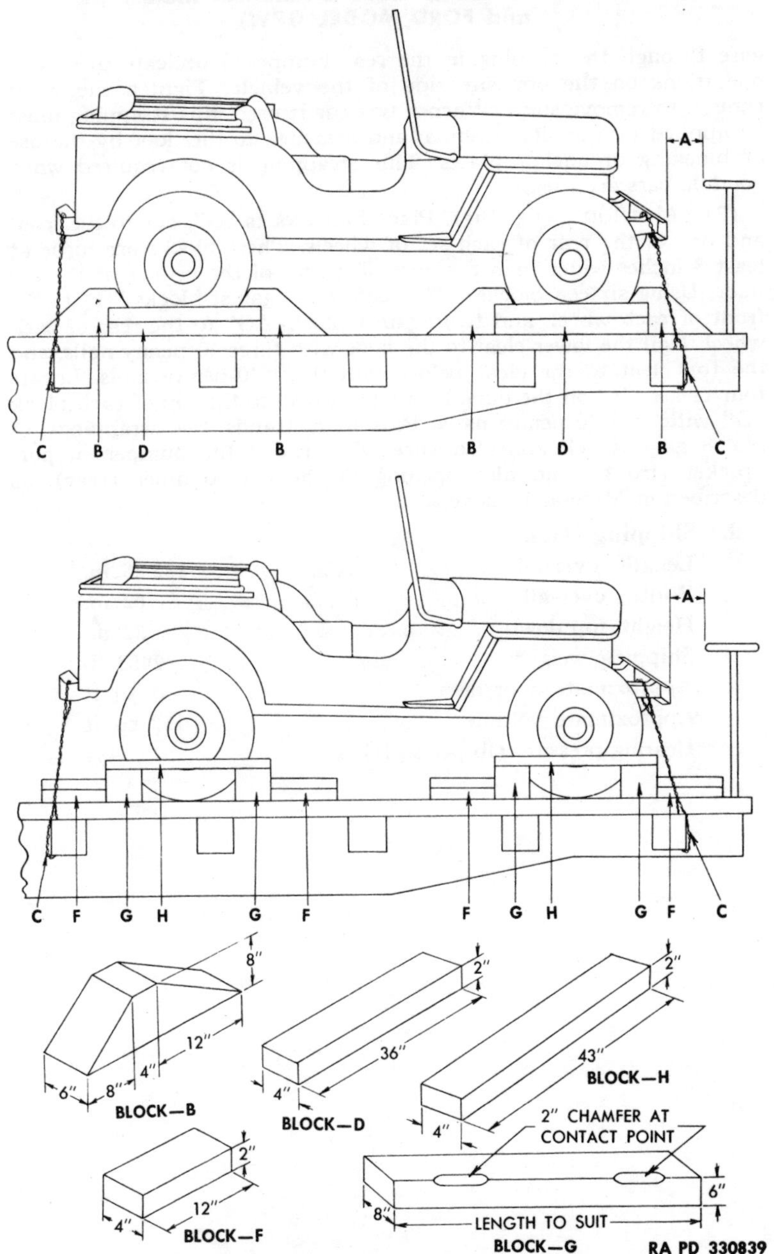

Figure 103—Blocking Requirements for Securing Wheeled Vehicles on Railroad Cars

wire through the opening in the rear bumper. Duplicate these two operations on the opposite side of the vehicle. Tighten the wires enough to remove slack. When a box car is used, this strapping must be applied in a similar fashion, and attached to the floor by the use of blocking or anchor plates. This strapping is not required when gondola cars are used.

(2) METHOD 2 (fig. 101). Place four blocks "G", one to the front and one to the rear of each set of wheels. These blocks are to be at least 8 inches wider than the over-all width of the vehicle at the car floor. Using sixteen blocks "F", locate two against blocks "G" to the front of each wheel, and two against blocks "G" to the rear of each wheel. Nail the lower cleat to the floor with three 40-penny nails, and the top cleat to the cleat below with three 40-penny nails. Locate four cleats "H" on the outside of each wheel to the top of each block "G" with two 40-penny nails. Pass four strands, two wrappings, of No. 8 gage, black annealed wire "C" around the bumper support bracket (front), and also opening in the rear bumper (rear), as described in Method 1 above.

d. Shipping Data.

Length, over-all	132.25 in.
Width, over-all	62 in.
Height, top down	32 in.
Shipping weight	2453 lb
Approximate floor area	57 sq ft
Approximate volume	152 cu ft
Bearing pressure (lb per sq ft)	4½

REFERENCES

PUBLICATIONS INDEXES.

The following publications indexes should be consulted frequently for latest changes to, or revisions of the publications given in this list of references and for new publications relating to materiel covered in this Manual:

Introduction to Ordnance Catalog (explains SNL system) .... ASF Cat. ORD-1 IOC

Ordnance publications for supply index (index to SNL's) .... ASF Cat. ORD-2 OPSI

Index to Ordnance publications (lists FM's, TM's, TC's, and TB's of interest to Ordnance personnel, MWO's, OPSR's, RSD, S of SR's, OSSC's, and OFSB's. Includes alphabetical listing of Ordnance major items with publications pertaining thereto) .... OFSB 1-1

List of publications for training (lists MR's, MTP's, T/BA's, T/A's, FM's, TM's, and TR's, concerning training) .... FM 21-6

List of training films, film strips, and film bulletins (lists TF's, FS's, and FB's by serial number and subject) .... FM 21-7

Military training aids (lists graphic training aids, models, devices, and displays) .... FM 21-8

STANDARD NOMENCLATURE LISTS.

Truck ¼-ton, 4 x 4, command reconnaissance (Ford and Willys) .... SNL G-503

Cleaning, preserving and lubrication materials, recoil fluids, special oils, and miscellaneous related items .... SNL K-1

Soldering, brazing and welding materials, gases and related items .... SNL K-2

Tool sets—motor transport .... SNL N-19

EXPLANATORY PUBLICATIONS.

Fundamental Principles.

Automotive electricity .... TM 10-580

Automotive lubrication .... TM 10-540

Basic maintenance manual .... TM 38-250

Driver's manual .... TM 10-460

Driver selection and training .... TM 21-300

Electrical fundamentals .... TM 1-455

Military motor vehicles	AR 850-15
Motor vehicle inspections and preventive maintenance service	TM 9-2810
Precautions in handling gasoline	AR 850-20
Standard Military Motor Vehicles	TM 9-2800
The internal combustion engine	TM 10-570

Maintenance and Repair.

Cleaning, preserving, lubricating and welding materials and similar items issued by the Ordnance Department	TM 9-850
Cold weather lubrication and service of combat vehicles and automotive materiel	OFSB 6-11
Maintenance and care of pneumatic tires and rubber treads	TM 31-200
Ordnance Maintenance: Engine and engine accessories for ¼-ton 4 x 4 truck (Ford and Willys)	TM 9-1803A
Ordnance Maintenance: Power train, chassis, and body for ¼-ton 4 x 4 truck (Ford and Willys)	TM 9-1803B
Ordnance Maintenance: Electrical equipment (Auto-Lite)	TM 9-1825B
Ordnance Maintenance: Hydraulic brake system (Wagner)	TM 9-1827C
Ordnance Maintenance: Carburetors (Carter)	TM 9-1826A
Ordnance Maintenance: Fuel pumps	TM 9-1828A
Tune-up and adjustment	TM 10-530

Protection of Materiel.

Camouflage	FM 5-20
Chemical decontamination, materials and equipment	TM 3-220
Decontamination of armored force vehicles	FM 17-59
Defense against chemical attack	FM 21-40
Desert operations	FM 31-25
Explosives and demolitions	FM 5-25

Storage and Shipment.

Ordnance storage and shipment chart, group G—Major items	OSSC-G
Registration of motor vehicles	AR 850-10
Rules governing the loading of mechanized and motorized army equipment, also major caliber guns, for the United States Army and Navy, on open top equipment published by Operations and Maintenance Department of Association of American Railroads.	
Storage of motor vehicle equipment	AR 850-18

INDEX

B—Cont'd

C

D

INDEX

¼-TON 4 x 4 TRUCK (WILLYS-OVERLAND MODEL MB and FORD MODEL GPW)

F—Cont'd

Page No.

G

H

Page No.

I

INDEX

R—Cont'd

S

INDEX

W

NOTES

TM 9-803 C1

WAR DEPARTMENT TECHNICAL MANUAL

¼-TON 4x4 TRUCK (WILLYS-OVERLAND MODEL MB and FORD MODEL GPW)

WAR DEPARTMENT • MAY 1950

TECHNICAL MANUAL

¼-TON 4 x 4 TRUCK (WILLYS-OVERLAND MODEL MB AND FORD MODEL GPW)

Changes No. 1

DEPARTMENT OF THE ARMY
WASHINGTON 25, D. C., *17 May 1950*

TM 9–803, 22 February 1944, is changed as follows:

The footnote at bottom of page 5 is rescinded.

1.1. (Added) Forms, Records, and Reports

a. GENERAL. Forms, records, and reports are designed to serve necessary and useful purposes. Responsibility for the proper execution of these forms rests upon commanding officers of all units operating and maintaining vehicles. It is emphasized, however, that forms, records, and reports are merely aids. They are not a substitute for thorough practical work, physical inspection, and active supervision.

b. AUTHORIZED FORMS USED WITH THE VEHICLE. The forms, records, and reports generally applicable to units operating and maintaining these vehicles are listed in SR 310–20–6. No forms other than approved Department of the Army forms will be used. Pending availability of all required forms, old forms may be used.

c. FIELD REPORT OF ACCIDENTS. The reports necessary to comply with the requirements of the Army safety program are prescribed in detail in the SR 385–10–40 series of special regulations. These reports are required whenever accidents involving injury to personnel or damage to matériel occur.

d. REPORT OF UNSATISFACTORY EQUIPMENT OR MATERIALS. Any suggestions for improvement in design, maintenance, safety, and efficiency of operation prompted by chronic failure or malfunction of the matériel, spare parts, or equipment or as to defects in the application or effect of prescribed petroleum fuels, lubricants, and/or preserving materials will be reported through technical channels as prescribed in SR 700–45–5 to the Chief of Ordnance,

*This change supersedes TB 9–803–FE–1, 17 August 1944; TB 9–803–FE–2, 19 October 1944; TB 9–803–5, 18 September 1944; TB 9–803–FE–5, 15 January 1945; TB 9–803–7, 7 February 1945; TB 9—803—FE-8, 19 April 1945; and those portions of TB ORD 44, 16 February 1944; TB ORD 205, 29 September 1944; and TB ORD 362, 30 March 1948, pertaining to the materiel covered herein.

Washington 25, D. C., ATTN: ORDFM, using DA AGO Form 468, Unsatisfactory Equipment Report. Such suggestions are encouraged in order that other organizations may benefit.

2. Description

*   *   *   *   *   *   *

b. IDENTIFICATION. The manufacturer's chassis serial number is stamped on a plate inside the left frame side member at the front end, and on the name plate **on the instrument panel** (fig. 6). The engine serial *** of the hood.

c. (Added) DIFFERENCES AMONG MODELS. The standard model is equipped with a 6-volt electrical system. In some models this was converted to 12-volts to supply current for radio equipment. Modification work order ORD G–503–W7 and changes thereto cover this conversion. This modification prescribes two 6-volt storage batteries connected in series to supply the current for the 12-volt system. All vehicle lights are changed from 6-volt to 12-volt lights, with the exception of the blackout driving light located on the left front fender. A series connected resistor installed on the dash reduces the 12 volts to 6 volts for operating the 6-volt blackout driving light. Shielding and filters are also installed to suppress radio interference. The 6-volt fuel gage, ignition coil, horn, generator, generator regulator, and cranking motor are also replaced by 12-volt units. Maintenance procedures for the 12-volt system are essentially the same as those for the 6-volt system with the exception of the removal and installation of the shielding and filters.

3. Data

a. VEHICLE SPECIFICATIONS.

*   *   *   *   *   *   *

Length over-all .... **131 in.**

*   *   *   *   *   *   *

Height, over-all—top up .... **72 in.**

*   *   *   *   *   *   *

Weights:

*   *   *   *   *   *   *

Shipping (less water and fuel) .... 2,337 lb

Crated .... **3,349 lb**

Maximum pay load .... 800 lb

*   *   *   *   *   *   *

b. PERFORMANCE. Maximum allowable speeds (mph) with transfer case in "HIGH" range:

High gear (3rd) **60**

*   *   *   *   *   *   *

Minimum turning radius—right .... **18 ft**
—left .... **18 ft**

* * * * * * *

Cruising range—(miles) average conditions..... **300**

c. CAPACITIES.

* * * * * * *

Transmission capacity—**early models** .... **¾ qt**
later models .... **1 qt**

* * * * * * *

4. Instruments and Controls

* * * * * * *

b. CONTROLS.

(1) *Blackout driving light switch (fig. 5).* The blackout driving *** light switch knob. **The blackout driving light switch is not furnished on vehicles equipped with a rotary type main lighting switch (fig. 9); on these, the rotary switch controls the blackout driving light.**

(2) (Superseded) *Blackout (main) light switches (figs. 9 and 62).*

(*a*) The blackout (main) light switch used on this vehicle is either a push-pull or a rotary type, and is installed on the left end of the instrument panel. This switch controls the entire lighting system, including the blackout driving, marker, tail and stoplights also the service head, tail and stoplights and the dash lights. A circuit breaker, on the back of the switches (fig. 62) opens when a short circuit occurs, and closes when the thermostatic element cools.

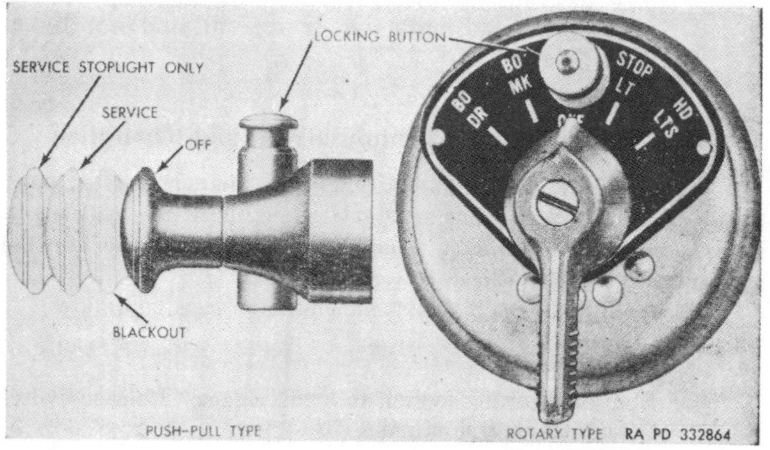

Figure 9. (Superseded) Blackout (main) light switch operating positions.

(*b*) The push-pull blackout (main) light switch (figs. 9 and 62) is a four-position type with a safety lock. When the control knob is pulled out to the first position, the blackout marker lights and blackout stop and tail lights are turned on. The blackout driving light can also be turned on with switch in this position ((1) above). The switch control knob is automatically locked in this position by the lock-out button to prevent accidental turning on of the service (bright) lights in a blackout area. To obtain service lights, push in on lock-out control button on the left side of the switch and pull out the control knob to the second position. In this position the service head lights, service stop and tail lights are turned on, and the panel lights can be turned on by pulling out the panel light switch knob marked "PANEL LIGHTS." To activate the regular stop light for daytime driving press in the lock-out control button and pull control knob to the last or stop light position.

(*c*) The rotary blackout (main) light switch (figs. 9 and 62) is a four-position type with a safety lock. In the first position to the left of the center or OFF position, it turns on the blackout marker lights and blackout tail and stop lights; in the second position to the left of the center or OFF position. it operates the blackout driving light, the blackout marker lights, and blackout tail and stop lights. In the first position to the right of center or OFF position, it operates the service stop light for daytime driving; in the second position to the right or OFF position, it operates the service (bright) head lights and service tail and stop lights.

* * * * * * *

5. Use of Instruments and Controls in Vehicular Operation

a. Before-Operation Service. Perform the services in paragraph 13 before attempting to start the engine **if the vehicle is in active service. Before putting a new or reconditioned vehicle in use, perform the services outlined in section X.**

b. Starting Engine. To start the engine proceed as follows:

* * * * * * *

(6) Step on starting switch to crank **engine.** Release switch as soon as engine starts.

* * * * * * *

7. Operation in Extreme Cold Weather

* * * * * * *

d. LUBRICATION.

(1) *Transmission and differential.*

(*a*) Rescinded.

* * * * * * *

(2) Rescinded.

(3) Rescinded.

(4) Rescinded.

* * * * * * *

g. STARTING AND OPERATING ENGINE.

* * * * * * *

(4) Rescinded.

* * * * * * *

8. Operation in Extreme Hot Weather

a. PROTECTION OF VEHICLE. In extremely hot *** adjust throttle control.

* * * * * * *

(2) *Lubrication.* Lubricate the vehicle for hot weather operation (par. 18).

* * * * * * *

10. (Superseded) Deep Water Fording

a. GENERAL. Refer to TM 9–2853 for information on application of deep water fording kits for preparation of ordnance matériel for a planned operation involving deep water fording and servicing vehicle after landing. The following instructions apply to *other* deep water fording operations where the deep water fording kit has *not* been applied.

b. OPERATING THE VEHICLE. Drive slowly and steadily, not over 3 or 4 mph, in order to prevent "bow-wave" from forming. Avoid using clutch because frequent use of clutch while driving through deep water may cause clutch to slip when reengaged. Fording water deep enough for the fan to touch water may short-out the ignition and stall the engine. The brakes will usually be completely "lost" but in some cases may "grab" after emerging. "Touching" the brakes will help to dry out the brake linings once dry land has been reached.

c. PRECAUTIONS AFTER PROLONGED FORDING. After fording, stop the vehicle at once, if tactical situation permits, and drain any accumulated water. If vehicle has forded through deep water for any appreciable length of time or has been completely submerged, appropriate precautions must be taken to avoid serious damage to the engine, clutch, transmission, transfer case, axles, universal joints, steering gear, battery, fuel tank, brakes, and wheel bearings.

(1) *Chassis.* After any prolonged fording operation, lubricate all chassis points to cleanse bearings of water or grit. Check the brakes and dry out the brake linings. Repack wheel bearings.

(2) *Engine.* Drain the engine crankcase oil. If water or sludge is found, drain and refill with engine oil OE–10. Run engine for 15 minutes at fast idle, stop engine, drain oil, and refill with proper grade engine oil. Before putting in new oil, clean the valve chamber, drain and clean the oil filter, and install a new filter element.

(3) *Fuel System.* Inspect and, if necessary, clean the carburetor bowl, fuel strainers, fuel pump, filter (on those vehicles equipped with a filter), fuel tanks, and lines. Clean the air cleaner and change the oil.

12. Purpose

* * * * * * *

e. Any defects or unsatisfactory operating characteristics beyond the scope of the first echelon **maintenance responsibilities** must be reported at the earliest opportunity to the designated individual **in charge, and should be noted in the appropriate place on AGO Form No. 48.**

13. Before Operation Service

* * * * * * *

b. Procedures. Before-Operation Service consists *** individual in authority.

* * * * * * *

(9) *Item 10, windshield wipers and horn.* Sound horn, tactical *** operation and tone. Check both wipers **(hand operated type)** for secure attachment and normal full contact operation through full stroke. **On those vehicles equipped with a vacuum motor type wiper, check both wipers to see that they are secure, and that wiper blades contact glass evenly and operate through their full range.**

* * * * * * *

(11) *Item 12, lights and reflectors.* Try switches in each position and see if lights respond, **provided the tactical situation permits.** Lights and warning *** of headlight beams.

* * * * * * *

16. After-Operation and Weekly Service

* * * * * * *

b. PROCEDURES. When performing the *** each applicable item.

* * * * * * *

(12) *Item 65, *air cleaner.*

* * * * * * *

(*b*) *Weekly*. (Superseded) If operating under extremely sandy and dusty conditions, inspect the air cleaners to see that they are in condition to deliver clean air properly. Service in accordance with instructions on the lubrication order (par. 18).

* * * * * * *

Section VI. LUBRICATION (Superseded)

17. Lubrication Order

a. LO 9–803 (fig. 13) prescribes organizational lubrication maintenance. This order is issued with each item of matériel and is to be carried with it at all times. In event the matériel is received without a copy, the using arm shall immediately requisition one in conformance with instructions in SR 310–90–1. Lubrication to be performed by ordnance maintenance personnel is prescribed in the NOTES on the lubrication order.

b. Instructions on the lubrication order are binding on all levels of maintenance and there will be no deviations.

c. Service intervals specified on the lubrication order are for normal operation during active service and where moderate temperature, humidity, and atmospheric conditions prevail. These intervals will be reduced under extreme conditions, such as high or low temperatures, prolonged periods of high speed operation, continued operation in sand or dust, immersion in water, or exposure to moisture. Any one of these conditions may quickly destroy the protective qualities of the lubricant. During inactive periods, intervals may be extended commensurate with adequate preservation.

d. Lubricants are prescribed in the "KEY" in accordance with four temperature ranges: above +32° F, from +32° to 0° F, from 0° F down to —40° F, and below —40° F. When to change grades of lubricants is determined by maintaining a close check on operation of the matériel during the approach to change-over periods, especially during initial action. Sluggish starting is an indication of lubricants thickening, and is the signal to change to grades prescribed for the next lower temperature range. Ordinarily, it will be necessary to change grades of lubricants only when air temperatures are consistently in the next higher or lower range.

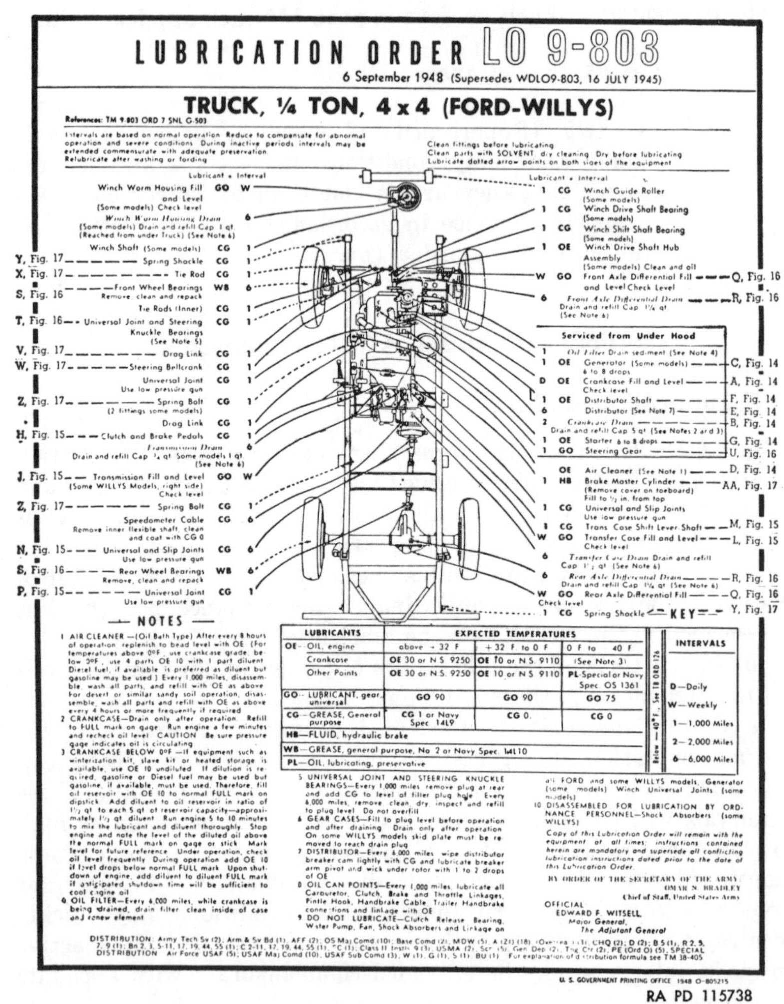

LUBRICATION ORDER LO 9-803

6 September 1948 (Supersedes WDLO9-803, 16 JULY 1945)

TRUCK, ¼ TON, 4 x 4 (FORD-WILLYS)

References: TM 9-803 ORD 7 SNL G-503

Intervals are based on normal operation. Reduce to compensate for abnormal operation and severe conditions. During inactive periods intervals may be extended commensurate with adequate preservation.
Relubricate after washing or fording.

Clean fittings before lubricating.
Clean parts with SOLVENT, dry cleaning. Dry before lubricating.
Lubricate dotted arrow points on both sides of the equipment.

Lubricant • Interval

Winch Worm Housing Fill and Level (Some models) Check level — GO W
Winch Worm Housing Drain (Some models) Drain and refill Cap 1 qt. (Reached from under Truck) (See Note 6) — 6
Winch Shaft (Some models) — CG 1
Y, Fig. 17 — Spring Shackle — CG 1
X, Fig. 17 — Tie Rod — CG 1
S, Fig. 16 — Front Wheel Bearings, Remove, clean and repack — WB 6
Tie Rods (Inner) — CG 1
T, Fig. 16 — Universal Joint and Steering Knuckle Bearings (See Note 5) — CG 1
V, Fig. 17 — Drag Link — CG 1
W, Fig. 17 — Steering Bellcrank — CG 1
Universal Joint, Use low pressure gun — CG 1
Z, Fig. 17 — Spring Bolt (2 fittings some models) — CG 1
Drag Link — CG 1
H, Fig. 15 — Clutch and Brake Pedals — CG 1
Transmission Drain Drain and refill Cap ¾ qt. Some models 1 qt. (See Note 6) — 6
J, Fig. 15 — Transmission Fill and Level (Some WILLYS Models, right side) Check level — GO W
Z, Fig. 17 — Spring Bolt — CG 1
Speedometer Cable, Remove inner flexible shaft, clean and coat with CG 0 — CG 6
N, Fig. 15 — Universal and Slip Joints, Use low pressure gun — CG 6
S, Fig. 16 — Rear Wheel Bearings, Remove, clean and repack — WB 6
P, Fig. 15 — Universal Joint, Use low pressure gun — CG 1

Lubricant • Interval

1 CG Winch Guide Roller (Some models)
1 CG Winch Drive Shaft Bearing (Some models)
1 CG Winch Shift Shaft Bearing (Some models)
1 OE Winch Drive Shaft Hub Assembly (Some models) Clean and oil
W GO Front Axle Differential Fill and Level Check Level — Q, Fig. 16
6 *Front Axle Differential Drain* Drain and refill Cap 1¼ qt. (See Note 6) — R, Fig. 16

Serviced from Under Hood

1 *Oil Filter* Drain sediment (See Note 4)
1 OE Generator (Some models) 6 to 8 drops — C, Fig. 14
D OE Crankcase Fill and Level Check level — A, Fig. 14
1 OE Distributor Shaft — F, Fig. 14
6 Distributor (See Note 7) — E, Fig. 14
2 *Crankcase Drain* Drain and refill Cap 5 qt (See Notes 2 and 3) — B, Fig. 14
1 OE Starter 6 to 8 drops — G, Fig. 14
1 GO Steering Gear — U, Fig. 16

OE Air Cleaner (See Note 1) — D, Fig. 14
1 HB Brake Master Cylinder (Remove cover on toeboard) Fill to ½ in. from top — AA, Fig. 17
1 CG Universal and Slip Joints, Use low pressure gun
1 CG Trans. Case Shift Lever Shaft — M, Fig. 15
W GO Transfer Case Fill and Level Check level — L, Fig. 15
6 *Transfer Case Drain* Drain and refill Cap 1½ qt. (See Note 6)
6 *Rear Axle Differential Drain* Drain and refill Cap 1¼ qt (See Note 6) — R, Fig. 16
W GO Rear Axle Differential Fill Check level — Q, Fig. 16
1 CG Spring Shackle — Y, Fig. 17

KEY

LUBRICANTS		EXPECTED TEMPERATURES		
OE—OIL, engine		above +32 F	+32 F. to 0 F	0 F to −40 F
	Crankcase	OE 30 or N.S. 9250	OE 10 or N.S. 9110	(See Note 3)
	Other Points	OE 30 or N.S. 9250	OE 10 or N.S. 9110	PL-Special or Navy Spec. OS 1361
GO—LUBRICANT, gear, universal		GO 90	GO 90	GO 75
CG—GREASE, General purpose		CG 1 or Navy Spec. 14L9	CG 0.	CG 0
HB—FLUID, hydraulic brake				
WB—GREASE, general purpose, No. 2 or Navy Spec. 14L10				
PL—OIL, lubricating, preservative				

Below —40° F., See TB ORD 126

INTERVALS

D—Daily
W—Weekly
1—1,000 Miles
2—2,000 Miles
6—6,000 Miles

— NOTES —

1. AIR CLEANER—(Oil Bath Type) After every 8 hours of operation, replenish to bead level with OE. (For temperatures above 0°F., use crankcase grade; below 0°F., use 4 parts OE 10 with 1 part diluent. Diesel fuel, if available, is preferred as diluent but gasoline may be used.) Every 1,000 miles, disassemble, wash all parts, and refill with OE as above. For desert or similar sandy soil operation, disassemble, wash all parts and refill with OE as above every 4 hours or more frequently if required.
2. CRANKCASE—Drain only after operation. Refill to FULL mark on gage. Run engine a few minutes and recheck oil level. CAUTION: Be sure pressure gage indicates oil is circulating.
3. CRANKCASE BELOW 0°F.—If equipment such as winterization kit, slave kit or heated storage is available, use OE 10 undiluted. If dilution is required, gasoline or Diesel fuel may be used but gasoline, if available, must be used. Therefore, fill oil reservoir with OE 10 to normal FULL mark on dipstick. Add diluent to oil reservoir in ratio of 1½ qt. to each 5 qt. of reservoir capacity—approximately 1½ qt. diluent. Run engine 5 to 10 minutes to mix the lubricant and diluent thoroughly. Stop engine and note the level of the diluted oil above the normal FULL mark on gage or stick. Mark level for future reference. Under operation, check oil level frequently. During operation add OE 10 if level drops below normal FULL mark. Upon shutdown of engine, add diluent to diluent FULL mark if anticipated shutdown time will be sufficient to cool engine oil.
4. OIL FILTER—Every 6,000 miles, while crankcase is being drained, drain filter, clean inside of case and renew element.
5. UNIVERSAL JOINT AND STEERING KNUCKLE BEARINGS—Every 1,000 miles remove plug at rear and add CG to level of filler plug hole. Every 6,000 miles, remove, clean, dry, inspect and refill to plug level. Do not overfill.
6. GEAR CASES—Fill to plug level before operation and after draining. Drain only after operation. On some WILLYS models skid plate must be removed to reach drain plug.
7. DISTRIBUTOR—Every 6,000 miles, wipe distributor breaker cam lightly with CG and lubricate breaker arm pivot and wick under rotor with 1 to 2 drops of OE.
8. OIL CAN POINTS—Every 1,000 miles, lubricate all Carburetor, Clutch, Brake and Throttle Linkages, Pintle Hook, Handbrake Cable, Trailer Handbrake connections and linkage with OE.
9. DO NOT LUBRICATE—Clutch Release Bearing, Water Pump, Fan, Shock Absorbers and Linkage on all FORD and some WILLYS models, Generator (some models), Winch Universal Joints (some models).
10. DISASSEMBLED FOR LUBRICATION BY ORDNANCE PERSONNEL—Shock Absorbers (some WILLYS).

Copy of this Lubrication Order will remain with the equipment at all times; instructions contained herein are mandatory and supersede all conflicting lubrication instructions dated prior to the date of this Lubrication Order.

BY ORDER OF THE SECRETARY OF THE ARMY:

OMAR N. BRADLEY
Chief of Staff, United States Army

OFFICIAL:
EDWARD F. WITSELL,
Major General,
The Adjutant General.

DISTRIBUTION: Army Tech Sv (2); Arm & Sv Bd (1); AFF (2); OS Maj Comd (10); Base Comd (2); MDW (5); A (21) (18); (Overseas) (3); CHQ (2); D (2); B 5 (1); R 2, 5, 7, 9 (1); Bn 2, 3, 5-11, 17, 19, 44, 55 (1); C 2-11, 17, 19, 44, 55 (1); FC (1); Class II Instls 9 (3); USMA (2); Sch (5); Gen Dep (2); Tng Ctr (2); PE (Ord O) (5). SPECIAL DISTRIBUTION: Air Force USAF (5); USAF Maj Comd (10); USAF Sub Comd (3); W (1); G (1); S (1); BU (1). For explanation of distribution formula see TM 38-405.

U. S. GOVERNMENT PRINTING OFFICE 1948 O-805215

RA PD 115738

Figure 13. (Superseded) Lubrication order 9–803.

18. General Lubrication Instructions

a. LUBRICATION EQUIPMENT. Each vehicle is supplied with lubrication equipment adequate for its maintenance. This equipment will be cleaned both before and after use. Lubrication gun will be operated carefully and in such a manner as to insure a proper distribution of the lubricant.

b. POINTS OF APPLICATION.

(1) Lubricating fittings, grease cups, oilers and oil holes are indicated in figures 14 to 17 and may be referenced to the lubrication order. Wipe these devices and the surrounding surfaces clean before lubricant is applied.

(2) A ¾-inch red circle should be painted around all lubricating fittings and oil holes.

(3) Where relief valves are provided, apply new lubricant until lubricant is forced from the vent. (Exceptions are specified in NOTES on the lubrication order.)

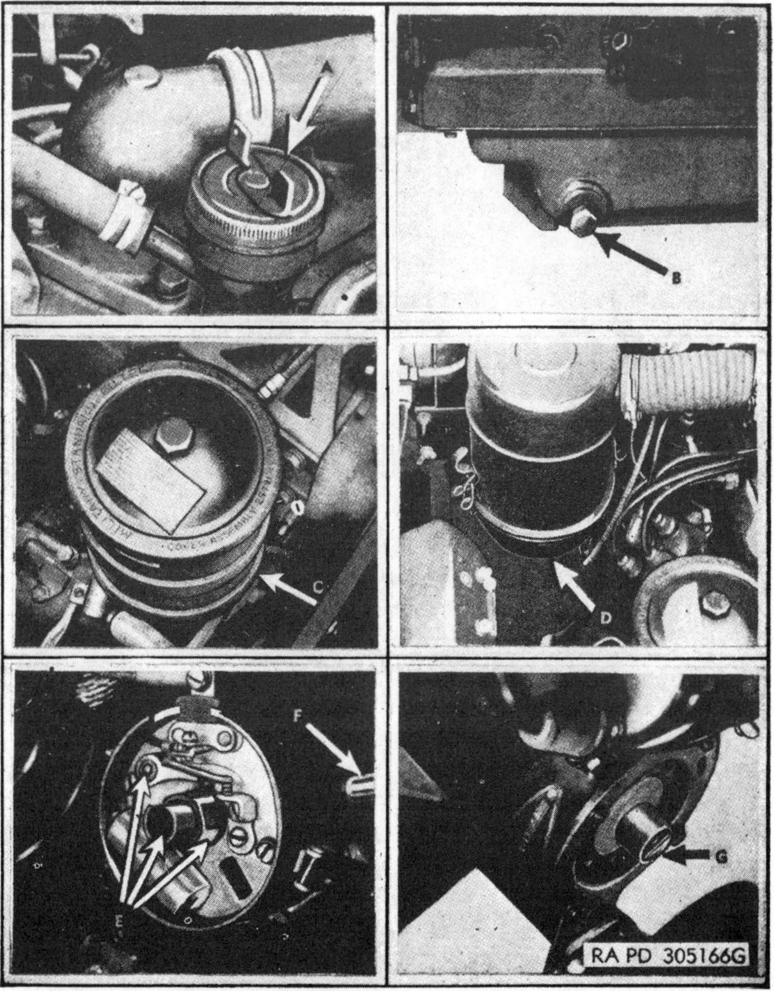

Figure 14. (Superseded) Localized lubrication points A through G.

c. Reports and Records.

(1) Report unsatisfactory performance of matériel or defects in the application or effect of prescribed petroleum fuels, lubricants, and preserving materials, using DA AGO Form 468, Unsatisfactory Equipment Report.

(2) Maintain record of lubrication for the vehicle on DA AGO Form 460, Preventive Maintenance Roster.

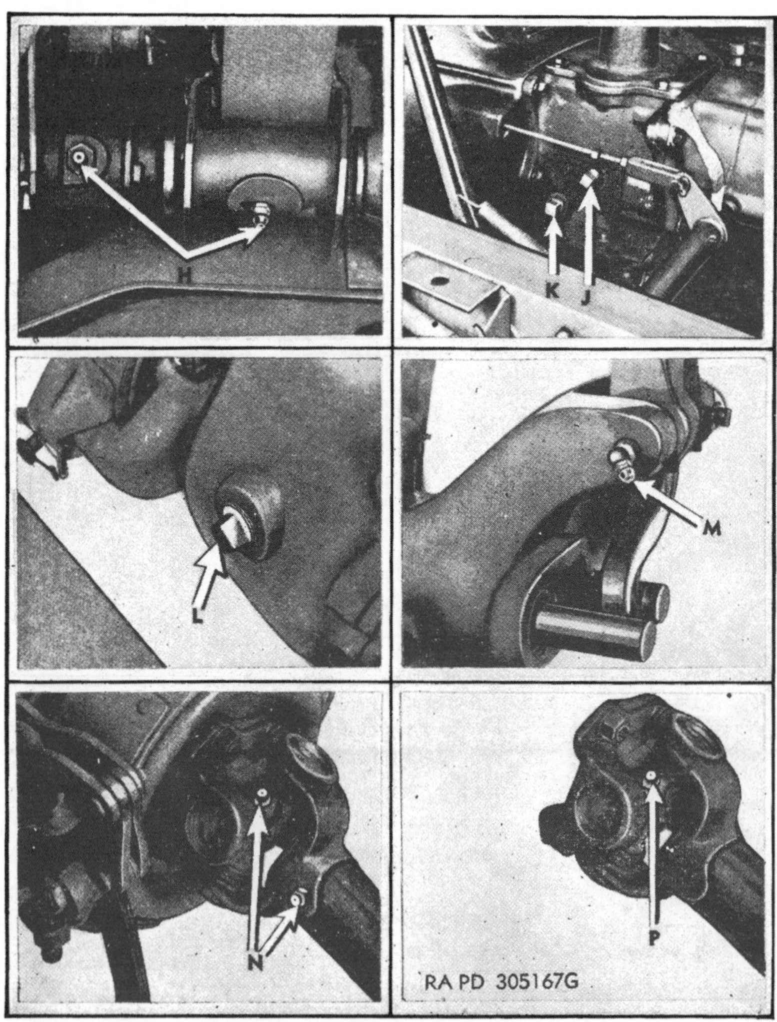

Figure 15. (Superseded) Localized lubrication points H through P.

23. Second Echelon Preventive Maintenance Services

a. Regular scheduled maintenance *** of operating organizations.

* * * * * * *

(5) *Specific procedures.* The procedures for performing each item in the **semiannual and monthly** maintenance procedures, are described in the following chart. Each page of the chart has two columns at the left edge corresponding to the **semiannual and monthly** maintenance respectively. Very often it will be found that a particular procedure does not apply to both scheduled maintenance **services.** In order to determine which procedure to follow, look down the column corresponding to the **particular** maintenance due, and wherever **a number** appears, perform the operations indicated opposite the number.

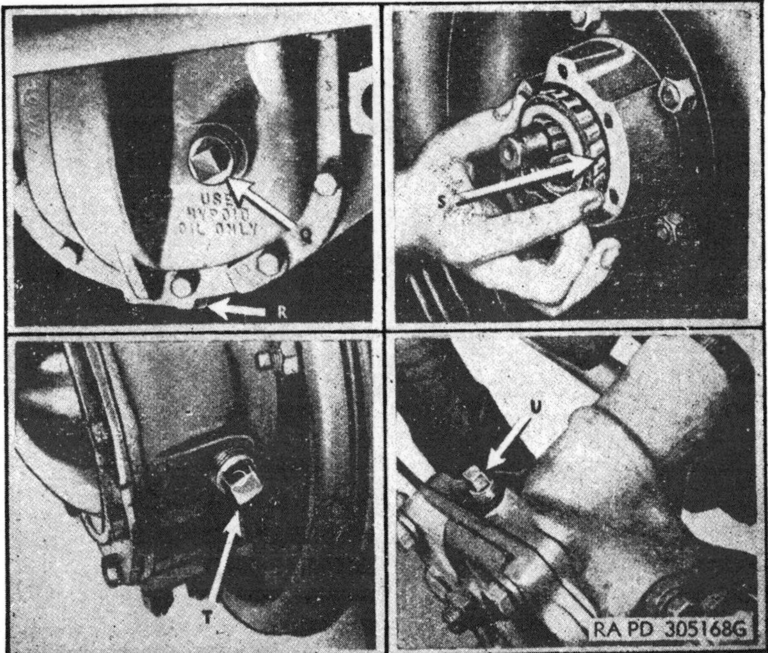

Figure 16. (Superseded) Localized lubrication points Q through U.

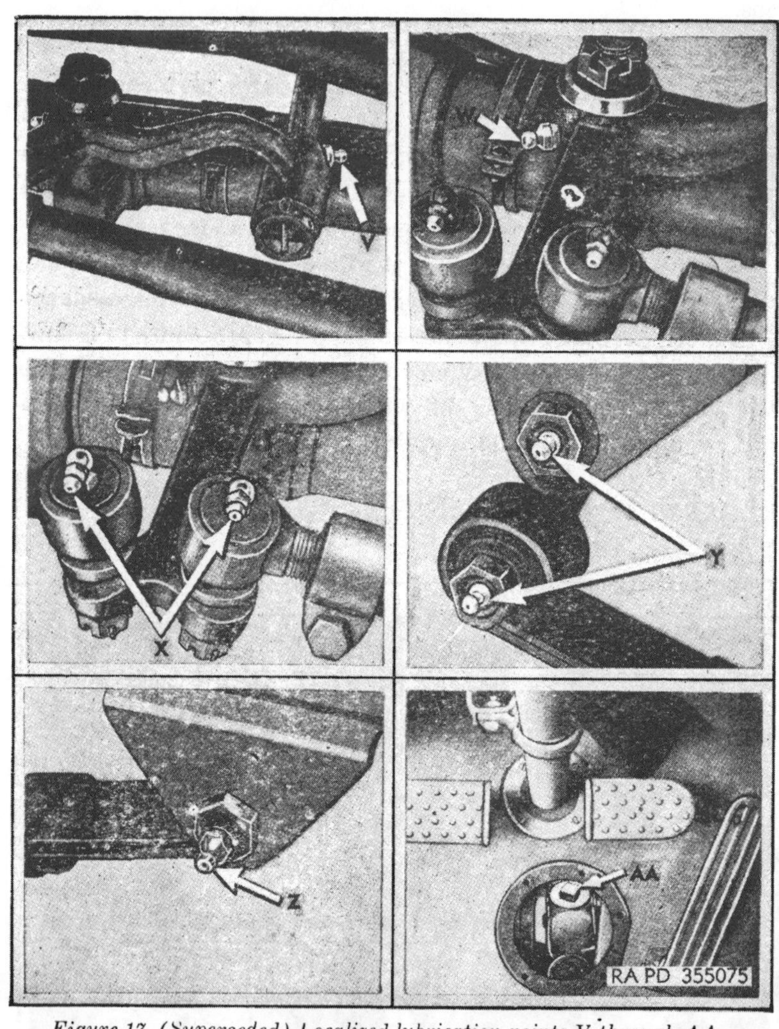

Figure 17. (Superseded) Localized lubrication points V through AA.

Section VII. Rescinded.
Section VIII. Rescinded.

ROAD TEST

*   *   *   *   *   *   *

Maintenance		
6000 mile *or Semi-annual**	1000 mile *or monthly**	
*	*	* * * * *
4	4	*Horn, mirror, and windshield wiper.* Test horn for *** or discolored glass. **(Hand type wipers.)** Wiper should have *** throughout entire stroke. **(Vacuum motor type wipers.) Check both motors to see that they are secure, and that wiper blades contact glass evenly and operate through their full range.**
*	*	* * * * *
16	16	*Gear oil level and leaks.* Examine lubricant levels *** with filler plug. If an oil change is due, drain and refill, according to Lubrication **Order** (par. 18).
		MAINTENANCE OPERATIONS
		Raise vehicle and block safely (Added)
		Caution (Added): Use necessary precautions to block the vehicle so it may be operated safely in gear at reasonable speeds. If facilities are not available for adequately and safely jacking up and blocking vehicle, omit the services below which require running the engine in gear.
*	*	* * * * *
35	35	*Crankcase Ventilating System* (Added). Remove and disassemble the crankcase ventilator valve and clean in dry cleaning solvent. Be sure that spring operates freely. Assemble and install valve (par. 59).
*	*	* * * * *
47	47	*Tires and rims.* Inspect valve stems *** and missing caps. **Tube valve stems must be equipped with mounting sleeves. The mounting sleeve screws onto valve stem.** Inspect tires for *** to 35 pounds (cold).
*	*	* * * * *
134	134	*First aid kit.* Examine contents of *** Report any deficiency.
*	*	* * * * *

Section X. SERVICE UPON RECEIPT OF MATÉRIEL

24. Purpose

When a new *** and correctly adjusted. In addition, they will perform a run-in of at least 50 miles **on new or reconditioned vehicles and a sufficient number of miles on used vehicles to completely check their operation** according to procedures in paragraph 26.

*Whichever is earlier.

25. Correction of Deficiencies

Deficiencies disclosed during the course of the run-in will be treated as follows:

* * * * * * *

26. Run-In Procedures

* * * * * * *

b. RUN-IN. Perform the following *** during the test.

* * * * * * *

(2) *Brakes: Foot and hand.* Test service brakes *** rod-to-piston resistance. Parking brake should hold vehicle on reasonable incline, leaving one-third lever ratchet travel in reserve.

Caution: Avoid long application *** seated to drums.

* * * * * * *

Section XI. (Superseded) SPECIAL TOOLS AND EQUIPMENT FOR ORGANIZATIONAL MAINTENANCE

27. General

Tools and equipment are issued to the using organization for maintaining the matériel. Tools and equipment should not be used for purposes other than prescribed and, when not in use, should be properly stored in the chest and/or roll provided for them. Spare parts are supplied to the using organization for replacement of those parts likely to become worn, broken, or otherwise unserviceable when such operations are within the scope of organizational maintenance. Spare parts, tools, and equipment supplied for the ¼-ton 4 x 4 truck (Willys-Overland Model MB and Ford Model GPW) are listed in the Department of the Army Supply Catalog ORD 7 SNL G–503, which is the authority for requisitioning replacements. Standard and commonly used tools and equipment having general application to this matériel are listed in the ORD 7 pamphlet but are not specifically identified in this manual.

28. Specially Designed Tools and Equipment

Certain tools and equipment specially designed for organizational maintenance, repair, and general use with the matériel are listed in table I for information only. This table is not to be used for requisitioning replacements.

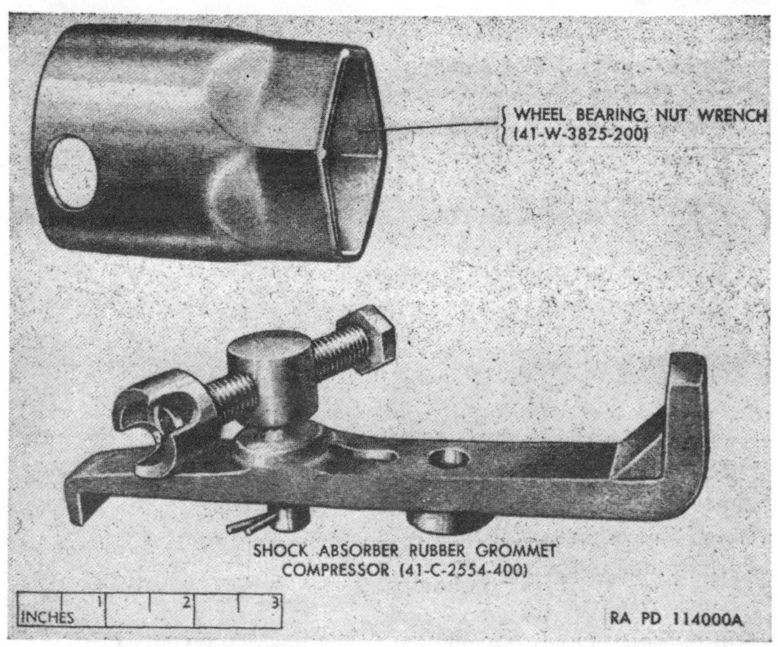

Figure 19.1. (Added) Special tools for ¼-ton 4 x 4 truck.

Table I. Special Organizational Tools and Equipment

Item	Federal stock No.	References Fig.	References Par.	Use
COMPRESSOR, shock absorber rubber grommet.	41–C–2554–400	19.1	157	For compressing rubber bushings on mounting pins.
WRENCH, engrs., angle 15 deg., dble-end., alloy-S, size of opngs. 3/16 and 1/4 in.	41–W–986		148	For manipulating brake eccentrics and anchor pins in making brake adjustment.
*WRENCH, wheel bearing nut sgle-end, tubular, hex., size of opng. 2-1/8 in., length 3.56 in.	41–W–3825–200	19.1, 78	128	Removing wheel bearing nut.

*On-Vehicle tools.

*   *   *   *   *   *   *

c. ENGINE WILL NOT START.

*   *   *   *   *   *   *

(2) *Weak spark.*

*   *   *   *   *   *   *

(Added) Low or partially discharged battery.	(Added) Replace or recharge battery (par. 97).

*   *   *   *   *   *   *

(4) *Backfiring.*

*   *   *   *   *   *   *

Valve holding open.	Adjust valves; report stuck valves to higher authority.

(5) (Added) *Ammeter indicates constant normal discharge.*

Distributor breaker points do not open.	Clean or replace and adjust (par. 64).
Primary wire from coil to distributor grounded.	Repair or replace.
Condenser shorted.	Replace condenser (par. 64).
Ignition coil primary grounded.	Replace coil (par. 66).

*   *   *   *   *   *   *

e. ENGINE STALLS ON IDLE.

*   *   *   *   *   *   *

(Added) Oil level too high in air cleaner.	(Added) Check oil level in air cleaner and remove excess oil (par. 73).

*   *   *   *   *   *   *

g. ENGINE DOES NOT IDLE PROPERLY (ERRATIC).

*   *   *   *   *   *   *

(Added) Too high oil level in air cleaner cup.	(Added) Check cleaner for proper oil level.
(Added) Improper seating of ventilator valve plunger (on vehicles equipped with positive crankcase ventilation).	(Added) Replace crankcase ventilator valve.

*   *   *   *   *   *   *

n. LOW OIL MILEAGE.

*   *   *   *   *   *   *

(Rescinded) Oil filter clogged.	(Rescinded) Clean; replace element (par. 58).

(Superseded) Faulty pistons, or rings or rear bearing oil return clogged; excessive clearance of intake valves in guides; cylinder bores worn (scored, out-of-round, tapered); excessive bearing clearance.	Report to higher authority.

* * * * * * *

p. LOW OIL PRESSURE.

* * * * * * *

(Rescinded) Oil too heavy (funneling in cold weather).	(Rescinded) Dilute engine oil (par. 18).

* * * * * * *

(Rescinded) Oil pressure too high.	(Rescinded) Faulty oil pump regulator valve stuck closed or improperly adjusted, report to higher authority.

* * * * * * *

38. Transfer Case

* * * * * * *

b. HARD SHIFTING.

* * * * * * *

(Rescinded) Low or uneven tire pressure; add tires on (front and rear) wheels.	(Rescinded) Service.

* * * * * * *

42. Brake System

* * * * * * *

c. ONE BRAKE GRABS (VEHICLE PULLS TO ONE SIDE).

(Rescinded) Tires underinflated.	(Rescinded) Inflate tires (par. 13).
(Rescinded) Tires worn unequally.	(Rescinded) Replace.
(Rescinded) Weak or broken shoe return spring.	(Rescinded) Replace.

* * * * * * *

e. BRAKES LOCKED.

* * * * * * *

Brakes frozen to drums (cold weather).	**Carefully apply heat to outside of drums.**

* * * * * * *

g. EXCESSIVE PEDAL TRAVEL.

* * * * * * *

Low fluid level in master cylinder or air in brake system.	Fill master cylinder and bleed lines (par. 151).

(Rescinded) Scored brake drums.	(Rescinded) Replace (par. 131 and 144).
(Rescinded) Incorrect brake lining.	(Rescinded) Replace with correct shoe and lining assemblies.
Pedal goes to floor board (disconnected from master cylinder).	Correct or replace faulty part (par. 149).

* * * * * * *

43. Wheels, Wheel Bearings, and Related Parts

* * * * * * *

Wheel out of balance.	Balance wheel, tire, or both.

* * * * * * *

45. Steering System

a. STEERING DIFFICULT.

* * * * * * *

Tight steering gear; misalined front wheels.	Adjust (par. 163). Report to higher authority for other adjustments.

* * * * * * *

b. WANDER OR WEAVING.

* * * * * * *

Steering gear worn out of adjustment.	Adjust or replace (par. 163). Report to higher authorit for other adjustments.

* * * * * * *

c. LOW SPEED SHIMMY OR WOBBLE.

* * * * * * *

Steering gear worn, or adjustments too loose.	Adjust or replace (par. 163). Report to higher authorit for other adjustments.

* * * * * * *

g. ROAD SHOCK.

* * * * * * *

Looseness in steering gear.	Adjust (par. 163). Report to higher authority for other adjustments.

* * * * * * *

h. Rescinded.

i. UNEQUAL STEERING (RIGHT AND LEFT).

* * * * * * *

(Added) Steering stop screws improperly set.	(Added) Report to higher authority.

46. Body and Frame (Superseded)

a. BODY.

Windshield wiper faulty.	Service or replace.

b. FRAME.

Damaged frame.	Report to higher authority.

47. Battery and Lighting System

* * * * * * *

e. LIGHTS DO NOT LIGHT.

* * * * * * *

(Added) Battery low.	(Added) Charge or replace battery.

f. LIGHTS DIM.

* * * * * * *

(Added) Battery low.	(Added) Charge or replace battery.

* * * * * * *

50. Description and Tabulated Data

* * * * * * *

b. TABULATED DATA.

* * * * * * *

Net horsepower.	60 at 4,000 rpm.

* * * * * * *

Maximum torque.	**105 ft-lb at 2,000 rmp.**

* * * * * * *

55. Valve Cover Gasket (Superseded)

a. REMOVAL. Remove front valve spring cover bolt or nut (figs. 26, 26.1, and 26.2).

Note. On Ford GPW engine cylinder blocks having serial numbers 232051 to 243405 inclusive or casting dates K10–4 to L29–4 inclusive, a change in the design of the valve cover bolt boss caused a weakness at this point. When too much force is exerted on the valve cover bolt, a crack may occur, allowing water to enter the crankcase. Whenever bolts are found on a Ford GPW engine cylinder block of the above serial numbers or casting dates, they should be replaced by shoulder type studs FM GPW6547 and FM GPW6548 and two 5/16–24NF–2 hexagonal nuts (stock No. H001–4027521).

When installing shoulder type studs, apply a coat of white or red lead to the shoulder ends of the studs before installing in cylinder block. Remove crankcase ventilator tube at ventilator valve and remove tube and cap. Remove rear valve spring cover bolt or nut and slide valve spring cover forward, up, and out over fuel pump Discard gasket.

b. Installation. Clean cover and gasket seat on cylinder block. Cement cork gasket to cover. Position cover on cylinder block by sliding it to the rear over fuel pump. Place copper gasket on rear bolt and install bolt through cover and turn in bolt, but do not tighten (if studs are used, loosely install nut on rear stud). Place copper gasket, ventilator body, body gasket, and baffle on front bolt and install bolt (if studs are used, install baffle, body gasket, and ventilator body on front stud and then install nut). Connect ventilator tube to valve and tighten both cover bolts (or nuts) evenly. Start engine and check for oil leaks.

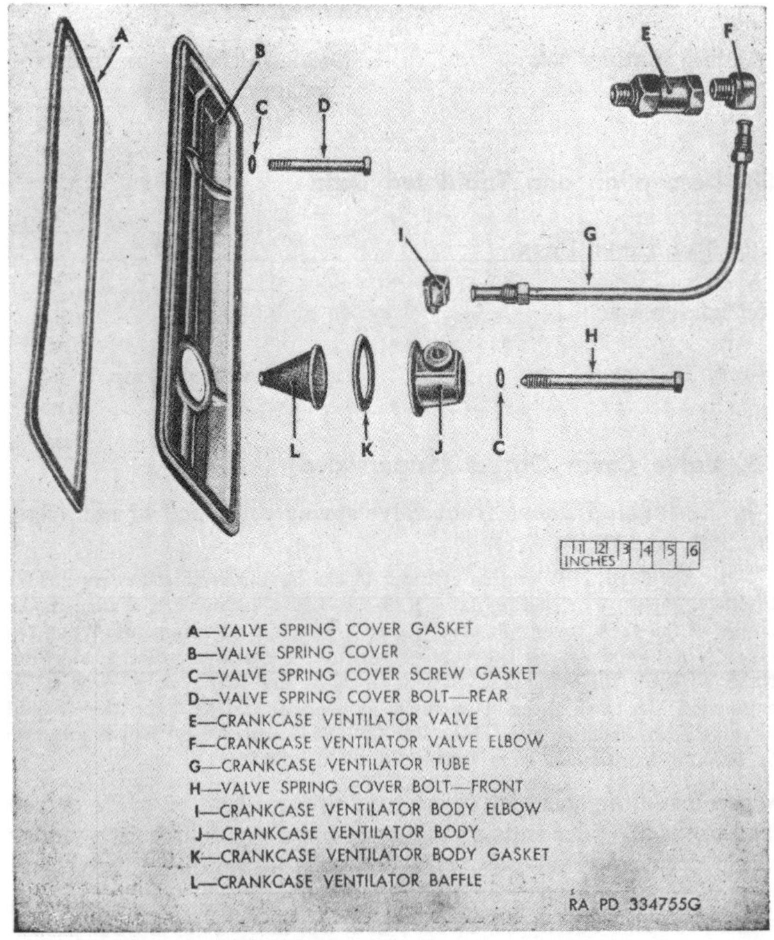

Figure 26. Valve spring cover, disassembled.

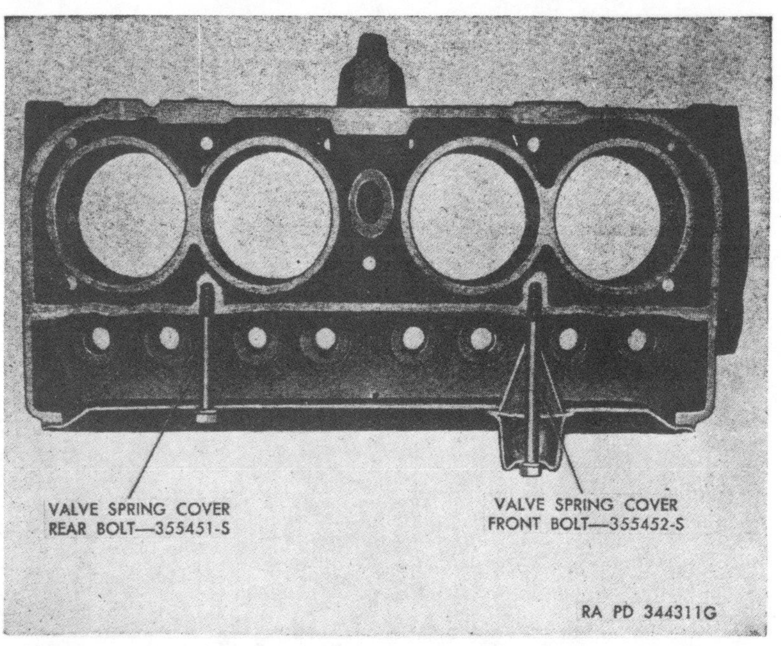

Figure 26.1. Section through engine block showing old type bolts.

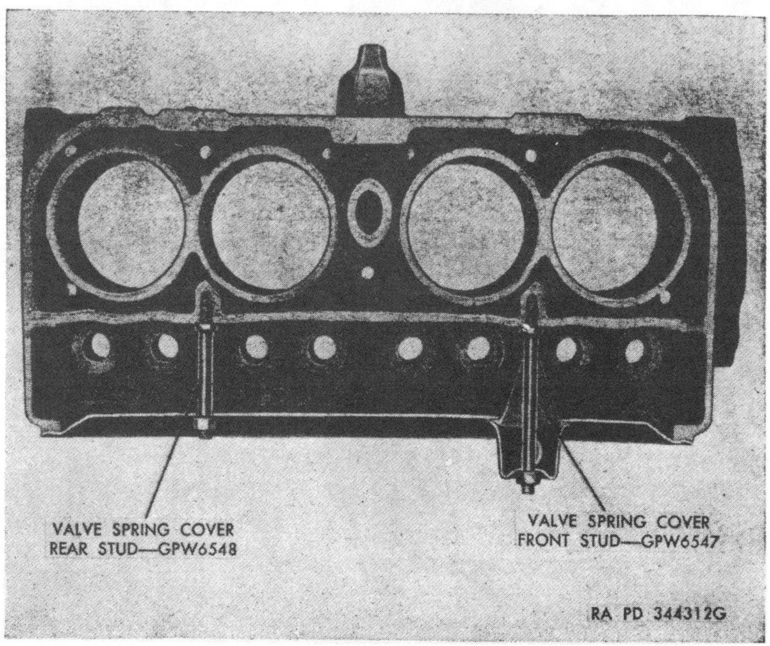

Figure 26.2. Section through engine block showing shoulder type studs.

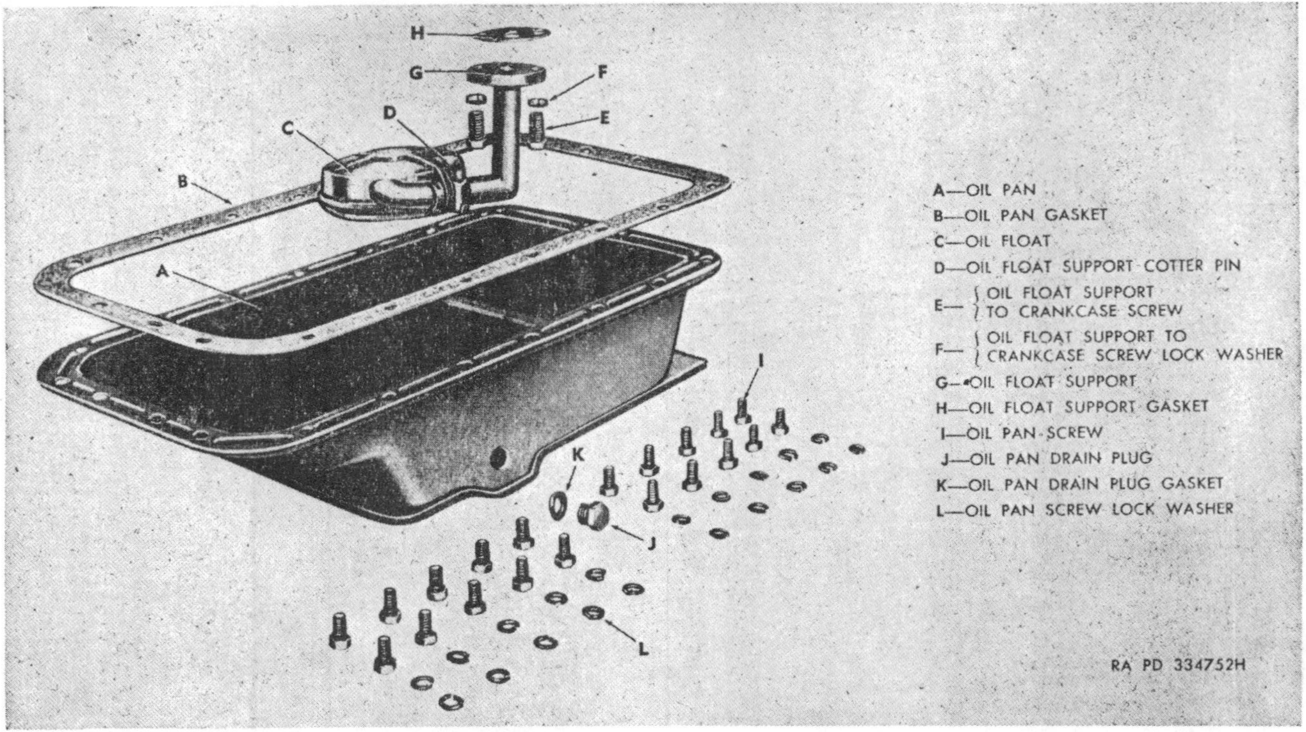

A—OIL PAN
B—OIL PAN GASKET
C—OIL FLOAT
D—OIL FLOAT SUPPORT COTTER PIN
E—OIL FLOAT SUPPORT TO CRANKCASE SCREW
F—OIL FLOAT SUPPORT TO CRANKCASE SCREW LOCK WASHER
G—OIL FLOAT SUPPORT
H—OIL FLOAT SUPPORT GASKET
I—OIL PAN SCREW
J—OIL PAN DRAIN PLUG
K—OIL PAN DRAIN PLUG GASKET
L—OIL PAN SCREW LOCK WASHER

RA PD 334752H

Figure 28. Floating oil intake and oil pan (Superseded).

56. Valve Tappet Adjustment (Superseded)

Remove the valve spring cover (par. 55). Adjust the self-locking tappet screws (fig. 27) while they are cold *(intake valves to 0.014 inch, exhaust valves 0.014 to 0.016 inch)*. Set tappet screws, starting with No. 1 cylinder on compression stroke at top center, then adjust valves in cylinder firing order 1–3–4–2, turning the crankshaft one-half turn for each cylinder.

Note. The valve tappets will then be on the heel of the cam.

After adjusting, replace valve spring cover (par. 55).

58. Oil Filter

* * * * * * *

b. REMOVE ELEMENT. Unscrew cover bolt in top of unit and remove cover. **discarding the gasket** (fig. 29). Remove drain plug *** lift out element.

c. INSTALLING ELEMENT. Clean filter thoroughly *** element in filter. **Replace cover gasket.** Install cover and *** mark on gage.

* * * * * * *

59. Crankcase Ventilator Valve

a. DESCRIPTION. The crankcase ventilator *** (manifold vacuum high). When the engine speed is increased the manifold vacuum is lowered, and the valve opens to allow clean air to be drawn from the air cleaner tube through the engine oil filler pipe **and crankcase, and then through the ventilator tube, elbow and valve, G, F, and E respectively (fig. 26)** to ventilate the crankcase. If this valve *** leaky intake manifold.

b. REMOVE VALVE. Loosen valve spring cover front **bolt or nut on stud.** Remove ventilator tube *** ventilator valve (fig. 22).

c. INSTALLING VALVE. Place ventilator valve *** and attach tube. Tighten valve spring cover front **bolt or nut on stud.**

61. Installation

* * * * * * *

b. ON RIGHT SIDE OF VEHICLE. Install cranking motor *** air flexible connection.

Note. **If the engine being removed from the vehicle is equipped with positive crankcase ventilation and the engine being installed is not so equipped, seal the tube projecting from the air cleaner to carburetor tube. If both engines are equipped with the positive crankcase ventilation system, be sure that the hose between the oil filler pipe and the carburetor air cleaner tube is properly connected so that no dust or dirt can be drawn into crankcase.**

Install battery, and *** to battery posts.

* * * * * * *

62. Description and Data

* * * * * * *

c. TESTS. The following procedure *** use of instruments:

* * * * * * *

(4) **With the ignition switch turned on,** open distributor points and notice if a slight spark is obtained. If spark occurs, *** faulty, as follows:

(5) Remove switch wire at ignition coil, **turn ignition switch on,** and strike wire against cylinder block. If no spark *** faulty. Replace coil.

70. Description and Data

* * * * * * *

c. OPERATION. Fuel in the *** or damaged lines. **Later vehicles have a permanently mounted filter in the gas tank instead of the strainer mounted on the dash.**

72. Carburetor

* * * * * * *

b. ADJUSTMENT. The idle adjustment *** requires other attention. **Improper idling of engine can be caused by a too high oil level in air cleaner oil cup; check cleaner for proper oil level. On those vehicles equipped with a positive crankcase ventilation system, improper idling can be caused by improper seating of the ventilator valve plunger; replace valve (par. 59).**

* * * * * * *

73. Air Cleaner

* * * * * * *

b. REMOVAL OF OIL CUP. Hold one hand *** two retaining clamps. Remove cup, clean, and refill to indicated oil level **carefully because too high a level can cause improper idling and excessive fuel consumption.**

* * * * * * *

e. INSTALLATION. Install the element *** with retaining bolt. Clean and refill oil cup to indicated level **(too high an oil level in air cleaner oil cup can cause improper engine idling and excessive fuel consumption)**, and clamp into place on cleaner. Mount cleaner on *** clamp in place.

78. Exhaust System

a. DESCRIPTION. The exhaust system *** with fabric inserts. **On later vehicles, muffler is located under rear of body.**

* * * * * * *

93. Generator

* * * * * * *

c. INSTALLATION. Place generator in *** adjust if necessary (par. 83). Attach wires, filter, and ground strap **and polarize the generator with the battery by momentarily connecting a jumper wire from the positive terminal of the battery to the armature (large) terminal on the generator.** Start engine and *** in instrument panel (fig. 5).

95. Description and Data

a. DESCRIPTION. The lighting system *** the instrument panel When the **push-pull type** blackout light switch is set in the proper operating position, other light switches, such as blackout driving light, instrument panel, stop lights and dimmers, are controlled by the respective switches. **There is no separate blackout driving light switch installed on vehicles equipped with the rotary type blackout (main) light switch. (See par. 4 b.)** The lighting system *** the blackout switch.

b. DATA.

* * * * * * *

Lamps:

Headlights................Sealed unit **(Mazda No. 4031)**

Blackout headlights........................Mazda No. **63**

* * * * * * *

97. Battery

a. DESCRIPTION. The battery (fig. 36) is *** 15 plates each. **Later vehicles are equipped with a 17 plate, 120 ampere-hour battery.** The battery is *** specific gravity is 1.275 to 1.285.

* * * * * * *

99. Headlights

a. DESCRIPTION. Two headlights (fig. 52) *** the engine compartment. The headlights are of the double filament sealed beam-unit type consisting of reflector, lamp, and lens, which can be replaced only as a unit (Mazda No. **4031**). The headlights light *** of the road.

* * * * * * *

100. (Superseded) Blackout Marker Lights

a. DESCRIPTION. **There are two blackout marker lights (fig. 55) with lens which permit only horizontal rays to pass through. These lights are illuminated only when the blackout (main) light switch is in blackout position. Mazda No. 63 lamps are used.**

b. REMOVAL OF LAMP. Remove door screw in lower side of rim and remove door by pulling out on lower side (fig. 56).

Note. The door and lens are in one unit.

Push in on lamp, turn lamp to left, and remove.

c. INSTALLATION OF LAMP. Insert lamp in socket, push in, and turn lamp to right. Replace door gasket if damaged. Replace door and tighten door screw.

d. REMOVAL OF MARKER LIGHT. Pull wire out of connection just behind left light. (For right light remove three clips across bottom of grille.) Remove mounting nut by reaching in from rear and lift out light.

e. INSTALLATION OF MARKER LIGHT. Put light in position and tighten in place with mounting nut. (Attach three clips for right light.) Attach wire in connector.

Figure 55. Blackout marker light.

Figure 56. Blackout marker light, disassembled.

104. Blackout (Main) Light Switch (Superseded)

a. DESCRIPTION. Either a push-pull type or a rotary type blackout (main) light switch (fig. 62) is mounted in the instrument panel to the left of the steering gear. This switch controls all the lights and has four positions (fig. 9). A thermal type overload breaker switch is mounted on the rear of these switches. When a short circuit occurs in the lighting system, the bimetal strip bends from the heat of the heavy current, and opens the contacts. As soon as the bimetal strip cools, the contacts close, completing the circuit.

b. REMOVAL.

(1) *Push-pull type.* Disconnect ground cable at negative post of battery. Loosen set screw in switch knob and unscrew knob. Loosen hexagon head screw at side of switch bushing on front of panel, press lockout control button, and pull off bushing. Remove mounting nut, and take switch out from under panel. Remove wire terminal screws. Mark the wires, as they are removed, for identification.

(2) *Rotary type.* Remove screw in lever. Pull off lever. Remove mounting nut, lockwasher, and escutcheon plate and remove switch from under panel. Remove wire terminal screws. Mark wires, as they are removed, for identification.

c. INSTALLATION.

(1) *Push-pull type.* Attach cables to proper terminals. *Note.* Switch terminals are marked for easy identification. Cables are to be attached as follows:

Terminal	*Circuit*	*Cable Color or Circuit No.*	
A	Extra	Not used	
B	Ammeter	Red-white tr.	10
BHT	Blackout marker lights	Yellow-black tr.	20
BHT	Blackout taillights	Yellow-black tr.	24
BHT	Blackout driving light	Black-white tr.	19
BS	Blackout stoplight	White-black tr.	23
HT	Service headlight	Blue-white tr.	16
HT	Service taillight	Blue-white tr.	21
HT	Panel lights	Blue-white tr.	40
S	Service stoplight	Red-white tr.	22
SS	Stoplight switch	Red-white tr.	75
SS	Trailer coupling socket	Red-black tr.	84
SW	Stoplight switch	Green-black tr.	75
TT	Trailer coupling socket	Green-black tr.	83

Install switch in panel and secure in place with mounting nuts. Install bushing and tighten screw. Install knob and tighten set screw. Attach ground cable to battery.

(2) *Rotary type.* Attach cables to proper terminals. *Note.* Switch terminals are marked for easy identification. Cables are to be attached as follows:

Terminal	*Circuit*	*Cable Color or Circuit No.*	
BAT	Ammeter	Red-white tr.	10
BHT	Blackout marker lights	Yellow-blue tr.	20
BHT	Blackout taillight	Yellow-blue tr.	24
BOD	Blackout driving light	Black-white tr.	19
BS	Blackout stoplight	White-black tr.	23
HT	Service taillight	Blue-white tr.	16
HT	Instrument light switch	Blue-white tr.	40
HT	Service headlight dimmer switch	Blue-white tr.	16
S	Service stoplight	Red-white tr.	22
SS	Trailer coupling socket	Red-black tr.	84
SS	Stoplight switch	Red-white tr.	75
SW	Stoplight switch	Green-black tr.	75
TT	Trailer coupling socket	Green-black tr.	83

Push switch shaft through instrument panel and place escutcheon plate over shaft. Secure in place with lockwasher and nut; install lever and tighten in place with screw. Attach ground cable to battery.

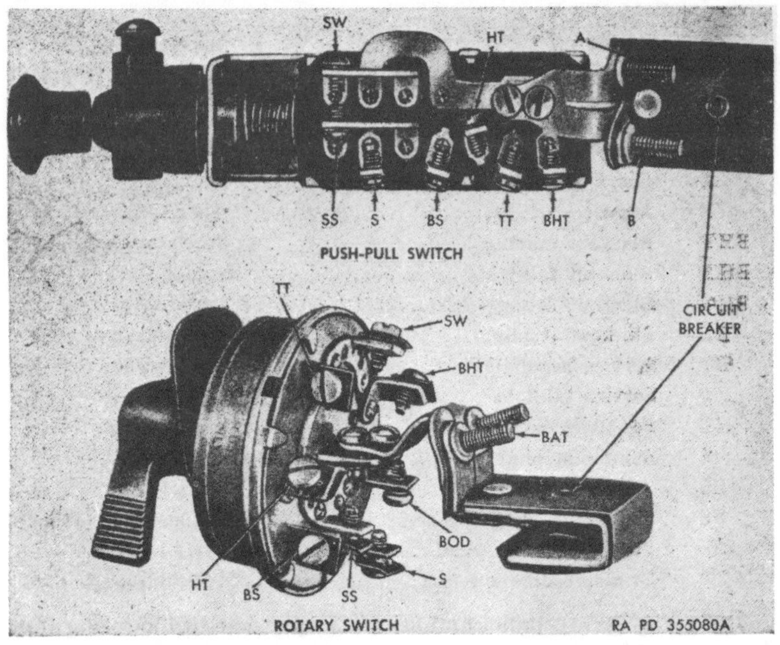

Figure 62. (Superseded) Blackout (main) light switches.

105. Panel and Blackout Driving Light Switch

a. DESCRIPTION. The panel and *** in blackout position. **No blackout driving light switch is used on vehicles equipped with a rotary type blackout (main) light switch.**

* * * * * * *

114. Maintenance

The transmission requires *** and securely tightened. The vent hole in **left side of** transmission control housing, **just below control housing cap,** must be kept clean at all times. Report transmission gear noise to higher authority.

118. Maintenance

The transfer case *** and filler plugs. **Breather assembly must be free from dirt and grit.** Report failure to *** to higher authority.

127. Maintenance

* * * * * * *

b. (Added) In an emergency, where difficulty is experienced with the front axle differential, making the vehicle inoperative,

remove the axle drive flanges (par. 128), put front wheel drive shift lever in forward (disengaged) position, and drive vehicle in regular manner.

128. Wheel Bearings

a. ADJUSTMENT. Raise front of *** away from nut. Remove lock nut with **wheel bearing nut wrench (41–W–3825–200) (figs. 19.1 and 78).** Remove lock washer *** new hub cap. **After a short period of road operation, recheck bearing adjustment.**

* * * * * * *

135. Wheel Alinement

* * * * * * *

b. (Superseded) TOE-IN AND TOE-OUT. Inflate tires to correct pressure and place vehicle on a smooth, level surface with the wheels in a straight-ahead position. Place gage (41–G–510) between the wheels ahead of the axle, with the ends of the gage bearing against the tire side walls and with both pendant chains just touching the ground. Set gage so pointer reads zero, move the vehicle forward until gage is brought into position in back of the axle, with both pendant chains just touching the ground. The pointer will indicate the amount of toe-in or toe-out. Set toe-in of front wheels at 3/64 inch to 3/32 inch.

139. Maintenance

* * * * * * *

b. (Added) In an emergency, should difficulty be experienced with the differential or propeller shaft, remove the rear axle shafts and propeller shaft, place front wheel drive shift lever in rear (engaged) position, and operate vehicle in regular manner.

141. Wheel Bearings

a. ADJUSTMENT. Place jack under *** vehicle to floor. **After a short period of road operation, recheck all bearing adjustments and readjust if necessary.**

* * * * * * *

146. Description and Data

a. DESCRIPTION. The service, or *** the instrument panel. Pulling out on the lever draws a flexible cable through a conduit to actuate the brake at the rear of the transfer case. **Some vehicles have an external contracting type brake in which** the brake cable is of a predetermined length, and cannot be adjusted. When adjustment is *** the release action. **The later type vehicles have an internal expanding type hand brake which is fully adjustable (figs. 91.1 and 91.2).**

*   *   *   *   *   *   *

148. Service (Foot) Brakes

a. ADJUSTMENT (MINOR). Adjust brake pedal *** one brake (fig. 86). Place wrench (**41–W–986**) on eccentric so that handle extends up. Rotate wheel, and *** to test brakes.

b. ADJUSTMENT (MAJOR). Adjust brake pedal *** forward brake shoe. Place wrench (**41–W–986**) on eccentric so that handle is up, and turn wrench handle toward wheel rim, or forward, until 0.008-inch clearance is obtained by feel of gage. Hold wrench on *** vehicle to floor.

*   *   *   *   *   *   *

152. Parking (Hand) Brake (Superseded)

a. EXTERNAL CONTRACTING TYPE.

(1) *Adjustment.* Place hand brake grip in released position. Check brake levers to see that cable is free and released. Remove lock wire from anchor adjusting screw (fig. 91). Place 0.005-inch thickness gage between band and drum at anchor screw, and adjust screw to secure clearance. Install lock wire. Tighten adjusting nut until brake band is tight around drum. Loosen bracket bolt lock nut and rear nut. Back nut off two turns and set lock nut. Loosen adjusting nut so that brake band has approximately 0.010-inch clearance on drum.

(2) *Removal.* Remove anchor bolt lock wire. Remove anchor bolt. Remove bracket bolt. Remove cotter pin from brake cam clevis pin and remove pin. Remove brake band adjusting nut. Remove brake adjusting bolt and spring. Remove retracting spring and remove brake band assembly.

(3) *Installation.* Install brake band on drum. Install brake release spring and adjusting bolt. Install clevis pin in brake cam and head of adjusting bolt. Install cotter pin in clevis pin. Install brake band adjusting nut. Install bracket bolt and nuts. Install anchor bolt. Adjust brake ((1) above). Install retracting spring.

b. INTERNAL EXPANDING TYPE.

(1) *Adjustment.*

(*a*) *Brake Shoes.* Place hand brake grip in released position. Check brake lever to see that cable is free and released. Rotate brake drum until two holes in the drum expose two adjusting screws (fig. 91.2). Use the edge of the holes as a fulcrum for a suitable tool or screw driver and rotate each adjusting screw by moving the handle of the tool away from the drive shaft until the shoes are snug in the drum. Back off seven notches on each adjusting wheel to secure correct running clearance.

(b) *Brake operating lever.* The correct clearance of the brake operating lever is 3/16 inch from the brake backing plate. This is set by the manufacturer and does not change even though new shoes or linings are installed. The position of the lever should be checked and if found altered, adjust the operating link by means of the lever clearance adjusting nut.

(2) *Removal* (figs. 91.1 and 91.2). Disconnect the propeller shaft at the forward end. Remove cotter pin, nut and washer from transfer case output shaft. Use a suitable puller to remove the brake drum. Remove the retracting spring link, clevis pin and spring clip, two brake shoe retracting springs and the shoes. (The brake backing plate and shoes can be removed as an assembly.)

(3) *Installation* (figs. 91.1 and 91.2). Turn both adjusting screws to the center or "all off" position. Place a light film of grease on the brake actuating cam and install the shoes. Install the black colored shoe retracting spring next to the cam and the yellow spring next to the notched adjusting wheel screws. Place the brake drum in posi-

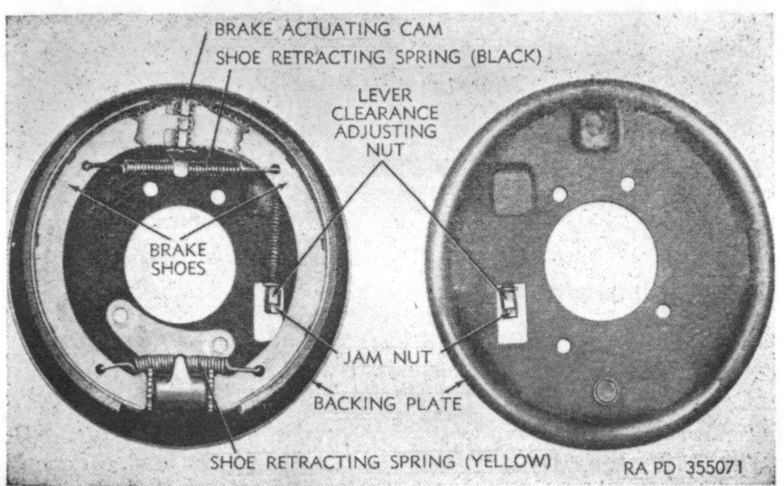

Figure 91.1. Internal expanding parking brake (removed).

tion and install transfer case output shaft washer, nut and cotter pin. Adjust the brake adjusting screws ((1) (*a*) above), leaving the brake tight. Adjust the clevis on the brake end of the operating cable until the clevis pin will just go through the hole in the clevis and brake operating lever. Tighten the clevis lock nut. After the cable is connected, back off seven notches on each of the adjusting screws for proper running clearance of the brake. Attach the propeller shaft. Install retracting spring clip, clevis pin and cotter pin. Install the retracting spring link and spring.

Figure 91.2. Internal expanding parking brake (cut-away view).

153. Description and Data

a. DESCRIPTION. The springs (figs. 92 and 93) *** first (main) leaf. **The older vehicles were equipped with eight-leaf front springs and nine-leaf rear springs. Later vehicles are equipped with ten-leaf front springs and eleven-leaf rear springs.** The front **eight-leaf** springs appear to be identical, but have different load carrying ability. The left **eight-leaf** spring has an "L" painted on the underside of the second leaf at the front end. **The ten-leaf front springs are identical and can be installed on either right or left side. The nine-leaf rear springs are identical. The eleven-leaf rear springs are identical.** Four spring leaf *** extremely rough service.

***Caution:* Springs must be matched pairs. No vehicle will be operated with an eight-leaf and a ten-leaf spring installed on the front of the vehicle; neither will it be operated with a nine-leaf and an eleven-leaf spring installed on the rear of the vehicle.**

The shock absorbers *** adjustable, and refillable.

b. DATA.

Front Springs

*   *   *   *   *   *   *

Number of leaves............................ 8 **or 10**

*   *   *   *   *   *   *

Rear Springs

*   *   *   *   *   *   *

Number of leaves............................ 9 **or 11**

*   *   *   *   *   *   *

157. Shock Absorbers

*   *   *   *   *   *   *

b. INSTALLATION. Check shock absorber *** and flat washer. Use **shock absorber rubber grommet** compressor (41–C–2554–400) to compress bushing, and install cotter pin. Spread both ends *** in proper position.

163. Steering Gear

*   *   *   *   *   *   *

c. ADJUSTMENT. (Superseded)

(1) *Binding.* Disconnect steering connecting rod at steering gear arm. Turn steering wheel slowly through the full range of travel. If roughness or erratic binding is felt, report to higher authority.

(2) *Cam and shaft end play.* Loosen lock nut on the side adjusting screw and loosen screw approximately one turn to relieve any binding between cam and lever shaft. Remove three screws in housing upper cover. Pry up cover, carefully cut and remove one shim. Re-install cover and tighten cover screws. Check by turning steering wheel. When properly adjusted, wheel must turn freely with no end play in shaft. Add or remove shims as necessary until proper adjustment is obtained.

(3) *Lever shaft backlash.* Turn steering wheel as far as possible in one direction. Mark wheel with chalk, then turn wheel in opposite direction as far as possible, counting the full and part revolutions, then turn wheel

back exactly half the total number of revolutions to locate center or straight ahead position. Turn side adjusting screw in until a slight drag can be felt when the steering wheel is turned back and forth past center or straight ahead position. Tighten the adjusting screw lock nut and recheck adjustment. **For other adjustments, report to higher authority.**

164. Description and Data

a. DESCRIPTION. The body (figs. 1 to 4) is *** of the body. The windshield is equipped with dual, hand-operated, **or vacuum-operated** wipers, and can be opened forward or folded down on top of hood. A fire extinguisher *** a trailed load.

* * * * * * *

Section XXXII. (Superseded) DOMESTIC SHIPMENT AND LIMITED STORAGE

180. Domestic Shipping Instructions

a. PREPARATION. When shipping unboxed ordnance vehicles domestically, the officer in charge of preparing the shipment *will be responsible* for furnishing vehicles to the carriers for transport properly cleaned, preserved, painted, lubricated, etc., as prescribed in SB 9–4.

b. REMOVAL OF PRESERVATIVES FOR SHIPMENT. Personnel withdrawing vehicles from a limited storage status for domestic shipment *must not remove preservatives* other than to insure that the vehicles are complete and serviceable. The removal of preservatives is the responsibility of depots, ports, or field installations (posts, camps, and stations) receiving the shipments.

c. ARMY SHIPPING DOCUMENTS. Prepare all Army shipping documents in accordance with TM 38–705.

181. Limited Storage Instructions

a. GENERAL. When matériel is out of use, it must be turned over to ordnance personnel, or placed in a limited storage status for periods not to exceed 90 days.

Note. Storage of matériel for periods in excess of 90 days will normally be handled by ordnance personnel only.

b. RECEIVING INSPECTIONS. Immediately upon receipt of vehicles for storage, inspect and service as prescribed in SB 9–63, replacing or repairing all missing or damaged parts. If repairs cannot be made prior to placing vehicle in storage, attach a tag to the vehicle specifying the repairs needed and furnish a written report of these items to the officer in charge.

c. PREPARATION FOR STORAGE. Completely process vehicles before storage if it is determined from the previous processing recorded on DA AGO Form 9–3, that such has been rendered ineffective by operation, use, or damage to the vehicles, or upon receipt of vehicles directly from manufacturing facilities. Preparation for storage must be in accordance with SB 9–63.

d. STORAGE SITE. Whenever practicable, the preferred type of storage is in buildings or sheds. Where it is found necessary to store vehicles outdoors, the storage site must be selected in accordance with AR 700–105.

e. PERIODIC INSPECTIONS. Make a visual inspection periodically to determine general conditions. If corrosion is found on any part, remove the rust spots, clean, and treat with the prescribed preservative.

f. REMOVAL FROM LIMITED STORAGE.

(1) If the matériel is not shipped or issued upon expiration of the limited storage period, the matériel must be further treated for stand-by storage (matériel out of use for periods in excess of 90 days up to 3 years). (See Note *a* above.)

(2) Vehicles to be shipped will not be reprocessed unless inspection reveals it to be necessary.

(3) When it has been ascertained that matériel is to be placed into immediate service, any item noted by a tag attached to matériel as still needing repairs must be repaired and matériel will be given complete inspection, plus any repairs which are indicated by this inspection. Matériel will be serviced as prescribed in section V and lubricated as prescribed in section VI.

182. Method of Loading ¼-Ton, 4 x 4 Trucks for Rail Shipment

a. LOADING RULES. For general loading rules pertaining to rail shipment of ordnance vehicles, refer to TB 9–OSSC–G.

b. FLATCAR LOADING. Provided slinging equipment is not available, the most common and effective method of loading vehicles on flatcars is to load the vehicles onto the rearmost flatcar by use of a runway and ramp and then move vehicles along the length of the train to its respective flatcar by the use of spanning platforms placed between cars. This method requires careful planning as to the order of loading, so that vehicles are arranged on the flatcars in their desired order.

Note. Lower the brake wheel to the floor of the flatcar to allow the vehicles to pass.

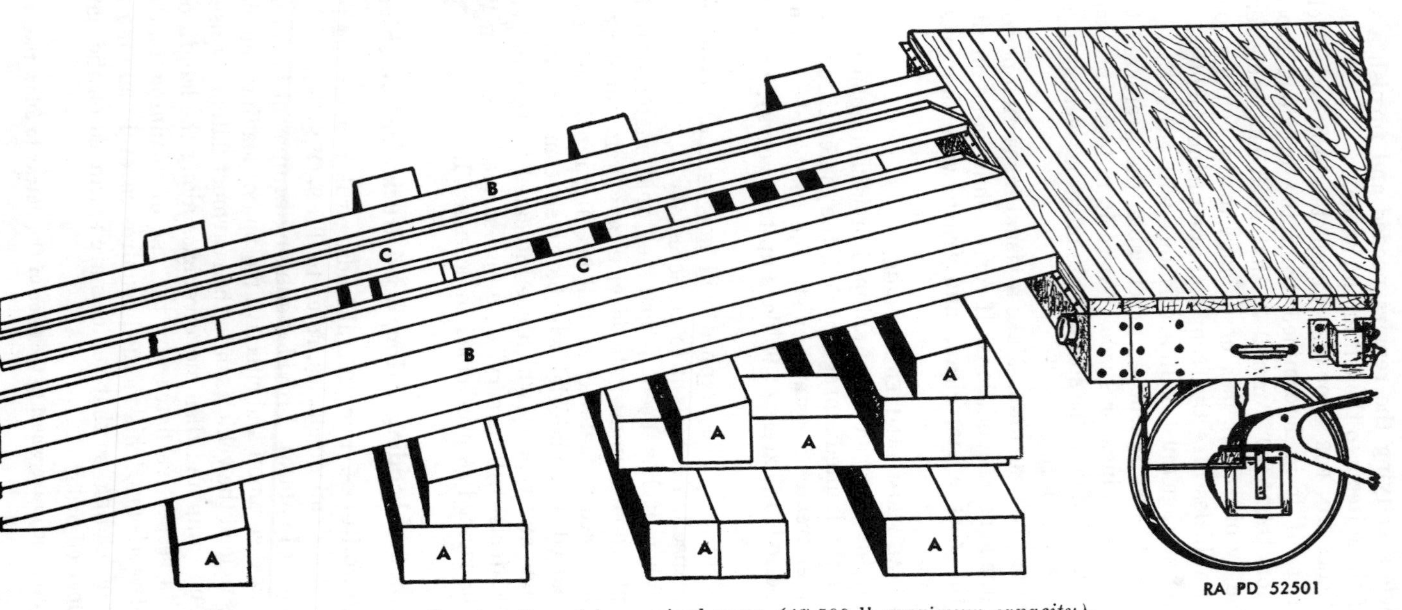

Figure 103. Construction of improvised ramp (17,500 lb maximum capacity).

(1) *Runways.* Level the road bed at the loading end of the rearmost flatcar to the top of rails, using 6- x 8-inch timbers. When such timbers are not available, use dirt and cinders to make a level approach or runway.

(2) *Ramps.* Use permanent ramps for loading the vehicles when available. When such ramps are not available, use improvised ramps (17,500 lb maximum capacity), constructed of railroad ties and other available lumber.

Note. Unless it is certain that the destination of the vehicles will provide unloading facilities, the improvised ramps must be shipped with the vehicles.

(*a*) *Railroad ties "A" (fourteen ties required.)* Bevel the four ties on which the runner boards "B" rest so that the boards are not resting on the edges of the ties. Locate the ties across the tracks as shown in figure 103. Secure the lower ties with stakes when positioned on a dirt runway or with nails when positioned on a timber runway.

(*b*) *Runner boards "B" (six 3-in. x 10-in. x 16-ft. boards required).* Bevel both ends of boards to permit ease in loading. Locate across the beveled ties "A" as shown in figure 103. Three boards will constitute each runner (30-in. width). Space the two runners approximately 36 inches apart. Nail all boards to railroad ties "A."

(*c*) *Guide boards ."C" (two 1-in. x 6-in. x 16-ft. boards required).* Nail the guide boards on the inner side of each runner to guide vehicles during loading.

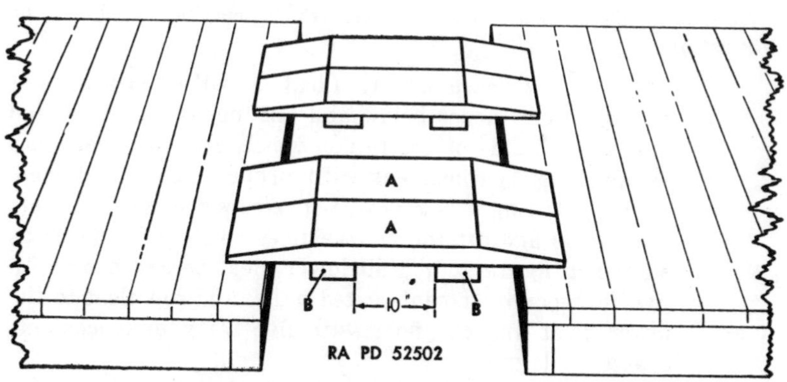

Figure 104. Construction of spanning platforms (17,500 lb maximum capacity).

(3) *Spanning platforms.* Use two spanning platforms between cars to move vehicles along the length of the train. The distance between the two platforms will be governed by the width of vehicle to be moved. Construct spanning platforms (17,500 lb maximum capacity) as illustrated in figure 104.

(*a*) *Spanner boards "A" (two 3- x 12- x 48-in. boards required).* Bevel each end of boards as shown in figure 104. Nail to cleats "B" as prescribed in (*b*) below.

(*b*) *Spanner cleats "B" (two 2- x 6- x 30-in. cleats required).* Nail cleats to boards "A" approximately 10 inches apart.

183. Method of Blocking ¼-Ton, 4 x 4 Trucks for Complete Troop Train Movement

a. General. All blocking instructions specified herein are minimum and are in accordance with Special Supplement No. 1 of the Association of American Railroads "Rules Governing the Loading of Commodities on Open Top Cars Transported in Complete Troop Trains, Accompanied By, and Under Direct Supervision of Military Personnel." Additional blocking as required, may be added at the discretion of the officer in charge.

Note. Any loading methods or instructions developed by any source, which appear in conflict with this publication or existing loading rules of the carriers, must be submitted to the Chief of Ordnance, Washington 25, D. C.

b. Method of Securing Vehicles Crosswise on Flatcars. After vehicles are positioned on flatcar, apply brakes and place the transmission gear shift lever in the neutral position. All item reference letters given below refer to the details and location in figure 105.

Note. With this method of loading, seven vehicles may be loaded on a 40-foot flatcar.

(1) *Brake wheel clearance "A."* Load car with a clearance of at least four inches below and six inches above, behind and to each side of the brake wheel. Increase clearance as much as is consistent with proper location of load.

(2) *Cleats "B" (eight 2- x 4- x 18-in. cleats required).* Locate two cleats against the end vehicles two outer wheels as shown in figure 105. Nail lower cleat to car floor with five fortypenny cement-coated nails, and top cleat to the lower cleat and car floor with five fortypenny cement-coated nails.

(3) *Cleats "C" (eight 2- x 4- x 12-in. cleats required).* Locate two cleats, lengthwise of car, against the center of cleats

"B." Nail lower cleat to car floor with three fortypenny cement-coated nails and top cleat to the lower cleat and car floor with three fortypenny cement-coated nails.

(4) *Cleats "D" (twenty-four 2- x 4- x 12-in. cleats required).* Locate two cleats, crosswise of car, between and against the front and rear wheels of adjoining units. Nail lower cleat to car floor with three fortypenny cement-coated nails and top cleat to the lower cleat and car floor with three fortypenny cement-coated nails.

(5) *Cleats "E" (eight 2- x 4- x 18-in. cleats required).* Nail cleats to car floor before vehicles are placed on car. Locate two cleats, lengthwise of car, against the end vehicle's two outer wheels as shown in figure 105. Nail lower cleat to car floor with three fortypenny cement-coated nails and top cleat to the lower cleat and car floor with three fortypenny cement-coated nails.

(6) *Cleats "F" (twenty-four 2- x 4- x 36-in. cleats required).* Nail to car floor before vehicles are placed on car. Locate two cleats against the inside tread of each pair of wheels on adjoining vehicles. Nail lower cleat to car floor with five fortypenny cement-coated nails and top cleat to the lower cleat and car floor with five fortypenny cement-coated nails.

(7) *Strapping "G" (four wires each consisting of four strands, No. 8 gage, black annealed wire, or wires of equivalent strength, required for each unit).* Attach wires to the four corners of each unit and to stake pockets. After truck springs have been compressed as much as possible, bring both ends of wire together and twist taut with rod or bolt just enough to take up slack.

c. METHOD OF SECURING VEHICLES LENGTHWISE ON FLATCARS. After vehicles are positioned on flatcar, apply brakes and place the transmission gear shift lever in the neutral position. All item reference letters given below refer to the details and location in figures 106 and 108.

Note. Units must be loaded so that distance between center line of car and outer edge of units is equal.

(1) *For car floors 10 feet wide or more.* With this method of loading, eight vehicles may be loaded on a 50-foot flatcar.

(*a*) *Brake wheel clearance "A."* See *b* (1) above.

(*b*) *Chock blocks "B" (forty-eight 6- x 9- x 12-in. blocks required).* Locate the 53-degree portion of blocks against the front and rear of outer wheels, against the front of inner front wheels, and in back of the inside rear wheels. Nail heel of blocks to car floor with three

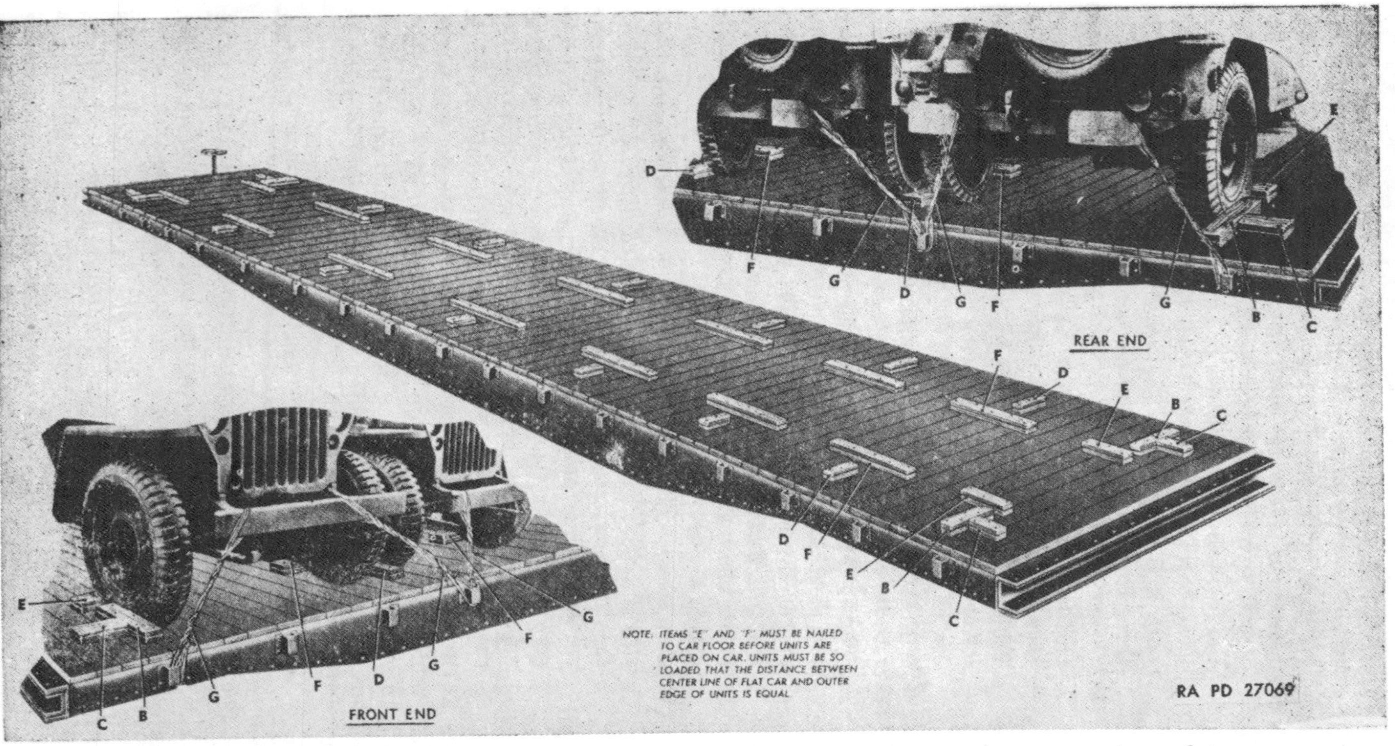
REAR END
FRONT END
NOTE: ITEMS "E" AND "F" MUST BE NAILED TO CAR FLOOR BEFORE UNITS ARE PLACED ON CAR. UNITS MUST BE SO LOADED THAT THE DISTANCE BETWEEN CENTER LINE OF FLAT CAR AND OUTER EDGE OF UNITS IS EQUAL
RA PD 27069

Figure 105. Method of securing ¼-ton 4 x 4 trucks for complete troop train movements—crosswise on flatcars.

fortypenny cement-coated nails. Toenail one side of blocks to car floor with two fortypenny cement-coated nails, (see figs. 106 and 108).

(c) *Chock blocks "C" (thirty-two 6- x 9- x 12-in. blocks required).* Locate blocks with 9-inch surface against the inside of each wheel. Nail heel of blocks to car floor with three fortypenny cement-coated nails. Toenail one side of blocks to car floor with one fortypenny cement-coated nail (see figs. 106 and 108).

(d) *Strapping "D" (two wires, each consisting of six strands, No. 8 gage, black annealed wire, or wires of equivalent strength, required for each vehicle).* Pass wires around each front bumper and cleat "E". Pass wires through each pintle and around cleat "E". After cleats "E" have been secured and truck springs compressed as much as possible, bring both ends of wires together and twist taut with rod or bolt just enough to take up slack.

(e) *Cleats "E" (sixteen 2- x 4- x 12-in. cleats required).* Locate one cleat under center of front bumper and one cleat under rear pintle. Position strapping "D" and nail each cleat to car floor with four thirtypenny cement-coated nails.

(2) *For car floors less than 9 feet 4 inches wide.* With this method of loading, eight vehicles may be loaded on a 50-foot flatcar.

(a) *Blocks "F" (sixteen 4- x 6-in. blocks required, cut length to extend beyond outer tires of units loaded side by side).* Bevel the inside edge of block (approximately 2 inches) where it contacts tires. Locate against front and rear of tires. Toenail to floor with four thirtypenny cement-coated nails.

(b) *Cleats "G" (one hundred twenty-eight 2- x 4- x 18-in. cleats required).* Locate one cleat assembly consisting of two cleats near each end and two assemblies near center of blocks "F". Nail lower cleats to car floor, lengthwise of car, with four thirtypenny cement-coated nails, and top cleats to the lower cleats with four twentypenny cement-coated nails.

(c) *Cleats "H" (sixteen 2- x 4-in. cleats required, cut length to extend 1 in. beyond outside face of blocks "F").* Locate 2-inch edge against edge of car floor, under blocks "F". Secure each end to blocks "F" with ½ inch diameter bolt, nuts and washers. Multiple length pieces may be used provided they protect two or more

Figure 106. Method of securing ¼-ton 4 x 4 trucks for complete troop train movements—lengthwise on flatcars

complete units and are secured to each block "F" throughout their length.

(*d*) *Cleats "J" (thirty-two 2- x 4-in. cleats required, cut length to extend to outside face of blocks "F").* Locate against inside face of each wheel on top of blocks "F". Nail to blocks "F" with three thirtypenny cement-coated nails at each location.

(*e*) *Strapping "K."* Strap units as prescribed in (1) (*d*) above.

(*f*) *Cleats "L."* Secure as prescribed in (1) (*e*) above.

184. Method of Blocking ¼-Ton 4 x 4 Trucks for Regular Freight Train Service

a. GENERAL.

(1) All blocking instructions specified herein are minimum and are in accordance with Special Supplement No. 2 of the Association of American Railroads "Rules Governing the Loading of Commodities on Open Top Cars *Not* Transported in Complete Trains, Accompanied By and Under Direct Supervision of Military Personnel". Additional blocking as required may be added at the discretion of the officer in charge. (See note, par. 183 *a.*)

(2) After vehicles are positioned on flatcar, apply brakes and place the transmission gear shift lever in the neutral position. All item reference letters given below refer to the details and location in figure 107.

Note. With this method of loading, eight vehicles may be loaded on a 10- by 50-foot flatcar.

b. PREFERRED METHOD.

(1) *Brake wheel clearance "A."* See paragraph 183 *b* (1).

(2) *Chock blocks "B" (sixty-four 6- x 9- x 12-in. blocks required).* Locate the 53-degree portion of blocks against front and rear of wheels. Nail heel of blocks to car floor with three fortypenny cement-coated nails. Toenail one side of blocks to car floor with two fortypenny cement-coated nails. See figures 107 and 108.

(3) *Inside wheel blocking "C" (thirty-two 6- x 9- x 12-in. blocks required).* Locate 9-inch face against inside of each wheel. Nail heel of block to car floor with three fortypenny cement-coated nails and toenail at side, to car floor with one fortypenny cement-coated nail. See figures 107 and 108.

(4) *Strapping "E" (sixteen straps required)*. Locate one 1-inch, No. 14 B. W. gage, hot rolled steel banding wire over front bumper and through rear pintle, and secure to car floor with anchor plates (fig. 108). Nail anchor plate to car floor with eight twentypenny cement-coated nails. See figures 107 and 108.

c. ALTERNATE METHODS.

(1) *Chock blocks "B–1" (sixty-four blocks required)*. Chock blocks "B–1" may be substituted at each location for chock blocks "B". Nail each block to car floor, at rear of support brace, with three thirtypenny cement-coated nails and toenail at front of support brace to car floor with two fortypenny cement-coated nails, one on each side. See figures 107 and 108.

(2) *Chock blocks "B–2" (sixty-four blocks required)*. Chock blocks "B–2" may be substituted at each location for chock blocks "B". Nail the rear of each block to car floor with four twentypenny cement-coated nails. See figures 107 and 108.

(3) *Inside wheel blocking "C–1" (sixty-four 2- x 4- x 18-in. blocks required)*. L shaped assemblies (consisting of two pieces) may be substituted for each block "C". Nail the face of one cleat "C–1" to the edge of the other cleat "C–1" with four twentypenny cement-coated nails. Nail to car floor with four thirtypenny cement-coated nails after cushioning material "D" is applied.

(4) *Cushioning material "D" (thirty-two pieces required for "C–1" blocks only)*. Place suitable cushioning material, such as waterproof paper, burlap, etc., between tires and blocks "C–1". The bottom edge of material must be under blocking "C–1" and the top portion of material must extend 2 inches above blocking.

(5) *Strapping "E–1."* One wire (consisting of four strands, No. 8 gage, black annealed wire, or wires of equivalent strength) may be substituted for steel banding "E". Pass one over front bumper and one through rear pintle and around cleats "F". After cleats "F" have been nailed to car floor, bring both ends of wires together and twist taut with rod or bolt just enough to take up slack.

(6) *Cleats "F" (sixteen 2- x 4- x 18-in. cleats required)*. Locate one under front bumper at center of unit and one under rear pintle. Position strapping "E–1" and nail each cleat to car floor with four thirtypenny cement-coated nails.

Figure 107. Method of securing ¼-ton 4 x 4 trucks for regular freight train service—lengthwise on flatcars.

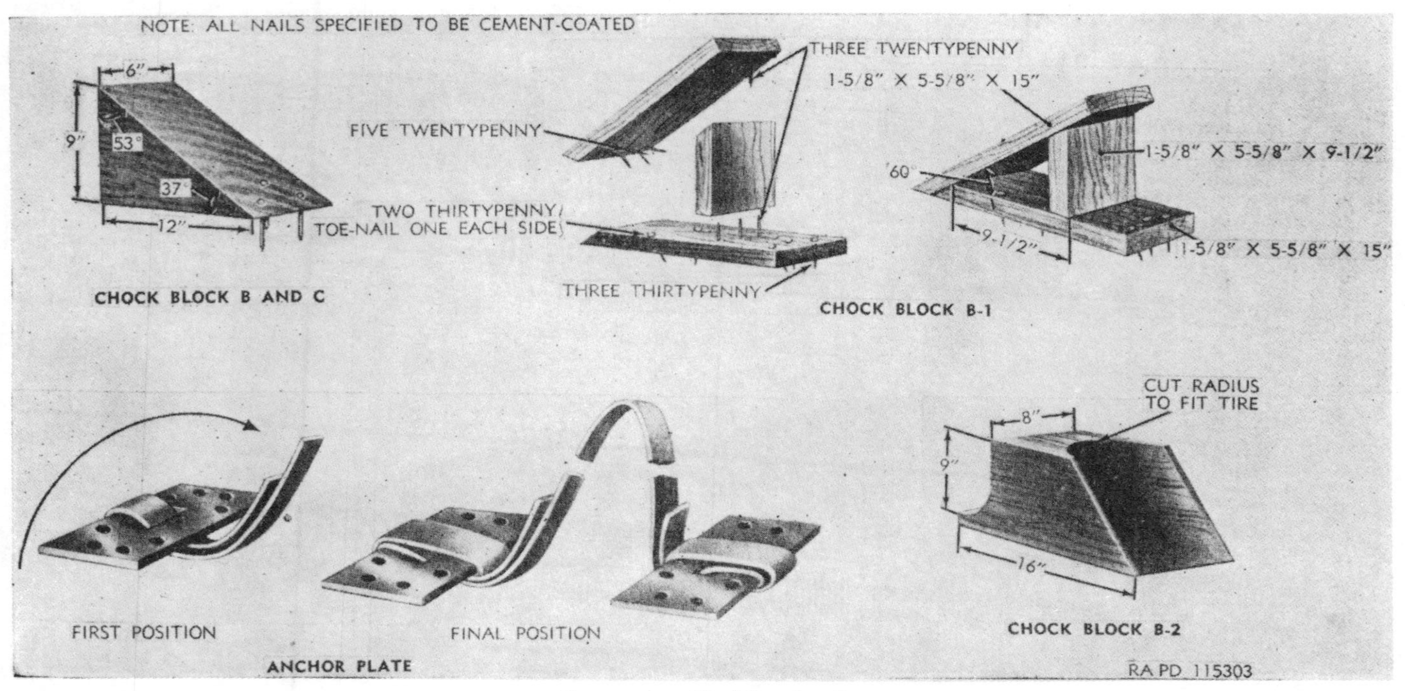
NOTE: ALL NAILS SPECIFIED TO BE CEMENT-COATED
6"
9"
53°
37°
12"
CHOCK BLOCK B AND C
FIVE TWENTYPENNY
TWO THIRTYPENNY
TOE-NAIL ONE EACH SIDE
THREE TWENTYPENNY
1-5/8" X 5-5/8" X 15"
THREE THIRTYPENNY
60°
9-1/2"
1-5/8" X 5-5/8" X 9-1/2"
1-5/8" X 5-5/8" X 15"
CHOCK BLOCK B-1
FIRST POSITION
FINAL POSITION
ANCHOR PLATE
CUT RADIUS
TO FIT TIRE
8"
9"
16"
CHOCK BLOCK B-2
RA PD 115303

Figure 108. Blocking details.

Section XXXIII. (Added) DEMOLITION TO PREVENT ENEMY USE

185. General

The demolition procedures outlined in paragraphs 186 through 188 will be used to prevent the enemy from using or salvaging this equipment. Destroy or damage beyond repair *all* parts essential to the operation of the vehicle, including essential spare parts. Select a point of destruction that will cause greatest obstruction to enemy movement and also prevent hazard to friendly troops from fragments or ricocheting projectiles. Observe appropriate safety precautions.

186. Methods of Destruction

a. Smash. Use sledges, axes, handaxes, pickaxes, hammers, crowbars, and heavy tools.

b. Cut. Use axes, handaxes, and machetes.

c. Burn. Use gasoline, kerosene, oil, flame throwers, and incendiary grenades.

d. Explosives. Use firearms, grenades, and TNT.

e. Other. Use anything immediately available for destruction of this equipment.

f. Disposal. Bury in slit trenches, fox holes, and other holes. Throw in streams. Scatter.

187. Destruction of Vehicle

a. General. Three methods of destroying the vehicle are outlined below in their order of effectiveness. Whichever method is used, the sequence outlined will be followed to assure uniformity of destruction among a group of similar vehicles.

b. Method No. 1.

(1) Remove and empty portable fire extinguishers. Puncture fuel tanks.

(2) Using an ax, pick, sledge or any other heavy object, smash all vital elements, such as distributor, carburetor, air cleaner, generator, ignition coil, fuel pump, spark plugs, lights, instruments, and controls. If time permits, and a sufficiently heavy object is available, smash the engine cylinder block and head, crankcase, transmission, and axles. Slash and destroy tires.

(3) Pour gasoline or oil over entire vehicle and ignite.

c. Method No. 2.

(1) Remove and empty portable fire extinguisher. Puncture fuel tanks.

(2) Fire on the vehicle using gun motor carriages, tanks, artillery or antitank rockets or grenades. Aim at the engine compartment, axles, and wheels. If a good fire is started, the vehicle may be considered destroyed.

(3) Destroy the last remaining vehicle by the best means available.

d. Method No. 3.

(1) Remove and empty portable fire extinguishers. Puncture fuel tanks.

(2) Prepare two 4-block charges of ½-pound blocks of TNT or equivalent explosive, with a nonelectric blasting cap and about 6 feet of safety fuse for each 2-pound charge. Place one charge on top of the clutch housing and one as low as possible on the left side of the engine.

***Caution:* If charges are prepared beforehand and carried in the vehicle, keep the blasting caps and safety fuses separated from the TNT charges until they are to be used.**

(3) Ignite the TNT charges and take cover. The danger zone is approximately 200 yards. The fuse will burn approximately 3½ minutes.

188. Destruction of Tires

a. An attempt to destroy pneumatic tires, including the spare, must always be made even if time will not permit destruction of any other part of the vehicle.

b. Tires can be destroyed by incendiary grenades. Ignite one grenade under each tire. When this method is combined with the destruction of the vehicle by TNT, the incendiary fires must be well started before the TNT is detonated.

c. Tires may be damaged with an ax, pick, or by heavy machine gun fire; they should be deflated first, if possible. Gasoline may be poured on the tires and then ignited.

REFERENCES
(Superseded)

1. Publication Indexes

The following publication indexes and lists of current issue should be consulted frequently for latest changes or revisions of the references given herein and for new publications relating to matériel covered in this manual:

a. Index of administrative publications.........SR 310–20–5.
b. Index of blank forms and Army personnel classification tests ....SR 310–20–6.
c. Introduction and index...........................ORD 1.
d. Ordnance major items and combinations, and pertinent publications........................SB 9–1.
e. List and index of Department of the Army publications ....FM 21–6.
f. List of Department of the Army films, film strips, and recognition film slides......................FM 21–7.

2. Supply Catalogs

The following Department of the Army Supply Catalogs pertain to this matériel:

a. MAINTENANCE.
Cleaners, preservatives, lubricants, recoil fluids, special oils, and related maintenance materials ....ORD 3 SNL K–1.
Items of soldering, metallizing, brazing and welding materials; gases and related items ....ORD 3 SNL K–2.
Lubricating equipment, accessories and related dispensers ....ORD (*) SNL K–3.
Ordnance maintenance sets ....ORD 6 SNL N–21.
Tool-sets (common), specialists' and organizational ....ORD 6 SNL G–27, Sec. 2.
Tool-sets (special), motor vehicles ....ORD 6 SNL G–27, Sec. 1.

b. VEHICLE AND EQUIPMENT.
Gun, machine, cal. .30, Browning, M1919A4, fixed and flexible; M1919A5, fixed; and M1919A6; and ground mounts ....ORD (*) SNL A–6.

*See ORD 1, Introduction and Index, for published catalogs of the Ordnance Section of the Department of the Army Supply Catalog.

Gun, machine, cal. .50, Browning, M2,
heavy barrel, fixed and flexible; and
ground mounts ....ORD (*) SNL A–39.

Mount, machine gun, cal. .30,
M48 ....ORD (*) SNL A–55, Sec. 32.

Mount, truck pedestal, M31
and M31C ....ORD (*) SNL A–55, Sec. 18.

Rifle, automatic, cal. .30, Browning,
M1918A2 ....ORD (*) SNL A–4.

Rifle, cal. .30, U. S. M1, M1C, and
M1D ....ORD (*) SNL B–21.

Truck, ¼-ton, 4 x 4 (Ford model GPW
and Willys model MB)..........ORD (*) SNL G–503.

3. Other Publications

The following publications contain information pertinent to this matériel:

a. AMMUNITION.

Ammunition, general ....TM 9–1900.

Small arms ammunition........................TM 9–1990.

b. ARMAMENT.

Browning automatic rifle, cal. .30, M1918A2....FM 23–15.

Browning machine gun, cal. .30, M1917A1,
M1919A4, and M1919A6...................FM 23–55.

Browning machine gun, cal. .50, HB, M2
(mounted in combat vehicles)...............FM 23–65.

Machine gun mounts for trucks...............TM 9–224.

U. S. rifle, cal. .30, M1.........................FM 23–5.

c. CHEMICAL WARFARE.

Decontamination ....TM 3–220.

Decontamination of armored force vehicle......FM 17–59.

Defense against chemical attack...............FM 21–40.

Military chemistry and chemical agents........TM 3–215.

d. FUNDAMENTAL PRINCIPLES.

Automotive electricity ....TM 10–580.

Auxiliary sighting and fire control instruments..TM 9–575.

Principles of automotive vehicles.............TM 9–2700.

e. MAINTENANCE AND REPAIR.

Basic maintenance manual....................TM 38–650.

Cleaning, preserving, sealing and related
materials issued for ordnance matériel.......TM 9–850.

Installation of radio equipment in truck,
¼-ton, 4 x 4............................TM 11-2715.

*See ORD 1, Introduction and Index, for published catalogs of the Ordnance Section of the Department of the Army Supply Catalog.

Instruction Guide: Care and maintenance of ball and roller bearings....................TM 37-265.
Maintenance and care of pneumatic tires and rubber treads ....TM 31-200.
Motor vehicle inspection and preventive maintenance services ....TM 37-2810.
Painting instructions for field use.............TM 9-2851.
Supplies and equipment, motor vehicles.......AR 700-105.

f. MISCELLANEOUS.
Camouflage, basic principles...................FM 5-20.
Dictionary of United States Army terms.......TM 20-205.
Distribution and supply of publications and blank forms........................SR 310-90-1.

g. STORAGE AND SHIPMENT.
Instruction Guide: Ordnance packaging and shipping (posts, camps, and stations).......TM 9-2854.
Ordnance storage and shipment chart—Group C—Major items.................TB 9-OSSC-G.

[AG 300.7 (15 Feb 49)]

BY ORDER OF THE SECRETARY OF THE ARMY:

J. LAWTON COLLINS
Chief of Staff, United States Army

OFFICIAL:
EDWARD F. WITSELL
Major General, USA
The Adjutant General

DISTRIBUTION:

Tech Sv (2) except 9 (50); Arm & Sv Bd (2); AFF (2); OS Maj Comd (10); Base Comd (2); MDW (3); A (20); CHQ (2); D (2); B 5, 7, 44 (1); R 2, 5-8, (1), 9 (2), 10, 11, 17, 19, 55 (1); Sep Bn 2, 3, 5-8, 10, 11, 17, 19, 44, 55 (1); Bn 9 (2); Sep C 2, 3, 5-8, 10, 11, 17, 19, 44, 55 (1); C 9 (2); FC (1); Sch (5) except 9 (50); Gen Dep (1); Dep 9 (3); PE (Ord O) (5), OSD (1); PG 9 (3); Ars 9 (3); Dist 9 (3); SPECIAL DISTRIBUTION.

For explanation of distribution formula see SR 310-90-1.

U.S. GOVERNMENT PRINTING OFFICE: 1950—881712

TM 9-1803A

WAR DEPARTMENT TECHNICAL MANUAL

ORDNANCE MAINTENANCE

Engine and Engine Accessories For 1/4-Ton 4x4 Truck

(Willys-Overland Model MB and Ford Model GPW)

WAR DEPARTMENT • 24 FEBRUARY 1944

WAR DEPARTMENT TECHNICAL MANUAL

TM 9-1803A

ORDNANCE MAINTENANCE

Engine and Engine Accessories For $^1/_4$-Ton 4x4 Truck

(Willys-Overland Model MB and Ford Model GPW)

WAR DEPARTMENT • *24 FEBRUARY 1944*

WAR DEPARTMENT
Washington 25, D. C., 24 February 1944

TM 9-1803A, Ordnance Maintenance: Engine and Engine Accessories for 1/4-ton 4 x 4 Truck (Willys-Overland model MB and Ford model GPW), is published for the information and guidance of all concerned.

[A.G. 300.7 (9 Oct 43)
O.O.M. 461 Rar. Ars. (2-25-44)]

BY ORDER OF THE SECRETARY OF WAR:

G. C. MARSHALL,
Chief of Staff.

OFFICIAL:
J. A. ULIO,
Major General,
The Adjutant General.

DISTRIBUTION: R 9 (4); Bn 9 (2); C 9 (5).

(For explanation of symbols, see FM 21-6.)

CONTENTS

★ For supersession of Quartermaster Corps 10-series Technical Manuals, see paragraph 1 j.

ORDNANCE MAINTENANCE — ENGINE AND ENGINE ACCESSORIES FOR ¼-TON 4x4 TRUCK (WILLYS-OVERLAND MODEL MB AND FORD MODEL GPW)

CHAPTER 1

INTRODUCTION

1. SCOPE.

a. The instructions contained in this manual are for the information and guidance of personnel charged with the maintenance and repair of the 4-cylinder engine used in the Willys MB and Ford GPW ¼-ton 4 x 4 Trucks. These instructions are supplementary to field and technical manuals prepared for the using arms. This manual does not contain information which is intended primarily for the using arms, since such information is available to ordnance maintenance personnel in 100-series TM's or FM's.

b. This manual contains a description of, and procedure for inspection, removal, disassembly, repair, and rebuilding of the engine.

c. TM 9-803 contains information and guidance for the using arms and first and second echelons.

d. TM 9-1803B contains information for removal, inspection, repair, rebuild, assembly, and installation of the power train and chassis.

e. TM 9-1825B contains information for the maintenance of the Auto-Lite electrical equipment used on this vehicle.

f. TM 9-1826A contains information for the maintenance of the Carter carburetor used on this vehicle.

g. TM 9-1827C contains information for the maintenance of the Wagner hydraulic brake system used on this vehicle.

h. TM 9-1828A contains information for the maintenance of the A. C. fuel pump used on this vehicle.

i. TM 9-1829A contains information for the maintenance of the speedometer used on this vehicle.

j. This manual includes engine ordnance maintenance instructions from the following Quartermaster Corps 10-series technical manuals. Together with TM 9-803 and TM 9-1803B, this manual supersedes them:

(1) TM 10-1103, 20 August 1941.

(2) TM 10-1207, 20 August 1941.

(3) TM 10-1349, 3 January 1942.

(4) TM 10-1513, Change 1, 15 January 1943.

INTRODUCTION

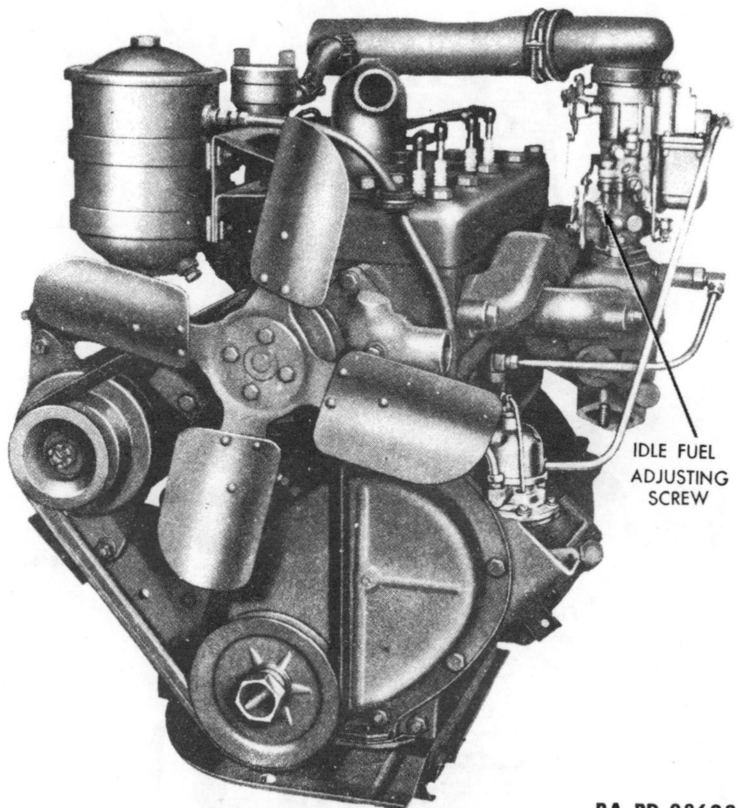

Figure 1 — Front View of Engine

2. MWO AND MAJOR UNIT ASSEMBLY REPLACEMENT RECORD.

a. **Description.** Every vehicle is supplied with a copy of AGO Form No. 478 which provides a means of keeping a record of each MWO (FSMWO) completed or major unit assembly replaced. This form includes spaces for the vehicle name and U.S.A. registration number, instructions for use, and information pertinent to the work accomplished. It is very important that the form be used as directed, and that it remain with the vehicle until the vehicle is removed from service.

b. **Instructions for Use.** Personnel performing modifications or major unit assembly replacements, must record clearly on the form a

RA PD 28665

Figure 2 — Left Side View of Engine

RA PD 28664

Figure 3 — Right Side View of Engine

description of the work completed, and must initial the form in the columns provided. When each modification is completed, record the date, hours and/or mileage, and MWO number. When major unit assemblies, such as engines, transmissions, transfer cases, are replaced, record the date, hours and/or mileage, and nomenclature of the unit assembly. Minor repairs and minor parts and accessory replacements need not be recorded.

c. **Early Modifications.** Upon receipt by a third or fourth echelon repair facility of a vehicle for modification or repair, maintenance personnel will record the MWO numbers of modifications applied prior to the date of AGO Form No. 478.

ORDNANCE MAINTENANCE – ENGINE AND ENGINE ACCESSORIES FOR ¼-TON 4x4 TRUCK (WILLYS-OVERLAND MODEL MB AND FORD MODEL GPW)

CHAPTER 2

ENGINE

Section I

DESCRIPTION AND DATA

3. DESCRIPTION.

a. The engine used in the ¼-ton 4 x 4 Truck is the 4-cylinder, L-head, gasoline-type (figs. 1, 2, and 3), equipped with a counter-balanced crankshaft. The camshaft is operated off the crankshaft through a timing chain (fig. 40). The oil pump and distributor operate off the camshaft.

4. DATA.

Type	L-head
Numbers of cylinders	4
Bore and stroke	3.125 x 4.375 in.
Piston displacement	134.2 cu in.
Compression ratio	6.48 to 1
Max. brake horsepower	54 at 4,000
Compression (lb per sq in. at 185 rpm)	111
SAE horsepower	15.63
Maximum torque	105 ft-lb at 2,000 rpm
Firing order	1-3-4-2

Section II

ENGINE REMOVAL FROM VEHICLE

5. REMOVAL FROM VEHICLE.

a. General. Unhook the two nood clamps, raise the hood, and lay it against the windshield. Drain the coolant from the radiator and the engine by opening the radiator drain cock and the drain cock

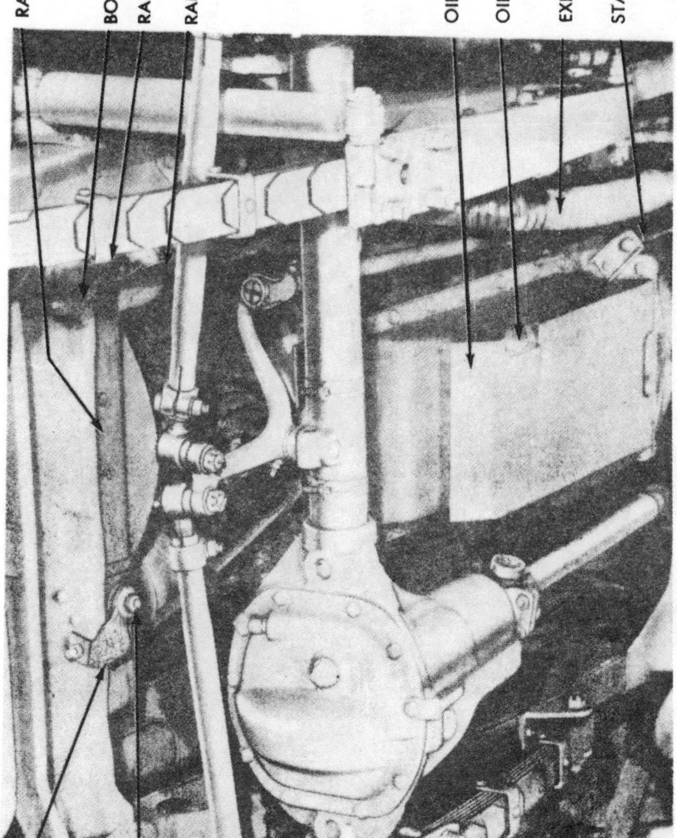

RA PD 28748

Figure 4 — Underside View of Engine Installed in Vehicle

Figure 5 — Right Side View of Engine Installed in Vehicle

Figure 6 — Side View of Engine Compartment

located on the right-hand side of the engine. Remove the oil pan drain plug and drain the engine oil. Some variation exists in the location of the various bond straps used to eliminate radio interference on these vehicles. Disregard references to bond straps in the following instructions if they are not present on the particular vehicle being worked on. If bond straps are found in locations other than those mentioned in the following procedure, they should be disconnected, if they prevent removal of the engine.

b. **Remove Battery.** Loosen the two battery cable bolts, and disconnect both cables. Loosen the battery brace wing nut on the fender. Remove the two battery hold-down frame wing nuts (fig. 5). Move the battery brace to one side, and remove the battery hold-down frame. Lift the battery from the vehicle.

c. **Remove Radiator.** Remove the nut and lock washer from the front and rear of the radiator brace, and remove the brace. Loosen the two front outlet radiator hose clamps, and slide the hose back on the metal tubing. Loosen the rear radiator outlet hose clamp, and remove the hose. Loosen the radiator hose clamps on the inlet hose at the water pump, also the one on the radiator and remove the radiator inlet hose. Working from underneath the vehicle, remove the two nuts, flat washers, and bond straps from the radiator bolts (fig. 4). Remove the two nuts and flat washers from the radiator bolts. Lift the radiator from the vehicle and remove the two radiator pads.

d. **Disconnect Oil and Water Temperature Gages.** Disconnect the oil gage line at the flexible oil line, located at the left-hand side of the engine. Disconnect the water temperature gage (engine unit) at the right-hand side of the cylinder head (fig. 5).

e. **Remove Air Cleaner Hose** (fig. 6). Loosen the hose clamps on the carburetor air cleaner and oil filler pipe, and remove the air cleaner hose.

f. **Disconnect Electrical Wires and Bond Straps.** Disconnect the field, armature, and ground wires at the generator. Disconnect the primary wire running from the dash to the coil, at the coil. Disconnect the bond strap at the rear of the cylinder head. Disconnect the ground strap at each front engine support. Disconnect the cranking motor cable at the cranking motor.

g. **Remove Cranking Motor.** Remove the cap screw that holds the cranking motor bracket to the cylinder block. Remove the two cap screws that hold the cranking motor to the clutch housing, and slip the cranking motor from the engine.

RA PD 28817

Figure 7 — Lifting Engine from Vehicle

h. Disconnect Choke and Throttle Controls. Remove the nut and bolt on the choke and throttle hold-down bracket. Loosen the set screw on the carburetor choke lever, and remove the choke control cable. Loosen the set screw on the throttle control cable and remove the throttle control cable. Disconnect the throttle control at the accelerator pedal in the driver's compartment.

i. Disconnect Exhaust Pipe. Remove the nut, bolt, and cap screw that hold the exhaust pipe to the exhaust manifold. Pry the exhaust pipe from the exhaust manifold.

j. Disconnect Front Engine Supports. Remove the two nuts and bolts from each front engine support.

k. Remove Stay Cable and Clutch Housing Bolts. Remove the two engine stay cable nuts at the front crossmember, and remove the stay cable (fig. 4). Remove the 10 cap screws and bolts from the clutch housing.

l. Remove Engine From Vehicle. Install a suitable lifting sling or rope on the engine (fig. 7). Raise the engine high enough to release the weight on the front engine supports. Pull the engine forward until it is free from the clutch housing, and lift the engine from the vehicle (fig. 7).

Section III

DISASSEMBLY OF ENGINE INTO SUBASSEMBLIES

6. PRELIMINARY OPERATIONS.

a. General. If the clutch housing was removed with the engine, start the procedure beginning with subparagraph **b** below. If the clutch housing was not removed with the engine, remove the cranking motor (par. 5 **g**), remove the rest of the clutch housing bolts or cap screws, and remove the clutch housing from the engine.

b. Remove Carburetor (fig. 6). Remove the fuel line connecting the carburetor and fuel pump. Remove the accelerator return spring from the careburetor and accelerator lever. Remove the two carburetor hold-down nuts, lock washers, and accelerator return spring clip.

c. Remove Fuel Pump (fig. 6). Disconnect the other fuel line at the fuel pump. Remove the two cap screws and lock washers that hold the fuel pump to the cylinder block, and remove the fuel pump.

d. Remove Distributor (fig. 5). Pull the spark wires off the spark plugs, and slide the wires out of the air filter tube bracket. Remove the primary and secondary wires from the ignition coil. Remove the distributor hold-down screw, and lift the distributor and wires from the cylinder block.

e. Remove Oil Filter (fig. 5). Disconnect the inlet oil line on the left-hand side of the cylinder block, and the outlet oil line on the engine front cover. Remove the cap screw that holds the oil filler pipe to the oil filter bracket. Remove the three cylinder head nuts

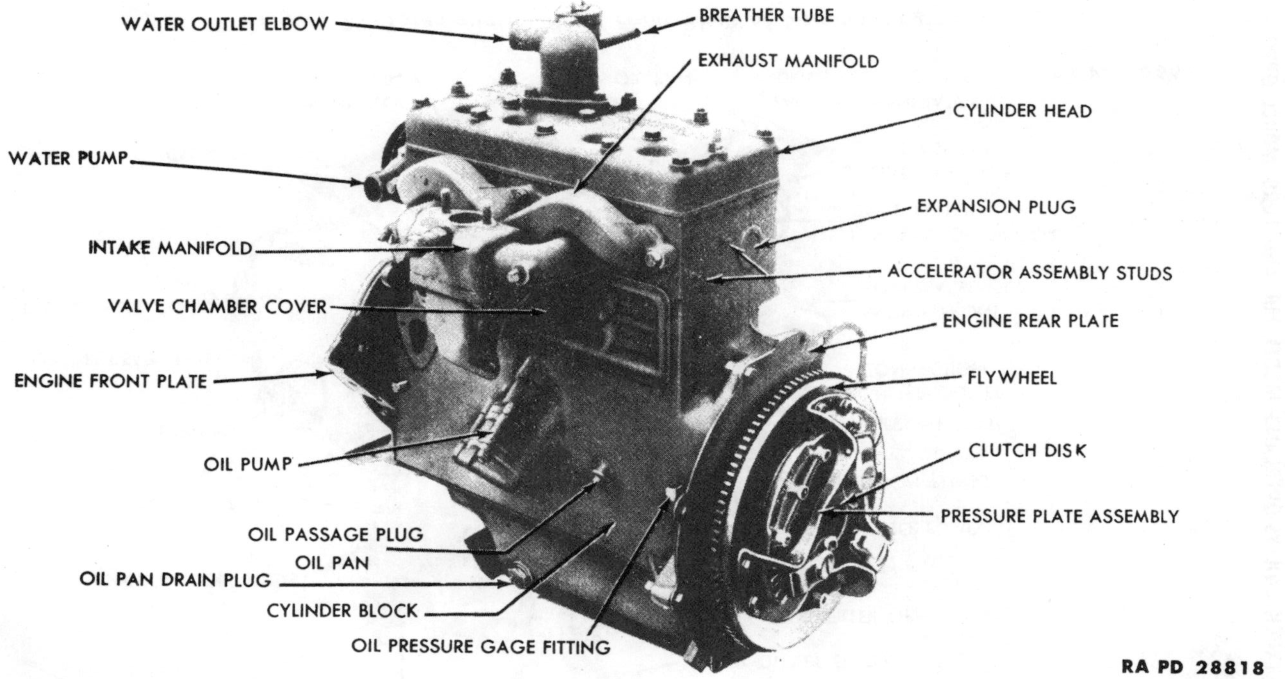

Figure 8 — Three-quarter Left Rear View of Stripped Engine

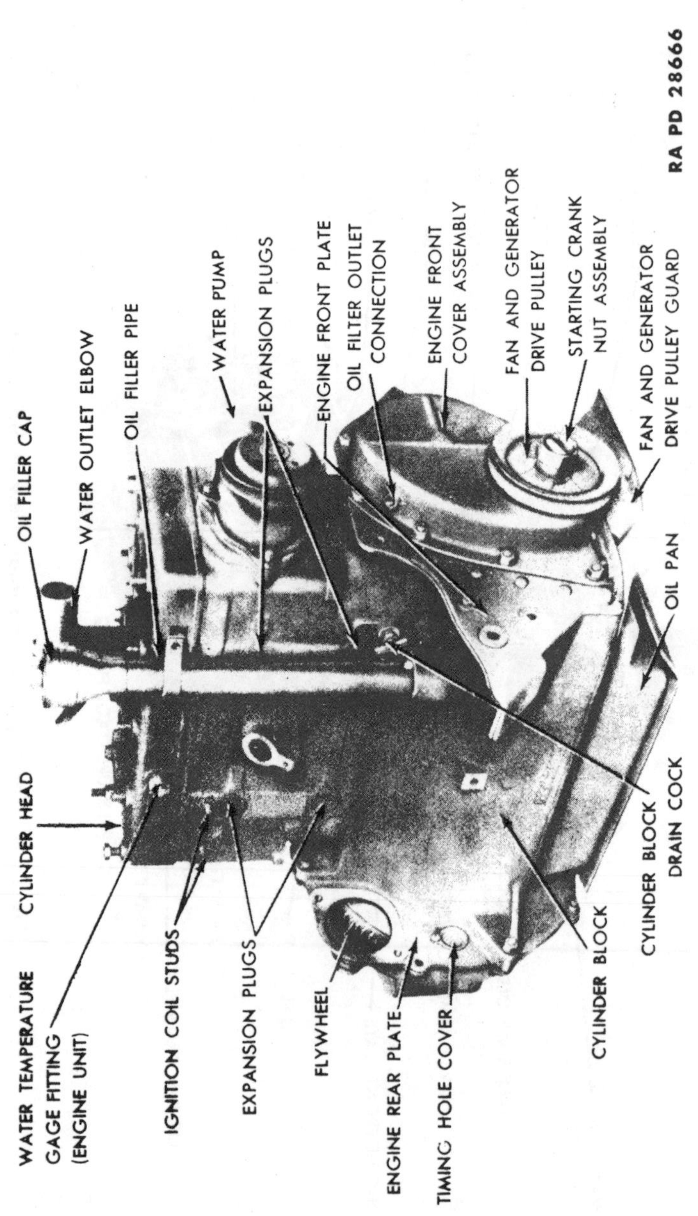

Figure 9 — Three-quarter Right Front View of Stripped Engine

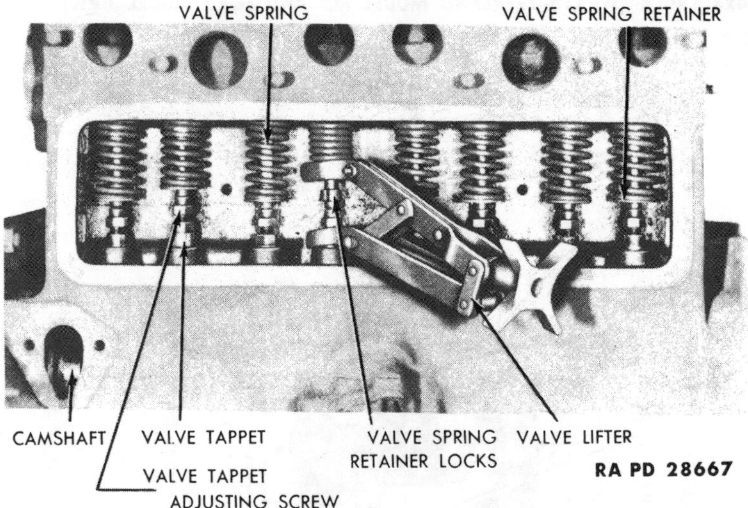

Figure 10 — Removing Valve Spring Retainer Locks, Using Valve Lifter (41-L-1410)

that hold the oil filter bracket to the cylinder head, and remove the oil filter.

f. Remove Generator and Generator Support Bracket. Pull up on the generator adjusting bracket, raise the generator to release the tension on the fan belt, and remove the belt. Remove the two bolts that hold the generator to the support bracket, and remove the generator. Remove the two cap screws that hold the generator support bracket to the cylinder block, and remove the generator support bracket.

g. Remove Ignition Coil. Remove the two nuts and lock washers that hold the ignition coil to the cylinder block, and remove the ignition coil and bond strap.

h. Remove Fan. Remove the four cap screws and lock washers that hold the fan to the water pump, and remove the fan.

7. DISASSEMBLY OF STRIPPED ENGINE.

a. Remove Water Pump (fig. 9). Remove the four cap screws and lock washers that hold the water pump to the cylinder block, and remove the water pump.

b. Remove Intake and Exhaust Manifold (fig. 8). Remove the ventilating tube that connects the intake manifold and valve chamber cover. Remove the seven nuts, and lift the intake and exhaust manifold off the engine.

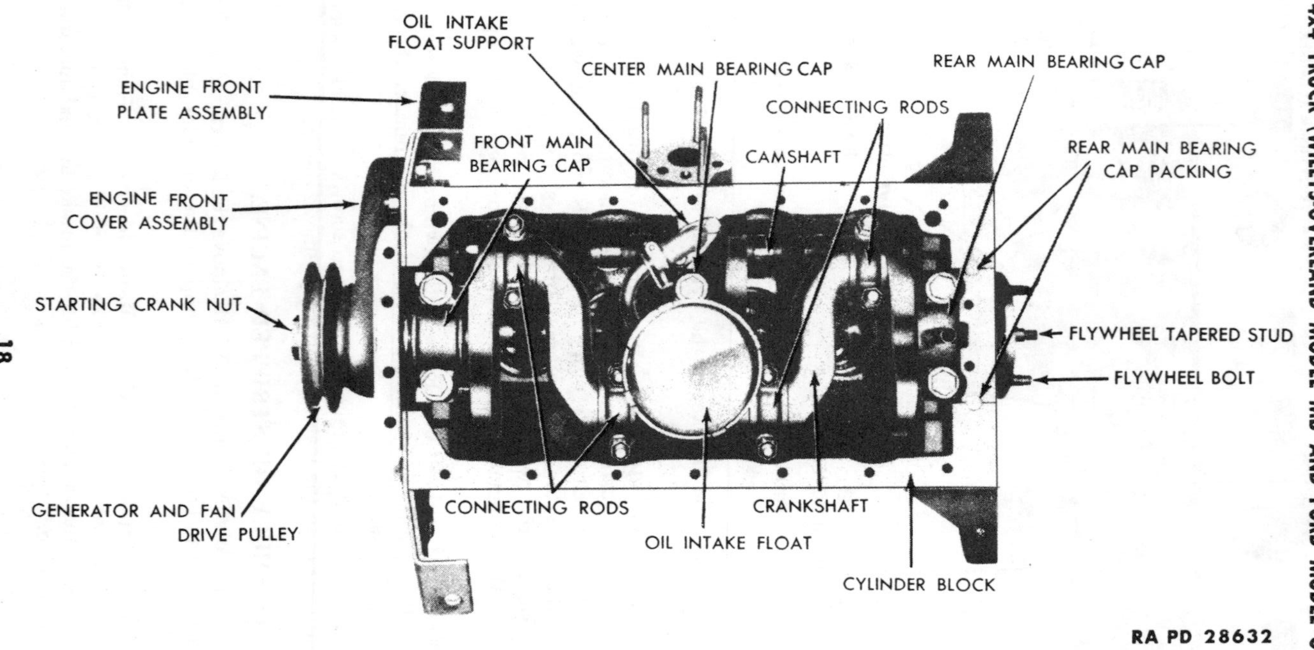

Figure 11 — Underside View of Engine with Oil Pan Removed

c. **Remove Water Outlet Elbow** (fig. 8). Remove the three nuts that hold the water outlet elbow to the cylinder head, and remove the water outlet elbow and thermostat. Remove the thermostat retainer and thermostat.

d. **Remove Clutch Disk** (fig. 8). Loosen the six pressure plate bracket cap screws in sequence, a little at a time, to prevent distortion of the pressure plate bracket. Remove the six cap screws, pressure plate, and clutch disk.

e. **Remove Flywheel** (fig. 8). Remove the six nuts and lock washers that hold the flywheel to the crankshaft. Tap the flywheel off the crankshaft with a brass hammer. Lift the rear engine plate from the engine.

f. **Remove Cylinder Head** (fig. 9). Remove the remaining cap screws that secure the head to the cylinder block, and remove the cylinder head.

g. **Remove Valves and Springs** (fig. 10). Remove the two cap screws and crankcase ventilator assembly from the valve chamber cover, and remove the cover. With a valve lifter (41-L-1410) inserted between the valve tappet and valve spring retainer, raise the valve springs that are in closed position, and remove the valve spring retainer locks (fig. 10). Turn the crankshaft until those valves which are open become closed, and remove the rest of the valve spring retainer locks. Remove the valves and place them in a valve carrying board, so that they can be identified as to cylinders from which they were removed. Compress the valve spring with the valve lifter on each valve tappet that is in the closed position, and pull the spring off the valve guide. Turn the crankshaft until the tappets are in a closed position, and remove the rest of the valve springs.

h. **Remove Oil Pan and Oil Intake Float.** Turn the engine on its side, and remove the cap screws that secure the oil pan and fan pulley guard to the cylinder block. Remove the fan pulley guard and oil pan. Remove the two cap screws from the oil intake float (fig. 11), and remove the oil intake float.

i. **Remove Camshaft Sprocket and Camshaft.** Remove the eight nuts and bolts that secure the engine front cover and engine front plate to the cylinder block and remove the cover. Remove the camshaft thrust plunger and spring. Straighten the tabs on the four camshaft sprocket cap screw lock washers (fig. 25), and remove the four cap screws and lock washers. Lift the camshaft sprocket and the camshaft drive link chain off the camshaft. Remove the camshaft thrust washer. Lay the cylinder block on its side. Pull all the valve tappets toward the top of the cylinder block. Pull the cam-

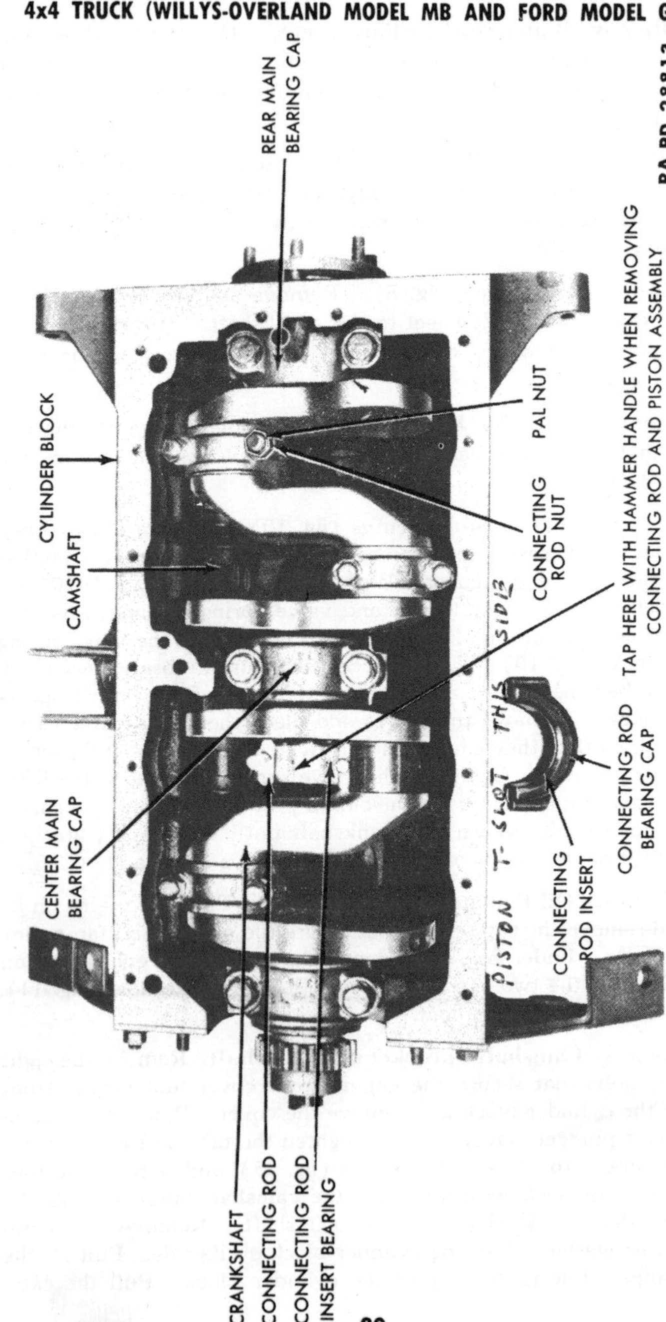

Figure 12 — Connecting Rod and Piston Assembly Removal

shaft out of the cylinder block, and remove the valve tappets. Remove the three cap screws that hold the engine front plate to the cylinder block, and remove the plate.

j. Remove Piston and Connecting Rod Assemblies (fig. 12). Remove the two pal nuts, connecting rod nuts, and connecting rod bearing cap from each connecting rod. Remove all carbon from the top of the cylinder walls. Tap the connecting rod and piston assembly out of the cylinder block with the handle end of a hammer (fig. 12). Install the connecting rod bearing caps on the rods in same position as originally installed, to prevent later improper mating of parts.

k. Remove Crankshaft. Remove the two cap screws from each main bearing cap (fig. 11), and remove the three main bearing caps. Lift the crankshaft from the cylinder block.

Section IV

DISASSEMBLY, CLEANING, INSPECTION, REPAIR, AND ASSEMBLY OF SUBASSEMBLIES

8. CYLINDER BLOCK, HEAD, AND OIL PAN.

a. Cleaning. Strip off all old gaskets and sealing compound from all machined surfaces. Remove plugs, and clean all oil passages in the cylinder block with steam or compressed air. Scrape the carbon from the cylinder block and head. Clean the cylinder block, head, and oil pan thoroughly with dry-cleaning solvent.

b. Inspection and Repair.

(1) OIL PAN (fig. 13). An oil pan with stripped threads in the drain plug opening, or an oil pan that is badly dented or deformed, must be replaced.

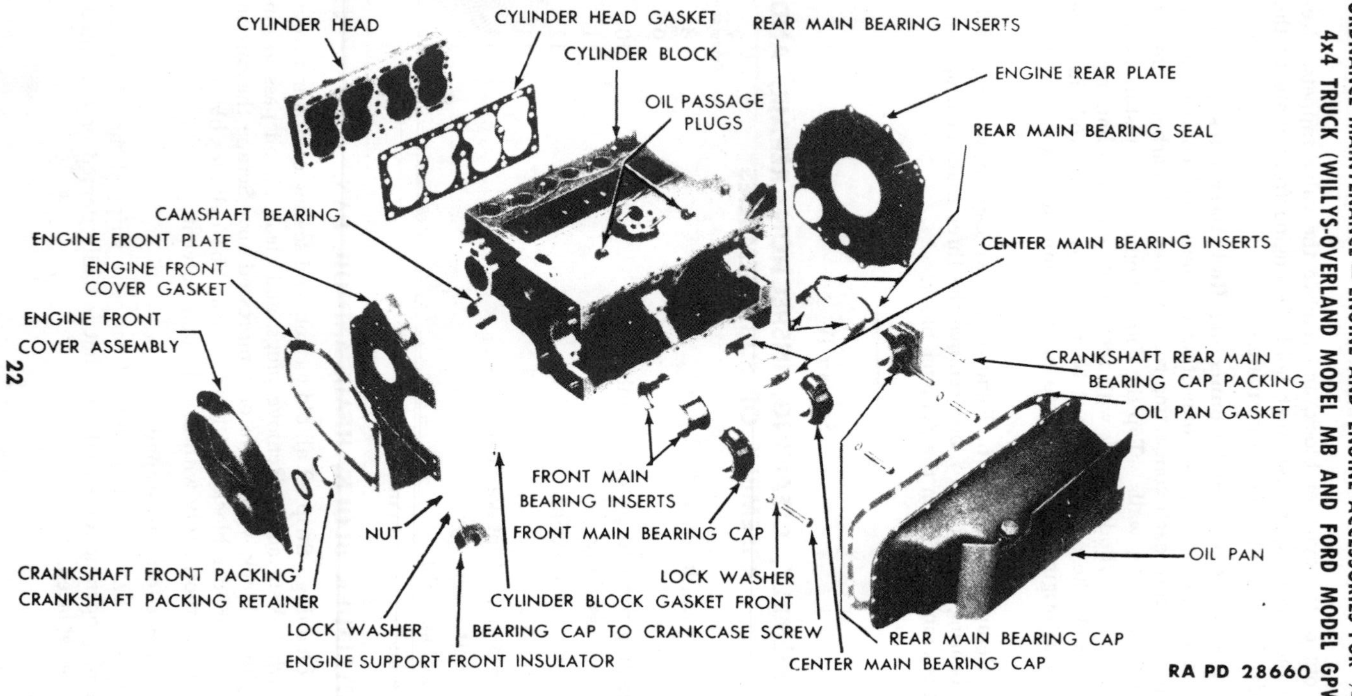
CYLINDER HEAD
CYLINDER HEAD GASKET
CYLINDER BLOCK
OIL PASSAGE PLUGS
REAR MAIN BEARING INSERTS
ENGINE REAR PLATE
REAR MAIN BEARING SEAL
CAMSHAFT BEARING
ENGINE FRONT PLATE
ENGINE FRONT COVER GASKET
ENGINE FRONT COVER ASSEMBLY
CENTER MAIN BEARING INSERTS
CRANKSHAFT REAR MAIN BEARING CAP PACKING
OIL PAN GASKET
FRONT MAIN BEARING INSERTS
NUT
FRONT MAIN BEARING CAP
OIL PAN
CRANKSHAFT FRONT PACKING
CRANKSHAFT PACKING RETAINER
LOCK WASHER
CYLINDER BLOCK GASKET FRONT
LOCK WASHER
BEARING CAP TO CRANKCASE SCREW
REAR MAIN BEARING CAP
ENGINE SUPPORT FRONT INSULATOR
CENTER MAIN BEARING CAP
RA PD 28660

Figure 13 — Cylinder Block, Head, Oil Pan, and Bearings, Disassembled

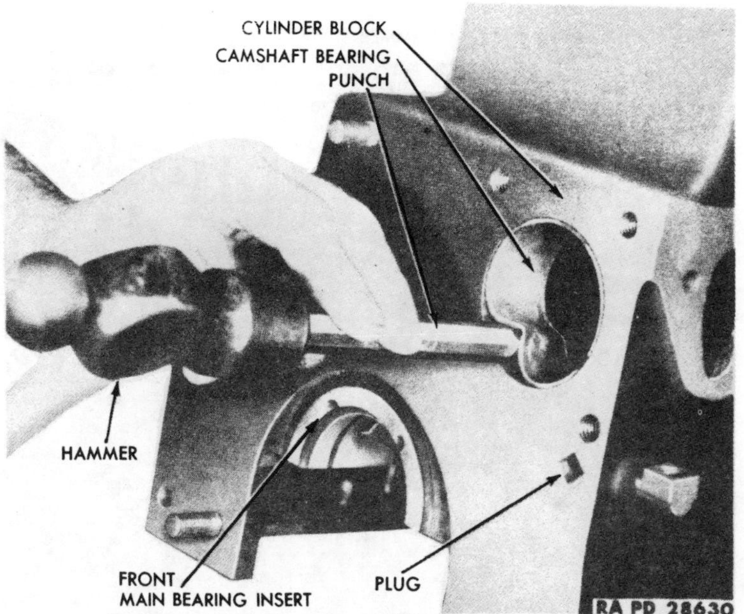

Figure 14 — Driving Camshaft Bearing from Cylinder Block

(2) CYLINDER HEAD (fig. 13). A cracked or warped cylinder head, or a cylinder head with stripped threads in the spark plug holes, must be replaced.

(3) CYLINDER BLOCK (fig. 13). A cracked or damaged cylinder block must be replaced. All loose expansion plugs (fig. 9) or damaged studs must be replaced (step (4) below). A scored, ridged, discolored, or excessively worn, front camshaft bearing (fig. 13) (worn to more than 2.190 in. inside diameter) must be replaced (step (5) below). Measure the other three camshaft bearings with a micrometer caliper. If the bearings are larger than 2.128 inches for the front intermediate, 2.1395 inches for the rear intermediate, or 1.628 inches for the rear bearing, the cylinder block must be replaced. Measure the cylinder bores with a micrometer caliper and telescope gage. If any of the cylinders has a taper of more than 0.010 inch, or an out-of-round condition of more than 0.005 inch, the cylinders must be rebored to 0.020 or 0.030 inch oversize. If cylinder walls will not clean up at 0.030 inch, the cylinder block must be replaced. Pitted, burned, or nicked valve seats must be reseated. Check the clearances of the valve guides with new valves. If the clearance ex-

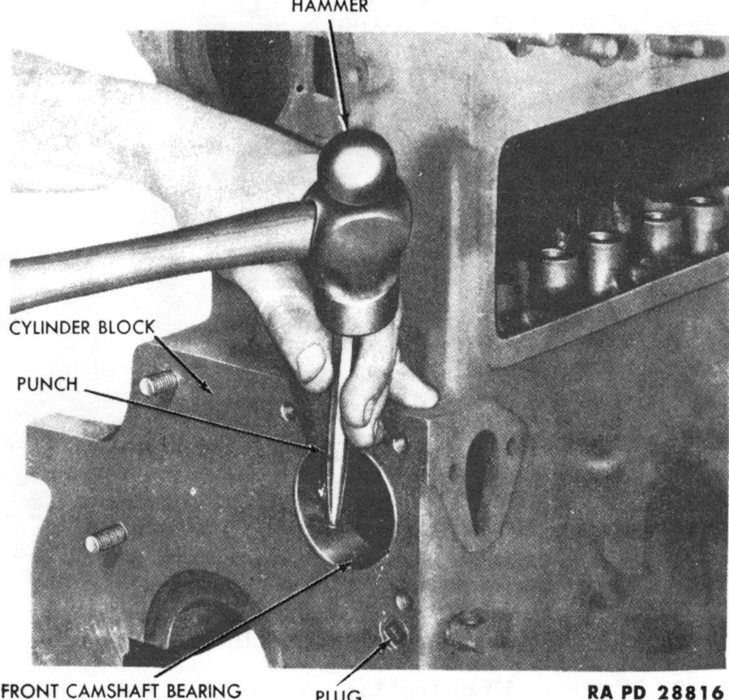

Figure 15 — Staking Camshaft Bearing in Place

ceeds 0.0045 inch in an intake valve guide (using a new intake valve as a gage), or 0.005 inch in an exhaust valve guide (using an exhaust valve as a gage), the valve guides must be replaced (step (6) below). If the clearance exceeds 0.003 inch between valve tappet and valve tappet bore, the valve tappet bores must be reamed to 0.004 inch oversize, and 0.004-inch oversize valve tappets must be installed when assembling engine. If valve tappet bore will not clean up at 0.004 inch oversize, the cylinder block must be replaced.

(4) REPLACE STUDS. Remove all damaged studs with a standard stud puller. To remove a broken stud, indent the end of the broken stud exactly in the center with a center punch. Drill approximately two-thirds through the broken stud with a small drill, then follow up with a larger drill. However, the drill selected must leave a wall thicker than the depth of the threads. Select an extractor (EZ-Out) of the proper size, insert it into the drilled hole, and screw out the

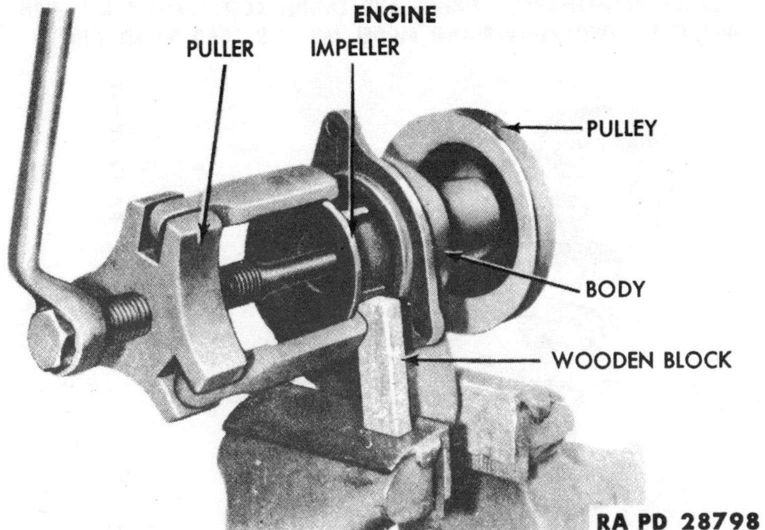

Figure 16 — Removing Water Pump Impeller, Using Puller (41-P-2912)

remaining part of the broken stud. Install the studs with a standard stud driver. Drive all studs until no threads show at the bottom of the studs.

(5) Replace Camshaft Bearing. Drive a punch between the camshaft bearing and cylinder block (fig. 14), and tap the camshaft bearing from the cylinder block. To install the camshaft bearing, drive it in place with a fiber block, making sure the oil hole in the bearing is in line with the oil passage in the cylinder block. Stake the camshaft bearing in place with a punch (fig. 15). Line-ream the camshaft bearing to 2.3145 inches.

(6) Replace Valve Guides. Remove the guides with a suitable valve guide remover. When installing valve guides, drive all intake and exhaust valve guides into the block with a valve guide replacer, leaving a distance of 1 inch from the top of the guide to the top of the cylinder block for exhaust valve guides, and a distance of $1\frac{5}{16}$ inches for the intake guides.

9. WATER PUMP.

a. Disassembly. Pull the water pump bearing retaining wire (fig. 17) from the water pump. Remove the water pump impeller with a puller (41-P-2912) as in figure 16, or press it off in an arbor press. Remove the water pump seal assembly, and water pump seal washer. Press the water pump bearing and shaft assembly, and water pump

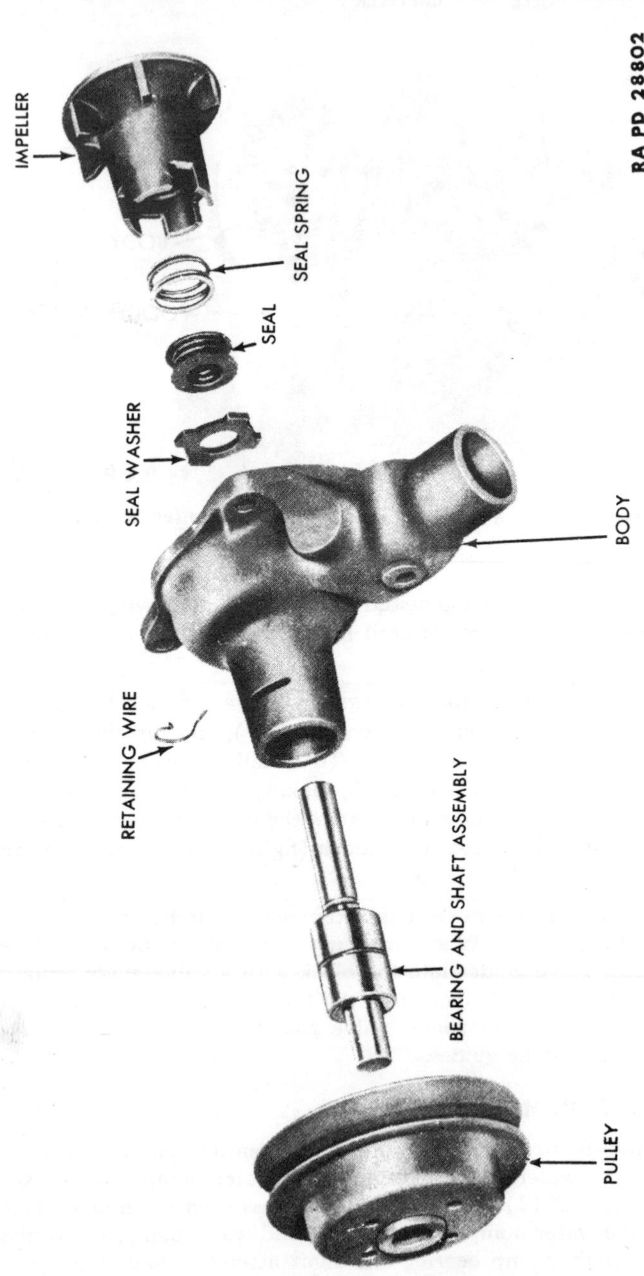

Figure 17 — Water Pump Disassembled

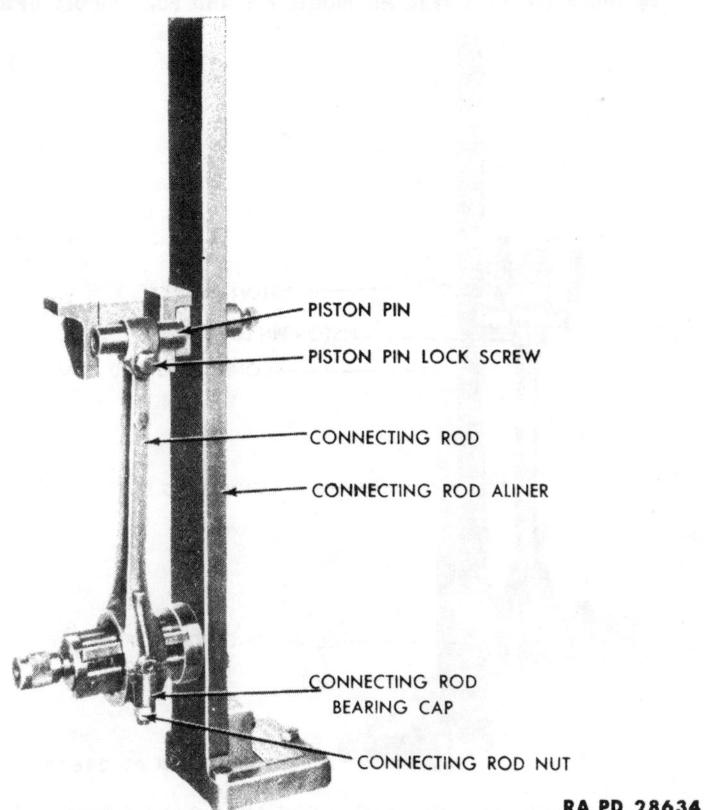

Figure 18 – Checking Connecting Rod Alinement for Twist, using Aliner (41-A-135)

pulley from the water pump body. Press the water pump pulley off the water pump bearing and shaft assembly.

b. Cleaning. Clean all parts thoroughly in dry-cleaning solvent.

c. Inspection and Repair.

(1) WATER PUMP BODY (fig. 17). A cracked or damaged water pump body must be replaced.

(2) WATER PUMP IMPELLER (fig. 17). A water pump impeller that is cracked or that has a broken fin must be replaced.

(3) WATER PUMP PULLEY (fig. 17). A distorted or damaged water pump pulley must be replaced.

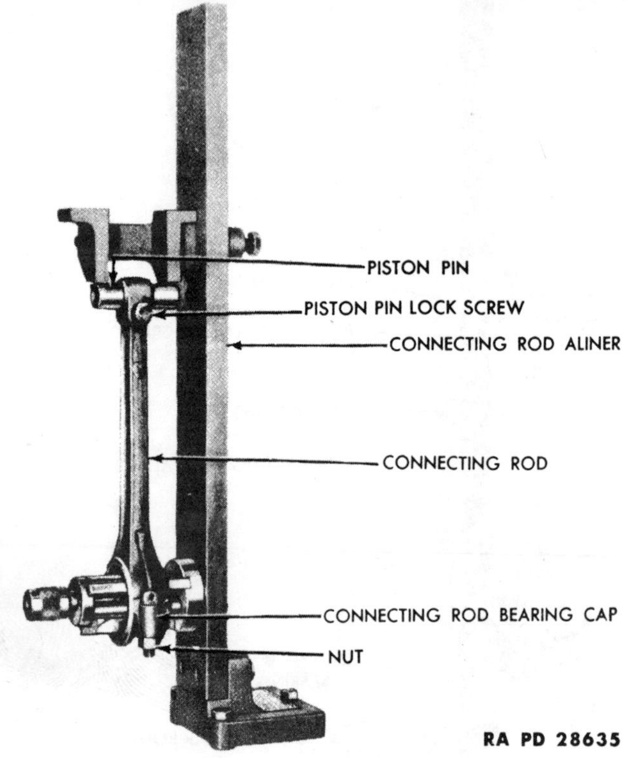

Figure 19 — Checking Connecting Rod Alinement for Bend, Using Aliner (41-A-135)

(4) WATER PUMP BEARING AND SHAFT ASSEMBLY (fig. 17). Rotate the water pump bearing; if the bearing binds or has a tendency to stick, it must be replaced. Bearings that have side or end play must be replaced.

d. **Assembly.** Press the front (short) end of the water pump bearing and shaft assembly into the water pump pulley. Press the water pump pulley and water pump bearing and shaft assembly into the front end of the water pump body until the groove on the bearing is in line with the small slot in the water pump body. Dip a new water pump seal assembly and water pump seal washer in hydraulic brake fluid, and install them in the water pump impeller. Place the impeller in a press, and press the shaft into the impeller until the end of the shaft is flush with the end of the water pump impeller. Install the water pump bearing retaining wire in place.

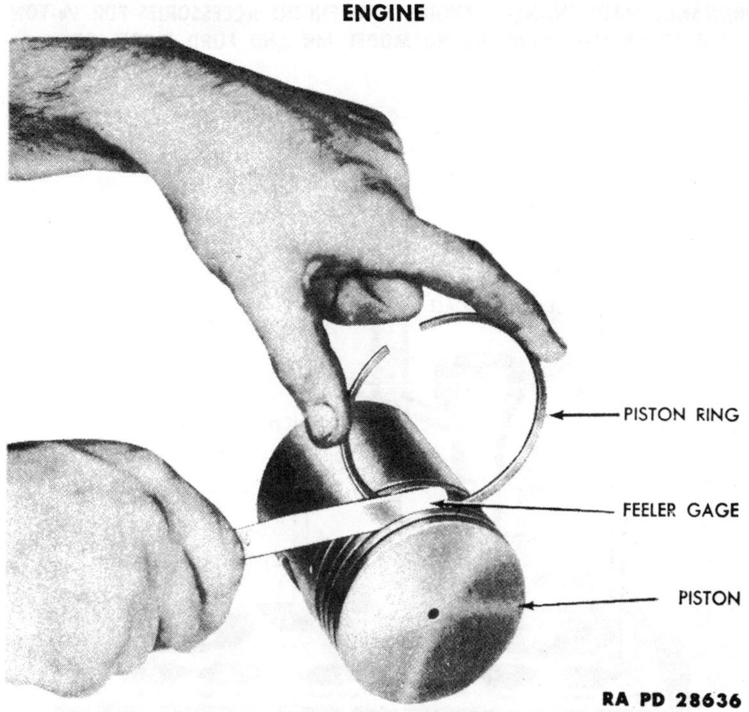

Figure 20 – Checking Clearance of Ring Groove with Feeler Gage

10. CONNECTING ROD AND PISTON ASSEMBLY.

a. **Disassembly.** Remove the piston rings with a standard ring remover. Remove the piston pin lock screw, and push the piston pin out of the piston.

b. **Cleaning.** Scrape the carbon from the ring grooves in the piston, and from the dome. Remove all foreign matter from the oil holes in the oil ring (lower) groove. Clean the complete assembly in dry-cleaning solvent.

c. **Inspection and Repair.** Pistons with cracks, scores, or damage of any kind must be replaced. Determine the wear on the skirt of each piston at the bottom at right angles to the piston pin. If the wear is 0.010 inch less than the original size, or if the piston is out-of-round more than 0.005 inch, the piston must be replaced. Check the width of the ring grooves with new rings and a feeler gage (fig. 20). If the piston ring groove wear exceeds 0.003-inch clearance between the piston ring and ring groove, the piston must be replaced. Measure the piston pin hole. If the inside diameter of the piston pin hole is more than 0.813 inch, the piston must be replaced. Piston pins worn to less than 0.8115-inch

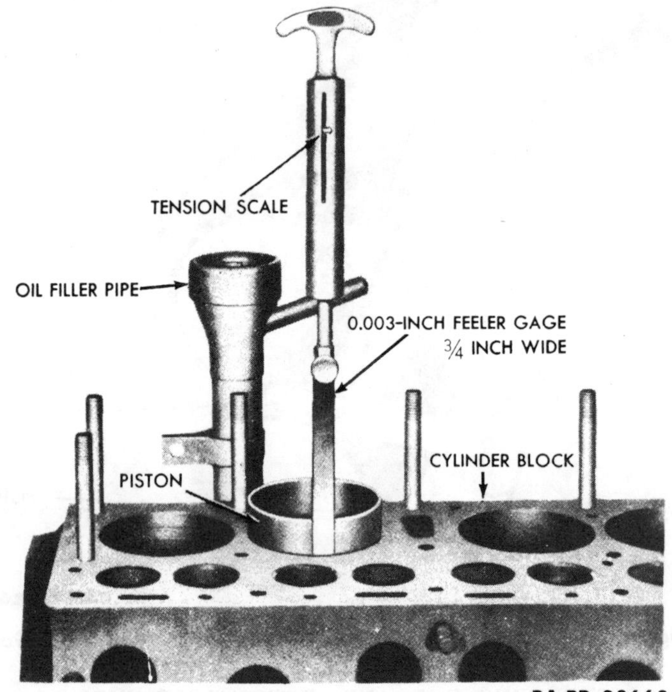

Figure 21 — Fitting Piston in Cylinder Bore, Using Scale w/feelers (41-S-498)

diameter must be replaced. Check the connecting rods for alinement, using aliner (41-A-135) (figs. 18 and 19). Bent or twisted connecting rods must be correctly alined. Damaged connecting rod bolts must be replaced. If connecting rods are fitted with studs, and studs are damaged, the complete connecting rod must be replaced. Excessively worn, scored, discolored, or pitted connecting rod insert bearings must be replaced.

d. Fit Piston. The normal clearance of the piston to the cylinder bore is 0.003 inch. Place a piston fitting scale with feelers (41-S-498) into the cylinder bore, making sure the feeler gage is long enough to cover the entire length of a piston. Push a piston into the cylinder bore with the T-slot in the piston opposite the feeler gage (fig. 21). Lift up on the tension scale; if more than 10 pounds is required to pull the feeler gage from the cylinder bore, the piston is too tight. Select a

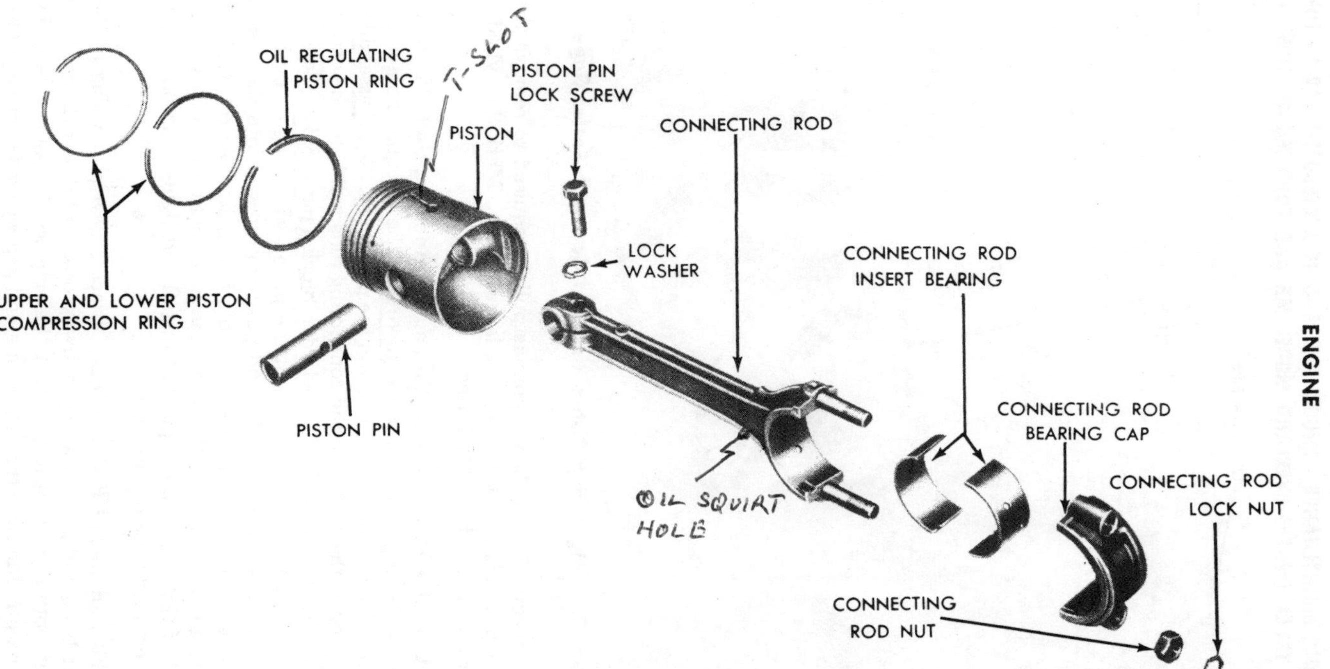

Figure 22 — Connecting Rod and Piston Assembly, Disassembled

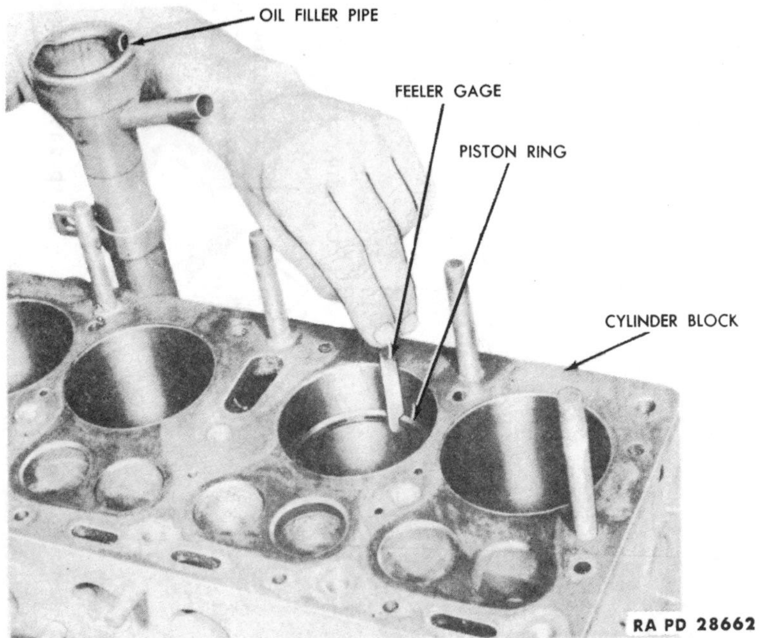

Figure 23 — Measuring Piston Ring End Gap with Feeler Gage

smaller piston. If less than 5 pounds pull is required to remove the gage, the piston is too loose. Select a larger piston. Mark the cylinder number on each piston after fitting.

e. **Assemble Piston, Piston Pin, and Connecting Rod.** When installing connecting rods on pistons, make sure the oil squirt hole in the connecting rod is opposite the T-slot in the piston (fig. 36). If assembled in this manner, the off-set on the connecting rods will be in the correct position when installed in the cylinder block (par. 18 f). Select a piston pin which can be inserted in the piston with a light "push" fit (piston temperature at 70° F), and push it part way into the piston pin hole, with the groove in the piston pin facing downward. Hold the connecting rod in line with the piston pin hole, and push the piston pin the rest of the way into the piston. Install and tighten the piston pin lock screw in the connecting rod.

f. **Fit and Install Piston Rings.** Place a new piston ring in the cylinder bore, and press it about halfway down into the cylinder bore with the bottom of a piston, so that the ring will be square with the cylinder wall. Measure the piston ring end gap with a feeler gage (fig.

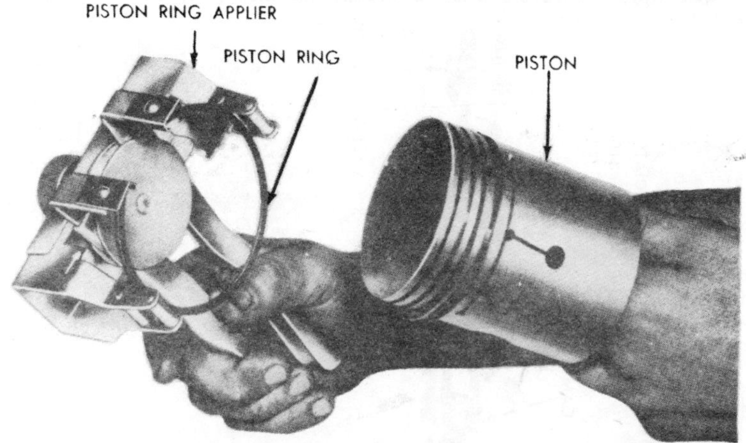

Figure 24 — Installing Piston Ring on Piston, Using Applier (41-A-329-500)

23). If the gap is less than 0.008 inch, remove the ring, and file with a fine-cut file until the correct gap (0.008 to 0.013 inch) is obtained. If end gap exceeds 0.013 inch, an oversize ring must be used. Repeat the same procedure for all piston rings. Roll the new piston ring around its particular groove in the piston. The ring should roll freely, and not have a clearance of more than 0.003 inch (fig. 20). Repeat the same procedure on each piston ring. Install the piston rings on the piston with a piston ring applier (41-A-329-500) (fig. 24), making sure that the beveled edge of both compression rings are towards the top.

11. CAMSHAFT ASSEMBLY.

a. Cleaning. Clean the camshaft, camshaft sprocket, camshaft thrust washer, and camshaft thrust spring and plunger, in dry-cleaning solvent.

b. Inspection and Repair. A camshaft with excessively scored or damaged cams, or with worn, corroded, scored, or discolored journals, must be replaced. Inspect the camshaft oil pump drive gear. If the teeth are worn, broken, or chipped, the camshaft must be replaced. Measure the four camshaft journals (fig. 25), and record the readings. If reading is less than 2.185 inches for the front journal, 2.122 inches for the front intermediate journal, 2.0595 inches for the rear intermediate journal, and 1.622 inches for the rear journal, the camshaft must be replaced. A camshaft gear with worn, broken, or chipped teeth must be replaced. Small nicks can be honed, and then polished

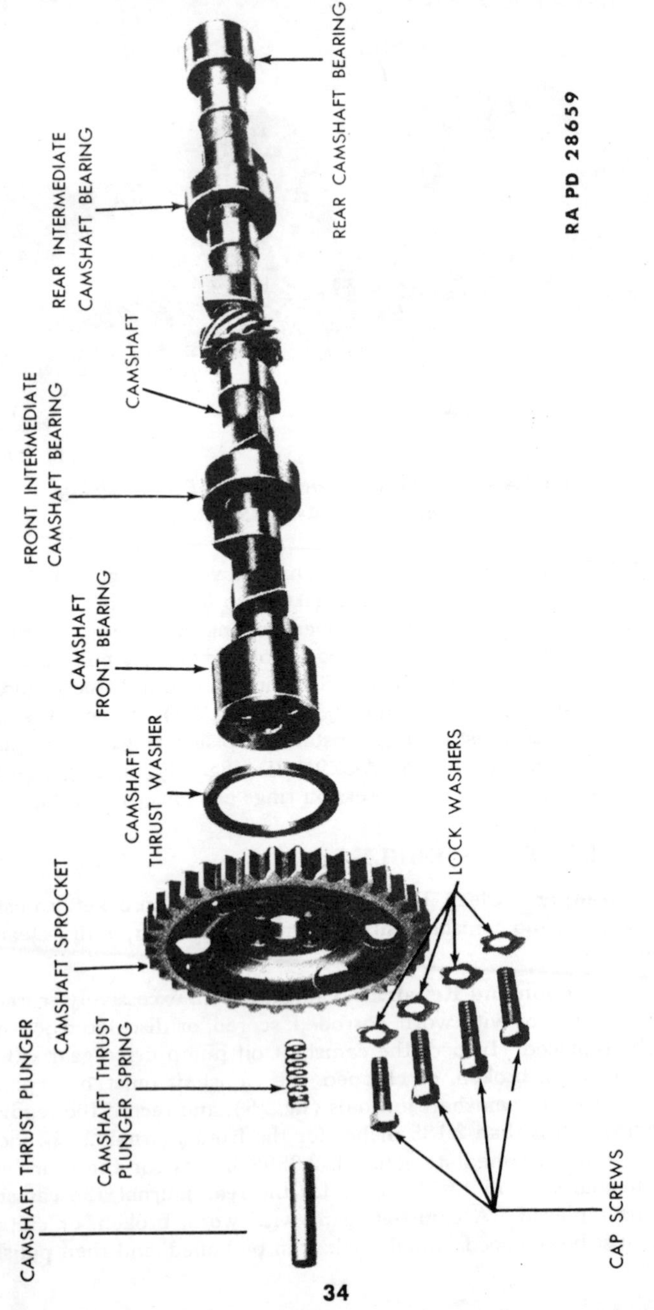

Figure 25 — Camshaft Assembly Disassembled

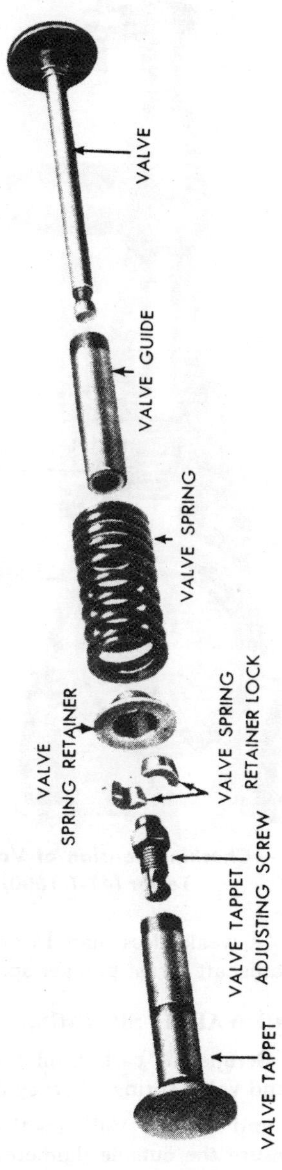

Figure 26 — Valve Assembly Disassembled

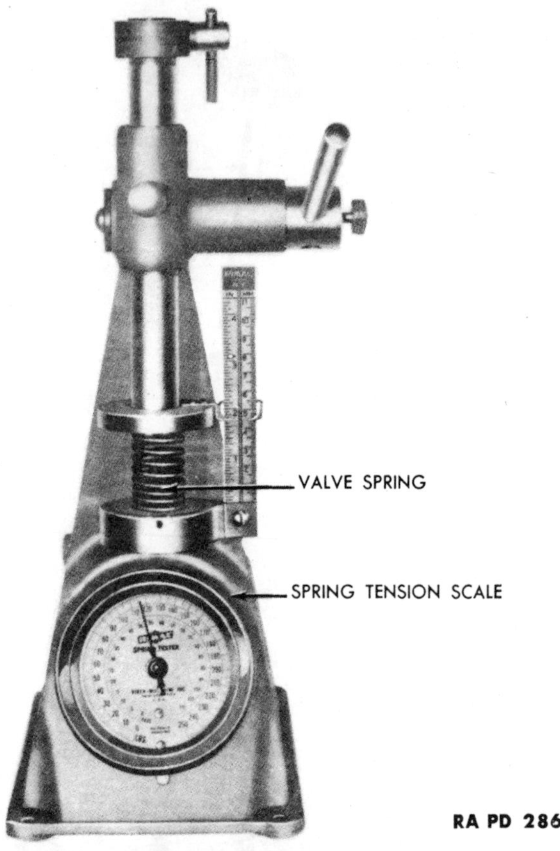

Figure 27 — Checking Tension of Valve Spring, Using Tester (41-T-1600)

with a fine stone. A weak (less than 15 pounds compressed to $^{29}/_{32}$ inch) or broken camshaft thrust plunger spring must be replaced.

12. VALVE AND VALVE SPRINGS.

a. Cleaning. Scrape the carbon off the valve heads and stems. Clean the valves and valve springs thoroughly in dry-cleaning solvent.

b. Inspection and Repair. Valves with bent or scored stems must be replaced. Measure the outside diameter of each valve stem (fig. 26). If measurement is less than 0.3685 inch for the exhaust valve, or 0.368 inch for the intake valve, the valves must be replaced. Pitted, corroded, or burned valves must be refaced. Valves that are burned, warped, or pitted, and will not clean up with a light cut of the grinding wheel, must be replaced. Measure the free length of each valve spring; if less than 2½ inches in length, the spring must be replaced. Check the tension of each valve spring (fig. 27), using tester (41-T-1600). If the valve spring registers less than 50 pounds when compressed to 2$\frac{1}{16}$ inches, or 116 pounds when compressed to 1¾ inches in length, it must be replaced.

13. VALVE TAPPETS.

a. Cleaning. Clean the valve tappets thoroughly in dry-cleaning solvent.

b. Inspection and Repair. Cracked, scored, or excessively worn valve tappets (fig. 26) must be replaced. Valve tappets, or valve tappet adjusting screws (fig. 26) with worn or damaged threads, must be replaced.

c. Disassembly. Unscrew the valve tappet adjusting screw from the tappet.

d. Assembly. Screw the valve tappet adjusting screw approximately three-quarters of the way into the valve tappet.

14. OIL PUMP AND OIL INTAKE FLOAT.

a. Disassembly. Remove the screw that holds the oil pump cover assembly to the oil pump, and remove the cover. Remove the oil pump relief spring retainer, gasket, shims, spring, and plunger from the oil pump cover (fig. 28). File either side of the oil pump driven gear pin (fig. 28), until the pin is flush with the driven gear sleeve. Drive the pin out of the sleeve and shaft with a small punch. Pull the oil pump shaft assembly out of the housing. Remove the cotter pin that holds the intake oil float to the oil float support, and remove the float (fig. 11). Straighten the four tabs on the oil intake float sump, and remove the sump. Lift the screen from the oil intake float.

b. Cleaning. Clean all parts and drilled passages thoroughly with dry-cleaning solvent, and blow out the oil intake float screen and all oil passages in the oil pump and oil intake float.

c. Inspection and Repair. A cracked or damaged oil pump housing or cover must be replaced. Measure the small pinion shaft on the oil pump cover. If less than 0.372 inch, the cover must be replaced. Measure the inside diameter of the oil pump housing (shaft end) (fig. 28). If larger than 0.505 inch, the oil pump housing must be replaced. An oil pump shaft assembly with broken teeth, or with a shaft measuring under 0.495 inch, must be replaced. An oil pump shaft assembly with a distributor slot worn more than three-sixteenths inch, must be

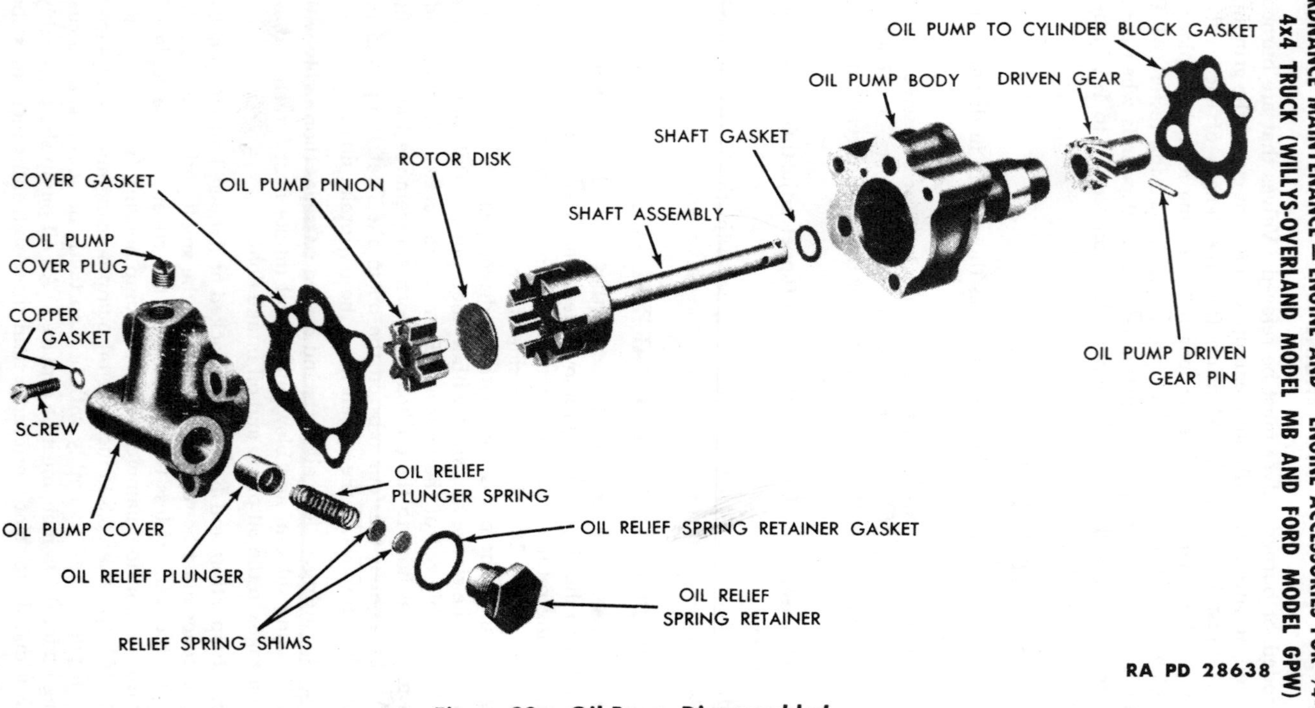

Figure 28 — Oil Pump Disassembled

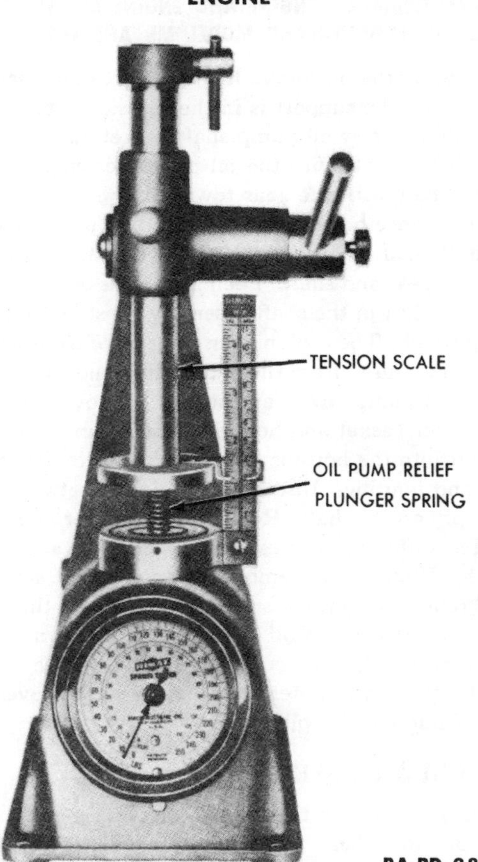

RA PD 28815

Figure 29 — Checking Oil Pump Relief Valve Spring Tension, Using Tester (41-T-1600)

replaced. An oil pump pinion gear with broken or worn teeth, or with an inside diameter of more than 0.378 inch, must be replaced. Measure the rotor disk (fig. 28); if less than 0.069 inch thick, it must be replaced. An oil pump driven gear with broken or chipped teeth must be replaced. Compress the oil pump relief valve spring to $1\frac{1}{16}$ inches (fig. 29), using tester (41-T-1600). If the tension is less than $5\frac{1}{2}$ pounds, the spring must be replaced. Replace a broken or cracked oil intake float support; also a distorted or leaking intake float support.

d. Assembly. Place the screen in the oil intake float. Place the sump on the oil intake float, and bend the four tabs to lock the sump to the float. Slide the oil intake float support onto the float, making sure the tongue on the support is in the recess. Install a cotter pin in the support. Slide a new oil pump shaft gasket on the shaft assembly. Slide the shaft assembly into the oil pump housing. Tap the driven gear onto the shaft with the gear toward the oil pump, until there is 0.0312-inch clearance between the gear and oil pump body. If installing a new shaft, drill a hole for the pin, and install a new driven gear pin through the gear and shaft. Peen both ends of the driven gear pin. Install the rotor disk in the shaft assembly. Install the pinion gear on the oil pump cover. The pinion gear must have from 0.001- to 0.003-inch end play, measured from the end of the pinion shaft. Place a new gasket on the oil pump cover, and install the cover onto the housing. Install the copper gasket and hold-down screw in the cover. Tap the oil pump shaft into the housing, and check the clearance between the driven gear and housing. Insert a screwdriver between the gear and housing, and pry on the shaft. Remove screwdriver and again measure clearance. The difference represents the end play, and must be 0.002- to 0.004 inch. If sufficient, remove cover and add sufficient gaskets. Drop the oil relief plunger and spring (fig. 28) into the opening in the oil pump cover. Place two oil relief spring shims into the oil relief spring retainer (fig. 28). Place a new gasket on the oil relief spring retainer, and install and tighten the retainer to the cover. Install and tighten the oil pump cover plug.

15. CRANKSHAFT ASSEMBLY.

a. **Cleaning.** Clean out the drilled holes on the crankshaft journals with a piece of wire. Clean the crankshaft thoroughly with dry-cleaning solvent.

b. **Inspection and Repair.** Inspect all crankshaft journals. If worn or scored, the crankshaft must be replaced or reworked. Measure the outside diameter of each crankshaft journal. If the diameter is less than 1.9365 inches on the crankpin journals (fig. 30), or 2.3325 inches on the main bearing journals (fig. 30), or if any of the journals are out-of-round more than 0.0005 inch, the crankshaft must be reworked to 0.010-, 0.020-, or 0.030-inch undersize, whichever the case may be. Light scores and scratches can be honed, and then polished with crocus cloth. Crankshafts that will not clean up at 0.030-inch undersize must be replaced If a new crankshaft or flywheel is being used, it must be fitted as outlined in paragraph 16 e.

c. **Remove Crankshaft Sprocket** (fig. 30). Install a standard puller on the crankshaft sprocket and remove the sprocket. Remove the Woodruff key, spacer, thrust washer, and shims.

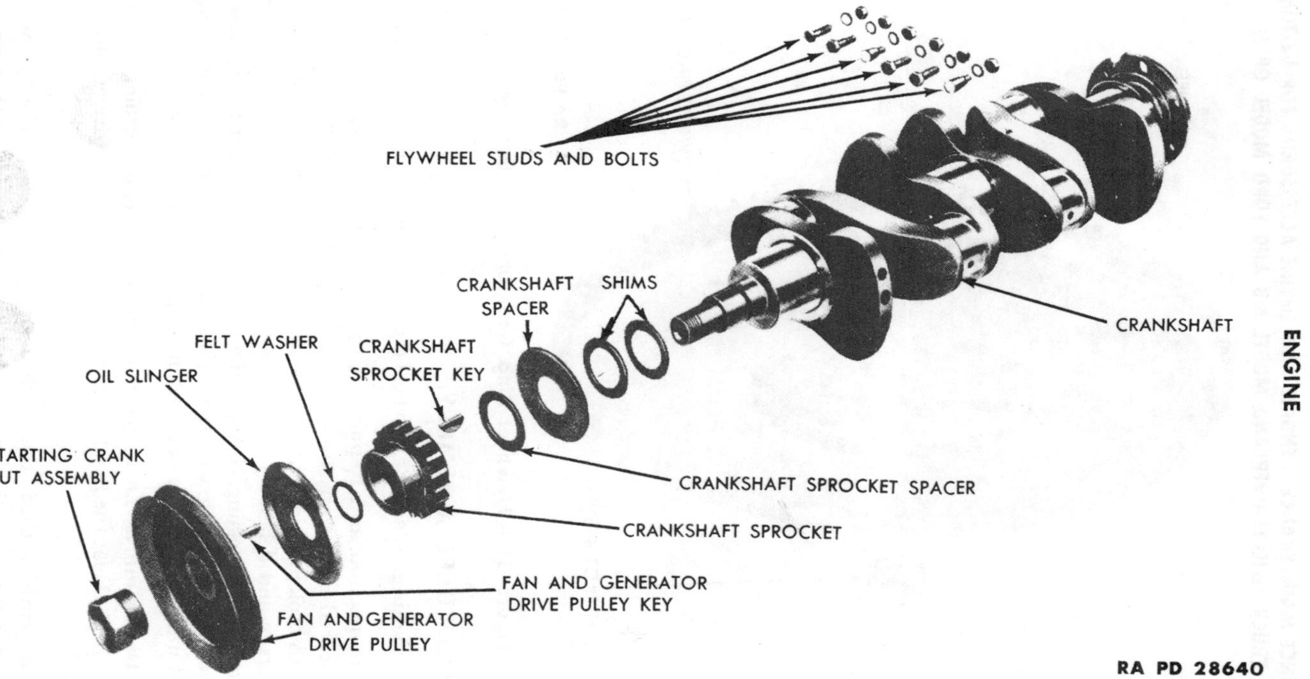

Figure 30 — Crankshaft Assembly Disassembled

Figure 31 — Flywheel Ring Gear and Pilot Bushing

16. FLYWHEEL ASSEMBLY.

a. **Cleaning.** Wash the flywheel thoroughly in dry-cleaning solvent.

b. **Inspection and Repair.** A flywheel (fig. 31) with an excessively scored or worn friction face must be replaced. A flywheel ring gear with broken, chipped, or excessively worn teeth must be replaced (subpars. c and d below). Measure the inside diameter of the main drive gear pilot bushing. If more than 0.632 inch, it must be replaced (subpars. c and d below). If a new crankshaft or flywheel is being used, it must be fitted as outlined in subparagraph e below.

c. **Disassembly.** Drive the main drive gear pilot bushing out of the flywheel. Heat the flywheel ring gear until it can be driven off the flywheel.

d. **Assembly.** Clean the flywheel ring gear recess on the flywheel. Apply heat evenly to the ring gear. When the ring gear is thoroughly heated, place it on the cold flywheel, making sure it is firmly seated in its recess. Drive a main drive gear pilot bushing in place with a fiber block.

e. **Fit Crankshaft to Flywheel When Either Part Is New.** Install the flywheel onto the crankshaft with the four crankshaft bolts, lock washers and nuts, making sure the index mark on the crankshaft is in line with the index mark on the flywheel. Drill the two tapered (stud) holes with a $^{35}/_{64}$-inch drill, and ream the two holes with a $^{9}/_{16}$-inch (0.5625-inch) reamer. Install the two bolts that are supplied with each crankshaft and/or flywheel.

17. INTAKE AND EXHAUST MANIFOLDS.

a. **Disassembly.** Remove the four cap screws that secure the intake manifold to the exhaust manifold, and separate the two manifolds. Remove the nut and bolt that hold the heat control valve shaft. Pull the counterweight lever, heat control lever, washer, and spring off the shaft.

b. **Cleaning.** Scrape all the old gaskets and carbon from the manifolds. Wash the manifold and parts in dry-cleaning solvent.

c. **Inspection and Repair.** Cracked or broken manifolds must be replaced. Damaged or broken studs must be replaced. An exhaust manifold with a damaged exhaust valve control or shaft must be replaced (par. 7 **b**).

d. **Assembly.** Slide the heat control valve spring onto the shaft, making sure the end of the heat control valve spring is resting on top of the stop. Slide the washer, counterweight, and control lever onto the shaft; install the nut and bolt through the counterweight. Place a new gasket between the two manifolds, and install the four cap screws and heat control spring stop.

Section V

ASSEMBLY OF ENGINE

18. ASSEMBLY.

a. **Install Valves.** Place a valve tappet in each valve tappet bore. Slide the camshaft into the cylinder block. Install a valve spring and valve spring retainer on each tappet, making sure the closed coils of the valve springs are against the cylinder block. Install the valves

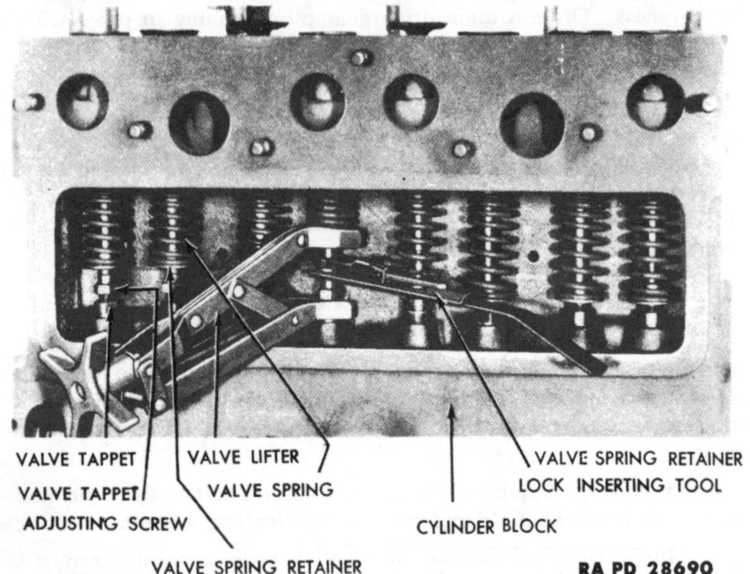

Figure 32 — Installing Valve Spring Retainer Locks, Using Lifter (41-L-1410) and Replacer (41-R-2398)

in their respective valve guides. Compress the valve springs on all valves that are in closed position using valve lifter (41-L-1410), and install the lower valve spring retainer locks (fig. 32), using replacer (41-R-2398). Turn the camshaft to close the other valves, and install the lower valve spring retainer locks on the rest of the valves.

b. Adjust Valve Tappets. Turn the camshaft until No. 1 valve is in a closed position, and the tappet is on the heel of the cam. Hold the valve tappet with one wrench, and turn the valve tappet adjusting screw with another wrench (fig. 33) clockwise or counterclockwise until 0.014-inch clearance is established between the valve and the valve tappet adjusting screw. Repeat the same procedure on each valve.

c. Install Crankshaft. If a new crankshaft or flywheel is being used, refer to paragraph 16 e. Install the three upper halves of the main bearing inserts in the cylinder block (fig. 13). Press the rear main bearing crankshaft packing into the recess provided at the rear main bearing (fig. 13), and in the rear main bearing cap. Cut the ends of the crankshaft packing flush with the crankcase and with the bearing cap. Install the four bolts and the two tapered studs in the

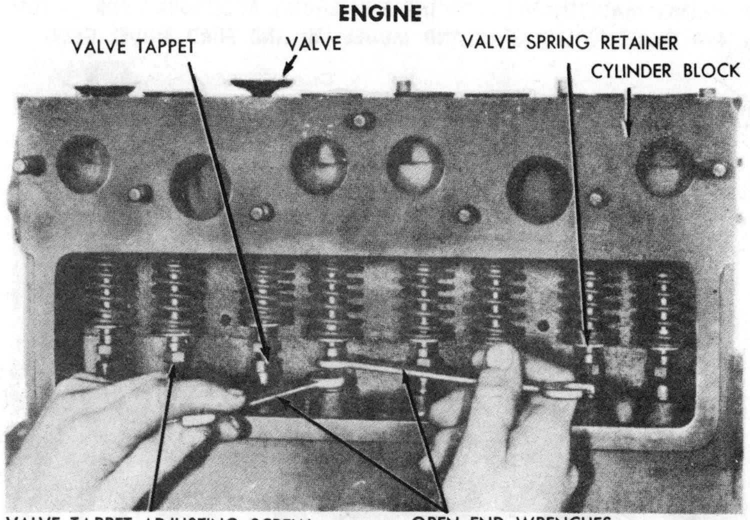

Figure 33 – Adjusting Valve Tappers, Using Wrenches (41-W-3575)

flywheel flange on the crankshaft. Install the three lower halves of the main bearing inserts in the three main bearing caps. Oil the main bearing inserts with a light oil. Place the crankshaft in place in the cylinder block. Install the front and center bearing caps, and tighten the bolts until they are just snug. Coat the rear bearing cap with joint and thread compound on both sides and top. Install the rear bearing cap in the cylinder block. Tighten the six main bearing bolts with a torque wrench to from 65 to 70 foot-pounds. Slip the rear bearing cap packing into the hole on each side of the rear main bearing cap, leaving ¼ inch of the packing to protrude from the crankcase.

d. Fit Crankshaft. Place a 0.006-inch feeler gage between the front main bearing cap and the crankshaft, and pull the crankshaft toward the front of the engine as far as possible. Place a straightedge across the front main bearing, and measure the distance between the straightedge and crankshaft to determine the amount of shims to be used (fig. 34).

e. Check Crankshaft End Play. Install the necessary amount of shims on the crankshaft to take up the space between the straightedge and crankshaft (fig. 35). Install the crankshaft thrust washer and spacer washer (fig. 30). Tap the large Woodruff key in the crankshaft, and slide the crankshaft sprocket, felt, and crankshaft oil slinger (fig. 30) on the shaft. Tap the small Woodruff key in the crankshaft, install the generator and fan belt drive pulley and cranking nut,

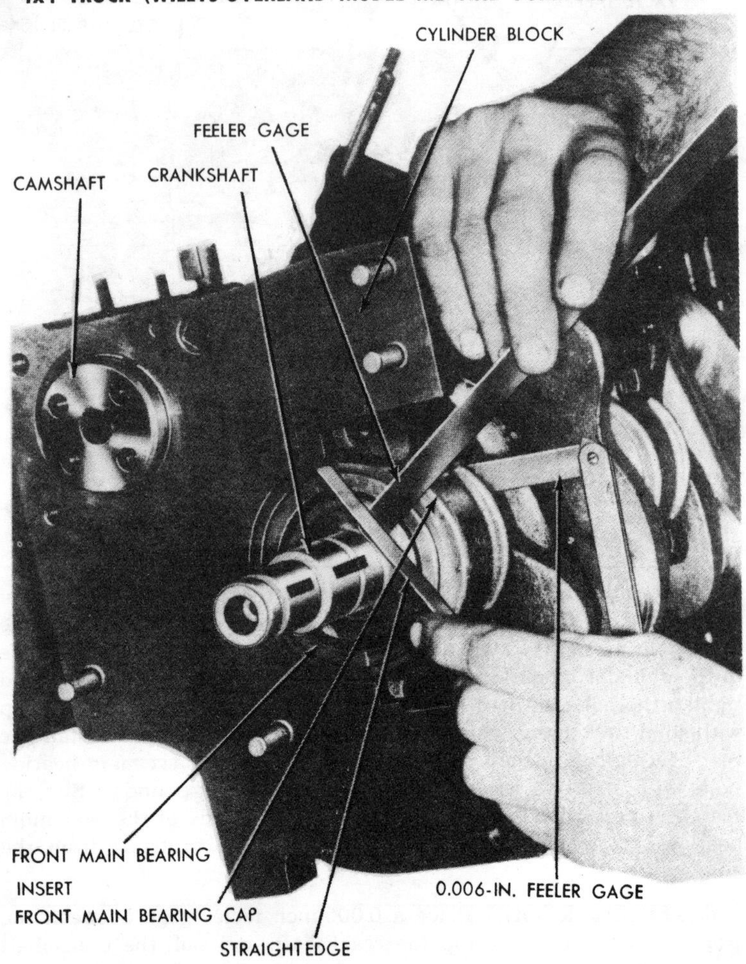

Figure 34 — Measuring Crankshaft End Play

and tighten the cranking nut. Place a feeler gage between the front main bearing cap and crankshaft. If more than 0.006-inch end play exists, shims must be removed. If less than 0.004 inch, shims must be added (fig. 35).

f. Install Connecting Rod and Piston Assemblies. (Piston assemblies will have previously been selected for each cylinder as outlined in paragraph 10 **d**). Oil the piston rings and install a ring compres-

Figure 35 — Shims in Place on Crankshaft

sor (41-C-2550) on the piston rings. Place the No. 1 connecting rod and piston assembly in the No. 1 cylinder with the offset on the connecting rod away from the nearest main bearing (fig. 36). With the T-slot of the piston to the left, and the oil squirt hole in the connecting rod facing toward the right-hand side of the engine, tap the piston down into the cylinder with the handle end of a hammer (fig. 37). Place one-half of a connecting rod insert bearing in the connecting rod, and the other half in the connecting rod bearing cap. Coat the connecting rod insert bearings with a light film of oil. Connect the rod to the crankshaft and install, but do not tighten, the two connecting rod nuts. Repeat the same procedure when installing the other rods, making sure the offset on each connecting rod is away from the nearest main bearing, and the oil squirt hole facing toward the left-hand side of the engine. Tighten all the connecting rod nuts to from 50 to 55 foot-pounds pull with a torque wrench. Install a

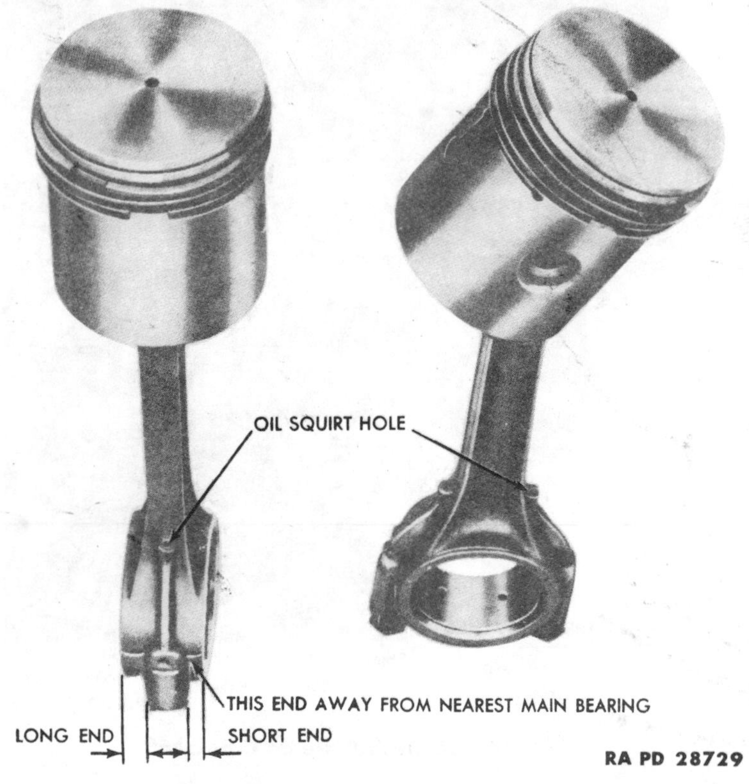

Figure 36 — Position of Connecting Rod Off-set and Oil Squirt Hole When Installed in Engine

pal nut on each connecting rod stud or bolt. Turn the pal nuts down on the stud or bolt until sealed, then turn one complete turn.

g. Install Flywheel. If installing a new flywheel or crankshaft, fit the crankshaft to the flywheel as outlined in paragraph 16 **e**. Fasten the engine rear plate temporarily to the engine with two bolts. Turn the crankshaft until the No. 1 and No. 4 pistons are at top center. Place the flywheel on the crankshaft flange so that the letters "TC" on the flywheel are lined up with the index mark at the center of the timing hole (fig. 38) in the engine rear plate, and the index mark on the crankshaft flange and on the flywheel are in line with each other. Install and tighten the six lock washers and nuts on the flywheel from 36 to 40 foot-pounds with a torque wrench. Check run-

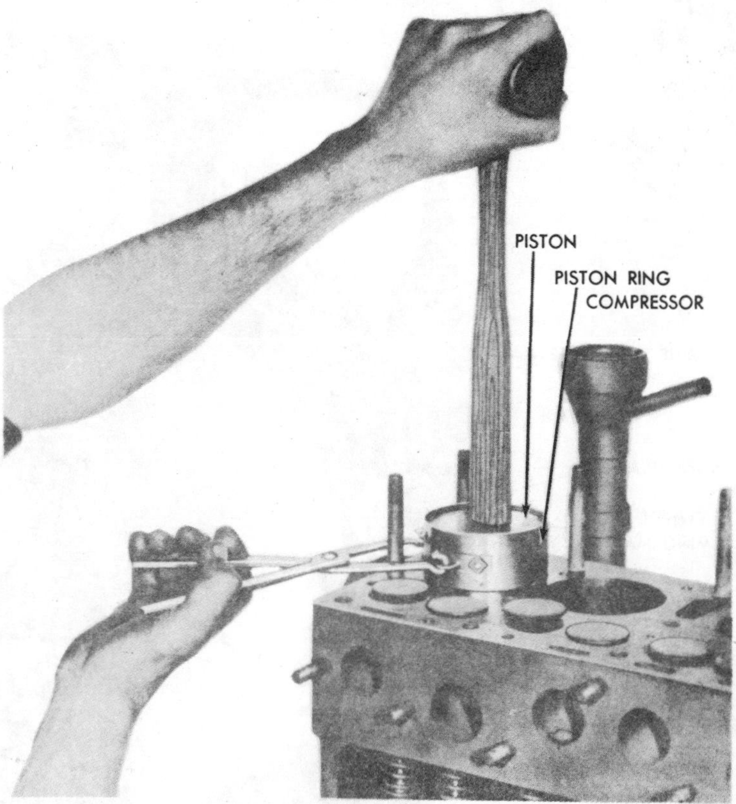

Figure 37 — Installing Piston and Connecting Rod Assembly in Cylinder Block, Using Ring Compressor (41-C-2550)

out on the flywheel with a dial gage. If the run-out exceeds 0.008 inch at the outer edge, the flywheel or crankshaft flange must be refaced.

h. Install Clutch Disk and Pressure Plate. Hold the clutch disk on the flywheel, and install a clutch pilot tool in the flywheel and the disk. Hold the pressure plate on the flywheel and install, but do not tighten, six lock washers and cap screws (fig. 39). Tighten the six cap screws evenly to prevent bending the pressure plate frame. Remove the clutch pilot.

i. Install Camshaft Sprocket. Place a gasket and the engine front plate on the engine, and install the three cap screws. Turn the crankshaft until No. 1 piston is at top center (fig. 38). Install the camshaft

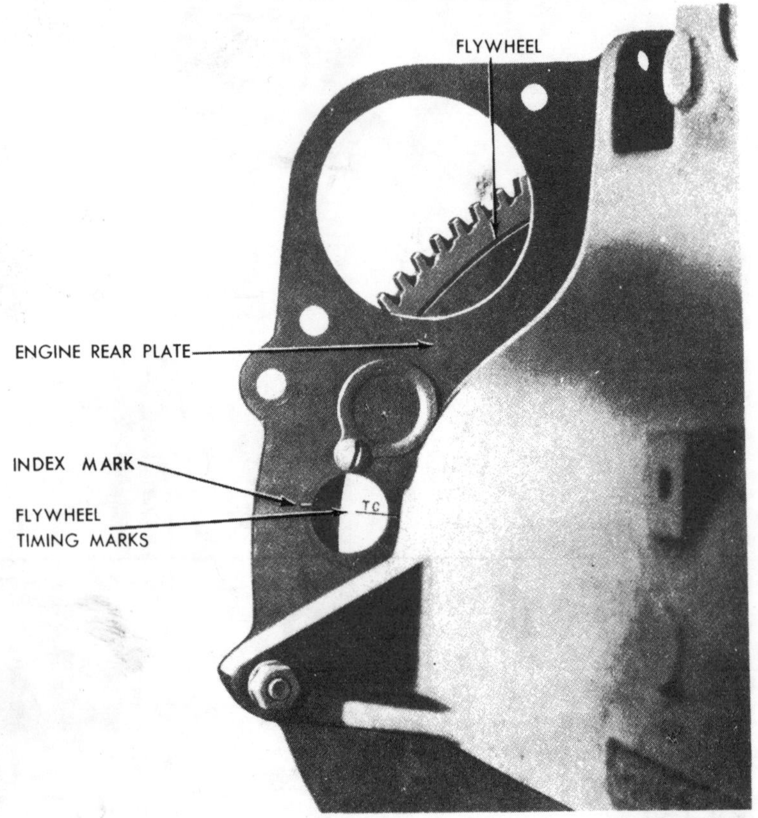

Figure 38 — Flywheel Timing Marks, T.C. (Top Center)

sprocket on the camshaft temporarily with two cap screws. Turn the camshaft sprocket until the punch mark on the camshaft sprocket is opposite the punch mark on the crankshaft sprocket (fig. 40). Remove the camshaft sprocket from the camshaft, being careful not to move the camshaft. Place the camshaft thrust washer on the camshaft. Place the camshaft drive chain on the crankshaft sprocket and camshaft sprocket, and install the camshaft sprocket on the camshaft with four lock washers and cap screws. Tighten the four cap screws, and bend the lock washer tabs down on the cap screws.

j. **Install Front Engine Cover.** Place the camshaft thrust plunger spring and plunger in the camshaft (fig. 25). Place a gasket on the engine front cover, and also install an oil seal in the recess provided in the cover. Install the cover on the engine.

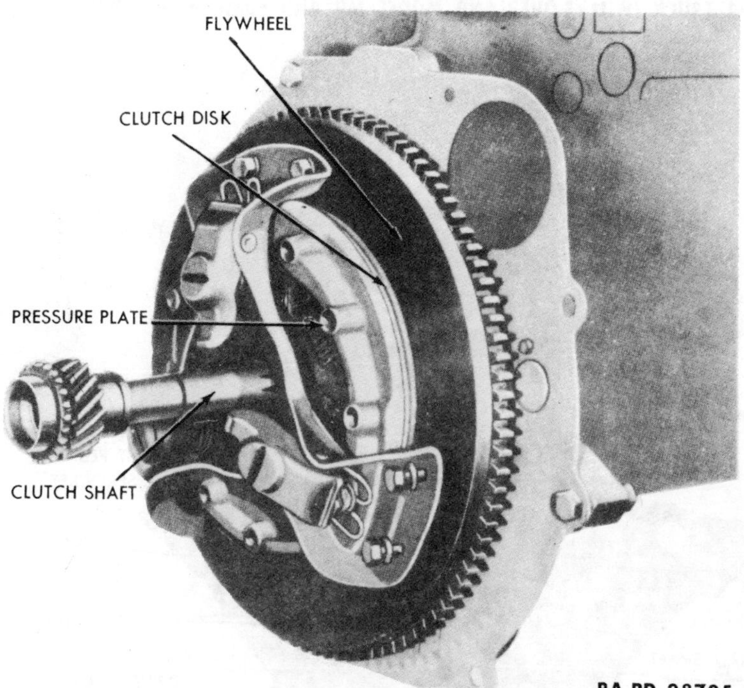

Figure 39 — Installing Clutch Disk and Pressure Plate on Flywheel

k. Install Oil Pan. Hold a gasket and the oil intake float in place (fig. 11), and install the two lock washers and cap screws. Coat the bottom (machined surface) of the crankcase with grease, and install the oil pan gasket. Hold the oil pan in place, and install all the lock washers and cap screws except the six front cap screws. Hold the generator and fan drive pulley guard in place, and install the remaining six lock washers and cap screws. Tighten all the oil pan cap screws.

l. Install Cylinder Head. Install a cylinder head gasket on the cylinder block. Making sure there is no foreign material in the cylinders, place the cylinder head on the cylinder block, and install and tighten the cylinder head bolts to from 65 to 75 foot-pounds with a torque wrench. (Start with a centrally located bolt, and work alternately each way.)

m. Install Intake and Exhaust Manifold. Place an intake and exhaust manifold gasket in place on the cylinder block. Install the intake and exhaust manifold on the cylinder block. Install the seven

ORDNANCE MAINTENANCE — ENGINE AND ENGINE ACCESSORIES FOR ¼-TON 4x4 TRUCK (WILLYS-OVERLAND MODEL MB AND FORD MODEL GPW)

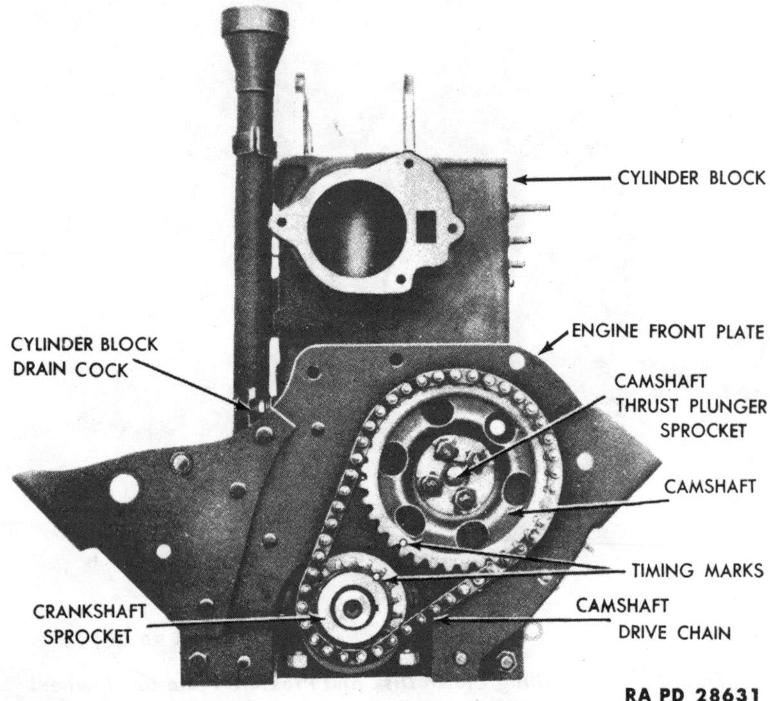

Figure 40 — Camshaft Timing Marks

flat washers and nuts. Connect the crankcase ventilation tube at the intake manifold, and at the crankcase ventilator assembly (fig. 41).

n. Install Oil Pump. Place a finger in No. 1 spark plug hole, and turn the crankshaft until No. 1 piston is coming up on compression stroke. Continue turning the crankshaft until the timing mark "IGN" appears on the flywheel and is in line with the index mark in the center of the timing hole on the engine rear plate (fig. 42). Install the distributor in the cylinder block (par. 19 e) temporarily. Set the rotor on No. 1 firing position (fig. 43) with the ignition points just breaking. Immerse the oil pump in a container of oil (same grade as used in engine), and turn the oil pump shaft assembly until the oil flows from the outlet hole in the oil pump body. Place a gasket on the oil pump and, with the wide side of pump shaft up, install the oil pump on the engine, making sure the slot in the oil pump shaft engages with the distributor shaft while the rotor is on No. 1 firing position with ignition

ENGINE

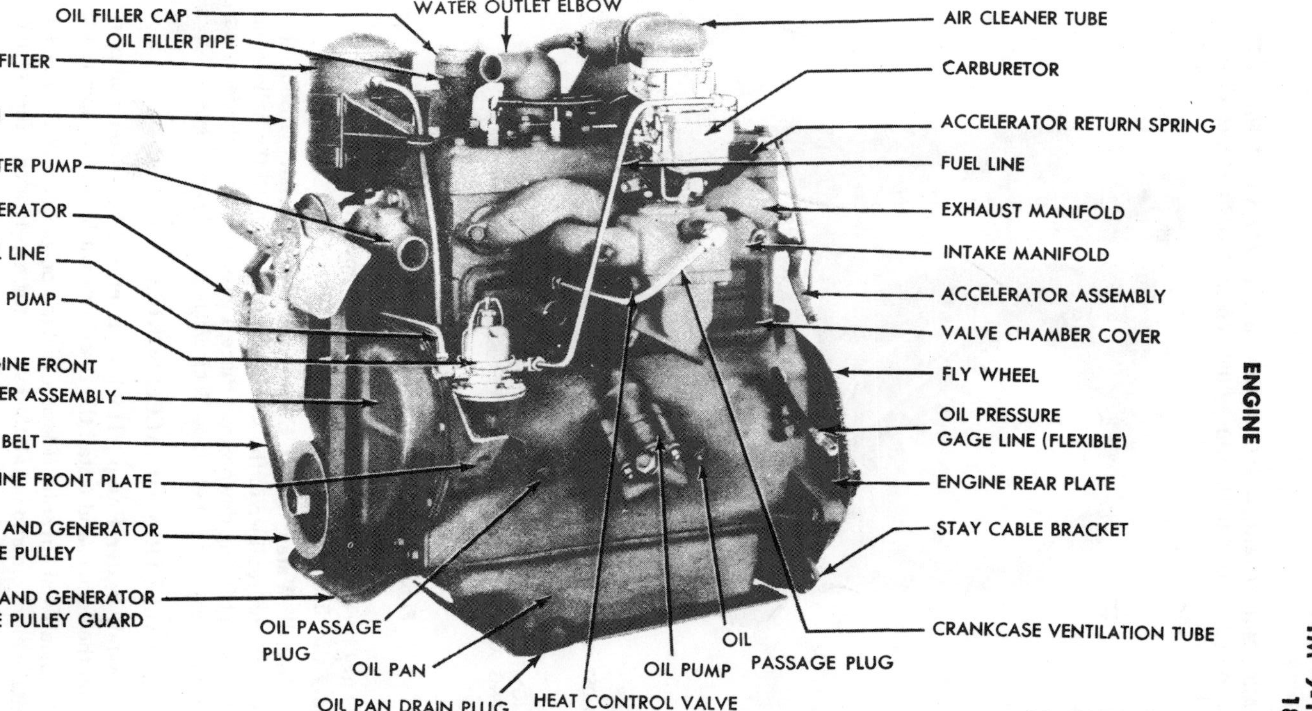
OIL FILLER CAP
OIL FILLER PIPE
OIL FILTER
FAN
WATER PUMP
GENERATOR
FUEL LINE
FUEL PUMP
ENGINE FRONT COVER ASSEMBLY
FAN BELT
ENGINE FRONT PLATE
FAN AND GENERATOR DRIVE PULLEY
FAN AND GENERATOR DRIVE PULLEY GUARD
WATER OUTLET ELBOW
OIL PASSAGE PLUG
OIL PAN
OIL PAN DRAIN PLUG
HEAT CONTROL VALVE
OIL PUMP
OIL PASSAGE PLUG
AIR CLEANER TUBE
CARBURETOR
ACCELERATOR RETURN SPRING
FUEL LINE
EXHAUST MANIFOLD
INTAKE MANIFOLD
ACCELERATOR ASSEMBLY
VALVE CHAMBER COVER
FLY WHEEL
OIL PRESSURE GAGE LINE (FLEXIBLE)
ENGINE REAR PLATE
STAY CABLE BRACKET
CRANKCASE VENTILATION TUBE
RA PD 28730

Figure 41 — Left Front View of Engine

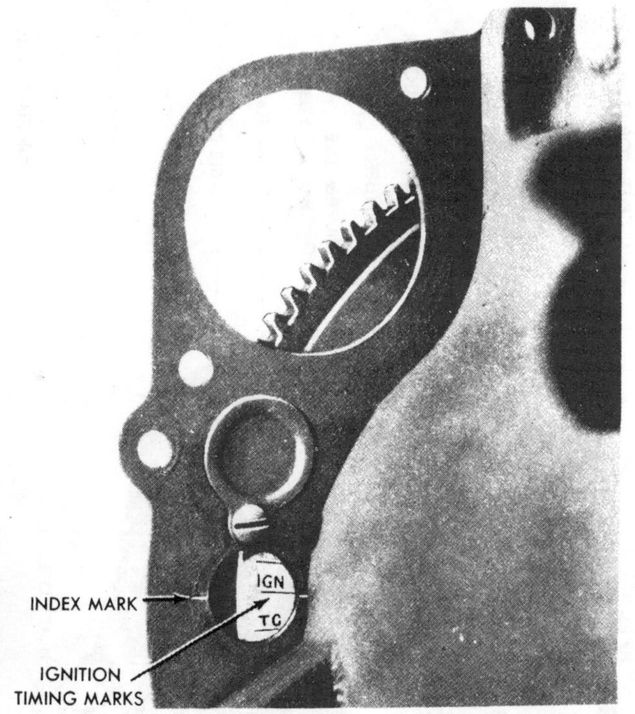

RA PD 28793

Figure 42 — IGN Timing Marks on Flywheel

points just breaking. Install the lock washers and nuts on the oil pump. Remove the distributor.

o. Install Water Outlet Elbow and Thermostat. Install the thermostat and retainer in the water outlet elbow with the bellows of the thermostat facing downward. Place a gasket on the cylinder head and install the water outlet elbow, lock washers, and cap screws.

19. INSTALLATION OF ACCESSORIES.

a. Install Water Pump. Hold a gasket and the water pump in place on the engine, and install the three lock washers and cap screws.

b. Install Carburetor. Place a carburetor gasket and diffuseı on the intake manifold and install the carburetor, accelerator return spring clip, lock washers, and nuts (fig. 41).

c. Install Oil Filter (fig. 43). Hold the oil filter in place, and install and tighten the three head nuts with a torque wrench to from 60 to 65 foot-pounds pull. Connect the oil filler pipe bracket to the oil filter bracket with a cap screw. Connect the outlet oil line to the engine front cover, and the inlet line to the elbow fitting located on the left-hand side of the engine in front of the fuel pump opening.

d. **Install Fuel Pump.** Place a gasket on the fuel pump. Hold the fuel pump in place on the engine, making sure the fuel pump rocker arm is on top of the camshaft. Install the two lock washers and cap screws in the fuel pump. Install the fuel line that connects the fuel pump and carburetor. Connect the generator brace and fuel line to the engine front plate. Connect the fuel line to the fuel pump.

e. **Install Distributor.** Place a thumb over No. 1 spark plug hole, and turn the crankshaft until No. 1 piston is coming up on compression stroke, and the timing mark "IGN" on the flywheel is in line with the index mark in the center of the timing hole on the engine rear plate (fig. 42). Install the distributor in the engine, and rotate the rotor until the distributor shaft engages in the oil pump shaft. Install the cap screw in the distributor hold-down clamp. Loosen the bolt in the distributor hold-down clamp, and turn the distributor until the points are just breaking. Tighten the bolt in the distributor hold-down clamp.

f. **Install Ignition Coil.** Install the ignition coil on the engine, making sure the bond strap is in place behind the ignition coil bracket (fig. 43). Connect the primary wire to the coil and distributor.

g. **Install Fan.** Hold the fan in place on the water pump pulley, and install the four lock washers and cap screws.

h. **Generator.** Install the generator bracket on the cylinder block with two lock washers and cap screws. Install the generator on the engine with the generator bolts, making sure there is a flat washer on each side of the rubber bushing in the generator bracket and engine front plate. Install a flat washer, lock washer, and nut on the generator front mount. Install a flat washer, bond strap, lock washer, and nut on the generator rear mount.

i. **Install Spark Plugs, Wires, and Air Cleaner Tubing.** Install air cleaner tube and bracket assembly, and tighten the head nuts from 60 to 65 foot-pounds. Connect the air cleaner tubing at the oil filler pipe (fig. 43) and carburetor. Install the distributor cap on the distributor. Pull the spark plug wires through the air cleaner tube bracket (fig. 43). Set the spark plug gap at 0.030 inch, and install the spark plugs and new spark plug gaskets in the cylinder head. Connect the spark plug wires.

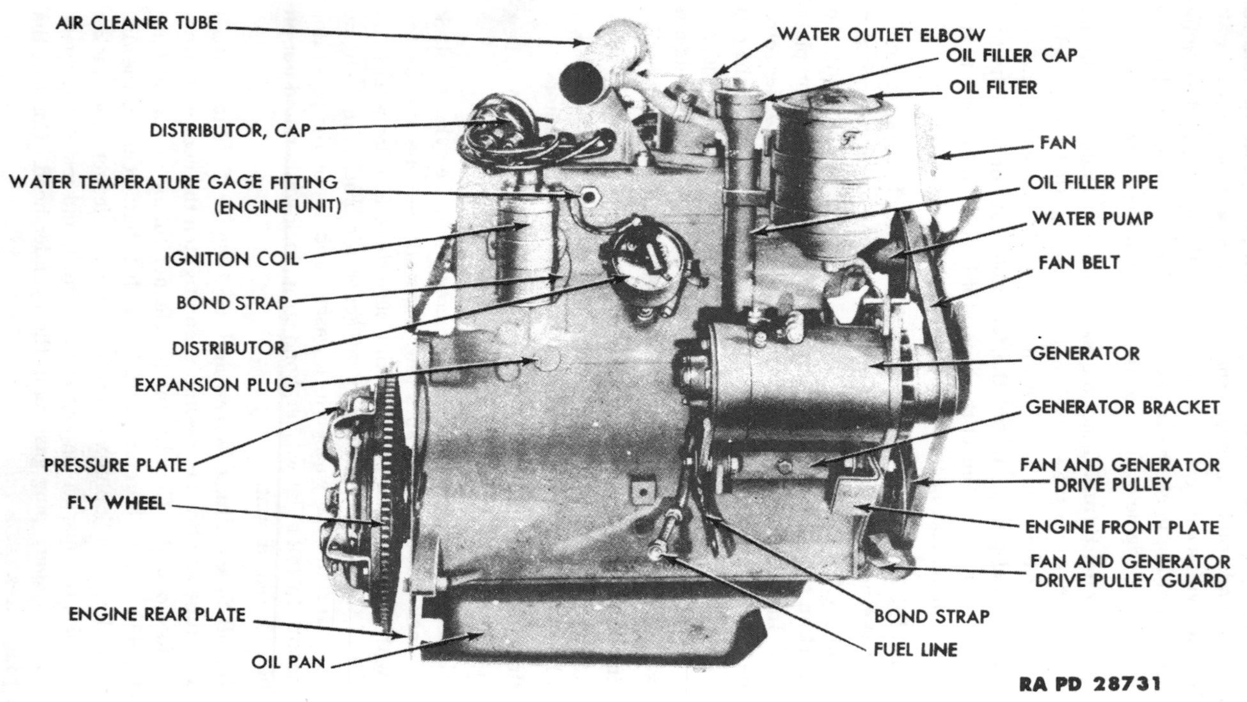

Figure 43 — Right Side View of Engine

j. Install Accelerator Linkage. Install the accelerator (throttle linkage) on the engine with two lock washers and nuts. Connect the accelerator linkage to the carburetor throttle lever with a cotter pin. Connect the accelerator return spring (fig. 41) to the accelerator return spring clip.

k. Install Engine Front Supports. Install an engine front support on each side of the engine front plate.

Section VI

INSTALLATION OF ENGINE

20. INSTALLATION.

a. General. If the clutch housing was not removed with the engine, start the installation procedure, beginning with subparagraph **b** below. If the clutch housing was removed with the engine, assemble the clutch housing onto the engine, and install the clutch housing bolts; then proceed with the installation as outlined, starting with subparagraph **b** below. Some variation exists in the location of the various bond straps used to eliminate radio interference on these vehicles. Disregard references to bond straps in the following instructions, if they are not present on the particular vehicle being worked on. If bond straps are found in locations other than those mentioned in the following instructions, they must be connected when installing the engine.

b. Place Engine in Vehicle. Install a suitable engine sling or a rope on the engine (fig. 7). Lift the engine into the vehicle with a hoist, and lower the engine until the clutch disk in the engine is in line with the main drive gear shaft in the transmission. Place the gearshift lever in low speed position, and roll the vehicle forward and backward, at the same time pushing in on the engine until the splines on the main drive gear shaft are engaged with the splines in the clutch disk. Push the engine back onto the clutch housing, and install the clutch housing bolts. Lower the engine until the two hold-down bolts and bond strap can be installed loosely in the engine front support insulator. Lower the engine the rest of the way, and remove the engine sling or rope. Slide the stay cable through the bracket on the engine rear plate (fig. 4), and through the front crossmember. Install a nut on the stay cable, tighten it until all slack is removed, and install and tighten the stay cable lock nut. Tighten the two hold-down bolts in each engine front support insulator. Tighten the nut on each engine front support insulator.

c. **Install Clutch Control Lever and Cable.** Install the four lock washers and cap screws that hold the clutch housing to the transmission. Working through the inspection opening on top of the clutch housing, install the clutch control lever on the clutch release bearing carrier, and on the ball joint located on the main drive gear bearing retainer (fig. 44). Slide the clutch control lever cable through the hole in the clutch housing, and connect the clutch control lever cable yoke end to the clutch control lever and tube assembly with a clevis pin and cotter pin. Press the ball and socket joint end of the clutch control lever inward, and slide the clutch control lever cable in place on the clutch control lever (fig. 44).

d. **Install Cranking Motor.** Hold the cranking motor in place on the clutch housing, and install and tighten the two cranking motor cap screws on the clutch housing. Hold the cranking motor support bracket in place on the engine and install a lock washer, flat washer, generator bond strap, and cap screw; do not tighten the cap screw. Install and tighten a lock washer, flat washer, and cap screw in the cranking motor and cranking motor support bracket. Tighten the cap screw in the cranking motor support bracket. Connect the cranking motor cable to the cranking motor.

e. **Connect Oil Pressure and Water Temperature Gages.** Connect the water temperature gage (engine unit) at the right-hand side of the cylinder head (fig. 5). Connect the oil pressure gage line at the flexible oil line on the left-hand side of the engine.

f. **Connect Electrical Wires and Bond Straps.** Connect the field wire on the small post of the generator, and the armature wire and condenser on the large post. Connect the ground wire at the rear of the generator at the fillister-head cap screw. Connect the bond strap at the rear of the cylinder head. Connect the primary wire to the ignition coil.

g. **Connect Choke and Throttle Controls.** Slide the choke control cable and conduit through the choke lever carburetor bracket assembly on the carburetor, and the choke control cable through the collar on the choke lever. Push in the choke control button on the instrument panel. Pull the choke lever forward as far as possible, and tighten the set screw in the collar. Connect the throttle control cable and conduit to the choke lever carburetor bracket assembly with the carburetor air cleaner clamp, nut, and bolt. Run the throttle control cable and conduit to the left of the carburetor choker link between the link and the carburetor. Run the throttle control cable

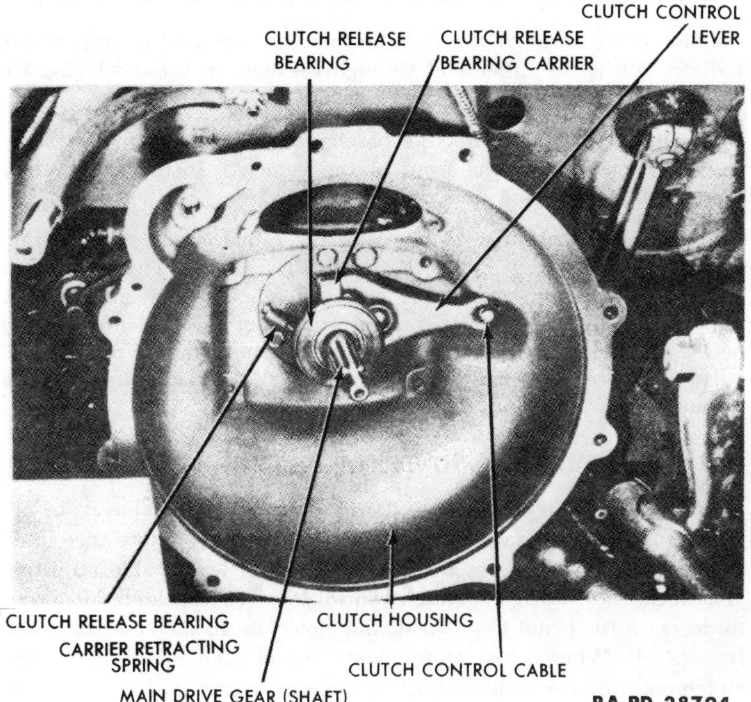

Figure 44 — Clutch Housing Installed in Vehicle

through the carburetor throttle shaft arm and screw assembly. Push the throttle control cable on the instrument panel all the way in. Tighten the screw on the carburetor throttle shaft arm.

h. Install Air Cleaner Hose. Slide the crankcase ventilation flexible hose on the oil filler pipe, and tighten the hose clamp. Slide the air cleaner flexible hose onto the metal tube, and tighten the clamp.

i. Connect Exhaust Pipe. Place a new exhaust gasket on the exhaust manifold, and attach the pipe to the manifold with a cap screw, lock washer, and bolt.

j. Install Radiator. Install the two carriage head bolts in the bottom of the radiator. Place a radiator pad on each of the two radiator mounting brackets. Lower the radiator into place in the vehicle. Install and tighten a flat washer and nut on each radiator bolt. Place a radiator bond strap on each radiator bolt, and install a flat washer and nut. Slide the radiator hose in place on the engine and radiator, and tighten the radiator hose clamps. Slide the straight end of the radiator brace through the radiator bracket mounted on top of the radiator; press the other end through the hole in the cowl (fig. 5), and install the lock washers and nuts.

k. Install Battery. Set the battery in the battery tray with the negative post toward the front of the vehicle. Install the battery hold-down frame, wing nuts, and battery cables.

l. Final Operations. Make sure the radiator and engine drain cocks are closed, and install the specified coolant. Tighten the oil pan drain plug, and install the specified amount and grade of oil. Start the engine. If the oil pressure does not register immediately on the oil pressure gage, stop the engine. Remove the oil pump relief valve retainer and prime the oil pump. Make adjustments and tests as outlined in paragraph 21.

21. ADJUSTMENTS AND TESTS IN VEHICLE.

a. Adjust Clutch. The free travel of the clutch pedal must be adjusted so that the pedal will have 3/4-inch free travel before the clutch starts to disengage. Loosen the clutch control lever cable adjusting yoke lock nut. Turn the clutch control lever cable counterclockwise to decrease the pedal free travel, and clockwise to increase the pedal free travel. When a 3/4-inch free pedal travel is obtained, tighten the clutch control lever cable adjusting yoke lock nut.

b. Set Timing With Neon Light.

(1) PRELIMINARY WORK. Loosen the screw in the timing hole cover, and move the cover to one side. Make certain the ignition switch is in the "OFF" position, then turn the engine with a crank until the timing mark "IGN" (fig. 42) on the flywheel is in line with the index mark on the engine rear plate. Mark the line under the timing mark "IGN" with chalk or white paint.

(2) CONNECT TIMING LIGHT (fig. 45). Attach the high tension lead of the timing light to the terminal of No. 1 spark plug. Attach the positive low tension lead to the positive terminal of the battery, and connect the negative low tension lead to the negative battery terminal.

(3) USE THE TIMING LIGHT. Start the engine, and allow it to warm up. Set the engine idle speed at 600 revolutions per minute. Point the timing light at the timing mark opening so that it can flash on the flywheel. If the timing mark "IGN" on the flywheel appears at the index mark on the opening in the engine rear plate, the timing is correct. If the timing mark "IGN" on the flywheel appears lower than the index mark, the timing is too far advanced.

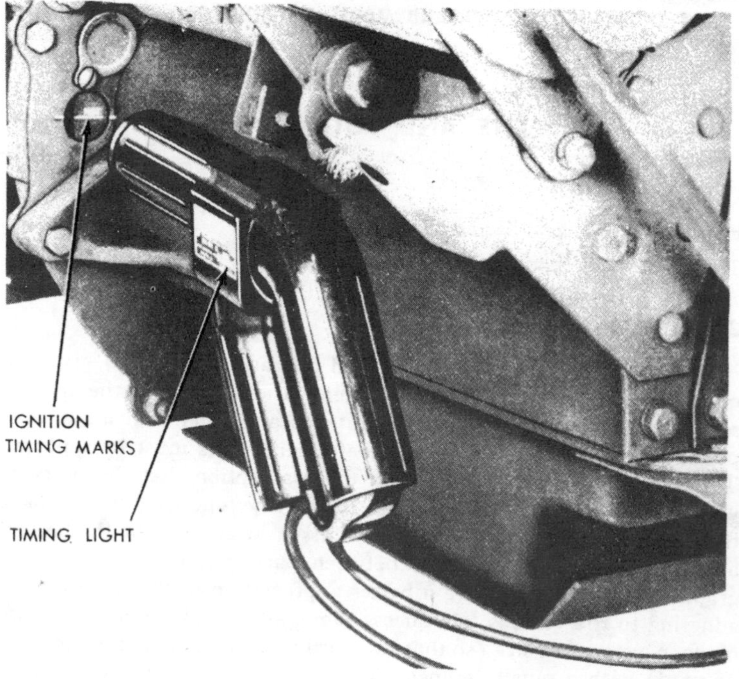

Figure 45 — Timing Engine, Using Timing Light (41-L-1440)

(4) ADJUST DISTRIBUTOR TO CORRECT TIMING. Loosen the bolt in the advance control arm, and turn the distributor clockwise to advance the ignition timing. Turn the distributor counterclockwise to retard the ignition timing. When the correct timing is obtained, tighten the bolt in the advance control arm. If the correct timing cannot be obtained by turning the distributor, set the timing as outlined in paragraph 19 **e**, but do not remove the distributor.

c. Adjust Carburetor. Start the engine, and allow it to run until it reaches normal operating temperature. Turn the idle fuel adjustment screw (fig. 1) clockwise, or counterclockwise, until all indications of vibration and roll are eliminated from the engine. Set the idle speed adjustment screw so that engine will idle at 400 revolutions per minute.

Section VII

FITS AND TOLERANCES

22. DEFINITION OF FITS.

a. General. The table of fits and tolerances (par. 23) gives the original clearance established between various parts at the time of manufacture, as well as wear and limit clearances that indicate to what point the clearance may increase before the parts must be replaced. These clearances all are based on the assumption that the parts involved are both at a temperature of 70° F. The following definitions of the various types of fits are given to assist in arriving at the correct amount of clearance required between parts not included in paragraph 23, as well as to give a better appreciation of the necessity for adhering to the various tolerances. Generally speaking, all bores are made to a standard size (so that standard reamers, plug gages, etc. may be used) with a plus tolerance. The maximum size of male parts is usually a standard size, less the minimum clearance required for the type of fit desired. The minimum size for male parts is the maximum size, minus the tolerance.

b. Ring Fit. A ring fit is the type of fit obtained when the two parts are of identical size. This is the type of fit required between a bore and a plug gage when using the plug gage to determine the inside diameter of the bore. With a ring fit, it is necessary to turn or ring the plug gage or part to force it through the bore. This type of fit does not provide space for film of oil.

c. Slip Fit. A slip fit exists when the male part is slightly smaller than the female part, and involves less clearance than a running fit (subpar. **d** below). An example of the minimum allowable clearance for a slip fit would be a piston pin that from its own weight would pass slowly through the connecting rod bushing (bushing and pin both in a vertical position). In most cases (except where only a limited movement of the parts is involved) slip fits are specified, when, due to anticipated expansion (subpar. **g** below) of the female part, enough additional clearance will result to change this type of fit to a running fit (subpar. **d** below), and provide adequate clearance for a film of oil.

d. Running Fit. A running fit is a fit providing enough clearance for a continuous film of oil between the two parts. A running fit usually requires 0.001 inch for the oil film plus a minimum of 0.001 inch clearance for each inch of diameter (subpar. g below).

e. **Press Fit.** A press fit is one that requires force to enter the male part into the bore. Accepted practice for press fits is to have the male part larger by 0.001 inch for each inch of diameter, than the bore into which it is to be pressed

f. **Shrink Fit.** Generally speaking, a shrink fit is tighter than a press fit. The amount of the shrink ranges from 0.001 inch to 0.002 inch for each inch of diameter, and in some cases even more. There are two methods of shrinking two parts together, either one of which may be used (both may be used in some instances). One eethod involves expansion of the female member by heating. The second method involves contracting the male member by chilling with dry ice or liquld air.

g. **Effect of Expansion on Fits.** Allowances are made in establishing fits on parts that are exposed to high temperatures in order to provide for the anticipated expansion of the part during operation, and still provide adequate clearance for the type of fit required. Absolute minimum allowances for expansion of parts exposed to flame or exhaust gases (pistons, piston rings, and valves) is 0.001 inch for each inch of diameter or length. In anticipating the expansion of a valve stem or piston ring to make allowances for the additional gap required between the end of the valve and the push rod, or between the ends of the piston ring, 0.001 inch for each linear inch of the part is added.

23. FITS AND TOLERANCES.

CYLINDER BLOCK

Fit Location Name	Manufacturers Fit Tolerance	Fit Wear Limit	Type of Fit
Cylinder bore out-of-round	———	0.005 in.	———
Cylinder bore taper	———	0.010 in.	———
Clearance between camshaft and (front) bearing	0.002 in. to 0.0035 in.	0.006 in.	Running
Clearance between camshaft and intermediate and rear bearings	0.002 in. to 0.0035 in.	0.008 in.	Running
Valve guide and cylinder block	———	———	Press
Clearance between valve stem and valve guide (exhaust)	0.002 in. to 0.004 in.	0.005 in.	———
(intake)	0.0015 in. to 0.0035 in.	0.0045 in	———
Clearance between valve tappet and valve tappet bore	0.0005 in. to 0.002 in.	0.003 in.	———

ORDNANCE MAINTENANCE – ENGINE AND ENGINE ACCESSORIES FOR ¼-TON 4x4 TRUCK (WILLYS-OVERLAND MODEL MB AND FORD MODEL GPW)

Fit Location Name	Manufacturers Fit Tolerance	Fit Wear Limit	Type of Fit
CONNECTING ROD AND PISTON ASSEMBLY			
Connecting rod side clearance	0.005 in. to 0.009 in.	0.013 in.	—
Connecting rod clearance on crankshaft	0.0005 in. to 0.001 in.	0.001 in.	Running
Piston pin clearance in connecting rod.	Locked in connecting rod	—	—
Piston pin clearance in piston	0.0001 in. to 0.0005 in.	0.0015 in.	Slip
Piston and cylinder at skirt	5-pound to 10-pound pull with 0.003-in. feeler	5-pound to 10-pound pull with 0.010-in. feeler	—
Piston top land and cylinder	0.0205 in. to 0.0225 in.	—	—
Piston ring to groove clearance (all rings)	0.0005 in. to 0.0015 in.	0.003 in.	—
Piston ring gap (all rings)	0.008 in. to 0.013 in.	0.013 in.	—
VALVES AND VALVE SPRINGS			
Intake valve stem diameter	0.373 in.	0.368 in.	—
Valve seat angle	45 degree	—	—
Exhaust valve stem diameter	0.3725 in.	0.3685 in.	—
Valve seat angle	45 degree	—	—
Spring tension at 2 7/64 inches (all springs)	50 pounds	—	—
Spring tension at 1¾ inches (all springs)	116 pounds	—	—
OIL PUMP			
Clearance between pinion shaft and pinion gear	0.001 in. to 0.003 in.	0.003 in.	Running
Clearance between oil pump housing and oil pump shaft	0.002 in. to 0.004 in.	0.005 in.	Running
Oil pump relief plunger spring tension at 1 1/16 in.	5½ pounds	—	—
CRANKSHAFT			
Crankshaft end play	0.004 in. to 0.006 in.	0.006 in.	—
Main bearing clearance (all main bearings)	0.0005 in. to 0.001 in.	0.001 in.	Running

24. TORQUE WRENCH READINGS.

Main bearing nuts .... 65 to 70 ft-lb
Connecting rod nuts .... 50 to 55 ft-lb
Flywheel to crankshaft cap screws .... 36 to 40 ft-lb
Cylinder head nuts .... 60 to 65 ft-lb
Cylinder head bolts .... 65 to 75 ft-lb

CHAPTER 3

CLUTCH ASSEMBLY

25. DESCRIPTION AND DATA.

a. **Description.** The clutch is of the single-plate automotive type, composed of two major units (fig. 46); the pressure plate assembly, and the driven plate or disk. The pressure plate is adjusted at the factory, and requires no other adjustments, except where it is necessary to install new clutch pressure springs, clutch fingers, or pressure plate.

b. **Data.**

Type	Single dry plate
Torque capacity	132 ft-lb
Clutch disk:	
Make	Borg and Beck
Facings	1 woven, 1 molded asbestos
Facing diameter	Inside 5⅛ in. Outside 7⅞ in.
Facing thickness	0.125 in.
Pressure plate:	
Make	Atwood
Number of springs	3
Spring pressure at 1$\frac{9}{16}$ in.	220 to 230 lb

26. PRESSURE PLATE DISASSEMBLY.

a. **Remove Clutch Adjusting Screw** (fig. 47). Place the pressure plate in a press with a wood block 2½ inches square on top of the clutch fingers (fig. 48). Depress the clutch fingers, and remove the three clutch adjusting screws, lock nuts, and lock washers. Release the pressure on the clutch fingers slowly to prevent the clutch pressure springs from flying out from under the clutch fingers.

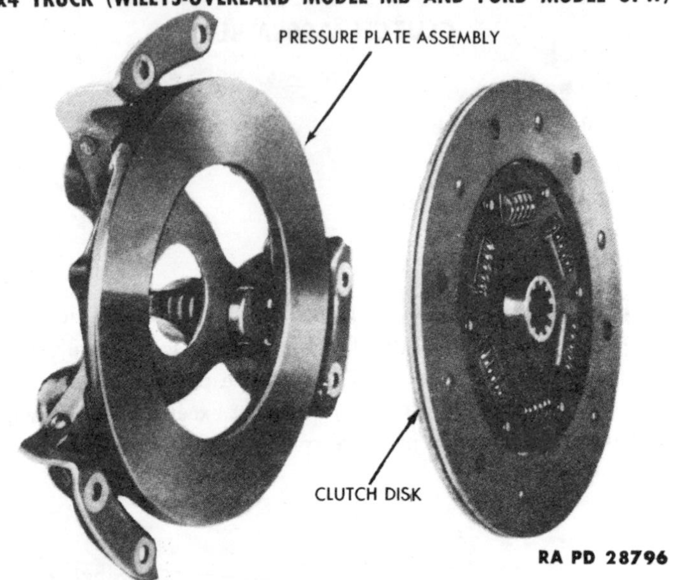

Figure 46 — Clutch Disk and Pressure Plate

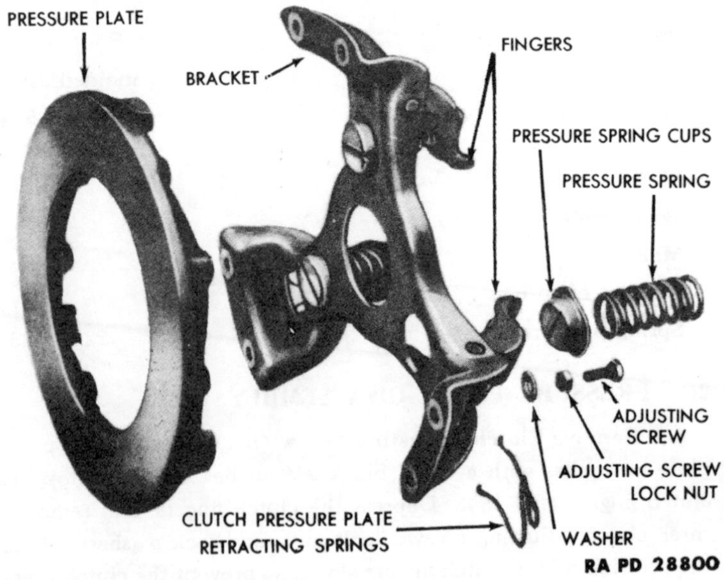

Figure 47 — Pressure Plate Disassembled

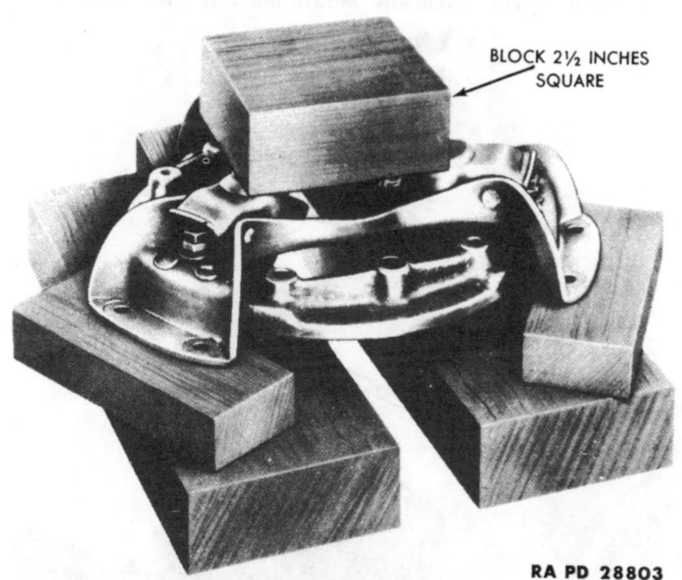

Figure 48 – Pressure Plate Blocked Up in Press for Disassembling or Assembling

b. **Remove Clutch Pressure Spring Cups and Springs.** Push the clutch pressure spring cups and clutch pressure springs from the pressure plate bracket with a screwdriver or punch (fig. 49). Remove the clutch pressure plate return springs from the clutch pressure plate bracket.

27. CLEANING, INSPECTION, AND REPAIR.

a. **Cleaning.** Clean all parts thoroughly in dry-cleaning solvent.

b. **Inspection and Repair.**

(1) CLUTCH PRESSURE PLATE (fig. 47). A ridged, scored, radial cracked, or burned pressure plate must be replaced.

(2) PRESSURE PLATE BRACKET (fig. 47). A distorted pressure plate bracket or a pressure plate bracket with worn clutch fingers must be replaced.

(3) CLUTCH PRESSURE SPRINGS. Place each clutch pressure spring in a tension scale, and depress it to 1$\frac{9}{16}$ inches (fig. 50). If

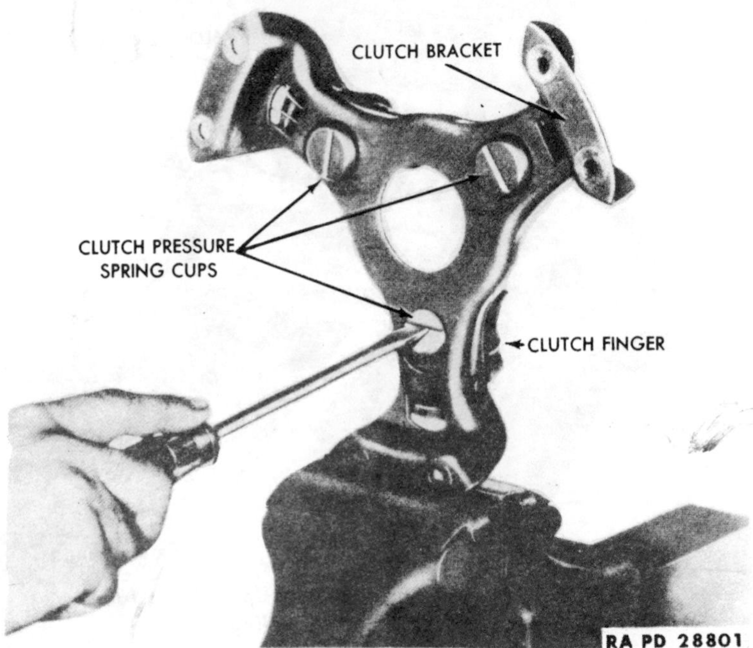

Figure 49 — Removing Clutch Pressure Spring Cups and Clutch Pressure Springs

the spring tension is less than 220 pounds on any clutch pressure spring, it must be replaced.

28. ASSEMBLY OF PRESSURE PLATE.

a. Install Clutch Pressure Spring Cups and Springs. Install the clutch pressure spring cups and clutch pressure springs in the pressure plate bracket (fig. 51), making sure the indentation of each clutch pressure spring cup is toward the center of the pressure plate bracket (fig. 51).

b. Install Pressure Plate on Pressure Plate Bracket. Slide a pressure plate return spring in place under each clutch finger on the pressure plate bracket (fig. 47). Place the pressure plate bracket in a press, blocking it up as shown in figure 48. Place a wood block 2½ inches square on top of the clutch fingers, and depress the fingers (fig. 48). Install the three clutch adjusting screws, lock nuts, and flat washers in the pressure plate.

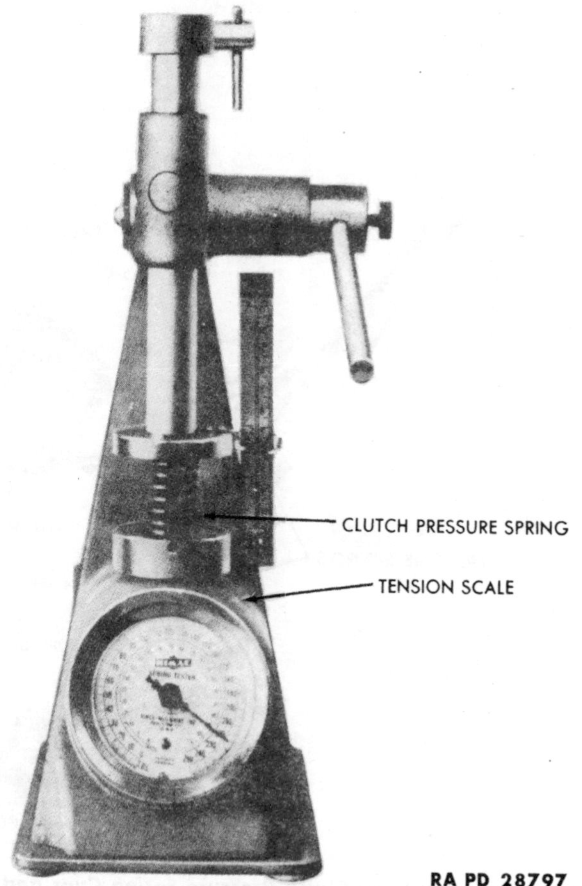

Figure 50 — Testing Spring Tension of Clutch Pressure Spring, Using Tester (41-T-1600)

c. **Adjust Pressure Plate.** Install the clutch disk and pressure plate onto the flywheel (par. 18 **h**). Hold a straightedge across the clutch fingers, and measure the distance from the straightedge to the face of the pressure plate bracket (fig. 52). Turn each clutch adjusting screw until a distance of $2\frac{7}{32}$ inches is established between the straightedge and the face of the pressure plate bracket. Hold the clutch adjusting screws with a wrench, and tighten each clutch adjusting screw lock nut. Recheck the distance between the straightedge and the face on the pressure plate bracket.

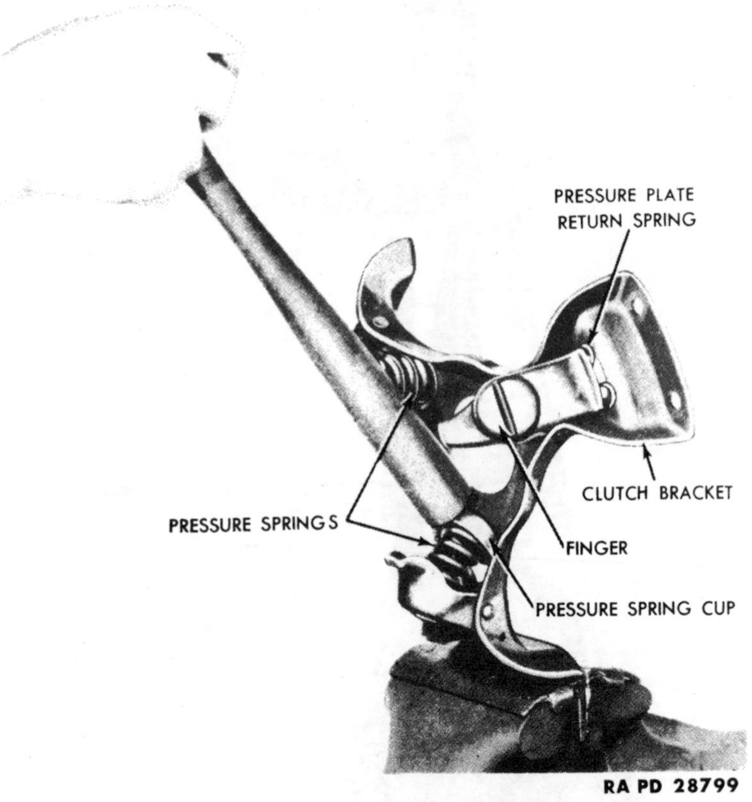

Figure 51 — Installing Clutch Pressure Spring Cups and Pressure Springs in Pressure Plate Bracket

---

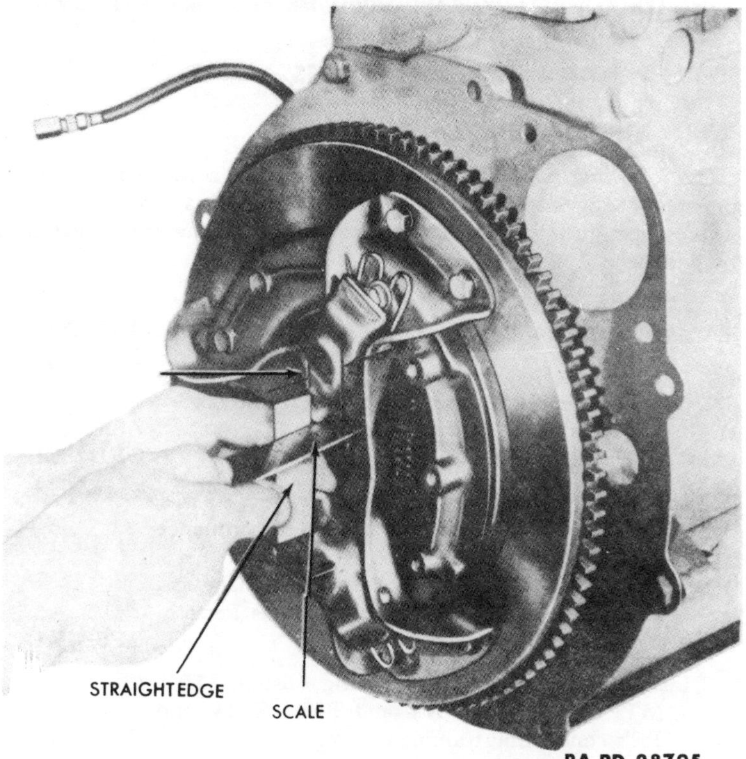

Figure 52 — Adjusting Pressure Plate

ORDNANCE MAINTENANCE — ENGINE AND ENGINE ACCESSORIES FOR 1/4-TON 4x4 TRUCK (WILLYS-OVERLAND MODEL MB AND FORD MODEL GPW)

REFERENCES

PUBLICATIONS INDEXES.

The following publications indexes should be consulted frequently for latest changes to or revisions of the publications given in this list of references and for new publications relating to materiel covered in this manual:

Introduction to Ordnance Catalog (explaining SNL system)	ASF Cat. ORD1 IOC
Ordnance Publications for Supply Index (index to SNL's)	ASF Cat. ORD2 OPSI
Index to ordnance publications (listing FM's, TM's, TC's, and TB's of interest to ordnance personnel, MWO's, OPSR, BSD, S of SR's, OSSC's and OFSB's and includes Alphabetical List of Major Items with Publications Pertaining Thereto)	OFSB 1-1
List of Publications for Training (listing MR's, MTP's, T/BA's, T/A's, and FM's, TM's, and TR's concerning training)	FM 21-6
List of Training Films, Film Strips, and Film Bulletins (listing TF's, FS's, and FB's by serial number and subject)	FM-21-7
Military Training Aids (listing Graphic Training Aids, Models, Devices, and Displays)	FM 21-8

STANDARD NOMENCLATURE LISTS.

Cleaning, preserving and lubrication materials, recoil fluids, special oils, and miscellaneous related items	SNL K-1
Soldering, brazing and welding materials, gases and related items	SNL K-2
Tools, maintenance for repair of automotive vehicles	SNL G-27 Volume 1.

REFERENCES

Tool-sets, for ordnance service command automotive shops .... SNL N-30

Tool-sets, motor transport .... SNL N-19

Truck, ¼-ton, 4x4, command reconnaissance (Ford and Willys) .... SNL G-503

EXPLANATORY PUBLICATIONS.

Fundamental Principles.

Automotive electricity .... TM 10-580

Automotive lubrication .... TM 10-540

Basic Maintenance Manual .... TM 38-250

Driver's Manual .... TM 10-460

Electrical fundamentals .... TM 1-455

Military motor vehicles .... AR 850-15

Motor vehicle inspections and preventive maintenance service .... TM 9-2810

Precautions in handling gasoline .... AR 850-20

Standard Military Motor Vehicles .... TM 9-2800

The internal combustion engine .... TM 10-570

Maintenance and Repair.

Cleaning, preserving, lubricating and welding materials and similar items issued by the Ordnance Department .... TM 9-850

Cold weather lubrication and service of combat vehicles and automotive materiel .... OFSB 6-11

Maintenance and care of pneumatic tires and rubber treads .... TM 31-200

Ordnance Maintenance: Power train, chassis, and body for ¼-ton 4x4 truck (Ford and Willys) .... TM 9-1803B

Ordnance Maintenance: Electrical equipment (Auto-Lite) .... TM 9-1825B

Ordnance Maintenance: Hydraulic Brake System (Wagner) .... TM 9-1827C

Ordnance Maintenance: Carburetors (Carter) .... TM 9-1826A

Ordnance Maintenance: Fuel Pumps .... TM 9-1828A

Ordnance Maintenance: Speedometers and Tachometers (Stewart-Warner) .... TM 9-1829A

Tune-up and adjustment .... TM 10-530

Protection of Materiel.

Camouflage .... FM 5-20

Chemical decontamination, materials and equipment .... TM 3-220

Decontamination of armored force vehicles .... FM 17-59

Defense against chemical attack .... FM 21-40

Explosives and demolitions .... FM 5-25

Storage and Shipment.

Ordnance storage and shipment chart, group G—Major items .... OSSC-G

Registration of motor vehicles .... AR 850-10

Rules governing the loading of mechanized and motorized army equipment, also major caliber guns, for the United States Army and Navy, on open top equipment published by Operations and Maintenance Department of Association of American Railroads.

Storage of motor vehicle equipment .... AR 850-18

INDEX

ORDNANCE MAINTENANCE — ENGINE AND ENGINE ACCESSORIES FOR ¼-TON 4x4 TRUCK (WILLYS-OVERLAND MODEL MB AND FORD MODEL GPW)

C — Cont'd

INDEX

INDEX

DEPARTMENT OF THE ARMY
TECHNICAL MANUAL

DEPARTMENT OF THE AIR
FORCE TECHNICAL ORDER

TM 9-1826A

TO 19-75CCA-6

ORDNANCE MAINTENANCE

CARBURETORS (CARTER)

(Willys-Overland Model MB and Ford Model GPW)

CONTENTS

DEPARTMENTS OF THE ARMY AND THE AIR FORCE

DECEMBER 1952

CHAPTER 6

TYPE W-O CARBURETOR, MODELS 450S, 450SA, 539S, 567S, 572S, AND 698S

Section I. DESCRIPTION AND DATA

38. Description

The type W-O carburetors (fig. 27) are of the outside vented "unbalanced" type. Models 539S, 572S, and 698S differ from the others in that the metering rod seats in the metering rod jet when the throttle is in the normal idling position. This seals off the high speed passage from the float bowl and prevents any discharge of fuel from the high-speed nozzle which might otherwise occur if the engine were operated on a steep incline. This feature also serves as an antipercolator (par. 41*b* (2)). Descriptions of the low-speed, high-speed, float, pump, and choke circuits are given in paragraphs 39 through 43.

39. Float Circuit
(fig. 28)

The float circuit consists of a needle and seat, float pin, float, and bowl cover gasket. The needle and seat used in these carburetors differs from the conventional type in that the needle is made hollow for a portion of its length and a spring and pin are inserted. When the carburetor is assembled, the lip of the float bears on the spring loaded pin in the needle. This device helps to prevent needle chatter and consequent flooding of the carburetor under conditions of excessive vibration. It is very important that the specified float level be maintained since even a slight deviation will result in unsatisfactory high speed performance.

40. Low-Speed Circuit
(fig. 29)

a. General. The low-speed circuit supplies fuel for idle and early part throttle operation. In most carburetors, the fuel must first pass through the main metering jet to get to the low speed circuit. However, this is not the case in the type W-O carburetor. Fuel from the bowl flows directly to the low-speed circuit through the calibrated idle well jet. This feature causes the circuit to be termed "inde-

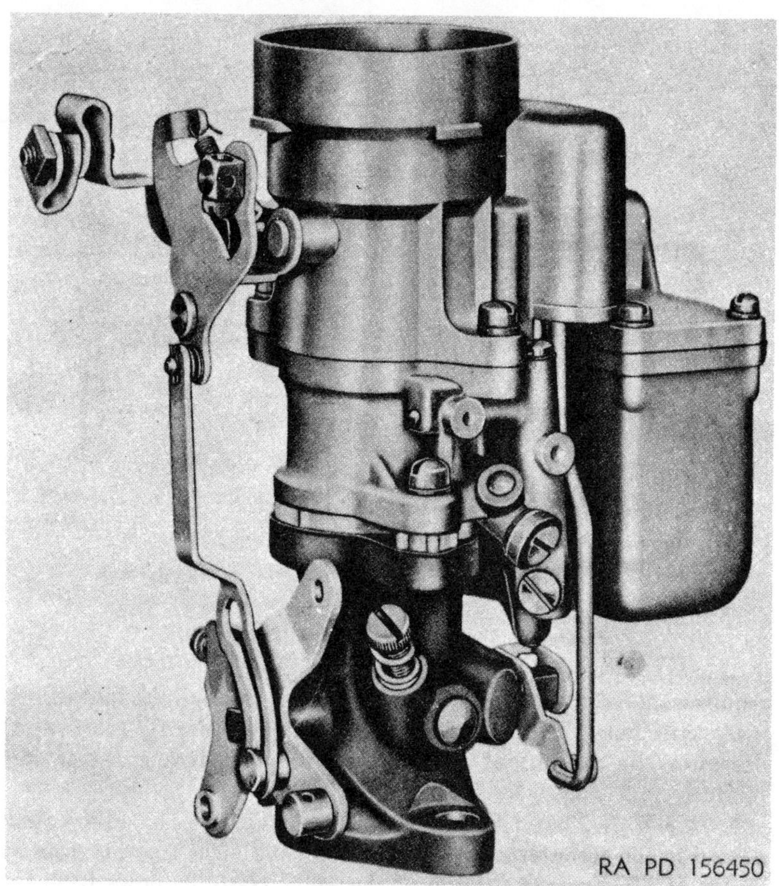

Figure 27. Typical W-O carburetor.

pendent" or "isolated." Adjacent to the bowl is the idle-well passage in which the low-speed jet is installed. Fuel from the bowl flows through the idle-well jet to the well from which it flows through the calibrated orifice in the low-speed jet and up into the low-speed passage. Here air is admitted from the carburetor throat through the bypass, and the resulting mixture of fuel and air passes through the economizer, which is a restriction in the cross passage. An additional amount of air enters the low-speed passage at this point, through the idle bleed hole, and the mixture flows down the passage terminating at the idle port and idle adjustment screw hole. Most of the fuel is discharged from the idle port. This port is made in the shape of a slot so that as the throttle valve is opened to admit more air it also uncovers a greater portion of the idle port and permits additional gasoline to mix with the air to maintain the necessary air-fuel ratio. It is by this means that a smooth transition is made from the idling

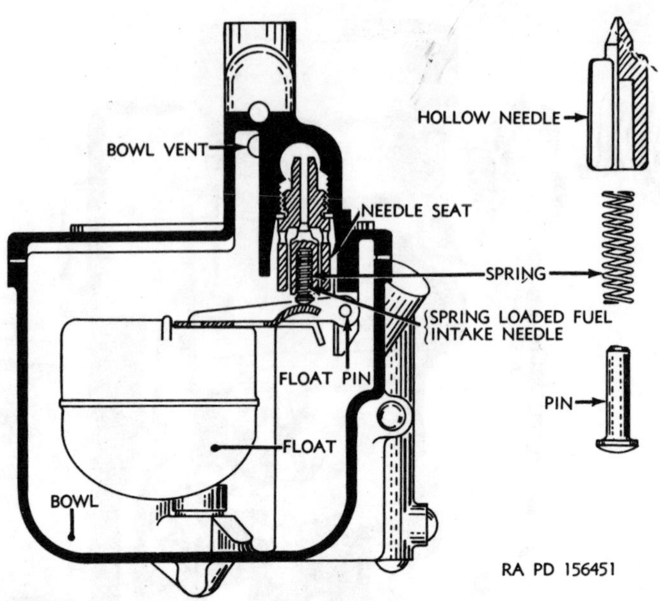

Figure 28. Type W-O carburetor, float circuit.

requirements of the engine. Fuel is admitted through the idle adjustment screw hole. Turning the adjustment screw inwardly (clockwise) decreases the amount of fuel discharged and gives a leaner idle mixture.

b. Idle-Well Vent (Models 450S and 450SA). The idle well is vented to the carburetor bowl in the 450S and 450SA carburetors by means of a passage at the top of the well. Gasoline flows from the bowl to the idle well through the idle-well jet by the force of gravity. Thus, when the demands of the idle circuit are greater than the fuel flowing through the idle-well jet, the balance of the demand is met by admitting air through the idle-well vent. This well vent passage is not included in carburetor models 539S, 567S, 572S, and 698S. Consequently, only gasoline is admitted to the low-speed jet.

c. Idle-Well Jet. Since there is no connection between the low-speed circuit and the high-speed circuit, the low-speed circuit delivers gasoline throughout the entire range, even at wide open throttle. The purpose of the idle-well jet is two-fold:

(1) At part throttle and higher speeds, it aids in the metering of the fuel from the low-speed circuit, however, it does not meter the fuel during idle operation.

(2) On bumpy ground, where the vehicle has extreme side sway, the idle-well jet prevents the gasoline from readily draining out of the idle well, thus assuring constant idle circuit operation regardless of terrain.

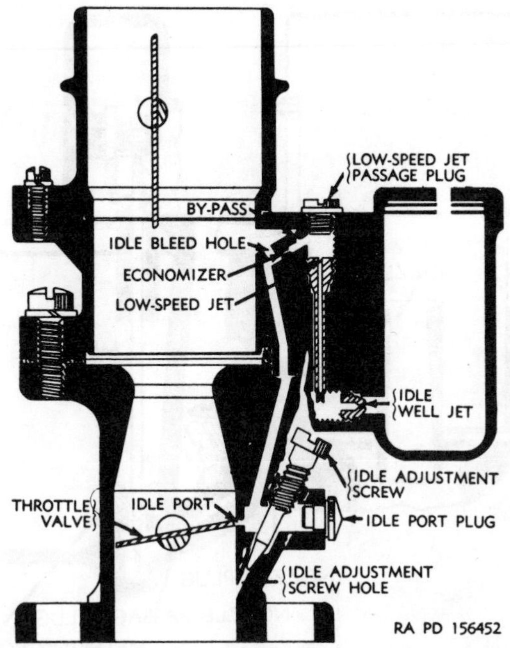

Figure 29. Type W-O carburetor low-speed circuit.

41. High-Speed Circuit
(fig. 30)

a. General. Fuel from the bowl is metered to the high-speed circuit through the calibrated orifice provided by the metering rod jet and the metering rod within it. From this point, the fuel is conducted through a passage to the nozzle extending into the small venturi. The upper tip of this nozzle is flush with the inner wall of the venturi and the nozzle is, therefore, known as a "flush type" nozzle. When the fuel level in the carburetor bowl is correct, the level of the fuel in the nozzle is just below the lower lip. The metering rod has several steps or tapers machined on the lower end, and as it is raised in the jet it makes the effective size of the fuel orifice greater, thus, permitting more fuel to flow through the circuit to meet the load demand imposed upon the engine. At wide open throttle position, the smallest step of the metering rod is in the circular opening of the jet, thus permitting the maximum amount of fuel to flow through the circuit to meet the requirements of maximum power.

b. Metering Rod Seat (Models 539S, 572S, and 698S). On these W-O carburetors, the metering rod seats in the metering rod jet when the throttle is closed (idle position). To insure the seating of the rod in the jet, the metering rod eye is elongated on these models; the

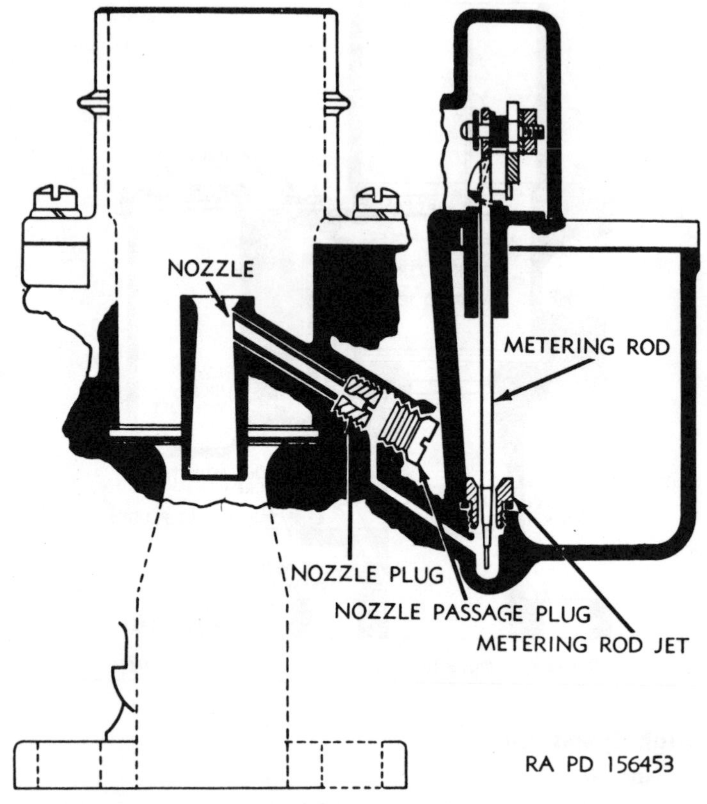

Figure 30. Type W-O carburetor high-speed circuit.

metering rod spring which is hooked through a hole in the rod rather than around it, exerts a downward pressure on the rod. The seating of the metering rod in the jet has two purposes:

(1) It prevents fuel in the bowl from spilling over the nozzle and stalling the engine when the vehicle is operated at extreme angles on rough terrain.

(2) It acts as an antipercolator. When a hot engine is idled or stopped the heat of the engine tends to vaporize the fuel in the high-speed nozzle passage. These bubbles of vapor will force fuel out of the nozzle and cause flooding of the engine. This is known as percolation. The seating of the metering rod in the metering jet prevents any large amount of fuel from being forced into the engine by isolating the high-speed circuit from the carburetor bowl.

c. Adjustable Throttle Stop (Models 567S, and 572S). Models 567S and 572S have an adjustable throttle stop on the throttle lever in order to limit the maximum throttle opening.

42. Pump Circuit
(fig. 31)

a. General. As the throttle is closed, the linkage raises the plunger toward the top of the pump cylinder. On this stroke of the pump, a quantity of fuel from the bowl flows through the intake check valve into the pump cylinder. At this time the discharge check valve is seated preventing air from entering the pump circuit through the pump jet. The check valves are protected from dirt by a strainer located directly beneath them. When the throttle is opened, the plunger is forced downward and the fuel below it is pushed out of the pump cylinder back to the check valve passage. The pressure of the fuel seats the intake check valve ball, preventing the return of the fuel to the bowl. The discharge check valve disk is forced off its seat and the fuel passes through it to the pump jet where it is metered and discharged.

b. Delayed Action. It is necessary to provide a delayed action for the discharge of fuel from the pump circuit. This action is achieved in the type W-O carburetors by means of the pump arm spring. This spring connects the pump arm and collar to the pump lever. Therefore, when the throttle is opened, the linkage drives the pump plunger

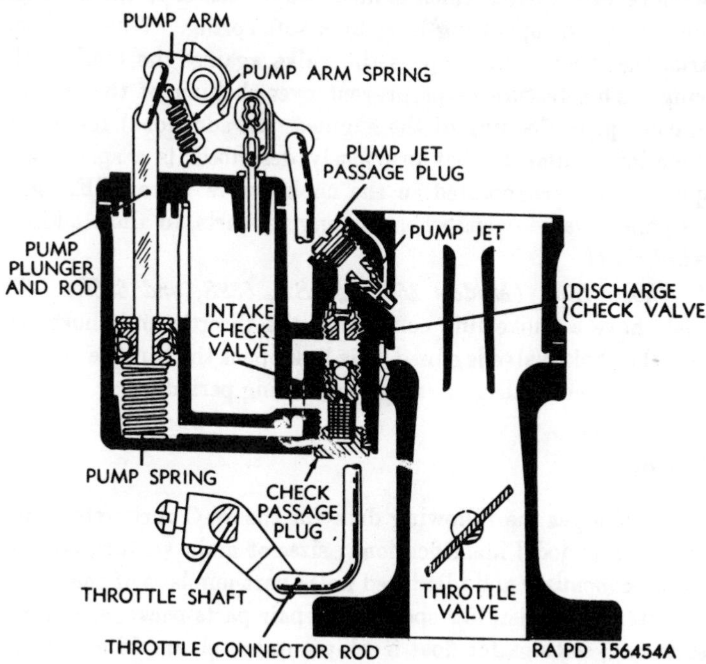

Figure 31. W-O pump circuit.

through the pump arm spring. This provides a continuous discharge from the pump circuit for the necessary time interval.

c. Pump Jet Relief Hole. In the pump circuit of these carburetors "pump bleed" is not allowed to occur. "Pump bleed" is the term used to describe the delivery of fuel from the pump jet during constant throttle operation (par. 11*c*). In the W-O carburetors, the discharge end of the pump jet is extended; both ends of the pump jet have shoulders which seat in the casting. A small hole, from the outside of the casting, vents a cross-drilling between the two seating surfaces in the jet. This vent to the atmosphere destroys the low pressure effect at the pump jet, hence no fuel can bleed from the pump circuit during constant-throttle operation.

43. Choke Circuit
(fig. 32.)

a. General. These carburetors employ a manual type choke. When the choke is used, the mixture is enriched by cutting down the amount of air admitted through the carburetor and by lowering the pressure in the throat causing a greater amount of fuel to be discharged. These carburetors use a choke valve with a semiautomatic feature, the choke valve plate, which is mounted off center in the air horn, is connected to the operating lever by a soft spring. When the engine starts, the incoming air opens the valve against the tension of the spring. This feature helps prevent over-choking of the carburetor and consequent flooding of the engine. An additional feature, with a function similar to that previously described, is a spring loaded poppet valve incorporated in the choke valve plate (BF, fig. 33). This poppet valve opens when the engine starts, to allow additional inward relief.

b. Choke Link (Models 450S, 450SA, 539S, and 698S). These models have a choke link connecting the throttle and choke levers. When the choke valve is closed, this link opens the throttle slightly in order to prevent stalling during the choking period.

44. Data

Table V gives the following data for the W-O carburetors: flange number (for model identification); sizes of main venturi, bowl vent, bypass, economizer and idle bleed hole; part numbers of the metering rod, metering rod jet, low-speed jet, repair parts package, and gasket assortment; settings for float level, pump travel, and idle adjustment screw; and numbers of the metering rod and float level gages.

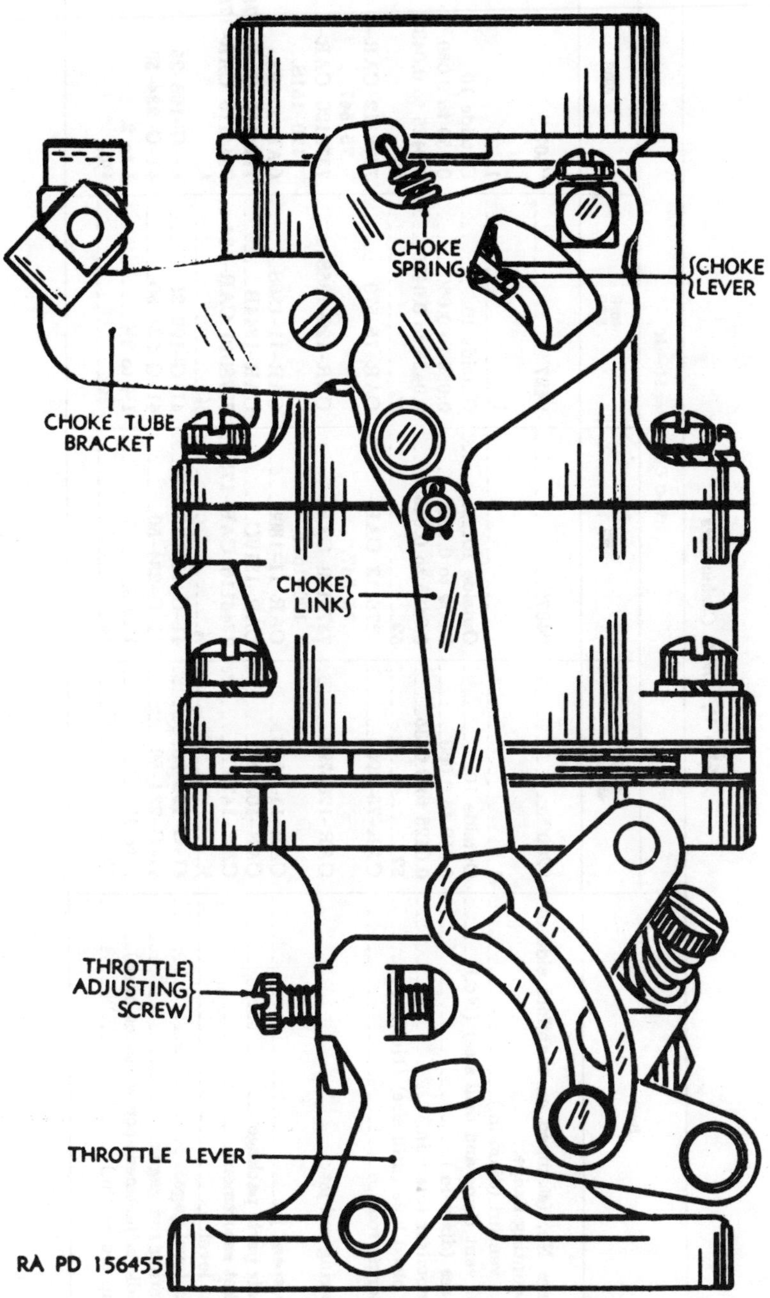

Figure 32. Type W-O carburetor choke circuit.

Table V. W-O Carburetors

Item	W-O Carburetor Models			
	450S 450SA	539S	567S 572S	698S
Flange No. (stamped on manifold side of mounting flange).	"200"	"407"	"427"	"407."
Main venturi (diam-in.)	1	1	¾	1.
Bowl vent (type and drill size) (No.)	Outside 10	Outside 10	Outside 10	Outside 10
Bypass (diam-in.)	0.059 to 0.060	0.059 to 0.060	0.059 to 0.060	0.059 to 0.060.
Economizer (diam-in.)	0.0425 to 0.0435	0.0425 to 0.0435	0.0425 to 0.0435	0.0425 to 0.0435.
Idle bleed hole (drill size) (No.)	52	52	52	52.
Metering rod	CAR–75–390	7378112 CAR–75–547.	CAR–75–570	7378112 CAR–75–547.
Metering rod jet	CAR–120–79S	7378120 CAR–120–1518	CAR–120–135S	7378120 CAR–120–151S.
Low speed jet	CAR–11–163S	CAR–11–180S	CAR–11–180S	CAR–1389A.
Repair parts package	CAR–1087B	CAR–1319C	CAR–1344B	7744116 CAR–175A.
Gasket assortment	CAR–147A	7744116 CAR–175A	7378040 CAR–184	7744116 CAR–175A.
Float level	⅜	⅜	⅜	⅜.
Float level gage	41–G–196–25	41–G–196–25	41–G–196–25	41–G–196–25.
Metering rod gage	41–G–234–50	41–G–234–50	41–G–234–50	41–G–234–50.
Set idle adjustment screw (turns open)	½ to 2½	1 to 2	1½ to 2½	1 to 2.
Pump travel (in.)	17/64	17/64	17/64	17/64.

Section II. REBUILD OF TYPE W-O CARBURETORS

45. General

Due to the close tolerances of carburetor parts (as little as 0.00025 inch for the metering rod and metering rod jet), it is not possible to repair most of the individual parts. The instructions following cover the procedure for completely cleaning and adjusting the carburetor. If the carburetor is to be rebuilt, new parts furnished in repair parts package (table V, par. 44) must be installed. Obviously, if this is done, those parts which are to be replaced need not be cleaned and inspected. When the carburetor is disassembled for any reason, a new gasket assortment (table V, par. 44) should be installed.

46. Disassembly
(fig. 33)

a. Remove and Disassemble Air Horn.

(1) Remove pin spring (AL), choke link (AS), and choke link spring (AR).

(2) Remove air horn lock washer screw (BH) and air horn (BE) with all parts attached.

(3) Remove choke valve plate screws (BG) and choke valve plate (BF).

(4) Remove choke tube bracket (AV) and choke shaft and lever (AY).

b. Remove and Disassemble Bowl Cover (ZZ).

(1) Remove throttle arm screw (F), rod retainer (H), throttle arm (G), and throttle connector rod (J).

(2) Remove bowl cover lock washer screw (AC) and bowl cover (ZZ) with all parts attached.

(3) Remove pin spring (AQ), connector link (AP), and plunger and rod (RR).

(4) Remove metering rod pin nut (AF), metering rod pin washer (AG), metering rod spring (AH), metering rod (AE), metering rod disk (AD), pump arm spring (AM), pump arm and collar (AN), and pump operating lever (AJ).

(5) Remove float pin (AB), float (SS), fuel intake needle (VV), needle seat (WW), needle seat gasket (XX), and bowl cover gasket (YY).

c. Disassemble Main Body.

(1) Remove pump spring (LL).

(2) Remove low-speed jet passage plug (NN), low-speed jet passage plug gasket (MM), and low-speed jet (FF).

(3) Remove pump jet passage plug (KK), pump jet passage plug gasket (JJ), and pump jet (HH).

A—THROTTLE VALVE PLATE SCREW
B—THROTTLE VALVE PLATE
C—THROTTLE BODY
D—THROTTLE SHAFT AND LEVER
E—THROTTLE ADJUSTING DOG POINT SCREW
F—THROTTLE ARM SCREW
G—THROTTLE ARM
H—ROD RETAINER
J—THROTTLE CONNECTOR ROD
K—IDLE PORT PLUG
L—MAIN BODY GASKET
M—INSULATOR
N—IDLE ADJUSTMENT SCREW SPRING
P—IDLE ADJUSTMENT SCREW
Q—PIN SPRING
R—CHECK VALVE PASSAGE PLUG
S—CHECK VALVE PASSAGE PLUG GASKET
T—STRAINER
U—INTAKE CHECK VALVE
V—DISCHARGE CHECK VALVE
W—NOZZLE GASKET
X—NOZZLE
Y—NOZZLE RETAINER PLUG
Z—NOZZLE PASSAGE PLUG GASKET

AA—NOZZLE PASSAGE PLUG
BB—IDLE-WELL JET
CC—IDLE-PASSAGE PLUG GASKET
DD—IDLE-PASSAGE PLUG
EE—MAIN BODY
FF—LOW-SPEED JET
GG—MAIN BODY LOCK WASHER SCREW
HH—PUMP JET
JJ—PUMP JET PASSAGE PLUG GASKET
KK—PUMP JET PASSAGE PLUG
LL—PUMP SPRING
MM—LOW-SPEED JET PASSAGE PLUG GASKET
NN—LOW-SPEED JET PASSAGE PLUG
PP—METERING ROD JET GASKET
QQ—METERING ROD JET
RR—PLUNGER AND ROD
SS—FLOAT
TT—NEEDLE PIN
UU—NEEDLE SPRING
VV—FUEL INTAKE NEEDLE
WW—NEEDLE SEAT
XX—NEEDLE SEAT GASKET
YY—BOWL COVER GASKET
ZZ—BOWL COVER
AB—FLOAT PIN
AC—BOWL COVER LOCK WASHER SCREW

AD—METERING ROD DISK
AE—METERING ROD
AF—METERING ROD PIN NUT
AG—METERING ROD PIN WASHER
AH—METERING ROD SPRING
AJ—PUMP OPERATING LEVER
AK—METERING ROD PIN
AL—PIN SPRING
AM—PUMP ARM SPRING
AN—PUMP ARM AND COLLAR
AP—CONNECTOR LINK
AQ—PIN SPRING
AR—CHOKE LINK SPRING
AS—CHOKE LINK
AT—WIRE CLAMP SCREW
AU—PIN SPRING
AV—CHOKE TUBE BRACKET
AW—TUBE CLAMP
AX—TUBE CLAMP NUT
AY—CHOKE SHAFT AND LEVER
AZ—CHOKE SCREW
BC—CHOKE SPRING
BD—TUBE CLAMP SCREW
BE—AIR HORN
BF—CHOKE VALVE PLATE
BG—CHOKE VALVE PLATE SCREW
BH—AIR HORN LOCK WASHER SCREW

Figure 33. Type W-O carburetor, model 698S—exploded view.

RA PD 156456A

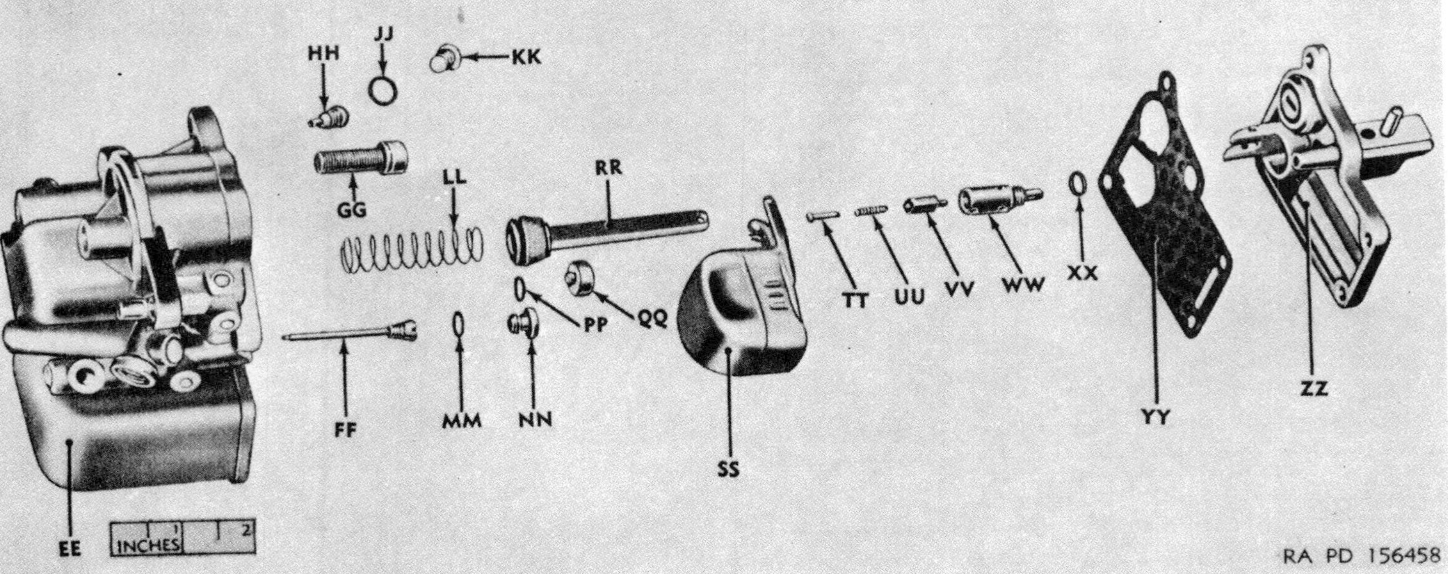
HH
JJ
KK
GG
LL
RR
FF
MM
NN
PP
QQ
SS
TT
UU
VV
WW
XX
YY
ZZ
EE
INCHES 1 2
RA PD 156458

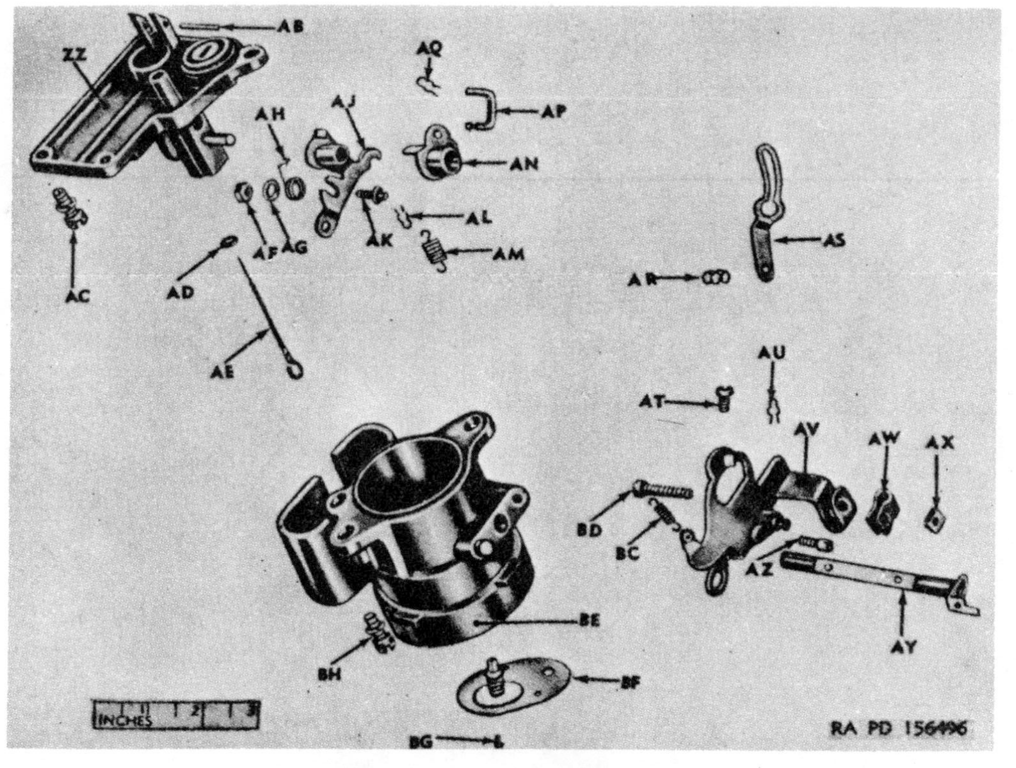

Figure 33. Type W-O carburetor, model 698S—exploded view—Continued

(4) Remove nozzle passage plug (AA), nozzle passage plug gasket (Z), nozzle retainer plug (Y), nozzle (X), and nozzle gasket (W). Use puller 41-P-2951-10 (fig. 18) to remove nozzle.

(5) Remove metering rod jet (QQ) and metering rod jet gasket (PP).

(6) Remove check valve passage plug (R), check valve passage plug gasket (S), strainer (T), intake check valve (U), and discharge check valve (V).

(7) Remove idler passage plug (DD), idler passage plug gasket (CC), and idle well jet (BB).

d. Remove and Disassemble Throttle Body (C).

(1) Disassemble throttle body (C) from main body (EE) and remove insulator (M) and main body gaskets (L).

(2) Remove throttle valve plate screws (A), throttle valve plate (B), and throttle shaft and lever (D).

(3) Remove idle adjustment screw (P), idle adjustment screw spring (N), idle port plug (K), fuel intake needle (VV), needle spring (UU), and needle pin (TT).

47. Cleaning

Soak all parts in dry-cleaning solvent or volatile mineral spirits for at least 20 minutes. (The use of a wire basket for the small parts will facilitate their handling.) Blow out all castings with compressed air. Blow out all passages by applying the tip of the blow gun directly to the opening of the passages. Remove any carbon accumulation from the bore of the throttle body by scraping or with wet or dry flint paper.

Caution: Do not use emery cloth.

Blow out all jets, nozzles, and check valves. By either blowing or visual inspection, see that all openings in jets and nozzles are clear and that check valves are undamaged.

48. Inspection and Repair

(fig. 33)

a. Bowl Cover, Air Horn, Throttle Body and Main Body.

(1) Check bowl cover (ZZ) for warpage and wear on countershaft pin. Replace cover if warped or worn.

(2) Check air horn (BE) for out of roundness and wear in choke shaft bearings. Replace if defective.

(3) Inspect throttle body (C) for wear on throttle shaft bearings. Replace if worn.

(4) Be sure that the old nozzle gasket (W) has been removed from the high-speed passage.

(5) Be sure that all passages are clear of carbon and dirt.

(6) Check all shoulders for seats of check valves, low-speed jet (FF), idle well jet (BB) and pump jet (HH) to see that they are not damaged.

(7) If bottom of float bowl in main body (EE) shows oxidation, remove all deposit with a wire brush and paint inside of bowl with a good grade of auto body lacquer.

b. Float Circuit.

(1) Check fuel intake needle and needle seat (VV and WW) for wear (par. 32*b*.(1)). Replace if worn.

(2) Check float (SS) for loading damage and wear. If lip of float is worn it may be smoothed with fine emery cloth.

Note.—Do not file.

Replace float if damaged or loaded.

c. Low-Speed Circuit.

(1) Inspect low-speed jet (FF) and idle well jet (BB) for damage or obstructions. Replace if damaged.

(2) Inspect idle adjustment screw (P) for wear or damage. Replace if necessary.

d. High-Speed Circuits.

(1) Inspect metering rod (AE) and metering rod jet (QQ) for wear. Replace if worn.

(2) Inspect nozzle (X), nozzle retainer plug (Y), and nozzle passage plug (AA) for damage. Replace if necessary. (Note particularly the seating surfaces.) Be sure that the old nozzle gasket (W) is removed from the nozzle.

(3) Inspect throttle connector rod (J) and throttle arm (G) for wear. Replace if worn.

e. Pump Circuit.

(1) Inspect plunger and rod (RR) for wear or damage to the leather. Replace if necessary.

(2) Inspect intake check valve (U) and discharge check valve (V) for proper operation and for damage to the seating surfaces. Inspect pump jet (HH) for damage to seating surfaces. Replace if necessary.

(3) Inspect connector link (AP) and hole in pump operating lever (AJ) for wear. Replace link or shaft and lever if worn.

f. Choke Circuit. See that choke spring (BC) is not stretched or weak. Replace if necessary.

49. Assembly

(fig. 33)

a. Group Parts.

Note.—**Parts for the five circuits listed in (1) through (5) below when grouped as directed will greatly facilitate assembly of the carburetor.**

(1) Group float circuit parts including bowl cover gasket (YY), fuel intake needle (VV), needle seat (WW), needle seat gasket (XX), needle spring (UU), needle pin (TT), float (SS), and float pin (AB).

(2) Group low-speed circuit parts including throttle shaft and lever (D), throttle valve plate (B), throttle valve plate screws (A), idle adjustment screw (P), idle adjustment screw spring (N), idle port plug (K), insulator (M), main body gaskets (L), idle well jet (BB), idle passage plug (DD), idle passage plug gasket (CC), low-speed jet (FF), low-speed jet passage plug (NN) and low-speed jet passage plug gasket (MM).

(3) Group high-speed circuit parts including throttle arm (G), throttle connector rod (J), nozzle (X), nozzle passage plug gasket (Z), nozzle retainer plug (Y), nozzle passage plug (AA), and nozzle passage plug gasket (Z).

(4) Group pump circuit parts including pump jet (HH), pump jet passage plug (KK), pump jet passage plug gasket (JJ), discharge check valve (V), intake check valve (U), strainer (T), check valve passage plug (R), check valve passage plug gasket (S), pump spring (LL), plunger and rod (RR), pump arm and collar (AN), pump arm spring (AM), pump operating lever (AJ), and connector link (AP).

(5) Group choke circuit parts including choke shaft and lever (AY), choke valve plate (BF), choke valve plate screws (BG), choke link (AS), choke link spring (AR), and pin spring (AU).

b. Install Float Circuit Parts.

(1) Install bowl cover gasket (YY), needle seat (WW), needle seat gasket (XX), needle, needle spring, and pin.

(2) Install float (SS) and float pin (AB).

c. Install Pump Circuit Parts.

(1) Install pump jet (HH), pump jet passage plug (KK), and pump jet passage plug gasket (JJ).

(2) Install discharge check valve (V) and intake check valve (U).

(3) Push strainer (T) into recess in check valve passage plug (R) and install strainer (T), check valve passage plug (R), and check valve passage plug gasket (S) as assembled.

(4) Install pump spring (LL) and plunger and rod (RR).

d. Assemble Low-Speed Circuit.

(1) Install throttle shaft and lever (D) and throttle valve plate (B). Install valve with "O" trademark toward idle port and facing manifold. Insert throttle valve plate screws (A) loosely. Close throttle and tap valve lightly to centralize the plate in the bore. Hold in place and tighten screws.

(2) Install idle adjustment screw (P) and idle adjustment screw spring (N) and set to specifications (table V, par. 44).

(3) Install new idle port plug (K).

(4) Assemble throttle body (C) to main body (EE). Place a new main body gasket (L) above and below insulator. Be sure that the holes are alined. Aline insulator (M) and main body gaskets (L) with throttle body and main body. Insert screws main body lock washer (GG) and tighten.

(5) Install idle well jet (BB), idle passage plug (DD) and idle passage plug gasket (CC).

(6) Install low-speed jet (FF), low-speed jet passage plug (NN), and low-speed passage plug gasket (MM).

e. Install High-Speed Circuit Parts.

(1) Install bowl cover (ZZ) as assembled. Tighten bowl cover lock washer screws (AC) evenly.

(2) Install pump arm and collar (AN) and pump operating lever (AJ).

(3) Install connector link (AP) with pin spring (AL) at top and away from bore.

(4) Install throttle arm (G) and throttle connector rod (J), secure with rod retainer (H).

(5) Install nozzle (X) and new nozzle gasket (W). Have flat side of nozzle facing up.

(6) Install nozzle retainer plug (Y), nozzle passage plug (AA), and nozzle passage plug gasket (Z).

(7) Adjust pump stroke and metering rod (pars. 52 and 53).

(8) Install metering rod (AE) and metering rod disk (AD). On models 539S, 572S, and 698S, the metering rod spring is inserted through the hole in the metering rod. The spring should exert a downward pressure on the rod when it is seated. If it does not, bend it slightly to accomplish this.

f. Assemble Choke Circuit.

(1) Install choke shaft and lever (AY) and choke valve plate (BF). Centralize valve by tapping lightly against bore before tightening choke valve plate screws (BG).

(2) Assemble air horn (BE) to body with air horn lock washer screw (BH).

(3) Install choke tube bracket (AV) with choke screw (AZ).

(4) Install connector link (AP), choke link spring (AR), and pin spring (AQ).

(5) Adjust fast idle (par. 54).

Section III. ADJUSTMENT OF TYPE W-O CARBURETORS

50. General

Whenever a W-O carburetor is repaired, the float level, pump stroke metering rod, and fast idle should be adjusted. The methods of adjusting these for the W-O carburetors are given in paragraphs 51, 52, 53, and 54. Specifications are given in table V (par. 44).

51. Float Level Adjustment

Swing gasket wide so that float level gage may be placed on machined surface of bowl cover. Adjust float level to specifications (table V, par. 44) by bending lip of float until float just touches gage.

Note.—Due to the use of the spring and pin in the needle of this model carburetor, the float must be kept level and be allowed to rest on needle by its own weight only or a correct adjustment will not be obtained.

52. Pump Stroke Adjustment (fig. 34)

a. Back out throttle adjustment screw and hold throttle in fully closed position.

b. Place base of gage 41–G–256 on raised portion of bowl cover with notch against plunger rod.

c. Turn knurled nut on gage until projecting finger rests on top of plunger rod.

d. Remove gage and note figure closest to index mark on beveled edge of knurled nut.

e. Open throttle wide and repeat *c* and *d* above.

f. Subtract wide open throttle reading from closed throttle reading. The difference is pump stroke in sixty-fourths of an inch.

Note.—A tolerance of plus or minus one-sixty-fourth of an inch from specified plunger stroke (table V, par. 44) is permitted. Adjust stroke by bending throttle connector rod at lower angle next to throttle arm (fig. 34). To increase pump stroke, bend throttle connector rod to raise starting position of plunger. To decrease pump stroke, bend throttle connector rod to lower the starting position of plunger.

Caution: Pump must be adjusted before metering rod is adjusted.

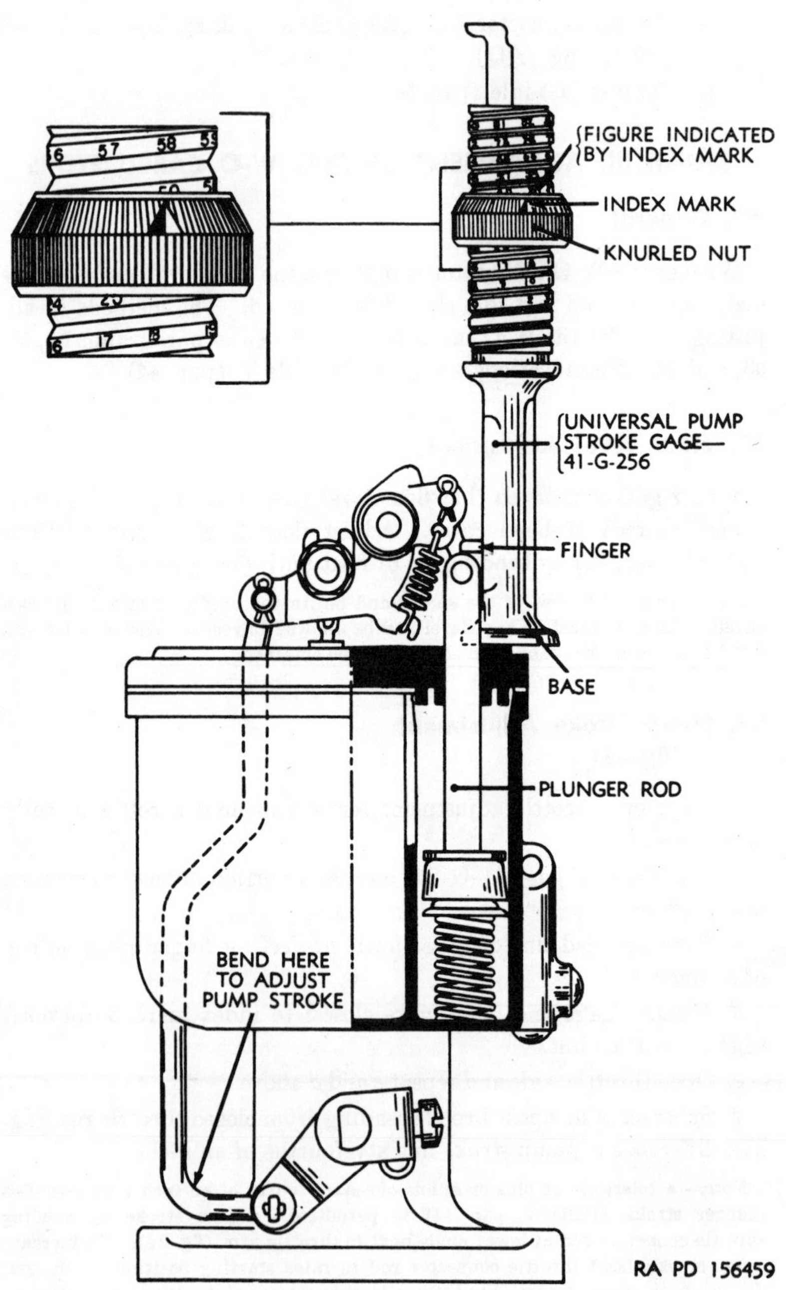

Figure 34. Gaging pump stroke with gage 41–G–256.

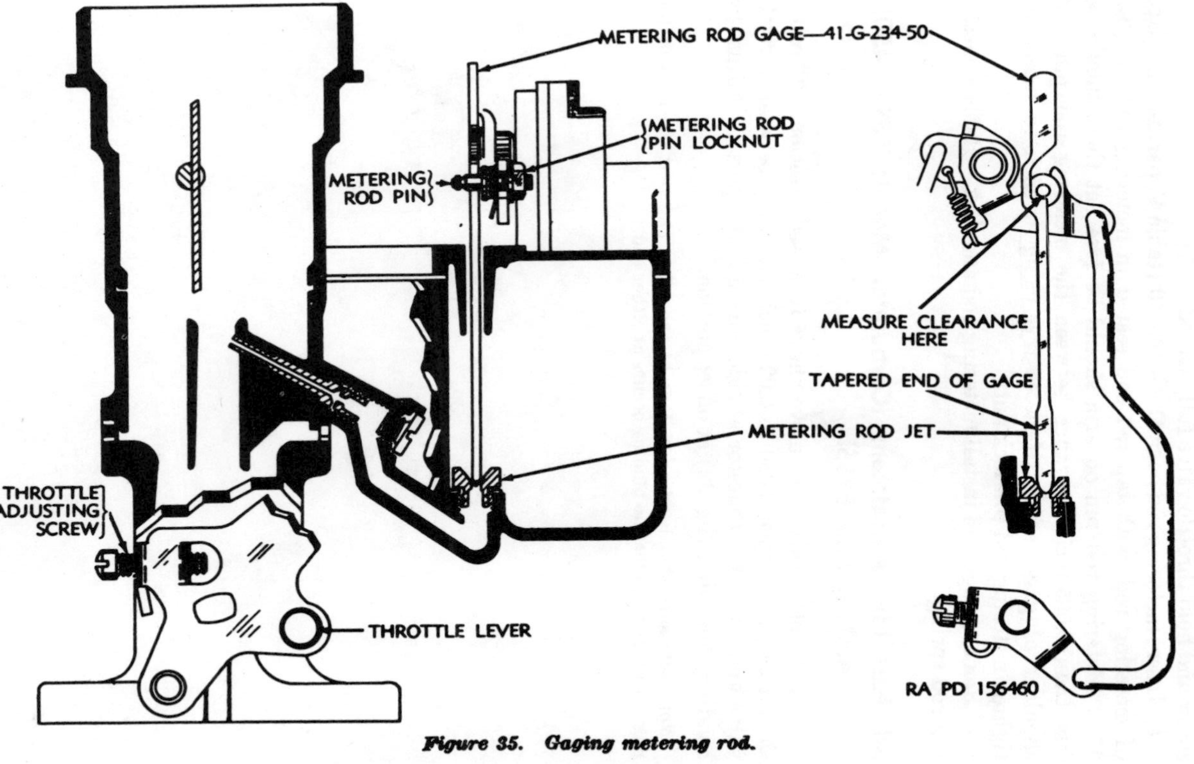

Figure 35. Gaging metering rod.

53. Metering Rod Adjustment

a. See CAUTION in paragraph 52. Back out throttle adjusting screw and hold throttle valve fully closed.

b. Insert metering rod gage 41–G–196–50 (table V, par. 44), in place of metering rod, with tapered end seated in metering rod jet (fig. 35). Metering rod pin on arm should be free but there should be less than 0.005-inch clearance between the metering rod pin and shoulder of gage, adjust if necessary, using wrench to loosen or tighten metering rod pin lock nut.

c. Remove gage and install metering rod and disk. Replace metering rod spring.

54. Fast Idle Adjustment (Carburetor Models 539S, 450S, 450SA, and 698S)

Close throttle valve and move choke to closed position. Throttle should be pulled open 0.080 to 0.090 inch (distance between throttle valve and bore of carburetor at side opposite idle port). Adjust by bending choke link (fig. 32) at offset portion.

Note.—Be sure that bending is done at the offset and that the ends of the link are parallel, so that no binding occurs at either end.

TM 9-1803B

WAR DEPARTMENT TECHNICAL MANUAL

ORDNANCE MAINTENANCE

Power Train, Body, and Frame for 1/4-Ton 4x4 Truck

(Willys-Overland Model MB and Ford Model GPW)

WAR DEPARTMENT • APRIL 1944

WAR DEPARTMENT TECHNICAL MANUAL

ORDNANCE MAINTENANCE

Power Train, Body, and Frame for 1/4-Ton 4x4 Truck

(Willys-Overland Model MB and Ford Model GPW)

This is a reprint of TM 9-1803B, Power Train, Body, and Frame for 1/4-Ton 4x4 Truck. (Willys-Overland Model MB and Ford Model GPW). No distribution will be made to personnel possessing the original publication.

WAR DEPARTMENT • APRIL 1944

WAR DEPARTMENT
Washington 25, D. C., 8 April 1944

TM 9-1803B, Ordnance Maintenance: Power Train, Body, and Frame for ¼-ton 4 x 4 Truck (Willys-Overland Model MB and Ford Model GPW), is published for the information and guidance of all concerned.

[A.G. 300.7 (17 Nov 43)
O.O.M. 461/(TM-9) Rar. Ars. (4-15-44)]

BY ORDER OF THE SECRETARY OF WAR:

G. C. MARSHALL,
Chief of Staff.

OFFICIAL:
J. A. ULIO,
Major General,
The Adjutant General.

DISTRIBUTION: R 9 (4); Bn 9 (2); C 9 (5).

(For explanation of symbols, see FM 21-6.)

CONTENTS

★This Technical Manual supersedes TB 1803-1, dated 8 December 1943. For supersession of Quartermaster Corps 10-series Technical Manuals, see paragraph 1 j.

ORDNANCE MAINTENANCE — POWER TRAIN, BODY, AND FRAME FOR ¼-TON 4 x 4 TRUCK (WILLYS-OVERLAND MODEL MB AND FORD MODEL GPW)

CHAPTER 1

INTRODUCTION

1. SCOPE.

a. The instructions contained in this manual are for the information and guidance of personnel charged with the maintenance and repair of the power train, body, and frame of the ¼-ton 4 x 4 truck. These instructions are supplementary to field and technical manuals prepared for the using arms. This manual does not contain information which is intended primarily for the using arms, since such information is available to ordnance maintenance personnel in 100-series TM's or FM's.

b. This manual contains a description of, and procedure for, removal, disassembly, inspection, and repair of the transmission, transfer case, axles, body, and frame.

c. TM 9-803 contains operating instructions and information for the using arms.

d. TM 9-1803A contains instructions for the information and guidance of personnel charged with the maintenance and repair of the 4-cylinder engine used in these vehicles.

e. TM 9-1825B contains information for the maintenance of the Auto-Lite electrical equipment.

f. TM 9-1826A contains information for the maintenance of the Carter carburetor.

g. TM 9-1827C contains information for the maintenance of the Wagner hydraulic brake system.

h. TM 9-1828A contains information for the maintenance of the A. C. fuel pump.

i. TM 9-1829A contains information for the maintenance of the speedometer.

j. This manual includes pertinent ordnance maintenance instructions from the following Quartermaster Corps 10-series Technical Manuals. Together with TM 9-803 and TM 9-1803A, this manual supersedes them:

(1) TM 10-1103, dated 20 August 1941.

(2) TM 10-1207, dated 20 August 1941.

(3) TM 10-1349, dated 3 January 1942.

(4) TM 10-1513, Changes 1, dated 15 January 1943.

INTRODUCTION

RA PD 28742

Figure 1 — ¼-ton Truck 4 x 4 — Three-quarter Front View

2. MWO AND MAJOR UNIT ASSEMBLY REPLACEMENT RECORD.

a. **Description.** Every vehicle is supplied with a copy of AGO Form No. 478 which provides a means of keeping a record of MWO's completed or major unit assemblies replaced. This form includes spaces for the vehicle name and U. S. A. Registration Number, instructions for use, and information pertinent to the work accomplished. It is very important that this form be used as directed and that it remain with the vehicle until the vehicle is removed from service.

b. **Instructions for Use.** Personnel performing modifications or major unit assembly replacements must record clearly on the form, a description of the work completed, and must initial the form in the columns provided. When each modification is completed, record the date, hours and/or mileage, and MWO number. When major unit assemblies, such as engine, transmission, transfer case, are replaced, record the date, hours and/or mileage and nomenclature of the unit assembly. Minor repairs and minor parts and accessory replacements need not be recorded.

c. **Early Modifications.** Upon receipt of a vehicle for modification or repair, by a third or fourth echelon repair facility, maintenance personnel will record the MWO numbers of modifications applied prior to the date of AGO Form No. 478.

CHAPTER 2
POWER TRAIN

Section I
POWER TRAIN DESCRIPTION

3. POWER TRAIN DESCRIPTION.

a. The power from the engine is transmitted to the driving wheels through a transmission and a transfer case, each of which provides a means of selecting the gear reduction. The power from the transfer case is transmitted to the front and rear axles through propeller shafts equipped with universal joints. The transmission is located at the rear of the engine and is secured to the clutch housing (fig. 2). The various gears in the transmission (par. 4) are controlled by a shift lever. The transfer case is mounted directly onto the rear of the transmission. The transmission output shaft extends from the rear of the transmission into splines of the main drive gear in the transfer case. The transfer case is provided with two levers, one to select the transfer case ratio, and the other to engage or disengage the front axle (fig. 5). A hand brake drum is mounted on the rear axle output shaft. Each axle is of the spiral bevel hypoid gear full-floating type, equipped with the conventional differential.

Section II
TRANSMISSION

4. DESCRIPTION AND DATA.

a. Description. The transmission (fig. 3) is of the 3-speed type with synchronized second and high speed gears. The transmission and transfer case are mounted on rubber on the frame center cross-member. The gearshift lever is incorporated in the gearshift housing.

b. Data.

Make	Warner
Model	T84J
Type	Synchronous Mesh
Speeds:	
Forward	3
Reverse	1
Ratios:	
Low	2.665 to 1
Second	1.564 to 1

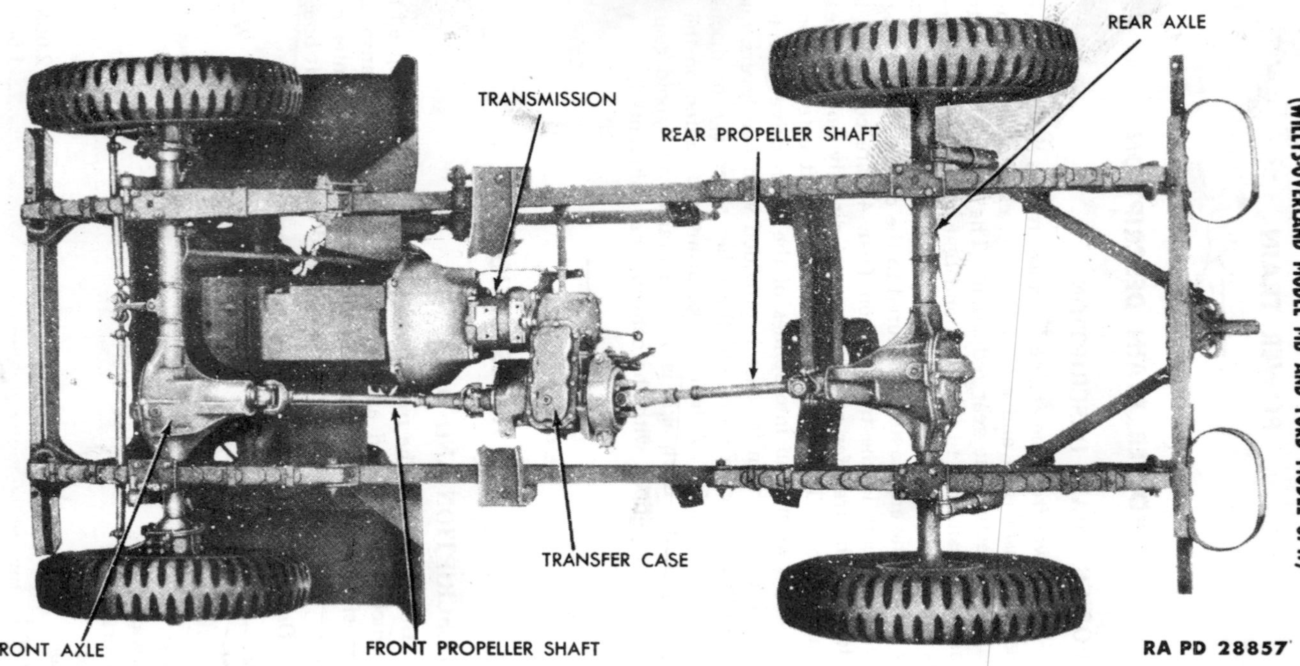

Figure 2 — Power Train

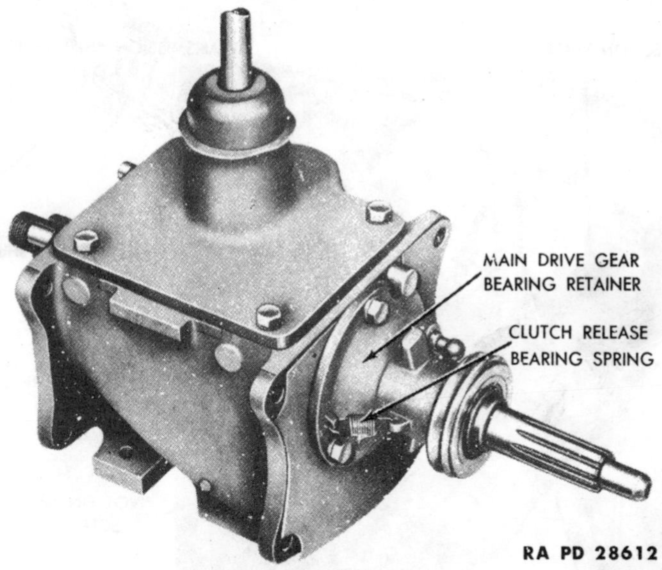

Figure 3 — Transmission — Three-quarter Front View

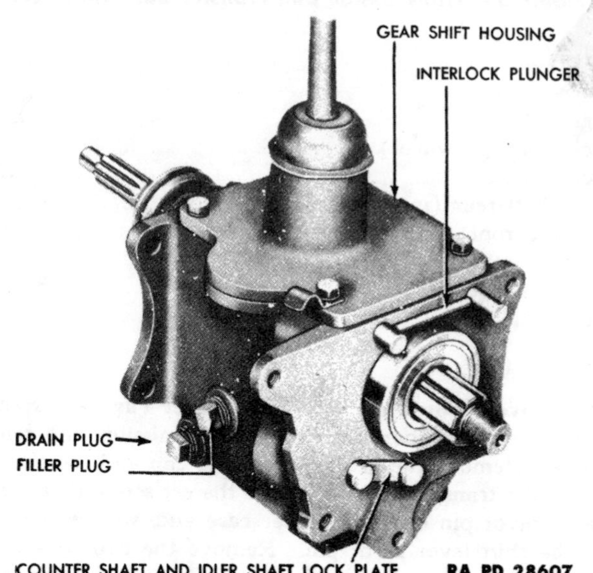

Figure 4 — Transmission — Three-quarter Rear View

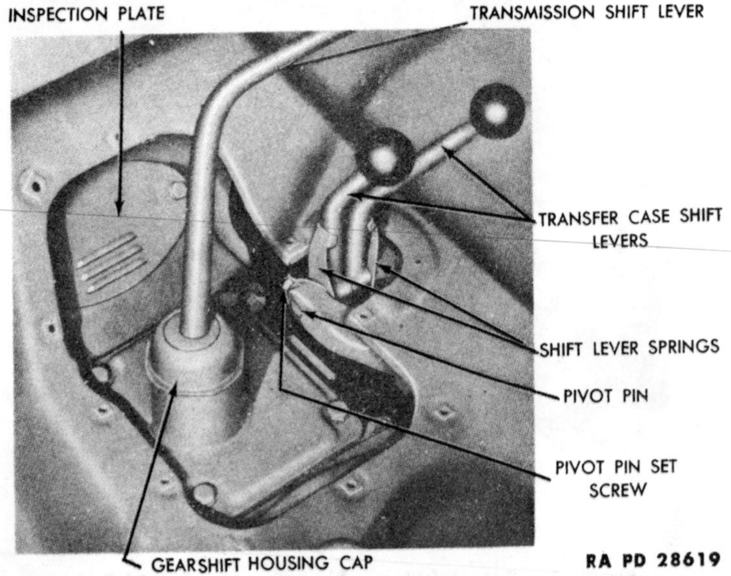

Figure 5 — Transmission and Transfer Case Shift Levers

High	1 to 1
Reverse	3.554 to 1
Bearings:	
Clutch shaft (flywheel)	Bushing
Clutch release	Ball
Clutch shaft rear (main drive gear)	Ball
Mainshaft front	13 rollers
Mainshaft rear	Ball
Countershaft gear	Bushings (2)
Reverse idle gear	Bushing

5. REMOVAL.

a. **Remove Floor Plate and Shift Lever** (fig. 5). Remove the cap screws from the floor plate at the transmission, and remove the floor plate. Remove the gearshift housing cap and remove the shift lever from the transmission. Remove the set screw that secures the shift lever pivot pin on the transfer case and, with a suitable drift, remove the shift lever pivot pin. Remove the two shift levers and shift lever springs from the transfer case. Remove the two cap screws that secure the clutch housing inspection plate and remove the inspection plate.

Figure 6 — Under Side of Chassis

b. **Remove Transmission Shield** (fig. 6). Remove the cap screws that secure the exhaust pipe clamp to the shield, and remove the clamp. Remove the five bolts that secure the transmission shield to the transmission support crossmember. Remove the transmission shield.

c. **Remove Brake Springs and Speedometer Cable** (fig. 6). Remove the hand brake spring. Remove the foot brake spring leading from the bottom of the brake pedal to the transmission support crossmember. Disconnect the speedometer cable at the transfer case.

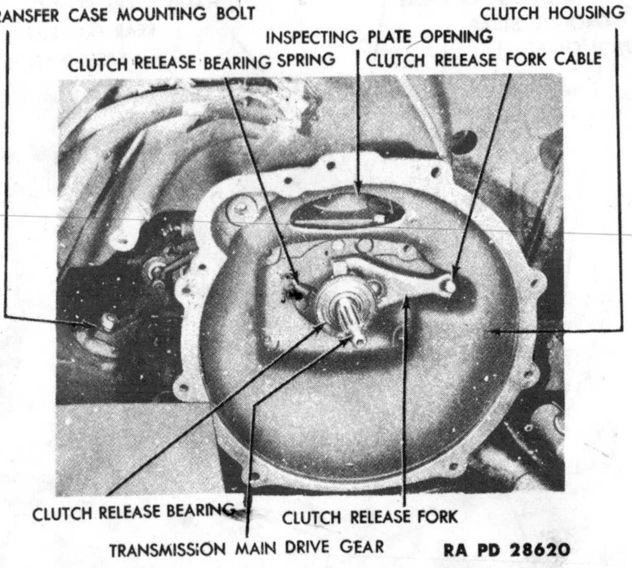

Figure 7 — Clutch Release Fork

d. Remove Hand Brake Cable, Clutch Cable, and Engine Stay Cable (fig. 6). Remove the clevis pin that secures the hand brake cable to the brake band. Remove the hand brake cable clamp at the transfer case. Disconnect the clutch cable at the clutch shaft. Remove the two nuts from the engine stay cable on the transmission support crossmember and remove the engine stay cable.

e. Remove Propeller Shafts (fig. 6). Disconnect the front propeller shaft at the transfer case (par. 17 **a**). Disconnect the rear propeller shaft at the transfer case (par. 17 **b**).

f. Remove Ground Strap (fig. 6). Remove the ground strap leading from the transfer case to the floor plate.

g. Remove Clutch Release Fork (fig. 7). Working through the inspection plate opening on the clutch housing, remove the clutch cable from the clutch release fork, and remove the clutch release fork from the clutch housing.

h. Disconnect Radiator Hose. Drain the coolant from the radiator. Loosen the radiator hose clamp at the radiator end, and remove the hose from the radiator.

i. Disconnect Transmission at Clutch Housing (fig. 6). Place a jack under the oil pan shield at the rear of the engine. Remove

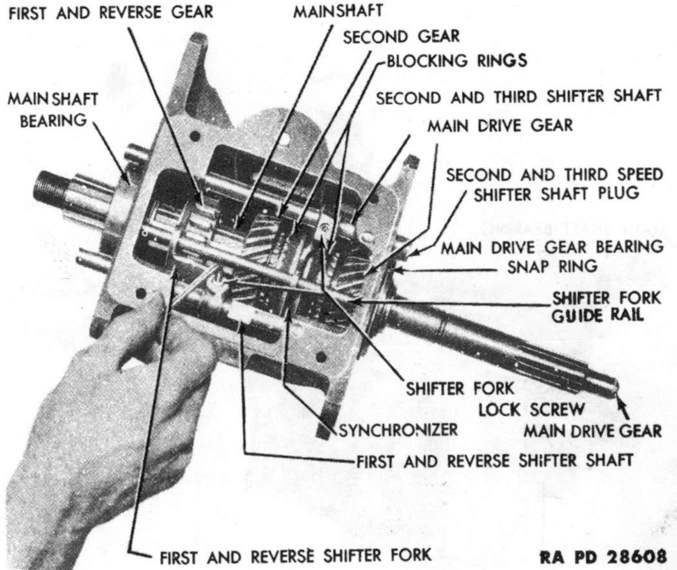

Figure 8 — Removing Shifter Fork Lock Screws

three cap screws from each side of the transmission support crossmember. Place another jack under the transmission. Remove the four bolts that secure the transmission to the clutch housing. Lower both jacks evenly until the transmission support crossmember is approximately 2 inches from the frame. Push the transmission and transfer case to the right so as to free the clutch shaft from the ball joint on the transfer case. Pull the transfer case with transmission straight back until the transmission main drive gear is out of the clutch housing and remove the transfer case and transmission.

j. **Remove Transmission Support Crossmember** (fig. 6). Remove the five mounting bolts that secure the transmission and transfer case to the transmission support crossmember. Remove the transmission support crossmember.

k. **Remove Transmission From Transfer Case** (fig. 27). Drain the oil from the transmission and transfer case. Remove the rear cover from the transfer case. Remove the castellated nut and flat washer that secure the drive gear on the transmission mainshaft and remove the drive gear and oil baffle from the transmission mainshaft, using a suitable puller, if necessary. NOTE: *Vehicles of early manufacture were not supplied with this oil baffle.*

Long shifter shaft goes on pin side

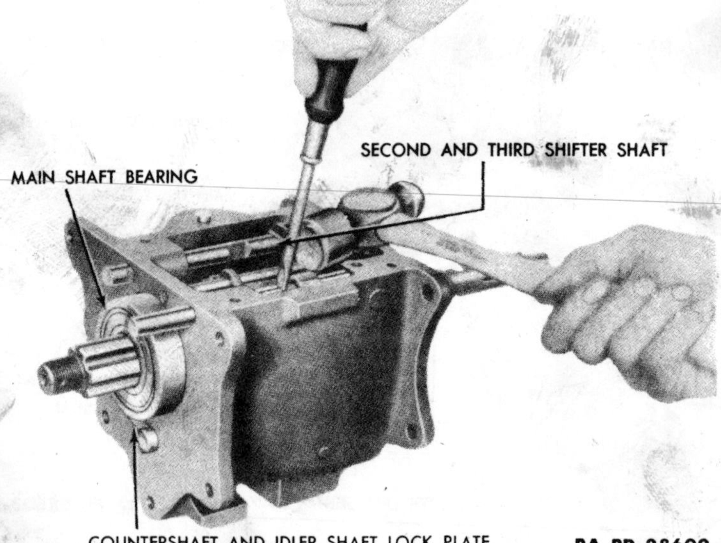

Figure 9 — Removing Shifter Shafts

6. DISASSEMBLY.

a. **Remove Gearshift Housing.** Remove the four cap screws that secure the gearshaft housing to the transmission (fig. 4). Lift the housing, shifter shaft plate, and spring washer from the transmission (fig. 17).

b. **Remove Main Drive Gear Bearing Retainer** (fig. 3). Unhook the clutch release bearing return spring and slide the bearing assembly off the bearing retainer. Remove the three cap screws from the bearing retainer. Slide the bearing retainer and cork gasket off the main drive gear.

c. **Remove Shifter Fork Guide Rail** (fig. 8). Push the shifter fork guide rail out of the transmission.

d. **Remove the Low and Reverse, and the Second and High Shifter Forks.** Remove the shifter fork lock screw from each fork (fig. 8). Tap the shifter shafts part way out of the transmission (fig. 9), being careful not to lose the interlocking ball in each shaft. Hold the shifter fork and pull the shafts from the transmission.

e. **Remove Main Drive Gear.** Tap the countershaft and idle reverse shaft lock plate out of the two shafts (fig. 4). With a long

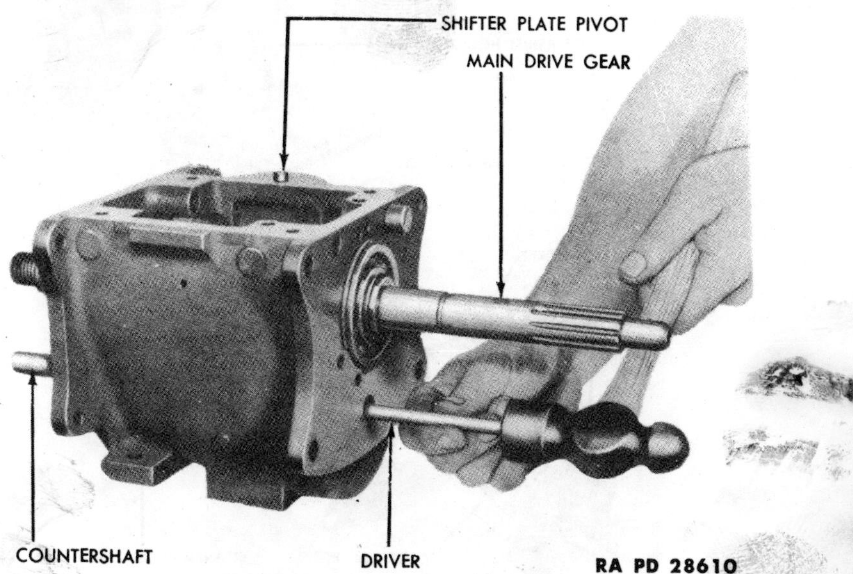

Figure 10 — Removing Countershaft

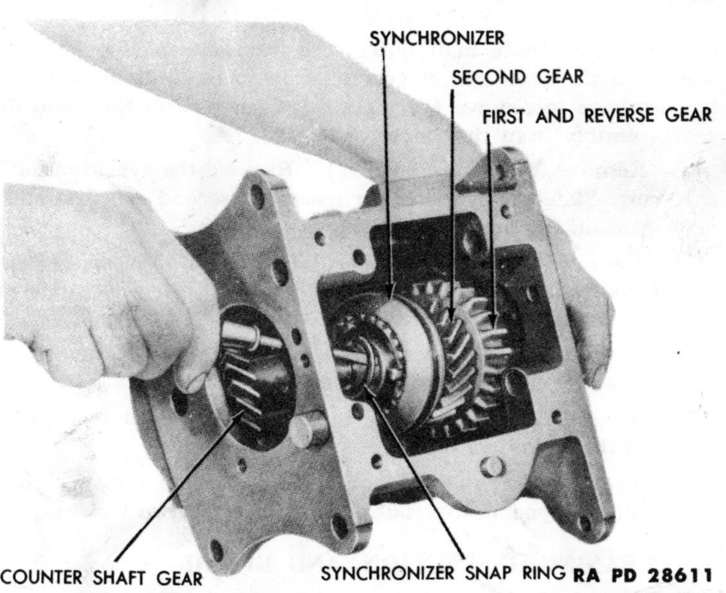

Figure 11 — Removing Synchronizer Hub Snap Ring

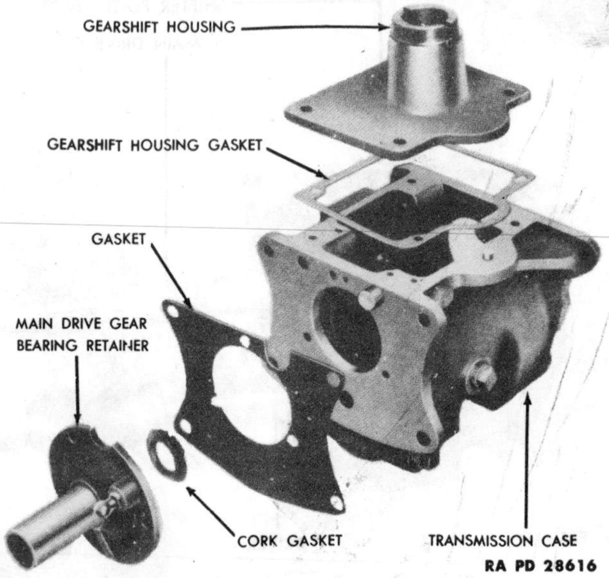

Figure 12 – Transmission Case and Gearshift Housing – Exploded View

drift, tap the countershaft out of the transmission (fig. 10). This will allow the countershaft gear to drop to the bottom of the case for clearance to remove the main drive gear. Pull the main drive gear assembly from the transmission.

f. Remove Mainshaft (fig. 11). Remove the synchronizer hub snap ring. Slide the synchronizer assembly, second and first and reverse gear off the mainshaft. Remove the shaft.

g. Remove Idle Reverse Gear. Tap the idle reverse gear shaft out of the transmission and remove the gear. Lift the countershaft gear and both thrust washers out of the transmission.

h. Disassemble Countershaft Gear (fig. 14). Remove the two bushings and spacer from the countershaft gear.

i. Disassemble Main Drive Gear (fig. 13). Remove the snap ring and the 13 rollers from the main drive gear.

j. Disassemble Synchronizer (fig. 13). Slide the synchronizer sleeve off the synchronizer hub and remove the two lock rings.

7. CLEANING, INSPECTION, AND REPAIR.

a. Cleaning. Wash all parts thoroughly in dry-cleaning solvent until all trace of old lubricant has been removed. Oil the bearings

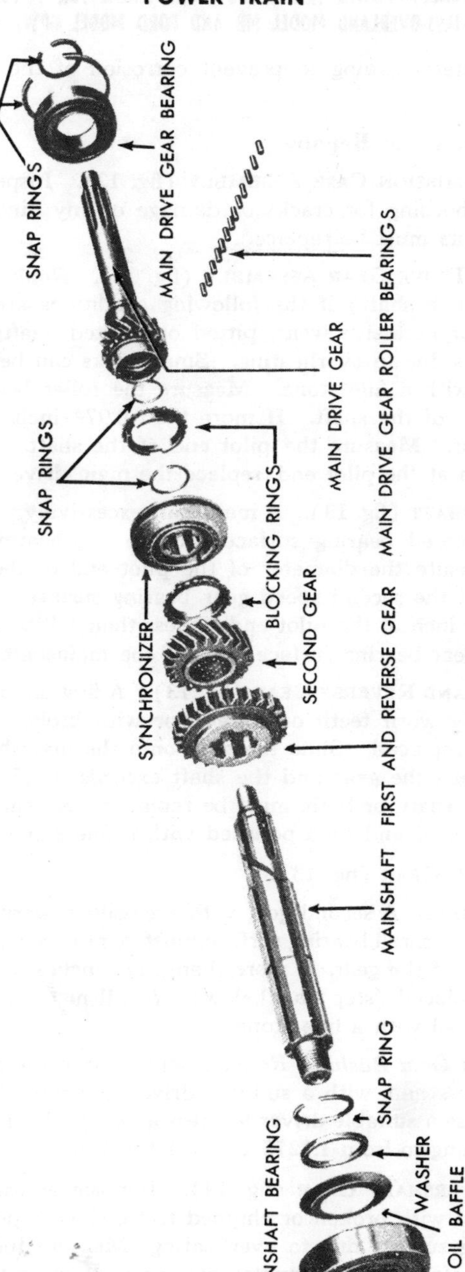

Figure 13 — Mainshaft Assembly — Exploded View

immediately after cleaning to prevent corrosion of the highly polished surfaces.

b. Inspection and Repair.

(1) TRANSMISSION CASE ASSEMBLY (fig. 12). Inspect the case and gearshaft housing for cracks or damage of any kind. Cracked or damaged units must be replaced.

(2) MAIN DRIVE GEAR ASSEMBLY (fig. 13). Replace the main drive gear (clutch shaft) if the following conditions are apparent: Broken teeth or excessive wear; pitted or twisted shaft; discolored bearing surfaces due to overheating. Small nicks can be honed and then polished with a fine stone. Measure the roller bearing recess in the gear end of the shaft. If more than 0.974 inch, replace the main drive gear. Measure the pilot end of the shaft. If it is less than 0.595 inch at the pilot end, replace the main drive gear.

(3) MAINSHAFT (fig. 13). A mainshaft excessively worn, or with pitted or discolored bearing surfaces due to overheating, must be replaced. Measure the diameter of the pilot end of the shaft and the diameter of the second speed gear bearing surface. If they are less than 0.595 inch at the pilot end, or less than 1.126 inches at the second speed gear bearing surface, replace the mainshaft.

(4) FIRST AND REVERSE GEAR (fig. 13). A first and reverse gear with excessively worn teeth or splines, or with broken or chipped teeth must be replaced. Slide the gear onto the mainshaft. If the backlash between the gear and the shaft exceeds 0.005 inch, either the gear or the shaft, or both, must be replaced. A gear with small nicks can be honed and then polished with a fine stone.

(5) SECOND GEAR (fig. 13).

(a) Inspection. A second gear with excessively worn, broken, or chipped teeth, or scored bearing surface must be replaced. Measure the inside diameter of the gear. If more than 1.129 inches the gear bushing must be replaced (step *(b)*, below). Small nicks can be honed and then polished with a fine stone.

(b) Second Gear Bushing Replacement. Place the second gear in an arbor press and, with a suitable driver, press the bushing out of the gear. Use a suitable driver to press a new bushing in the gear. Ream the bushing to from 1.1275 to 1.1280 inches.

(6) COUNTERSHAFT GEAR (fig. 14). Replace excessively worn gears, and gears with broken or chipped teeth, or with pitted or discolored bearing surface due to overheating. Measure the front and rear bearing surfaces of the countershaft gear. If more than 0.7625 inch on either end, replace.

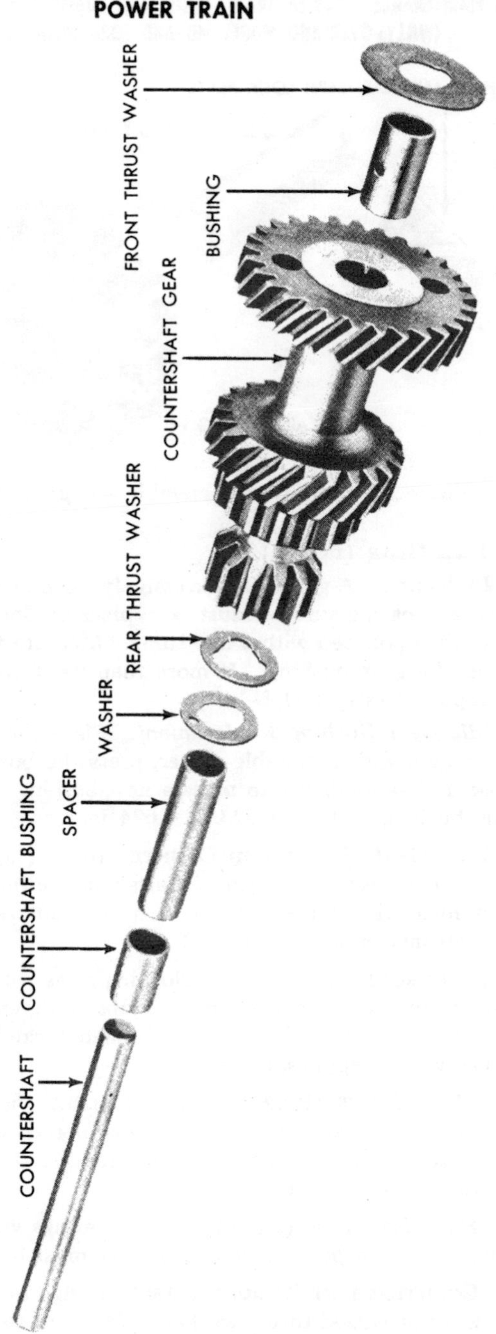

Figure 14 — Countershaft Gear Assembly — Exploded View

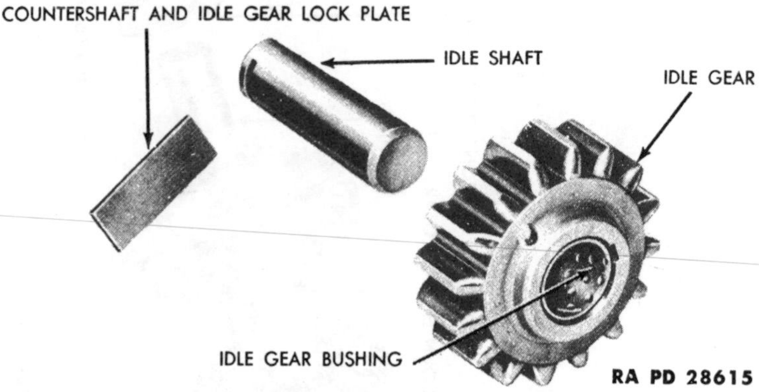

COUNTERSHAFT AND IDLE GEAR LOCK PLATE
IDLE SHAFT
IDLE GEAR
IDLE GEAR BUSHING
RA PD 28615

Figure 15 — Idle Gear Assembly — Exploded View

(7) IDLE GEAR (fig. 15).

(a) Inspection. A gear with excessively worn or broken teeth, or with a scored bearing surface must be replaced. Small nicks can be honed and then polished with a fine stone. Measure the inside diameter of the idle gear bushing. If more than 0.626 inch, the bushing must be replaced (step *(b)*, below).

(b) Idle Gear Bushing Replacement. Place the idle gear in an arbor press and, with a suitable driver, press the bushing out of the gear. Use a suitable driver to press a new bushing in the idle gear. Ream the bushing to from 0.623 to 0.624 inch.

(8) IDLE GEAR SHAFT AND COUNTERSHAFT (figs. 14 and 15). Ridged, scored, or excessively worn, shafts must be replaced. An idle gear shaft measuring under 0.6185 inch or countershaft measuring under 0.7490 inch must be replaced.

(9) SYNCHRONIZER (fig. 13). Blocking rings with worn, broken, or nicked teeth, must be discarded. Hubs with excessively worn splines must be replaced. Sleeves with broken, nicked, or worn teeth, or excessively worn splines, must be replaced.

(10) MAIN DRIVE GEAR BEARING ROLLERS (fig. 13). Needle bearing rollers with flat spots, pitted, or discolored surfaces must be replaced. Measure the diameter of each roller. If less than 0.187 inch, the rollers must be replaced.

(11) BALL BEARINGS (fig. 13). Ball bearings with loose or discolored balls, or with pitted or cracked races must be replaced.

(12) COUNTERSHAFT THRUST WASHERS (fig. 14). Replace excessively worn or ridged thrust washers. Measure each thrust wash-

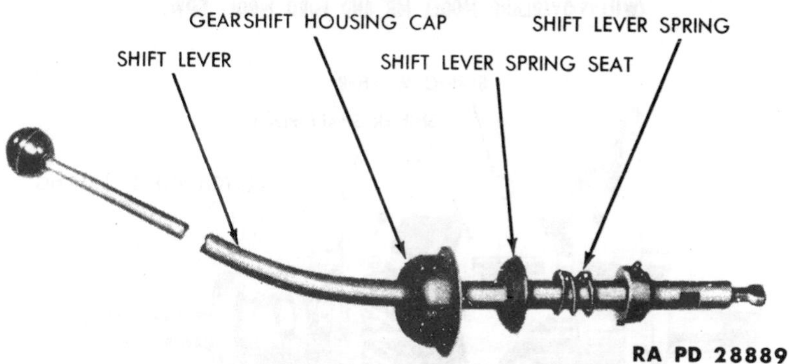

Figure 16 — Transmission Shift Lever

er. If the front washer is less than 0.029 inch, or if either of the rear washers are less than 0.060 inch, they must be replaced.

(13) COUNTERSHAFT BUSHINGS (fig. 14). Excessively worn, scored, or ridged countershaft bushings must be replaced. Measure the inside and outside diameter of the bushings. If the outside diameter is less than 0.759 inch, or if the inside diameter is more than 0.6225 inch, the bushings must be replaced.

(14) SHIFT LEVER (fig. 16). Replace the shift lever if it is excessively worn or bent. Check the gearshift housing cap for stripped threads. Replace the shift lever spring, if it is cracked.

8. ASSEMBLY.

a. Install Idle Gear. Hold the idle gear (fig. 15) in place in the case with the cone end of the hub toward the front, and push the idle gear shaft into the case.

b. Install Countershaft Gear (fig. 14). Dip the countershaft bearings into SAE 90 oil. Slide the spacer into the countershaft gear and install a bushing in each end of the countershaft gear. Coat the front thrust washer, rear thrust washer, and steel washer with a light film of grease to hold them in place while installing the gear. Lay the countershaft gear in the case with the large gear toward the front.

c. Install Mainshaft Assembly (fig. 13). Insert the mainshaft in the case through the opening in the rear of the case. Slide the first and reverse gear onto the shaft, with the shifter fork channel toward the rear. Slide the second gear onto the mainshaft with the tapered end of the gear toward the front. Install a blocking ring onto the second gear. Slide the synchronizer onto the mainshaft with the long end of the hub toward the front and install the snap ring.

d. Install Main Drive Gear Assembly (fig. 13). Place the other blocking ring in the synchronizer and install the main drive gear assembly in the case.

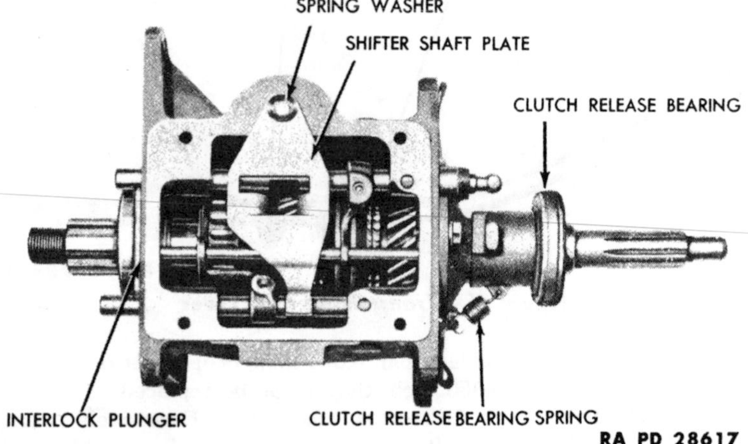

Figure 17 — Gears Installed in Transmission — Top View

e. **Install Countershaft.** Raise the countershaft gear into position. Making sure the three washers are in line, push the countershaft into the case and tap the lock plate between the countershaft and idle gear shaft (fig. 4).

f. **Install First and Reverse Shifter Fork** (fig. 8). Hold the first and reverse shifter fork in position on the first and reverse gear, and slide the low and reverse shifter shaft (short shaft) into the case about half way. Drop an interlock spring and ball in the pocket. Press down on the ball and push the shifter shaft all the way in the case. Line up the groove of the shaft with the shifter fork and install the lock screw.

g. **Install Second and Third Shifter Fork** (fig. 8). Repeat the same procedure as used in installing the low and reverse shifter fork, and then push the guide rail into the case and through both shifter forks.

h. **Install Gearshift Housing on Case** (fig. 17). Place the transmission in neutral position. Lay the shifter shaft plate on the pivot and on the shifter shafts. Lay the spring washer on the pivot. Place a new gearshift housing gasket on the case. Place the shift lever in neutral position. Lay the housing on the transmission and install the four lock washers and cap screws in the housing.

i. **Install Clutch Release Bearing** (fig. 3). Slide the clutch release bearing assembly onto the main drive gear bearing retainer and install the clutch release bearing return spring.

9. INSTALLATION.

a. Install Transmission to Transfer Case. Place the transmission in position on the transfer case. Be sure the interlock plunger (fig. 4) is in position between the two shifter shafts on the transmission. Install the bolts that secure the transmission to the transfer case. Slide the oil baffle and mainshaft gear on the transmission mainshaft through the rear cover opening on the transfer case. (The oil baffle was not supplied on vehicles of early manufacture. If grease is found to have been leaking from the transfer case into the transmission on vehicles without this baffle, reverse the rear mainshaft bearing (fig. 13) so that the open side of the bearing faces the front of the transmission. Leave the oil baffle in front of the bearing in its original position. Install another oil baffle at the rear of the bearing.) Install the flat washer and nut that secure the mainshaft gear to the transmission mainshaft. Install a new gasket and the rear cover on the transfer case (fig. 27).

b. Place Transmission in Position on Vehicle. Place a jack under the transmission and raise the transmission and transfer case up until the shaft of the main drive gear is lined up with the splines in the clutch disk.

c. Install Transmission Main Drive Gear to Clutch Housing. Insert the shaft of the main drive gear into the clutch splines carefully, do not use force. Slide the transmission in flush with the clutch housing. Install the four bolts that secure the transmission to the clutch housing.

d. Install Clutch Shaft to Transfer Case (fig. 6). Push the transfer case to the right until the clutch shaft has enough clearance to enter the ball joint on the transfer case.

e. Install Transmission Support Crossmember (fig. 6). Place the transmission support crossmember in position on the transmission. Install the four bolts that secure the crossmember to the transmission. Raise the transmission up with a jack until the crossmember is flush with the frame. With a long nosed drift, line up the holes on the crossmember with the holes in the frame. Install the three nuts and bolts on each end of the crossmember and remove the jack. Install the transfer case mounting bolt.

f. Install Clutch Release Fork (fig. 7). Working through the inspection plate opening on the clutch housing, insert the clutch release fork in the clutch housing. Place the release fork behind the clutch release bearing. Slide the clutch release fork cable in the slot on the opposite end of the clutch release fork. Install the clutch release fork cable to the clutch shaft at the transfer case.

g. Install Hand Brake Cable (fig. 6). Install the hand brake cable to the brake band at the transfer case. Install the hand brake spring leading from the brake band linkage to the body floor plate. Install the clamp that secures the hand brake cable to the transfer case.

h. Install Engine Stay Cable and Ground Strap (fig. 6). Install the engine stay cable leading from the engine rear plate to the transmission support crossmember. Install the ground strap leading from the transmission to the floor plate.

i. Install Propeller Shafts and Speedometer Cable (fig. 6). Install the rear propeller shaft to the transfer case (par. 21 **a**). Install the front propeller shaft to the transfer case (par. 21 **b**). Install the speedometer cable to the transfer case.

j. Install Transmission Shield (fig. 6). Install the five nuts and bolts that secure the shield to the transmission support crossmember. Install the clamp that secures the exhaust pipe to the shield.

k. Lubricate and Adjust Clutch. Fill both the transmission and transfer case to proper oil level with specified oil. Adjust the clutch pedal free travel (refer to TM 9-803).

Section III

TRANSFER CASE

10. DESCRIPTION AND DATA.

a. Description. The transfer case (figs. 28 and 29) is located at the rear of the transmission. The transfer case is essentially a 2-speed transmission, which provides two gear ratios and a means of distributing the power from the transmission to the two axles.

b. Data.

Make	Spicer
Model	18
Mounting	Unit with transmission
Shift lever	Floor
Ratio:	
High	1 to 1
Low	1.97 to 1

Bearings:

Transmission mainshaft	Ball
Idle gear	2 rollers
Output shaft	Taper rollers
Front axle clutch shaft front bearing	Ball
Rear pilot in output shaft	Bronze bushing

11. REMOVAL.

a. Remove Transmission Shield (fig. 6). Remove the two cap screws that secure the exhaust pipe clamp to the shield. Remove the exhaust pipe clamp. Remove the five bolts that secure the transmission shield to the transmission support crossmember and remove the shield.

b. Remove Hand Brake Cable and Clutch Cable (fig. 6). Remove the hand brake spring at the transfer case. Remove the clevis pin that secures the hand brake cable at the brake on the transfer case. Remove the hand brake cable clamp on the transmission. Remove the clevis pin from the clutch cable at the transmission support crossmember.

c. Remove Mounting Bolt and Rear Cover (figs. 7 and 27). Remove the mounting bolt that secures the transfer case to the transmission support crossmember at the right side of the transfer case. Remove the five cap screws that secure the rear cover to the transfer case.

d. Remove Rear Propeller Shaft (fig. 7). Disconnect the rear propeller shaft at the transfer case (par. 17 **b**).

e. Remove Mainshaft Gear (fig. 27). Through the opening at the rear of the transfer case, remove the castellated nut that secures the mainshaft gear to the transmission mainshaft. Remove the flat washer mainshaft gear and oil retainer.

f. Remove Transfer Case. Place a jack under the transfer case. Remove the five cap screws that secure the transfer case to the transmission. Move the transfer case straight back until the transmission mainshaft is out of the transfer case. Remove the transfer case.

12. DISASSEMBLY.

a. Remove Brake Band and Drum Assembly (fig. 28). Remove the two anchor screws from the brake band. Remove the brake band adjusting nut and adjusting screw. Remove the clevis pin from the hand brake linkage. Remove the brake band assembly. Remove the castellated nut that secures the universal joint flange to the output shaft. Install puller 41-P-2912 on the universal joint flange and remove the flange and brake drum (fig. 18). NOTE: *The puller illustrated in figure 18 is similar to puller 41-P-2912.*

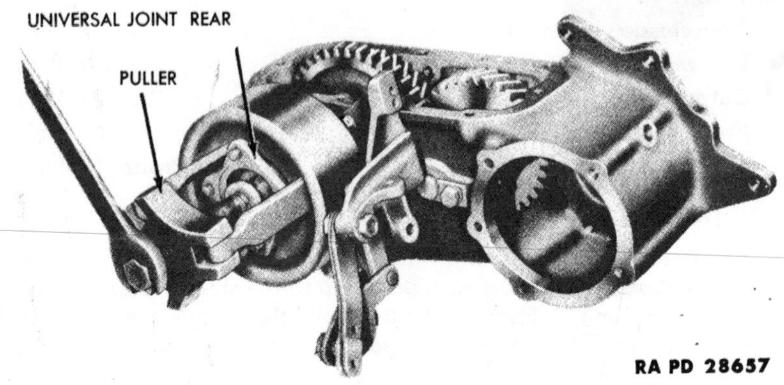

Figure 18—Removing Rear Universal Joint Flange With Puller Similar to Puller 41-P-2912

b. Remove Rear Output Shaft Bearing Cap (fig. 26). Remove the four cap screws that secure the rear output shaft bearing cap to the transfer case housing. Remove the rear output shaft bearing cap. Remove the rear bearing cap shims. Remove the speedometer drive gear from the output shaft.

c. Remove Intermediate Gear and Bottom Cover (figs. 25 and 27). Remove the 10 cap screws that secure the bottom cover to the transfer case and remove the bottom cover. Remove the cap screw that secures the lock plate. Remove the lock plate. With a suitable driver, remove the intermediate gear shaft. Remove the intermediate gear, thrust washers, and roller bearings through the bottom of the transfer case.

d. Remove Shifter Shaft and Front Output Shaft Bearing (fig. 29). Shift front axle drive to the engaged position. Remove the poppet plug, spring, and ball on both sides of the output shaft bearing cap. Remove the five cap screws that secure the front output shaft bearing cap to the transfer case. Remove the front output shaft bearing cap as an assembly with the universal joint flange, clutch shaft, bearing, clutch gear, shifter fork, and shifter rod. Be careful not to lose the interlock in the front bearing cap.

e. Remove Output Shaft (fig. 19). Insert a screwdriver between the snap ring and output shaft bearing and pry the output shaft bearing away from the snap ring. Remove the snap ring from the groove in the output shaft. Pull the output shaft out from the rear of the housing. The output shaft bearing, snap ring thrust washer, output shaft sliding gear, and output shaft gear can now be removed through the bottom of the transfer case.

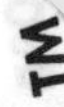

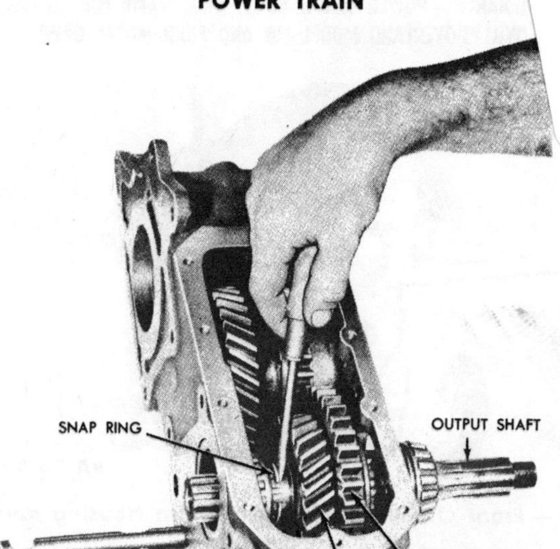

Figure 19 – Removing Snap Ring From Output Shaft

f. Disassemble Front Output Shaft Bearing Cap (fig. 21). Remove the set screw that secures the shifter fork to the front wheel drive shifter shaft. Slide the shifter shaft out of the shifter fork. Remove the shifter fork and clutch gear from the bearing cap. Remove the snap ring that secures the output shaft bearing and remove the output shaft bearing from the bearing cap.

13. CLEANING, INSPECTION, AND REPAIR.

a. Cleaning. Cleaning all parts thoroughly in dry-cleaning solvent. Clean the bearings by rotating them while immersed in dry-cleaning solvent until all trace of lubricant has been removed. Oil the bearings immediately to prevent corrosion of the highly polished surface.

b. Inspection.

(1) TRANSFER CASE ASSEMBLY (fig. 27). Inspect the transfer case housing for cracks or damage of any kind. Inspect the bottom and rear cover for bent or damaged condition. Replace the gaskets on the bottom and rear covers.

(2) FRONT OUTPUT SHAFT BEARING CAP ASSEMBLY (fig. 21).

(a) *Front Output Shaft Bearing Cap Housing* (fig. 20). Replace the front bearing cap, if it is cracked or damaged. Shifter shaft and output shaft oil seals must be replaced (subpar. c, below).

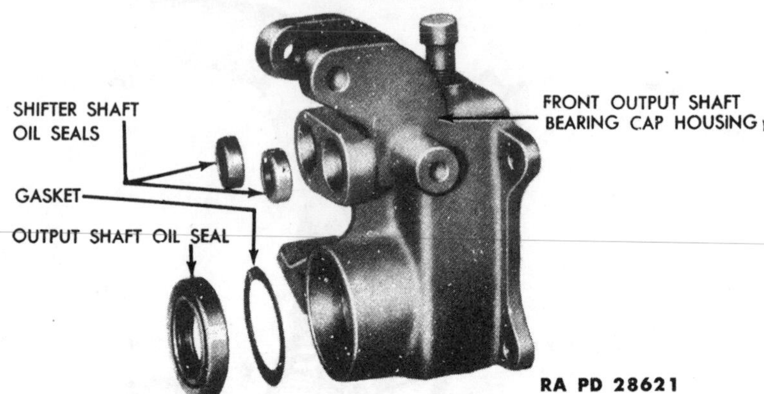

Figure 20 — Front Output Shaft Bearing Cap Housing and Oil Seals

(b) *Front Wheel Drive Shifter Shaft and Fork* (fig. 21). Replace the front wheel drive shifter shaft, if bent or damaged. Replace the fork if it has stripped set screw threads, if it is cracked or has bent forks.

(c) *Clutch Shaft and Gear* (fig. 21). Replace the clutch shaft if the splines or gear teeth are chipped or worn, if the gear has any teeth missing. Check the diameter of the pilot end of the clutch shaft. If the diameter is less than 0.625 inch, replace the clutch shaft. Replace the clutch gear, if it is worn or has any broken teeth.

(d) *Output Shaft Bearing* (fig. 21). Ball bearings with loose or discolored balls or with pitted or cracked races must be replaced.

(3) INTERMEDIATE GEAR ASSEMBLY (fig. 25). Replace the intermediate gear if excessively worn, or if any teeth are damaged. Check the thickness of the thrust washers. If the thrust washers are less than 0.093 inch in thickness, replace them. Check the diameter of the intermediate gear shaft. If the diameter is less than 0.750 inch, replace the intermediate gear shaft. Replace the roller bearing, if the rollers are scored or have flat spots.

(4) REAR OUTPUT SHAFT BEARING CAP ASSEMBLY (fig. 26). Replace the output shaft bearing cap if cracked or damaged. Replace the speedometer drive gear if it is worn or has damaged teeth. Replace the oil seal in the output shaft bearing cap housing (subpar. c, below). Replace the brake drum if it is worn or bent. Replace the universal joint rear flange, if the splines are worn. Replace the dust shield on the flange if bent.

(5) OUTPUT SHAFT ASSEMBLY (fig. 24). Replace the output shaft if the splines are worn. Small nicks can be removed by honing and then polishing with a fine stone. Measure the inside diameter of

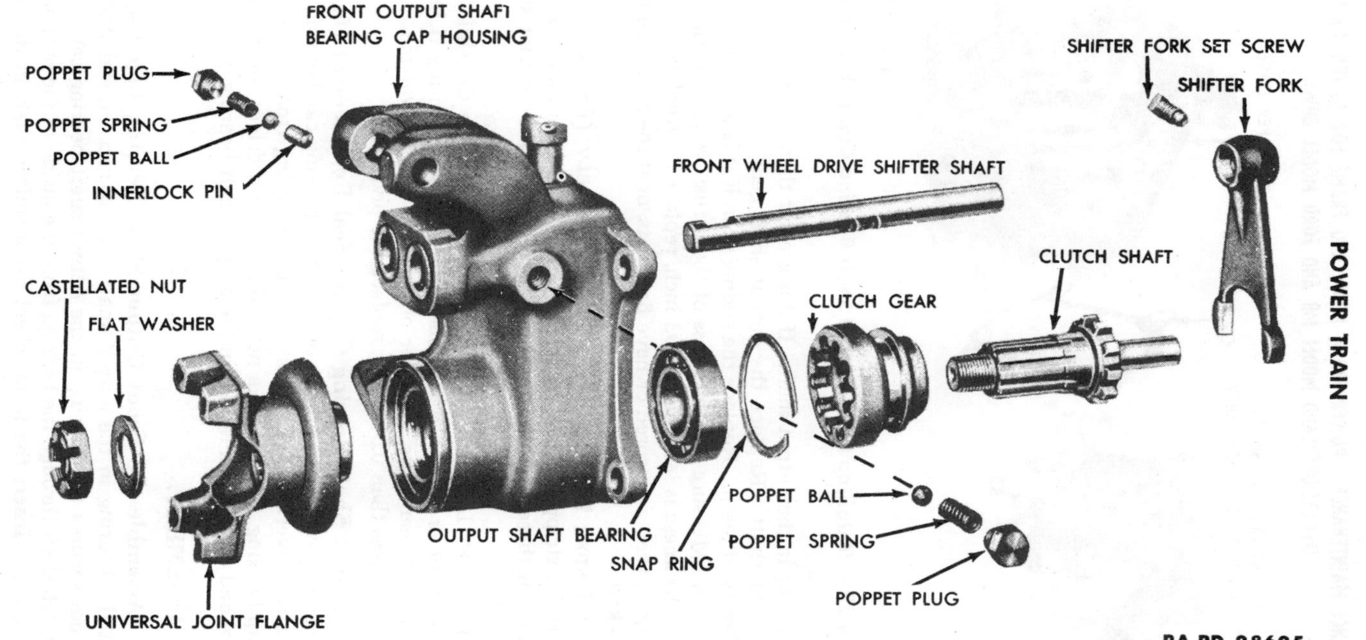

Figure 21 — Front Output Shaft Bearing Cap — Exploded View

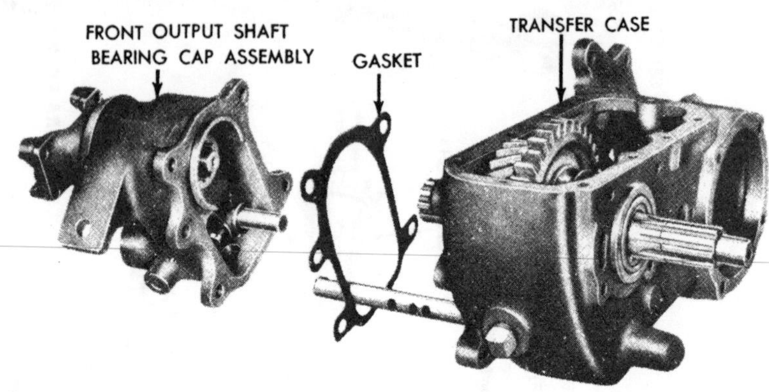

Figure 22 — Installing Front Output Shaft Bearing Cap to Transfer Case

the bushing in the output shaft. If it is greater than 0.627 inch, replace the output shaft. Replace the output shaft gear if it is worn or has any damaged teeth. Replace the sliding gear, if it is worn or has damaged teeth. Measure the thickness of the thrust washer. If the thrust washer thickness is less than 0.103 inch, replace it. Replace the roller bearings if they are scored or have flat spots, or if the races are nicked or cracked.

(6) Under Drive Shifter Fork Assembly (fig. 24). Check the fork for stripped set screw threads, cracked or bent forks. Replace if in any of these conditions. Replace the under drive shifter shaft if it is bent.

(7) Shift Lever Assembly (fig. 29). Replace the shift levers if found bent or damaged. Replace the shift lever spring if bent or cracked. Measure the diameter of the shift lever pivot pin. If the diameter is less than 0.500 inch, replace the pivot pin.

c. **Output Shaft Bearing Cap Oil Seal Replacement** (fig. 20). Drive the old oil seal out of the output shaft bearing cap housing, using a suitable driver. Drive the oil seals out, working from the inside of the cap housing. To install a new oil seal, use a driver the size of the oil seal and drive the new seal in the output shaft bearing cap housing.

14. ASSEMBLY.

a. **Assemble the Front Output Shaft Bearing Cap** (fig. 21). Insert the bearing in the output shaft bearing cap. Install the snap ring that secures the bearing in the output shaft bearing cap. Insert the clutch shaft through the bearing from the inside of the output shaft bearing cap. Insert the front wheel drive shifter shaft in the output

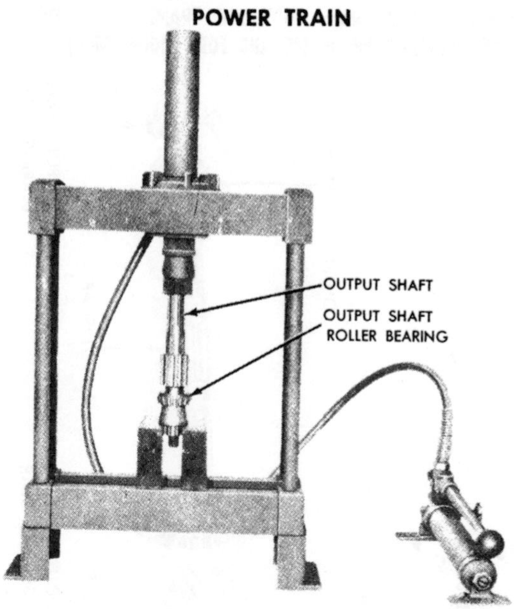

Figure 23 — Pressing Output Shaft Bearing on Output Shaft

shaft bearing cap through the outer side of the output shaft bearing cap. Place the front wheel drive shifter fork in position on the clutch gear. Slide the shifter fork on the shifter shaft and clutch gear on the clutch shaft together. Install the set screw in the shift fork and secure with a lock wire. Install the universal joint flange on the clutch shaft. Install the washer and castellated nut that secure the universal joint flange to the clutch shaft.

b. Install Under Drive Shifter Fork (fig. 20). Place the under drive shifter fork in the transfer case housing. Insert the under drive shifter shaft in the transfer case and shifter fork. Install the shifter fork set screw that secures the fork to the shifter shaft. Secure the set screw with lock wire.

c. Install Output Shaft in Transfer Case (figs. 23 and 24). Press the rear output shaft bearing on the output shaft (fig. 23). Set the output shaft sliding gear in the transfer case with the shifter fork in the channel of the sliding gear. Place the output shaft gear in the transfer case with the shoulder of the output shaft gear facing the sliding gear. Insert the output shaft in the transfer case and through the gears. Slide the thrust washer on the output shaft. Install the snap ring that secures the output shaft gear on the shaft. Slide the front output shaft roller bearing on the output shaft and, using a suitable driver, tap the roller bearing snug against the snap ring. Tap the front roller bearing cup

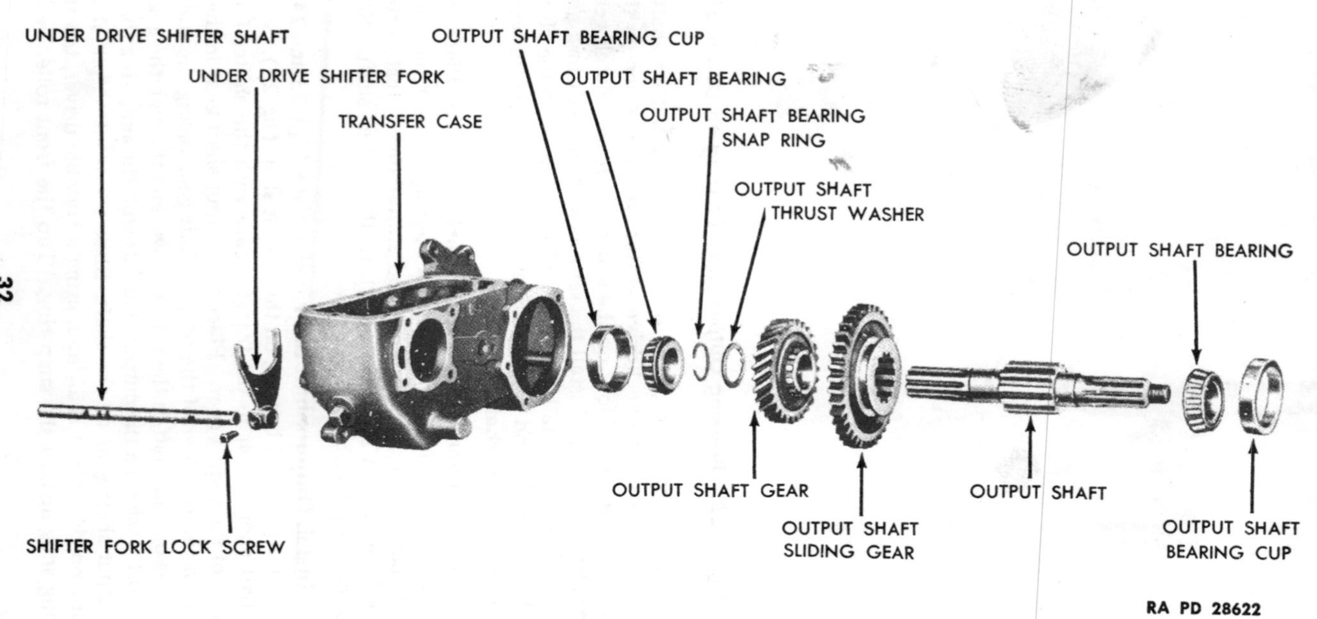

Figure 24 —Output Shaft — Exploded View

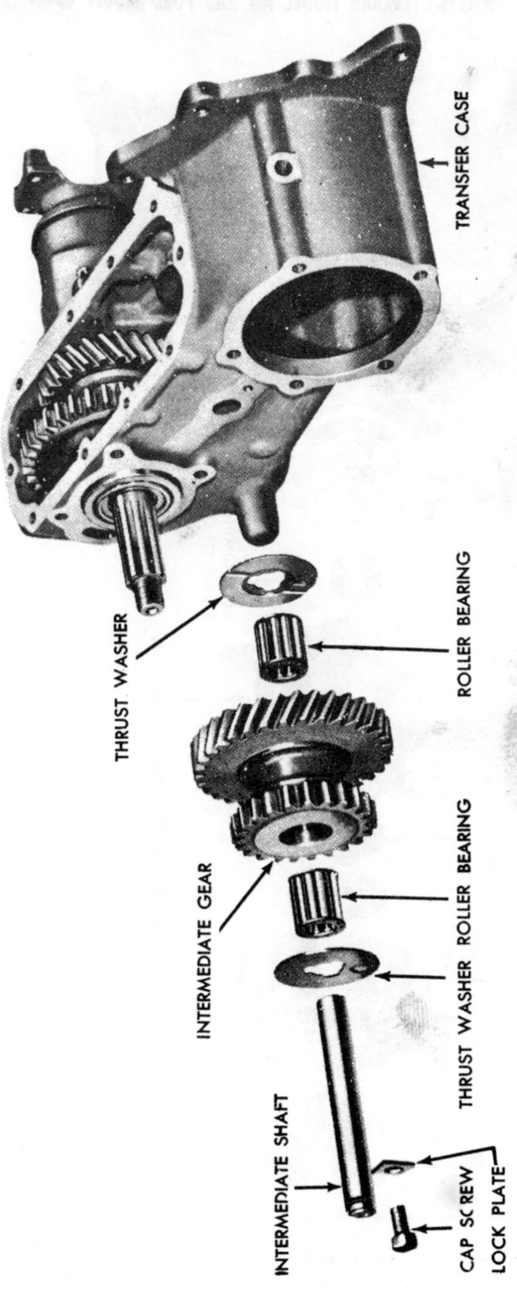

RA PD 28624

Figure 25 — Intermediate Gear Assembly — Exploded View

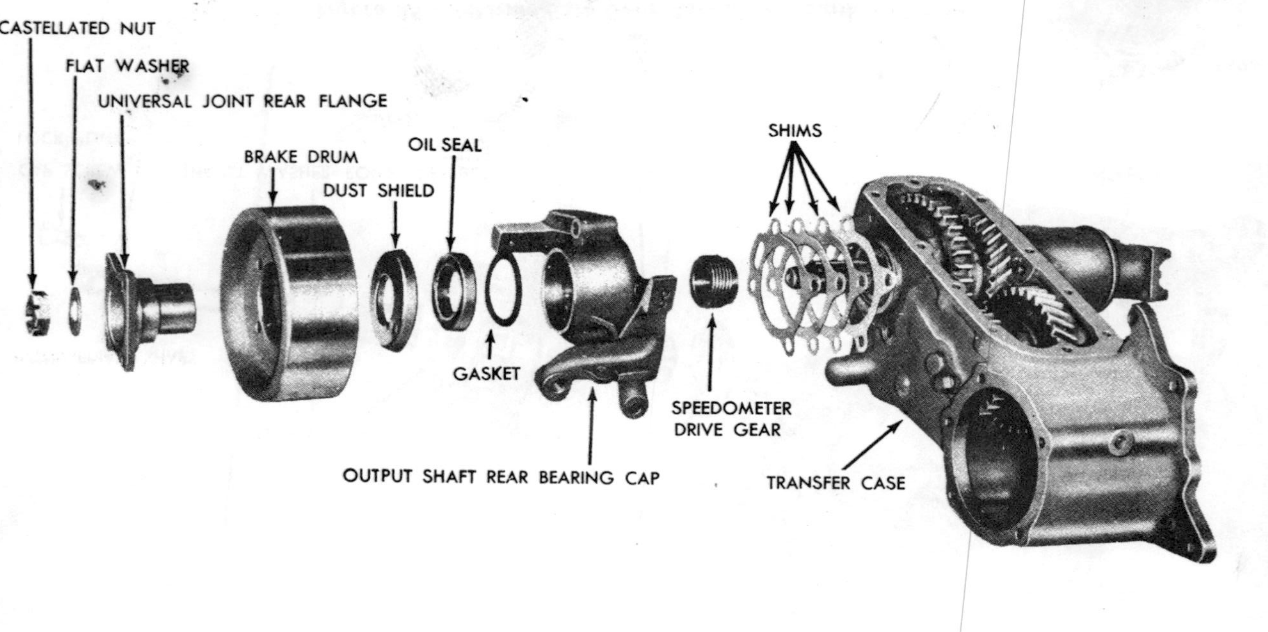

RA PD 28627

Figure 26 — Rear Output Shaft Cap — Exploded View

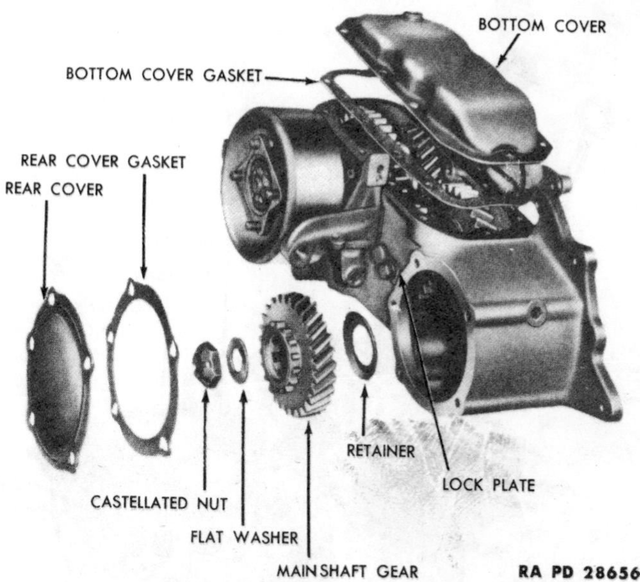

Figure 27 — Bottom Cover and Mainshaft Gear — Exploded View

in the transfer case until the cup is slightly below flush with the transfer case. Tap the rear bearing cup in the transfer case until the cup is approximately ⅛ inch from the transfer case surface.

d. **Install Front Output Shaft Bearing Cap to Transfer Case** (figs. 21 and 22). Place a new gasket in position on the transfer case. Install the interlock (fig. 21) in the interlock opening on the bearing cap. Slide the front output shaft bearing cap on the under drive shifter shaft, being careful not to damage the oil seal in the output shaft bearing cap. Install the five bolts that secure the front bearing cap to the transfer case. Install the poppet ball, poppet spring and poppet plug on both sides of the front bearing cap (fig. 21).

e. **Install Intermediate Gear** (fig. 25). Insert the roller bearings in the intermediate gear. Place the thrust washers in the transfer case, with the side having the bronze facing, toward the intermediate gear. Apply grease to the thrust washers to hold them in position, if necessary. Place the intermediate gear between the thrust washers in the transfer case. Install the intermediate gear shaft in the transfer case. Install the lock plate that secures the intermediate gear shaft to the transfer case.

f. **Install Rear Output Shaft Cap to Transfer Case** (fig. 26). Slide the speedometer drive gear on the output shaft. Install the oil seal in

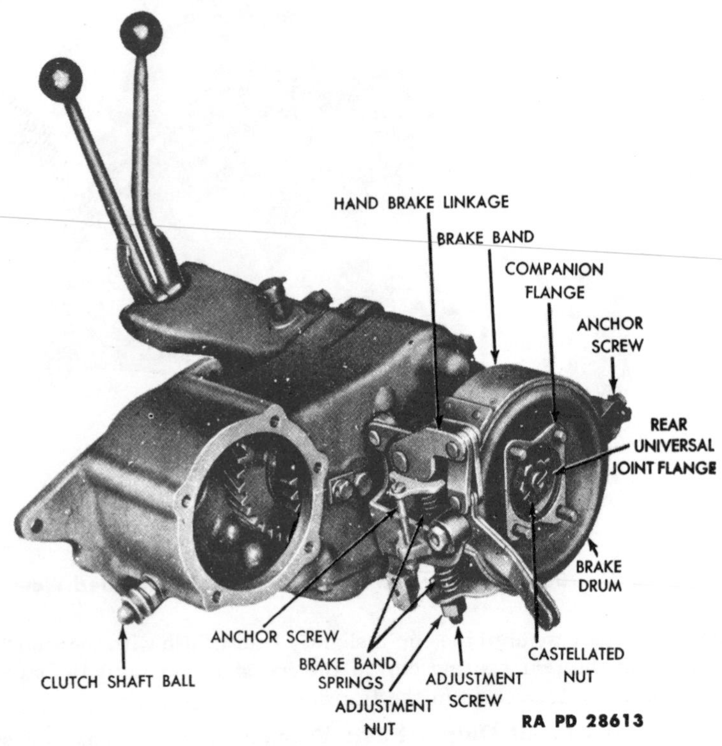

Figure 28 — Transfer Case

the rear output shaft cap (par. 13 c). Install the rear output shaft cap, shims and gasket on the transfer case. Tighten the four cap screws evenly to prevent cracking the output shaft cap. Shims are to be added or removed until the output shaft has no end play, but turns freely. When adjusting the bearings, each time shims are added, the shaft must be free before attempting to tighten the output shaft cap again. Insert the rear universal joint flange in the brake drum. Place the four cap screws in the brake drum and universal joint flange, using a suitable driver, drive the dust shield on the universal joint flange. Install the rear universal joint flange on the output shaft, and install the flat washer and nut.

g. **Install Bottom Cover to Transfer Case** (fig. 27). Install a new gasket in position on the transfer case. Place the bottom cover on the transfer case. Install the cap screws that secure the bottom cover to the transfer case.

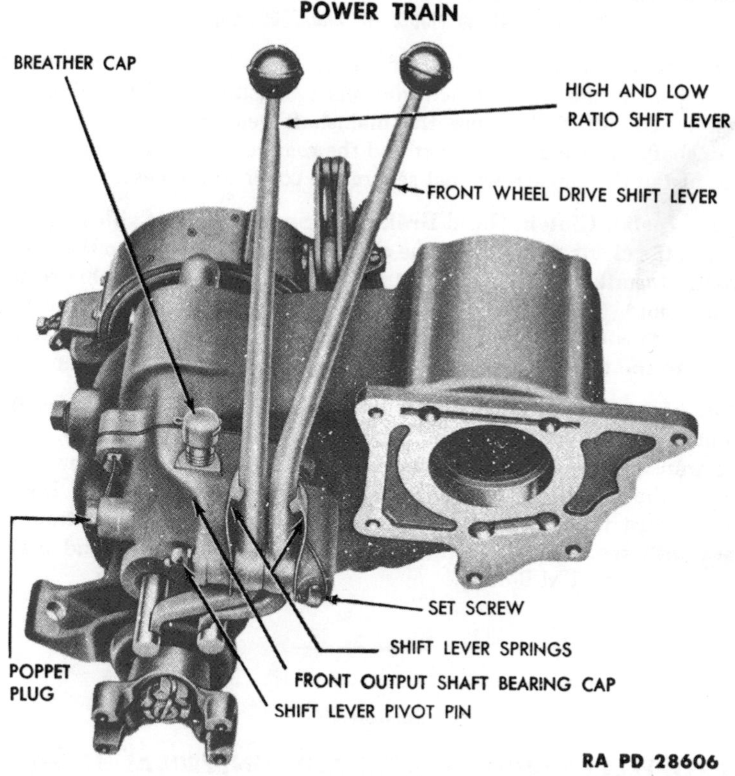

Figure 29 — Transfer Case Shift Levers

h. **Install Brake Band to Transfer Case** (fig. 28). Place the brake band on the brake drum. Place the brake band springs between the rear output shaft bearing cap and the ends of the brake band. Install the nut and bolt that secure the hand brake linkage to the rear output shaft bearing cap. Insert the adjusting screw through the brake band linkage, brake band springs, and install the adjusting nut. Install the two anchor screws on the brake band.

15. INSTALLATION.

a. **Raise Transfer Case.** Raise the transfer case and line up the clutch shaft ball joint in the transfer case. Line up the transfer case with the transmission. Be sure the interlock is in position on the rear of the transmission case before installing the transfer case to the transmission (fig. 4). Install the five cap screws that secure the transfer case to the transmission. Install the mounting bolt that secures the transfer case to the transmission support crossmember.

b. Install Mainshaft Gear (fig. 27). Insert the retainer and mainshaft gear on the transmission mainshaft. Install the flat washer and castellated nut that secure the mainshaft gear on the transmission mainshaft. Place a new gasket and the rear cover on the transfer case and install the cap screws that secure the cover to the case.

c. Install Clutch, Hand Brake and Speedometer Cables (fig. 6). Install the clevis that secures the clutch release fork cable to the clutch shaft. Install the clevis pin that secures the hand brake cable to the brake band. Install the cap screw that secures the hand brake clamp to the transfer case rear output shaft cap. Install the speedometer cable to the transfer case at the top of the rear output shaft cap.

d. Install Propeller Shaft and Transfer Case Shield (fig. 6). Connect the rear propeller shaft to the transfer case (par. 17 **b**). Place the transmission shield in position and install the five cap screws that secure the shield to the transmission support crossmember. Install the exhaust pipe clamp to the transmission shield. Fill the transfer case with specified oil to the proper level. Adjust the hand brake band (refer to TM 9-803).

Section IV

PROPELLER (DRIVE) SHAFTS AND UNIVERSAL JOINTS

16. DESCRIPTION AND TABULATED DATA.

a. Description (fig. 2). The power from the transfer case is carried through two propeller shafts. One propeller shaft runs from the front of the transfer case to the front axle, and a second propeller shaft runs from the rear of the transfer case to the rear axle. Each is equipped with two universal joints. The splined slip joint at one end of each shaft allows for variations in distance between the transfer case and the axle units due to spring action. Two types of universal joints are used; the U-bolt type and the solid yoke type.

b. Tabulated Data.

(1) PROPELLER SHAFTS.

Make .... Spicer
Shaft diameter .... 1½ in.
Length (front) .... 21$^{11}/_{16}$ in.
Length (rear) .... 20$^{1}/_{32}$ in.

(2) Front Propeller Shaft Forward Universal Joint.

Make .... Spicer
Type .... U-bolt and solid yoke
Model 1268
Bearings .... Needle roller

(3) Front Propeller Shaft Rear Universal Joint.

Make .... Spicer
Type .... U-bolt and solid yoke
Model 1261
Bearings .... Needle roller

(4) Rear Propeller Shaft Forward Universal Joint.

Make .... Spicer
Type .... Solid yoke slip joint
Model 1261
Bearings .... Needle roller

(5) Rear Propeller Shaft Rear Universal Joint.

Make .... Spicer
Type .... U-bolt and solid yoke
Model 1268
Bearings .... Needle roller

17. REMOVAL.

a. **Front Propeller Shaft** (fig. 33). Bend the ears of the lock plates off the U-bolt nuts. Remove the two nuts from each of the two U-bolts at the front axle and at the transfer case. Remove the U-bolts from the propeller shaft. Take care to hold the bearing races in place on the universal joint to avoid losing the rollers.

b. **Rear Propeller Shaft** (fig. 34). The rear propeller shaft is similar to the front propeller shaft with the exception of the solid yoke type connection at the transfer case. Remove the nuts from the U-bolts at the rear axle end. Remove the U-bolts. Slide the universal joint out of the universal joint rear flange. Care must be taken to hold the bearing races on the universal joint to avoid losing the rollers. Remove the four nuts that secure the universal joint flange yoke to the rear flange at the transfer case. Remove the rear propeller shaft from the vehicle.

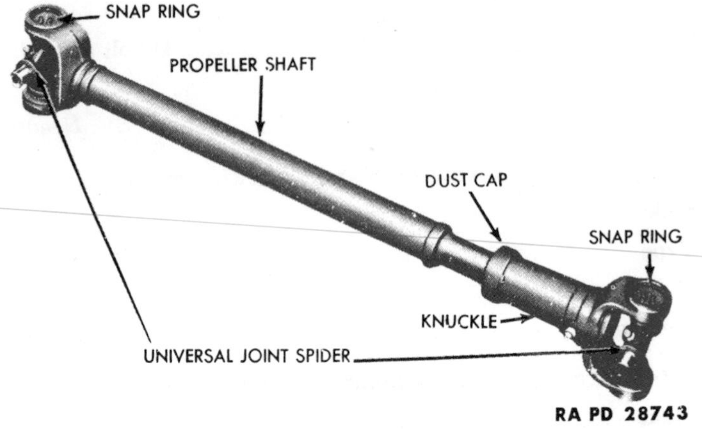

Figure 30 — Front Propeller Shaft

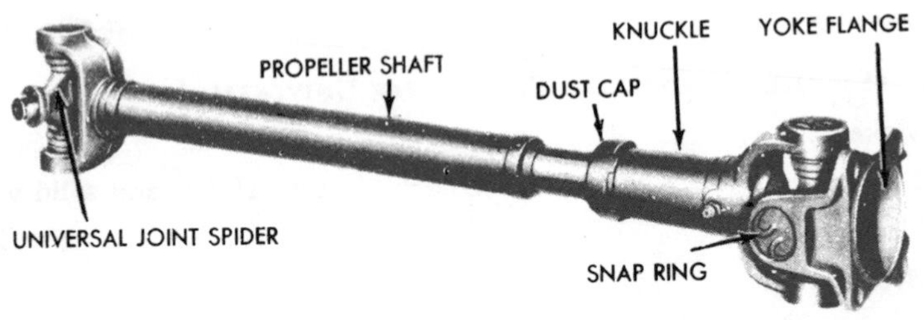

Figure 31 — Rear Propeller Shaft

18. DISASSEMBLY.

a. Front Propeller Shaft (fig. 30).

(1) Remove Snap Rings From Yoke (fig. 30). Place the propeller shaft in a vise. Remove the snap rings that secure the spider bearings in the yoke flange with a pair of pliers. If the snap ring does not snap out of the groove, tap the end of the bearing lightly. This will relieve the pressure against the snap ring.

(2) Remove Spider From Yoke (fig. 32). Drive lightly on the end of the spider bearing until the opposite bearing is pushed out of the yoke flange. Turn the assembly over in the vise and drive the first spider bearing back out of its lug by driving on the exposed end of the spider. Use a brass drift with a flat face about $\frac{1}{32}$ inch smaller

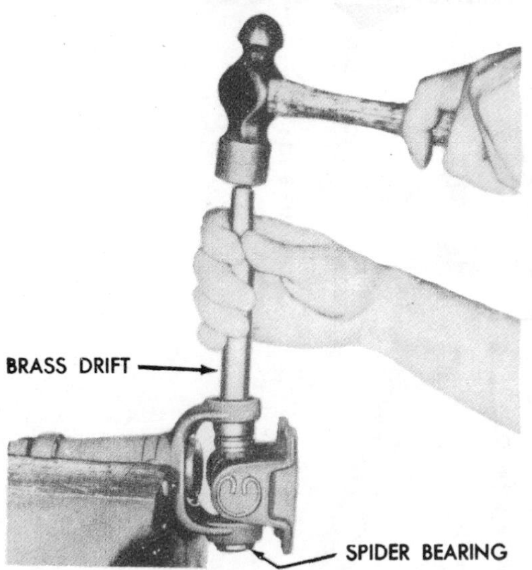

RA PD 28745

Figure 32 — Removing Spider Bearing

in diameter than the hole in the yoke, otherwise there is danger of damaging the spider bearing. Repeat this operation for the other two bearings, then lift out the spider, sliding to one side and tilting over the top of the yoke.

(3) REMOVE KNUCKLE FROM SHAFT (fig. 30). Bend the ears of the dust cap off the knuckle. Slide the knuckle off the drive shaft. Remove the split cork gasket from the bearing cap. Line up the slots in the dust cap with the splines on the drive shaft and remove the cap from the shaft.

b. Rear Propeller Shaft.

(1) REMOVE YOKE FLANGE (fig. 31). Place the propeller shaft in a vise. Remove the four snap rings that secure the spider bearings in the yoke flange and knuckle. Using a brass drift with a flat face about 1/32 inch smaller than the hole in the yoke, drive lightly on the end of the bearing until the opposite bearing is out of the yoke flange. Turn the assembly over in the vise and drive the first bearing out of its lug by driving on the exposed end of the spider. Remove the yoke flange from the spider.

(2) REMOVE SPIDER AND KNUCKLE (fig. 32). Remove the spider from the knuckle (subpar. a (2), above). Remove the knuckle from the propeller shaft (subpar. a (3), above).

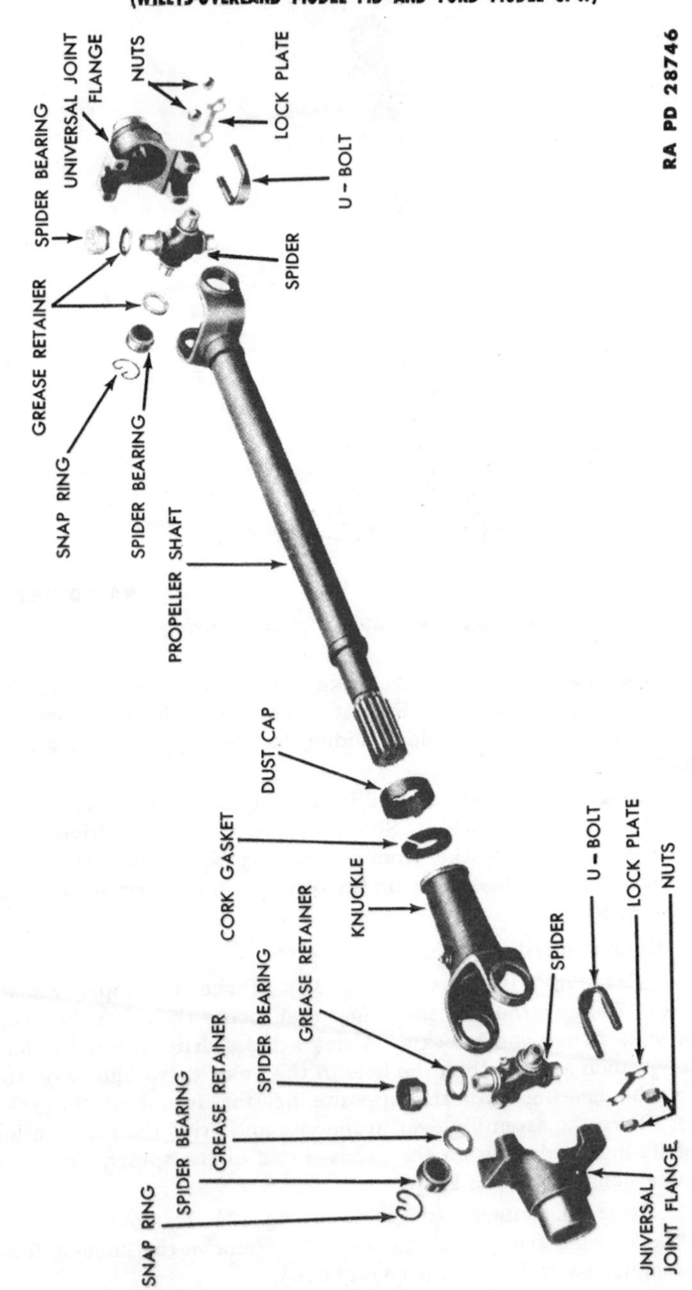

Figure 33 — Front Propeller Shaft — Exploded View

19. CLEANING, INSPECTION, AND REPAIR.

a. Clean all parts thoroughly with dry-cleaning solvent. Inspect the drive shafts for cracks, broken welds, scored spider bearing surfaces, or bent shafts. Parts with any of these faults must be replaced. Inspect the knuckle for worn splines, worn bearing surfaces and bearings and plugged lubricant fittings. Check the diameter of the machined surface of the spiders. If the diameter is less than 0.595 inch, replace the spider. Replace all grease seals regardless of their condition.

20. ASSEMBLY.

a. Front Propeller Shaft (fig. 33). Place the propeller shaft in a vise. Slide the dust cap on the drive shaft. Place a new cork gasket in the cap. Slide the knuckle on the shaft splines, being sure that the knuckle on the shaft is in the same angle as the yoke at the opposite end of the propeller shaft. Slide the dust cap on the shoulder of the knuckle and bend the ears of the cap over the shoulder of the knuckle.

b. Rear Propeller Shaft (fig. 34).

(1) INSTALL SPIDER IN YOKE FLANGE (fig. 34). Insert the spider into the yoke flange. Tap the spider bearing approximately 1/4 inch into the yoke flange, using a brass drift approximately 1/32 inch smaller than the hole in the yoke. Tap the other bearing into the opposite end of the yoke flange until the bearing is in line with the snap ring grooves. With a pair of pliers, install the snap rings on both ends of the yoke flange. Insert the flange assembly in the knuckle. Tap the bearing approximately 1/4 inch into the yoke. Place the other bearing into the opposite end of the yoke, and tap this bearing into the yoke until the bearing is in line with the snap ring groove. Install the snap rings on both ends of the yoke.

(2) INSTALL KNUCKLE AND SPIDERS (fig. 34). Install the knuckle on the propeller shaft (subpar. **a** (1), above).

21. INSTALLATION.

a. Rear Propeller Shaft. Place the propeller shaft with the yoke flange end toward the transfer case (fig. 6). Install the four nuts that secure the yoke flange to the transfer case. Insert the two spider bearings on the spider at the rear axle end. Place the spider in the universal joint rear flange. Install the two U-bolts that secure the propeller shaft to the rear axle flange. Lubricate the propeller shaft with specified lubricant.

b. Front Propeller Shaft. Place the propeller shaft with the knuckle end at the transfer case. Insert the bearings on the spider

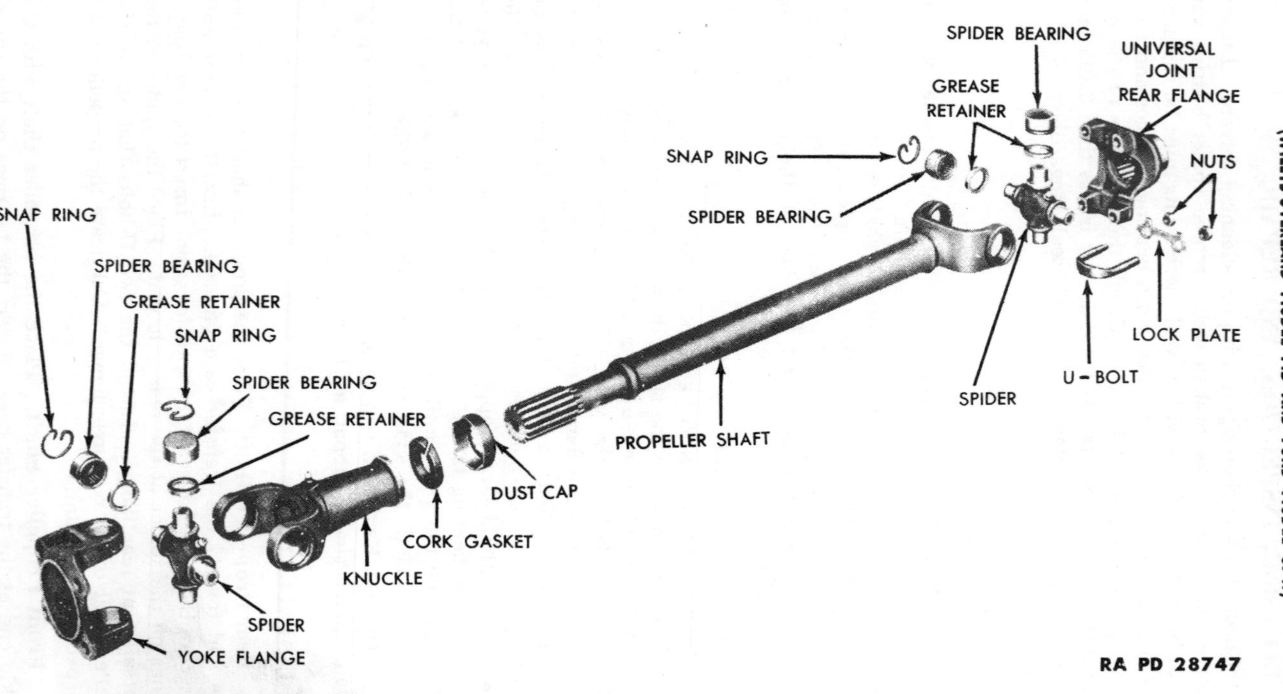

Figure 34 — Rear Propeller Shaft — Exploded View

and place the propeller shaft in the universal joint flange on the transfer case. Install the two U-bolts that secure the propeller shaft to the transfer case. Insert the two spider bearings on the spider at the front axle end. Place the propeller shaft in the front axle flange. Install the two U-bolts that secure the propeller shaft to the universal joint flange. Lubricate the propeller shaft with specified lubricant.

Section V

FRONT AXLE

22. DESCRIPTION AND DATA.

a. **Description** (fig. 2). The front axle assembly is a front wheel driving unit, with specially designed spindle housings, and has a conventional type differential with hypoid drive gears. The differential parts are interchangeable with those of the rear axle. The axle shafts are of the full-floating type. The differential is mounted in the housing similar to the rear axle, except that the drive pinion shaft is toward the rear instead of the front and to the right of the center of the axle. Three types of axle shafts and universal joints have been used (Rzeppa, Bendix, and Tracta). The vehicles using the different types of shafts are identified by an identification tag attached to the spindle housing (fig. 35).

b. **Data.**

(1) FRONT AXLE.

Make .... Spicer
Drive .... Through springs
Type .... Full-floating

(2) DIFFERENTIAL.

Drive .... Hypoid
Gear ratio .... 4.88 to 1
Bearings .... Timken roller 2
Adjustment .... Shims
Gears (pinion) 2

(3) OIL CAPACITY .... 2½ pt

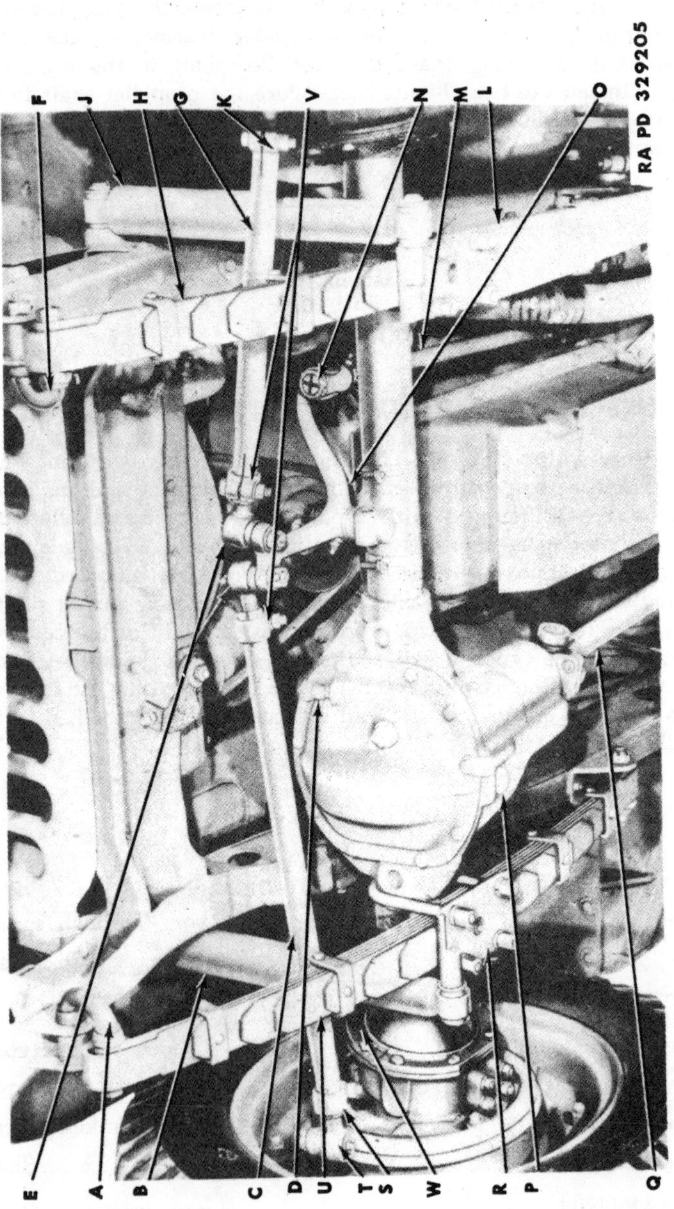

Figure 35 — Front Axle Assembly in Vehicle

A—SPRING SHACKLE
B—SHOCK ABSORBER
C—TIE ROD
D—BREATHER CAP
E—TIE ROD ENDS
F—SPRING SHACKLE
G—TIE ROD
H—LEFT FRONT SPRING
J—SHOCK ABSORBER
K—TIE ROD CLAMP
L—TORQUE REACTION SPRING
M—DRAG LINK
N—DRAG LINK PLUG
O—PIVOT ARM
P—DRAIN PLUG
Q—FRONT PROPELLER SHAFT
R—SPRING SEAT PLATE
S—TIE ROD CLAMP
T—TIE ROD ENDS
U—RIGHT FRONT SPRING
V—TIE ROD CLAMPS
W—AXLE SHAFT IDENTIFICATION TAG

RA PD 329205 -B

Legend for Figure 35 — Front Axle Assembly in Vehicle

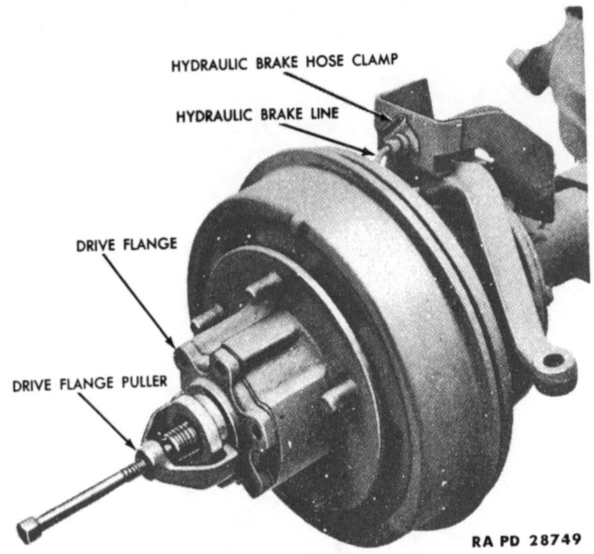

Figure 36 — Removing Drive Flange With Puller Similar to Puller 41-P-2912

23. REMOVAL.

a. **Preliminary Work.** Remove the drain plug at the differential housing and drain the oil. Raise the vehicle until the weight is off the front springs.

b. **Disconnect Shock Absorbers and Drag Link** (fig. 35). Remove the cotter pin and flat washer that secure the shock absorber to the spring seat plate at both front shock absorbers. Remove the drag link plug at the pivot arm. Remove the drag link from the pivot arm.

c. **Disconnect Front Propeller Shaft and Spring U-bolts** (fig. 35). Disconnect the front propeller shaft at the front anxle (par. 17 **a**). Remove the four nuts from the two U-bolts that secure the spring seat plate. Remove the spring seat plate and U-bolts. Remove the four nuts from the U-bolts at the torque reaction spring. Remove the two U-bolts.

d. **Disconnect Spring Shackles** (fig. 35). Remove the lower spring shackle bushing at the forward end of the front springs. Pull both springs out of the spring shackles and drop the forward end of the springs to the floor. Roll the front axle assembly from the vehicle.

RA PD 28750

Figure 37 — Removing Bearing Lock Nut With Wrench 41-W-3825-200

24. DISASSEMBLY.

a. **Remove Wheels.** Place the front axle assembly on two blocks. Remove the five nuts that secure the wheels to the brake drum. Remove the wheels.

b. **Remove Axle Shaft Assembly.** Using a screwdriver, pry the hub cap off the drive flange. Remove the cotter pin and castellated nut from the axle shaft. Remove the six cap screws that secure the drive flange to the hub. Install the puller 41-P-2912 or simiiar on the drive flange and remove the drive flange (fig. 36). Bend the ear of the lock washer off the bearing lock nut. Remove the bearing lock nut, lock washer, and bearing adjustment nut, using the wheel bearing nut wrench 41-W-3825-200 furnished with the vehicle (fig. 37). Slide the brake drum and hub assembly, including the wheel bearings, off the spindle. Disconnect the hydraulic brake line at the brake hose guard (fig. 36). Remove the six cap screws that secure the brake plate to the spindle housing. Remove the brake plate from the spindle. Slide the spindle off the axle shaft. The axle shaft can now be removed from the housing. If equipped with a Tracta universal joint axle shaft, see subparagraph c, below. Use the same procedure to disassemble the other end of the front axle shaft.

c. **Axle Shaft Disassembly.** Three types of axle shaft universal joints, as shown in figures 38, 42, and 44, are used in the front axle.

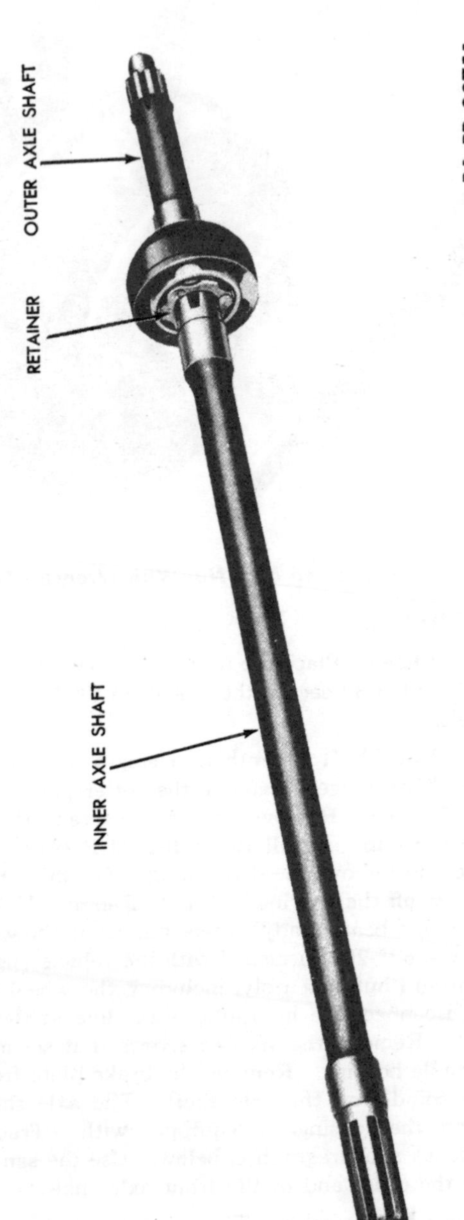

Figure 38 — Front Axle Shaft (Rzeppa Joint)

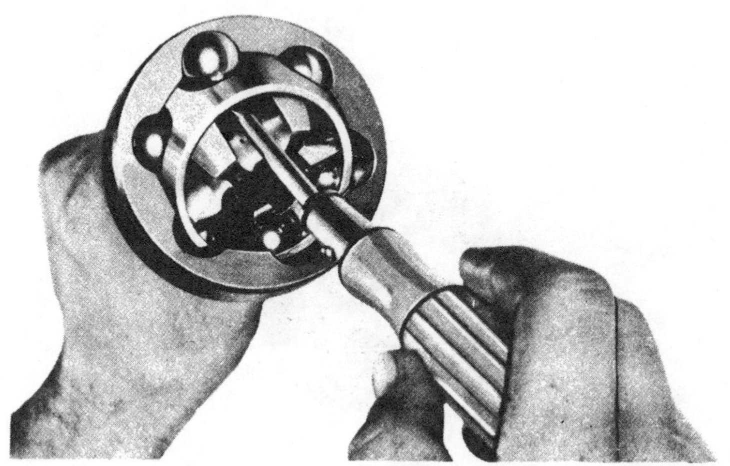

RA PD 28752

Figure 39 — Removing Balls From Cage

Disassembly procedures for each are given in steps (1), (2), and (3), below.

(1) Rzeppa Universal Joint.

(a) Remove Inner Axle Shaft (fig. 59). Remove the three flat head screws that secure the retainer to the inner ball race. Slide the inner axle shaft out of the universal joint. Remove the pilot pin from the outer axle shaft. If the pilot pin does not drop out of the outer axle shaft, hold the shaft upside down and tap the shaft on a piece of wood.

(b) Remove Balls From Cage (fig. 39). Tilt the cage in the axle shaft cup until the opposite side of the cage is out of the housing. It may be necessary to use a brass drift and hammer to tilt the cage. Use a screwdriver to pry the steel ball out of the cage. Repeat this operation until all the balls are removed.

(c) Remove Cage and Inner Race From Axle Shaft (fig. 40). Turn the cage in the axle shaft cup in line with the shaft and with the two larger elongated holes between two bosses in the shaft. Lift the cage and inner race from the axle shaft cup.

(d) Remove Inner Race From Cage (fig. 41). Turn the inner race in the cage so that one of the bosses on the inner race can be dropped into one of the two elongated holes in the cage. Remove the inner race from the cage.

(2) Bendix Universal Joint (figs. 42 and 43). Place the axle

RA PD 28754

Figure 40 — Removing Cage and Inner Race From Axle Shaft (Rzeppa Joint)

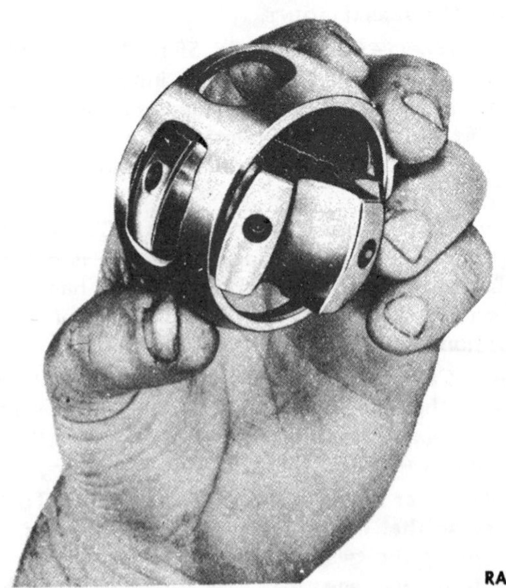

RA PD 28753

Figure 41 — Removing Inner Race From Cage (Rzeppa Joint)

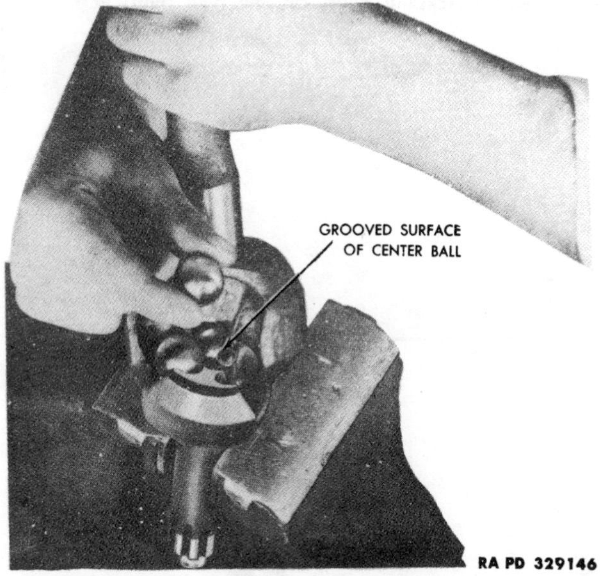

Figure 42 — Front Axle Shaft (Bendix Type)

shaft in a vise and with a long nosed drift remove the groove pin from the universal joint knuckle. Remove the axle shaft from the vise. Tap the knuckle end of the axle shaft on a wood block until the center ball pin drops in the groove pin hole. Place the axle shaft with the knuckle end (short end) in a vise. Bend the axle shaft so that the center ball can be rotated until the grooved surface of the center ball is facing the first ball that is to be removed. Holding the axle shaft in a bent position, raise the shaft until the first ball to be removed slides into the groove of the center ball, and remove the ball. Remove the axle shaft from the knuckle. The three remaining balls will drop out of the knuckle.

(3) TRACTA UNIVERSAL JOINT (fig. 45). Remove the outer portion of the axle shaft and the outer portion of the universal joint from the axle housing. Pull the inner portion of the axle shaft and the inner portion of the universal joint out of the housing.

d. **Remove Spindle Housing** (fig. 46). Remove the castellated nut that secures the tie rod ends to the two spindle arms. Remove the two castellated nuts that secure the two tie rod ends to the steering pivot arm and remove the two tie rods. Remove the hydraulic brake hose clamp from the hydraulic brake line at the brake hose guard. Remove the four nuts that secure the brake hose guard and spindle arm to the spindle housing. Remove the spindle arm and

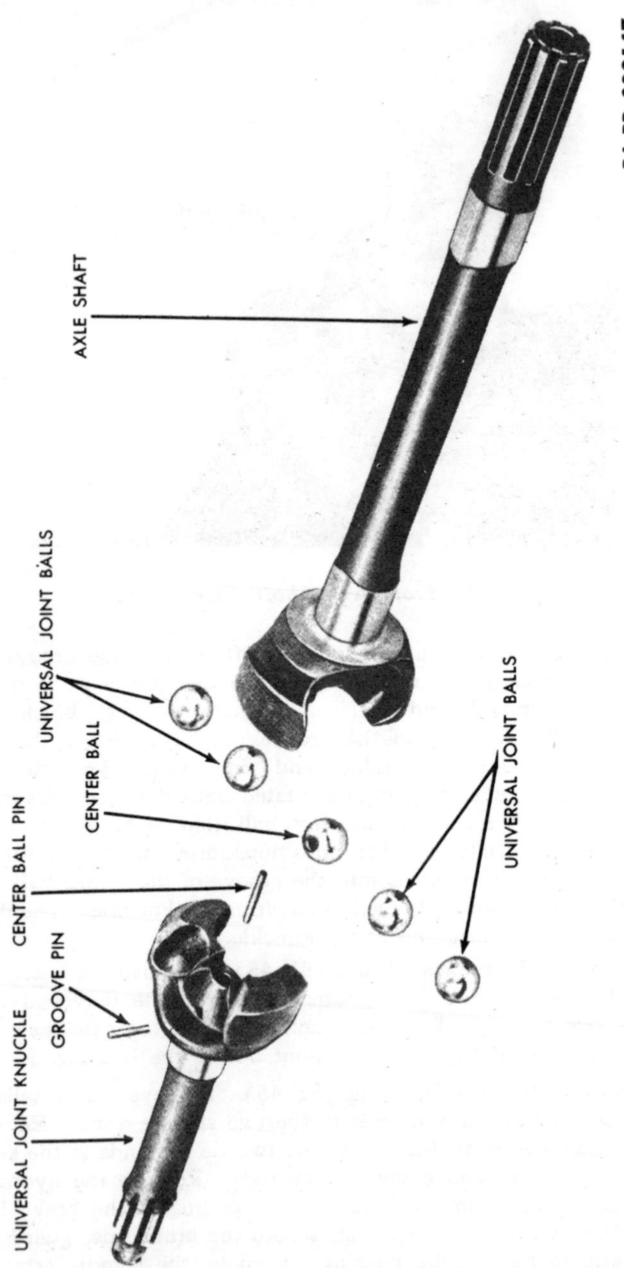

Figure 43 — Front Axle Shaft — Exploded View (Bendix Type)

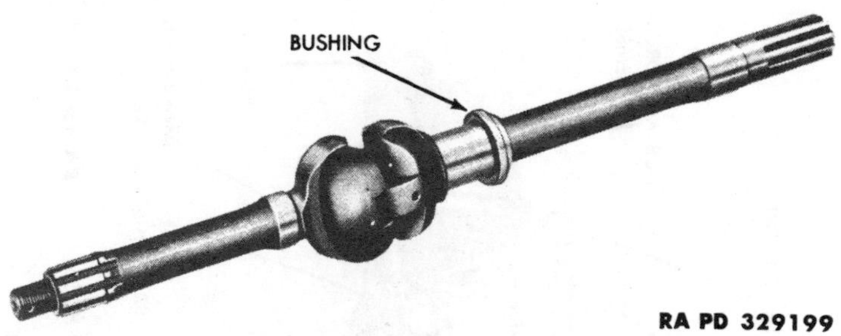

Figure 44 — Front Axle Shaft (Tracta Type)

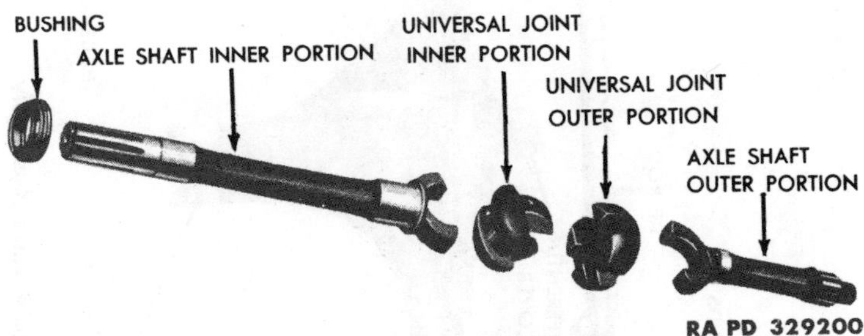

Figure 45 — Front Axle Shaft — Exploded View (Tracta Type)

shims from the spindle housing. Remove the four cap screws that secure the lower bearing cap to the spindle housing. Remove the bearing cap and shims. Remove the eight cap screws that secure the spindle housing oil seal retainer to the spindle housing. Remove the spindle housing from the axle housing. Use the same procedure for disassembling the other spindle housing.

e. **Remove Differential** (fig. 47). Remove the ten cap screws that secure the differential cover to the differential housing. Remove the differential cover and gasket. Remove the two cap screws from the bearing cap at each end of the differential gears and remove the caps. Remove the differential gear assembly from the housing, using a pry bar, if necessary. Reinstall the bearing caps in the housing, noting the markings (fig. 47) to assure their being installed in their correct location.

f. **Disassemble Differential.**

(1) Remove Differential Pinion Gears and Axle Shaft Gears (fig. 48). Place the differential assembly in a vise equipped with brass jaws. With a long nosed drift, drive the differential

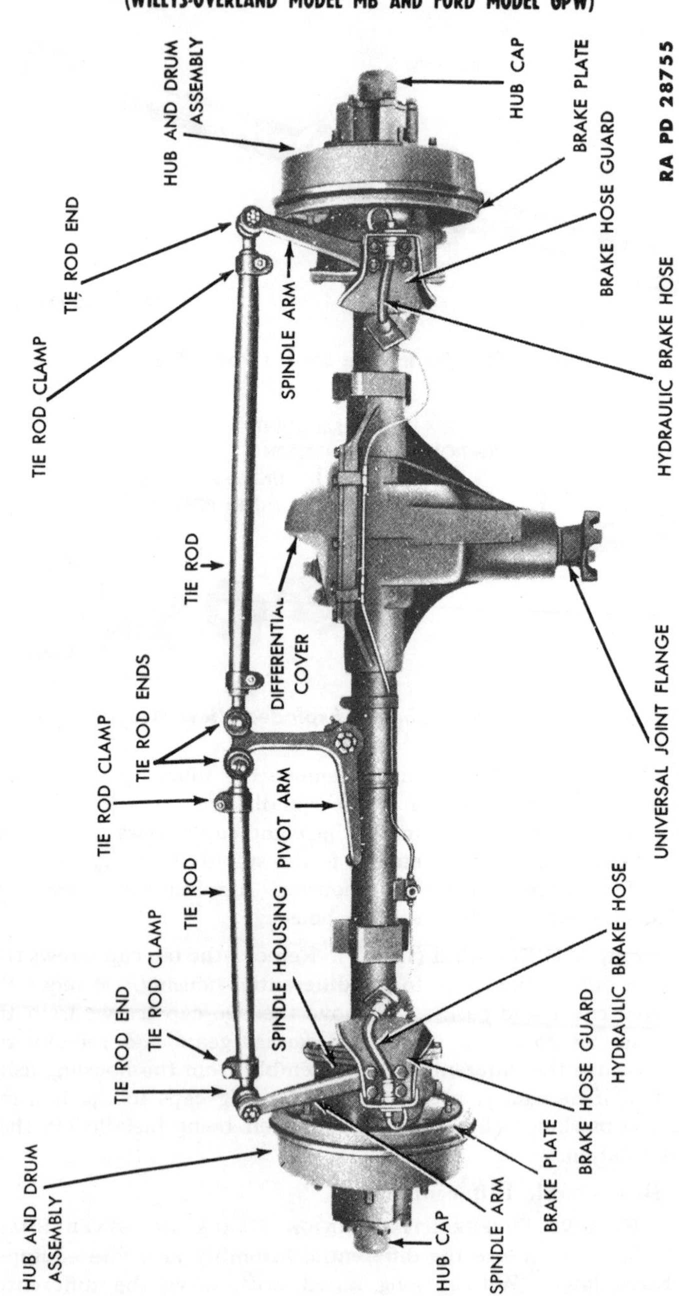

Figure 46 — Front Axle Assembly

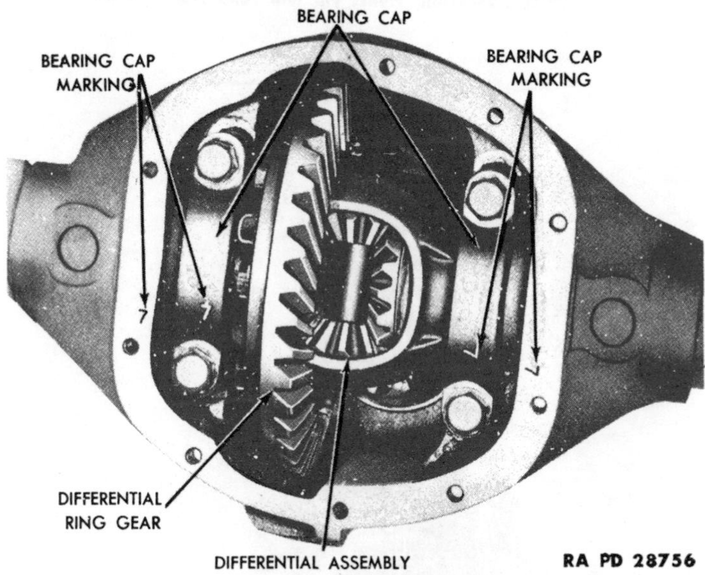

Figure 47 — Differential Assembly

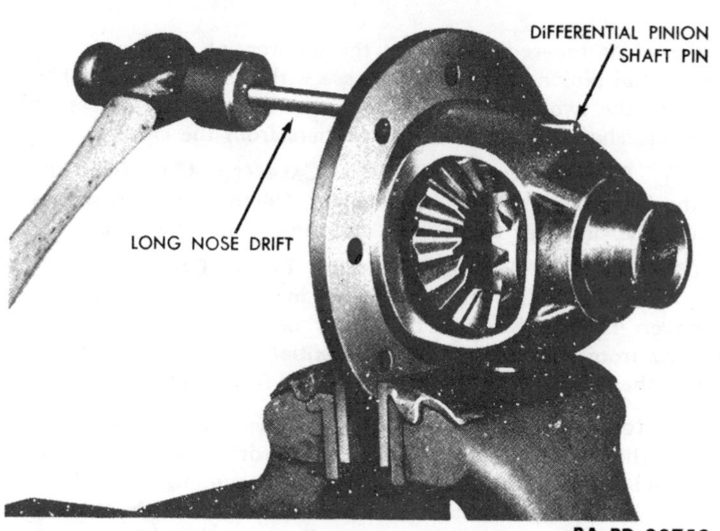

Figure 48 — Removing Pinion Shaft Lock Pin

RA PD 28757

Figure 49 — Removing Bearings From Differential Case With Special Tool 41-R-2378-30

pinion shaft tapered pin out of the differential gear case. Tap the differential pinion shaft from the case with a brass drift and hammer. Remove the two differential pinion gears and thrust washers and the two axle shaft gears and thrust washers from the case.

(2) REMOVE RING GEAR FROM CASE (fig. 47). Bend the ears of the lock plates off the cap screws. Remove the cap screws that secure the ring gear to the case, and remove the ring gear.

(3) REMOVE ROLLER BEARING FROM DIFFERENTIAL CASE (fig. 49). Place the differential case in a vise. Install the bearing remover 41-R-2378-30 to the roller bearing. Remove the roller bearing from each end of the differential case. Remove the shims, noting the thickness of the shims removed from each end.

g. **Remove Drive Pinion.** Remove the nut and flat washer that secure the universal joint flange to the drive pinion. Install the puller 41-P-2905-60 to the universal joint flange (fig. 50) and remove the flange. Using a brass drift and hammer, drive the drive pinion out of the axle housing (fig. 51). Remove the shims and spacer from the drive pinion, noting the thickness of the shims removed from the pinion.

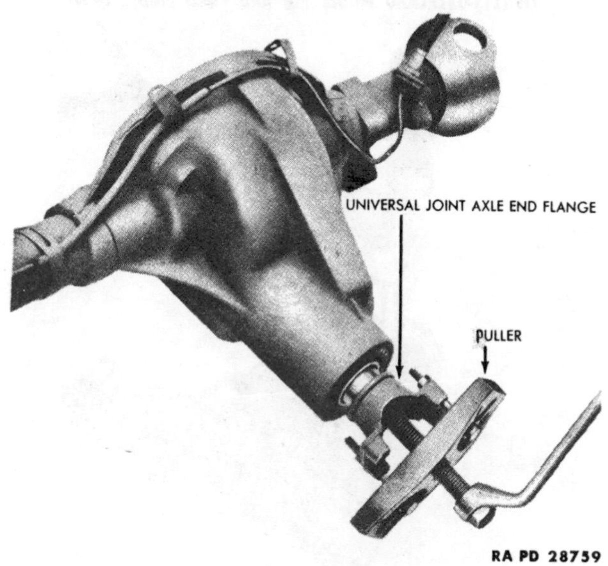

Figure 50 – Removing Universal Joint Axle End Flange With Puller 41-P-2905-60

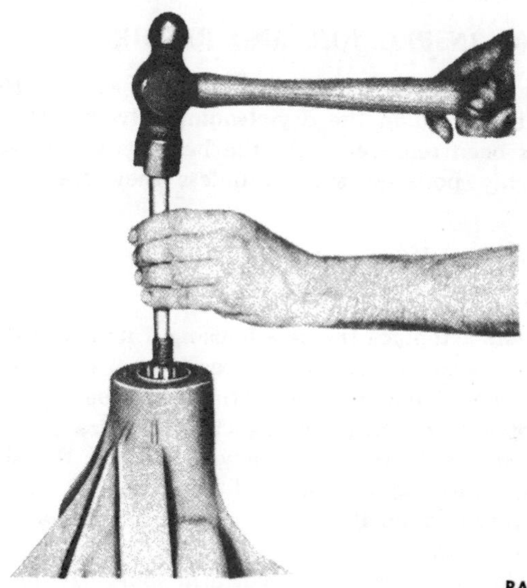

Figure 51 – Removing Drive Pinion

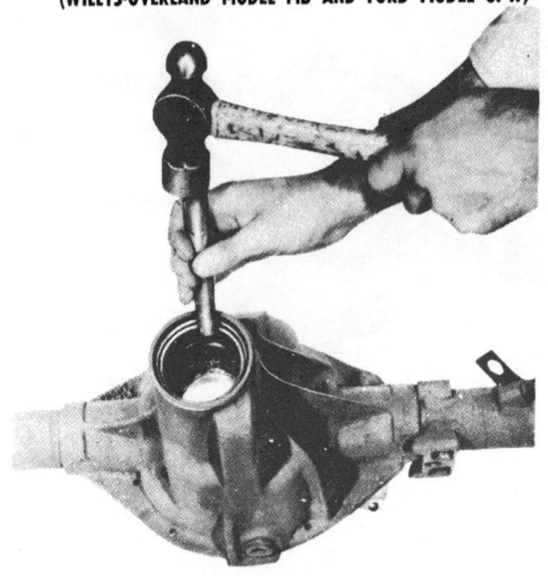

RA PD 28761

Figure 52 — Installing Pinion Outer Bearing Cup

25. CLEANING, INSPECTION, AND REPAIR.

a. Cleaning. Clean all parts in dry-cleaning solvent. Rotate the bearings while immersed in the dry-cleaning solvent until all trace of lubricant has been removed. Oil the bearings to prevent corrosion of the highly polished surface unless they are to be used immediately.

b. Inspection and Repair.

(1) AXLE HOUSING (fig. 53).

(a) Inspection. Replace the axle housing if it is bent or has any broken welds or cracks. Drive pinion bearing cups that are pitted, corroded or discolored due to overheating must be replaced (step *(c)*, below). Spindle housing bearing cups that are pitted or corroded must be replaced (step *(d)*, below). Replace the oil seals in the axle housing regardless of their condition (step *(e)*, below). Replace the differential cover, if cracked or if it has damaged threads in the filler plug hole. Check the cover for missing or damaged breather cap. Check the steering pivot arm shaft. If the diameter is less than 0.747 inch, replace the pivot shaft (step *(b)*, below). If the front axle is equipped with a Tracta type axle shaft, measure the

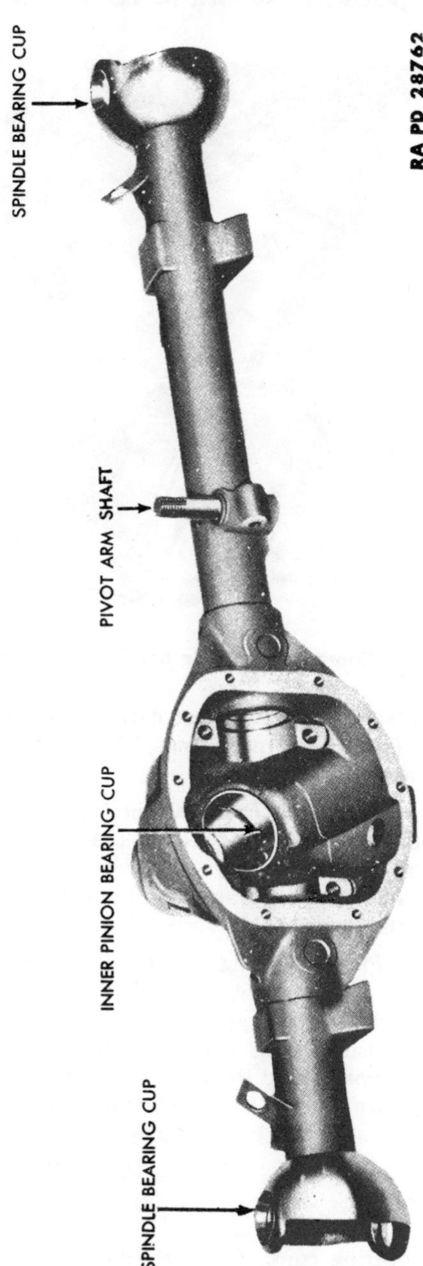

Figure 53 — Front Axle Housing

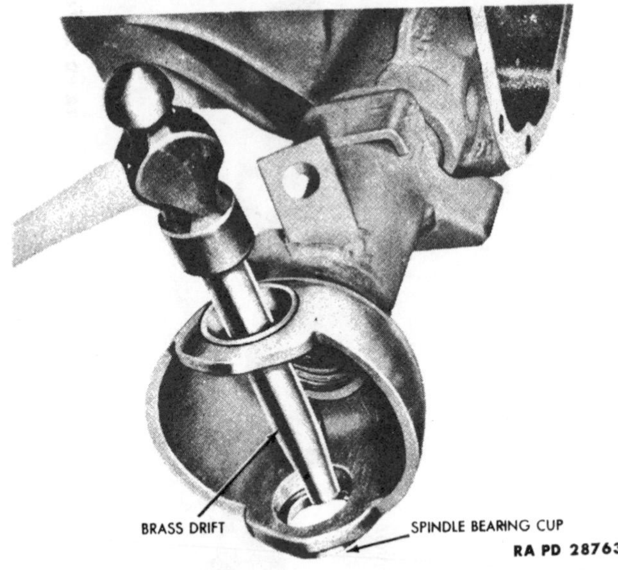

Figure 54 — Removing Spindle Bearing Cup From Axle Housing

inside diameter of the housing at each end of the axle housing. If the bushing is worn to more than 1.285 inch, replace the bushing (step *(f)*, below).

(b) Pivot Arm Shaft Replacement (fig. 53). With a long nosed drift, drive out the dowel that secures the pivot arm shaft to the axle housing. Tap the shaft out of the housing. To install a new pivot arm shaft, insert it in the bracket on the housing with the dowel slot in line with the dowel hole. Drive dowel in place.

(c) Drive Pinion Bearing Cup Replacement. Remove the inner and outer bearing cups, using a standard puller, noting the thickness of the shims when removing the inner bearing cup. To install new bearing cups, use a brass drift and hammer. Place the original thickness of shims behind the inner bearing cup and tap the bearing cups lightly around the entire circumference until flush with the shoulder in the axle housing (fig. 52).

(d) Spindle Housing Bearing Cup Replacement. Working through one of the bearing cups, tap the opposite bearing cup out of the axle housing, using a brass drift and hammer (fig. 54). To install new bearing cups, place the bearing cup in position and tap the cup lightly until it is flush with the shoulder in the axle housing.

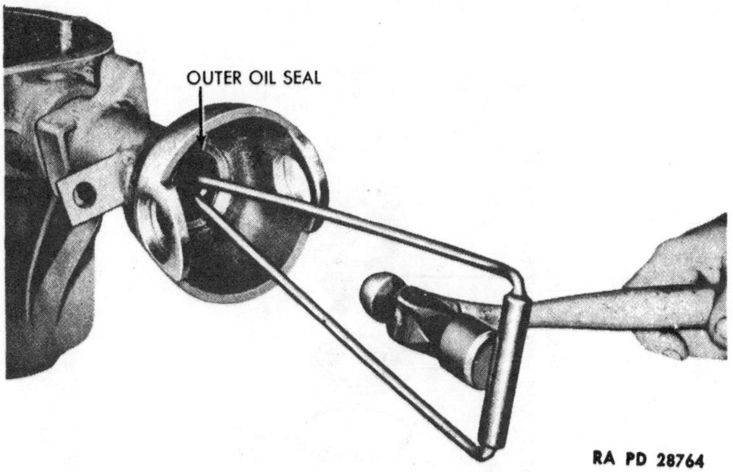

Figure 55 — Removing Oil Seal From Outer End of Axle Housing With Remover 41-R-2384-38

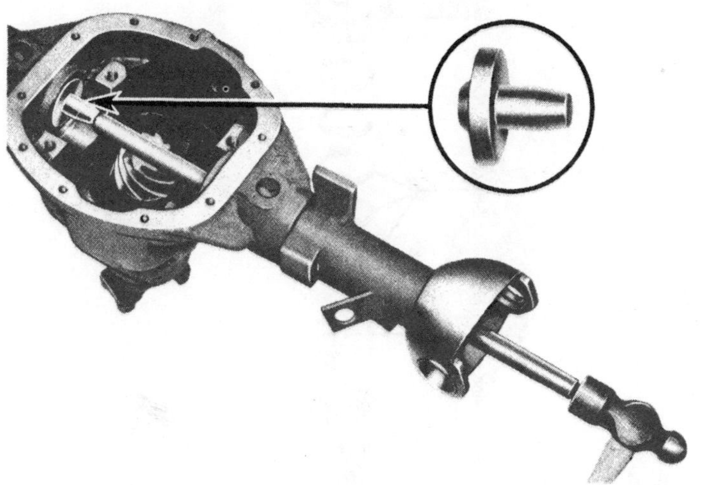

Figure 56 — Installing Oil Seal, With Replacer 41-R-2391-20

(*e*) *Oil Seal Replacement* (fig. 55). To remove the outer axle shaft oil seal, remove the oil seal retainer. Use a screwdriver to pry the retainer out of the housing. Use the oil seal remover 41-R-2384-38 to remove the inner and outer oil seals (figs. 55 and 80). To install the inner and outer oil seals, use the oil seal replacer

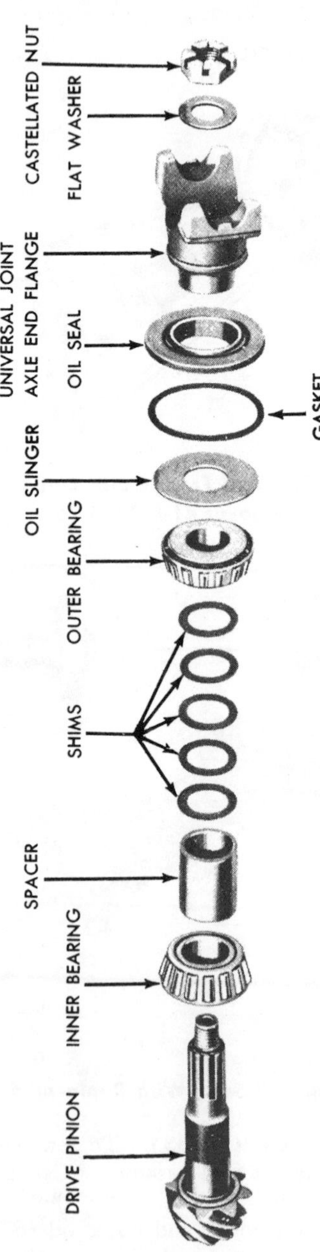

Figure 57 — Drive Pinion Assembly — Exploded View

41-R-2391-20 and tap the oil seals in the inner and outer ends of the axle housing (fig. 56). Using a brass hammer, tap the oil seal retainer in the outer end of the axle shaft housing.

(f) Axle Housing Bushing Replacement (For Tracta Type Axle Shafts Only). Remove the bushing from the outer end of the axle housing, using a standard puller. To install a new bushing, place the bushing in position in the axle housing and using a suitable driver, drive the bushing in the housing until it is flush with the shoulder in the axle housing.

(2) DRIVE PINION ASSEMBLY (fig. 57). Roller bearings that are pitted, corroded or discolored due to overheating must be replaced. Replace the drive pinion if it has worn or broken teeth. The differential ring gear and the drive pinion assembly are furnished only in matched sets and if either is found damaged, both must be replaced. Small nicks can be removed from the pinion gear with a fine stone.

(3) DIFFERENTIAL ASSEMBLY (fig. 58). Replace any gear that is excessively worn or has any broken teeth. The differential ring gear and the drive pinion assembly are furnished only in matched sets and if either is found damaged, both must be replaced. Replace the differential pinion gears, if the inside diameter is worn to more than 0.627 inch. Replace the differential pinion shaft if the diameter is less than 0.623 inch. Replace the axle shaft gears if the outside diameter of the hub is worn to less than 1.498 inches. Replace the differential pinion gear and axle shaft gear thrust washers if the thickness is worn to less than 0.32 inch. Roller bearings and races that are pitted, corroded or discolored due to overheating must be replaced. All shims that were damaged during the disassembly must be replaced.

(4) AXLE SHAFTS. Three different types of axle shaft universal joints as shown in figures 38, 42, and 44 are used in front axles. Inspection of each of these three types is covered in steps *(a)*, *(b)*, and *(c)*, below.

(a) Rzeppa Universal Joint (fig. 59). Replace the inner axle shaft if it is bent or has worn splines. Using a new axle shaft gear as a gage, slip it on the inner axle shaft and check the backlash. If the backlash is more than 0.005 inch, replace the axle shaft. Replace the outer axle shaft if it has worn splines or nicked ball bearing surfaces. Replace the inner race if it is found to be excessively worn. Small nicks or scratches can be removed with a fine stone. Replace steel balls that have flat spots. Replace the cage if it is cracked.

(b) Bendix Universal Joint (fig. 43). Replace the inner axle shaft if it is bent or has worn splines or worn universal joint ball surface. Replace the universal joint knuckle if it has worn splines or

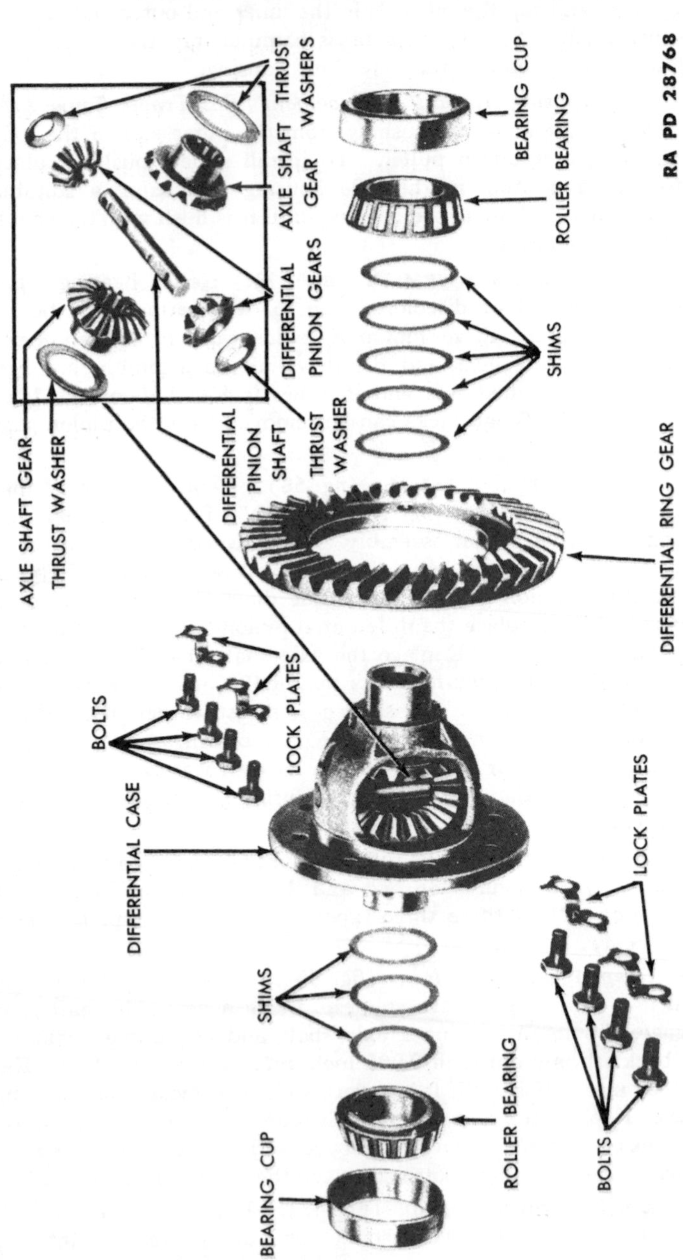

Figure 58 — Differential Assembly — Exploded View

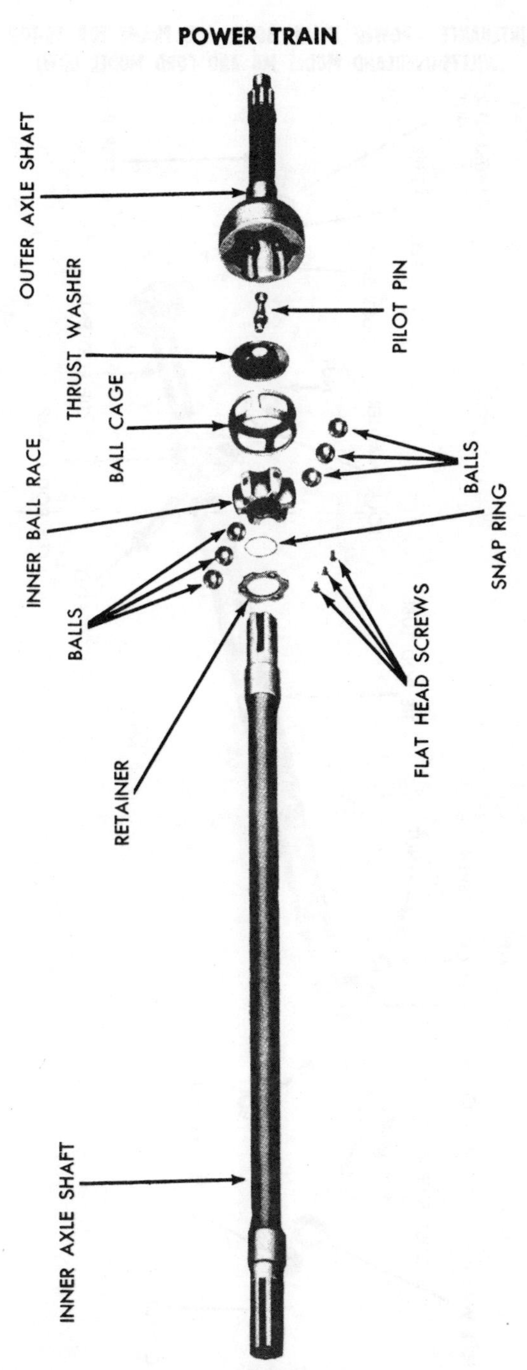

RA PD 28769

Figure 59 — Axle Shaft — Exploded View (Rzeppa Type)

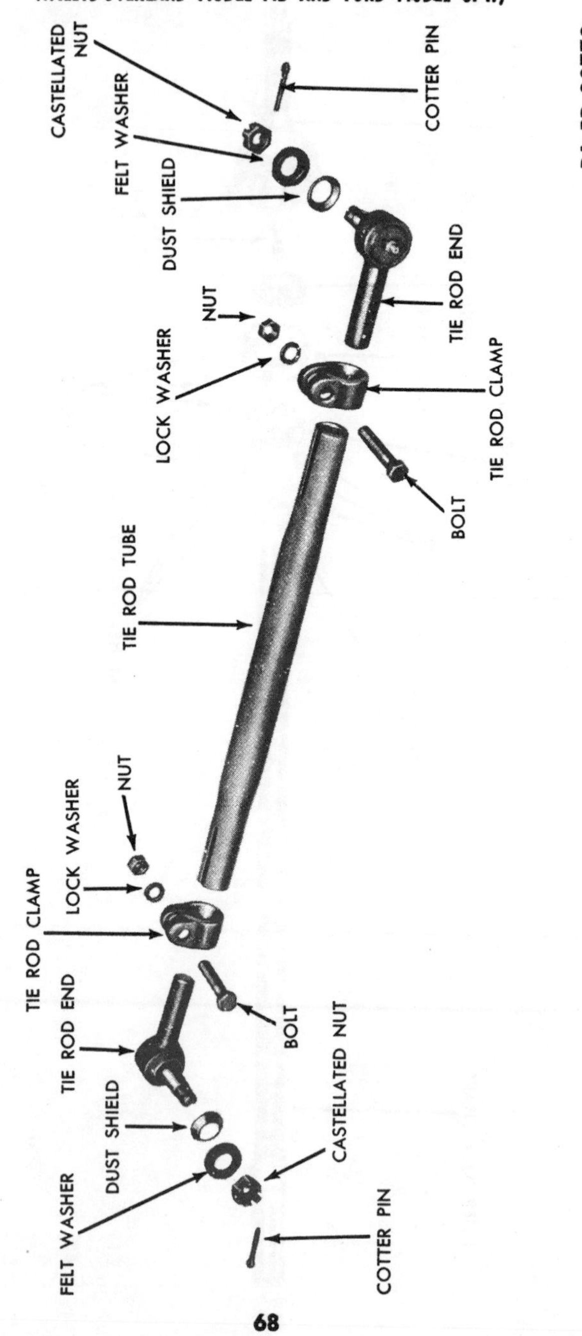

Figure 60 — Tie Rod, Right Side — Exploded View

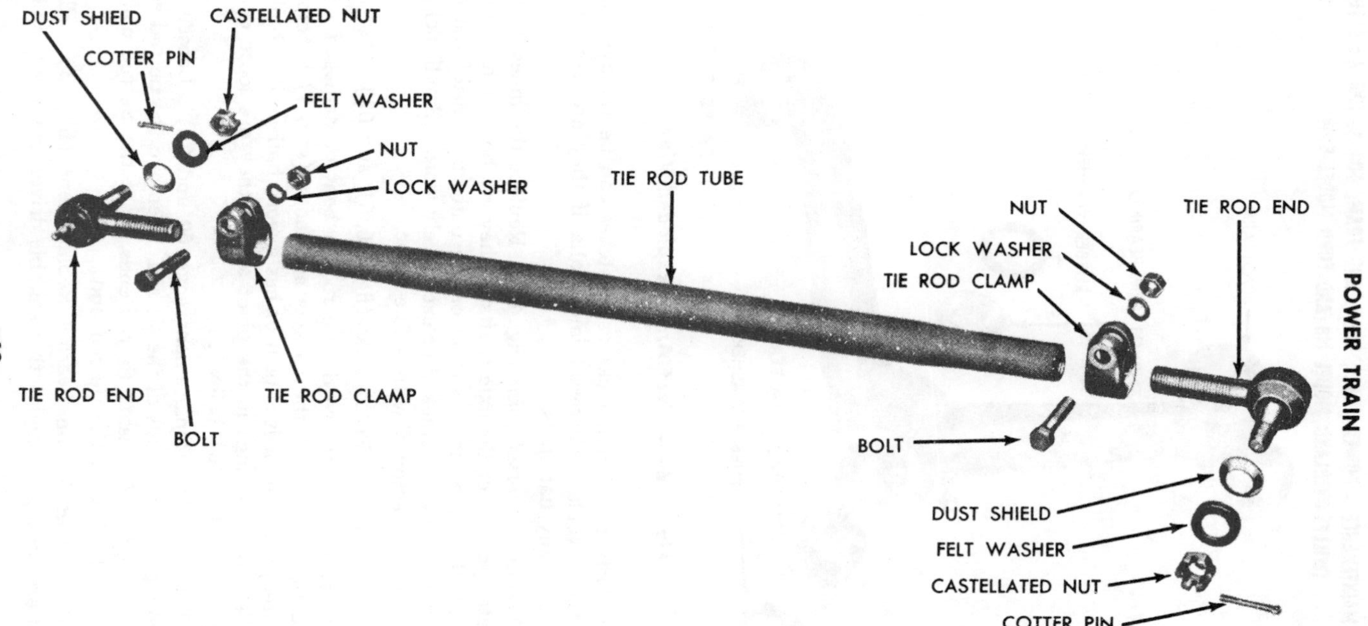

Figure 61 — Tie Rod, Left Side — Exploded View

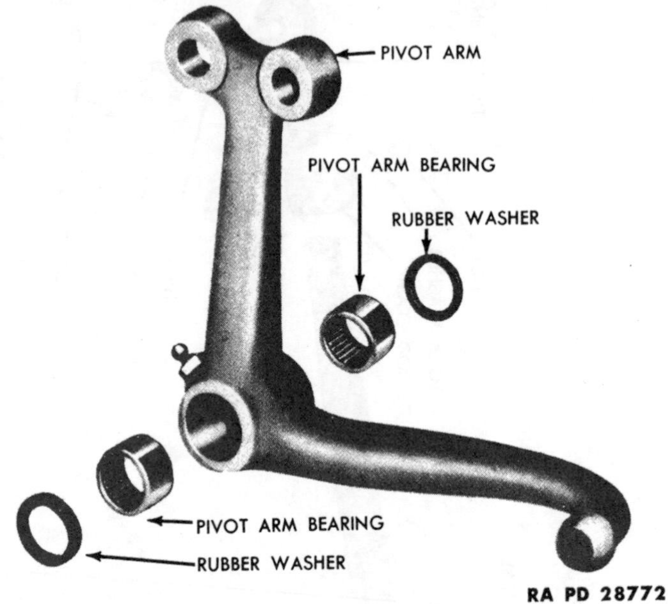

Figure 62—Pivot Arm—Exploded View

worn ball surfaces. Small nicks or scratches can be removed with a fine stone. Replace universal joint balls, if they are excessively worn or have any flat spots.

(c) Tracta Universal Joint (fig. 45). Replace the inner portion or the outer portion of the axle shafts, if they are bent or have worn splines. Replace the inner portion or the outer portion of the universal joints, if they are cracked or excessively worn. Small nicks or scratches can be removed with a fine stone.

(5) TIE RODS AND PIVOT ARM (figs. 60, 61, and 62).

(a) Inspection. Replace the tie rods if bent or damaged. Replace the tie rod ends if the sockets are loose (step *(b)*, below). Replace the pivot arm, if it is bent or has a worn ball joint. Replace the needle roller bearings in the pivot arm if they are loose or excessively worn (step *(c)*, below).

(b) Tie Rod End Replacement (figs. 60 and 61). Loosen the tie rod clamps at both ends of the tie rod. Remove the tie rod ends from the tie rods. To install tie rod ends, place the tie rod clamps on the tie rod. Install the tie rod ends.

(c) Pivot Arm Needle Bearing Replacement (fig. 62). Place the pivot arm in a press and with a suitable driver, press out the two

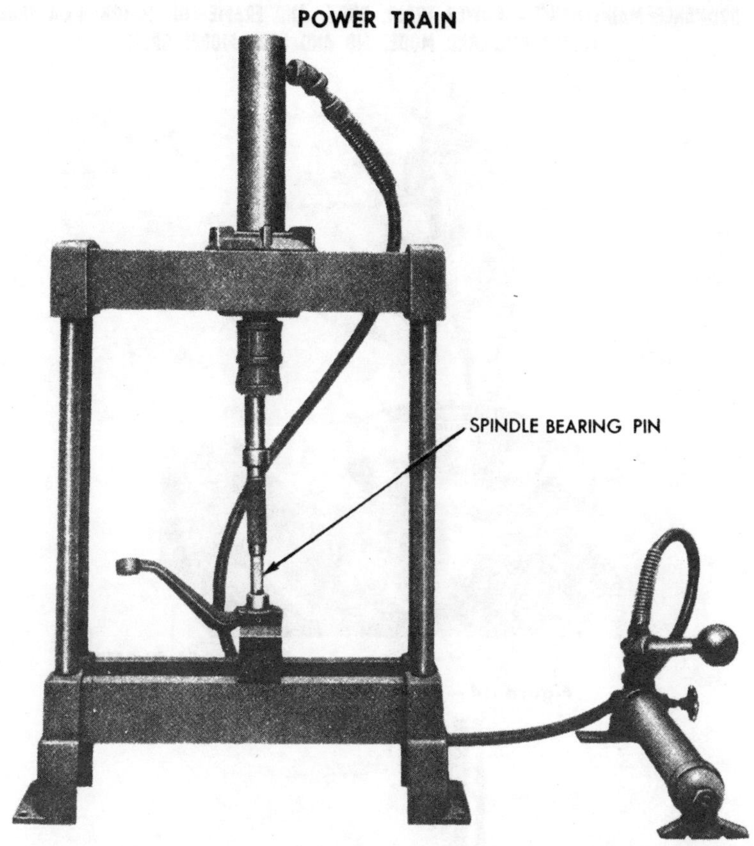

Figure 63 — Replacing Spindle Bearing Pin in Spindle Arm

needle bearings. To install the needle bearings, press one needle bearing in the pivot arm about $\frac{1}{16}$ inch below the shoulder of the pivot arm, then turn the pivot arm over and press the other bearing in the arm about $\frac{1}{16}$ inch below the shoulder of the pivot arm.

(6) SPINDLE ARM AND SPINDLE HOUSING BEARING CAP.

(a) Inspection. Replace the spindle arm if bent. Replace the spindle arm bearing pin if the diameter of the pin is worn to less than 0.623 inch. Replace the spindle housing bearing cap pin if it is worn to less than 0.625 inch (step *(b)*, below).

(b) Spindle Bearing Pin Replacement. Place the spindle housing bearing cap or the spindle arm (fig. 76) in a press and with a suitable driver, press out the bearing pin. To install a new pin, use a suitable driver and press the pin in until it is flush with the outer

Figure 64 — Removing Spindle Bushing

Figure 65 — Pressing New Bushing in Spindle

RA PD 28776

Figure 66 — Installing Inner Bearing on Pinion

shoulder. The same procedure applies to both the spindle housing bearing cap and the spindle arm (fig. 63).

(7) SPINDLE HOUSING AND SPINDLE (fig. 76).

(a) Inspection. Replace the spindle housing if it is cracked. If the studs on the spindle housing are bent, broken or damaged, replace them (step *(b)*, below). Replace the spindle, if it has damaged threads or grooved bearing surfaces. If the inner diameter of the spindle bushing is more than 1.225 inch, replace the bushing (subpar. *(c)*, below).

(b) Broken Stud Replacement. Indent the end of the broken stud exactly in the center with a center punch. Drill approximately two-thirds through the broken stud, using a small drill, then follow up with a larger drill (the size of the drill depending on the size of the stud to be removed). The drill selected, however, must leave a wall thicker than the depth of the threads. Select an extractor of the proper size. Insert it into the drilled hole and screw out the remaining part of the broken stud. To install a new stud, use a standard stud driver and drive all studs until no threads show at the bottom of the stud. If the stud is too tight or too loose in the stud hole, select another stud.

(c) Spindle Bushing Replacement. The spindle bushing can be removed with a center punch as shown in figure 64. To install a

Figure 67 — Checking Pinion in Differential Housing With Gage 41-G-176

new bushing, use a suitable driver and press the bushing in the spindle (fig. 65).

26. ASSEMBLY.

a. **Install Inner Bearing on Pinion** (fig. 66). Press the inner bearing on the pinion, using an arbor press. Make sure the bearing is seated against the shoulder of the pinion gear when installed.

b. **Adjust Pinion in Housing** (fig. 67). Place the pinion in the differential housing. Install the 41-G-176 gage to check the setting from the back face of the pinion to the center line of the differential case bearing. The standard setting is 0.719 inch. If the gage reading is more than 0.179 inch, shims will have to be added to the inner bearing cup (par. 25 **b** (1) *(c)*). If the gage reading is less than 0.719 inch, shims will have to be removed from the inner bearing cup (par. 25 **b** (1) *(c)*).

c. **Install Outer Bearing on Pinion** (fig. 57). After the correct pinion setting has been obtained, install the spacer and the original amount of shims on the pinion. If the thickness of the original shims is unknown, install the shims totaling approximately 0.060 inch thick

Figure 68 — Installing Differential Bearing, Using Special Replacer 41-R-2391-65

before installing the outer bearing. Start the outer bearing on the pinion. Install the oil slinger on the pinion.

d. **Adjust the Outer Bearing.** Place the universal joint flange on the pinion. Install the nut on the universal joint flange and draw the flange down tight. Turn the universal joint flange, if there is a slight drag, the pinion bearing adjustment is correct. If the pinion turns with difficulty or can't be turned by hand, shims will have to be added behind the outer bearing. If the pinion turns loosely, shims will have to be removed. If the pinion bearing adjustment is not correct, remove the universal joint flange, and add or remove shims until the correct adjustment is obtained. After the correct adjustment is obtained, again remove the universal joint flange and install the oil seal on the pinion. Install the universal joint flange. Install the nut and cotter pin.

e. **Install Gears in Differential Case** (fig. 58). Place the axle shaft gear thrust washers on the two axle shaft gears. Place the axle shaft gears in the case. Place the two differential pinion thrust washers and gears in the case. Install the differential pinion gear shaft in the case. Install the pinion shaft lock pin in the case and stake the pinion shaft lock pin to prevent the pin from coming out.

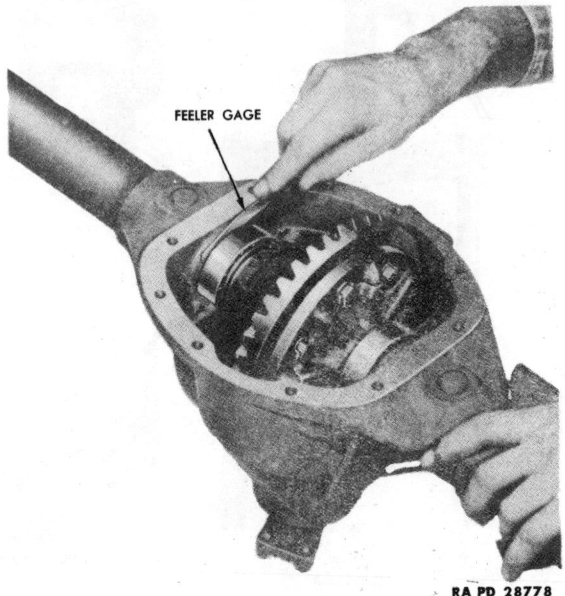

Figure 69—Checking Clearance Between Differential Case and Bearing

f. **Install Differential Ring Gear** (fig. 58). Place the differential ring gear in position on the case. Install the lock plates and cap screws that secure the ring gear to the case. Bend the ears of the lock plates on the cap screws.

g. **Install Roller Bearings on Case** (fig. 68). If all the original parts have been used in the differential assembly, add the same thickness of shims as originally used and press the roller bearings on the case, then proceed with subparagraph **h**, below. If the original parts are not being used, or if the original shim thickness is not known, install the roller bearings on the case without the shims, and proceed with subparagraph **i**, below.

h. **Install Differential Assembly in Housing** (fig. 47). Place the bearing cups on the roller bearings. Tilt the bearing cups in order to start the assembly in the housing. Tap the bearing cups lightly until the assembly is seated firmly in the housing. Install the two bearing caps so the numbers on the caps and the housing face the same way and match in every way as shown in figure 47. If the differential assembly being used is not the one originally in the axle, proceed with subparagraph **i**, below.

i. **Adjust Differential Assembly** (fig. 69). Place the bearing cups on the differential assembly and place the assembly in the housing.

RA PD 28780

Figure 70 — Checking Ring Gear Backlash With Dial Indicator 41-I-100

Slide the assembly to one side of the housing. Check the clearance between the bearing cup and differential housing with a feeler gage. After this clearance has been determined, add 0.008 inch. This will give the thickness of shims required for proper bearing adjustment. Remove the differential assembly from the housing. Remove the bearings from the differential case (par. 24 f (3)). Install the amount of shims determined above in equal amounts on each side of the case and install the bearings back on the case (subpar. g, above). Tilt the bearing cups and place the differential in the housing. Tap the bearing cups lightly until the assembly is seated firmly in the housing. Install the two bearing caps so the numbers on the caps and the housing face the same way, and match in every way.

j. **Check Backlash** (fig. 70). Install a dial indicator 41-I-100 on the differential housing so that the indicator contact is resting on the surface of a ring gear tooth as shown in figure 70. Rotate the ring gear back and forth to determine the backlash. If the backlash is less than 0.005 inch or more than 0.007 inch, remove the differential from the housing (par. 24 e) and remove the bearings from the differential case (par. 24 f (3)). If the backlash was more than 0.007 inch, the ring gear must be brought closer to the pinion. If the backlash was less than 0.005 inch, the ring gear must be moved away from the pinion. This is accomplished by moving shims equal to the

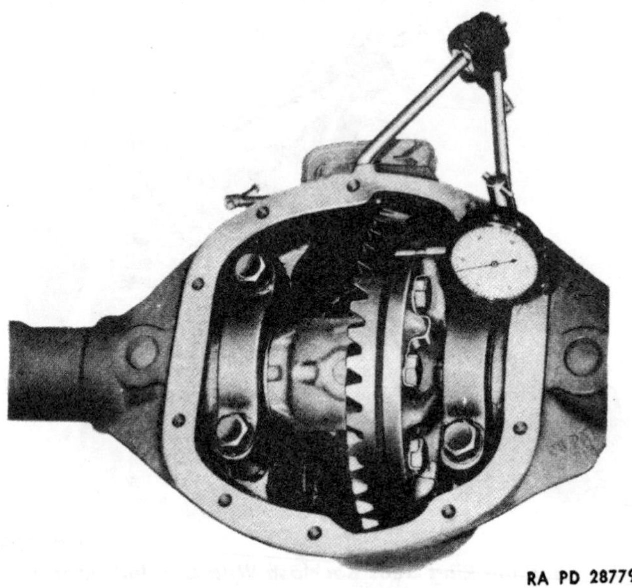
RA PD 28779

Figure 71 —Checking Ring Gear Run-out With Dial Indicator 41-I-100

error in backlash from one side of the case and adding them to the other side. Install the bearings on the case (subpar. **g**, above). Install differential in housing (subpar. **h**, above) and recheck the backlash.

k. Check Ring Gear Run-out (fig. 71). Install a dial indicator on the differential housing so that the indicator contact is resting on the flat side of the ring gear as shown in figure 71. Turn the pinion drive flange by hand to determine the run-out on the ring gear. The run-out should not exceed 0.003 inch. If the run-out is more than 0.003 inch, remove the differential assembly from the housing (par. 24 **e**), and remove the ring gear from the differential case. Check the surface of the differential case and the ring gear for chips or small nicks, which might have occurred during the assembly of the differential. If any small nicks are found, remove them with a fine stone, also check the flange on the differential case for being sprung. Reinstall the differential assembly in the housing (subpar. **h**, above) and recheck the ring gear run-out.

l. Install Differential Cover (fig. 46). Place a new gasket and the differential cover in place on the axle housing. Install the 10 cap screws that secure the cover to the housing.

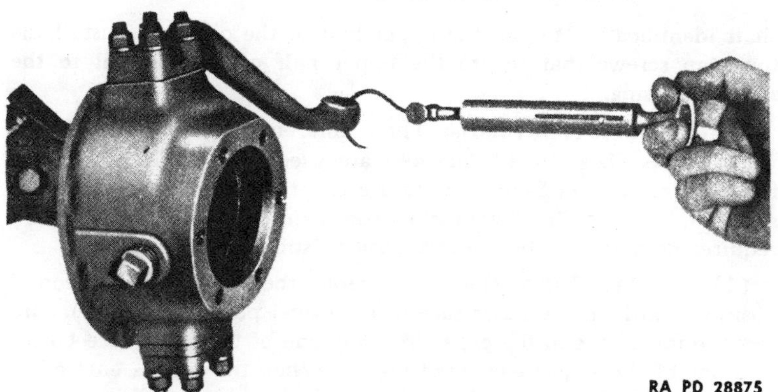

RA PD 28875

Figure 72 — Checking Tension of Spindle Housing

m. **Install Pivot Arm** (fig. 46). Insert the two rubber seals in the pivot arm. Place the flat washer on the pivot arm shaft. Place the pivot arm on the shaft with the ball joint of the arm facing downward. Place the flat washer and dust shield on the shaft. Install the castellated nut and cotter pin.

n. **Install Spindle Housing** (fig. 76). Dip the two spindle housing bearings in grease. Place the bearings in the bearing cups on the axle housing. Place the spindle housing on the axle housing with the grease plug to the rear of the vehicle. Install shims totaling 0.048 inch thick on the spindle bearing cap and the spindle arm. Shims are available in thicknesses of 0.003 inch, 0.005 inch, 0.010 inch and 0.030 inch. Install one of each size on the top and bottom of the spindle housing. Place the lower bearing cap on the spindle housing and install the four nuts that secure the cap to the spindle housing. Place the spindle arm on the spindle housing and install the four nuts that secure the spindle arm to the spindle housing.

o. **Adjust Spindle Housing** (fig. 72). Check the tension of the spindle housing by hooking a scale to the end of the spindle arm. The tension should not be more than 6 pounds or less than 4 pounds. If the tension is over 6 pounds, shims must be removed from the spindle housing. If the tension is less than 4 pounds, shims must be added. When removing or adding shims, be sure the same thickness is removed from, or added to, both ends of the spindle housing. Remove, or add, shims until the correct tension is obtained.

p. **Install Spindle Housing Oil Seal** (fig. 76). Place a new gasket on the spindle housing. Place the upper and lower halves of the oil seal on the spindle housing. Install the four cap screws that secure the lower half of the oil seal to the spindle housing. Place the axle shaft identification tag on the upper half of the oil seal. Install the four cap screws that secure the upper half of the oil seal to the spindle housing.

q. Assemble Axle Shafts. Three different types of front axle universal joints (figs. 38, 42, and 44) are used. Assembly procedures for the Rzeppa and Bendix types are covered in subparagraphs (1) and (2), below. The Tracta type front axle universal joint (fig. 43) requires no assembly before installation (subpar. **r** (2), below).

(1) RZEPPA JOINT (fig. 38). Hold the cage in a horizontal position and hold the inner race in a vertical position (fig. 41). Insert the inner race in the cage, dropping one of the inner race bosses into one of the larger elongated holes. When the race is entered in the cage, turn the race so that it is entirely in the cage. Line up the two larger elongated holes with the bosses on the axle shaft (fig. 40). Slide the cage in the axle shaft. Holding the cage in this position, insert the thrust washer (fig. 59) behind the cage. Tilt the cage so that it is flush with the shaft. Tilt the cage so that a steel ball can be inserted in the elongated hole (fig. 39). After the steel ball is in position, push the cage down until the opposite side of the cage is exposed. Insert another steel ball in the elongated hole on the cage and push the cage down. Repeat this operation until all the steel balls are in the cage. Insert the pilot pin (fig. 59) in position. Insert the retainer on the axle shaft and secure the retainer with the snap ring. Insert the inner shaft in the outer shaft. Install the three flat head screws that secure the retainer to the inner race.

(2) BENDIX JOINT (figs. 42 and 43). Place the universal joint knuckle in an upright position in a vise. Insert the center ball in the hole of the knuckle. Place the center ball in its race on the center ball pin hole. Arrange the center ball so that the grooved side of the center ball is away from the pin hole. Insert the three universal joint balls in their races. Arrange the center ball so that the grooved side is in line with the race of the last ball to be installed as shown in figure 42 and drop the ball in its race. Rotate the center ball in its race until the hole in the ball is in line with the center ball pin. Remove the assembly from the vise. Turn the assembly over so that the pin may drop in the hole of the center ball. Install the grooved pin in the knuckle and stake the pin to prevent it from coming out.

r. Install Axle Shaft.

(1) BENDIX AND RZEPPA JOINTS. Slide the axle shaft in the axle housing. It will be necessary to turn the axle shaft until the splines on the axle shaft are in line with the axle shaft gear in the differential.

Figure 73 — Checking Clearance Between Drive Flange and Hub

(2) Tracta Joint (fig. 45). Slide the inner portion of the axle shaft and the inner portion of the universal joint into the axle housing. Turn the axle shaft so as to line up the splines of the axle shaft with the axle shaft gear in the differential. Slide the outer portion of the universal joint on the outer portion of the axle shaft. Line up the slots of the two universal joints and slide the outer axle shaft in place on the axle.

s. **Install Brake Plate and Spindle.** Place the spindle on the spindle housing. Place the brake plate on the spindle with the wheel cylinder toward the top of the brake plate. Line up the holes in the brake plate and spindle with the spindle housing. Install the six cap screws that secure them to the spindle housing.

t. **Install Hydraulic Brake Hose** (fig. 46). Install the brake hose to the brake line on the axle housing. Install the clamp to the brake hose at the bracket on the axle housing. Insert the brake hose through the guard and connect the hose to the brake line on the brake plate. Install the brake hose clamp at the guard.

u. **Install Hub and Brake Drum** (fig. 46). Pack the wheel bearings with the specified lubricant. Insert the hub and brake drum on the spindle with the inner wheel bearing and grease retainer in the hub. Insert the smaller thrust washer on the spindle and install the bearing adjusting nut. Tighten the adjusting nut until the brake

RA PD 28868

Figure 74 — Checking Wheels With Straightedge

drum binds when turned; then back off the adjusting nut one-eighth turn. This will give the correct wheel bearing adjustment. Install the lock washer and lock nut on the spindle. Bend the ears of the lock washer over the lock nut.

v. **Install Drive Flange** (fig. 73).

(1) RZEPPA TYPE AXLE SHAFTS. Install a 0.060-inch thickness of shims between the drive flange and the hub. Place the drive flange on the axle shaft. Install the six cap screws that secure the drive flange to the hub. Install the castellated nut on the axle shaft. Install the hub cap on the drive flange.

(2) BENDIX OR TRACTA TYPE AXLE SHAFT (fig. 73). Place the drive flange on the axle shaft. Install the castellated nut on the axle shaft and draw it down tight. Turn the front wheels to the maximum left or right and measure the space between the drive flange and hub with a feeler gage (fig. 73) to determine the number of shims to be installed. Remove the nut from the axle shaft and remove the drive flange. Add the required thickness of shims between the drive flange and the hub. Install the six cap screws that secure the drive flange to the hub. Install the castellated nut on the axle shaft. Back off the nut on the axle shaft until a 0.50-inch feeler gage can pass between the nut and drive flange. Tap the nut on the axle shaft lightly. The axle shaft will move inward. Again check the space between the nut and drive flange. The space should not be less than 0.015 inch or more than 0.035 inch. If the space is less than 0.015 inch, add shims behind the drive flange and hub until this limit is obtained. If the space is more than 0.035 inch, remove shims from the drive flange until the above limit is obtained. Draw the nut on the axle shaft up tight. Install the hub cap.

w **Install Tie Rods** (fig. 46). Insert the ends of the tie rods in the spindle arms and pivot arm. Be sure the dust shield and felt washer are on the tie rod ends. Install the castellated nuts that secure the tie rod ends to the spindle arms and to the pivot arm.

27. INSTALLATION.

a. **Preliminary Work.** Place a hydraulic jack under the front axle assembly. Roll the assembly under the vehicle. Raise the assembly until the front springs can be raised and secure to the spring shackles. Lower the jack to allow the axle assembly to rest on the springs.

b. **Install Spring U-bolts** (fig. 35). Place the spring U-bolts in position on the axle housing. Install the spring seat plate on the U-bolts at the right side of the axle. Install the four nuts that secure the spring seat to the U-bolts. Raise the torque reaction spring in position on the U-bolts on the left side. Install the nuts that secure the torque reaction spring to the U-bolts.

RA PD 28869

Figure 75 — Adjusting Toe-in, Using Wheel Alining Gage 41-G-510

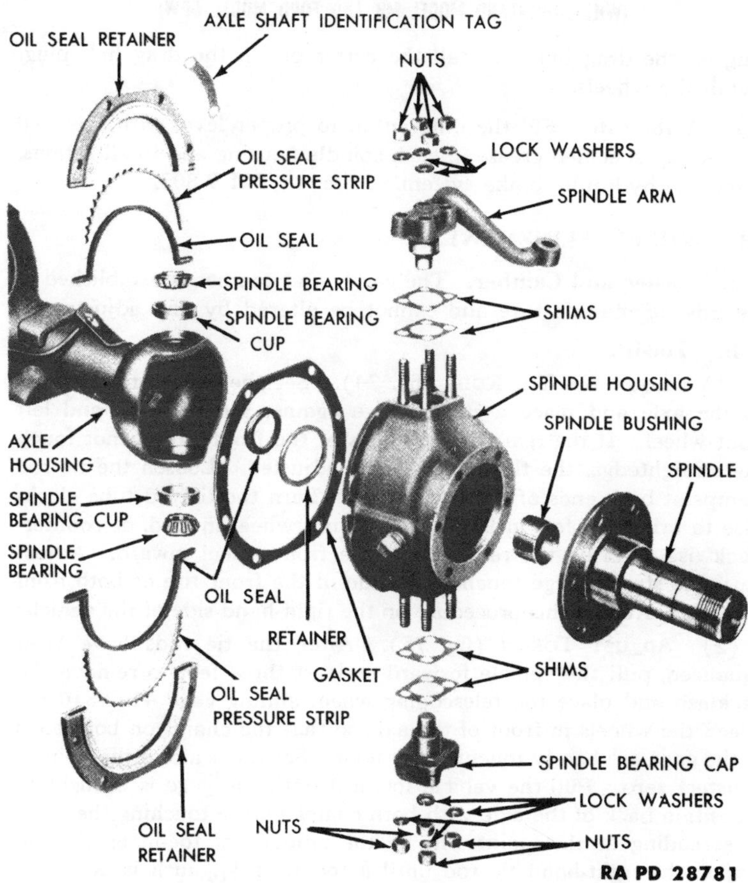

Figure 76 — Spindle Housing — Exploded View

c. **Install Shock Absorbers** (fig. 35). Insert a rubber mounting in each side of each shock absorber eye. Place the shock absorber on the mounting bracket at the spring seat plate. If new rubber mountings are being used, compress them with compressor 41-C-2554-400. Install the flat washer and cotter pin that secure the shock absorber to the spring seat plate. Place the left shock absorber on the mounting bracket at the torque reaction spring. Install the flat washer and cotter pin that secure the shock absorber to the torque reaction spring.

d. **Install Propeller Shaft, Drag Link, and Wheels** (fig. 35). Install the propeller shaft to the front axle (par. 21 **b**). Place the drag link in the ball joint on the pivot arm. Install the drag link plug on the drag link. Install the cotter pin in the drag link plug. Install the wheels.

e. **Lubricate.** Fill the differential to proper level with specified oil. Apply specified grease in each spindle housing and to all fittings. Bleed the hydraulic brake system. Refer to TM 9-803.

28. WHEEL ALINEMENT.

a. **Caster and Camber.** The caster and camber is established at the time of manufacture and cannot be altered by any adjustment.

b. **Toe-in.**

(1) EQUALIZE TIE RODS (fig. 74). Set the pivot arm parallel to the axle and place a straightedge against the left rear and left front wheel. If the rear or front sides of the front tire do not touch the straightedge, the tie rods must be adjusted. Loosen the tie rod clamps at both ends of the left tie rod. Turn the tie rod tube clockwise to bring the forward side of the front wheel inward, or counterclockwise to bring the rear side of the front wheel inward. Adjust until the straightedge touches the side of the front tire at both front and rear. Repeat this procedure on the right-hand side of the vehicle.

(2) ADJUST TOE-IN (fig. 75). After the tie rods have been equalized, pull the vehicle forward at least three feet to remove the backlash and place the telescoping wheel alining gage 41-G-510 between the wheels in front of the axle so that the chains on both ends of the gage are barely touching the floor. Set the scale so the pointer registers zero. Pull the vehicle forward until the gage is brought to a position back of the axle with both chains barely touching the floor. The reading at this point will be the amount of toe-in or toe-out. Adjust the right-hand tie rod until a toe-in of $\frac{1}{16}$ inch is obtained. Recheck the toe-in after making the adjustment. Tighten the tie rod clamps.

Section VI

REAR AXLE

29. DESCRIPTION AND DATA.

a. **Description** (fig. 78). The rear axle is the full-floating type, designed so that the axle shafts can be removed without disturbing the wheels. The differential drive is of the hypoid type. The differential parts are identical and are interchangeable with the front axle.

b. Data.

Rear Axle:

Type	Full-floating
Make	Spicer
Drive	Through springs
Road clearance	8 7/8 in.

Differential:

Type	Hypoid
Ratio	4.88 to 1
Bearings	Timken roller
Oil capacity (pt)	2.5

Pinion Shaft:

Bearings	Timken
Adjustment	Shims
Backlash	0.005 to 0.007 in.

30. REMOVAL.

a. Preliminary Work. Remove the differential drain plug and drain the oil. Raise the rear of the vehicle until the weight of the vehicle is off the rear springs.

b. Disconnect Propeller Shaft (fig. 77). Remove the four nuts and two U-bolts that secure the propeller shaft to the universal joint flange at the rear axle. Slide the propeller shaft off the universal joint flange. Wrap a piece of tape around the bearings on the propeller shaft to prevent losing the bearings.

c. Disconnect Shock Absorbers and Hydraulic Brake Line (fig. 77). Remove the cotter pin and flat washer that secure the two rear shock absorbers to the bracket on the spring seat plates. Pull the shock absorbers off the bracket. Disconnect the hydraulic brake line leading to the rear axle at the differential housing.

d. Remove Spring U-bolts (fig. 77). Remove the four nuts that secure the spring U-bolts at both rear springs. Remove the U-bolts and the spring seat plates from the axle.

e. Disconnect Springs (fig. 77). Remove the lower spring shackle bushings at the rear of both springs. Pull both springs off the spring shackles. Drop the springs to the floor and roll the rear axle assembly out from the vehicle.

Figure 77 — Rear Axle Assembly in Vehicle

31. DISASSEMBLY.

a. **Remove Wheels.** Remove the five nuts that secure each wheel to the hub. Remove the wheels.

b. **Remove Axle Shafts** (fig. 82). Remove the six cap screws that secure the drive flange to the hub. Install two of the cap screws that were removed from the drive flange in the two threaded holes on the drive flange. Draw the cap screws down until the drive flange is free from the hub. Remove the axle shafts from the axle housing.

c. **Remove Hub and Drum Assembly** (fig. 82). Bend the ears of the flat washer off the bearing lock nut. Remove the bearing lock nut and bearing adjusting nut off the housing, using the wrench furnished with the vehicle. Slide the hub and drum assembly with the wheel bearings off the housing.

d. **Remove Brake Plate** (fig. 82). Disconnect the hydraulic brake line at the brake plate. Remove the six cap screws that secure the brake plate to the axle housing. Remove the brake plate from the axle housing.

e. **Remove Differential Assembly.** Remove the 10 cap screws that secure the differential cover to the housing (fig. 78). Remove the differential cover. Remove the 4 cap screws from the 2 differential bearing caps (fig. 47), and remove the caps. Remove the differential assembly from the housing, using a pry bar if necessary. Reinstall the bearing caps in the housing, noting the markings (fig. 47) to assure their being installed in their correct location.

f. **Remove Differential Pinion Gears and Axle Shaft Gears From Differential** (fig. 48). Place the differential assembly in a vise equipped with brass jaws. With a long-nosed drift, drive the differential pinion shaft tapered pin out of the differential gear case (fig. 48). Tap the differential pinion shaft from the case with a brass drift and hammer. Remove the two differential pinion gears and thrust washers and the two axle shaft gears and thrust washers from the case.

g. **Remove Ring Gear From Case** (fig. 58). Bend the ears of the lock plates off the cap screws. Remove the cap screws that secure the ring gear to the case, and remove the ring gear.

h. **Remove Roller Bearings From Differential Case** (fig. 49). Place the differential case in a vise. Install the bearing remover 41-R-2378-30 to the roller bearing. Remove the roller bearings from both ends of the differential case. Remove the shims. Note the thickness of the shims removed from each side to assist in reassembly.

i. **Remove Drive Pinion.** Remove the nut and flat washer that secure the universal joint axle end flange to the drive pinion. Install

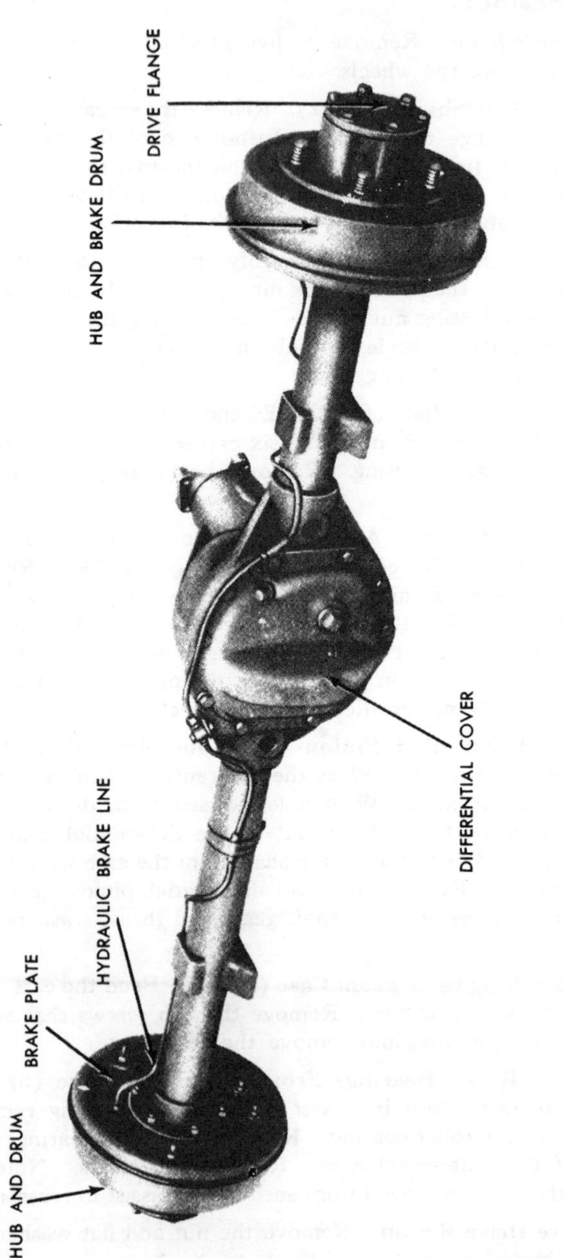

RA PD 28867

Figure 78 — Rear Axle Assembly

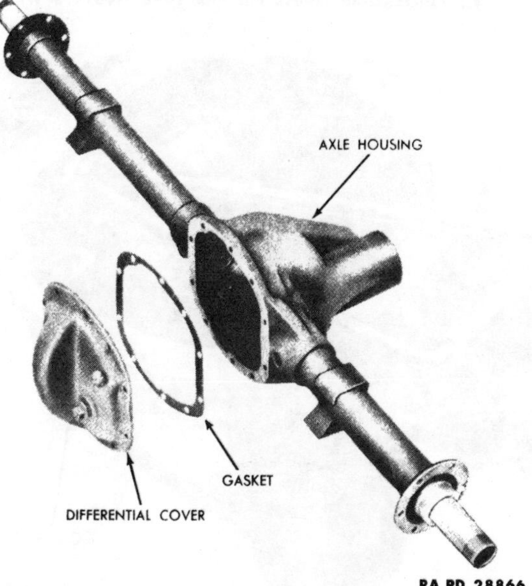

Figure 79 — Rear Axle Housing

the flange puller to the universal joint flange (fig. 50) and remove the flange. Using a brass drift and hammer, drive the drive pinion out of the axle housing (fig. 51). Remove the shims and spacer from the drive pinion. Note the thickness of shims removed from the pinion to assist in reassembly.

32. CLEANING, INSPECTION AND REPAIR.

a. Cleaning. Clean all parts in dry-cleaning solvent. Rotate the bearings in dry-cleaning solvent until all trace of lubricant has been removed. Oil the bearings immediately to prevent corrosion of the highly polished surface.

b. Inspection and Repair.

(1) AXLE HOUSING AND COVER (fig. 79).

(a) Inspection. Replace the axle housing if it is broken at any of the welds or if it is cracked or bent. Replace the drive pinion bearing cups if they are pitted, corroded, or discolored due to overheating (subpar. *(b)*, below). Replace the oil seals in the axle housing regardless of their condition (step *(c)*, below). Replace the differential cover if cracked or if it has damaged threads in the filler plug hole. Replace the breather cap on the cover, if it is missing or damaged.

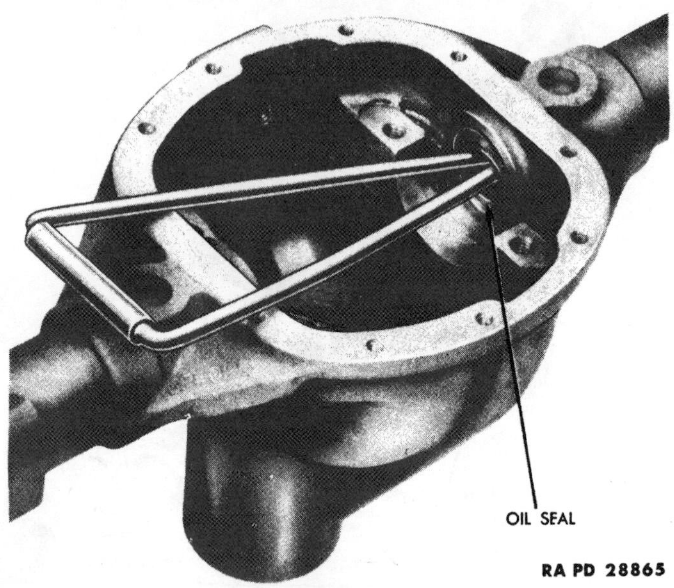

Figure 80 — Removing Oil Seal From Axle Housing, With Remover 41-R-2384-38

(b) Drive Pinion Bearing Cap Replacement. Remove the inner and outer bearing cups, using a standard puller. To assist in assembly, note the thickness of shims when removing the inner bearing cup. To install a new bearing cup, use a brass drift and hammer. Place the original thickness of shims behind the inner bearing cup and tap the bearing cup lightly around the entire circumference of the cup until it is flush with the shoulder in the axle housing (fig. 52).

(c) Oil Seal Replacement (fig. 80). Remove the inner oil seal with the remover 41-R-2384-38. To install a new oil seal, use special replacer 41-R-2391-20 and tap the oil seals in place (fig. 81).

(2) DRIVE PINION ASSEMBLY (fig. 57). Replace any roller bearings that are pitted, corroded, or discolored due to overheating. Replace the drive pinion gear if it has excessively worn, or broken teeth, or if the splines are worn or the threads damaged. The differential gear and the drive pinion are furnished in matched sets only, and if either is found damaged, both must be replaced. Small nicks can be removed from the pinion gear with a fine stone.

(3) DIFFERENTIAL ASSEMBLY (fig. 58). Replace any gears that are excessively worn or have any missing teeth. The differential ring gear and the drive pinion are furnished in matched sets only, and if

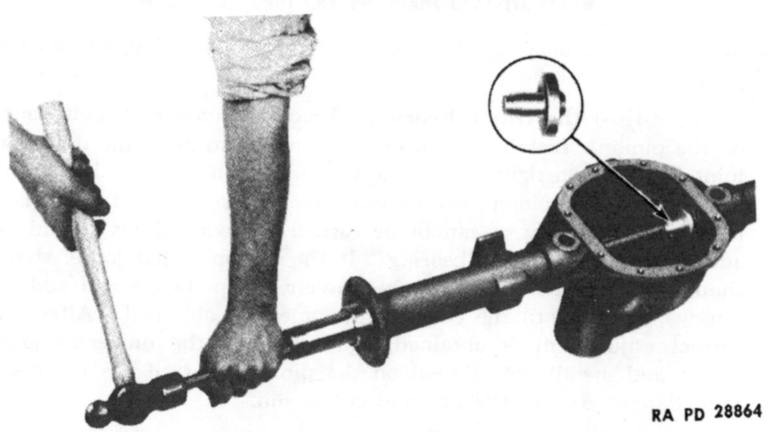

Figure 81 — Installing Oil Seal With Replacer 41-R-2391-20

either is found damaged, both must be replaced. Replace the differential pinion gear if its inside diameter is more than 0.625 inch. Replace the differential pinion shaft, if the inside diameter is worn to less than 0.625 inch. Replace the axle shaft gear if the hub is worn to less than 1.500 inches. Replace the differential pinion gear and the axle shaft gear thrust washer if the thickness is worn to less than 0.032 inch. Roller bearings and cups that are pitted, corroded, or discolored due to overheating must be replaced.

(4) AXLE SHAFT (fig. 82). Replace the axle shafts if they are bent or have any worn or broken splines.

33. ASSEMBLY.

a. **Install Inner Bearing on Pinion** (fig. 66). Press the inner bearing on the pinion, using an arbor press. Make sure the bearing is firmly seated on the shoulder of the pinion gear when installed.

b. **Adjust Pinion in Housing** (fig. 67). Place the pinion in the differential housing. Install the gage 41-G-176 to check the setting from the back face of the pinion to the center line of the differential case bearing. The standard setting is 0.719 inch. If the gage reading is more than 0.719 inch, shims will have to be added to the inner bearing cup (par. 32 **b**). If the reading is less than 0.719 inch, shims will have to be removed from the inner bearing cup (par. 32 **b**).

c. **Install Outer Bearing on Pinion** (fig. 57). After the correct pinion setting has been obtained, install the spacer and the original amount of shims on the pinion. If the thickness of the original shims is unknown, install shims totaling approximately 0.060 inch thick.

Start the outer bearing on the pinion. Install the oil slinger on the pinion.

d. **Adjust the Outer Bearing.** Place the universal joint flange on the pinion. Install the nut on the pinion and draw the universal joint flange down tight. Turn the universal joint flange. If there is a slight drag, the pinion bearing adjustment is correct. If the pinion turns with difficulty or cannot be turned by hand, shims should be added behind the outer bearing. If the pinion is too loose, shims should be removed. Remove the universal joint flange and add, or remove, shims, until the correct adjustment is obtained. After the correct adjustment is obtained, again remove the universal joint flange and install the oil seal on the pinion. Install the universal joint flange. Install the nut and cotter pin.

e. **Install Gears in Differential Case** (fig. 58). Place the axle shaft gear thrust washers on the two axle shaft gears. Place the axle shaft gears in the case. Place the two differential pinion thrust washers and gears in the case. Install the differential pinion gear shaft that secures the two differential pinion gears in the case. Install the pinion shaft lock pin in the case.

f. **Install Differential Ring Gear** (fig. 58). Place the differential ring gear in position on the case. Install the lock plates and cap screws that secure the ring gear to the case. Bend the ears of the lock plate on the cap screws.

g. **Install Roller Bearings on Case** (fig. 68). If all the original parts have been used in the differential assembly, add the same thickness of shims as originally used, and press the roller bearings on the case, then proceed with subparagraph **h**, below. If the original parts are not being used, or if the original shim thickness is not known, install the roller bearings on the case without the shims, and proceed with subparagraph **i**, below.

h. **Install Differential Assembly in Housing** (fig. 47). Place the bearing cups on the bearings. Tilt the bearing cups in order to start the assembly in the housing. Tap the bearing cups lightly until the assembly is seated firmly in the housing. Install the two bearing caps so that the numbers on the caps, and the housing face the same way, and match in every way as shown in figure 47. If the differential assembly being used is not the one originally in the axle, proceed with subparagraph **i**, below.

i. **Differential Assembly Adjustment** (fig. 69). Place the differential assembly in the housing with the bearing cups on the assembly. Slide the assembly to one side of the housing. Check the clearance between the bearing cup and differential housing with a feeler gage. After this clearance has been determined, add 0.008 inch. This will give the thickness of shims required for proper bearing adjustment. Remove the differential assembly from the housing. Remove the bearings from the differential case (par. 24 **f** (3)). Install the number of shims, determined above, on each side of the case and install the bearings back on the case (par. 26 **e** (3)). Tilt the bearing cups in order to start the assembly in the housing. Tap the bearing cups lightly until the assembly is seated firmly in the housing. Install the two bearing caps so the numbers on the bearing caps and housing face the same way and match in every way.

j. Check Backlash (fig. 70). Install a dial indicator on the differential housing so that the indicator contact is resting on the surface of a ring gear tooth as shown in figure 70. Rotate the ring gear back and forth to determine the backlash. If the backlash is less than 0.005 inch or more than 0.007 inch, remove the differential from the housing (par. 24 **e**) and remove the bearings from the differential case (par. 24 **f** (3)). If the backlash was more than 0.007 inch, the ring gear must be brought closer to the pinion. If the backlash was less than 0.005 inch, the ring gear must be moved away from the pinion. This is accomplished by removing the shims, equal to the error in backlash, from one side of the case, and adding them to the other side of the case. Install the bearings on the case (subpar. **g**, above). Install the differential in the housing (subpar. **h**, above).

k. Check Ring Gear Run-out (fig. 71). Install a dial indicator on the differential housing so that the indicator contact is resting on the flat side of the ring gear as shown in figure 71. Turn the pinion drive flange by hand to determine the run-out of the ring gear. The run-out should not exceed 0.003 inch. If the run-out is more than 0.003 inch, remove the differential assembly from the housing (par. 24 **e**) and remove the ring gear from the differential case. Check the surface of the differential case and the ring gear for chips or small nicks which might have occurred during the assembly of the differential. If any small nicks are found, remove them with a fine stone; also check the flange on the differential case for being sprung. Reinstall the differential assembly in the housing (subpar. **h**, above) and recheck the ring gear run-out.

l. Install Differential Cover (fig. 78). Place a new gasket and the differential cover in place on the axle housing. Install the ten cap screws that secure the cover to the housing.

m. Install Brake Plate (fig. 82). Place the brake plate on the housing, with the brake cylinder on the brake plate toward the top. Line up the holes in the brake plate with the axle housing. Install the six cap screws that secure it to the axle housing. Install the hydraulic

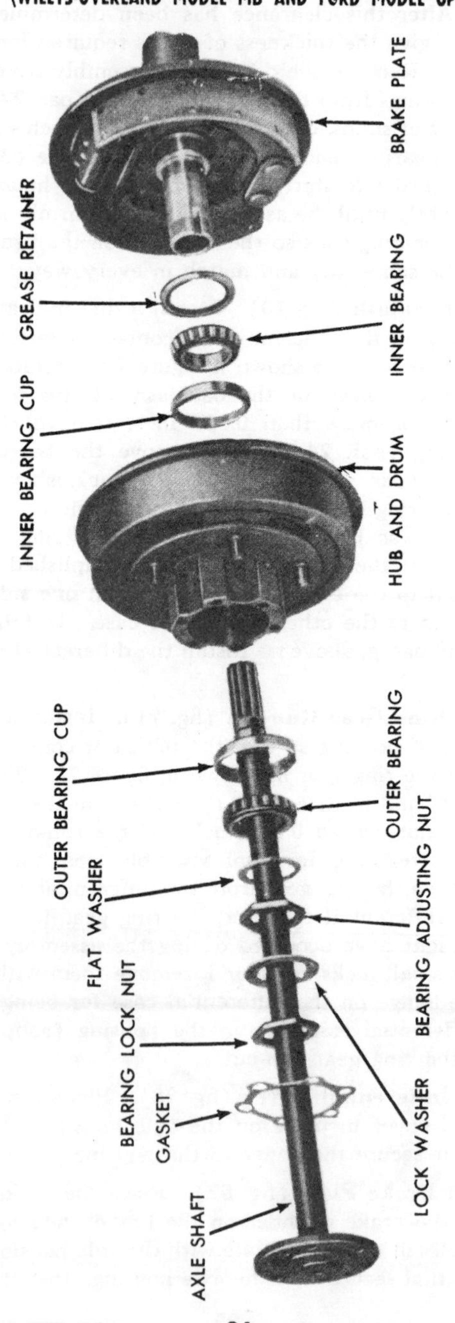

Figure 82 — Axle Shaft — Exploded View

brake line at the connection on the brake plate. Install the flexible hydraulic brake line leading from the frame crossmember at the connection at the differential housing.

n. Install Hub and Brake Drum (fig. 82). Pack the wheel bearings with the specified lubricant. Install the inner bearing in place in the hub and install the hub and brake drum on the housing. Install the outer wheel bearing and thrust washers. Install and tighten the bearing adjusting nut until the brake drum binds, then back it off one-sixteenth turn. This will give the correct wheel bearing adjustment. Install the lock washer and lock nut. Bend the ears of the lock washer over the lock nut.

o. Install Axle Shafts (fig. 82). Insert the axle shaft in the axle housing. Turn the axle shaft to line up the splines on the axle shaft with the gear in the differential. Install the six cap screws that secure the drive flange to the hub.

p. Install Wheels. Place the wheel in position on the hub and secure it with five cap screws.

34. INSTALLATION.

a. Preliminary Work. Place the rear axle assembly under the vehicle. With a hydraulic jack, raise the rear axle high enough so that the spring shackles can be connected.

b. Install Springs (fig. 77). Raise the two rear springs and install them on the spring shackles. Install the spring shackle bushings in the spring shackles. Lower the jack until the axle assembly is resting on the springs, making sure that the spring tie bolt is in line with the hole on the axle housing.

c. Install Spring U-bolts (fig. 77). Place the spring U-bolts in position on the axle housing. Install the spring seat plate on the U-bolts and secure it to the spring with four nuts. The same procedure applies for installing the U-bolts on the other spring.

d. Install Shock Absorbers (fig. 77). Insert a rubber mounting in each side of each shock absorber eye. Place the lower end of the shock absorber on the bracket at the spring seat plate. If new shock absorber rubber mountings are being used, compress them with compressor 41-C-2554-400. Install the flat washer and cotter pin that secure the shock absorber to the bracket on the spring seat plate.

e. Install Hydraulic Brake Line and Propeller Shaft. Install the flexible hydraulic line to the connection at the differential housing (fig. 77). Connect the propeller shaft at the axle (par. 21 **a**).

f. Lubricate. Fill the differential to proper level with specified oil. Apply specified grease to all fittings. Bleed the hydraulic brake system. Refer to TM 9-803.

Section VII

FITS AND TOLERANCES

35. FITS AND TOLERANCES.

Fits Location and Name	Manufacturers Fit Tolerance	Fit Wear Limit	Type of Fit
a. Transmission.			
Second speed gear bushing	—	—	Press
Second speed gear and mainshaft	0.001-0.002 in.	0.004 in.	Running
Idle gear bushing	—	—	Press
Idle gear and idle gear shaft	0.003-0.0045 in.	0.005 in.	Running
Countershaft end play	0.004-0.016 in.	0.016 in.	—
Countershaft gear bushings and countershaft gear	0.0015-0.003 in.	0.005 in.	Running
Countershaft gear bushings and countershaft	0.0015-0.0025 in.	0.005 in.	Running
b. Transfer Case.			
Intermediate gear end play	0.006-0.017 in.	0.017 in.	—
Output shaft bushing and clutch shaft	0.0015-0.003 in.	0.003 in.	Running
Shift lever pivot pin and shift levers	0.001-0.005 in.	0.010 in.	Slip
Output shaft and output shaft gear	0.0015-0.0025 in.	0.003 in.	Running
c. Front Axle.			
Differential pinion gears and differential pinion shaft	0.0019-0.0044 in.	0.005 in.	Running
Axle shaft gear and differential case	0.003-0.006 in.	0.006 in.	Running
Differential pinion adjustment	0.719 in.	0.719 in.	—
Differential ring gear backlash	0.005-0.007 in.	0.005-0.007 in.	—
Differential ring gear run-out	0.003 in.	0.003 in.	—
Spindle housing tension	4 to 6 lb	4 to 6 lb pull scale	—
Bendix or Tracta axle shaft backlash	0.015-0.035 in.	0.015-0.035 in.	—
d. Rear Axle.			
Differential pinion gears and differential pinion shaft	0.0019-0.004 in.	0.005 in.	Running
Axle shaft gear and differential case	0.003-0.006 in.	0.006 in.	Running
Differential ring gear backlash	0.005-0.007 in.	0.005-0.007 in.	—
Differential pinion adjustment	0.719 in.	0.719 in.	—
Differential ring gear run-out	0.003 in.	0.003 in.	—

CHAPTER 3

BODY AND FRAME

Section I

SPRINGS AND SHOCK ABSORBERS

36. SPRINGS.

a. Description and Data.

(1) DESCRIPTION. The front and rear springs are the semi-elliptic type. The front end of the front springs and the rear end of the rear springs are shackled, using the U-bolt type shackle with a threaded core bushing. The rear ends of the front springs and the front ends of the rear springs each have a bronze bushing and are each pivoted by a pivot bolt mounted to a bracket on the frame. A torque reaction spring, mounted on the left front spring, stabilizes the torque of the front axle. The front springs appear to be identical in construction but are different in load carrying ability. The left spring can be identified by the letter "L" stamped on the No. 8 leaf.

(2) DATA.

Front spring:

Make	Mather
Type leaf	Parabolic
Length (center to center of eye)	36¼ in.
Width	1¾ in.
Number of leaves	8
Front eye (center to center bolt)	18⅛ in.
Rear eye (center to center bolt)	18⅛ in.
Left camber under 525 lb	5/16 in.
Right camber under 390 lb	5/16 in.
Rear eye	Bushing
Rebound clips	4

Rear springs:

Make	Mather
Type leaf	Parabolic
Length	42 in.
Width	1¾ in.
Number of leaves	9
Rebound clips	4
Camber under 800 lb	¾ in.
Eye to center bolt	21 in.
Front eye	Bushing

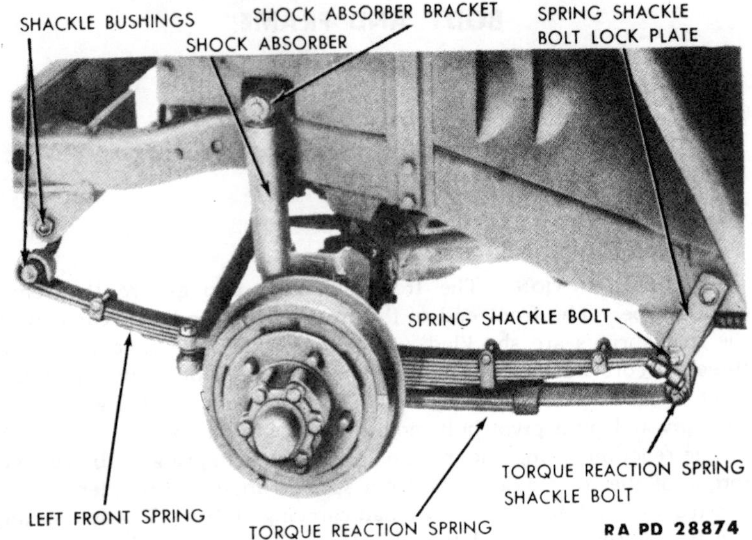

Figure 83 — Left Front Spring With Torque Reaction Spring

b. Removal.

(1) RIGHT FRONT SPRINGS (fig. 35). Raise the vehicle frame until the weight is off the springs but the wheels are still on the floor. Remove the cotter pin and flat washer that secure the shock absorber to the spring seat plates. Remove the shock absorbers from the spring seat plates. Remove the four nuts from the spring U-bolts and remove the U-bolts and spring seat plates. Remove the two front shackle bushings from the spring shackles at the forward end of the frame. Remove the cotter pin and nut from the shackle bolt at the rear of the spring. Remove the shackle bolt from the spring. Remove the spring from the vehicle.

(2) LEFT FRONT SPRING (fig. 83). Raise the vehicle frame until the weight is off the springs but the wheels are still on the floor. Remove the cap screw that secures the shackle bolt lock plate to the left side of the frame. Remove the nut and bolt from the clamping end of the lock plate and remove the lock plate from the shackle bolt. Remove the cotter pin and flat washer that secure the lower end of the shock absorber to the torque reaction spring. Pull the shock absorber off the reaction spring. Remove the cotter pin and nut from the reaction spring shackle bolt and remove the shackle bolt. Remove the cotter pin and nut from the spring shackle bolt and remove

the shackle bolt and shackles from the spring. Remove the four nuts from the U-bolts and remove the torque reaction spring. Remove the two spring shackle bushings from the spring shackle at the forward end of the spring. Remove the spring from the vehicle.

(3) REAR SPRINGS (fig. 77). Raise the rear of the vehicle frame until the weight is off the spring but the wheels still are on the floor. Remove the cotter pin and flat washer that secure each shock absorber to the spring seat plate. Remove the shock absorbers from the spring seat plates. Remove the four nuts from the spring U-bolts at both springs. Remove the U-bolts and spring seat plates. Remove the two shackle bushings from the spring shackle at the rear of the spring. Remove the spring shackles from the spring. Remove the cotter pin and castellated nut from the two shackle bolts at the front of the rear spring. Remove the two shackle bolts from the springs. Remove the rear springs from the vehicle.

c. Cleaning, Inspection, and Repair.

(1) CLEANING AND INSPECTION (figs. 85 and 86). Clean all parts in dry-cleaning solvent. Replace spring leaves or spring clips that are cracked or bent (step (2) *(b)*, below). Replace spring shackles or shackle bolts that are bent or excessively worn. Replace the shackle bolt if the diameter is worn to less than 0.055 inch. Replace the spring bushing in the spring if the inside diameter is worn to more than 0.565 inch (step (2) *(a)*, below). Replace the torque reaction leaves if they are cracked or bent. Replace the bushing in the torque reaction spring if worn to more than 0.566 inch (step (2) *(a)*, below). Replace the inner shackle bushing if the inside diameter is worn to more than 0.570 inch. Replace the outer shackle bushing if the inside diameter is worn to more than 0.630 inch.

(2) REPAIR.

(a) Front and Rear Spring and Torque Reaction Spring Bushing Replacement (fig. 84). Place the spring in a press and, with a suitable driver, press out the bushing. Press a new bushing in the spring, using the same driver.

(b) Spring Leaf Replacement (fig. 86). Remove the nut and bolt from each of the four spring clips and remove the clips. Install a C-clamp next to the spring tie bolt to hold the tension of the spring leaves before removing the tie bolt. Remove the nut from the spring tie bolt and remove the spring tie bolt from the spring. Remove the C-clamp and separate the spring leaves. Replace the damaged or broken spring leaves. To reassemble the spring, place the spring leaves on the spring tie bolt, starting with the shortest leaf. Pull the leaves together in a vise or a suitable press and install the nut on the tie bolt. Install the four spring leaf clips on the spring.

Figure 84 — Pressing Bushing Out of Spring

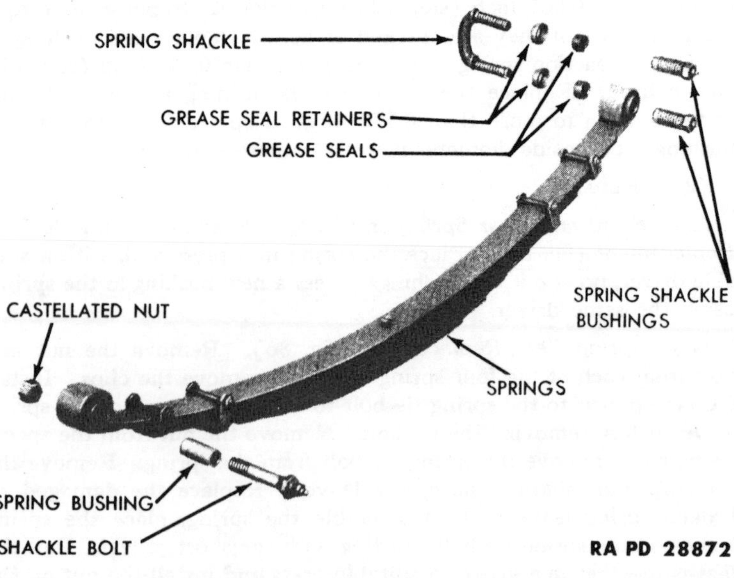

Figure 85 — Rear Spring and Shackles

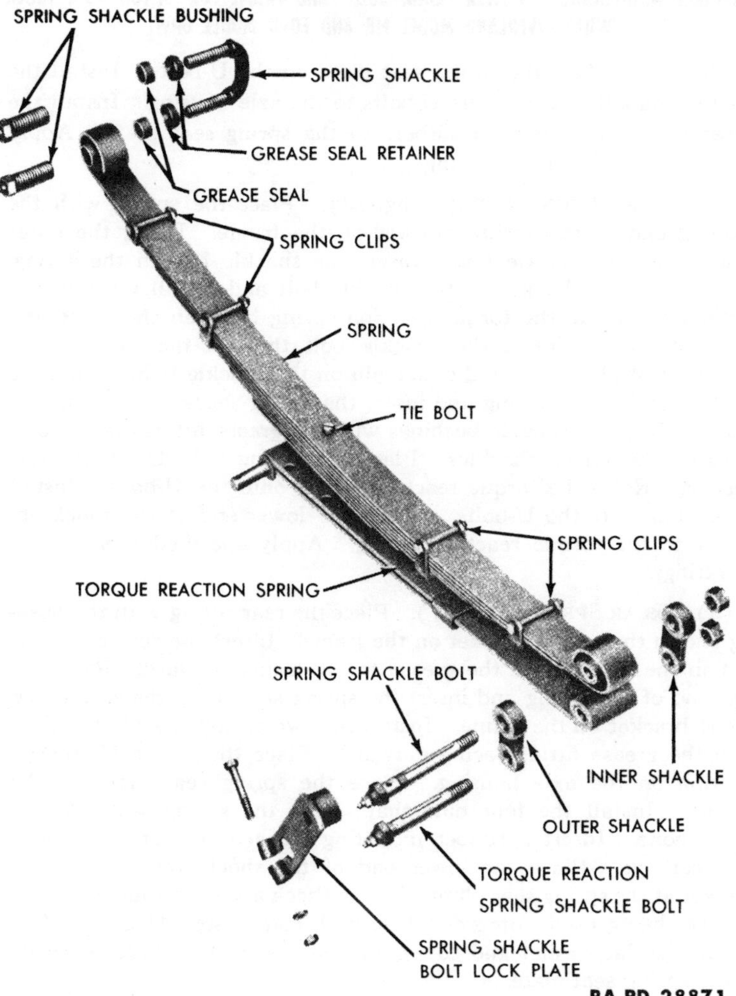

Figure 86 — Front Spring — Exploded View

d. Installation.

(1) RIGHT FRONT SPRING (fig. 35). Place the front spring with the bushing end in the spring bracket on the frame. Insert the spring shackle bolt in the spring with the grease fitting facing outward. Install the nut and cotter pin on the shackle bolt. Raise the forward end of the spring and insert the spring shackle in the bracket on the frame and in the spring. Install the spring shackle bushing with the grease fittings facing outward. Place the spring U-bolts in position

on the axle. Place the spring seat plate on the U-bolts. Install the the four nuts that secure the U-bolts to the axle housing. Install the lower end of the shock absorbers to the spring seat plate. Apply specified lubricant to all fittings.

(2) LEFT FRONT SPRING (fig. 83). Place the spring with the bushing end in the spring bracket on the frame. Insert the outer shackle on the shackle bolt. Insert the shackle bolt in the spring. Place the inner shackle on the shackle bolt and install the nut and cotter pin. Place the torque reaction spring between the inner and outer shackles. Insert the shackle bolt through the shackle and spring. Install the nut and cotter pin on the shackle bolt. Raise the forward end of the spring and insert the spring shackle in the spring. Install the spring shackle bushings with the grease fittings facing outward on the spring shackles. Place the spring U-bolts on the axle housing. Raise the torque reaction spring onto the U-bolts. Install the four nuts to the U-bolts. Install the lower end of the shock absorber to the torque reaction spring. Apply specified lubricant to all fittings.

(3) REAR SPRINGS (fig. 77). Place the rear spring with the bushing end in the spring bracket on the frame. Insert the spring shackle bolt in the spring with the grease fitting facing outward. Raise the rear end of the spring and insert the spring shackle in the spring and in the bracket on the frame. Install the two spring shackle bushings with the grease fitting facing outward. Place the spring U-bolts in position on the axle housing. Place the spring seat plate on the U-bolts. Install the four nuts that secure the spring seat plate to the U-bolts. Insert a rubber mounting in each side of each shock absorber eye. Place the lower end of the shock absorber on the bracket at the spring seat plate. If new shock absorber rubber mountings are being used, compress them with compressor 41-C-2554-400. Install the flat washer and cotter pin that secure the shock absorber to the spring seat plate.

37. GABRIEL SHOCK ABSORBER.

a. Description and Data.

(1) DESCRIPTION. The Gabriel shock absorbers used on some of the vehicles can be distinguished from the Monroe type (par. 38) in that the upper tube has no cutaway section (fig. 87). Four of these direct-acting shock absorbers are used, one at each side of each axle. These shock absorbers are sealed at the factory with the proper amount of fluid and are non-refillable. These shock absorbers are adjustable (subpar. e, below).

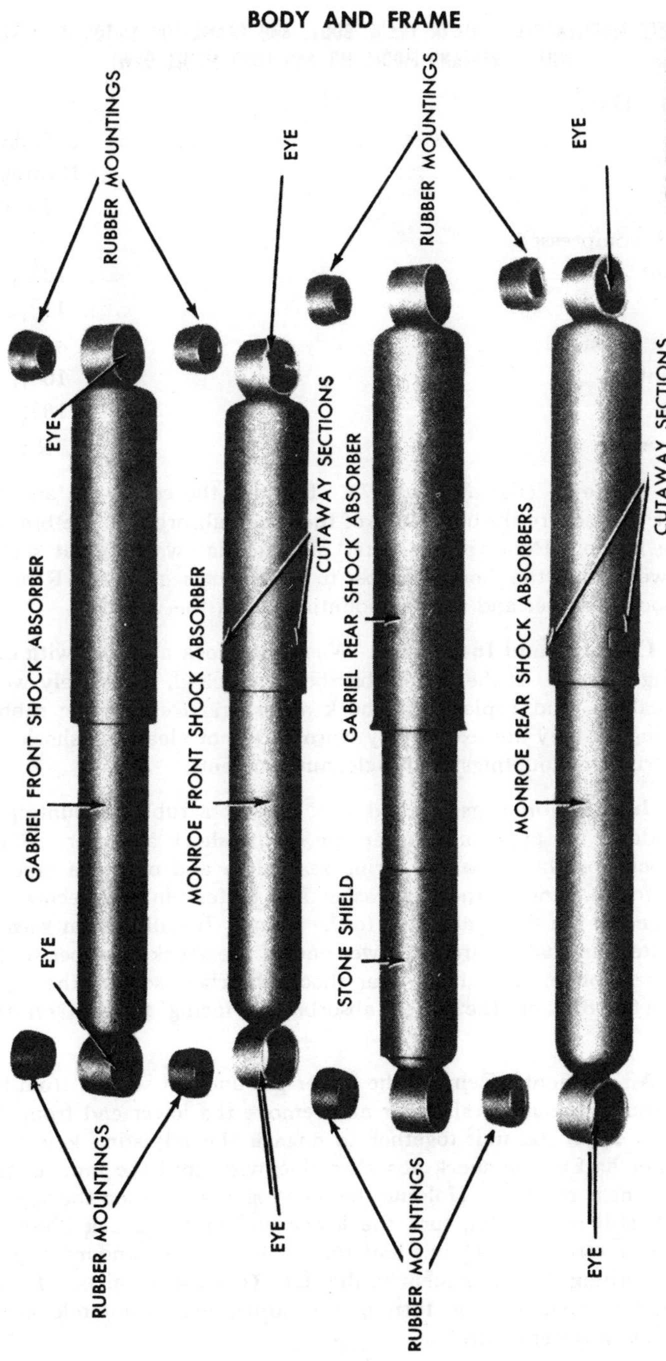

Figure 87 — Monroe and Gabriel Shock Absorbers

(2) DATA.

Make .... Gabriel
Type .... Hydraulic
Action .... Double
Length compressed:
Front .... $10\frac{5}{16}$ in.
Rear .... $11\frac{5}{16}$ in.
Length extended:
Front .... $16\frac{5}{16}$ in.
Rear .... $18\frac{5}{16}$ in.
Mountings .... Rubber

b. Removal (figs. 35 and 77). Remove the cotter pin and flat washer that secure the upper end of the shock absorber to the bracket on the frame. Remove the cotter pin and flat washer that secure the lower end of the shock absorber to the spring seat plate. Remove the shock absorber and rubber mountings from the vehicle.

c. Cleaning and Inspection. Wash the shock absorber with dry-cleaning solvent. If the shock absorber is cracked, excessively worn or is leaking fluid, replace the shock absorber. Replace the rubber mountings if they are excessively worn. Do not clean the shock absorber rubber mountings in dry-cleaning solvent.

d. Installation (figs. 35 and 77). Insert a rubber mounting in each side of the upper and lower eye of the shock absorber. Place the shock absorber onto the spring seat plate and onto the bracket on the frame. Install the flat washer and cotter pin that secure the upper end of the shock absorber to the frame. Install the flat washer and cotter pin that secure the lower end of the shock absorber to the spring seat plate. Install the rear shock absorbers so that the stone shield (fig. 87) on the shock absorber is facing forward on the vehicle.

e. Adjustment. Remove the cotter pin and flat washer from the lower end of the shock absorber and remove the lower end from the bracket. Push the unit together to engage the adjusting key, turn the lower half of the shock absorber clockwise until the limit of the adjustment is reached. Holding the unit together to keep the adjusting key still in the slot, turn the lower end of the shock absorber back (counterclockwise) one-half turn. This is the standard adjustment. Turning the adjustment to the right (clockwise) gives a firmer control for rough terrain, turning the adjustment counterclockwise establishes a softer control.

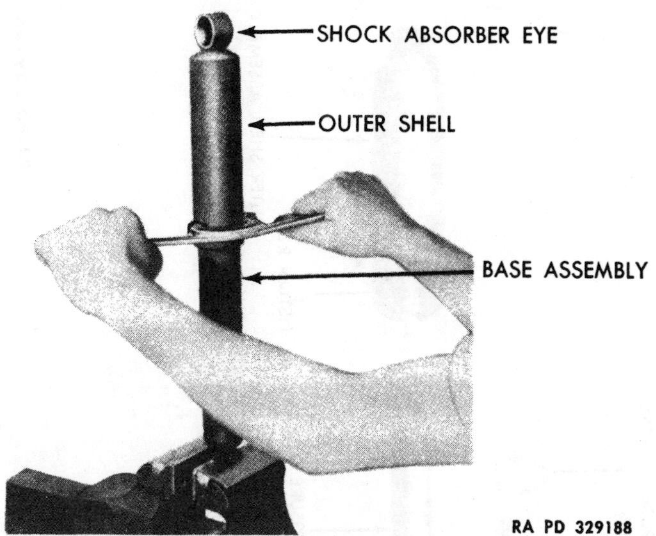

Figure 88 — Removing Seal Assembly With Special Spanner Wrench 41-W-3336-745

38. MONROE SHOCK ABSORBER.

a. Description and Data.

(1) DESCRIPTION. The Monroe type shock absorber used on some of the vehicles can be distinguished from the Gabriel shock absorber by the cutaway sections on the outer shell of the shock absorber (fig. 87). Four of these direct-acting shock absorbers are used, one on each spring. These shock absorbers are refillable (subpar. **e** (5), below) and can be disassembled for repairs. They are also adjustable (subpar. **e** (3), below).

(2) DATA.

Make	Monroe
Type	Hydraulic
Action	Double
Length, compressed:	
Front	10 9/16 in.
Rear	11 9/16 in.
Length, extended:	
Front	16 1/8 in.
Rear	18 1/8 in.
Mountings	Rubber

ORDNANCE MAINTENANCE — POWER TRAIN, BODY, AND FRAME FOR ¼-TON 4 x 4 TRUCK (WILLYS-OVERLAND MODEL MB AND FORD MODEL GPW)

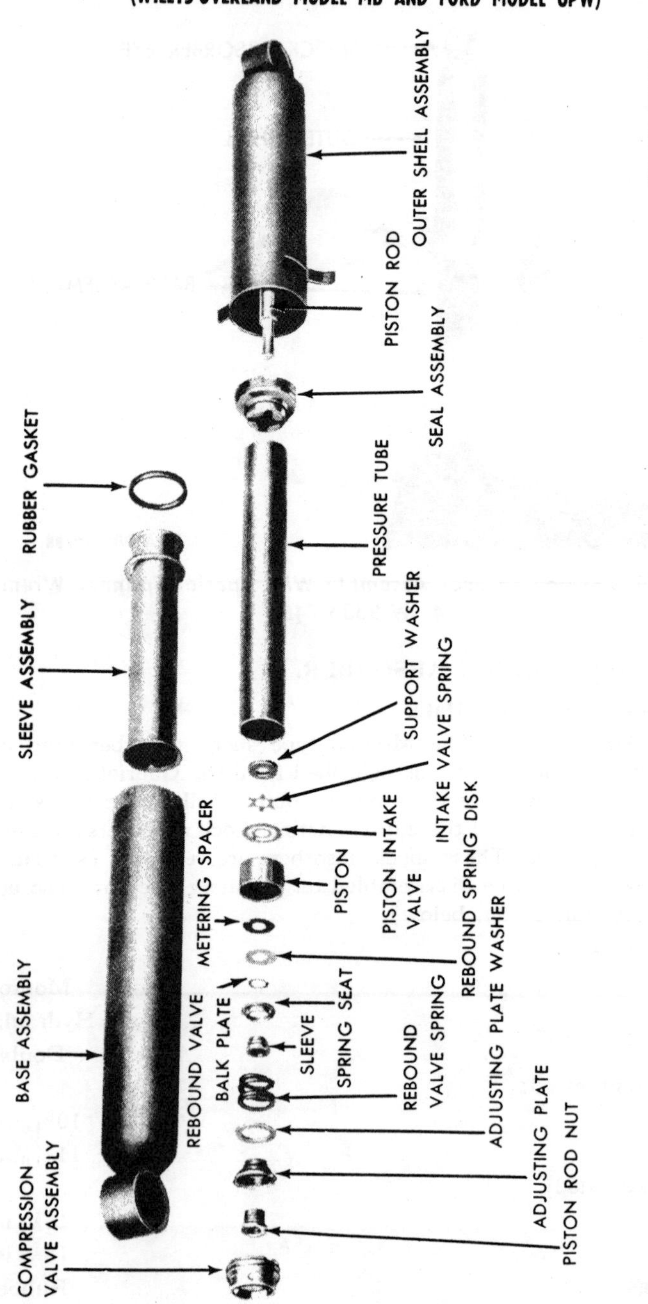

Figure 89 — Monroe Shock Absorber — Exploded View

b. Removal. Remove the cotter pin and flat washer that secure the upper end of the shock absorber to the bracket on the frame. Remove the cotter pin and flat washer that secure the lower end of the shock absorber to the spring seat plate. Remove the shock absorber and rubber mountings from the vehicle. The same procedure applies to all four shock absorbers.

c. Disassembly (figs. 88 and 89). Place the eye of the base assembly in a vise. Pry open the two metal punch-out openings at the lower end of the outer shell. Install the special spanner wrench 41-W-3336-745 in the slots of the seal assembly and unscrew the seal assembly from the base. Pull the outer shell and pressure tube out of the base. Remove the base assembly from the vise and install the eye of the outer shell in the vise. Pry the compression valve assembly off the pressure tube, using a pair of pliers. Remove the shock absorber from the vise. Turn the pressure tube upside down and remove the fluid. Place the eye of the outer shell back in the vise in its original position. Push the pressure tube down into the outer shell. Remove the piston rod nut. Pull the pressure tube off the piston rod. Remove all of the internal parts from the pressure tube. Place a long drift in the pressure tube and tap the seal assembly out of the pressure tube.

d. Cleaning and Inspection (fig. 89). Clean all parts in dry-cleaning solvent. Replace the rubber gasket and seal assembly regardless of its condition. Replace all parts that are cracked, bent or excessively worn. Replace the piston if the diameter is worn to less than 0.997 inch. Replace the pressure tube if the inside diameter is worn to more than 1.001 inches. Replace the outer shell if the piston rod is bent or excessively worn. Replace the compression valve assembly if the valve spring is broken or if the adjustment slots are excessively worn. Replace the base assembly if there are any bad dents in the casing or if the threads are damaged. Replace the sleeve assembly if it is bent or out of shape.

e. Assembly.

(1) INSTALL PRESSURE TUBE AND INTERNAL PARTS (fig. 89). Place the eye of the outer shell in a vise. Place the seal assembly at either end of the pressure tube and press the seal assembly in the tube. Install the special thimble 41-T-1657 on the threaded end of the piston rod. Push the pressure tube down into the outer shell and remove the pilot tool from the piston rod. Place the following parts on the piston rod in the order given; piston support washer with the flat surface facing down; intake valve spring with the bent ends facing up; piston intake valve; piston with the skirt of the piston facing up; metering spacer; rebound spring disk; rebound valve back plate; spring seat with the flat surface facing down; sleeve with the tapered

end facing down; rebound valve spring; and adjusting plate washer. Screw the piston rod nut all the way into the adjusting plate. Install the nut and adjusting plate on the piston rod. Stake the rod and nut to prevent the nut from loosening.

(2) FILL SHOCK ABSORBER WITH FLUID. Pull the pressure tube out of the outer shell to its fullest extent. If working on a front shock absorber, measure 5 ounces of shock absorber fluid and put it in a clean container or 5¾ ounces if working on a rear shock absorber. Fill the pressure tube with fluid from this container to within ⅜ inch from the top. Pour the remaining amount of the measured fluid into the base assembly. Hold the pressure tube firmly and place the compression valve assembly on the tube. Tap the valve lightly until it is seated firmly in the pressure tube. Remove the outer shell from the vise and install the loop end of the base in the vise. Insert the sleeve assembly into the base assembly. Insert a new rubber gasket into the base assembly. Place the outer shell on the base. Using the special spanner wrench 41-W-3336-745, tighten the seal assembly into the base assembly (fig. 88).

(3) ADJUST. Push the unit together to engage the adjusting key, turn the base assembly (lower half) of the shock absorber clockwise until the limit of the adjustment is reached. Holding the unit together to keep the adjusting key still in the slot, turn the lower end of the shock absorber back (counterclockwise) two turns. This establishes the standard adjustment. Turning the adjustment to the right (clockwise) gives a firmer control for rough terrain, turning the adjustment counterclockwise establishes a softer control.

(4) INSTALL. Insert the rubber mountings in the upper and lower ends of the shock absorber. Install the shock absorber to the spring seat plate and to the frame. Install the flat washer and cotter pin that secure the upper end of the shock absorber to the frame. Install the flat washer and cotter pin that secure the lower end of the shock absorber to the spring seat plate.

(5) REFILL SHOCK ABSORBER. Remove the shock absorber (subpar. **b**, above). Place the eye end of the shock absorber base assembly in a vise. Pry open the two metal punch-out openings at the lower end of the outer shell. Install the special spanner wrench 41-W-3336-745 in the slots of the seal assembly (fig. 88). Unscrew the seal assembly from the base assembly. Pull the outer shell with the pressure tube out of the base assembly. Remove the base assembly from the vise and install the eye end of the outer shell in the vise. Pry the compression valve assembly off the pressure tube, using a pair of pliers. Fill the shock absorber with fluid as outlined in step (2), above.

Section II

STEERING GEAR AND DRAG LINK

39. STEERING GEAR ASSEMBLY.

a. Description. The Ross Model T-12 steering gear (fig. 90) is of the cam and twin lever, variable ratio type, having a ratio of 14-12-14 to 1. The steering gear sector shaft is serrated for attachment of the Pitman arm, and the steering wheel is serrated for attachment to the worm and shaft assembly. The steering wheel is of the safety type, having three spokes and is 17¼ inches in diameter.

b. Removal.

(1) REMOVE LEFT FRONT FENDER. Remove the 12 bolts that secure the left front fender to the body, frame and radiator guard. Remove the bolt that secures the fender to the top of the frame in the engine compartment. Remove the wing nut that secures the headlight bracket to the fender. Disconnect the wires leading from the fender to the junction block on the cowl. Disconnect the wires leading from the junction block on the fender to the headlight and blackout light. Remove the fender from the vehicle.

(2) REMOVE STEERING WHEEL. Remove the steering wheel nut, horn button nut and horn button. Pull the steering wheel off the shaft with a steering wheel puller.

(3) REMOVE STEERING COLUMN TUBE AND BEARING ASSEMBLY. Remove the two nuts and bolts that secure the steering column support clamp at the instrument panel and remove the clamp. Remove the four metal screws that hold the steering column cover plate to the floor plate in the driver's compartment. Remove the two screws that hold the horn wire contact brush to the steering column and remove the brush. Loosen the bolt at the steering column clamp and slide the steering column tube and bearing assembly off the shaft.

(4) DISCONNECT DRAG LINK AT PITMAN ARM (fig. 104). Remove the cotter pin from the Pitman arm end of the drag link. Loosen the drag link socket plug and lift the drag link off the Pitman arm.

(5) REMOVE STEERING GEAR (fig. 104). Remove the three bolts that hold the steering gear to the frame. Slide the steering gear assembly down through the floorboard and out over the frame.

c. Disassembly.

(1) REMOVE PITMAN ARM (fig. 92). Remove the nut and lock washer that hold the Pitman arm on the sector shaft assembly. Pull the Pitman arm off the steering sector shaft assembly with a standard Pitman arm puller.

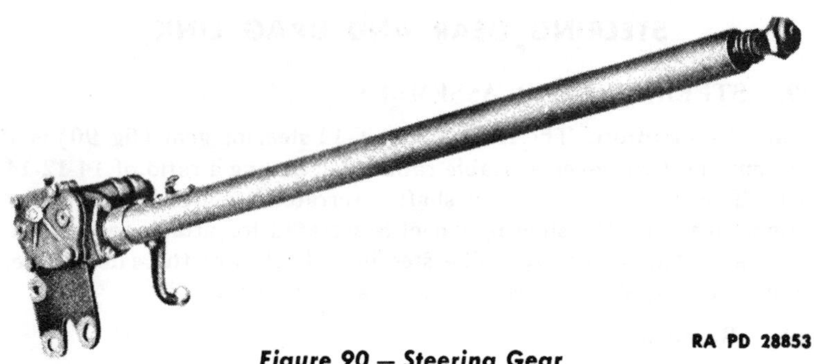

Figure 90 — Steering Gear

(2) REMOVE STEERING SECTOR SHAFT ASSEMBLY (fig. 92). Remove the four cap screws that hold the side cover to the housing and remove the side cover and gasket. Slide the sector shaft assembly from the housing.

(3) REMOVE STEERING GEAR WORM AND SHAFT ASSEMBLY FROM HOUSING (fig. 92). Remove the three cap screws that secure the housing end cover and shims to the housing. Slide the housing and shims off the worm and shaft assembly.

(4) REMOVE STEERING GEAR WORM BEARINGS (fig. 91). Remove the retainer ring that secures the steering gear worm lower bearing cup at the end of the shaft assembly. Remove the bearing cup and balls. Remove the retainer ring that secures the worm upper bearing cup to the shaft assembly. Slide the worm bearing cup up on the shaft and remove the balls.

d. Cleaning, Inspection, and Repair.

(1) CLEANING AND INSPECTION (figs. 91 and 97). Clean all parts thoroughly in dry-cleaning solvent. Replace a housing assembly or side cover that is cracked or damaged. Replace the expansion plug in the lower end of the housing if it is loose. Replace the inner and outer bushings in the housing (step (2) *(c)*, below) if worn larger than 0.876 inch inside diameter. Replace a sector shaft assembly that has flat spots on the tapered studs or that has chipped studs. Replace the sector shaft if the shaft measures less than 0.870 inch at the bearing surfaces. Replace the worm and shaft assembly if the worm is excessively worn, ridged, scored, or chipped. Replace a worn, pitted, or cracked worm upper and lower bearing cup (step (2) *(b)*, below). Replace a broken or damaged horn wire (step (2) *(a)*, below). Replace a steering column tube that is bent or damaged. Replace the whole assembly if it is damaged. Replace

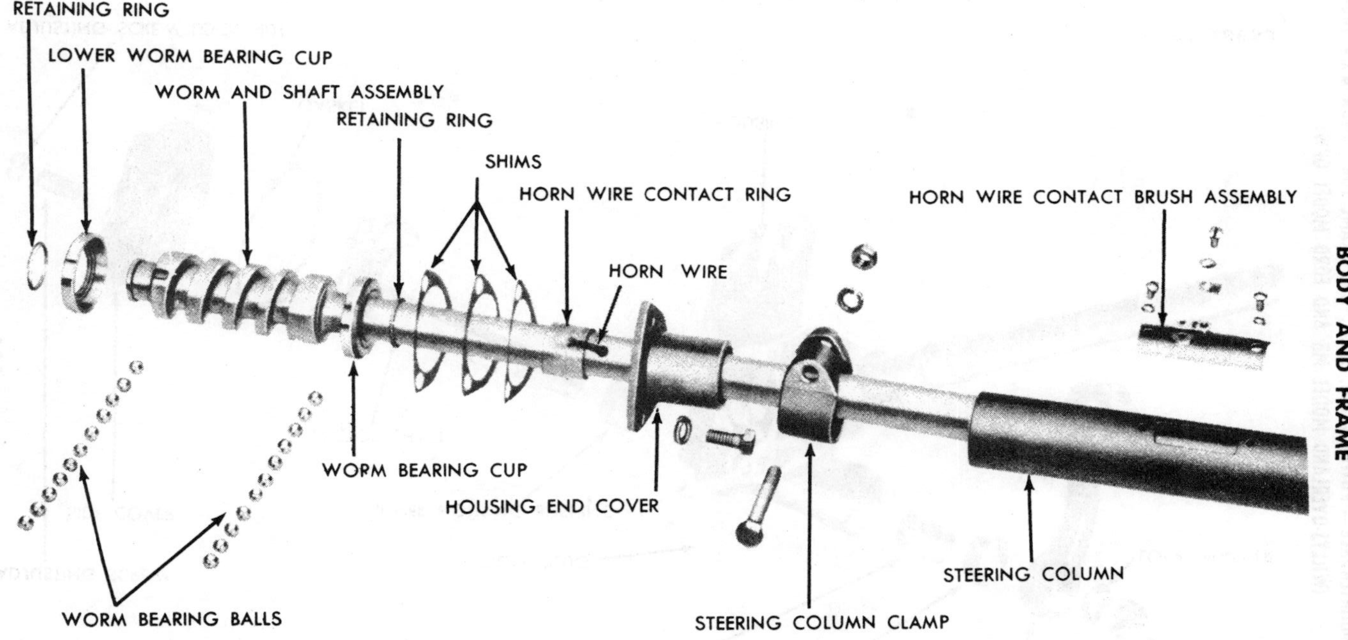

RA PD 28858

Figure 91 — Worm and Shaft Assembly — Exploded View

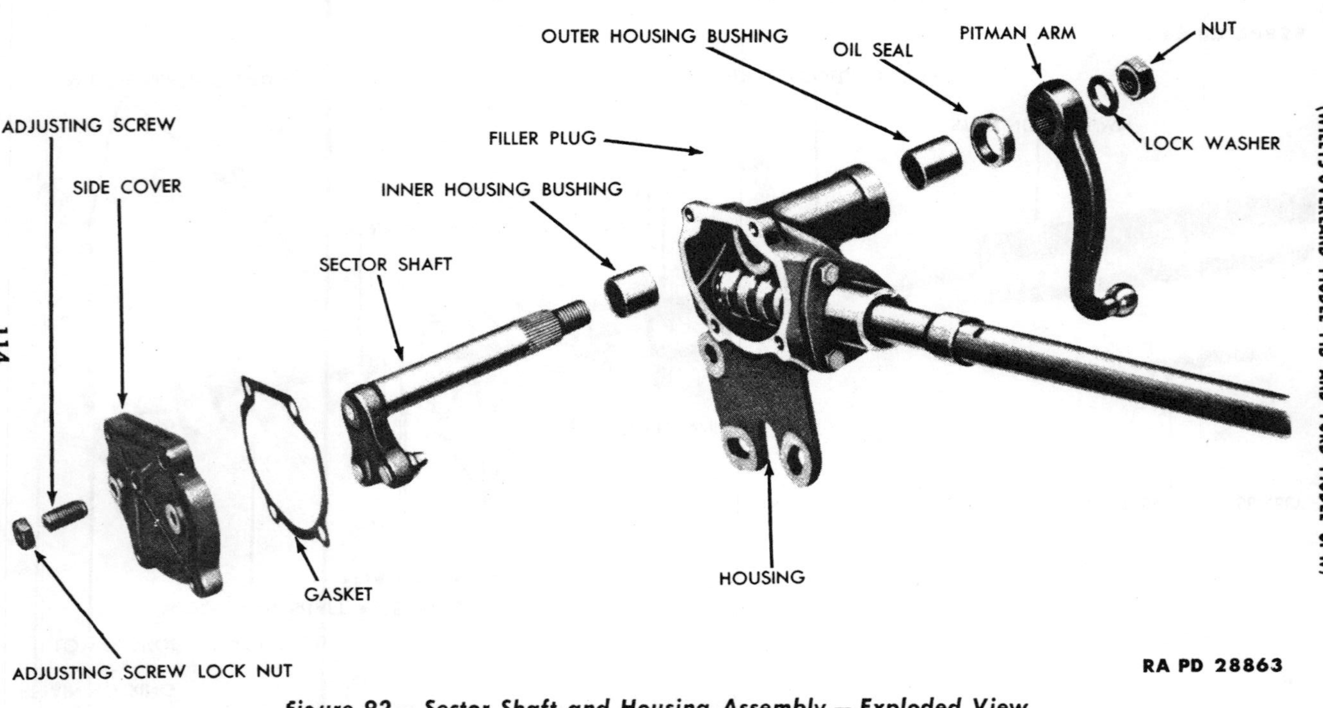

Figure 92 — Sector Shaft and Housing Assembly — Exploded View

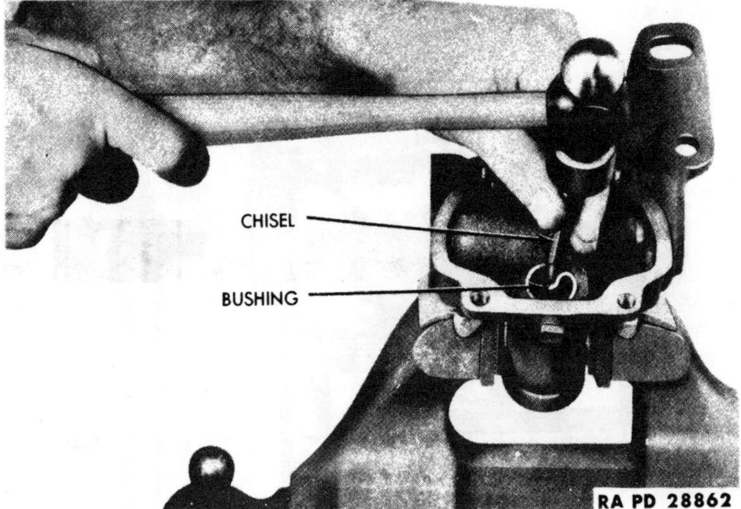

Figure 93 – Removing Housing Bushings

any balls with flat spots. Replace the steering column tube bearing if it is excessively worn.

(2) REPAIR.

(a) Horn Wire Replacement (fig. 96). Unsolder the horn wire at the horn wire contact ring and pull the wire assembly from the shaft. To install the horn wire, slide the contact washer, insulating ferrule, horn button spring and horn button spring cup onto the horn wire. Push the horn wire down through the shaft and out of the hole in the lower end of the shaft. Solder the horn wire onto the horn wire contact ring, making sure that none of the strands of wire or the solder are touching the shaft.

(b) Worm Upper Bearing Cup Replacement. Remove the horn wire (step *(a)*, above). Unsolder the horn wire from the contact ring (fig. 96) and slide the ring off the shaft. Slide the worm upper bearing cap and retaining ring off the shaft. To reinstall the worm bearing cup on the shaft, slide the cup onto the shaft with the concave side toward the worm. Slide the retaining ring onto the shaft. Select a heavy flat washer that will slide onto the shaft, but will not slide over the horn wire contact ring. Make a mark on the lower part of the shaft with a file ½ inch below the horn wire hole. Slide the horn wire contact ring onto the shaft. Place the flat washer on the shaft and place the shaft assembly loosely in a vise (fig. 98). Using a fiber block to protect the shaft, drive down on the shaft until the mark on the shaft is even with the upper part of the horn

RA PD 28861

Figure 94 — Pressing Bushing in Steering Gear Housing

wire contact ring. Install the horn wire in the shaft (step *(a)*, above).

(c) Housing, Inner, and Outer, Bushing Replacement. Remove the housing oil seal with a small punch or chisel. Drive a small punch or chisel between the housing and the joint in the bushings (fig. 93), until the ends of the bushings overlap. Tap the bushings out of the housing. To install the bushings, press the outer bushing into the housing (fig. 94) until it is flush with the oil seal shoulder in the housing assembly. Press the inner bushing into the housing. Ream the bushings to 0.875 inch diameter (fig. 95) with reamer 41-R-1220.

e. Assembly.

(1) ASSEMBLE WORM AND SHAFT ASSEMBLY. Place the 11 worm bearing balls in the upper worm bearing cup. Slide the cup and retainer ring in place. Place the balls in the lower worm bearing cup and install the cup and retainer ring on the lower end of the shaft.

(2) INSTALL WORM AND SHAFT IN HOUSING. Slide the worm and shaft assembly in the housing. Install shims approximately 0.024 inch thick and the housing end cover on the shaft (fig. 91).

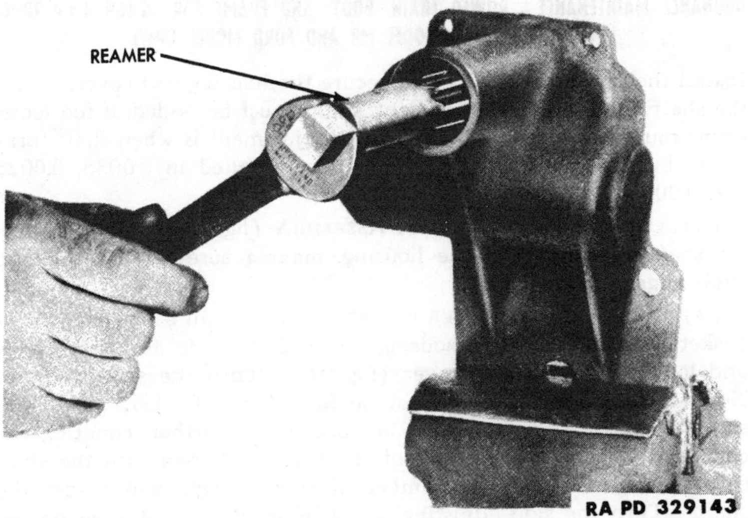

Figure 95 — Reaming Steering Gear Housing Bushing With Reamer 41-R-1220

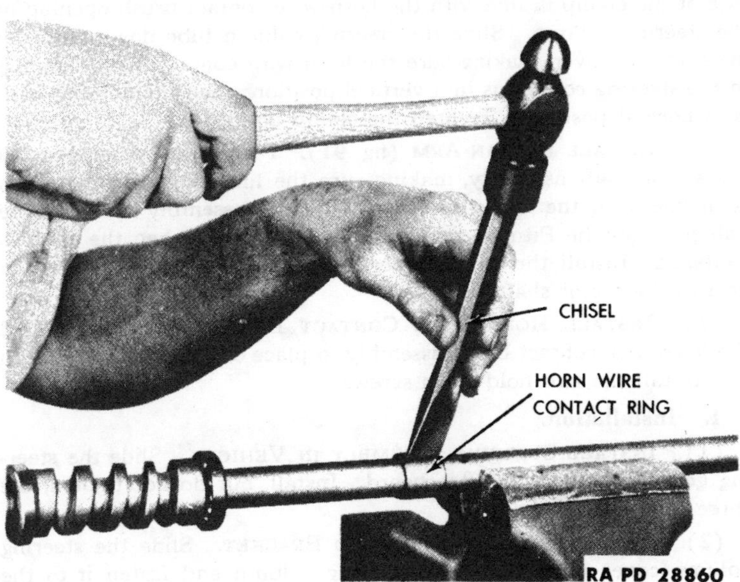

Figure 96 — Removing Horn Wire Contact Ring

Install the three cap screws that secure the housing end cover. Turn the shaft by hand, if it is too tight, shims must be added, if too loose, shims must be removed. The correct adjustment is when shaft turns freely but has no end play. Shims are supplied in 0.0035, 0.0025 and 0.0065 inch thicknesses.

(3) INSTALL SECTOR SHAFT ASSEMBLY (fig. 92). Slide the sector shaft assembly into the housing, making sure the two tapered studs engage in the worm.

(4) INSTALL SIDE COVER ON HOUSING. Install a new side cover gasket and cover on the housing. Install the side adjusting screw and lock nut in the side cover (fig. 92). Turn the shaft counterclockwise until the shaft cannot be turned any farther. Turn the shaft clockwise until it cannot be turned any farther, counting the complete and part revolutions of the shaft and then turn the shaft counterclockwise half the number of turns. This will center the shaft. Turn the side adjusting screw in, until a slight drag on the shaft can be felt at this point. Tighten the adjusting screw lock nut and recheck the adjustment.

(5) INSTALL STEERING COLUMN TUBE ON SHAFT (fig. 91). Install the steering column clamp on the steering column with the bolt side of the clamp in line with the horn wire contact brush opening in the steering column. Slide the steering column tube down onto the housing end cover, making sure the horn wire contact brush opening in the steering column is in a vertical position when the housing base is in normal position. Tighten the clamp bolt.

(6) INSTALL PITMAN ARM (fig. 91). Place the Pitman arm on the sector shaft assembly, making sure the line on the Pitman arm is in line with the mark on the sector shaft assembly and that the ball joint on the Pitman arm is facing downward when the shaft is centered. Install the lock washer and nut that secure the Pitman arm to the sector shaft.

(7) INSTALL HORN WIRE CONTACT BRUSH ASSEMBLY. Hold the horn wire contact brush assembly in place on the steering column and install the two hold-down screws.

f. Installation.

(1) INSTALL STEERING ASSEMBLY IN VEHICLE. Slide the steering gear up through the floorboard. Install, but do not tighten, the three steering gear bolts.

(2) CONNECT STEERING GEAR TO BRACKET. Slide the steering column cover plate down the steering column and fasten it to the floorboard with four metal screws. Install the two bolts that secure the steering column clamp to the instrument panel in the driver's compartment.

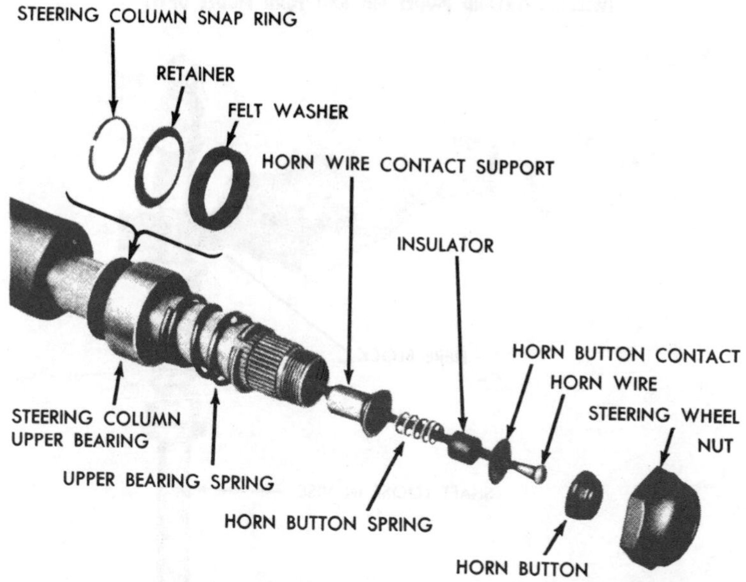

Figure 97 — Horn Button Assembly — Exploded View

(3) CONNECT DRAG LINK (fig. 104). With the front wheels in a straight ahead position, connect the drag link to the Pitman arm, making sure the ball socket on the Pitman arm is between the socket and ball seat (fig. 99). Tighten the socket plug and install the cotter pin. Tighten the three steering gear hold-down bolts at the frame.

(4) INSTALL HORN WIRE CONTACT BRUSH (fig. 91). Hold the horn wire contact brush in place on the steering column and install the two hold-down screws. Connect the horn (live) wire to the contact brush.

(5) INSTALL STEERING WHEEL (fig. 97). Slide the steering column bearing spring and spring seat on the shaft. With the front wheels in a straight ahead position, place the steering wheel on the shaft with the center spoke in a vertical position and facing downward. Install the horn button and horn nut.

(6) INSTALL FENDER AND REPLENISH LUBRICANT. Place the fender in position on the vehicle. Install the 12 bolts that secure the fender to the frame, body, and radiator guard. Install the bolt that secures the fender on the frame in the engine compartment. Install the wires leading from the fender to the junction block on the cowl. Install the wires leading from the junction block on the

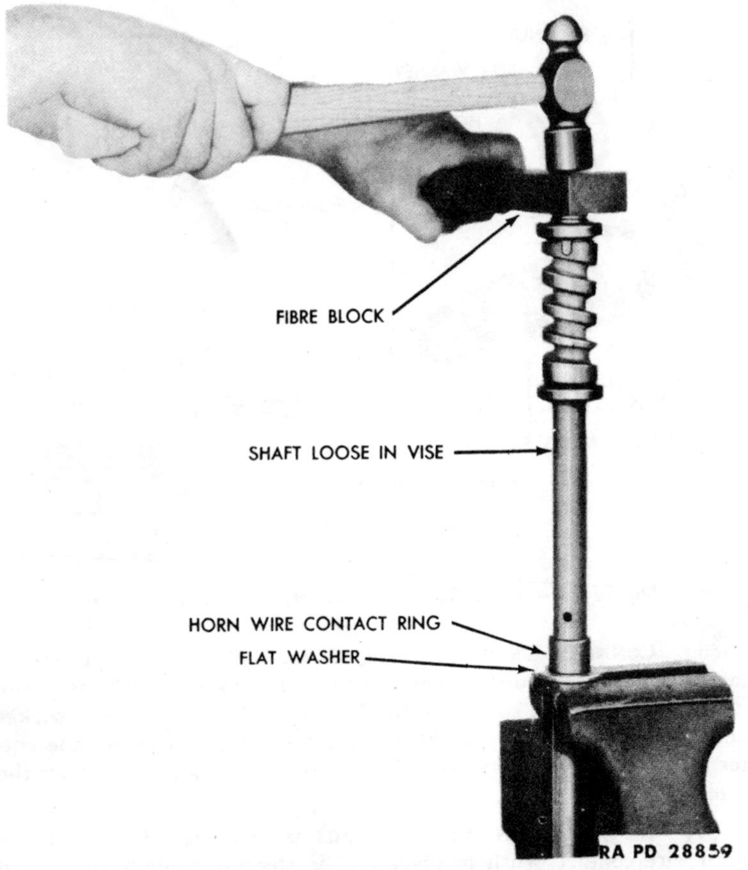

Figure 98 — Installing Horn Wire Contact Ring

fender to the headlight and blackout light. Replenish the lubricant, using the specified amount and grade (refer to TM 9-803).

40. DRAG LINK.

a. **Removal.** Remove the cotter pin from each end of the drag link. Loosen the adjusting plug at each end of the drag link. Lift the drag link from the vehicle.

b. **Disassembly.** Remove the dust seal shield and dust seal from each end of the drag link. Remove the adjusting plug, ball seat, spring, and spring seat from the front end of the drag link. Remove

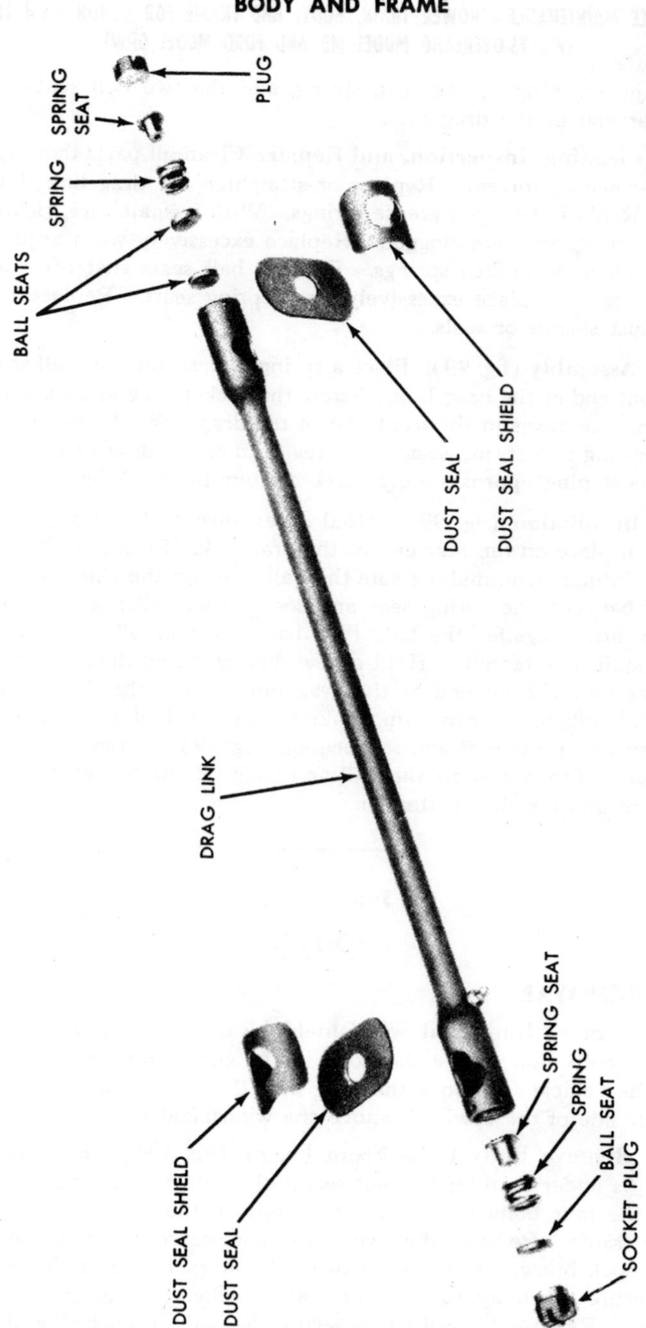

Figure 99 — Drag Link — Exploded View

the adjusting plug, spring seat, spring, and the two ball seats from the rear end of the drag link.

c. Cleaning, Inspection, and Repair. Clean all parts thoroughly in dry-cleaning solvent. Replace or straighten the drag link if it is bent. Replace damaged grease fittings. With a small wire, clean all grease fittings that are clogged. Replace excessively worn adjusting socket plugs or broken springs. Replace ball seats that are excessively worn. Replace excessively worn spring seats. Replace damaged dust shields or seals.

d. Assembly (fig. 99). Place a spring seat, spring and ball seat in the front end of the drag link. Screw the socket plug approximately three or four turns in the front end of the drag link. Place two ball seats, spring and spring seat in the rear end of the drag link. Screw the socket plug approximately three or four turns in the drag link.

e. Installation (fig. 99). Hold a new dust seal and a dust seal shield in place on the rear end of the drag link. Place the drag link on the Pitman arm, making sure the ball joint on the Pitman arm is seated between the spring seat and socket plug. Screw the socket plug in firmly against the ball, then back the plug off one full turn and install a cotter pin. Hold a new dust seal and dust seal shield in place on the front end of the drag link. Place the drag link on the intermediate steering arm, making sure the ball joint is seated between the spring seat and socket plug (fig. 99). Screw the adjusting plug in firmly against the ball and back off the socket plug one-half turn and install a cotter pin.

Section III

BODY

41. REMOVAL.

a. Remove Hood and Windshield. Raise the hood and remove the five bolts that secure the hood to the cowl. Remove the hood from the vehicle. Remove the wing nuts that secure the windshield at each side of the cowl. Remove the windshield from the vehicle.

b. Remove Body Bolts From Frame (fig. 100). Remove the five bolts under each fender that secure the fender to the body. Remove the four bolts that secure the body to the rear crossmember of the frame. Remove the two bolts that secure the body to the pintle hook brace. Remove the two bolts at each side of the frame that secure the body to the rear body brackets on the frame side member. Remove the bolts that secure the body at each side of the

A REAR CROSSMEMBER
B PINTLE HOOK BRACE
C REAR PROPELLER SHAFT
D BODY BRACKETS
E GROUND STRAP
F SPEEDOMETER CABLE
G MUFFLER
H FRONT FENDER
J FRONT PROPELLER SHAFT
K EXHAUST PIPE
L FRONT FENDER
M TRANSMISSION SUPPORT CROSSMEMBER
N TRANSMISSION SHIELD
O HAND BRAKE CABLE
P HAND BRAKE SPRING
Q BODY BRACKETS

RA PD 329148

Figure 100 — Under Side of Body

Figure 101 — View of Electrical Wires and Tubes on Cowl

transmission support crossmember. Remove the bolts that secure the body at each side of the frame at the forward end of the body.

c. Disconnect Hand Brake Cable and Speedometer Cable (fig. 100). Remove the hand brake spring at the transfer case. Remove the clevis pin that secures the hand brake cable at the brake on the transfer case. Remove the hand brake cable clamp on the transmission. Disconnect the speedometer cable at the transfer case.

d. Disconnect Ground Straps and Muffler (fig. 100). Disconnect the ground strap at the left side of the transmission. Disconnect the ground strap leading from the body to the right side of the frame at the muffler. Remove the two nuts and bolts that secure the muffler to the body.

e. Remove Air Cleaner. Loosen the hose clamp that secures the air cleaner hose at the air cleaner. Remove the hose from the air cleaner. Remove the four wing nuts that secure the air cleaner to the brackets on the cowl.

f. Remove Clutch and Brake Pedal Pads and Steering Wheel. Remove the cap screw from the clamp at the bottom of the clutch pedal under the floor plate and remove the clutch pedal pads. Remove the cap screw from the clamp under the floor plate at the bottom of the brake pedal and remove the brake pedal. Remove the nut that secures the steering wheel to the steering shaft and remove the steering wheel, using a steering wheel puller. Disconnect the foot accelerator in the driver's compartment.

g. Disconnect Miscellaneous Wires and Tubes in Engine Compartment (fig. 101). Disconnect the positive cable at the battery. Disconnect the wire leading from the junction block at the left side of the cowl to the generator regulator. Disconnect the wire leading from the ignition coil to the junction block. Disconnect the battery cable at the starting switch. Disconnect the ground strap leading from the cylinder to the cowl. NOTE: *When removing the wires, tag them for later identification.* Disconnect the fuel outlet line at the fuel filter. Disconnect the three wires leading from the left fender to the junction block at the left side of the cowl. Disconnect the blackout light wire at the connection at the cowl. Disconnect the two wires at the hydraulic brake master cylinder. Disconnect the wire at the bottom of the steering tube. Disconnect the choke and throttle cable at the carburetor. Disconnect the oil line leading to the oil gage at the flexible connection at the left side of the engine. Disconnect the radiator stay rod at the radiator and cowl and remove the stay rod. Drain the coolant from the radiator and remove the heat indicator (engine unit) at the right-hand side of the cylinder head.

RA PD 28856

Figure 102 — Raising Body From Chassis

h. Remove Body From Frame (fig. 102). Install a rope on the two forward lifting handles on the body and raise the body slowly off the frame. While raising the body, move it toward the rear of the vehicle until the steering tube is clear of the body. Remove the body from the vehicle.

42. INSTALLATION.

a. Place Body in Position on Frame (fig. 102). Install a rope on the two lifting handles at the forward end of the body. Position the body over the chassis. Line up the steering post with the hole provided in the floor plate of the body. Lower the body slowly and at the same time roll the chassis under the body so as to follow the angle of the steering post until the body is resting on the frame.

b. Install Body Bolts (fig. 100). Install the two bolts that secure the body to each side of the frame at the forward end of the body. Install the four bolts that secure the body to the rear crossmember of the frame. Install the two bolts that secure the body to the pintle hook brace. Install the two bolts that secure the body to the two brackets on each frame side member. Install the bolt that secures the body to each side of the transmission support crossmember.

c. Connect Hand Brake Cable and Speedometer Cable (fig. 100). Connect the speedometer cable to the transfer case. Install the clevis pin that secures the hand brake cable at the brake linkage on the transfer case. Install the hand brake cable clamp to the transmission. Install the spring leading from the hand brake to the floor plate.

d. Connect Muffler and Ground Straps (fig. 100). Install the two nuts and bolts that secure the muffler to the right hand side of the body. Connect the ground strap leading from the left side of the transmission to the floor plate. Connect the ground strap leading from the body to the right-hand side of the frame.

e. Install Miscellaneous Wires and Tubes in Engine Compartment (fig. 101). Install the heat indicator (engine unit) at the right-hand side of the cylinder head. Install the radiator stay rod to the radiator and at the cowl. Connect the gage oil line at the flexible connection on the left side of the cylinder block. Connect the choke and throttle cables at the carburetor. Connect the horn wire at the bottom of the steering post. Connect the two stop light wires at the hydraulic brake master cylinder. Connect the blackout light wire at the connection at the cowl. Connect the three headlight wires on the left fender to junction block at the left side of the cowl. Connect the ground strap leading from the rear of the cylinder head to the cowl. Connect the battery cable at the starting motor switch. Connect the wire leading from the coil to the junction block at the right-hand side of the cowl. Connect the wire leading from the junction block at the left side of the cowl to the generator regulator. Connect the positive cable at the battery. Connect the fuel line at the fuel filter.

f. Install Clutch and Brake Pedal Pads and Steering Wheel. Place the clutch and brake pedal pads in the clutch and brake pedals so that the raised ends of the pedal pads are toward the steering post. Install the two cap screws that secure the pedals to the levers. Install the steering wheel on the steering shaft. Connect the foot accelerator to the accelerator rod. Install the transmission gear shift lever on the transmission.

g. Install Air Cleaner. Install the air cleaner with four wing nuts securing it to the brackets on the cowl. Connect the air cleaner hose to the air cleaner.

h. Install Hood and Windshield. Place the hood in position on the vehicle and install the five cap screws that secure the hood to the cowl. Place the windshield in position on the cowl and install the wing nuts that secure the windshield at each side of the cowl.

Section IV

FRAME

43. INSPECTION BEFORE REMOVAL.

a. Position the vehicle on a clean level floor. Attach a plumb bob to the grease fittings at the forward ends of the front spring shackle brackets. Mark the floor at the point indicated by the plumb bob. Attach the plumb bob to the grease fittings at the rear of the rear spring shackle brackets and mark the floor at the point indicated by the plumb bob. Move the vehicle off the markings on the floor. Measuring from the markings on the floor, compare the distance between the front shackle and the rear shackle on the one side of the vehicle with the same measurement on the opposite side of the vehicle, and compare the diagonal distance between each of the front shackles and the rear shackles on the opposite side of the vehicle. Differences of more than ¼ inch in these measurements indicate misalinement that must be corrected. If these comparative measurements are the same within ¼ inch, the frame is not misalined.

44. REMOVAL.

a. Remove Battery (fig. 101). Disconnect the positive and negative cables from the battery. Remove the two wing nuts that secure the battery hold-down rack and remove the rack from the battery.

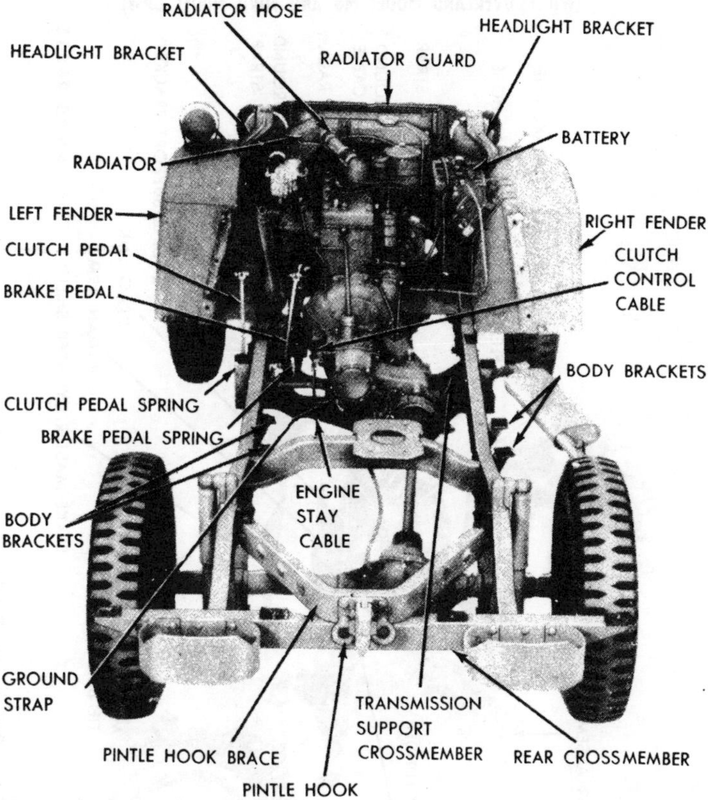

Figure 103 — Chassis

b. **Remove Body and Fenders.** Remove the body (par. 40). Loosen the wing nuts that secure the headlight support bracket to the top of the fenders. Remove the seven bolts that secure the right-hand fender to the frame and to the radiator guard and remove the fender. Remove the eight bolts that secure the left fender to the frame and to the radiator guard, and remove the fender.

c. **Remove Radiator and Radiator Guard** (fig. 103). Drain the coolant from the radiator. Disconnect the hose connections at the top and bottom of the radiator. Remove the two bolts that secure the radiator to the frame front crossmember and remove the radiator. Remove the three nuts that secure the radiator guard to the frame front crossmember and remove the radiator guard.

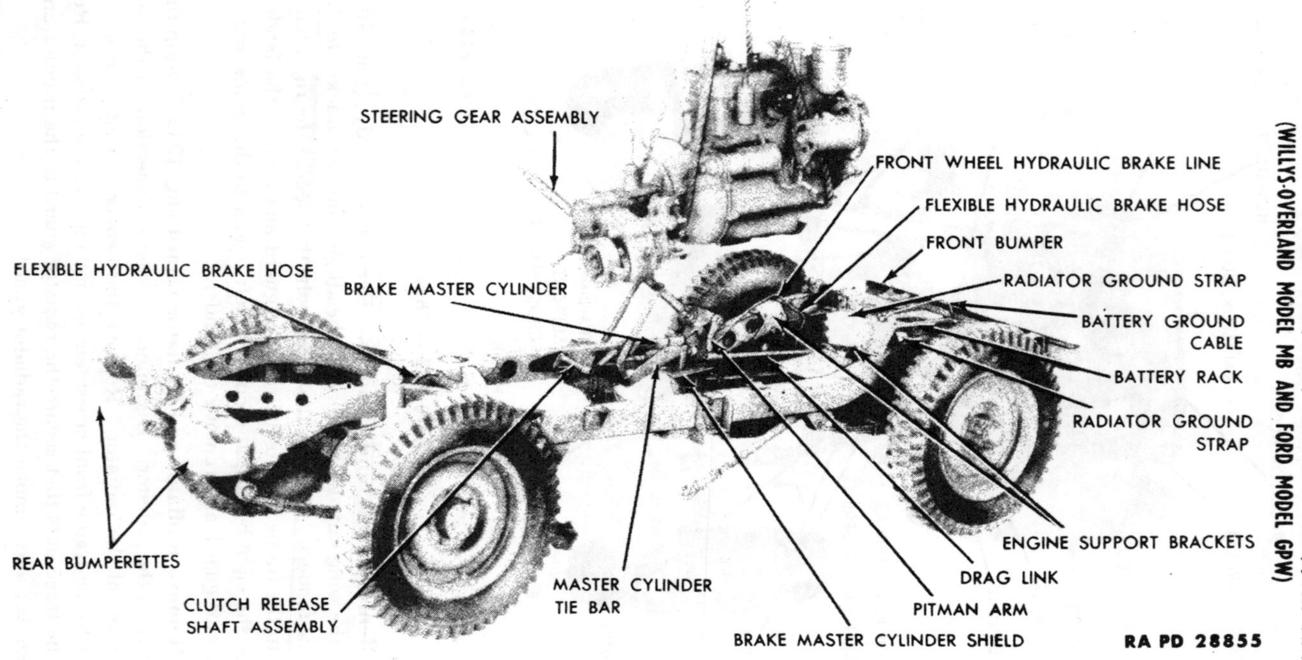

Figure 104 — Removing Engine From Chassis

d. Remove Exhaust Pipe and Transmission Shield (fig. 100). Remove the two bolts that secure the exhaust pipe at the exhaust manifold. Remove the five bolts that secure the transmission shield to the transmission support crossmember. Remove the exhaust pipe and shield from the vehicle.

e. Disconnect the Propeller Shafts (fig. 100). Remove the two U-bolts that secure the front propeller shaft to the transfer case. Remove the propeller shaft from the universal joint flange on the transfer case. Remove the four nuts that secure the rear propeller shaft to the transfer case. Remove the propeller shaft from the transfer case.

f. Remove Front and Rear Bumpers (fig. 104). Remove the eight nuts and bolts that secure the two rear bumperettes to the rear crossmember of the frame and remove the bumperettes. Remove the four nuts and bolts that secure the front bumper bar to the frame and remove the bumper bar.

g. Remove Engine From Vehicle (figs. 103 and 104). Remove the two nuts that secure the transmission to the transmission support crossmember. Remove the ground strap leading from the transmission support crossmember to the transmission. Remove the two nuts that secure the engine stay cable to the transmission support crossmember. Remove the clevis pin that secures the clutch control cable to the clutch release shaft. Remove the two nuts and cap screws that secure the engine mounting to the engine support brackets on each side of the frame. Remove the two ground straps leading from both engine support brackets to the engine. Install a suitable lifting sling on the engine and remove the engine from the frame.

h. Remove Steering Gear Assembly (fig. 104). Disconnect the drag link at the Pitman arm. Remove the cap screw that secures the brake master cylinder shield to the master cylinder. Remove the three nuts and bolts that secure the steering gear assembly to the frame. Remove the steering gear assembly and master cylinder shield from the vehicle.

i. Remove Clutch and Brake Levers (fig. 103). Remove the cotter pin from the clutch and brake pedal shaft at the clutch end of the shaft. Remove the nut and bolt that secure the clutch pedal to the shaft. Remove the clutch pedal and Woodruff key from the shaft. Remove the clutch and brake pedal return springs leading from the pedals to the transmission support crossmember. Remove the two cap screws that secure the master cylinder tie bar to the brake master cylinder. Remove the clutch and brake pedal shaft with the brake pedal and the clutch release shaft from the frame as a unit.

j. Remove Brake Master Cylinder (fig. 104). Disconnect the hydraulic brake line leading to the flexible connection at the forward

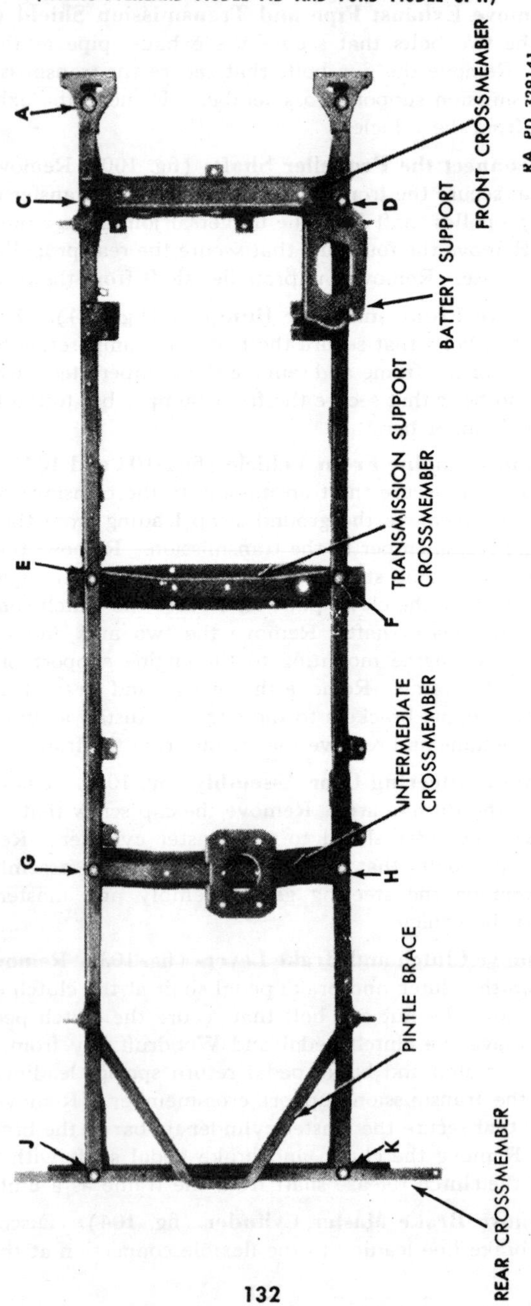

Figure 105 — Frame Assembly

end of the frame. Remove the lock plate that secures the flexible hose to the frame. Disconnect the hydraulic brake line leading to the rear wheels at the master cylinder. Remove the two bolts that secure the master cylinder to the frame and remove the master cylinder. Disconnect the hydraulic brake line at the flexible connection on the center crossmember. Remove the lock plate that secures the flexible hose to the center crossmember.

k. Remove Front Axle (fig. 35). Remove the cotter pin from the upper end of the two front shock absorbers. Pull the shock absorbers off the brackets on the frame. Remove the two spring shackle bushings from the forward end of each front spring and remove the spring shackles. Remove the shackle bolt that secures the rear ends of the front springs to the frame. Remove the front axle from the frame.

l. Remove Rear Axle (fig. 77). Remove the cotter pin from the upper ends of the two rear shock absorbers and pull the shock absorbers off the brackets on the frame. Remove the two spring shackle bushings at the rear end of the frame from each spring. Remove the shackle bolts that secure the forward end of the rear springs to the frame. Remove the rear axle from the frame.

m. Remove Ground Straps (fig. 104). Remove the two radiator ground straps at the front crossmember of the frame. Remove the ground strap at the transmission support crossmember. Remove the battery ground cable at the front crossmember.

45. INSPECTION AND REPAIR.

a. Inspection.

(1) CHECK FRAME ALINEMENT (fig. 105). The extent of misalinement of the frame can be determined by taking measurements at the various points as indicated in figure 105. Measure the distance from A to D and from B to C. The distance between these two points should not vary more than ⅛ inch. Measure the distance from C to F and D to E. The distance between these two points should not vary more than ⅛ inch. Measure the distance from E to H and F to G. The distance between these two points should not vary more than ⅛ inch. Measure the distance from H to J and G to K. The distance between these two points should not vary more than ⅛ inch. If the frame is found to be out of alinement, in most cases it can be corrected by straightening or replacing the damaged frame members or sections.

(2) INSPECT FRAME FOR LOOSE RIVETS. Replace any rivets that are loose or missing. Replace the battery support bracket if bent.

46. INSTALLATION.

a. **Install Ground Straps** (fig. 104). Install the two radiator ground straps at the front crossmember of the frame. Install the ground strap at the transmission support crossmember. Install the battery ground cable at the front crossmember.

b. **Install Rear Axle** (fig. 77). Place the rear axle in position under the frame. Install the rear spring forward shackle bolts with the grease fittings facing outward. Install the two castellated nuts and cotter pins that secure the shackle bolts. Install the rear spring rear shackles with the shackle ends facing outward. Install the two shackle bushings to each spring shackle. Install the shock absorbers to the brackets at each side of the frame.

c. **Install Front Axle** (fig. 35). Place the front axle in position under the frame. Install the two front spring rear shackle bolts with the grease fittings facing outward. Install the two castellated nuts and cotter pins that secure the shackle bolts. Install the spring shackle at the forward end of the frame with the shackle ends facing outward. Install the two spring shackle bushings to each spring shackle. Install the shock absorbers to the brackets at each side of the frame.

d. **Install Brake Master Cylinder** (fig. 104). Install the lock plate that secures the hydraulic brake flexible hose to the center crossmember of the frame. Connect the hydraulic brake line at the flexible connection on the center crossmember. Install the two bolts that secure the hydraulic brake master cylinder to the side of the frame. Install the brake line leading from the rear wheels to the brake master cylinder. Install the lock plate that secures the brake flexible hose at the bracket on the frame. Install the brake line leading from the flexible hose to the master cylinder.

e. **Install Clutch and Brake Pedals** (fig. 103). Install the clutch and brake shaft with brake pedal and clutch release shaft onto the frame. Install the two cap screws that secure the master cylinder tie bar to the master cylinder. Insert the brake pedal rod in the master cylinder. Install the clutch and brake return springs leading from the clutch and brake pedals to the transmission support crossmember. Install the Woodruff key on the clutch and brake pedal shaft. Slide the clutch pedal on the clutch shaft. Install the lock bolt that secures the clutch pedal to the shaft and install the cotter pin.

f. **Install Steering Assembly and Bleed Brakes** (fig. 104). Place the steering assembly in position on the frame. Install the three nuts and bolts that secure the steering assembly to the frame. Connect the drag link at the Pitman arm. Bleed the hydraulic brake system. (Refer to TM 9-803.)

g. **Install Engine in Vehicle** (fig. 104). Install a suitable lifting sling on the engine and place the engine in position on the frame. Move the rear of the engine slightly to the right-hand side so as to allow the ball joint on the transfer case to enter in the clutch release shaft. Install the two nuts and bolts that secure the engine mounts to the engine support brackets on each side of the frame. Install the two ground straps leading from the engine support brackets to the engine. Install the two nuts that secure the transmission to the transmission support crossmember. Install the ground strap leading from the transmission to the transmission support crossmember. Install the clevis pin that secures the clutch control cable to the clutch release shaft. Install the engine stay cable to the transmission support crossmember.

h. **Install Front and Rear Bumpers** (fig. 104). Place the front bumper in position on the frame. Install the four nuts and bolts that secure the bumper to the ends of the frame. Place the two bumperettes in position on the rear crossmember of the frame and install the eight cap screws that secure the bumperettes to the rear crossmember of the frame.

i. **Install Propeller Shafts** (fig. 100). Place the front propeller shaft in the universal joint flange at the transfer case. Install the two U-bolts that secure the propeller shaft to the transfer case. Place the rear propeller shaft yoke flange in position on the transfer case. Install the four nuts that secure the propeller shaft to the transfer case.

j. **Install Exhaust Pipe and Transmission Shield** (fig. 100). Install the two nuts that secure the exhaust pipe to the exhaust manifold. Place the transmission shield in position under the vehicle. Install the five bolts that secure the transmission shield to the transmission. Install the clamp that secures the exhaust pipe to the shield.

k. **Install Radiator and Radiator Guard** (fig. 103). Place the insulators on the radiator brackets on the frame. Place the radiator in position in the brackets on the frame. Install the flat washers, ground straps, and flat washers on the two radiator studs. Install the nuts that secure the radiator to the frame. Install the upper and lower radiator hose connections. Install the radiator guard in the bracket in front of the radiator. Install the three nuts and bolts that secure the guard to the frame.

l. **Install Fenders and Body** (fig. 102). Place the fenders in position on the vehicle. Install the seven cap screws that secure each fender to the radiator guard and to the frame. Install the body on the chassis (par. 41).

m. Install Battery (fig. 101). Place the battery in the battery rack. Install the hold-down bracket on the battery. Install the two wing nuts that secure the hold-down bracket. Connect the negative and positive cables to the battery.

n. Lubricate. Lubricate the chassis of the vehicle with specified lubricants. Fill the radiator to proper level with coolant.

Section V

FITS AND TOLERANCES

47. FITS AND TOLERANCES.

Fit Location and Name	Manufacturer's Fit Tolerance	Fit Wear Limit	Type of Fit
a. Front Springs.			
Spring bushing and shackle bolt	—	0.010 in.	Running
Torque reaction spring and shackle bolt	—	0.010 in.	Running
Torque reaction spring shackle inner bushing and lower shackle bolt	—	0.010 in.	Running
Torque reaction spring shackle outer bushing and lower shackle bolt	—	0.010 in.	Running
b. Rear Springs.			
Rear spring bushing and shackle bolt	—	0.010 in.	Running
c. Steering Gear.			
Sector shaft bushing and sector shaft	—	0.001 in.	Running
d. Monroe Shock Absorber.			
Piston and pressure tube	0.002 in.	0.004 in.	Running

CHAPTER 4

SPECIAL TOOLS

48. PURPOSE.

a. The special tools required for maintenance and repair of the ¼-ton 4 x 4 Truck are listed in SNL G-27.

b. The following list, extracted from SNL G-27, contains those special tools required to perform the operations described in this manual. The list is supplied for identification purposes only; it is not to be used as a basis for requisition.

49. LIST OF SPECIAL TOOLS.

a. Special Tools for Power Train.

Name	Federal Stock Number	Mfr's Number	Figure Number
Gage, drive pinion setting (set)	41-G-176	KM-J-589-S	67 and 106
Locator, idle gear thrust washer	41-L-1570	KM-J-1758	106
Remover, drive pinion flange and side bearing	41-R-2378-30	KM-J-872-S	49 and 106
Remover, drive pinion oil seal	41-R-2378-40	KM-J-1742	106
Remover, front axle outer oil retainer	41-R-2384-38	KM-J-943	55-80
Remover, mainshaft front cone, transmission	41-R-2368-200	KM-J-1749	106
Replacer, axle shaft, front and rear oil seal	41-R-2391-20	KM-J-1753	56 and 106
Replacer, differential side bearing cone	41-R-2391-65	KM-J-1763	68 and 106
Tool, oil seal assembly shifter shaft (set)	41-T-3280	KM-J-1757	106
Tool, universal joint, assembly and disassembly	41-T-3379	KM-J-881-A	—
Wrench, wheel bearing nut	41-W-3825-200	GP-17033	—

b. Special Tools for Shock Absorbers (Monroe).

Name	Federal Stock Number	Mfr's Number	Figure Number
Compressor, shock absorber grommet	41-C-2554-400	MAS-1148	—
Filler cup, Monroe shock absorber	41-F-2985-200	—	106
Remover, base valve	41-R-2373-340	—	106
Remover, rod guide and seal assembly	41-R-2373-115	—	106
Replacer, pressure tube	41-R-2399-350	—	106
Spanner wrench, special piston rod guide and seal assembly	41-W-3336-745	—	88 and 106
Thimble, piston rod	41-T-1657	—	106

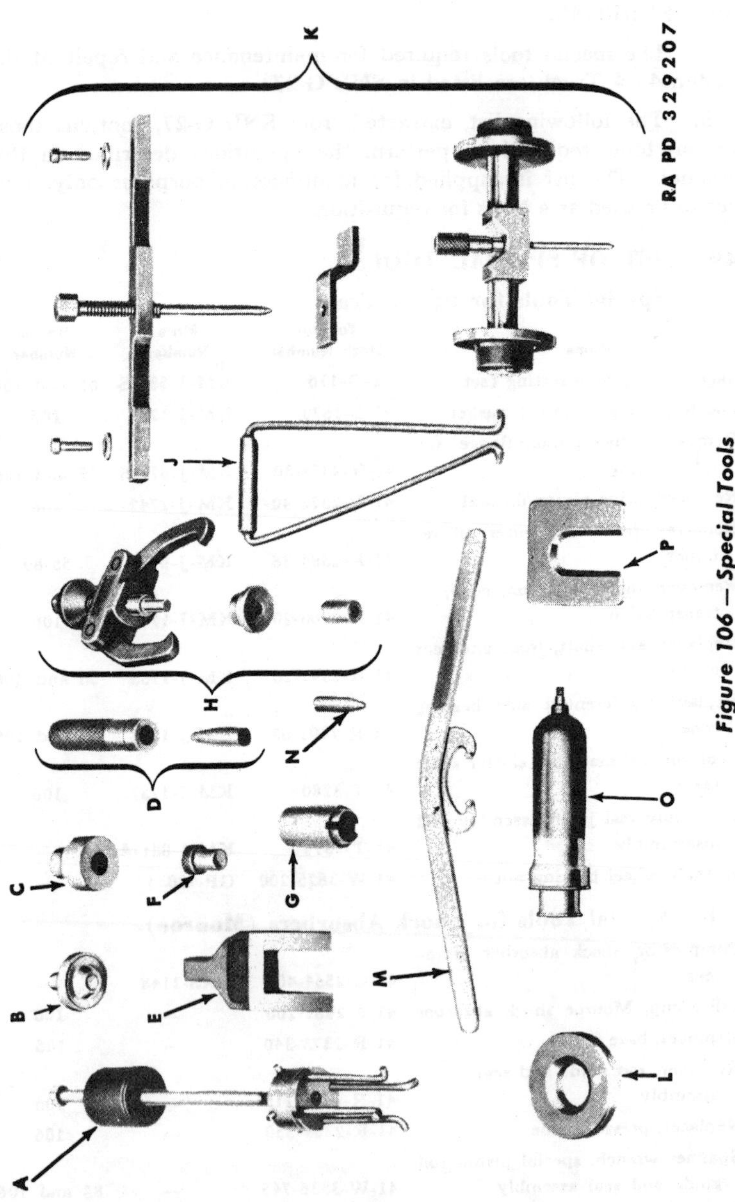

Figure 106 — Special Tools

	Federal Stock No.
A—REMOVER, DRIVE PINION OIL SEAL	41-R-2378-40
B—REPLACER, AXLE SHAFT FRONT AND REAR OIL SEAL	41-R-2391-20
C—REPLACER, DIFFERENTIAL SIDE BEARING CONE	41-R-2391-65
D—TOOL, OIL SEAL ASSEMBLY, TRANSFER CASE SHIFTER SHAFT SET	41-T-3280
E—REMOVER, MAINSHAFT FRONT CONE	41-R-2368-200
F—LOCATOR, IDLER GEAR THRUST WASHER	41-L-1570
G—REPLACER, PRESSURE TUBE	41-R-2399-350
H—REMOVER, DRIVE PINION FLANGE AND DIFFERENTIAL SIDE BEARING	41-R-2378-30
J—REMOVER, FRONT AXLE OUTER OIL RETAINER	41-R-2384-38
K—GAGE, DRIVE PINION SETTING (SET)	41-G-176
L—REMOVER, ROD GUIDE AND SEAL ASSEMBLY	41-W-2373-115
M—SPANNER WRENCH, SPECIAL PISTON ROD GUIDE AND SEAL ASSEMBLY	41-W-3336-745
N—THIMBLE, PISTON ROD	41-T-1657
O—FILLER CUP, SHOCK ABSORBER	41-F-2985-200
P—REMOVER, PRESSURE VALVE	41-R-2373-340

RA PD 329207-B

Legend for Figure 106 — Special Tools

ORDNANCE MAINTENANCE — POWER TRAIN, BODY, AND FRAME FOR ¼-TON 4 x 4 TRUCK (WILLYS-OVERLAND MODEL MB AND FORD MODEL GPW)

REFERENCES

PUBLICATIONS INDEXES.

The following publications indexes should be consulted frequently for latest changes or revisions of references given in this section and for new publications relating to materiel covered in this manual:

a. Introduction to Ordnance Catalog (explaining SNL system) .... ASF Cat. ORD 1 IOC

b. Ordnance Publications for Supply Index (index to SNL's) .... ASF Cat. ORD 2 OPSI

c. Index to Ordnance Publications (listing FM's, TM's, TC's, and TB's of interest to ordnance personnel, OPSR, MWO's, BSD, S of SR's, OSSC's, and OFSB's; and includes Alphabetical List of Major Items with Publications Pertaining Thereto) .... OFSB 1-1

d. List of Publications for Training (listing MR's, MTP's, T/BA's, T/A's, FM's, TM's, and TR's concerning training) .... FM 21-6

e. List of Training Films, Film Strips, and Film Bulletins (listing TF's, FS's, and FB's by serial number and subject) .... FM 21-7

f. Military Training Aids (listing Graphic Training Aids, Models, Devices, and Displays) .... FM 21-8

STANDARD NOMENCLATURE LISTS.

Cleaning, preserving and lubricating materials; recoil fluids; special oils, and miscellaneous related items .... SNL K-1

Ordnance maintenance sets .... SNL N-21

Soldering, brazing and welding materials, gases and related items .... SNL K-2

Tools, maintenance for repair of automotive vehicles SNL G-27 Volume 1

Tool-sets, for ordnance service command automotive shops .... SNL N-30

Tool-sets, motor transport .... SNL N-19

Truck, ¼-ton, 4 x 4, command reconnaissance (Ford and Willys) .... SNL G-503

REFERENCES

EXPLANATORY PUBLICATIONS.

Fundamental Principles.

Automotive brakes	TM 10-565
Automotive electricity	TM 10-580
Automotive power transmission units	TM 10-585
Basic maintenance manual	TM 38-250
Chassis, body, and trailer units	TM 10-560
Electrical fundamentals	TM 1-455
Military motor vehicles	AR 850-15
Motor vehicle inspections and preventive maintenance service	TM 9-2810
Precautions in handling gasoline	AR 850-20
Sheet metal work, body, fender, and radiator repairs	TM 10-450
Standard military motor vehicles	TM 9-2800
The body finisher, woodworker, upholsterer, painter, and glassworker	TM 10-455
The machinist	TM 10-445

Maintenance and Repair.

Cleaning, preserving, lubricating and welding materials and similar items issued by the Ordnance Department	TM 9-850
Cold weather lubrication and service of combat vehicles and automotive materiel	OFSB 6-11
Maintenance and care of pneumatic tires and rubber treads	TM 31-200
Ordnance Maintenance: Electric equipment (Auto-Lite)	TM 9-1825B
Ordnance Maintenance: Engine and engine accessories for ¼-ton 4 x 4 truck (Ford and Willys)	TM 9-1803A
Ordnance Maintenance: Hydraulic brake system (Wagner)	TM 9-1827C
Ordnance Maintenance: Speedometers and tachometers (Stewart-Warner)	TM 9-1829A

Operator's Manual.

¼-ton 4 x 4 truck (Willys-Overland model MB and Ford model GPW)	TM 9-803

Protection of Materiel.

Camouflage .... FM 5-20

Chemical decontamination, materials and equipment .... TM 3-220

Decontamination of armored force vehicles .... FM 17-59

Defense against chemical attack .... FM 21-40

Explosives and demolitions .... FM 5-25

Storage and Shipment.

Ordnance storage and shipment chart, group G—Major items .... OSSC-G

Registration of motor vehicles .... AR 850-10

Rules governing the loading of mechanized and motorized army equipment, also major caliber guns, for the United States Army and Navy, on open top equipment published by Operations and Maintenance Department of Association of American Railroads.

Storage of motor vehicle equipment .... AR 850-18

INDEX

INDEX

ORDNANCE MAINTENANCE — POWER TRAIN, BODY, AND FRAME FOR ¼-TON 4 x 4 TRUCK (WILLYS-OVERLAND MODEL MB AND FORD MODEL GPW)

INDEX